Constructive Conflicts

Praise for
Constructive Conflicts

"This sweeping study explores conflict from every angle, with particular attention to the origins and cycles of the most destructive conflicts and the variety of roads available for conflict termination. Its lucid and accessible presentation makes the volume well-suited as a core text for coursework in conflict resolution as well as a practitioners' handbook of the ways in which conflict parties, as well as third parties, can deal with conflict constructively." —**Chester A. Crocker**, James R. Schlesinger Professor of Strategic Studies, Edmund A. Walsh School of Foreign Service, Georgetown University

"The mass protests, resulting violence, and intergroup tensions within communities around the world this past year have made this fourth edition of *Constructive Conflicts* an urgently needed addition to dispute resolution literature. The authors have reshaped the relevant theory and rigorous analysis of past editions, building in the learning from recent events. Of special interest is the new chapter 10, which recognizes that 'the 'end' of conflict simply marks its transformation from one state to another.'"—**John Murray**, senior consultant, CMPartners, LLC

"Any doubt about the social nature of conflict will be dispelled by *Constructive Conflicts*. The fourth edition gives us an updated version of Kriesberg's landmark work, placing social conflict in multiple contexts of history, politics, and institutional dynamics. Kriesberg's new collaboration with Bruce Dayton adds freshness to a book that counts among the foundational classics of the field." —**Beth Roy**, Peace and Conflict Studies, University of California, Berkeley

"Kriesberg has improved on his already excellent volume. His grasp of established research and new understandings is superb, and the book is a must-read for any scholar and student in the emerging field of conflict resolution." —**Andrea Bartoli**, Drucie French Cumbie Chair of Conflict Analysis and Resolution, George Mason University

"I wish I had had this book when I began my study of social conflict." —**Gene Sharp**, senior scholar and founder, Albert Einstein Institution

"Kriesberg and Dayton have done it again! Very rich, very social, very constructive, deep, and broad; a MUST in the field of conflict transformation!" —**Johan Galtung**, founder, TRANSCEND: A Network for Conflict Transformation by Peaceful Means

Constructive Conflicts

From Escalation to Resolution

Fourth Edition

Louis Kriesberg *and* Bruce W. Dayton

Viva Books

New Delhi | Mumbai | Chennai | Kolkata | Bengaluru | Hyderabad | Kochi | Guwahati

First Indian Edition 2012

VIVA BOOKS PRIVATE LIMITED

- 4737/23 Ansari Road, Daryaganj, New Delhi 110 002
  E-mail: vivadelhi@vivagroupindia.net, Tel. 42242200
- 76, Service Industries, Shirvane, Sector 1, Nerul, Navi Mumbai 400 706
  E-mail: vivamumbai@vivagroupindia.net, Tel. 27721273, 27721274
- Jamals Fazal Chambers, 26 Greams Road, Chennai 600 006
  E-mail: vivachennai@vivagroupindia.net, Tel. 28290304, 28294241
- B-103, Jindal Towers, 21/1A/3 Darga Road, Kolkata 700 017
  E-mail: vivakolkata@vivagroupindia.net, Tel. 22836381, 22816713
- 7, Sovereign Park Apartments, 56-58, K. R. Road, Basavanagudi, Bengaluru 560 004
  E-mail: vivabangalore@vivagroupindia.net, Tel. 26607409, 26607410
- 101-102 Mughal Marc Apartments, 3-4-637 to 641, Narayanguda, Hyderabad 500 029
  E-mail: vivahyderabad@vivagroupindia.net, Tel. 27564481, 27564482
- Beevi Towers, First Floor, SRM Road, Kaloor, Kochi 682 018, Kerala
  E-mail: vivakochi@vivagroupindia.net, Tel: 0484-2403055, 2403056
- 232, GNB Road, Beside UCO Bank, Silpukhuri, Guwahati 781 003
  E-mail: vivaguwahati@vivagroupindia.net, Tel: 0361-2666386

www.vivagroupindia.com

Published by arrangement with
Rowman & Littlefield Publishers, Inc.
4501 Forbes Boulevard, Suite 200
Lanham, Maryland 20706

ISBN : 978-81-309-2112-9

Published by Vinod Vasishtha for Viva Books Private Limited, 4737/23, Ansari Road Daryaganj, New Delhi-110 002. Printed and bound in India by Anand Sons, Delhi.

Contents

Figures and Tables

FIGURES

TABLES

Acronyms

ADR Alternative Dispute Resolution

ANC African National Congress

BATNA best alternative to a negotiated settlement

CBM confidence building measure

CIA Central Intelligence Agency

CODESA Convention for a Democratic South Africa

CORE Congress of Racial Equality

CSCE Conference on Security and Cooperation in Europe

DOP Declaration of Principles

ERA Equal Rights Amendment

EU European Union

EZLN Ejercito Zapatista de Liberacion Nacional (Zapatista Army of National Liberation)

FLQ Front de Liberation du Quebec (Quebec Liberation Front)

FMCS Federal Mediation and Conciliation Service

FMLN Farabundo Marti para la Liberacion Nacional (Farabundo Marti Liberation Front)

GNP gross national product

GRIT graduated reciprocation in tension-reduction

IFP Inkatha Freedom Party

IGO international governmental organization

IMF International Monetary Fund

IRA Irish Republican Army

LTTE Liberation Tigers of Tamil Eelam

NATO North Atlantic Treaty Organization

NGO nongovernmental organization

NOW National Organization for Women

NPA National Peace Accord

OSCE Organization on Security and Cooperation in Europe

PA Palestinian Authority

PAN Partido Accion Nacional (National Action Party)

PATCO Professional Air Traffic Controllers Association

PD prisoners' dilemma

PFLP Popular Front for the Liberation of Palestine

PIP Partido Independentista Puertorriqueno (Puerto Rican Independence Party)

PLO Palestine Liberation Organization

PRC People's Republic of China

PRI Partido Revolucionario Institucional (Institutional Revolutionary Party)

SALT Strategic Arms Limitation Treaty

SCLC Southern Christian Leadership Conference

TFT tit for tat

TRC Truth and Reconciliation Commission

TVA Tennessee Valley Authority

UDF United Democratic Front

UNHCR United Nations High Commissioner for Refugees

WMD Weapons of Mass Destruction

WTO World Trade Organization

Preface and Acknowledgments

Writing this fourth edition as coauthors has been exciting for both of us. It has ensured a fresh look at the fundamental concepts, particular formulations, and the numerous conflicts discussed in earlier editions. It has also permitted us to organize many of the ideas previously covered in new ways and to update, elaborate, and clarify many matters. As the fields of conflict resolution, peace and conflict studies, and security studies rapidly evolve and the world continues to undergo transformations of all sorts, we are gratified that many of the ideas examined in the earlier editions remain pertinent and at times seem prescient.

Throughout the revision process we have tried to keep in mind the various audiences for this book and the diverse uses to which its readers may make of it. For a casual curious reader it can provide a broad understanding of the conflict-filled world in which we all live. For students in higher education it offers a framework through which to analyze social conflicts of all kinds as well as an accounting of all kinds of conflicts that can be relevant for their particular field of study. For people who are considering careers as conflict resolvers or professionals in peace or security work, this book should provide a sound base of information and reasoning upon which further specialization can be built. Finally, for persons expecting to be engaged in serious conflicts as partisans or interveners in them, this book provides insights about how such conflicts can be waged constructively.

Although this fourth edition retains the general stages-of-conflict framework of earlier editions, there are changes that enhance the utility of the book. In clarifying the writing, we integrated chapters 10 and 11 from the earlier editions into a single chapter, reducing the number of book chapters from twelve to eleven. New technological, political, and social developments in the world pertaining to the waging of conflicts are discussed. This includes increased attention to conflicts following violent terminations, peace agreements, and transformations in relationships. We also give more attention to the realities that different social conflicts are frequently interlocked with each other and that various groups within each contending side may consider themselves to be at different conflict stages. These complexities provide opportunities for constructive actions by different people at various times throughout a conflict's trajectory. A list of acronyms used in the book appears on pages ix and x.

Currently debated issues relating to theory and practice in conducting conflicts constructively and minimizing destructive conflicts are discussed. These pertain to moral and ethical issues, ideological and religious developments, and the changing role of the United States in our ever-more-integrated world. Our views are stated forthrightly, but not dogmatically; we're hoping to stimulate readers' thinking.

This work has been aided by our engagement in several research and practitioner groups, which have tested our thinking and been a source of ideas, information, and stimulating exchanges. Some of these groups are part of Syracuse University's Maxwell School of Citizenship and Public Affairs, notably the Program for the Advancement of Research on Conflict and Collaboration (PARCC); the Moynihan Institute of Global Affairs; the Executive Education Program; the National Institute for National Security and Counterterrorism (INSCT); and the National Security Studies program. Some groups are based elsewhere, including the United States Institute of Peace, in Washington, D.C.; the Beyond Intractability Knowledge Base Project at the University of Colorado; the School for Conflict Analysis and Resolution at George Mason University; and the Syracuse Area Middle East Dialogue Group (SAMED).

In writing this edition, we have benefited from comments and exchanges with many colleagues and friends, particularly Pamela Aall, Heidi and Guy Burgess, John S. Burdick, Rebecca Stefan Dayton, Karen DeCrow, Esra Çuhadar Gürkaynak, Miriam F. Elman, Paula Freedman, Catherine Gerard, Tom Hastings, Peg Hermann, Neil Katz, Christopher R. Mitchell, John S. Murray, Thania Paffenholz, Marc H. Ross, Robert A. Rubinstein, Stuart J. Thorson, and Stephen Zunes.

We deeply appreciate the support that Catherine Gerard and the faculty, staff, and students of PARCC gave us in this undertaking. In particular we thank Joseph S. Jones Jr., who was a graduate assistant for this book, and Elizabeth Mignacca, who helped greatly in technical matters relating to converting the third edition into the fourth edition.

1

Analyzing Social Conflicts

This book examines the strategies that partisans and intermediaries can use to minimize the destructiveness of large-scale social conflicts and, indeed, to transform them so as to achieve significant mutual benefit. We regard conflicts waged with these strategies and the outcomes they engender to be relatively constructive. They include the well-known struggles for India's independence from Great Britain, for U.S. women's suffrage, and for U.S. trade unions' right to organize and bargain collectively, each of which demonstrated the effectiveness of nonviolent action and mutually agreed-upon settlements. They also include lesser-known struggles for mutual accommodation between former adversaries in post-war Mozambique and between native people, the state and federal governments, and private property owners through such provisions as the Maine Indian Claims Settlement Agreement.[1] We present these cases so that those studying and coping with social conflicts can learn about conflicts that have avoided extreme violence, that have had limited destructive trajectories, and that have resulted in the advancement of some of the interests of most parties impacted by the conflict.

Over the course of the next ten chapters we will introduce the reader to the stages through which conflicts move, the processes that can be used to transform them from a negative to a more positive state, and the strategies that can be used to keep the conflicts from reemerging destructively. We hope that readers will find inspiration in the cases examined in the following pages and that the book will provide them with an effective analytical framework through which to understand destructive escalation of social conflicts and constructive conflict transformation.

DEFINING SOCIAL CONFLICTS

The following chapters examine different ways of conducting diverse large-scale conflicts: class-based revolutions, civil rights struggles, community disputes about garbage disposal, border wars, communal confrontations, and labor-management struggles. We refer to all such struggles as "social conflicts." A social conflict arises when two or more persons or groups manifest the belief that they have incompatible objectives.

Nearly every word in that definition needs elaboration. "Social" indicates that we are concerned with conflicts among interacting people. "Two or more" means that the persons involved in a conflict view each other as adversaries in trying to achieve their goals. "Persons or groups" include individuals and organizations that claim to represent larger collectivities such as governments, classes, or ethnic communities. "Manifest" means that members of at least one of the contending groups engage in conduct attempting to change the other side's behavior in ways that bring them closer to their objectives; for example, they may urge the adversary to accept the justice of the goals they seek, they may offer material or symbolic benefits in exchange for achieving what they want, or they may arouse and mobilize their own group for the struggle and injure, threaten, or otherwise coerce an opponent to make the desired concessions.[2]

Finally, "belief that they have incompatible objectives" means that members of one or more of the parties think that another party thwarts some of their goals. The word "belief" is used here to denote that conflicts between groups do not exist independently of the way the members of the groups view their relationship. In other words, circumstances that some observers might regard as putting people in a competitive or exploitative relationship do not in themselves constitute a conflict.[3] For example, material inequalities between the Brahmin and the Harijan castes in India may support the emergence of caste-based conflict, but until that condition is perceived by one party to interfere with their ability to achieve their objectives the situation is not a manifest conflict. Competition may or may not involve awareness, while conflict does.[4] Competing actors generally strive for what they want, not directly from each other, but from other parties in their environment. We refer to such situations as objective, latent, underlying, or potential conflicts.

FIVE CORE IDEAS ABOUT SOCIAL CONFLICTS

As we explore social conflicts in the coming pages, we will often refer to five core ideas in conflict studies that guide our thinking. These are: social conflicts are universal and can be beneficial; social conflicts are waged with varying destructiveness; social conflicts entail contested social constructions; all social conflicts can be transformed; and social conflicts are dynamic and tend to move through stages. These five ideas are derived from several decades of research about many kinds of social conflicts. They are based particularly upon experience in conducting large-scale conflicts constructively, as illustrated by the cases of relatively constructive social conflict examined in this book.

Social Conflicts Are Universal, and Can Be Beneficial

The first idea that guides this book is that social conflicts are natural, inevitable, and essential aspects of social life. They serve to alert individuals, organizations, and communities about underlying tensions that exist in some degree in every social relationship. They provide a pathway through which challenges to an oppressive status quo can be articulated and they give individuals and groups a vehicle for achieving desired social change. In this sense, social conflicts can be beneficial for many people and even improve relations between erstwhile opponents. Without struggles exploitive hierarchies would remain unchallenged; organizations would remain stagnant; relationships could not mature and develop; and the problems confronting groups, organizations, and nations could not be comprehensively considered, debated, and solved. Not only would it be impossible to live in a world without social conflicts, but that world would not be a place in which most people or groups would want to live.

Take for example the U.S. judicial system, which is based on the adversary principle. The contest between lawyers for the prosecution and lawyers for the defense, arguing within a court setting, is regarded as the best way of achieving justice. In this setting, the contest between the accused and the accuser is encouraged in order to reveal guilt or innocence, uphold the value of accountability, and provide restitution to those that have been wronged. Similarly, for many decades in the United States both business management and trade unions have generally believed that the struggles between them, conducted through institutionalized collective bargaining, served the long-term interests of the American society as well as their own. The merits of collective bargaining are so enshrined in labor-management relations that they have become institutionalized in many industries, and come with an accepted set of norms, principles, and procedures that avoid the kind of violence, industry shut-downs, and campaigns of intimidation that marked such disputes during the first half of the twentieth century.

Social Conflicts Are Waged with Varying Destructiveness

Second, living in a world with inevitable social conflicts does not mean that people are inevitably locked into battles for survival in which they must resort to unconstrained violence to defeat an enemy. Partisans in every social conflict face choices about how constructively or destructively they wage their fight. Constructive forms of social conflict management are those that preserve relationships, maximize mutually satisfactory outcomes, and minimize reliance on violence. Examples include pursuing political objectives by forming a social movement, entering the political arena, providing cooperation or withdrawing support, enlisting the help of intermediaries, eliminating contact with an adversary, or applying economic pressure in one form or another. Destructive forms of fighting, on the other hand, occur when one or both parties see conflicts in zero-sum terms, dehumanize opponents to mobilize supporters, and rely largely on the use of extreme violence to achieve their ends.[5]

Everyone is all too familiar with destructive forms of contention. Stories of intra-state war, for instance, are most often stories of armed militias and governments seeking their objectives by militarily defeating the other side. Such was the case in Guatemala (1960–1996), in the Sudan (1962–2005), Sri Lanka (1976–2009), and in Somalia since 1991. In each of these cases opposition and resistance groups and the states they opposed became locked in cycles of violence where victory rather than mutually acceptable accommodation was the goal. Under such conditions the victory of one side over another, if it comes at all, rarely results in the kinds of integrated socioeconomic systems that are crucial to building lasting peace, especially where ethnic, cultural, or other identity-based differences are salient aspects of the conflict. There are, however, instances where the parties to such conflicts begin to shift and consider de-escalatory overtures and options, undertake to constructively engage with each other through negotiation, and devise mutually acceptable agreements, sometimes alone and sometimes with the help of mediators or other interveners. In these instances—which include the rise of the African National Congress to political power in South Africa, the moderation of the Renamo rebel group in Mozambique, and the incorporation of the Farabundo Martí National Liberation Front into the political process in El Salvador—opposition groups and the authorities they were fighting shifted their strategies toward less violent means of struggle.[6] A 2008 Rand report underscores this point by demonstrating that most so-called terrorist groups end not through defeat, but though engagement in a political process.[7]

Social Conflicts Entail Contested Social Constructions

Third, adversaries in a conflict usually differ in their views of who the opponents are and what they are fighting about. Members of each side tend to characterize the fight in ways that justify their goals and the means of struggle they use. Stakeholders in social conflicts most often start their struggle with contrasting and often incompatible models, metaphors, and understandings about the issue in contention. Each side tries to make its views of the conflict the dominant ones in the eyes of the opponent and of external observers and potential allies.

Even analysts of conflicts cannot avoid passing judgment about such matters. After all, it is our moral concern about many aspects of conflicts that motivates much of our interest in trying to understand them. Too often simplistic comparisons, which are misleading and harmful, are used to characterize a conflict. They are framed in reference to a salient past, but not precisely to the issue at hand. For example in 2011, as the Western world watched, democratization forces mobilized in many Arab countries. Some observers warned against assisting them, framing their argument in terms of the Iranian revolution of 1979, which resulted in an authoritarian theocracy that was hostile to Western interests. Other observers, however, urged support of various uprisings, pointing to secular Turkey as a model of what a transformed Arab world might someday become.

Long-term effectiveness of partisans and analysts alike can be enhanced by avoiding self-indulgent perspectives and by seeking instead to understand how an adversary understands the conflict. One safeguard against making handicapping assumptions is to keep in mind the many grounds of evaluation and consequently alternative judgments of the conflict. We cannot avoid having feelings and making judgments about a conflict, but we can also recognize other groups' concerns and assessments. Another way to reduce the dangers of thinking about conflicts from too narrow a perspective is to use a comprehensive framework of analysis. This book offers such a framework.

The adversaries in any large-scale conflict are not unitary actors. There are many different strata and groups with different interests, concerns, values, and beliefs. There are likely to be differences between hawks and doves. These variations are generally expressed in varied conceptions about what any particular conflict is about. Interestingly, factions in one side of a conflict may tend to share ways of thinking about a conflict with similar factions in the opposing camp. They may reinforce each other's views, as when extremists on opposing sides provide support for each other's views.

As will be discussed further in later pages, each conflict is interlocked with many others. Some conflicts are embedded in larger conflicts, historically and contemporaneously. Each adversary is also engaged in several other conflicts at any given time. The primacy of one or another conflict shifts over time, as one intensifies or moves to little relevance. Various groups within each side in a conflict may dispute which conflict should be given the greatest priority, which enemy is number one and which is number two.

All Social Conflicts Can Be Transformed

Fourth, even in the most intractable conflicts in the world, it is always conceivable for someone, somewhere, to do something that helps at least a bit to transform the conflict in a positive direction. Even so called "intractable" large-scale conflicts are rarely limited to the activities of the main partisans. They involve diverse actors including nongovernmental organizations (NGOs) and nonprofit groups; stakeholders at the local, national, or international level; financial organizations; social networks; and other stakeholders. Each of these actors has particular entry points and ways to influence the direction of the conflict. For example, even when the official representatives of antagonistic sides of a conflict are unwilling to communicate directly with each other about possible settlements, it may be possible for members of diaspora communities to apply leverage directly or by influencing the governments of their new countries of residence.[8]

Alternatively, social movements, interest groups, and other unofficial actors can also be used to advance peace initiatives in cases where states lack leverage, credibility, or will. Such actors have increasingly shown their capacity to engage partisans in unofficial diplomacy, provide conflict monitoring and early warning, utilize social network technologies, and advance the work of civil society organizations in conflict zones. Unofficial efforts by former Israeli and Palestinian officials Yossi Beilin and Yasser Abed Rabbo, for instance, resulted in the drafting of the Geneva Accords, which showed that a consensus-based solution to the major issues separating Palestinians and Israelis was conceivable and plausible. Similarly, the international NGO Search for Common Ground has initiated numerous dialogue projects in the United States over the past two decades to engage citizens in discussions about issues as diverse as abortion, health care reform, and race relations. Such bottom-up approaches to constructive conflict management can help initiate, conduct, and consolidate top-down actions in many ways at each conflict stage.

Waging conflicts constructively typically entails different stakeholders doing different things at different times. Sometimes elites may focus on transforming conflicts through new policies and laws; other times private parties can constructively transform conflicts by attending to the emotional wounds or problematic narratives that sustain conflicts. At still other times, the assistance of intermediaries may be necessary to convene meetings, to transmit information, or to guarantee the adherence to agreements that are made.

Social Conflicts Are Dynamic and Tend to Move Through Stages

Fifth, social conflicts are never static; rather they are fluid and move through various stages as partisans adopt new strategies, develop different perspectives, achieve some objectives, and fail to achieve others, or as the composition of the contending groups or the environment in which they are operating change. This book follows the course of a conflict, as it emerges, escalates, de-escalates, and is settled.[9] We believe that a "stages" approach to the study of social conflicts is essential because how the adversaries assess the course of a conflict has profound implications, as when the parties perceive a transition from one stage to another that permits new kinds of behavior.

Before a conflict emerges, its preconditions exist. It is assumed or hypothesized by many adversaries, intermediaries, observers, and theoreticians of conflict that particular underlying conditions are likely to result in an overt conflict. The persons making such interpretations, however, are likely to disagree about what those underlying conditions are. We examine the wide variety of possible bases for social conflicts in chapter 2.

Many circumstances that could result in a conflict becoming manifest do not have that result. The initial stage of a conflict is only reached when at least one potential adversary acts on the belief that its goals are incompatible with those of an adversary. This stage may include a period of time during which one or more parties probe and explore the reality of that belief. The processes of conflict emergence are examined in chapter 3.

An escalating stage is reached when the adversaries begin to actively pursue their incompatible goals. Escalation is expressed in increasing intensity of the means of conflict, often entailing coercion. The various ways a conflict may be pursued are discussed in chapters 4 and 5, and the processes of escalation are examined in chapter 6. A conflict in which adversaries threaten and try to damage each other is only one possible stage in the larger set of interactions among them. Figure 1.1 indicates that from all the relations between a set of parties, only a subset of those are potentially conflicting; and only a subset of those actually emerges as social conflicts; and of these, only some are pursued contentiously. Even in that subset, only some exhibit coercive acts; finally, only a subset of those conflicts becomes destructively waged for a period of time.

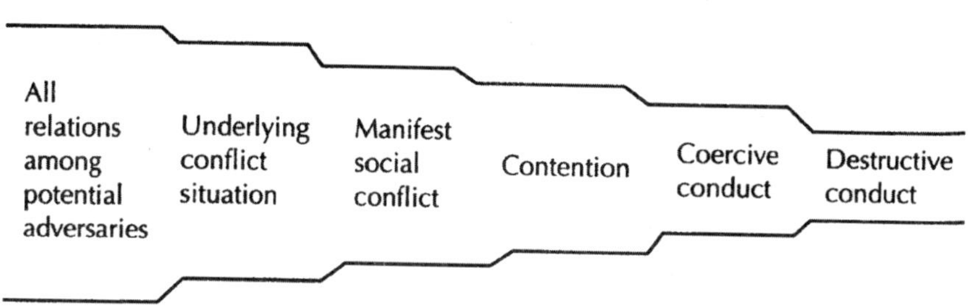

Figure 1.1. Conflict Funnel

Conflicts not only escalate; they also de-escalate after a brief or extended transition. A protracted conflict often has many escalating and de-escalating episodes of varying magnitude. Only in retrospect can we discern a long-term transformation from intractable antagonism to de-escalation leading to a resolution of a conflict. In chapter 7, transitions toward reduced antagonism and the processes of de-escalation are examined. In chapter 8, mediation in conflicts is explored. In chapter 9, we examine the settlement of conflicts through both negotiated and non-negotiated means. In chapter 10, the factors shaping the various outcomes and long-term termination sequences are analyzed. Finally, in chapter 11, the various elements developed in this study are applied to each conflict stage and the approach taken is specified for different kinds of conflicts. We also consider the implications of the interpretations made here for policies that are conducive to waging conflicts constructively.

Although all conflicts do not go in one sequence through all the stages identified here, without backsliding, it will prove helpful to consider these stages and why some conflicts move from one stage to the next more or less constructively. A diagram of the potential sequence of stages is shown in figure 1.2. The series of arrows forming the circle indicates that a conflict

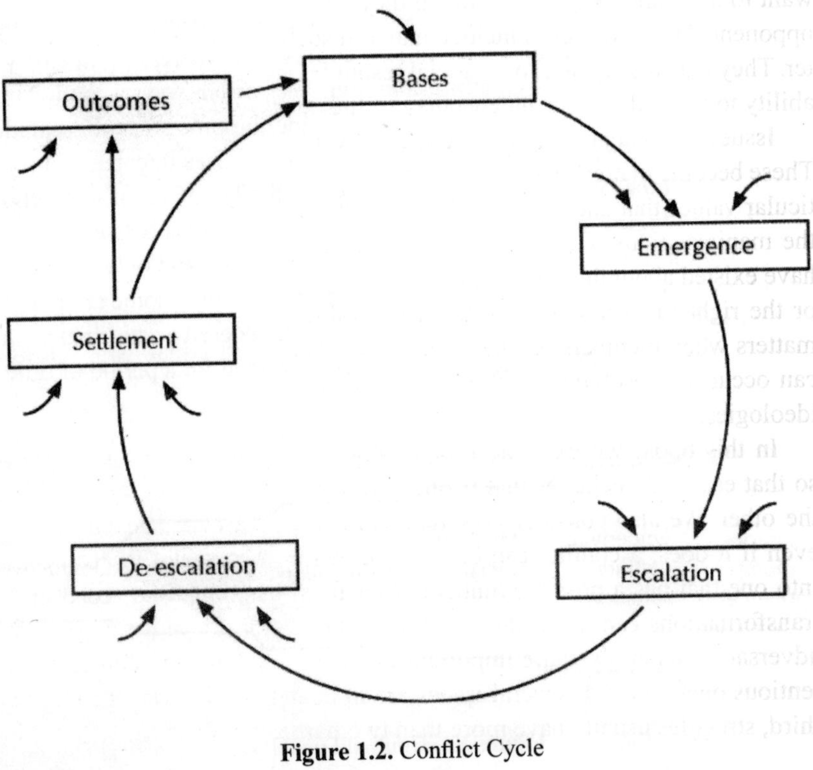

Figure 1.2. Conflict Cycle

emerges, escalates, de-escalates, terminates, and results in an outcome that becomes the basis for another conflict. How the previous stage is enacted heavily influences the next stage. The short arrows entering from outside and inside the circle indicate that factors internal to each adversary as well as social environmental factors also affect each stage.

VARIETIES OF CONFLICTS

Discerning how particular conflicts are like each other and unlike each other is critical in comparing one conflict with another and deciding what policy should be pursued. Conflicts vary in six relevant ways: the issues in contention, the characteristics of the contending parties, the relations between the adversaries, the context in which the adversaries contend, the means used to conduct the struggle, and the outcomes of the struggle.

Issues in Contention

Adversaries wage conflicts over two kinds of matters: interests and values. Thus, they may quarrel about resources, assets, or capabilities that they each want to have and believe how much they have must be at the expense of the opponent. These resources include material such as land, money, oil, and water. They may also quarrel over social resources, such as their prestige, or their ability to make decisions independent of the desires of others.

Issues in contention also arise from diverse values each side holds dear. These become matters in contention when one side insists on manifesting particular values that another party finds so objectionable that they try to forbid the manifestations. For example, in the United States strong disagreements have existed about the right to practice polygamy, the right to have abortions, or the right to own and carry firearms. Values may also become contested matters when members of one group insist that others adopt their values, as can occur in proselytizing efforts for particular religious beliefs or political ideologies.

In this book, we examine how conflicts come to be seen as zero-sum, so that each side believes that if one side wins, it must be at the expense of the other. We also consider how that sometimes does not happen and how, even if it does, a conflict can be transformed in the eyes of the antagonists into one that has a possible mutually beneficial outcome. Such constructive transformations can occur due to at least three widespread conditions: first, adversaries generally share important interests and value in addition to contentious ones; second, several issues are in contention in every conflict; and third, struggles usually have more than two parties involved.

First, adversaries usually share some common and complementary values and interests as well as opposing ones. Consequently, there are often grounds for collaboration and joint gains. For example, while trade union and management negotiators may be in conflict about the amount of money the workers should be paid, they may also believe that they have common interests in expanding the firm's share of the market and its profits and they have complementary interests in improving the motivation and skill that each party exercises. Similarly, some women's organizations and the religious right may not agree on most issues, but both express concern about the exploitation of women through Internet pornography.

Second, since every conflict has more than one matter of contention, it is likely that opponents will have different priorities for these various matters. This allows trading off one matter against another. Consider the terms of the 1979 peace treaty between Israel and Egypt. After the 1967 war in which Israel defeated Egypt together with its Arab allies, Syria and Jordan, Israel occupied the Sinai, which had been part of Egypt prior to the war. Sovereignty over the Sinai was of paramount importance to the Egyptian government. Security against an Egyptian military attack based in the Sinai was of vital importance to the Israeli government. Among the many provisions of the peace treaty, Egypt gained full sovereignty over the Sinai, and Israel was assured that only limited Egyptian military forces would ever be stationed or moved into the Sinai.

Third, since social conflicts generally involve many contending parties, a conflict may be transformed by changing the salience of the antagonism between a particular set of opponents. Every adversary has many groups within it, and there are many groups outside who are or might be induced to become allies. In addition, there are entities that cross-cut and transcend the adversaries. Thus, in a union-management struggle, the union consists of nationally elected leaders, staff persons, local union officials, and rank-and-file members at varying pay scales; management consists of the labor relations department heads and staff; sales, production, and advertising departments; and overall officers. In addition, each group has ties with political parties, government officials, consumers, and stockholders.

Given all these parties, what might seem like a zero-sum conflict can be transformed because it is embedded in a whole set of other relationships, including other conflicts. The dispute can then be seen as a mixed-motive game, in which some adversaries cooperate to gain benefits at the expense of other parties. For example, trade union and management leaders may agree to raise wages but cover the costs by raising prices to the consumers. In many fights, also, opponents become allies when facing attack from what they regard as a common enemy.

Adversary Characteristics

Conflicts are often distinguished according to the character of the adversaries: countries, persons, ethnic groups, or particular organizations. Large bodies of literature analyze conflicts among each of these kinds of adversaries. Adversaries also may be distinguished in terms of characteristics such as their culture, size, and available means to wage conflicts. Distinguishing the nature of adversaries in more abstract terms, three general features have implications for how destructively or constructively they conduct their conflicts. These are: the adversary's self-other conceptions; the clarity of the adversary's social boundaries; and the internal organization of a conflict party. These features not only vary but they also can change in the course of a conflict and affect its trajectory.

Self-Other Conceptions

Variations in the way adversaries view themselves and each other are an essential component of a conflict. Thus, religious, ethnic, or ideological identities can be important sources for such conceptions and are central to "identity conflicts." Social identity theory argues that the innate human capacity to categorize people and other phenomena contributes to the creation of what are often called "in-groups" and "out-groups." In-group/out-group categorization allows individuals to classify other people according to their similarity or dissimilarity to the self. When combined with the need for high personal and group esteem, in-group/out-group categorization may lead to stereotyping and ethnocentrism, which contributes to the emergence and persistence of conflicts.[10] Indeed, the degree to which individuals or groups regard themselves as superior to those that they are opposing has grave implications for the way a struggle is conducted.[11] In these kinds of conflicts, extreme dehumanization on one or both sides can justify the resort to extreme means of struggle. Many conflict resolution practitioners seek to overcome this dynamic by bringing such groups into closely supervised contact with each other. It is believed that through such contact individuals can overcome their parochial identities and develop a new superordinate identity that includes their former adversary. Such approaches will be discussed at length in chapter 8.

Boundary Clarity

The social boundaries of parties in a conflict vary in clarity, recognition, and permeability. For example, the boundaries between particular ethnic groups may be sharp and sustained by law and custom that restricts communication and movement across ethnic borders. These may be largely established and maintained by a dominant group. This was the case in the southern United States during the years of the Jim Crow laws and in South Africa during the years of apartheid. In other times and places, as in cosmopolitan cities, the boundaries between many ethnic groups have been vague and the realms of life governed by ethnic designation have been more limited.

The clarity of social boundaries has important implications for the emergence of a social conflict and for its course and resolution. The clarity of the boundaries often depends on social markers, such as clothing or dialect. Thus, boundaries are not inherent in the physical features of the members of the socially defined categories. Insofar as the distinctions are generally recognized, members of any of the distinguished categories are available to be mobilized for reasons of perceived self-interest.

Clear and strong boundaries between adversaries ease mobilization for waging a conflict and hamper the communication and shared interests that might limit escalation and hasten resolution. This dynamic is evident, for instance, in the history of modern interstate war where citizenship and nationalism has become a rallying cry for conflict and lack of contact across war zones has facilitated the dehumanization of each side by the other. By contrast, the growth of global civil society, the ease with which individuals can now traverse national borders, and the development of a horizontal global communication infrastructure may be leading to the erosion of overriding national identities and the development of regional, occupational, or new cosmopolitan identities.[12] Increasingly now, many people have multiple national identities and even dual citizenship, and they appreciate multicultural experiences.

In general, contending parties in a community or within a country are less clearly bounded. Sometimes it is difficult to distinguish the social categories that serve as recruiting grounds for the active participants in the contending groups. It is true there may be some established, tightly knit organizations engaged in a struggle, but they almost always need a broader and more loosely bounded body of supporters to survive and be effective.

The boundaries of different entities are becoming more porous as the world is undergoing globalization. Transnational social movements and governmental and nongovernmental organizations are increasing in number and significance, and they cross-cut traditional state borders. Conflicts can and do occur between entities that differ in the degree to which they have clear and impermeable boundaries. For example, al Qaeda at its height of strength consisted of a few thousand full members, from several different countries and scattered among a small number of countries; they were supported by more numerous people in many countries who supplied money and other resources. In addition, there were very many sympathizers in many regions who were influenced by al Qaeda and sometimes acted in solidarity with it. Al Qaeda remains in conflict with the United States, which includes people living, working, and voting within the territory of the United States of America; but it also includes military bases throughout the world, Americans working in multinational corporations, and people everywhere who appreciate and admire American entertainment, political ideas, technological innovations, and way of life.

Degree of Differentiation

Finally, adversaries vary in their degree of internal differentiation. That variation is important in accounting for the destructive or constructive course of a conflict. In highly differentiated parties, such as states, various persons or groups within them play specialized roles; the degree and character of the specialization for external relations are particularly significant in this regard. Some groups are essentially combat organizations and a large proportion of their members and resources are devoted to external conflicts. Other organizations have relatively few persons in roles specializing in conducting conflicts with adversaries. For example, compare national governments and city governments or compare ethnic separatist organizations and traditional religious denominational organizations.

The subgroups within an adversary that are assigned to conduct external conflict are likely to scan the environment searching for external enemies. The existence of external threats justifies their activities and the allocation of resources to them. They may exaggerate, even unwittingly, the threat from outside and garner prestige, dominance, and economic benefits for fending off an alleged enemy. Leaders of such groups or of countries may also use external threats to enhance group unity, to eviscerate internal opposition, or to distract members of their group from internally generated problems. For instance, the diversionary theory of war, popular in foreign policy analysis, cites numerous cases where leaders use a foreign enemy to divert public attention from domestic political crises that threaten that leader.[13]

Relations between Adversaries

The nature of the relationship between adversaries is another fundamental way of distinguishing among kinds of conflicts. Four variations in adversarial relations significantly affect the course of the conflict between them: (1) their shared past history, (2) the number of adversaries engaged in a struggle, (3) the degree to which the adversaries are integrated with each other, and (4) the degree of asymmetry between the adversaries.

Past History

Adversaries may share a history of being closely integrated or allied against a common enemy. On the other hand, they may have a history of past antagonistic relations, including one-sided oppression, bloody suppression, or genocidal attacks. Those past experiences and the memories of them influence the interpretation of current actions and future options. Past histories, however, are not permanent and unchanging. Past events are subject to new interpretations as ways of thinking change and as the groups with varying interpretations change their relations. This is notably the case in the years and decades after a civil war has ended.

Number

Commonly, the number of adversaries in a conflict is assumed to be two; indeed, some analysts argue that even if many conflict parties are engaged in a struggle, ultimately they form two sides. But the engagement of many parties in a conflict has significant consequences for the course of a struggle, often helping, sometimes hampering de-escalation and settlement.[14]

The adversaries may be two clearly bounded entities: persons, governments, or organizations. They also may be several independent parties, each seeking its own goals in a free-for-all fight. Typically, though, as the struggle goes on, many of the parties tend to coalesce into larger camps. Sometimes, conflicts are undertaken by two opposing sets of parties, each constituted as a coalition or alliance. If not at the outset, then as the conflict escalates in scope, other parties with links to those already engaged may join the fight.

In multiparty conflicts, even when two sides are formed, defections and shifts in allegiance often occur. Furthermore, each party in a conflict is engaged in conflicts with other adversaries, conflicts being intertwined over time and social space. Some of these conflicts are superimposed on each other, making the conflict more likely to destructively persist, while if the conflicting parties cross-cut each other, the destructiveness of any single conflict tends to be reduced. Therefore, increasing the salience of one conflict tends to reduce the salience of the interlocked others, which may help ease their de-escalation and settlement.

Integration

Integration refers to the degree of engagement and interdependence the parties normally have with each other. At one extreme, the parties may be so interdependent that neither could survive without the other; or in order for each to achieve what it wants, cooperation with the other is desirable or even necessary. Under these circumstances, conflicts are often about how to cooperate and work together. At the other extreme, the adversaries may be almost wholly independent of each other, each party normally functioning with little exchange or other kind of interaction with the other.

Generally, integration between adversaries helps constrain them from destructive escalation. They are inclined to avoid disrupting mutually beneficial relations and try to quickly settle disputes that emerge. Furthermore, they have more noncoercive inducements to employ to advance their interests in a nonprovocative manner. Thus, one of the main pillars of the so-called liberal peace thesis is that peace is more likely when states are tied together through common economic policies, which are overseen by established multilateral institutions. In such contexts, it is argued that states, particularly democratic ones, will be more likely to cooperate with other members of the international community and be less inclined to confrontation and destructive conflict with each other.[15]

Symmetry

The resources that adversaries have relative to each other vary from balanced or symmetrical to highly unequal or asymmetrical. Dominance refers to a high degree of asymmetrical interdependence. Thus, party B may be dependent on party A for goods or services that it needs while lacking alternative sources. Party A may be able to use coercion to deny alternative sources, as when management threatens to fire nonunionized workers for going on strike. A relationship of domination, then, depends on the alternatives available to each party, within the context of a particular social system.

Asymmetry comes in many forms.[16] One basis for asymmetry is a person's or group's ability to threaten or impose negative sanctions; these may include physical coercion and the denial of needed resources. Asymmetry also rests on the ability of one party to use positive sanctions to ensure compliance by the other party, creating dependency by the subordinate party. Asymmetry also arises by one side's control over interpretations of what is happening in a relationship between the dominating and dominated groups. This control may be carried out in the way ideas are expressed and communicated, as exemplified by totalitarian regimes.

When all of these forms of domination are combined, the dominant party (whether an ethnic group, ruling class, or political party) may be regarded as a hegemon.[17] Such asymmetry does not necessarily entail intentionality by the preeminent party. The inequality in resources and authority may be so great that both those dominating and those dominated accommodate to it with little self-awareness. Moreover, control is rarely total, even in the most hegemonic of organizations or societies. Some resistance is always possible and the dominating party may take that into account in the extent to which it imposes sanctions or takes advantage of its superior position. It may constrain itself from being overly exploitative, fearing a rise in resistance. Such was the case with many of the great colonial powers which often granted limited control to local leaders in order to better control potential opponents.

Power relations are generally regarded to have great relevance for analyzing social conflicts, but the notion of power has great conceptual ambiguity. The term *power* sometimes refers to a social system's capacity to accomplish an agreed-on task, but often it refers to the relationship between groups within a system in which one group directs the other.[18] Given the attention in this book to conflicts, the latter meaning is more pertinent. Power refers here to a person or group's ability to induce another party to act as the power wielder wishes, even (but not necessarily) against the resistance of those others. That ability may rest on actual or threatened negative sanctions (coercion). But it may also rest on the use of positive sanctions (the provision of benefits). Power may also rest on the sense of identity that the subordinates share with those exercising power, finding their persuasion convincing.[19]

Power wielders are obeyed in many social settings because they are regarded as having the right to give orders; authority is accorded them because of the office they hold and the way they came to occupy the office. In democratic organizations and societies, this reflects commitment to an electoral system. Legitimacy, however, is never unlimited and may be withdrawn by the followers when they believe the basis for it has been violated. Herein lies the great power of nonviolent resistance when masses of people stop according legitimacy to particular office holders.[20] Power is often conceived as implicit and latent in social relations. Its presence in various degrees then depends on theoretical assumptions, which are disputed. Given these many different understandings about power, in this work we will generally use more specific terms and ones that refer to relatively directly observable conduct. This is suitable here because of our focus on the way people act in manifest conflicts.

Asymmetry is multidimensional and subject to change in the course of a conflict.[21] Since it refers to the relationship between particular entities, if the parameters and capabilities of any one of the entities changes, asymmetry may be increased or reduced. Such changes of course are important for the way conflicts are transformed.

Contexts

Conflicts often are distinguished in terms of their context, as in references to family, community, nation, or world. As social systems, the characteristics of these larger contexts are related to the characteristics of the adversaries within these systems. Similarly, adversaries' relationships and their means of struggle are also shaped by the social systems in which they are embedded. Furthermore, social systems overlap each other and some small systems are nested in larger ones. Consequently, adversaries may contend with each other in many systems at the same time. In addition, there may be disagreement within an adversary group as to which system or systems encompass their conflict. For example, when Great Britain was at war against Germany from 1939 to 1945, some class, ethnic, and national liberation struggles within the United Kingdom or within the British Empire were put aside for the time; but some groups, for example, in India, saw this as an opportune time to increase their challenge, with support from the enemies of Great Britain.

As the earlier discussion about interdependency and asymmetry between two parties indicated, the degree of asymmetry depends on the extent to which the parties constitute a closed system. The kind of relations either adversary has with other parties, inside and outside of the system, provides alternatives that make one or another party believe it is strong or weak. The parties in a conflict frequently quarrel about what their relevant boundaries are. This is often evident in communal struggles. The Tamils in Sri Lanka may see themselves as a vulnerable minority relative to the Sinhalese, while the Sinhalese may feel threatened by the Tamils in Sri Lanka because of the many Tamils living in southern India.[22] The Catholics of Northern Ireland may see themselves as an oppressed minority dominated by the Protestants in Northern Ireland and the rest of the United Kingdom, while the Protestants may feel threatened as a minority within the island of Ireland encompassing Northern Ireland and the Republic of Ireland.[23]

Sometimes one of the adversaries views itself as representing the social system in which its adversary is a constituent part. Governments usually so regard themselves in conflicts with groups or organizations within the polity they claim to oversee and coordinate. Often, but not always, this claim is accepted by the adversary that regards itself as a part of the political order that is legitimately coordinated by the government. This often creates a dilemma for an ethnic minority in a society ruled by a dominant majority.

When parties do not agree about the nature of the system they constitute, the conflicts are particularly contentious and difficult to settle. Thus, a government claiming jurisdiction over the society as a whole may be attacked by one segment as being the agent of an opposing segment and not representative of the entire society. For example, trade union officials may charge that the city government is a tool of the firm they are striking against and that the police are aiding the firm's management.

Sometimes the contention is even more direct, as when a superordinate unit claims to represent all subordinate units, including one that challenges it.

For example, university administrators may argue that they represent the interests of all the components of the university community, but many students in the 1960s viewed them as serving the narrow interests of large business corporations.[24]

Adversaries are rarely alone in a fight. Usually, many parties have a stake in a given conflict and its course of development. They may become engaged in the conflict, sometimes to assist one or another opponent. They sometimes intervene to limit the conflict or to help resolve it. The norms they hold regarding appropriate means of struggle may influence the choices the antagonists make about how to wage their fight.

Means of Conflicting

Conflicts can also be distinguished by the means that the adversaries use to achieve their objectives. These range from mediation to negotiation to electoral politics to armed struggle to suicide bombing. More than one means can be used at the same time, and inevitably the mixture of means changes as the conflict dynamics change. Two dimensions of the means used in conflict are especially important here: the degree of regulation and the severity of enforcement. Regulation entails rules about how a conflict may be pursued and procedures for reaching decisions to settle a dispute. Such rules may be more or less institutionalized. Regulations are institutionalized insofar as they (1) have been internalized by the participants; (2) are expressed in tradition, formal writing, or some other embodiment external to the participants; and (3) are enforced by sanctions.[25] These rules may be quite effective in governing conflict conduct. They are effective insofar as the participants engaged in a conflict agree about the rules and believe the rules are legitimate enough that violating them would make the antagonists feel subject to condemnation. In addition, if the participants experience the rules as external to them, they are less free to interpret the rules as they would like. Finally, certainty of punishment if violations are committed also increases the likelihood of compliance.[26] Thus, organizations or systems that lack an overarching authority that is able to set the rules and police them are more prone to unruly conflict than those organizations or systems that have such an authority.

When disputes are highly institutionalized, they are often not even regarded as conflicts. For example, in long-established democratic societies, the issue of which political party will control the government for a coming term may be discussed using the metaphors of military campaigns, but they also are spoken of as sporting contests. On the whole, they are conducted according to generally accepted rules, and analysts and participants think of them as contests rather than as conflicts.

A major dimension of the level of severity of a conflict is the degree of injury suffered by those engaged in the conflict. The injuries may be equally shared, or, more likely, greater harm is endured by one of the parties than another. The injuries may result from violent or nonviolent coercion, such as firing guns, burning buildings, imposing economic sanctions, or excluding certain groups from political participation.

Sometimes the harm done in the course of a struggle is unintentional or even self-inflicted. Preparing for struggle, for example, exacts costs in resources ordinarily used for consumption or investment. The self-harm can also be more direct, as when military preparations result in accidental deaths or injuries. In waging the Cold War between the United States and the Soviet Union, for example, the development of nuclear weapons and their testing and production caused great environmental damage, resulting in extensive illness in the former Soviet Union and to a lesser degree in the United States.[27] Similarly, troops returning from military campaigns often suffer from psychological trauma and face great difficulty in reintegrating into society.

Severity of injury also includes harm done to those not engaged in the conflict. That may refer to noncombatants, such as the innocent civilians in a city suffering "collateral damage," and those who flee to avoid being killed. Such injuries result from military fighting, riots, and revolutionary struggles. Sometimes the harm done to noncombatants is intentional, meant to dry up support for the combatants, to drive people of the other side away, or to commit genocide. In recent violent conflicts, many more noncombatants than combatants have been killed.[28]

Another important dimension of severity is the degree of negative affect held by each side toward the other. Conflict parties vary in how strongly their members feel hostility and hatred toward their adversary, and how many of them have such feelings. Conflict parties also vary in their beliefs about their adversaries. Sometimes many of their members think that their opponents are inferior humans or not fully human, with destructive consequences, notably in the European Holocaust, the Rwandan genocide, and in the treatment of native peoples by European colonialists.

High negative affect often positively correlates with the manifestation of conflict behavior. However, there are reasons why the feelings and behavior may not coincide. On the one hand, feelings of hatred and resentment can be stifled when their expression might appear to be ineffective or counterproductive or when such behavior would be highly sanctioned by political authorities. On the other hand, great injury may be inflicted on an adversary without intense hostile feeling accompanying the violence. This is most likely when large collectivities are fighting, using complex technologies of violence with a high division of labor. Researchers studying the U.S. soldiers of World War

II concluded that even among combat infantrymen "hatred of the enemy, personal and impersonal, was not a major element in combat motivation."[29]

How antagonistically partisans feel and how hostilely they act vary greatly in struggles. Each varies somewhat independently of the other, as when soldiers use weapons that kill people they do not know or even see, explaining, "We are doing our job." But people's actions and feelings do affect each other, and people expect them to be associated, so that high levels of one justify high levels of the other. Moreover, they both are affected by similar conditions and so are likely to vary along similar trajectories.

This study focuses on relatively unregulated conflicts and on those that also entail great violence or the potentiality of becoming very destructive. Comparisons will also be made with relatively regulated conflicts to provide insights regarding the prevention and limitation of destructive conflicts.

The severity with which a conflict is waged is affected by the degree of regulation, but is not determined by it. The content of the rules governing conflict may allow for the use of various degrees of coercion, including violence. Severity also varies somewhat independently in relation to conflict regulation because there is more than one dimension of severity and they do not all vary in the same way. Generally, however, regulated conflicts tend to be less severe than unregulated ones.

Outcomes

Finally, some conflicts are chiefly characterized by their outcome. For example, part of the definition of a revolution is that it entails a fundamental change in social relations within a society, resulting from a popularly based struggle often using violence. How conflict outcomes are assessed varies considerably. In this analysis, three general qualities of outcomes are of particular interest.

First, one way to look at conflict outcomes is to assess winners and losers. For partisans in a fight, that is generally what matters: each side tries to defeat the adversary and gain what it sought. Yet many conflicts do not result in clear victories by one side over the other. Unfortunately, often both sides may lose a great deal; but in other cases, adversaries can discover constructive solutions that provide them both with much of what they sought.

Second, conflict outcomes differ in the degree to which adversaries become either more integrated or more separated. Some conflicts are waged with one side seeking greater separation from its adversary, for example, in wars of secession or wars of national liberation. Other conflicts are waged to gain more integration, for example, in the form of reduced segregation and free participation in governance. Even if not an intentional goal, the outcome may entail movement toward or away from increased integration.

The third relevant dimension of outcomes is the degree to which a settlement is sustainable. Intractable conflicts persist in destructiveness with only temporary easements and settlements. Some outcomes are imposed by one side and are experienced as a humiliation that must be revenged or as a harsh, costly burden that must be overthrown. Other outcomes are regarded as acceptable or perhaps beneficial to the principal adversaries, although in varying degrees. Sustainable conflict outcomes have been particularly challenging when it comes to civil wars. For instance, between 1989 and 2005, 40 percent of civil wars that ended in peace agreements saw a return to violence within five years.[30]

COMBINATIONS CONSTITUTING DESTRUCTIVENESS AND CONSTRUCTIVENESS

It is the combination of characteristics reviewed above that determines the extent to which a conflict becomes a highly destructive or a highly constructive struggle.[31] Conflicts are waged destructively insofar as the means of fighting result in severe damage and many participants suffer great harm. The harm may result from various forms of coercion and violence and also from expressions of hostility based on values and beliefs about the enemy. Furthermore, destructiveness increases as the scale of the conflict expands, with increased numbers of adversaries participating. In addition, destructiveness is greater insofar as the issues at stake involve threats to the very survival of the members of one or more of the adversary groups, or of the groups as collective entities. Finally, destructive conflicts tend to have characteristics that contribute to the perpetuation of the struggle. These components of destructiveness tend to co-vary together. The destructiveness may be asymmetrical, with one side waging a destructive campaign and the other suffering immense injury. This is especially true of genocidal attacks against a whole people.[32]

The constructive waging of a struggle is not simply the absence of destructive elements. Constructive conflicts are often pursued using persuasive efforts and promises of benefits, rather than relying wholly or largely on coercive threats or actions. The adversaries recognize each other as legitimate entities and do not threaten the other's existence. They interact to solve the problem they face together—their conflict—by seeking how best to construct a mutually acceptable outcome. Such problem-solving approaches may be taken by each side's representatives or by significant groups within each side in the struggle. Again, these qualities may characterize the conduct of members of one side more than another.

The outcome of conflicts are affected, but not determined, by the way they were fought. After a fight is ended, the adversaries may think and act in ways that shape the outcomes to be relatively constructive or destructive. Conflict outcomes tend to be destructive insofar as one side imposes them unilaterally, with little or no regard to the interests and needs of most members of the other side. The defeated party then regards the outcome as oppressive and requiring redress, and/or as humiliating and requiring revenge. The interpretations of the interests and needs of the imposed-upon party, however, are not always those of its proclaimed leaders, particularly if the leaders lack legitimacy. Unless a fundamental transformation of one or more of the adversaries occurs, imposed outcomes tend to be the basis for a renewed and destructive struggle. Sometimes, the imposition can lead to a transformation of the conflict when a defeated party changes its self-conception. The victor can help in that regard by honoring such changes and assisting them.

Conflict outcomes are constructive insofar as the parties regard them as mutually acceptable. Moreover, they are constructive insofar as they provide a basis for an ongoing relationship within which future conflicts are limited and tend to be waged constructively. Such outcomes may require an extended period of time, particularly after a bitter and destructive struggle.

Struggles generally consist of a sequence of conflict modes, with varying degrees of constructiveness and destructiveness. For example, a relatively constructively waged struggle may precede a constructive outcome; in many ways, this fits the struggle to end legal segregation in the U.S. South in the 1950s and 1960s and the struggle for Catalan autonomy in Spain after 1975. And a destructively waged struggle may result in a prolongation of destructiveness and finally result in a destructive outcome; in many ways, the struggle for Tamil separatism in Sri Lanka is illustrative. However, many other sequences also occur, including when a struggle is waged destructively at times and by some parties yet ultimately yield a relatively constructive outcome. In at least some regards, this fits the East-West Cold War, the struggle for Indian independence from Great Britain, and the struggle against apartheid in South Africa. Obviously, the terms "constructive" and "destructive" usually refer to extremely complex matters that cannot be captured wholly in one word. Furthermore, as long as the adversary parties survive, no outcome is final. Outcomes can take on new meanings decades or even centuries af.er they have formally ended.

The strategies that partisans and interveners might pursue that can foster constructive waging of conflicts cannot be the same for all conflicts since they vary in so many important ways. In the following chapters we will discuss what various actors have done in particular conflicts that have contributed to a more constructive, or destructive, conflict trajectory. We will also note some empirically grounded generalizations about the effects of some kinds of strategies, implemented by various kinds of actors, upon specific kinds of conflicts.

2

Bases of Social Conflicts

In this chapter, we examine various theoretical approaches to the bases of social conflicts, which underlie the emergence of manifest conflicts. These approaches are elucidated and debated among academic analysts; they also may be inferred from the statements and actions of political leaders and citizens at large. Political leaders and citizens need not and usually do not consciously locate their statements and actions in a comprehensive theory about the bases of conflicts in general. Nevertheless, they use concepts, make assumptions, and draw upon pieces of empirical evidence that together function as a theoretical explanation when they formulate pronouncements and policies.

Thus, U.S. presidents George W. Bush and Barack Obama differ in many of their statements and policies regarding U.S. engagement in foreign conflicts, thereby indicating different theoretical ideas. For example, in countering al Qaeda, the perpetrators of the 9/11 attacks on America, Bush more often referred to the perpetrators' hatred of American freedom and the evilness of their actions; he concluded that "the only way to defeat terrorism as a threat to our way of life is to stop it, eliminate it, and destroy it where it grows."[1] He called for the world to join the fight, asserting that those who were not with the United States were with the terrorists. Taking office seven years later, with wars in Afghanistan and Iraq bloodily underway, Obama seemed to view the enemies as less unitary than Bush viewed them and regarded some of them and their supporters to be susceptible to being won over by blandishments rather than by threats and intimidation. Despite differences, there are also similarities in the general approach they took to external threats. These include shared conventional understandings of what American values and interests are and a shared assessment of the institutional capabilities, responsibilities, constraints, and influences embodied in the military forces and intelligence agencies.

As this example illustrates, interpretations of the bases of social conflicts are almost always contested. Every individual, whether a policy maker, a grassroots organizer, or a conflict analyst has experiences and expectations that influence his or her interpretations of the conflict. These interpretations are usually shaped by an implicit theory. The theory may be unrecognized and inconsistent, but making it more explicit and coherent tends to improve the understanding of partisans and observers alike. Considering alternative theoretical explanations and determining which alternatives best fit the experience and the evidence is one of the most important tasks of constructive conflict management. While we cannot prove any explanation to be true, it is possible to prove some assertions false. Refuting some explanations strengthens our confidence in the explanations that remain consistent with our information. Throughout this book, alternative ideas will be considered in this light.

The partisans in conflicts offer explanations for their own conduct and for that of their enemies. The explanations they use are important in mobilizing support, in deciding which means will be effective, and ultimately in agreeing to settle the conflict. Therefore, those explanations cannot be ignored. But neither can they always be accepted as the full truth.

Would-be intermediaries, academic analysts, and other observers try to discover which conditions generate the partisans' belief that they are in conflict. Knowing these conditions would help predict the outbreak and course of a conflict and would help mitigate its destructiveness and attain a more just resolution.

Yet, how can we possibly know which conditions truly underlie a conflict without reference to the attitudes and injuries nurtured by people engaged in the conflict? Or if the conflict is not yet manifest, how can one know what conditions are simmering unseen below the surface? Such judgments often depend on having a general theory about the sources of conflicts and the conditions that turn potential conflicts into active ones.

Desirable as it may be, however, there is no one unifying theory that explains the phenomena of social conflicts as they occur across different levels of society, across different issue domains, or across different stages of development. Social conflicts are so complex and dynamic that theorists cannot unequivocally explain why one fight erupts and another lies dormant, how one escalates and another subsides. We can never have enough detailed information about a specific conflict to predict precisely whether, when, or how it will become transformed. As a result, theoretical propositions relating to social conflicts are more often expressed in terms of tendencies and probabilities. We can say with some certainty that political regimes that inhibit political freedoms and exclude minority groups from participating in governance tend to be "conflict-prone," but we have a harder time explaining why some of these societies spiral into civil war while others long remain relatively stable.

Moreover, theorizing about conflicts should be distinguished from acting in them. Theory generalizes about a set of conflicts and what they have in common. Action, however, is carried out in a specific fight, which always has unique qualities. This distinction is familiar to physicians who distinguish between knowing the general processes of physiology and pharmacology and knowing the background and circumstances of an individual patient. Good clinical practice utilizes both kinds of knowledge and does not rely on one alone.

These observations provide the context for reviewing different theoretical claims about the bases of social conflicts. Among the innumerable theories about the bases of conflicts, many stress conditions and processes that exist independently of the adversaries' subjective awareness. These are constructs of the theoretician. Other theories emphasize the subjective processes of actual and potential conflict adversaries. For this analysis, we will assume neither a "subjectivist" nor an "objectivist" view of truth but instead proceed from the premise that, as Putnam claims, the mind both "makes up" and "copies" the world.[2] Our minds interact with the world in complex ways. We cannot know objects in the world directly; rather, we use our senses, augmented by many kinds of instruments to perceive them. Furthermore, objects have dispositions or tendencies rather than fixed qualities. That is, our perception of objects or situations depends on their context, the conditions in which they function. This is obvious in the case of an object's color. For example, an object that appears red can be seen as differently colored depending on the light cast on it; furthermore, different objects that appear red may do so for quite different reasons.

Major social-scientific approaches differ in their emphasis upon factors internal to each potential adversary, factors relating to the system of which the potential antagonists are a part, and factors pertaining to the relationship between the possible adversaries. Each of these factors focuses on different aspects of the conflict environment. Internal approaches consider how characteristics of individuals, groups, or societies make them more or less conflict prone. Systemic approaches seek to understand how environmental constraints and structural norms, rules, and institutions create conditions more or less conducive to the outbreak of conflicts. Relational approaches focus on how the type and quality of interactions between adversaries creates conditions that are ripe for the emergence or dissipation of conflicts. Each of these approaches is reviewed in detail below. However, what is internal to an adversary, what system is encompassing the antagonists, and what the relationship between the antagonists is depends on the way that we frame the conflict. For example, if the United States as a country is viewed as a conflict party, then its domestic social structure is an internal quality. But if the conflict is between groups within the country struggling for greater social equality for African Americans and groups resisting that effort, the U.S. social structure is part of the context for their relations.

INTERNAL FACTORS

Many theoretical approaches stress internal features of potential adversaries as the source of their conflict. Of course, these are not the explanations usually proclaimed by the adversaries about themselves, but they often do attribute the cause of the conflict to the other side's internal characteristics.[3] Some theoretical approaches also point to conflict-generating features of specific individuals, groups, or societies, but many emphasize characteristics shared by all persons, groups, or societies.

Since social conflicts are ubiquitous, it might seem reasonable to look for the underlying bases of conflicts in universal characteristics of humans or their societies. This view may be seen in certain theories about human nature, theories about widely shared social psychological responses, and theories about particular features of social groups.

Human Nature

Popular thought frequently attributes conflicts among humans to "human nature," suggesting our helplessness in stopping or controlling these antagonisms. If human nature is understood to mean what is intrinsic to humans, independent of their socialization, it is unknowable. Humans cannot survive without being nurtured and socialized in social environments, which vary immensely.

Nevertheless, the search for underlying human nature persists, taking three major paths. One is the biological and evolutionary way, including the study of other animals, particularly those that are genetically close to humans. Another path is to research psychological and social psychological processes, ideally in a wide variety of societies. The third path is to study many different human societies, seeking to winnow out the commonalities among them.

Focusing on the biological nature of humans has recurrent attractiveness. Some of this work selects specific patterns of behavior found in several animal species, regards them as instinctive, and then attributes apparent similarities among humans to such instincts. For example, territoriality is to be found in a variety of animal species, and thus a "territorial imperative" may be attributed to humans.[4] But this ignores the absence of territoriality in many species and, even among those exhibiting it, research reveals that its occurrence depends on specific ecological conditions.[5] Furthermore, humans' sense of land is symbolically understood and socially constructed; once we understand that, the usefulness of positing a biological instinct of territoriality is undermined. Finally, it is important to remember that territory is an issue in many conflicts, including gang "turf" battles, jurisdictional disputes between government officials and citizens in religious communities, as well as border wars between sovereign states. Space, like power, can be conceived and used in many ways and permeates most relationships; consequently, a variety of issues may be socially framed as territorial.

Some research about sociobiological factors affecting social behavior restricts itself to phenomena within similar social organizational domains, for example, face-to-face groups. Comparisons among species should also take into account the degree of genetic similarity with humans. For example, research on status ranking in small, established groups among many primate species found ranking in all the groups.[6] This is expressed by overt threats and physical attacks among the species most distant from humans. However, among humans and our genetically closest primates, expressions of deference are exhibited subtly, and the dominant animals quietly perform control and service functions. This can be interpreted as indicating that humans establish dominant relationships not purely by threats and physical violence but by contributions to the group, for which they receive deference.

In addition to seeking human nature in biological and evolutionary evidence, studies of human psychology and social psychology may indicate fundamental human processes. The studies would have to demonstrate universality among humans, at least within specified social conditions. Although we lack such systematic demonstrations, some analysts have proposed several processes as universal, under certain conditions. Many developmental psychologists, for instance, claim that human beings are innately a pattern-recognition species and that the ability to distinguish among objects, sounds, and experiences extends to the social realm where human beings categorize people by defining who is "like me" (in-group) and who is "not like me" (out-group). This tendency to differentiate among people, coupled with the need to view the in-group in a positive light, is further postulated to lead to in-group favoritism and out-group bias as individuals denigrate the motivations and capabilities of outside groups in order to elevate the perceived merits of their own.[7]

Other psychological theories link unconscious emotions and contradictions to conflict behavior, as discussed by Sigmund Freud and others working in the psychoanalytic tradition. Thus, a person may have impulses or thoughts that are unacceptable and these may then be projected onto other persons or groups. For example, some people may resolve their feelings of guilt about being ambivalent toward their parents by idealizing authority figures and directing their hostile feelings toward out-groups.[8] This is the basis for the large body of research about the authoritarian personality.

More generally, in human societies infantile, primitive drives need to be controlled. This occurs through the internalization of a superego and the functioning of a strong ego. The emotion or affect that arises from frustrations of those primitive drives may be displaced onto a wide variety of objects, especially when the ego is inadequately functioning. For example, there is evidence that prejudice and animosity against members of a minority group are exacerbated by such displacement; this can become scapegoating.[9] This human capability of displacement, however, does not mean that it always occurs; people vary greatly in exhibiting this pattern, and social conditions largely determine its appearance and target.

Another widely held assumption about human nature is that individuals have a set of basic human needs, and if those are not satisfied, people will strive to fulfill them. For example, the U.S. Declaration of Independence, adopted on July 4, 1776, asserts "that all men are created equal, that they are endowed by their Creator with certain unalienable rights, that among these are life, liberty, and the pursuit of happiness." The denial of these rights would bring about a struggle to gain them.

Among contemporary writers, John Burton particularly emphasizes the necessity to satisfy basic human needs if a conflict is to be resolved.[10] He posits eight needs in the individual: a need for response, a need for security, a need for recognition, a need for stimulation, a need for distributive justice, a need for meaning, a need for rationality (and to be seen as rational), and a need for control.

The idea that there exist basic human needs or rights generally appears to rest on the belief that these are ordained by God or are inherent in human nature. To claim that they exist in particular manifestations and ranking and are independent of culture and social conditions subjects the assertions to the same criticisms as those leveled against assuming that there are human instincts or drives for aggression. In this analysis, human needs and rights will be regarded as dispositions, varying in intensity, preciseness, and independence from social conditions. For example, the human need to live in personal physical security, without threat of physical harm, is widely shared and less subject to cultural variations and interpretations than is the need to freely and openly express thoughts and feelings.

Anthropological and historical evidence reveals widespread violence perpetrated by humans against each other. But clearly, violence is not always present in all social relations, while cooperation also is universally exhibited among humans—within families and within larger social groups. Certainly, societies vary greatly in the levels of violence among their members and against nonmembers. Instances of homicides in major cities, for instance, not only vary significantly from year to year but also from city to city.

In 1989, a distinguished international group of geneticists, anthropologists, psychologists, biochemists, and other researchers summarized the state of scientific knowledge about the bases of violence and war in the Seville Statement. The statement was endorsed by the UN Educational, Scientific, and Cultural Organization (UNESCO) and was subsequently endorsed by many scientific and professional associations. The statement concludes that "it is not scientifically correct to say that war or any other violent behavior is genetically programmed into our human nature," or "that in the course of human evolution there has been a selection for aggressive behavior more than for other kinds of behavior."[11]

Social Psychological Responses

Various social psychological processes among the members of potential adversary parties may contribute to the emergence of destructive conflicts. Consider the idea that when people feel frustrated they will act aggressively, trying to harm those who are frustrating them.[12] If frustration always resulted in aggression and aggression was always caused by frustration, we would have a fundamental premise for a theory of conflicts. It is not, however, so simple.

Research on frustration and aggression makes it clear that the feeling of frustration depends on the intentions of those who might regard themselves as blocked, but their intentions often are not evident to the outside analyst. Research also indicates that the manifestation of aggression depends on the availability of a target that seems appropriate. Frustration may result in hostile behavior against a primary source of the blockage, but the attack may be directed elsewhere; that is, it may be displaced against a vulnerable scapegoat. The frustration may even be turned inward to self-blame. Consequently, while there may be a relationship between frustration and aggression, just how frustration is experienced and aggression is manifested depends on a great many social conditions that need to be specified.

In addition to processes relating to human emotions, cognitive processes play important roles in the emergence and course of conflicts. Thus, people tend to exaggerate the differences between themselves (however that is defined) and others. This occurs through several processes, including categorization, the tendency to simplify social reality and to impose dichotomies on continuous dimensions, and assimilation, the tendency to fit new information into prior understandings.[13] Furthermore, members of a group tend to evaluate their own attributes more positively than those of the other group, even when the attributes are the same. Thus, behavior viewed as steadfast or principled by one side is regarded as pigheaded or stiff-necked when exhibited by the adversary.[14]

In addition to such specific theories or hypotheses about sources of conflicts, a large body of evidence indicates that socialization may make persons and groups prone to conflict. Socialization occurs primarily through an infant's and a child's experience with parents, but also with siblings and other kin, with peers, and with institutions such as schools, churches, and the mass media. Depending on the nature of past experience and the current social context, the socialization processes have conflict-relevant effects.

Considerable research supports the idea that harsh socialization of the young produces aggressive adults who are prone to engage in overt conflict.[15] Harsh socialization includes severe physical punishment and also emotional deprivation. The connection between such experiences and later tendencies for aggression and violence may be explained by learning theory, encompassing imitation, modeling, and reinforcement. The processes previously noted, such as projection of unwanted feelings and frustration-generated aggression, may also explain it.

Research also supports the generalization that males in many societies tend to be conflict and violence prone. Differences between men and women in these regards result from socially constructed combinations of inborn, socialization, and situational factors as discussed in chapter 5. We only note here that they may occur in some societies as a result of confused male identity.[16] This pattern can happen when males grow up in a male-dominated society with fathers who are distant and therefore develop very strong bonds with their mothers, which they must break to meet expectations of proper male behavior. To sever those ties may be frustrating, and furthermore the way to do so may require behavior that is regarded as "masculine": tough, strong, and prideful.

The patterns of interaction that tend to generate hostility, aggression, and overt conflict do not fully account for even the internal factors that underlie social conflicts. Everyone also feels empathy, love, and solidarity with some other people and views them as friends, allies, and partners.[17] These feelings and views may counter or constrain the workings of the mechanisms generating conflict.

There is evidence that children whose rearing had been warm, affectionate, and loving are well prepared for cooperative relations later in life.[18] Open expression of affection toward children and close father-child relations foster the development of skills that are needed to nonviolently resolve conflicts.

Group Features and Processes

A society, an organization, or a family may have characteristics that impel its members to act in ways that generate and escalate conflicts with other social units. These characteristics include conditions that foster emotions and cognitions driving members of social groups to engage in external aggression. The characteristics include cultural values and norms that foster antagonistic behavior toward members of other social systems, and they also include social structures that engender external conflict.

Significant proportions of the members of those social systems must experience such psychological and social psychological processes similarly if they are to be relevant for the conduct of a social system. For example, a society undergoing disorienting rapid change or a deterioration of living standards tends to produce feelings of frustration in many society members.[19] The feelings of frustration may be expressed in great animosity against a vulnerable external social target, or a segment of the society who are redefined as nonmembers. This process helps account for the rise of Nazism in Germany, as high inflation and the worldwide depression worsened socioeconomic conditions and reduced many people's status and living conditions. But such channeling is not inevitable; it depends on the repertoire of possible responses and the alternatives presented by leaders. After all, the economic depression of the 1930s did not result in a fascist regime in the United States or in most other countries.

Some observers argue that the patterns of child rearing and other experiences of socialization when shared by society members tend to produce an enduring national character, which may include traits of aggressiveness.[20] For example, during World War II some U.S. and British analysts reasoned that the German national character was authoritarian. Germans were obedient to those above and arrogant to those below. After the war, however, the profoundly changed German policies and relations with the United States and allied governments contributed to the rejection of such attributions of an unchanging German national character.

A culture is never uniform and never unchanging.[21] Regional, class, organizational, gender, and other subcultures always exist, and every person has a unique variation. As circumstances change, so does the culture. All this should be kept in mind, even when it is not reiterated every time we discuss Americans, Arabs, South Africans, or Muslims.

The values and norms incorporated by people growing up with a given culture may promote external conflict or they may restrain it. Feminist analysts, for example, point out that most societies are patriarchal in values and structure.[22] They are dominated by men who are socialized to value competitiveness, dominance, honor, and toughness. The Spanish term *macho* is widely used to refer to this particular sense of masculinity, which stresses bravery and sensitivity to challenges of honor.

Finally, and most notably for large-scale conflicts, groups, organizations, and societies are differentiated, with members playing specialized roles, which often include defense of the systems' members from external attack. The status and resources of the incumbents of those roles depend in good part on the size of the threat and their success in countering it. Consequently, they have an interest in proclaiming a great external threat and perhaps even in provoking it to enhance their status and control over resources.

This reasoning underlies the warnings about the dangers of the military-industrial complex, as expressed by President Dwight D. Eisenhower in his 1961 farewell address.[23] There is much literature on the way the military establishments, defense industries, political leaders, and other groups on antagonistic sides advanced their interests by helping to sustain and even intensify military threats and engagements.[24]

In many ethnic and other intercommunal conflicts, persons seeking political or other forms of resource control try to mobilize support by claiming to be fighting to overcome past humiliations, to defend against enemy threats, and to reclaim past glories.[25] Slobodan Milosevic, for example, aroused and inflamed Serbian nationalist sentiments, which contributed greatly to the destructive violence that consumed so much of the former Yugoslavia. In international relations, state leaders are more likely to undertake military interventions in other countries when there is domestic unrest than when there is not, and such diversionary interventions occur by democratic as well as by autocratic regimes.

Implications

Conflicts can arise primarily as a result of one party's internally driven actions, often contributing to the outbreak of conflicts and their exacerbation. In these cases an individual or group, frustrated by internal social psychological forces, may simply seek out an external target for their frustration. Observers have regarded these conflicts as "unrealistic" in origins, if not in manifestation, as they are triggered by the need to release tension rather than by a desire to achieve a concrete demand.[26] Of course, the resulting manifest conflict will seem realistic when demands for resources or compliance are made upon another entity.

The role of internal factors in forming the basis for a conflict is greatly affected by the system context of the conflict and by the relations among the potential adversaries. The internal factors may provide some of the motive for antagonistic behavior, and at the same time other factors help channel that behavior. Furthermore, even leaders whose antagonism is largely internally driven must offer justifications that resonate and appear plausible to their supporters. Many other internal factors and processes, however, foster significant cooperation with people who might be regarded as adversaries. The outcome of those contrary social and psychological forces depends on the social context and the relations between possible adversaries.

SYSTEM CONTEXT

Many theories about wars, revolutions, and even fights between husbands and wives stress the importance of the social system within which the potential antagonists function. Among the many features of the system context, theoretical approaches varyingly emphasize the significance of its culture and institutions, the degree to which the system is characterized by scarcity of resources, the distribution of capacities, access to power among the system members, and the consistency and stability of the system.

Shared Culture and Institutions

Everything else being equal, insofar as members of different groups or societies share values and norms, they tend not to fight with each other.[27] Cultural variation in the degree to which direct confrontations are regarded as acceptable and in the rules for their expression and management also greatly affects the likelihood of an underlying conflict forming and erupting. Among some peoples or among particular segments of societies, the acknowledgment of particular kinds of conflicts may be considered improper. For example, in many cultures women are socialized to believe that they should subordinate their interests to those of their husbands and hence do not recognize many issues that in other cultures might be matters of contention.

Within countries, specialized legal institutions are the major instrument for managing conflicts. Insofar as society members regard these institutions as legitimate, matters that might otherwise become the subject of violent conflict are regarded as games or competitions, but not conflicts.[28] The paucity of legitimate international conflict management institutions with a capacity to set international rules and enforce them contributes to the widespread existence of latent international conflicts and their potential violent escalation.

Scarcity

Underlying conflicts tend to exist where potential adversaries are likely to come to view themselves as being in a zero-sum relationship, that is, situations where gains or losses are perceived by one side to be directly proportional to the losses and gains of the other. Zero-sum conflicts are most likely to appear in a social system where the resources its members seek are scarce and the system is small and closed. When the system includes many parties in addition to the possible adversaries and when system members interact readily with nonmembers, much of what the adversaries want may be obtained from others within the system or from people outside, and disputes do not erupt. Consider even a desired resource such as the income of two groups, one of which is employed by the other. The two sides would be in a zero-sum relationship if they constituted the entire system. But if they are producing a product for sale to customers, they might cooperate to pass on costs to the customer or produce a more attractive product and win additional customers, thus increasing the amount of income they have to distribute between themselves. Income also may be regarded as a symbol of relative status, and not simply as an amount of money needed to purchase goods. In that case, income relative to some other group's income is what is significant. If potential adversaries compare their incomes to each other and to no one else, they are in a zero-sum situation; the more one has relative to the other, the less the other has. But other conclusions are imaginable if other groups are used as the standard of reference.

Scarcity also has, of course, a material basis, as in the availability of clean water, arable land, petroleum, and many other resources. Competition for such resources is an important basis for interethnic as well as interstate conflicts. The failure to manage environmental challenges and fighting about them can lead to the collapse of the entire societal system, as evidently happened in the Easter Islands and as some conflict theorists maintain is happening today in many so-called failed states.[29]

Distribution of Domination Capacities

Rather than discuss relative power, given the noted ambiguities of that term, we will discuss the resources that each party has that can be used to affect the conduct of a specific other party or of the relative power of each party in the entire system to which they belong. Naturally, where one powerful actor dominates, weak potential adversaries tend not to become contentious. Evidence for this may be seen in the stability and absence of overt conflict among states in a region dominated by a great power, such as the former Soviet Union. Within the Soviet Union itself, when the central government's authority receded, many ethnic conflicts among different nationalities emerged. In a system where many actors have relatively equal capacities, conflicts are more likely to occur, since potential adversaries see possibilities of advancing their position; in trying to do so, overt conflicts erupt. These generalizations should be understood as tendencies that hold, everything else being equal.

Great inequality in control of resources or access to political power, insofar as it is regarded as illegitimate, tends to become a grievance. But the readiness of the subordinated groups to withdraw legitimacy from the power holders is affected by more than the degree of imbalance. The limited resources that the subordinated group can apply to fend off pressures by the dominators, to participate in collective decision making, and to legitimately replace the dominant power holders all contribute to members of the subordinate group granting legitimacy to the dominators.

Consistency and Stability

The various elements of a social system are never wholly consistent and stable. Inconsistencies are often found among the values that are shared by people in a social system, and these inconsistencies often lead to conflicts. For example, in 1944 Gunnar Myrdal concluded from a comprehensive study of the conditions of American Negroes that the United States faced a profound dilemma.[30] He found a widely and deeply held U.S. creed upholding the ideals of equality of opportunity and the rights of freedom and justice, but that blacks were denied elemental civil and political rights and a fair opportunity to make a living. This discrepancy constituted an unsustainable contradiction for whites as well as for blacks, as became manifest in the civil rights struggle a decade later.

Rapid change of any social system places strains on its members. Change never occurs at the same rate for all components of a system; consequently, some components inevitably lag behind others. Traditional attitudes may not keep up with new circumstances, or various segments of the system may develop differences in interests and values, which create new potential conflicts. This is true in communities where swift changes in population due to the entry of people from another part of the metropolitan area, country, or region of the world generate the basis for conflicts.[31] Some analysts regard social change that moves a society out of equilibrium as a condition leading to revolution.[32] For such reasons, societal transition from authoritarian rule to a democratic political order is often accompanied by intensified conflicts and violence, as became evident in North Africa and the Middle East in 2010–2011. The rise in fundamentalism within major religious traditions, including Christianity, Islam, Judaism, and Hinduism, is the basis for new cleavages within many countries. It also is the basis for transnational identities and organizations that are the basis for regional and global divisions. Those cleavages and divisions are the bases for many potential conflicts.

Finally, abrupt political, economic, or ideological changes in one part of the global system contribute to conditions that help generate large-scale conflicts. For example, a revolutionary regime generally alters the surrounding international system as it tries to create social and political space for itself. The probability of conflicts increases as other regimes see threats in the new situation or opportunities to settle old scores. The collapse of a large social system is another kind of abrupt change that generates grounds for numerous new conflicts, as occurred in Eastern Europe and the former Soviet Union in 1989–1992.

Implications

Systemic conditions likely to foster conflicts are more likely to be noted by outside analysts than by the adversaries themselves. Although its members shape many features of their social system, that process is not fully recognized by all members. Insofar as systemic factors strongly affect the bases of conflicts, controlling or preventing an emerging conflict may not be within the capability of any one of the potential adversaries.

RELATIONS BETWEEN ADVERSARIES

The third set of factors that generate underlying conflicts comprises the past and current relations between possible adversaries. The adversaries themselves frequently cite these factors, each side attributing the conflict to the other side's actions. Analysts frequently point to the relations between the adversaries as the crucial source of their conflict. However, in considering potential adversaries as a component of conflict bases, we should note their problematic quality.

Which set of actors will become adversaries is not easy to predict. People divide and define themselves and each other in infinite ways. Almost any division of people into two or more sets can be the basis for collective identity and be organized into contending groups.[33] Some divisions are well established, antedating the emergence of a particular conflict. They may have been formed in the course of a long-past fight. Or they may have arisen in another context, as is the case for organizations such as churches, trade unions, and governments. Such organizations have leaders who generally have authority to commit the organization or an even wider constituency to act in opposition to other organizations.

People also divide themselves into less clearly bounded and articulated groupings. These distinctions involve collective self-definitions and also efforts by some people to define and separate themselves from others. Such distinctions exist throughout the world, based on characteristics such as lifestyles, location in the labor market, religion, ethnicity, language, gender, age, and ideology.

Potential adversaries also may arise from analytically conceived categories. That is, a theorist constructs analytic distinctions that delimit quasi groups. These may become the recruiting grounds from which social groups are mobilized. For example, Ralf Dahrendorf argues that within hierarchically coordinated systems such as industrial corporations, there is a dividing line between those with authority and those without; the two categories are quasi groups from which, under certain conditions, social groups form and engage in conflict.[34]

Many aspects of the relations between potential adversaries may be the source of conflicts, and various theoretical approaches stress different aspects. Three important dimensions of the potentially adversarial relationship are discussed here: inequalities in class, status, and power; differences in values and beliefs; and differences in integration.

Inequalities in Class, Status, and Power

For many conflict analysts the unequal distribution of power, status, or access to goods and services or whatever else possible adversaries consider desirable is widely regarded as one of the primary bases of social conflicts of all kinds. Economic inequalities have been emphasized not only by Marxists, but also by critics of Marxism.[35] Marxists generally have stressed the preeminence of class differences in social conflicts, defining class in terms of the ownership of the means of production. The owners are the capitalists who expropriate the product of the labor of those they employ. Max Weber, writing in the early part of the twentieth century, emphasized other forms of market inequalities and also power and status inequalities.

Presumably, every person or group wants more of what it regards as good, and this desire brings it into competition and conflict with other persons or groups. Inequality may also generate conflicts when those with more believe they have a claim to even more, and in addition, they have the resources to try to get it. The idea that inequality universally produces conflict rests on assumptions about human nature. It may be assumed that people are not so pliable at birth that they can be socialized to accept their inferior power, status, or economic condition as proper and legitimate. Another assumption may be that people want more than others because of an innate competitive tendency; to have more confers status and power. They desire to have more relative to others regardless of any intrinsic worth of the items.

A conflict arises when people agree about what is desirable and then have different amounts of what they desire. This is a consensually based source of conflict.[36] What people want, how they are to obtain what is desired, and what claims they make for what is desired depend on social conditions. People must share a cultural upbringing or experience to agree about what is desirable to have or to be.

Consensus about what is desirable, however, may be the basis for cooperation as well as conflict. When two actors want the same thing and each can attain it only insofar as the other does, they have reason to cooperate. This may occur because they empathize with each other or they share an important common identity. Two parties may also have reason to cooperate because what they want can only be achieved by collaboration. Thus, they each may control part of what is needed to do the desired task. For example, governments controlling opposite banks of a river that might be used to supply irrigation or hydroelectric power need to cooperate to realize such projects.

Differences in Values and Beliefs

Dissensus, the lack of consensus about what is desirable, is another basis for conflict. This occurs when one party insists that the other agree with its preferences or believes that the other party threatens its way of life. Such dissensual conflicts arise from differences among religions, cultures, worldviews, values, and lifestyles. The idea that such phenomena are the bases for conflicts is consistent with the work of many contemporary analysts who emphasize that reality is socially constructed. That is, people use language and other symbolic systems to define and give meaning to their experience.[37] They do this by interacting with each other, and their resultant beliefs then become the reality to which all relate. Furthermore, these beliefs are transmitted across generations and through social space, giving them an even stronger appearance of external reality.

The people in the world, in each society or in any social system, however, are not homogeneous in their values and beliefs. Having varying perspectives or backgrounds engenders different visions of reality and of right. Such differences can also have profound effects on how stakeholders define a problem and what options seem viable at any point in time. One source of such diversity is the varying experiences that different generational cohorts have in their formative years.[38] For example, persons who come to political maturity while their country is suffering a severe depression or a major war develop enduring orientations from that historical experience, setting off their generation from others. They develop a common set of concerns, beliefs, values, and sometimes even identities. These ways of thinking, however, are not universal; within the same age cohort, subgroups in diverse circumstances may form differing interpretations of the same events. In any case, these intergenerational differences in collective mentalities are a frequent source of authority-challenging youth movements and other dissensual conflicts.

Differences among people in their views of themselves and of the social world they live in are the source of conflict only if certain other beliefs are also held. Thus, if members of a group are indifferent to the religious convictions of another group or think the convictions are simply harmless, no conflict will arise. If, however, one or more sets of people feel that the other's religious views are morally outrageous, then an underlying conflict exists. The outraged persons are likely to want to change the views and/or behavior of those holding such improper convictions. Or suppose that a group of people is so convinced of the virtue and validity of its views that it considers it urgent that others accept its views and learn the truth and so gain salvation. Certainly, political and religious revolutionary movements, on gaining control in one country, have often set out to proselytize and spread the good news to peoples in other countries. This has been true of advocates, for example, of the Russian, Cuban, and Iranian revolutions. Ideological proselytizing often is mixed with advancing economic interests and political domination of a powerful state, as appears to be the case in programs to spread American democracy in the Middle East and elsewhere in the world.[39]

Even internally, some groups trying to restore and others seeking to overthrow traditional ways of thinking and behaving may gain control of the state and then face resistance that unleashes severe conflicts, as has been the case in the Sudan, Afghanistan, and many other countries in recent years. Such nongovernmental organizations may operate transnationally in pursuit of their goals, as do Islamic organizations such as the Muslim Brotherhood and al Qaeda.

After the end of the Cold War, religious identities have become more salient and historical cleavages between peoples have been revived. Samuel P. Huntington emphasizes such cleavages as a kind of clash of civilizations, noting that many conflicts since 1990 are between Muslims and non-Muslims. Much of the time since Islam became established, Muslims and non-Muslims have lived side by side without violent conflicts. Quantitative studies of interstate wars do not find that wars along the Muslim-non-Muslim line of cleavage are uncommonly high.[40] This finding should not be surprising. Islam, like other major religions and civilizations, is immensely diverse and therefore varying in its implications for conflicts. Disagreements about values, beliefs, and other aspects of life abound; they need not be as broadly encompassing as a religion or political ideology to be the basis of a conflict. But what appear to be small differences to casual observers can be given great symbolic meaning by the partisans involved in a conflict.

Differences in worldviews or values may also foster misunderstanding, conflict escalation, and conflict perpetuation without the adversaries' awareness. Thus, disputes about environmental issues such as desirable land use or responding to global warming may be exacerbated by underlying differences in ways of thinking about nature, God, scientific knowledge, the role of humans in the natural world, and economic progress.[41]

Both consensual and dissensual factors are often intertwined as sources of conflicts. Consider the renewed struggle of women for greater equality, arising in the 1960s in the United States. For many women and men, the struggle was and is not only about equal work opportunities and equal pay for equal work. Disputants in the struggle for greater gender equality frequently also differ in their evaluation of characteristics associated with masculinity and femininity. Thus, some people feel that in business at least, it is good to be aggressive, dominating, competitive, stoic, risk taking, and physically tough. Those people label such characteristics masculine and assume that men possess them naturally. They further assume that feminine characteristics must be the opposite of masculine and that women are or should be feminine; it then follows that women are less highly regarded in a workplace that is considered competitive.

Feminists in the women's liberation movement do not concur with these values and beliefs.[42] Some argue that such stereotypical characterizations of male and female roles constrain and limit both men and women, forcing them to be less than they might otherwise be. The liberation of women from the restricted social role they learn and must play would also liberate men from their circumscribed masculine role. Other feminists agree that there are differences in the way men and women tend to think, feel, and act, but they invert the masculine evaluations. The feminine emphasis on human relationships, openness to emotional expressiveness, and aversion to hierarchy are esteemed by these partisans.

Differences in lifestyles, physical features, and values held can be the bases of differences in evaluation and ranking. People may be socialized to agree with the ranking, even if they themselves possess a characteristic that is accorded low status. This may result in low self-esteem or even self-hatred among people with those characteristics. For example, many African Americans in the past sought to lighten their skin color and straighten their hair; the assertion in the 1960s that "black is beautiful" was an effort to counter the feelings of self-denigration that underlay such conduct.

Differences in values and beliefs and the evaluations of characteristics possessed by a person or group often are the basis for dissensual conflicts. People tend to think their way of life and their characteristics are good and indeed better than those held by other people. This widespread phenomenon among different peoples is recognized in the term *ethnocentrism*, the tendency for people to regard themselves as the standard by which others should be evaluated.[43]

Integration

The degree to which possible adversaries are integrated might be expected to increase their likelihood of competing and fighting one another. After all, parties that have nothing to do with each other do not fight each other; conflict is a way of relating. Indeed, although the more parties interact with each other, the more matters they may have to quarrel about, it is also true that as parties are more involved with each other, each tends to derive benefits from the relationship, making conflict avoidance likely. So the degree and nature of the integration must be considered.

The previous discussions suggest that integration between parties who are relatively equal and whose differences are small tends to make conflicts unlikely. On the other hand, integration between parties who are relatively unequal, who are markedly different, and who are divided by their claims to scarce and valued resources tends to generate grievances.[44]

Insofar as one or more parties can easily leave the relationship, the chances of conflict are reduced. The would-be antagonists have options other than fighting. In some circumstances, everyone in each adversary unit may be able to leave and establish new relationships; this is typically the case in competitive market relations. Often, while individuals may leave, the units themselves cannot survive without continuing their relationship; this is the case, for example, in labor-management relations in a corporation. And sometimes the individuals constituting the unit find it almost impossible to leave; this is the case, for example, with prison inmates and sometimes for members of ethnic groups living alongside each other.

Finally, groups in any long-term relationship each have their own narratives about that relationship. Their narratives about past experiences help provide a context and a way of interpreting current inequalities and differences. If a group of people believes that in the past it has been exploited or humiliated by another, the group is likely to interpret current undesirable circumstances as a continuation of old injustices, be less willing to accommodate, and even seek retribution.

SYNTHESIS

The multitude of theoretical approaches to explaining the sources of conflicts raises four questions. First, how may the varied explanations be combined? Second, do the many explanations demonstrate that there are a multitude of potential conflicts? Third, how are these possible conflicts related to each other? Finally, why in a given situation, are conflicts so infrequent when so many are possible?

Combining Approaches

The various approaches we have discussed are best considered as complementary rather than as competing. One or another approach may be more helpful about some issues than others; for example, concerning the source of conflicts generally or the emergence of a particular conflict; about the predisposing conditions or the proximate cause of a conflict; or about one kind of conflict rather than another.

Many approaches stress factors and processes within a potential adversary, including psychological, cultural, and social structural conditions. But they in themselves are not sufficient to account for a struggle to ensue with any particular antagonist at any given time. The social context and the relationship with particular adversaries make necessary contributions. Whether or not these general factors result in a conflict at a particular time and place depends on the specific actions taken by the antagonists.

The relative contribution of these components to explaining the sources of conflicts varies with the kind of conflict being considered. For conflicts among large-scale, clearly bounded adversaries with enduring relationships, and functioning within the context of shared rules for conflicts, diffuse social psychological factors are likely to be less significant than in interpersonal or intragroup conflicts. Thus, the relative explanatory power of the approaches we have been discussing will differ, whether one seeks to account for variations in labor-management conflicts in an industry with collective bargaining or for variations in staff-line conflicts among managers in industrial corporations.

Since social conflicts must involve conscious formulations of adversaries and issues, we stress how the partisans themselves construct those formulations. But such formulations cannot just be made up by any of the partisans. These constructions are built up and negotiated by the contending parties, and they are constrained by social and nonsocial aspects of their world that have more or less strict dispositions.

The factors examined in this chapter are largely the necessary preconditions for conflicts to break out. They provide the fuel for conflicts; but it takes a spark and sometimes considerable tinder to get the fire started. Once ignited, the availability of fuel to sustain the conflict is important for its persistence and escalation.

Multiplicity of Possible Conflicts

Clearly, people have innumerable reasons to fight with each other. Some antagonisms arise from internal forces within one side, as when some people are inadequately socialized or suffer experiences that make them prone to see others as threatening. Some of these ill-adjusted persons even play leadership roles in protecting or advancing the interests and desires of the groups they claim to represent.

No social system functions with total harmony and stable equilibrium. Internal inconsistencies or rapid changes within a social system may be disruptive, damaging the well-being of many people and alienating some. This can provide an impetus to be aggressive, which may be channeled by leaders against external actors. Or particular factions may come to believe that their relative position within their own society or organization will be enhanced by conflict with a competing one. This may seem obviously true for the warriors within such social systems, but often it is also true for leaders beset by internal challengers or for ideologues seeking a special niche.

In addition, the overarching social context within which potential adversaries function is often a contributing and even a primary source of conflict among competing parties. Thus, the encompassing system may not provide adequate ways of reconciling the inequalities and differences among persons and groups, a frequent failing of nondemocratic political systems. International conflicts are often attributed to the anarchic nature of the world; it is full of inequities and lacks an overarching authoritative way to allocate resources or to adjudicate disputes.

The relations among possible adversaries are not only the most proximate factors in the sequence of conflict emergence, they are also particularly relevant for the way the actors themselves construct a conflict and may be most amenable to short-term conflict resolution. There are innumerable individual and collective identities and unlimited opportunities for groups to see themselves as an "us" being oppressed or threatened by a "them." In light of all the reasons for fights to occur, what is remarkable is their infrequency in so many domains. This book helps explain this remarkable reality.

Interlocking Conflicts

The vast number of conflicts in which every person or group may be engaged are not independent of each other; they are interlocked in many ways.[45] Some fights emerge and become salient, blocking the eruption of others. As new conflicts become salient, they may reduce the significance of a previously primary conflict, allowing the old one to de-escalate and even become transformed.

Analyzing how the variety of conflicts in which each adversary struggles are linked can help explain the shifts in the conduct of the conflict they have with each other. Understanding how the linkages shift as conditions and perceptions of them shift can help partisans and interveners act to transform a conflict. This discussion focuses on three dimensions of linkages: (1) the degree of connection over time, (2) the degree of connection through overlapping entities and issues, and (3) the degree of connection through the concurrence of conflicts.

Connections over Time

Partisans can view their conflict as a discrete episode, in the context of generally noncontentious relations. Often, however, the partisans and outside analysts consider the conflict to be an episodic escalation of an ongoing struggle.

The fight is seen to be essentially between the same adversaries about the same issues and is a link in a chain of fights, with a contentious past and future.

Members of each side in a conflict often disagree with each other about when their conflict began and about the original issue in contention. For example, in the United States what was called the Cuban missile crisis is generally thought to have started with the October 1962 discovery by a U.S. reconnaissance plane that Soviet missile bases were under construction in Cuba. In the Soviet Union, the episode was referred to as the Caribbean crisis and began in April 1961 with the failed U.S. efforts to forcefully overthrow the Castro-led government of Cuba.[46]

Whether an episode is regarded as discrete or as connected with others and therefore is a battle in an ongoing war has important implications for the handling of possible contentions. Viewed as an incident in a protracted struggle, a contention is likely to be regarded as momentous, but little noted if regarded as an isolated matter in an otherwise pacific environment. Thus, a labor-management difference can be regarded as more or less serious, depending on its context. For some analysts and partisans, it might be seen as a part of a long-enduring class struggle.[47]

Connections through Overlapping Entities and Issues

People have many characteristics that may be the basis for identity and for opposition to people with different characteristics. The characteristics often overlap; for example, people of one ethnicity may tend to reside in a particular region, generally have relatively high incomes, share the same religion, and speak the same language. If members of another ethnic community reside in another region, have relatively low incomes, practice a different religion, and use a different language, the lines of cleavage are superimposed. In some countries, however, the lines of cleavage do not coincide but cross-cut each other. For example, members of different ethnic communities may share the same language, not live in different localities, and be similarly diverse in their incomes.

These two kinds of structural conditions have different dispositions for conflicts. Where lines of cleavage are superimposed, people are more readily mobilized for struggle and conflicts tend to be more severe. Where lines of cleavage cross-cut each other, people are less easily mobilized for struggle; hence, conflicts do not tend to emerge and to be moderate if they do.[48]

In addition to these possibly overlapping bases of identity and organization, groups have characteristics that tend to be nested within each other, like wooden Russian matryoshka dolls. For example, Anwar al-Sadat as president of Egypt was also a member of the whole Arab nation, and also of the broader Islamic community. He could think of his policies as advancing the interests of his person, his government, his country, the Arab people, or the Islamic community. He could regard his adversary to be the head of the Israeli government, the State of Israel, world Jewry, or Western imperialism. It follows that conflicts themselves are often overlapping and embedded in each other. For example, the Cold War was superimposed on the Arab-Israeli conflict between the mid-1950s and mid-1980s, exacerbating both of them.[49]

Very large-scale conflicts are waged on many fronts, as was the case in World War II. Each front engages its own set of adversaries and their particular issues, as was the case for the United States in the European and in the Asian theaters. In addition, there is often an external and an internal front, as the czarist government of Russia found when it fought against German forces in World War I and also against revolutionary Russian movements opposing the war.

Connections through Concurrence

Each party in a conflict has its own set of possible adversaries. Each can be involved in many simultaneous fights or can subordinate or even deny most of them. Thus, leaders of almost any organized conflict party face threats from other adversaries in concurrent conflicts. Each party in a general conflict must emphasize one or more conflicts but minimize others. The adversaries in any given conflict may accord different priorities to that confrontation relative to others each faces. One adversary may even regard an enemy as a friend if an even worse enemy confronts them both.

This coexistence of concurrent potential conflicts helps account for the eruption and the termination of one rather than another fight as the salience of one of them changes. For example, consider the changing primary adversaries that the Iraqi government fought when Saddam Hussein was president: Syria, Iran, Kuwait, the United States, Iraqi Kurds, and so on. The eruption of one conflict may enflame some other conflicts but dampen still others.

Each party in large degree chooses which set of adversaries are to be characterized as part of the enemy camp, influenced by internal considerations as well as by the conduct of various external adversaries and opportunities. Thus, President George W. Bush and his administration tried to link Saddam Hussein's regime in Iraq with the threat of terrorism, which the United States was fighting globally. This helped President Bush rally enough domestic support to launch military operations in March 2003 to overthrow the Iraqi government. However, many Americans and the governments of many countries, including some long allied with the United States, disagreed. They argued that there was no evidence of any direct Iraqi links to the attacks on the United States on September 11, 2001, and attacking Iraq militarily without global consensus would weaken the fight against al Qaeda in Afghanistan and elsewhere. There were many other reasons for making war on Iraq, important for different segments of the United States, including concerns that Iraq had weapons of mass destruction (WMD) and maintaining American predominance in the region in line with domestic ideological convictions. The linkage was probably more a useful argument to win public support than a primary cause.

Absence of Overt Conflict

Most possible conflicts do not become manifest, and of those that do, most are managed using means regarded by the participants as legitimate. That needs to be recognized if we are to understand why conflicts do not erupt and when they do so that they are waged constructively. For example, considering the many possible conflicts between husbands and wives in their daily living together, the relative infrequency of fights can be understood in most societies by the wife's typical deference to her husband's preferences. This occurs even in the domain of preparing meals. As Marjorie DeVault observes, "The invisibility of the work that produces 'family,' the flexibility underlying perceptions of 'choice' about the work, and the association between caring work and the supposedly 'natural' emotions of a loving wife and mother all tend to suppress conflict over housework."[50]

Beginning in the early 1960s and continuing into the early 1970s, students in universities in South Korea, the United States, Mexico, France, Poland, and many other countries believed they were in conflict with the university administrators, but also with the dominant elites of their countries and with other symbols of authority. Students demonstrated in the streets, seized control of university buildings, and otherwise acted to change the policies they opposed, but this was a short episode. Most of the time in nearly all countries, students do not see themselves in conflict with university or government authorities. This acquiescence can be explained by the dominance of the authorities that is so pervasive as to be unrecognized. The argument is that prevailing ways of thinking are often actually components of hegemonic domination.[51] In such cases, according legitimacy to power inequality can be a denial of underlying conflicts.

Often, a conflict does not emerge simply because individuals find other means of coping with the inequalities and differences they find unsatisfactory. Seeking to escape from the relationship they find punishing, they emigrate, they divorce, or they quit their jobs. People also resist by using barely conscious ways to express their discontent. For example, in disliked employment relations, employees may arrive late, be absent, work slowly, or act ineptly. Individuals also frequently try to escape the unsatisfactory conditions by seeking personal advancement. Some curry favor with those with authority who can give them what they want. Others work hard, acting as they think their superiors want them to act.

In some situations, alternatively, people may deny that anyone else is responsible for their unsatisfactory conditions but see no way out. They think it is a matter of fate, luck, or God's will. Or they may believe their condition is the result of their own failings as a person and seek solace in alcohol and/or drugs. Others, seeing no exit and no way to change the reality, withdraw and passively accept what they deem to be immutable.

Finally, people may even engage in violent and hurting behavior against others while only marginally being engaged in a conflict as defined here. For example, a person may lash out against someone else to hurt that person, but the action is largely expressive and is not really directed to get that other person to do or give anything. This may occur in interpersonal relations and be driven by inner psychological processes.

Some people may regard one or more of these alternatives as better than conflict, and other people regard them as worse at times. That is why groups sometimes favor stirring up a conflict while at other times they try to prevent one from arising.

3

The Emergence of Conflicts

The outbreak of a fight often seems sudden but is usually the result of many gradual changes. The circumstances that produce an overt social conflict may have persisted for a long time; yet, some necessary component or the lack of a triggering event has kept the conflict from emerging. Thus, members of two ethnic communities may have interacted within a pattern of widespread individual acts of discrimination and of resistance for many years, but no group within either community had tried to change the relationship until an event occurs that makes collective resistance possible or necessary. At that point those suffering discrimination may coalesce and act on their demands to end that discrimination, thereby igniting a series of actions that make the struggle manifest.

If antagonisms are denied and divisive issues are unrecognized, the gravity of the underlying contradictions is likely to grow. Indeed, data suggest that leadership groups that are relatively insensitive to the political environment tend to be particularly "crisis-prone."[1] When the conflict finally erupts, it may do so in greater intensity than if it had been expressed earlier. For example, repressive governments often suppress expressions of dissatisfaction; unresponsive to popular wishes, they may be overwhelmed when the grievances do emerge and are openly displayed. The nonviolent uprisings in Tunisia and Egypt in 2010 and 2011 are illustrative.

In order for social conflicts to become manifest, four conditions must be minimally present.[2] Innumerable combinations of the four conditions may generate a social conflict, and a high level of one may compensate for the low level of another. The first condition is that members of at least one of the parties to the emerging conflict identify themselves as an entity separate from others they identify as opponents. Second, members of at least one of the parties must feel they have a grievance. Third, at least one of the parties must formulate goals to change another group's behavior so that the grievance will be reduced. Fourth, members of the aggrieved party must believe that they can indeed bring about the desired change in the antagonist. The character of the identities, grievances, goals, and means of struggles the adversaries adopt help determine the trajectory of their conflict. For example, a struggle that threatens or is perceived to threaten the very existence of one of the adversaries is very likely to be deeply destructive.

Before examining how these conditions arise, each one needs to be explicated, starting with self-other identities. For every individual, developing a sense of self is an essential part of becoming a person. Each person's self-conception is a unique combination of identifications, which may include terms as broad as "woman" or "man," "Catholic" or "Muslim," or as narrow as being a member of one particular family. Therefore, although a self-identity may be thought to coincide with a specific living person, the boundaries may be wider. Identities sometimes extend to regions, countries, or ethnic communities, so that people may sacrifice their individual lives in order to preserve their larger selves. People generally have more than one such wider identity that they have in common with others; people who share the same collective identity think of themselves as having a common interest and a common fate.

Furthermore, another group has to be identified as the opponent by members of the contending party for the conflict to be manifest. Adversaries tend to be characterized negatively and in terms contrasting to the self-identity of the contending party. The conception of the adversary group also tends to include negative ideas about the relationship with the contending collectivity.

The second condition of a manifest conflict is that members of a contending group must feel aggrieved. They believe they have less of a consensually valued resource, such as land, security, or income, than they should have. Or the grievance has a dissensual basis. That is, the members of a contending group feel that their values are not properly respected or supported by persons in another collectivity, or those persons adhere to values they regard as wrong and offensive.

The third condition necessary for a social conflict to emerge is that members of the aggrieved party develop goals that require changes on the part of the adversary. The goals need not necessarily be fully and clearly articulated. What is essential is that one group believes that another collectivity is responsible for its grievances, and if the other group would change, its dissatisfaction would be lessened.

Finally, members of the aggrieved party must believe that their actions can induce the other party to change. They may not have a clearly articulated strategy to bring about the desired change, but they think that they can act in ways that will improve their circumstances.

The way these four conditions change for each adversary and how the adversaries interact with each other largely determine the course of a conflict and the degree to which it becomes destructive or constructive. Furthermore, these four conditions are highly interdependent. Thus, the conceptions of who we are, what we have to complain about, who is responsible, and what we can do about it all help shape each other. Still, it is useful to distinguish among these conditions and examine how each comes into play and together account for the eruption of a conflict. These conditions provide the tinder and the spark that ignite a struggle, which is fueled by the underlying conditions discussed in the previous chapter.

IDENTITIES OF SELF AND OTHERS

Identities vary in expanse, from individuals to vast collectivities, and they may be long enduring or ephemeral. To understand how struggles erupt, then escalate, de-escalate, and become resolved, we must recognize that identities change in content and shift in salience. Everyone holds many identities, some of which are nested in each other, usually compatibly, as is the case for geographic ones, such as Parisians in France. But some collective identities are experienced as competing with each other, as occurs in civil wars.[3] For example, in the 1950s and 1960s many people living in what was then Yugoslavia felt pride in having stood up to the Soviet Union in 1948 and in creating a new economic system that seemed promising.[4] Although the identification was not universally primary, many citizens of Yugoslavia regarded themselves significantly as Yugoslavs, and this identity was growing in the 1960s and 1970s.[5] Yet in the 1990s, most people in Yugoslavia were led to believe that their identities as Serbs, Croats, Slovenes, Muslims, or Bosnians were more important than their identity as Yugoslavs.

Ethnic as well as other identities serve as a basis for mobilization and organization.[6] Claiming a shared identity can help generate resources that may be used to advance individual and common benefits. Choice of one or another identity depends upon the group members' characteristics, their relations with antagonists, and their larger social context.

Identities are socially constructed on the bases of various traits and experiences. Although characteristics and experiences are open to different interpretations, they are not equally susceptible to every interpretation, as evident from the debates about the nature of ethnicity. Some analysts regard ethnicity as a primordial phenomenon, relatively permanent and unchanging.[7] Many other analysts stress that identity is socially constructed, with people choosing a history and common ancestry and creating, as much as discovering, differences from others. Still others view identity from an instrumentalist vantage point, arguing that group identity is often nourished by elites in the pursuit of political objectives.[8] In the perspective taken here, most aspects of ethnicity are considered socially constructed, but some traits of ethnicity are not easily modifiable by social processes.

Ethnic traits are often socially regarded as set at birth, such as parental ancestry, religious origin, place of birth, and skin color. Other traits are seen to be acquired or modified later, requiring varying effort, such as language spoken, clothes worn, or food eaten. Insofar as the traits chosen to define membership in an ethnicity are of the former variety, ethnic status is ascribed; and insofar as they are acquired or modified in later life, ethnic status is achieved.[9]

Thus, skin color is an important marker of identity in some societies but not in all. In the United States, people have accorded great significance to skin color, and there has been a tendency to dichotomize color into black and white, asserting that having any black parentage makes a person black. But in some countries ethnicity is defined in terms of traits that may be acquired later in life; for example, in Mexico, "Indians" can become "Mestizos" by wearing Western clothing and speaking Spanish.[10]

Countries rely on varying combinations of ascribed and achieved characteristics in defining citizenship and in nonofficial designation of membership. Thus, in the United States citizenship is open to anyone who is born within the country or swears to support the U.S. Constitution and meets certain residence requirements. However, to some extent American citizens act as if some Americans do not "look American" or do not behave or think like Americans. In many countries, such as in Kuwait, Japan, Israel, Switzerland, and Saudi Arabia, citizenship is easier to obtain for those who by descent are Kuwaiti, Japanese, Jewish, Swiss, or Saudi, respectively. In the European Union the struggle between ascribed versus achieved identity is particularly pronounced as nations struggle to reconcile declining birthrates, increasing immigration, and the creation of a new pan-European identity.[11]

Identities characterized by ascribed traits are difficult to discard or escape. They are likely to be the basis of intergroup conflict, since individual solutions are less available. Qualifications to this tendency are enlightening. Sex and age are set at birth, but they are not a universal basis for the formation of groups frequently engaged in destructive struggles. This is true for sex differences, partly because individual men and women generally live in intimacy and complement each other in socially prescribed ways. Age differences are also peculiar in that everyone was young once, and nearly all young people want and expect to be older; besides, there are intimate intergenerational bonds. Nevertheless, in many societies and institutions men dominate women and the women in various ways often resist and struggle to reduce the domination. Political and economic struggles along generational lines also arise in particular societal circumstances.

Many identities are also based on shared values, beliefs, or concerns. As these are matters of contention, people often identify themselves with the side they take in a conflict. Thus, on specific matters such as abortion in the United

States, some people see themselves as protectors of the right to life, while others as defenders of freedom of choice. Some people think of themselves as defenders of the environment, and others as advocates of economic development. More generally, some people identify themselves as liberals and others as conservatives. Such identities may bring people together as partisans even without sharing a material self-interest in a conflict.[12]

Internal Characteristics

The formation of self-identified collectives derives from internal characteristics, social context, and adversary relations. Four internal factors are noteworthy: homogeneity, ease of communication, clear boundaries, and organizational potential.

Homogeneity of Members

Insofar as members of a social category perceive themselves to be similar in traits, the greater is their propensity to form a shared identity. Their perceived homogeneity tends to facilitate communication and to foster a sense of solidarity and shared fate. To illustrate, the French speakers of Quebec tended to share religion and class position within a particular region of Canada, which facilitated forming a strong Quebec identity and mobilization for Quebec autonomy or independence. On the other hand, in the United States, the ethnic heterogeneity of U.S. workers has hampered their class solidarity and their mobilization for trade union membership or for class-conscious political parties.[13] The high degree of occupational differentiation also hinders working-class solidarity.[14] Such heterogeneity may become the basis for ethnic conflicts within the social category, weakening the sense of identity for members of the category as a whole.[15]

Women's solidarity as a conflict group opposing men is also handicapped by their heterogeneity. Not only do they have the diversity of men in terms of ethnicity, region, and occupation, but in many societies their marital status and their husbands' occupational positions have great importance for them as well. These kinds of heterogeneity generate dissensual as well as consensual issues of contention among women, weakening their shared identity.[16]

Ease of Communication

A sense of common identity is highly dependent upon the ease of communication among the members of a particular group. Many factors affect the ease of communication, including the members' number, proximity, and density, their social and technical skills, sharing of a common language, and the social and nonsocial links among them.

Increased opportunities for effective communication among members of potential conflict groups also can increase the feeling of dissatisfaction and the belief that a grievance can be reduced. To illustrate, prior to the October 1917 Russian Revolution, the increasing concentration of workers in very large factories supported the growth of proletarian solidarity. Although the industrial proletariat was small, "it was disproportionately concentrated both in large-scale industrial enterprises and in major industrial centers."[17] This facilitated communication, mobilization, and organization and thus contributed to the emergence of militant organized opposition to the czar, and ultimately to the October Revolution.

A reduction of constraints on communication can liberate people to mobilize as a conflict group. This is why authoritarian and totalitarian governments fear that allowing a little freedom will undermine their rule. Nevertheless, to placate some dissenters or to use pressure from below against bureaucratic rigidity, government leaders or a faction of them may encourage the open expression of opinion, and the feared result sometimes follows. For example, in the late 1980s, Mikhail Gorbachev's glasnost policy encouraged open discussion in the former Soviet Union. Gradually, the expression of dissent and opposition to the previous policies of the Communist Party and the government it controlled built a momentum that became impossible to contain.

Populations vary greatly in possessing the social and technological resources that facilitate communication. Thus, one of the factors that accounts for the order in which trade unions were historically established in the United States was the ability of the workers to communicate and organize. Printers, for example, were among the first craftsmen to form trade unions. Dominant groups have often sought to deny or restrict the development of skills that would be helpful for communication among those they dominated. Consider how in the United States education was forbidden for slaves, and even after slavery African Americans were denied equal access to education. For generations, women too did not have equal educational opportunities.[18]

The rapidly increasing speed and accessibility of distant communication in the twenty-first century has profound consequences for transnational identities. So too does the creation of new media outlets with a global reach, such as Al Jazeera and the Xinhua News Agency, which increasingly compete with Western media outlets to report on and frame global events. Thus, today immigrants can maintain ongoing connections with their homeland and sustain various degrees of dual national identity.[19] Thus too, social movements struggling to defend human rights, protect the environment, or promote good working conditions can more easily mobilize across national borders.[20] Finally, globalized communication structures also contribute to the formation of and actions by transnational extremist Islamic organizations able to successfully export insecurity from remote and ungoverned portions of the globe.[21]

Clear and Stable Boundaries

Insofar as the social boundaries of population categories are clear and unchanging, their members tend to develop a sense of solidarity and common fate. Thus, members of a caste, as in India, are more likely to think of themselves as having a shared identity and fate than are members of a social class, whose boundaries are permeable. Of course, whether a social category is highly homogeneous or not depends on the boundaries used by an analyst or by the members themselves. Therefore the distribution of these characteristics may radically shift when the boundaries change, as people in a territory secede or are incorporated within another country.

Organizational Potential

The nature of a quasi group's organizational potential greatly affects the likelihood that the group will become mobilized as a collectivity. The more highly integrated and interdependent are the members of a quasi group, the more likely are they to see themselves as a collectivity with common interests. Variations in such self-conceptions can be noted among members of different occupations.[22] Miners, for example, are vitally interdependent in their work activities and historically have had a high sense of solidarity compared with other occupational groups. The solidarity of miners also is often reinforced by other factors, such as isolation and concentration of residency.

Research and experience demonstrate that networks linking persons and small groups are crucial in the development of collective identity in potential conflict groups. These preexisting groups and links facilitate communication and the creation of shared identities, giving certain issues salience. They are also crucial in mobilizing people, in developing a feeling of dissatisfaction, and in creating the belief that their dissatisfaction can be alleviated by their efforts.[23] This is illustrated by the rise of the U.S. civil rights movement against segregation in the U.S. South. The movement rested upon the local churches and other already-existing organizations and the interpersonal channels linking the people with those institutions.[24] Similarly, in Iran in 1979, mosques were important centers for the mobilization of the people who mounted the revolution against the government.

In the contemporary age of rapid communication and movement of goods and people, transnational networks linking small groups in many parts of the world can come together to wage large continuing campaigns. This is evident in the mobilization of public protests against the World Trade Organization (WTO), the International Monetary Fund (IMF), and the World Bank, for example, in Seattle in 1999, in Prague in 2000, and in Washington in 2009. The massive demonstrations in many world capitals against the U.S.-led war in Iraq in 2003 are also illustrative of links quickly forged.[25]

The emergence of al Qaeda, led by Osama bin Laden, provides another example.[26] In the 1980s, Muslims from several countries were drawn to join the struggle of Islamic traditional and fundamentalist groups to counter the Soviet military support of a secular Afghan government. Mosques in many Muslim countries were locales for airing grievances and bin Laden and others used videos and electronic means of communication to mobilize fighters. After the Soviets withdrew in 1989, the United States, which had supported the anti-Soviet Afghan forces, withdrew from major involvement in Afghanistan and terrible fighting among the Afghan warlords ensued. The Taliban succeeded in gaining power and provided a haven for al Qaeda's anti-U.S. activities. Jihadist militants came from many countries for training to attack Americans and American interests so as to liberate Arab lands from the regimes they believed were propped up by the United States. People joined militant jihadist or Salafist organizations through personal ties.[27] After the fall of the Taliban government, local groups have usually conducted operations in their own areas of residence, with varying transnational support.

Finally, it should be recognized that political and religious leaders play very important roles in guiding which identity is salient. Leaders articulate and use the resources they control to put forward identities that include certain people while excluding others. Their resources include the symbols of authority they are able to claim, the patronage they can offer, and the coercion they can threaten. Intellectuals are also influential, helping to construct and proclaim visions of present victimization and of past and future glory.

Social Context

The social setting within which conflict groups emerge greatly affects their members' collective identities. Thus, the prevailing ways of thinking in a culture, civilization, or period of history profoundly affect how people characterize themselves and others. Identifications in terms of religious beliefs, class relations, ethnicity, or lifestyles are more or less salient in different times and places. For example, class consciousness has been more prominent in many other societies than in the United States.

Prevailing ways of thought also provide the concepts by which people characterize themselves, and the shared understandings support some claims more than others. Thus, in an age sympathetic to nationalism, ethnic group members tend to claim the right of collective self-determination, and they find support for such claims from nonmembers.[28] The collapse of the Soviet Union undermined the appeal of the secular and universalistic communist ideology, while the rapid changes of the modern world created new sources of discontents. Religious faith and identities have been growing since the mid-1900s, as have fundamentalist interpretations in Islam, Christianity, Judaism, and Hinduism. Perhaps these are responses to failed secular nationalist efforts and unsatisfied needs for meaning, community, and hope. Even before the collapse of the Soviet Union, religious differences had begun to be more frequently associated with ethnic nationalist conflicts.

The social context provides a repertoire of possible identities to assume. Identities that others have taken and used to advance their interests serve as models, and similar identities then become attractive. Thus, in the United States, African Americans in the 1960s' civil rights struggle stressed their identity as blacks and served as models for other disadvantaged people. Many groups formed, using their disadvantaged position as a basis for identity and claim making. As women, gays, Hispanics, the deaf, and many other categories of people developed pride in that aspect of who they were, still other people felt free to find their identity in comparable experiences of discrimination and oppression.

Adversary Relations

In defining themselves, groups also define others; and in defining their opponents, they also define themselves. Each self-conscious collectivity defines nonmembers; indeed, identity is in good measure established in contrast to others.[29] We know who we are by emphasizing how we are not like others; thus, many former colonial peoples, such as Arabs, Africans, and Asians, define themselves by affirming their separation from Western ideals and values. Thus, too, during the Cold War many people in the United States partly defined themselves as being American by being anti-communist.

Absence of a clear contrast group hampers the formation of a collective identity. At the turn of the nineteenth century, workers in a locally owned mill or mine knew who the adversary was, and that helped them define themselves as workers. But since the turn of the twentieth century, when the mine or mill is owned by a vast conglomerate and the managers, too, are hired hands, the adversary is less clear.

People are generally inclined to evaluate their own group as superior to others. This universal tendency toward ethnocentrism contributes to the sense of each group to view relations with others as one of "us" against "them."[30] But it is important to note that this is not true for all collective identifications all the time. Some theorists argue that identity-based differences are not in and of themselves sufficient to trigger conflict but require additional structural inequalities or disagreements over scarce and valued resources to emerge.[31] Indeed, members of one people often find members of another interestingly different and enjoy their music, food, or other traditional products. Social psychological research indicates that positive attachment to one's country—patriotism—is separate from feelings of national superiority—nationalism.[32]

Self-identifications become salient in relationship to other persons and therefore are partly situational. For example, a person's identity as an American is less salient when in the United States than when visiting another country. There is evidence that persons living in ethnically heterogeneous neighborhoods take their ethnicity more seriously than do those in ethnically homogenous neighborhoods.[33] However, the derogatory content of stereotypes and the consequent feelings of antagonism can be greater and more resistant to change when people are isolated from each other and those views are inculcated without contradictions.

The content of a collective identity, then, is shaped by interaction between people sharing a particular identity with people having other identities. Such interaction, significantly, is never wholly symmetrical. If a group is relatively powerful, it will try to impose its definitions on other groups. The Nazis' violent imposition of their characterization of Jews stands as a grotesque example of that tendency. In most instances, the imposition of a definition and characterization is mitigated and less organized, but some degree of imposition is discernable in many relationships in ordinary life.

In cases with illegitimate power inequalities, the subordinate group usually will try to reject the definitions and characterizations superordinates seek to impose. What ensues is a struggle over who has the right to define membership and the perceived qualities of each group. But, interestingly, there are cases where under long-term domination, many members of the dominated group may internalize the evaluations of those who dominate them.[34] The result may be self-hatred and self-denigration, which inhibits challenging the system of domination.

Particular identifications are forged by specific kinds of domination. Thus, nationalist identification often emerges in the face of coercive treatment by foreign armies. For example, when Japanese troops invaded China in 1937 they took ruthless action against the entire rural population, arousing intense anti-Japanese feelings among the peasants.[35] That invasion and subsequent occupation raised the Chinese peasants' sense of citizenship and their interest in building and strengthening an independent Chinese state.

Changing Identities

Identities, because they are socially constructed, do change. Even "race" is a social construct. For example, in the United States "Hispanic" and "Asian" identities are relatively recent creations and the "white race" has expanded over the years to include Jews and others previously excluded.[36]

These identity shifts often significantly affect the outbreak of a conflict and help determine whether its course will be constructive or destructive. Thus, broad country identities may dissipate and the organizations that sustain them weaken so that religious or ethnic identities become more salient. This happened in the late 1980s for many people in Yugoslavia. Their identifications as communists and as Yugoslavs were undermined, and old ethnic and religious identities became more prominent. This occurred, too, in the former Soviet Union when the Soviet identity waned and national identities became salient.

Religious identities may also shift, generating new lines of social cleavages, as old ones fade. This is illustrated by the increased salience of religious identities after the decline of the secular ideologies of fascism and communism. The result may be sectarian cleavages within major religious faiths as well as among them.[37]

A sudden rise in migration can bring populations with different identities into closer relations and require higher levels of coordination. Shifts in political borders can also produce changes in the proportions of people with varying identities, making old solutions less applicable, as was the case within the former Soviet Union or former Yugoslavia. Such changes often contribute to the emergence of severe conflicts.

GRIEVANCE

The condition that receives most analytic and popular attention in explaining the emergence of a conflict is the grievance felt by at least one adversary, since contending groups usually account for their entering a conflict by referring to the injustices they suffer.[38] Consensual matters of contention occur when members of the adversarial groups agree about what is desirable but members of at least one group believe they have less than they should have while the opponents have more. Dissensual matters of contention occur when adversarial groups disagree about values and what is desirable; thus members of one group may be offended by another group's values and conduct, which they regard as immoral and in need of change. Naturally, that other group is likely to reject such views.

A sense of grievance arises from within each possible adversary, from their relations with each other and from their social context. Factors from all these sources combine to account for the content and the strength of the grievance.

Internal Developments

Various changes within a potential conflict party contribute significantly to the emergence of grievances. In consensual conflicts, grievances frequently arise from changes in the circumstances of one group's members or in their assessment of the justness of their conditions. This sense of dissatisfaction can arise when their perceived circumstances fall short of their expectations.[39] Discrepancies between attainments and expectations have three major sources. First, members of a society or a segment of the society experience a decline in what benefits they have had for a long time and had expected would continue. The decline may be due to an economic recession, or it may be due to a decline in autonomy, territorial control, or respect and deference from others.

Second, improving conditions produce the expectation of continuing improvement; consequently, when attainments decline, or simply stop rising, people are disappointed and feel aggrieved. This has been used to explain the outbreak of the French Revolution and many other major social convulsions.[40] The argument is that revolutions tend to follow a period of improving living conditions, not a long period of consistently bad times. The evidence for this has been indirect. Studies have related revolutionary efforts or domestic turmoil to changes in previous conditions, but the feeling of grievance has only been inferred.[41] Additional conditions are necessary to join a grievance with a goal to change others and undertake contentious behavior to correct the grievance.

The third source of discrepancy between expectations and attainments is rising expectations, which may occur for several reasons. One reason is that people learn, for example, from the mass media, that others have much more of what they also want. The ever-greater exposure of deprived people to knowledge of the lives of the advantaged in the world tends to raise their expectations. Shortly after World War II, some analysts argued that traditional societies would undergo modernization as people in underdeveloped countries discovered what was available in economically advanced countries.[42] The result would be rising expectations, a breakdown in the traditional order, and revolutionary demands if the expectations were not realized.

Indeed, there were many wars of national liberation against colonial powers, and many traditional regimes were overthrown in the Middle East and Asia. Leaders of the new governments drew from socialist, nationalist, and capitalist market ideas. People in many poor countries have experienced some improvement in their economic well-being and they do report feeling happy.[43]

However, many countries failed to grow economically and did not keep pace with the economic growth of the developed countries. At the same time, the economic, cultural, and military dominance of the United States and the economically developed countries seemed to increase. Religion, for some people in those countries, seemed the way to either overcome the past failures to meet raised expectations about Western goods and secular ideas or to reject them altogether.

Another reason expectations rise is that leaders promise future benefits and achievements, sometimes even initiating programs meant to attain those gains. The failure to achieve the promises, however, results in a discrepancy between the raised expectations and the reality. That discrepancy can be the source of conflict between the aggrieved and those they think are culpable for the failure. Perhaps the high expectations of many social movement activists in the early 1960s in the United States contributed later to more severe conflicts as the anticipated gains were not fulfilled.

Changes in expectations relative to attainments, however, provide a limited explanation for discontent resulting in conflict behavior. Poor conditions may be made endurable by promises of improvements in the future. The expectations of a glorious future do often induce people to accept current sacrifices. It is also plausible that if conditions have been improving, people are able to absorb a setback with less bitterness. Under other circumstances, a new deprivation may be interpreted as a personal failure that induces guilt or self-hate so that no outwardly directed efforts at redressing the grievance are taken. Finally, the partial improvement of conditions may be sufficient to satisfy rather than arouse appetites. For example, many European immigrants found U.S. working conditions much better than their previous conditions, and therefore they were more satisfied than their U.S.-born children and other U.S. workers.[44] A similar pattern occurs for workers who immigrated into Western European countries in the latter half of the twentieth century. Consequently, deprivation itself may not appreciably raise the level of conflict-generating discontent.

These various explanations for an emerging grievance have varying pertinence for different segments within a large-scale adversary. Leaders of a conflict party are a particularly important segment, and the sources and nature of their discontent are often different from the grievances of their followers. They therefore may stress other concerns, ones they believe will be effective in arousing a sense of grievance among the rank and file.

Religious, academic, and other intellectuals may elaborate and interpret historical or contemporary understandings to glorify their group's faith, values, or cultural life or to decry their unfair denigration or suppression by other groups. A linguistic minority in a particular country may begin to feel that the requirement of using a majority language in all judicial and educational institutions is a threat to their survival as a community or a denial of their rights. What had been accepted earlier without challenge then becomes a grievance.

Sometimes group members come to believe that their beliefs, faith, ideology, or particular values are so superior to those of another group that they should insist that those others conform to their preferences. They may insist that the others accept their superior faith or beliefs, live in subordination, be expelled, or even be killed. Within any large collectivity, members disagree about such matters and contend with each other about their differences. At times, particular groups of religious or political zealots have resorted to extreme violence to advance their ideas. In a country, they may seize control of the government; their victory then confirms the zealots' convictions and justifies a crusade, genocide, or invasion to spread their truth and morality.

A grievance often combines consensual and dissensual elements, as happens when members of a minority community feel that they suffer discrimination for their views or way of life. They are denied access to goods and resources they believe they should have unless they give up qualities they regard as central to their identity. In some social settings, even that choice is unavailable and they are unilaterally denied rights they believe they deserve. While the emergence of a grievance and its nature is affected by internal developments, they are also affected by the relationship and interaction between the potential adversaries.

Relationship Developments

A good way to begin considering how the relationship between adversaries affects their members' sense of grievance is to examine inequalities in class, status, and power.[45] Differences in class position, in status ranking, and in relative power are to be found in some degree within all social systems, and such differences are likely bases of grievances.

Class cleavages are to be found in varying degree in all large societies.[46] Class differences are based in the labor, capital, and other markets and affected by government tax and welfare policies. They are indicated by variations in income, wealth, and other measures of economic well-being.

People also vary in their ranking in status hierarchies. Thus, in many societies some people are accorded high regard due to their familial origins as aristocrats, while others are looked down upon due to their lowly origins. Variations in prestige and deference also may be accorded based on their occupations, educational level, ethnicity, religious adherences, lifestyles, or other qualities that are ranked according to culturally agreed-upon standards.

Power differences, in varying degrees, exist within all societies and other social systems. In light of the earlier discussion of the many meanings of the word *power*, we will refer to power here in terms of relative domination. Some persons and groups have more control over their own affairs than do others and more freedom from control by others. Furthermore, some people have more ability to affect collective decisions about the system as a whole and the allocation of its products, for example by influencing a country's government.

According to approaches emphasizing human nature and basic human needs, discussed in chapter 2, being low ranked would be experienced as a deprivation, and the more deprived people are, the worse they feel.[47] Despite the universality of social inequalities, manifest conflicts between low- and high-ranking persons and groups are not omnipresent. One reason for this is that hierarchies are often viewed as legitimate. Even low-ranking people may believe that the rank differences are proper and the people ranked above them in class, status, or power properly hold their position within their society, organization, or other social system.

There is much empirical data, as well as theoretical reasoning, regarding the relationship between inequalities and grievances. Survey data from many societies do indicate that persons with low occupational status or at low economic levels tend to be dissatisfied as measured by responses to several kinds of questions.[48] Similarly, occupational studies generally find that the lower the prestige, income, or work autonomy of an occupation, the more likely are its incumbents to be dissatisfied and want to leave it.[49] Furthermore, low rank in different dimensions, like education and income, has a cumulative negative effect.[50]

Dissatisfaction, however, is not always directly expressed in conflict or even a sense of grievance for a number of reasons. One is that people who rank low on a consensually valued dimension tend to think poorly of themselves and wish to avoid identifying themselves in terms of that dimension; consequently, the resulting weak solidarity interferes with collective recognition of dissatisfaction. In addition, severely deprived persons tend to be preoccupied with day-to-day efforts at coping rather than developing a shared sense of grievance. For example, a study in nine countries found that workers, compared with middle-class respondents, were less likely to identify with persons of their own nation who were not of their own class and also less likely to identify with members of their own class in other countries.[51] Accommodation to severe deprivation can even take the form of suppression and denial of hostile feelings and lead to placating and ingratiating behavior toward those of higher rank.[52]

A final difficulty with the idea of simple deprivation as an explanation of grievance must be noted. In many struggles, the party that initiates the pursuit of a contentious goal is relatively advantaged. It is often the stronger, the richer, or the higher-status groups that seek more of what they already have from those who have less.[53] Perhaps they do so because they can; but it also may be that by their standards, they feel that they not only deserve their high rank but that they deserve even more wealth, deference, and power. Their grievance, if we may call it that, derives from their claim that they are due even more than they already have. In addition, persons and groups ranking high in status or class, and particularly in power hierarchies, often fear that others will challenge and displace them. Some persons experience the perceived threat as a grievance that must be corrected by countering those who might attempt to knock them out of their high-rank position. In the early 1990s, a group of conservative American intellectuals, some of whom had been Democrats (and became known as neoconservatives, or neocons), asserted that U.S. preeminence must be maintained, which required military dominance that precluded the rise of a great-power rival.[54] Following the attacks of September 11, 2001, that became official American doctrine, President George W. Bush said in his speech to a joint session of Congress on September 20, 2001, "Our forces will be strong enough to dissuade potential adversaries from pursuing a military build-up in hopes of surpassing, or equaling, the power of the United States." In his speech at West Point on June 1, 2001, he went further, warning of the threats the United States now faced and declared, "To forestall or prevent such hostile acts by our adversaries, the United States will, if necessary, act preemptively."

For people to have a grievance, they must judge their circumstances to be inadequate by some criteria. One body of theory and research that suggests how those criteria are chosen relates to reference groups.[55] But the existence of many possible reference groups makes it difficult to posit which ones different persons will use as standards of reference. One way to predict which of many possible reference groups actually will be chosen stems from the work on rank disequilibrium, based on the fact that people are not ranked uniformly in diverse hierarchies.[56] People might be expected to use their high rank as a reference level, since that could be the basis of claims to be of higher rank in other dimensions in which they have lower ranks. Such a reference choice would well be a source of dissatisfaction, which might be a reason to choose their low rank as a reference level and feel good that they are high on another dimension. So the inference remains ambiguous. Recent work suggests that individual persons choose reference standards high enough to motivate efforts they feel capable of undertaking and low enough to avoid feeling deprived and a failure.[57] If so, group-shared grievances are not a likely consequence of adopting reference-group standards.

Studies have been made to specify the effects of different kinds of rank incongruence. Thus, some evidence supports the idea that persons ranked high on ascribed dimensions (e.g., ethnicity) or dimensions that are considered investments (e.g., education) but low on achieved or reward dimensions (e.g., income or occupational status) may be called "underrewarded." They tend to experience failure and feel disappointment and anger. The anger may be displaced, as indicated by the appeal to poor white Americans of nativist organizations that have been hostile to immigrants.[58] On the other hand, persons ranked low on ascribed or investment dimensions and high on achieved or reward dimensions would tend to feel successful and contented, and some may even feel guilt and obligated to assist the less advantaged.

Although there is evidence that rank inconsistency has effects, certain considerations limit its utility in explaining the emergence of large-scale unregulated social conflicts.[59] First, rank inconsistency may not uniformly contribute to feeling dissatisfied, since under some circumstances persons may use their low rank as a standard of reference. Second, for some people, at least, being high in certain hierarchies would compensate for being low in others. Finally, for collective action to emerge in large-scale conflicts, grievances must be experienced collectively.

On the whole, the simpler additive deprivation model provides the best accounting for a person's degree of dissatisfaction.[60] That is, the lower a group's ranking and the greater the number of low rankings, the greater will be the group members' dissatisfaction. However, certain kinds of rank inconsistencies, under specific conditions, may also affect the sense of personal grievance. Thus, rank disequilibrium may be a source of disturbance in a small group where it affects face-to-face interaction, but in a larger social system, such as a society, the resulting cross-cutting ties may be integrative.[61]

There is evidence that in rank systems within clearly marked boundaries, those toward the top of a low-ranking stratum tend to be satisfied. Yet it is usually from these levels that the leaders of the discontented emerge.[62] This is partly because the higher-ranking persons within each stratum have the social resources and skills that make them likely to be leaders of others within their stratum. Furthermore, such persons are in some ways marginal; they do not fit clearly into either the low-ranking or the high-ranking strata. Marginality can be a source of insight and understanding of different groups, which is useful for leaders.[63]

Leaders play critical roles in arousing discontent. Indeed, opponents of movements to redress grievances often argue that the movements are the result of "outside agitators." Influence does not go only from leaders to followers. In varying degrees, followers choose their leaders and accord them authority, and leaders must express views that make sense to their followers, given their experiences. Some experiences may be interpreted in diverse ways, but other experiences are usually interpreted similarly. For example, a study of black neighborhoods found that popular discontent with the police could be accounted for without recourse to the role of black community leaders, but feelings of economic exploitation by the local businesses were more dependent on the leaders' interpretation.[64]

Religious, intellectual, and political leaders can have transforming influences over the long term. Adapting traditional views to new conditions and drawing on current social conventions, they can revive dreams of past glories that make present conditions objectionable. Leaders of nationalist and religious movements have often done this effectively. The Sinhala Buddhist revivalism in Sri Lanka is illustrative.[65] It began in the late nineteenth century when Sri Lanka was a British colony known as Ceylon. Anagarika Dharmapala was one of its leaders, combining indigenous and colonial influences to claim that the Sinhala are a chosen people, with the mission of administering the island. The island, however, is peopled by the Tamils, a largely Hindu minority, as well as by the Sinhalese majority. Dharmapala asserted that the Sinhala people had flourished under Buddhism before Christianity, and polytheism, brought by barbaric vandals, corrupted the people. Clearly, the methods of the ancient days should be restored. Such a chauvinistic identity and fundamental grievance helped unleash a protracted struggle with the Tamils, which became highly destructive.

Besides the antagonistic interests arising from inequalities, however, possible adversaries often are interdependent and also share positive bonds, interests, and identities. The invigoration of such positive ties tends to inhibit feeling aggrieved, while their deterioration contributes to rising salience of dissatisfactions. One important positive aspect of the relationship between potential adversaries is the extent to which their members hold common identities. For example, most blacks and whites in the United States feel that they all are Americans. The loss of such a common identity creates the space for secondary antagonisms to become primary ones, as happened to many peoples in the former Soviet Union who suffered the loss of shared identity as supporters of communism and as Soviet citizens.

Another positive aspect of a relationship is the extent to which the potential adversaries share a common goal and work together cooperatively to attain it. This typically is a major cohesive force in social life. Within industrial organizations, for example, workers and managers collaborate to produce products that will be marketed to earn money for the organization, which is shared with owners and others, to varying degrees. Shared goals are based on consensus, on the similarities in values and beliefs that people have. Cooperative activities may also be aided by dissensus when people differ in what they enjoy doing and therefore complement each other's work.

The degree to which members of potential adversary groups have ties that cross-cut their lines of cleavage is another positive aspect of relations we must consider. These ties include interpersonal bonds or alliances against third parties. Thus, persons with friendships across possible conflict-group boundaries are less likely to construe potentially contentious issues between the groups antagonistically.

Finally, the degree of affection potential antagonists have toward each other is another positive aspect of a relationship. As Lewis A. Coser writes, "The closer the relationship, the greater the affective investment, the greater also the tendency to suppress rather than express hostile feelings."[66]

In short, changes in the relative balance between cooperative and antagonistic aspects of the relationship are crucial to the emergence of a social conflict. A deterioration of positive bonds and activities, as well as an increase in negative ones, contributes to the outbreak of a conflict.

Changes can occur in any of the three dimensions of relationships discussed in chapter 2: inequalities, differences in values and beliefs, and integration between possible adversaries. Increasing inequalities between potential adversaries tends to arouse a sense of grievance among the relatively disadvantaged, and the changes that make one party appear to benefit at the expense of another are particularly pertinent.

Thus, when a disadvantaged stratum is increasing in relative population or economic standing, its members are likely to regard their low standing as unjustified and seek more political power and/or social status. This is likely to be resisted by the previously advantaged stratum. Belgium, for example, was established in 1830 with a Walloon- or French-speaking area in the south and a Flemish- or Dutch-speaking area in the north.[67] At the outset, the French language was ascendant in a unified and centralized state. Gradually, however, the Flemish-speaking population, a majority of the country, gained parity for Flemish. In the post–World War II period, the Flemish region prospered relative to the French, and with growing Flemish nationalism a struggle for greater regional autonomy ensued.

The ending of colonial rule in a territory often has changed the relative standing of ethnic groups there and consequently has been a source of conflict. Colonial powers often awarded advantages to one ethnic group for various reasons, including presumed affinity. Furthermore, an advantage for the colonial power is that the favored group would be dependent and loyal to the colonial power. However, after independence, the favored group, often a minority community, is likely to face claims by the majority group for improved political and economic benefits. This was the case to some degree in Rwanda with the relations between the Hutus and Tutsis and in Sri Lanka with the relations between the Sinhalese and Tamils.[68]

The existence of different values and beliefs becomes a grievance when one side tries to impose its views on another, which may occur as a result of various developments. For instance, when people of one culture or civilization interact with people of another in a relationship of colonization, imperial control, or indirect domination, the subordinated people are likely to feel aggrieved. In addition to grievances about lower class, power, and status, some people will experience strong feelings of disruption, humiliation, and cultural violation, even when the dominant group's members act unwittingly in ways that members of the subordinated group experience as hurtful.[69] In some cultures, where a sense of honor is deeply embedded and retribution is required if a family member is dishonored, severe personal acts are needed to restore honor.

American military operations overthrowing Saddam Hussein in 2003 and occupying Iraq afterward made many Iraqis feel humiliated by Americans.[70] This feeling arose in part from the sense of honor men felt in relation to the women in their families; for example, U.S. troops breaking into their homes looking for fighters or arms and the lack of security in the streets resulted in daughters or wives feeling violated, even when not actually harassed or raped; Iraqi men were humiliated by not being able to protect their women. Retaliating against American soldiers was a way for some Iraqis to regain their honor.

Another development contributing to the emergence of dissensually derived grievances is an increase in the salience of religious or ideological views among adherents, and the adherents' efforts to convert other people to their views. This zealotry can result in proselytizing efforts that are rejected and resisted, constituting a severe social conflict.

Although a high level of integration between potential adversaries generally inhibits the emergence of a grievance, in particular circumstances it can actually contribute to developing a grievance. Thus, when mutual dependence is not equal, one side is easily subjected to threats based on its dependence. The dependence one party has for the goods or services provided by another makes it vulnerable to a reduction or withdrawal of those benefits.[71]

Furthermore, at high levels of involvement, parties may make high demands of responsiveness from each other and then find that these are not met. This evokes disappointment and sometimes anger and resentment. A related process is particularly relevant for dissensual conflicts. People tend to feel particularly outraged about disagreements with others who are supposed to be close. This is one reason for the vehemence in conflicts about doctrinal differences that outsiders may consider trivial. The intensity of struggles when one faction disagrees with the views of their religious or ideological co-believers is illustrative.

Decreases in the anticipated goods or services one party receives from the other can readily become a grievance. The denial of previously granted rights can trigger anger and forceful resistance. For example, Sri Lanka became independent in 1948, but in the elections of 1956, Dias Bandaranaike and the Sri Lanka Freedom Party came into power and pursued Buddhist revivalist policies. Tamil language and other rights were diminished and Tamil discontent grew, to be followed initially by nonviolent protest then by deadly violence.

Changes in the Social Context

The social context within which potential adversaries interact often changes in ways that enhance the partisans' sense of grievance. Those changes not only become possible sources of deprivation but also help provide the criteria by which circumstances are judged to be unsatisfactory and unjustified.

The social conditions discussed in chapter 2, which could be the source of dissatisfaction, are not static, and changes in the social and physical environment often result in groups feeling aggrieved. Thus, increased immigration tends to alter the demographic balance among ethnic, cultural, religious, and class categories. Some people in the host country may regard these immigrants as threatening their own economic position or political power. This is more likely when economic conditions are worsening. For instance, over the past two decades immigration from Muslim nations has played an important role in the expansion of the Dutch economy. However, the economic downturn of 2008–2010 has made these very same groups the object of intense political debate and targets of violence, making the future of immigration policy in the Netherlands a key issue in the 2010 parliamentary elections, which saw significant gains by the anti-immigration Freedom Party.

Changes in the global economy are a source of strain within and among societies. Shifts in investments, trade patterns, and labor flows often exacerbate inequalities and thereby provide the bases for grievances. The background to the eruption of violence in Chiapas, Mexico, on January 1, 1994, the day the North American Free Trade Agreement (NAFTA) took effect, is illustrative.[72] The state of Chiapas, on Mexico's southern border, has long been characterized by extreme inequality between privileged landowners and impoverished indigenous peoples. Changes in the 1980s and early 1990s worsened the conditions of the poor indigenous Mayan communities. Some of these changes were related to transnational developments and the Mexican government's economic liberalization policies, including the end of land reform and of price supports for agricultural products. Land pressures also increased as a result of migration into the area. At the same time, the Catholic bishop Samuel Ruiz and some priests in Chiapas preached liberation theology, criticizing the policies that further impoverished the poor. Many indigenous resistance groups were organized, and support grew for the emerging Ejército Zapatista de Liberación Nacional (EZLN).

Prevailing ways of thinking and communicating provide the language in which deprivations are articulated. They vary among organizations, societies, and civilizations and change from one historical period to another. The commonly shared sentiments and social norms may be expressed in the discourses of religion and spirituality, of class struggle, of ethnic and other communal traditions, of individualistic psychology, or of innumerable other discourses. They include various standards about core values, be they personal freedom, social equality, collective self-determination, or stable order.

In the 1960s and 1970s, in the United States and elsewhere in the world social equality was highly valued and groups that had been relatively disadvantaged believed they deserved remedial social action. Even those who were not disadvantaged generally regarded the demands as legitimate. Since then, however, there are signs of backlashes and of renewed importance given to individual rights. The view that individuals should maximize and retain their gains from the marketplace became more prevalent and legitimate. The widespread economic recession that began in 2008 reduced the confidence in the workings of unfettered markets. To a certain extent this tension between individual liberties and broader collective responsibilities is inherent in every social system. This tension continues today in much of the world, as the rights of collectivities and the appreciation of multicultural social systems come into conflict with individual freedoms.

Each claim of unjustified deprivation that is effectively voiced resonates with other groups, which then challenge the inequities and discrimination that had been accepted as "natural." This was evident in the United States especially in the 1960s and 1970s, with the demand for greater equity by blacks, women, the poor, and many other communities. Similarly, as indigenous peoples in one place in the world struggled to reclaim rights and compensation from the descendants of European settlers, other indigenous groups asserted claims prompted by their own histories in their lands.

Finally, standards may be raised by the actions and words of authorities recognized by the partisans in a conflict. For example, the 1954 U.S. Supreme Court decision in *Brown v. Board of Education*, which declared segregated schools unconstitutional, was made unanimously by the most authoritative interpreters of the fundamental law of the country. That decision reinforced and raised the expectations of blacks throughout the United States, as well as undercut the legitimacy of defenders of racial segregation.[73]

Structural characteristics of the social system in which possible adversaries interact also affect the rate of conflicts within the system. Studies of international conflicts, for example, examine the incidence of wars as related to different alliance structures and economic relations in the world system. Thus, status inconsistency can be regarded as a system characteristic, assessing the degree to which the countries in the world are inconsistent in military expenditures, economic strength, and prestige.[74] High disequilibrium might be conducive to international conflict since national leaders would seek to alter that status quo. On the other hand, high disequilibrium might contribute to international cross-cutting ties, while high consistency would reinforce lines of cleavage and make international conflict more likely.

Empirical studies for the years 1946–1964 found that the incidence of wars correlated moderately with the degree of status inconsistency. But a replication, covering the years 1950–1980, did not find this relationship.[75] Perhaps this is explained by the greater global dominance of the United States in the earlier period and a greater dispersal of power during the later years. Thus, during the earlier period the strong hegemonic capabilities of the United States and the deep political cleavage of the Cold War meant that status inconsistency tended to be related to the struggle between the hegemon's group and the challenging group. In the later period, status consistency would be more indicative of fundamental cleavages in the international order.

FORMING CONTENTIOUS GOALS

For a conflict to become overt, the cause of an adversary's grievance must be attributed to other persons. The members of an aggrieved party must formulate a goal directed at those they believe could reduce their grievance. The aggrieved may seek more money, more control over land, more autonomy, or other matters over which it is believed the other party has control.

Although contentious goals are infinitely various, three major dimensions of goals are usefully distinguished. First is the degree to which the change sought is toward greater integration or toward greater separation. The second dimension is the magnitude of the changes being sought. The left-right continuum is the third dimension to be considered.

Along the dimension of integration-separation, goals to achieve greater integration include attaining equal opportunities for educational and occupational positions, becoming assimilated, imposing conformity, or converting the other side. At the opposite extreme, goals to achieve greater separation include autonomy, independence, or the expulsion or destruction of the adversary. The scale of the change sought depends on the degree of integration or separation that already prevails.

The magnitude of the changes sought may be small, such as modifications in allocating resources or altering the policies being implemented by the adversary. These reform goals are often of an aggregate rather than a collective character. That is, the goals pertain to opportunities for members of the quasi group as individuals, rather than for the group as a whole. At the other extreme, a revolutionary change in who has the authority to make allocations may be the objective. These goals often have a relatively collective character, as when a transformation is sought so that new groups or classes come to dominate. In between the extremes are goals to reform relationships, alter policies, or change leaders. Leaders of an ethnic minority, for example, may seek increased representation by its members in policy making. Even a coup by a military junta taking over the highest government offices from another junta (regarded as a palace revolution) often does not entail a radical change in the society. In a sense, the magnitude of the change sought is a function of the discrepancy between the goals of the adversary camps. The greater the difference between their goals, the more radical each side's goals will be regarded by their opponent.

Finally, the left-right dimension is a frequently discussed variation in goals. Seeking to restructure the relationship or change the policy between social strata is generally considered "left" insofar as the objective is to increase equality in economic well-being, social status, and political power.[76] Another characterization of this dimension stresses who is making claims on whom. Thus, when the disadvantaged make claims against those who have relative advantage, their objectives are considered leftist. When members of the dominant group seek to maintain or enhance their position, their objectives are regarded as rightist or even reactionary.[77]

Certainly, the nature of the goals being pursued has implications for the course of a conflict. For example, conflicts about the allocation of resources are relatively amenable to compromise, especially when the resources are sufficient and divisible. This is typically the case in consensual disputes. Some consensual conflicts, however, involve radical restructuring of the adversary relationship and are not easily settled. As when a revolutionary group seeks to end private ownership of large agricultural estates, such goals are unitary and not easily divisible.[78]

Dissensual conflicts are often about issues that each side views as requiring significant changes by the adversary and are relatively difficult to settle via compromise. This is typically the case when one party tries to convert the other to its way of believing. However, a group's goal, for example, to attain greater autonomy for its members to practice their religion, is more amenable to negotiation.

A group's goals incorporate mental constructs of desired future conditions and usually are embedded in a set of ideas about the partisans' plight and what can be done about it. These goals and ideas are varyingly shared and deeply held by group members. They also are varyingly well articulated, sometimes being only implicit and inferred from indirect verbal expressions and from conduct. Thus, E. J. Hobsbawm observes that the classical city mobs, acting before they had access to formal political processes, manifested ideas in their actions.[79] Mob participants expected to achieve something, assumed that the authorities would be responsive to their actions, and directed their activities selectively against the rich and powerful. The focus here is on sustained intergroup struggles and adversaries with explicit goals, often formulated by leaders.

Turning to the construction of contentious goals, three sources of determinants are usefully distinguished: the character of possible adversary groups, their social contexts, and the relations between them.

Membership Characteristics

Three aspects of the quasi group's membership that are particularly important for the formation of goals are: leadership, culture and social system, and the members' grievances. Leaders of a conflict group play a primary role in formulating contentious goals. Discontent may be widespread among the members of a quasi-group but be dormant and festering. A leader, to mobilize followers for a struggle, must convince them that their grievances are attributable to the actions of other people. Leaders explain that view and help formulate the specific demands whose satisfaction would reduce or even end their grievance. Leaders holding offices of authority generally have advantages in making persuasive arguments. Thus, explanations by government or church officials tend to be accorded credence by those recognizing their legitimacy.

The leaders' assertion that a particular group is the cause of their grievance is often contested, particularly by those who are blamed. Indeed, feelings arising from internal sources may be displaced on some scapegoat, as in the case of attributing conspiracies to vulnerable minority groups, but also to elite groups or external foes. Government officials who attribute responsibility for a problem to a foreign power can usually count on the loyalty of their constituency in accepting the attribution. An extensive review of the U.S. public's response to foreign policy crises concludes, "It appears that, almost regardless of prior attitudes of the public, regardless of the popularity of the president and regardless of how well [or poorly] the president handles the crisis, a large proportion of the population will support him."[80] This is illustrated by the degree of support President George W. Bush was able to rally for a preemptive war against Iraq in 2003, despite the wide range of critics noting the lack of evidence of an imminent threat.[81] This dynamic, sometimes called the "rally around the flag" effect, is particularly pronounced during the peak of a crisis and tends to dissipate in intensity as the crisis ebbs.[82] The task for would-be leaders of opposition groups is more difficult. They must rely more on charisma or use their legitimate authority based in a subunit of the social system whose leadership they would challenge. For example, Martin Luther King Jr. drew on his authority as the minister of the Dexter Avenue Baptist Church in Montgomery, Alabama, in helping to arouse and mobilize the blacks of Montgomery to carry out the bus boycott initiated in 1955; and he drew on his broader charisma to arouse the widening general support.[83]

In addition to leadership, culture and social context are additional aspects of a group's membership affecting the formation of goals. Which goals seem convincing depends in part on the experiences and belief systems of an adversary group's members. Thus, members who believe that they previously improved their condition by formulating goals that blamed particular others for their unsatisfactory conditions and also changed the others' conduct are likely to replicate that formulation. For example, trade union members who have improved their working conditions by making claims against corporate employers are likely to try that formula again.

Conversely, having formulated and pursued goals that were unsuccessful in the past discredits those goals from being pursued in the future. The goal is then reformulated, becoming more reformist and attainable, but sometimes becoming more extremist and radical; in the Middle East, changes in goals of Palestinian, Israeli, Islamic, and Arab groups illustrate both kinds of changes. At times, however, advocates on both sides argue that the goal had not been attained simply because it had not been pursued with sufficient vigor and persistence. Such differences in interpretation are often debated within each contending party.

Sociocultural and psychocultural qualities within a quasi group help shape the emergence of contentious goals, as noted in chapter 2. These are usually relatively stable features of a group. Therefore, the formulation of a contentious goal requires new developments, which mesh with the established sociocultural and psychocultural tendencies.

Furthermore, the emergence and character of a contentious goal is greatly affected by the grievance to be redressed. By considering how different types of grievances affect the formulation of goals, we can resolve some of the apparent contradictions about the importance of different sources of discontent.

People who feel they are generally deprived or who suffer further deterioration of their condition tend to support more radical goals than do people with status inconsistency or whose improving conditions were halted. During the Great Depression of the 1930s, voices calling for radical change emerged within the U.S. labor movement. When economic conditions later improved, however, trade union members advocating more reformist goals regained influence. African Americans in the United States during the 1960s provide another example. Blacks with higher education and income usually agitated for integration, while those with low education and income tended to support black separatist objectives.[84] The increasing proportion of African Americans who are in the middle and upper-middle classes broadens the range of goals pursued by African American groups, some of which can be quite conservative. Among persons who are not greatly deprived, status inconsistency may be associated with utopian goals. Thus, in the 1960s college students with status inconsistency tended to belong to organizations with utopian goals, while those with more consistent backgrounds tended to belong to more conventional political groups.[85]

The direction of goals, whether to the left or right, toward increasing or decreasing inequalities, also depends on the nature of the discontent. Even moderately deteriorating conditions for those who had been well-off dispose them to favor goals that restore previous inequalities. Thus, reactionary political movements have drawn disproportional support from such persons. Persons with ascribed or investment statuses that are higher than their achieved or reward statuses, such as persons with high ethnic ranking and low incomes, tend to support conservative or reactionary goals; while persons with over-rewarded kinds of inconsistencies, such as persons with low ethnic standing but high incomes, tend to support more egalitarian aims.[86]

The pattern of status inconsistency affects the content of contentious goals in other ways. People are inclined to raise themselves along the dimensions in which they have relatively low status and therefore tend to challenge those who are above them on those dimensions. This challenge helps shape their goal. Thus, persons with low ethnic and high occupational and income levels try to raise the status of their ethnicity by campaigns against prejudice directed at their ethnic group. Jewish Americans organized effective organizations to wage such campaigns, and as Arab Americans have become more numerous and prosperous, they have similarly organized.[87]

Contexts

The prevailing ways of thinking within the social environment also help channel the formulation of goals, pointing at who is to blame and what they must do to rectify the injustice. Thus, in some eras and civilizations economic forces and class struggles are widely thought to be the predominant forces shaping social relations. Consider that in many parts of the world during much of the twentieth century Marxist analyses of domestic and international relations were widely used to account for the injustices people experienced and to point to solutions. With the evident failures, immense social costs, and final collapse of the Soviet Union, Marxist analysis was widely discredited. The capitalist class was less often seen as the oppressor and a strong government less often regarded as a necessary counterforce.

For more than a decade, starting in the mid-1970s, the take-home pay of many U.S. workers declined; and increasingly, families needed two earners to compensate for this decline.[88] Responsibility for the declining disposable income was variously attributed. Some people pointed to decreased worker productivity due to worker incompetence and laziness, to managerial short-sightedness and greed, or to the diversion of research and development investment into military projects. Others blamed the government for increasing taxes to support government bureaucrats, unnecessary military expenditures, give-aways to those who shirk working, or corruption and waste. Still others pointed to increasing competition within the U.S. economy by the growth of women's participation in the labor force and by new waves of immigration. Others emphasized the increasing globalization of the economy, pitting U.S. workers against the lower-paid workers in less economically developed countries; this was framed either as the necessary working of impersonal market forces or the machinations of international corporations. Clearly, the nature of the goals formulated by members of an adversary group will be quite different depending on which combination of explanations they choose. Some of the variations in goals are presented and argued within the context of the institutionalized political system. Others fall outside of politics, erupting into the severe social conflicts of particular concern here. For example, in much of the world, for many decades grievances had become politicized and attributed to the persons who exercised power, particularly state power, rather than to impersonal social forces or to immoral conduct.[89] In the 1970s, women's oppression also came to be explained in terms of patriarchal thinking, differential control of resources, and state power.[90]

Politicization has often been combined with ideologies of a universalistic nature, such as Marxism, liberalism, and conservatism, which are universalistic in their applicability and in their openness, with believers trying to convince everyone to share their beliefs. Recent decades have seen a renewed attraction of more particularistic ideologies. This may be partly a response to the impersonality of universal ideologies and to their failures to satisfy felt needs relating to communal and moral concerns. The collapse of the Soviet Union and the evident failure of communist ideology as manifested there enhanced the credibility of alternative worldviews.

The attraction of particularistic ways of thinking is evident in the emphasis on ethnicity and some kinds of religious fundamentalism. Ethnic and religious communities celebrate their own ways and experiences, and some of them have significant restrictions on accepting persons who do not come from their community.

Nationalism combines ethnic and other communal identities with political claims, including having an independent state, and nationalism has long been an important influence in the formulation of contentious goals. Revolutionary challenges to a government can be aided by cloaking them in nationalistic claims. For example, a government may be charged with being the instrument of foreign powers; this has been the message of many revolutionary movements in Third World countries. This charge contributed to the mobilization of Iranian resistance to Shah Mohammad Reza Pahlavi, his government's collapse, and the coming to power of Ayatollah Ruhollah Khomeini in 1979.[91] Also, when the Soviet Union invaded Afghanistan in 1979 to maintain a Marxist-secular government there, the Afghan resistance flourished, drawing on nationalist and religious convictions.[92] Similar resistance has often occurred countering U.S. interventions in Latin America, the Middle East, and elsewhere.

The social environment helps each conflict group determine who its adversary is, and so influences its goals. Thus, the visibility and the vulnerability of different groups in a society make them more or less likely adversaries. Some groups, such as governments, are likely targets since they presume to be responsible for a wide range of social and economic as well as political conditions. Other groups, such as ethnic minorities, may be vulnerable to attack and available to be blamed for grievances arising from many sources. For example, traditions of anti-Semitism have made Jews such targets at various times in history.[93]

Another important aspect of the social context is the extent to which a social system appears to be closed and contracting. Insofar as potential adversaries regard themselves to be in a zero-sum situation, they formulate goals to redress their grievances in those terms. There may be predispositions, based on experience, for some groups of people to view their world as a limited one.[94] Experiencing expanding opportunities, conversely, tends to dampen the belief that contending parties are in a zero-sum relationship. This tendency is exemplified by the reduced incidence of wars among European states when their colonial empires were expanding elsewhere.[95] In the nineteenth century, the United States' expanding economy and open frontier offers another example. Those conditions probably reduced the sense that people were living in a zero-sum society. Conversely, the economic stagnation of many African countries, even at the beginning of the twenty-first century, contributes greatly to the internal wars in Africa.

Third parties and their possible evaluations also significantly influence the goals adversaries formulate. Contending groups often consider the reactions of such third parties in order to gain their support or lessen their opposition, and this sometimes gives a reason to moderate the goals in order to rally wider support.[96] The increasing globalization of the world tends to foster the engagement of more external parties in more conflicts; thus, domestic conflicts are becoming increasingly internationalized.

Importantly, the degree and form of institutionalized conflict regulation strongly affects the formulation of goals, particularly their lessened radicalism. Units that are part of a larger system with legitimate means of reaching collective decisions tend to construct reformist goals. Democracies provide mechanisms for resolving small- and large-scale conflicts and help moderate the goals of various ethnic and other communal groups. The United Nations and other international organizations increasingly provide the venues for global and regional decision making on contentious matters.

Finally, the globalization of the world itself helps shape the formulation of goals, locating responsibility for grievances at the global level. Thus, environmental problems, such as global warming, are increasingly viewed as requiring global policies.[97] In addition, the growth of economic integration and multinational corporations raises issues of control that cannot be managed at the national level.[98] Furthermore, the growth of international governmental bodies such as the IMF, the World Bank, and the WTO locates power at the global level in regard to matters of widespread impact.[99] Partly as a result of these developments, as well as technological advances, transnational social-movement organizations proliferate and formulate goals to affect the conduct of each other and of multinational corporations and international governmental organizations.[100]

Adversary Relations

Adversaries significantly affect each other's goals. A potential conflict group may formulate objectives that in some ways mimic those of its opponent or develop ones that magnify the differences. An illustration of the former process may be seen in the formation of Zionist goals in response to the intensified persecution of Jews in Russia toward the end of the nineteenth century. Zionists aimed to establish a national home and have a social and economic life like the Russians and others among whom they lived, emphasizing productive labor, especially on the land. This was one kind of response to persecution and the denial of the right to own land and to farm. If they could not be accepted as Russians or Germans because they were Jews, then as Jews they would have their own country. When Zionism began to focus on Palestine, under British mandate, Palestinian nationalism, in turn, was aroused and was strongly affected by Palestinians' experience with Zionism and the establishment of Israel.[101]

The demands one party makes on another are also shaped by the structure of their relations with each other. For example, an analysis of agrarian revolutions demonstrates how certain agricultural relations generate particular revolutionary or reform goals. Noncultivators derive their income from the ownership of the land and the cultivators earn their income in the form of wages, as migratory workers. Revolutionary nationalist movements are likely to erupt in such migratory estate systems, and often did in colonial areas. Of course, certain other conditions must exist for such movements to emerge. For instance, if the migratory workers return to village subsistence holdings when the harvest ends, traditional tribal or peasant leadership can provide the resources needed for organization and workers have the time they need to collectively mobilize. Traditional village authorities will join the migratory laborers in the revolutionary nationalist movements "only when their own economic base of support is being ended by the same estate system that is exploiting the poor laborers."[102] This resulted in the rise of revolutionary movements in Vietnam and in Angola during the 1950s and 1960s.

The leaders and intellectuals who seek to formulate a goal for their group often do so taking into account the goal's utility not only for mobilizing their group but also for influencing the adversary. If members of the enemy side can be induced to question the morality and justice of their position, then the chances of arousing feelings of guilt or shame, acts of defection, and readiness to yield will increase. Consequently, aims are often formulated in terms shared with the opponent—values such as justice, freedom, or equality, as when leaders of national independence movements lay claim to the rights of a people to rule themselves.

This reasoning also suggests that the immediate aims a contending group selects from among the array of possible goals are those deemed feasible and possible to be yielded by the adversary. During the street protests that followed the contested 2009 Iranian presidential election, for instance, opposition groups appealed to Supreme Leader Ali Khamenei to cancel the election results and hold new elections rather than pursue more extreme goals, such as securing the resignation of President Ahmadinejad.

Finally, the attractiveness of pursuing a particular goal is affected by the group's feelings toward the adversary.[103] If one group hates another, it will derive extra pleasure by pursuing an aim that humiliates its adversary. Vengeance can be sweet. The gratification from extracting retribution, however, may lead a group to pursue goals that become self-defeating or inflict self-losses. On the other hand, if positive feelings are strong enough, a goal may be chosen that minimizes the harm to the opponent, even if it fails to maximize the group's own benefits. The result may be mutually beneficial in the long term. For example, the transformation in South Africa in the early 1990s was managed with less destructiveness than many anticipated because the primary adversaries set goals that allowed each side to gain or retain minimal safeguards.[104]

BELIEVING REDRESS IS POSSIBLE

The fourth condition to be present for a conflict to emerge is the belief by at least one party's members that they can act to change an adversary and/or the adversary's conduct, thereby attaining more of what they want. Analysts of social conflicts increasingly recognize the importance of attaining this condition. This recognition reflects the change in emphasis in theories about the emergence of social movements. For many decades, the strain, alienation, or dissatisfaction experienced by some population groups was used to explain the rise of a social movement or revolutionary challenge. Beginning in the 1960s, such theories drawing from ideas about collective behavior were superseded by theories stressing how groups mobilize resources to seek redress for their grievances.[105] Discontent is taken for granted, but the ability to change conditions that are unsatisfactory explains the rise of challenging social movements. Even terrible conditions may be endured without contention if those who suffer them believe that they cannot correct the behavior of those they hold responsible.

The availability of legitimate and credible means of seeking redress provides alternatives to coercive contention. Within many societies, electoral politics or a judicial system may seem effective, which may keep the kinds of struggles examined in this book from emerging. Members of an adversary group come to believe that they can improve their unsatisfactory conditions by changing their antagonist when they believe either that their capabilities have grown stronger or that the capabilities of those they would change have weakened. Such new beliefs follow changes within the adversaries, changes in their social context, or changes in the relations among the adversaries.

Membership Characteristics

Among the many features of the quasi group that contribute to its members' sense that they can act to reduce their grievances, two are particularly noteworthy: changing capabilities and leadership.

As members of a potential adversary group improve their conditions, their dissatisfaction may be expected to decline. But their improved conditions also tend to give them resources that prompt them to believe that their conditions can be improved even more. The earlier discussion of status inconsistency generating grievances is relevant here. If people have high ranks along particular dimensions, they are likely to have some resources that give them reason to believe they might raise their low rankings. On the other hand, research findings also indicate that status inconsistency does not always result in contentious behavior but may instead subject people to inconsistent claims and directives.[106] This would diminish the belief that unsatisfactory conditions could be corrected, and that dampens recognizing dissatisfaction. Furthermore, the discomfort of some kinds of rank inconsistencies may be expressed in anxiety, which also interferes with believing that unsatisfactory conditions can be imp·oved.[107]

Leaders play a major role not only in shaping an identity, developing a sense of grievance, and formulating a conflict goal but also in convincing their constituents that they can achieve their goals. This in part depends on offering an analysis of the opposing sides' relative weakness, claiming the sympathy of those not yet engaged in the struggle, and finally stressing their own significant resources.

Goals differ in the time needed to attain them. Leaders can help develop a long-term strategy with a sequence of sub-goals, starting with relatively immediate and attainable ones that then provide the basis for reaching larger goals. For a conflict organization to mobilize support and sustain itself, the succession of goals must be closely related to the group's capacities relative to its opposition. Particularly for emerging conflict organizations, the formulation of short-term attainable goals is important in building confidence and gaining more support.[108] If the organization is to persevere and win its larger goals the immediate goals should be feasible and if reached should not end the sense of grievance.

Leaders also play an important role in attracting allies, forming coalitions of diverse interests.[109] This may be done by promising future benefits after victory, by offering side payments, and by appealing to shared values and interests. Those coalitions enable a conflict to be undertaken with a prospect of victory, and they also shape the goals of the conflict. For example, after the Iraqi invasion of Kuwait in August 1990, President George H. W. Bush was able to quickly construct a coalition including nearly all the Arab governments and the permanent members of the UN Security Council. This gave international legitimacy and the capability of threatening and waging a land war from Saudi Arabia. It also put constraints on the conflict; the coalition probably could not be held together for long without decisive action and a goal limited to driving the Iraqi forces from Kuwait.

Leaders often try to convince their followers that they have the capability to wage a successful struggle by pointing to the past when they had what they now propose to achieve. For example, a feminist leader may argue that in early human history women were socially superior to men and were worshipped by them.[110] An ethnic leader may argue that in the past members of their ethnicity were much more advanced than the barbarian peoples around them. In addition, leaders often argue that the opposition is weak and getting weaker while their side is strong and getting stronger.

Leaders agitate, then, not only by trying to increase their followers' discontent but also by raising the hope that this can be changed, and by their own efforts. That seems paradoxical. To emphasize how exploited and victimized people are seems to contradict their possibility of bettering themselves. One solution to the paradox is to use the power of weakness. Desperation can engender determination and recklessness; having little, there is little that can be withheld from those who appear weak. Thus, Karl Marx and Friedrich Engels, in the *Communist Manifesto*, exhorted the workers of the world to unite in struggle, since "The proletarians have nothing to lose but their chains. They have a world to win."[111]

The task is often easier for leaders of a group with considerable resources in some arenas but dissatisfied in certain other arenas. An economically advantaged community may believe it can use its resources to gain more political autonomy and so not be required to share its resources with the disadvantaged of the larger society. Thus, in Spain the two regions with particularly strong movements for autonomy have long been Catalonia and the Basque country; both regions have been relatively advanced economically.[112]

Contexts

Various aspects of the adversaries' context affect a potential party's belief that it can change another group and so better its condition. For one, successes by other groups in making improvements against opposition provide models of what might be accomplished by struggle. They also may contribute to reinforcing belief in the efficacy of particular means of struggle, such as nonviolent resistance. Thus, surges of reliance on nonviolent action have followed significant applications, as occurred in Eastern Europe in 1989 and in North Africa and the Middle East in 2010 and 2011.

The social context includes people who are not clearly members of the adversary parties. They are an audience that the partisans address, pointing to the inequities they suffer in order to justify their action and to win support. Some members of that audience may actually be drawn into the struggle, and as they are, the conflict expands. An aggrieved party may seek redress, therefore, if its members believe their cause can be made visible and will win sympathy and support from persons not yet engaged in the struggle. For example, in 1994 the indigenous peoples of Chiapas had reason to expect wide support from the burgeoning NGOs in Mexico, particularly relating to human rights and to indigenous rights.[113] These were linked to other NGOs in the hemisphere and throughout the world.

Outsiders sometimes take the initiative in entering an emerging conflict situation. They tend to enter to help those with whom they feel linked by class, religion, ethnicity, ideology, or other interests or identities. Such "outside agitators" or would-be exporters of revolution, however, will be unable to ignite a flame if there is no dry tinder. They often help provide the means to sustain the struggle and so fuel the fight. This was evident as resistance to the Soviet-supported Afghan government grew, leading to the Soviet invasion of Afghanistan, which resulted in the increased flow of mujahidin, assisted by the U.S. government.[114]

Adversary Relations

A conflict is often initiated when a group with a grievance perceives that their opponent is in a position of weakness. An opponent may expose such weakness in several ways. It may act inconsistently, hesitantly, and incompetently, and reveal disunion and lack of conviction in its own positions. That may give credence to the view that a deterioration of conditions is due to that party's failures, which also indicates its vulnerability to pressure. Thus, analysts of revolutions generally agree that one of the immediate causes of revolts is the appearance of uncertainty and of self-doubt among the authorities. This may be signaled by verbal signs of panic and by defections. Such signals invite more radical goals if they indicate that fundamental restructuring of authority relations rather than reforms are needed and are becoming possible.

Changes in the relative power of potential antagonists are often the prelude to conflict emergence. For example, analyses of the great revolutions of France, Russia, and China reveal that the state in each case had been strained beyond its capacity by its international ventures.[115] More recently, a number of scholars have argued that the United States' extensive foreign policy commitments, coupled with its eroding global economic position, has subjected it to bold challenges from other states or nonstate actors in the international community.[116]

Finally, it should be noted that a powerful group believing that it has overwhelming dominance may exploit that dominance and so provoke strong resistance from the exploited, subordinated, or vulnerable party. Consequently, extreme acts of repression may fail to be effective, convincing groups previously unengaged in a struggle that they have no alternative but to resist and resort to desperate methods. That can set the stage for a destructive conflict escalation.

CONCLUSIONS

A conflict emerges when members of one or more potential antagonistic parties develop a shared identity, generate a sense of grievance, form a goal to change another party so as to reduce the grievance, and finally believe that they can bring about that change. These four conditions are highly interdependent, affecting each other as a struggle emerges.[117] Each is necessary, but none is sufficient alone; furthermore, various combinations of different levels of each can result in the initiation of a conflict. Together, they provide the impetus for at least one side to move against another, igniting a struggle. The characteristics of the identity, grievance, goal, and method used to redress the grievance greatly affect how destructive the conflict becomes; as those characteristics change, so does the destructiveness of the conflict as it moves through its trajectory.

The judgment of a party's members about their ability to gain what they seek is critical in their decision to engage in a conflict. But that does not mean that a conflict results simply from a rational calculation by each party to get as much as it thinks it can get. An overwhelming sense of grievance may result in acts of desperation that appear to an outside observer as irrational and self-destructive.

Three sources of determinants for each condition have been mapped out. One source is internal to each potential conflict party. These internal factors and processes may result in beliefs among members of a conflict party about who is responsible for their troubles, and they may target scapegoats so that the observers and analysts regard the resulting conflict as unrealistic.

The internal features and the contexts of potential adversaries affect each of the conditions necessary for the emergence of a conflict. In this analysis, however, the ways adversaries affect each other's conduct is emphasized. This is important because it means that no one party is totally in charge of a struggle's outbreak or its course. It also means that each party affects the behavior of its possible adversary in the emergence and development of a conflict. This can be an empowering insight for any adversary.

This analysis has wide-ranging implications for reducing conflict destructiveness. The multiplicity of factors and processes that account for identities, grievances, goals, and means of struggle indicate that many ways exist for partisans and intermediaries to restructure a conflict so that it is waged more constructively. The analysis suggests several strategies for preventing the eruption of destructive social conflicts: inhibiting the development of intensely antagonistic identities, ameliorating the grounds for severe grievances, diverting the formulation of goals that attribute responsibility for the grievance to others, or inhibiting the development of the belief that a sense of grievance will be redressed by acting violently against another person or group. These possibilities also suggest that often people do not want to prevent a conflict from emerging. In particular instances, justice is served and liberty is won if a conflict is waged. In order to avoid new injustices and new denials of freedom, the conflicts are best fought constructively.

4

Alternative Conflict Strategies

The conventional understanding among many partisans and observers of conflicts is that injurious coercion is needed to induce an adversary to change against its will. Apply enough pressure, so the logic goes, and one's adversary will eventually yield. Certainly coercion sometimes does result in getting an adversary to back down. This is evidenced by the ability of repressive regimes to stifle political opposition in locations as diverse as Myanmar, Iran, and Guatemala. Other times, however, the use of violence to defeat an adversary results not in their capitulation but in their heightened devotion to their cause. This appears particularly true where existential issues or core values are at stake. In these cases, which include the Israeli Palestinian conflict and efforts to control the nascent civil rights movement in the United States in the 1950s, injurious coercion only seems to strengthen the cohesion and willingness to fight of the group that is subjected to the violence. During even such conflicts, however, it is always possible for one or both sides to choose more nonviolent and noncoercive modes of contention. For instance, one side may promise future benefits to an opponent if the opponent yields what it seeks. Or one party may try to convince its adversary that to provide what it requests would be in the adversary's own true interests. Such noncoercive inducements are often combined with some coercion, but often the coercion is limited and not necessarily destructive of positive relationships between the adversaries.

A contending party's choice of conflict strategy is often a product of trial and error and generally shifts over time. In large-scale conflicts each side generally consists of many groups employing many different strategies, some of which may be complementary, others of which may be contradictory. Moreover, since every conflict is interlocked with many others, a group within one contending party is likely to use different strategies with various antagonists, within and outside its camp, and with parties that have diverse stakes in the conflict.

A party's selection of a conflict management strategy does not require that alternatives be consciously considered, their likely effectiveness assessed, or their costs weighed before being selected. At times, a tactic may be used simply because it appears to be the only reasonable one available, a similar strategy worked in the past, or because so many resources have been dedicated to the current strategy that changing course seems unthinkable.[1] Moreover, no single party wholly determines how a struggle is conducted; rather, the adversaries jointly shape their mode of struggle. Sometimes conflicts are highly institutionalized and the adversaries mutually agree to employ one particular mode of conflict management, as occurs in cultures with norms regarding duels, feuds, strikes, judicial proceedings, and so on. Other times the parties disagree about what mode is being used; one side may proclaim it is engaging in respectful petition or protest, while the other regards the conduct as an unlawful threat to authority and violently represses it, as occurred at Tiananmen Square, Beijing, in June 1989.

But whatever the circumstances, alternative conflict strategies are always conceivable and an analyst should consider what they might be and why the parties did not choose them or even consider them.

TYPES OF INDUCEMENTS

To examine the adoption and the consequences of different conflict modes, it is useful to consider three basic inducements available to conflicting parties: coercion, reward, and persuasion.[2]

Coercive Inducements

Coercion is a major element of the struggles examined here. It refers to actions, including symbolic ones, that injure or threaten to injure the adversary; they are presented as efforts to intimidate and deter the opponent or to force the opponent to comply with the demands made by the coercer. The cessation of coercive action, then, is conditional on the opponent's compliance and is not carried out for its intrinsic satisfaction only.

One significant difference in the form that coercion can take is between threatened and actualized coercion. Coercion is generally threatened before being applied in the hope that the threat will suffice. Another important distinction lies between violent and nonviolent coercion. The term *violent coercive inducement* refers to threatened or actual direct physical death or injury to people or destruction of part of their valued material world. This conventional notion is useful for the present analysis, but other conceptions should be recognized. Johan Galtung argues for broadening the concept of violence to include actions or inactions by some people such that "human beings are being influenced so that their actual somatic and mental realizations are below their potential realizations."[3] Galtung influentially reasons that "if people are starving when that is objectively avoidable, then violence is committed."[4] On the other hand, for many people, even killings may not be regarded as violent when they are done by legitimate authorities.[5] For some members of the public, the use of force is regarded as necessary to maintain law and order and consequently is not considered to be violent. In our analysis, however, the use or threatened use of force to injure others is called violence, whoever does it.

The magnitude of coercive inducements varies greatly, but not along a single dimension. A high level of coercion is evident when force is used to change the conditions of the target group. At the most extreme this would include, for instance, the widespread killing of group members, as in cases of bombing cities or of genocide. More typically, coercion is used against only some members of the opposing sides, thus weakening and intimidating enough of the other side so that the entire body is obliged to comply. This would include attacks against the other side's armed forces, leading figures, or even non-engaged members of the opposing collectivity. Violent coercion includes police repression of influential elites and torture or "disappearances" of political activists. Nonviolent coercion, such as boycotts or economic sanctions, is generally considered to be of lower magnitude than violent coercion.[6] For instance, a threat may be made to withhold payment or services on which the other party depends, as often occurs in labor-management disputes. In valued personal relations, the mere expression of disapproval or anger is also an example of nonviolent coercion. Nonviolent action also can take the form of massive demonstrations and withdrawal of the legitimacy formerly accorded to office holders.

For threats to be effective they must appear credible to the threatened. That means the party making the threat must seem capable and willing to execute it. For example, a government threatening warfare must build and maintain a powerful military force that is perceived by the other side as having a capability to inflict serious harm and the readiness to bear the costs of the likely counter blows. Carrying out a threat can have high costs, both in terms of exercising the coercion and suffering the consequences of retribution. Failing to follow through with a threat, when compliance is not won, is also costly, damaging future credibility with constituents as well as external adversaries and allies. Such risks have a great impact on the choice of strategies adopted by each side.

Furthermore, coercion can be an uncertain and imprecise means of inducing an adversary to change. In large-scale conflicts, trying to induce the leaders of the adversary to change may involve subjecting their constituents to massive violent coercion. Such coercion, however, may turn counterproductive as the initially wavering constituency rallies to support their leadership against the outside attacker. The use of broad and unselective coercion, then, tends to widen the conflict, add to its destructiveness, and sometimes prolong it. Finally, the resulting animosities and destruction severely hampers the attainment of mutually agreeable relations afterward.

Rewards as Inducements

Rewards as a form of inducement are commonly used but are relatively neglected in thinking about social conflicts. In child rearing and learning generally, an extensive body of theory and research indicates the value of using rewards rather than punishments when seeking to alter the behavior of another.[7] This principle is also observable in large-scale conflicts. For example, in the early 1990s the U.S. government had become deeply concerned about North Korea's nuclear program and sought UN approval for strong economic sanctions. By June 1994, plans to attack North Korea's nuclear facilities were prepared. The danger of a war was averted when former president Jimmy Carter went to North Korea and persuaded Kim Il Sung, North Korea's leader, to freeze the nuclear program. The U.S. and North Korean governments then conducted negotiations leading to the October 1994 Agreed Framework, according to which North Korea would roll back its nuclear arms program and the United States would gradually normalize political and economic relations, help replace nuclear reactors, and supply heavy fuel oil.[8] The effectiveness of this strategy was not fully tested since the policy was changed by the incoming administration of President George W. Bush early in 2001 and remains in flux under the administration of President Barack Obama. In South Korea itself a similar debate over strategy toward the North has occurred with the "Sunshine Policy" of dialogue and reconciliation toward North Korea initiated by South Korean president Kim Dae Jung following his election in 1992, which was replaced by a much harder-line strategy favored by President Lee Myung-bak, who was elected in December 2007.

Positive sanctions are more likely to be used and to be effective in the closing stages of a conflict than during a period of escalation or of intense antagonism. Offers of benefits while a conflict is being waged with great coerciveness tend to be regarded with suspicion by the recipient.[9] An exchange of benefits, such as of prisoners on each side, however, may be a way of signaling the possibility of eventually normalizing relations and are sometimes followed by confidence-building measures, which are discussed in chapter 7.

Even while a conflict is in progress, one party may offer or provide material benefits as an inducement to obtain what it seeks. Benefits may include money, land, or promises of access to occupational positions. In addition, positive sanctions include intangible benefits such as approbation or status recognition. This means that the side with greater resources is more capable of using positive sanctions, possessing "soft power."[10] The U.S. government is particularly strong in this regard.

As is true for negative sanctions, the recipients of positive sanctions vary in susceptibility. To complicate matters, certain individuals or factions within the opposing side in large-scale conflicts are more likely to obtain the benefits than are others. In addition, some factions may choose to accept positive inducements while other factions steadfastly refuse them, leading some to call those that refuse peaceful overtures "spoilers" of peace processes.[11] Often benefits may be covertly offered to the leaders of the opposing side, knowing that exposed acceptance would be regarded as corruption or treason. In collective bargaining situations, some agreements are considered "sweetheart contracts" because they offer little to the workers and imply that the union negotiator has received side payments from the management.

Over time, rewards can be part of a powerful strategy for constructive conflict transformation. In many capitalist countries, in the nineteenth and twentieth centuries, class conflict erupted between workers and the owners of the industries where the workers were employed, sometimes leading to bloody revolutions, many of which were violently suppressed. Yet gradually in most of these countries, governments began to implement social welfare policies and laws to protect workers, largely with the acquiescence of the dominant economic class. Members of the wealthy class in those countries saw that the stability of the society so purchased would be to their benefit as well as to the workers' benefit. In part this recognition was the result of coercion, but also of the persuasive efforts of the workers and their middle-class allies.

Persuasive Inducements

Persuasive inducements are efforts to influence an opponent by normative arguments, factual information, or appeals designed to alter the other side's feelings or perceptions of the conflict.[12] Since conflicts arise and persist only because adversaries believe they have incompatible goals, persuasion can play a significant role in the emergence, escalation, and transformation of conflicts. Although they are frequently used, they are often accompanied by some degree of coercion. Persuasive inducements are also difficult to assess, perhaps because antagonists rarely acknowledge that the enemy has convinced them of anything. Nevertheless, persuasive inducements can have transforming effects. This is evident in the decades since the 1970s, during which the women's movements and feminist thinking have overcome resistance to bring about immense changes in the relations between men and women in much of the world. This struggle, which has relied heavily on persuasive inducements, has produced a profound social-cultural transformation that continues to spread.

Persuasive efforts are likely to be more effective at the initial stages of conflict emergence, before mutual mistrust has intensified. Later, as a conflict enters a de-escalating phase, they may be renewed as one or both sides try to convince the other that belief in the incompatibility of their goals is misguided or that their common interests should be given higher priority. The resulting reframing of the conflict marks its transformation and may be aided by a mediator's redefinitions and restructuring.[13]

Persuasive inducements vary widely in content, depending on who is trying to influence whom, what the issues in contention are, and the stage the struggle has reached. Such efforts may be couched in appeals to shared values about justice, fairness, or freedom, where the other side is urged to concede what is being sought. Persuasive inducements may also be applied by other parties with a stake in the fight or even by intermediary groups, some of whom may try to convince the adversaries that they have common or complementary interests and that those interests would be well served by making what previously had been regarded as concessions.[14]

Adversaries who become convinced that they have a common enemy have a reason to moderate or even settle their conflict with each other and form a coalition to confront their shared enemy. One of the adversaries may persuade the other of the salience of this shared antagonist, or an intermediary may try to persuade two antagonists about the dangers from a third party. It is also possible that the adversaries become convinced that they have an opportunity for mutual gain by cooperation, such as joint exploitation of petroleum or water resources. Finally, the adversaries may be persuaded to recognize they share a problem that can best be overcome by their joint efforts; the problem may be an environmental risk or the waste of their resources in a mutually destructive struggle. Thus, although labor unions and environmental organizations often are in contention, pitting interests in jobs against protecting the environment, collaborative alliances sometimes are made between them. This happened during a strike of the United Paperworkers International Union against a papermaking company in Jay, Maine, 1987–1988. The townspeople had long endured the effects of toxic waste from the company's paper mills when two disasters caused grave environmental damage, revealing links between the company's environmental and labor policies. The UPIU and Greenpeace formed a lasting alliance, which resulted in passage of the state's first environmental ordinance enabling the town of Jay to enforce environmental regulations.[15]

Another kind of persuasive argument a contending party may use is that what it wants does not endanger the adversary. For example, it may argue that the autonomy or access to resources that it seeks would not adversely affect the other party. This might be argued in terms of shared values or norms of fairness, pointing out that in similar circumstances, the adversary would make the same claims. The contending party's leaders may ask the adversary to consider what its claim looks like from its perspective.

Finally, persuasive inducements may provide information to convince the opponent that agreement would be advantageous to them. The information is likely to be expressed as predictions of future losses or forgone gains if the other side does not change as desired. Predictions of future losses, generally called warnings, foretell terrible consequences, but only if those matters are not under the persuader's control. If they are, the predictions are regarded as threats. For example, leaders of a protesting organization may point out that if they fail to get what they seek, another leadership or a rival organization will take over and be even more hostile. Information may also come in the form of forecasting future benefits if the opponent changes and agrees to concede; for example, other groups would praise them. If what is predicted is under the control of the party making the predictions, it is a promise; when it is not, it has been called a mendation.[16]

In conflict relations, partisans often say that actions speak louder than words. Indeed, appeals, arguments, and information frequently are more convincingly conveyed by the contending party's behavior than by what it says. The gestures, policies, and a thousand other kinds of actions by members of a contending party are observed and interpreted by the other side and provide credibility to the words uttered. Thus, we cannot fully separate persuasive inducements from other kinds of inducements. In any particular mode of waging a conflict, positive and negative sanctions tend to be combined with persuasive efforts. Thus, in a war, psychological techniques are used to encourage enemy soldiers to surrender.[17] During the East-West Cold War, each side used various propaganda methods to undermine support of the other's leadership. In the American struggle against al Qaeda and allied Islamic groups, persuasive efforts are widely recognized as vital to deny those groups support from mainstream Muslims. Since President Obama came into office, official support for these efforts, often called public diplomacy, has expanded, with total public diplomacy appropriations in 2008 at nearly $900 million.[18]

The three kinds of inducements—coercion, reward, and persuasion—have been discussed as direct and explicit ways of trying to affect an opponent. But these efforts may also be indirect, in which case we speak of covert actions and of efforts to manipulate the opposing side. For example, one side may try to subvert or reduce adversary leaders' constituency support by covert operations such as secretly supporting publications and organizations opposing the leaders on the other side. Or one side may try to influence a third party to reduce its support for the opposing side, as may be undertaken in a public relations campaign.

STRATEGIES AND MODES OF STRUGGLE

Coercive and noncoercive inducements are combined in many ways to construct particular tactics, strategies, and modes of conflict. They may be short-term tactics such as a protest march or long-term strategies such as a guerrilla war. The long-term strategy incorporates many tactics, sets of them generally conducted in sequence. Each adversary adopts particular strategies, sometimes with little reflection, and as the adversaries struggle against each other, they fashion a specific mode of conflict.

Many modes have been socially constructed and contain generally recognized and familiar characteristics. Adversaries may agree, for example, that a particular action is part of "collective bargaining." They then share certain expectations about what the other side will do, and both feel constrained not to act outside the mutually understood rules. Similarly, legal systems are collectively enacted to provide procedures by which many disputes and conflicts are conducted and settled within a society. Even wars may be considered social constructs; as Margaret Mead observes, war is an institution that was invented.[19] Sometimes adversaries disagree about what mode of struggle is being used; one side may say it is engaged in a struggle for national liberation, and the other asserts that a small terrorist band is challenging legitimate authorities. When there are such disagreements, the adversaries are little constrained by shared rules. The degree to which conflict means are regulated and institutionalized, then, can affect how destructive or constructive a struggle becomes.

Institutionalized Conflict Regulation

Since social conflicts are omnipresent, every social system has contrived ways to manage them.[20] Within all societies, there are rules for conducting and settling conflicts that become institutionalized over time. The judicial system in most countries upholds regulations regarding disputes between individuals and/or corporate entities. The decision makers in these systems tend not to be the disputants themselves, but authorities such as judges, juries, or heads of religious or political organizations. Adversaries generally pursue and resolve conflicts by their own actions within the confines of such institutionalized regulations, as when conflicts between developers and environmentalists are conducted by the parties according to laws regarding zoning, wetland protection, and endangered species. Sometimes institutionalized modes of conflict management become so ingrained that the conflicts being managed are regarded as games more than as fights. In democratic societies, for instance, electoral politics may be so habitual and so well regulated that contesting political parties are not regarded as being in a social conflict, except metaphorically. By the definition used in this book, however, they are in conflict.

Degree of Regulation

As previously noted, rules often govern in great detail many aspects of adversarial conduct, which can be true even for conflicts waged with deadly violence. Thus, in many societies quarreling men have fought duels in which careful protocol was followed that might result in a death. Wars, too, may be quite limited, as were European wars between about 1640 and 1740 when fighting was halted to gather the harvest, compared with the relatively unlimited wars of the prior two centuries.[21]

With the establishment of large armies of conscripts at the end of the eighteenth century and the development of mechanized war fighting in the nineteenth and twentieth centuries, the scale of wars, the capabilities of killing people, and the deaths inflicted upon civilians grossly increased, reaching extreme levels in World War I. More war horrors followed. World War II was waged as a "total" war, with "terror" bombing of cities in Poland, Great Britain, Germany, and Japan, culminating in the use of nuclear bombs against Hiroshima and Nagasaki. Populations were forced into extremely harsh labor camps, and millions were murdered, reaching the horrors of the Holocaust.

In response to the horrors of World War I, World War II, and the large-scale killings in internal wars and genocides, numerous treaties, international resolutions, and other efforts were made during the twentieth century to prevent and restrain particular ways of killing people. These treaties and understandings have been widely accepted, and they have been largely observed.[22] Thus, since the dropping of two atom bombs in 1945, neither nuclear nor bacteriological weapons have been employed in warfare. Chemical weapons have generally not been used since World War I; however, in 1988 during the Iraqi-Iranian war, Saddam Hussein used chemical weapons on Kurdish citizens of Iraq.[23] Chemicals were also used as a defoliating agent by U.S. military forces in the war in Vietnam.

Normative constraints and institutionalized regulations have helped contain the development, deployment, and use of potentially horrific weapons. In addition, the widely agreed-upon constraints are sustained by threats of sanctions and fear of retaliation, as well as doubts about the effectiveness of chemical and bacteriological weapons. The importance of broadly recognized legitimate authority in constraining gross human rights violations is also evident by the violations that occur in the absence of such authority. This is evident during civil wars and revolutions, as illustrated by the grotesque brutality of genocidal attacks in Rwanda in 1994, the "ethnic cleansing" by rape, torture, and killing in Croatia and Bosnia in the former Yugoslavia in 1993–1995, and the large-scale killings of non-Arabs in the Darfur region of Sudan in the first years of the twenty-first century.[24] The existence of a government exercising control in a country does not in itself ensure the protection of human rights for the people in that country. Many of the worst atrocities in modern human experience have been conducted by government leaders against their own people, claiming legitimate authority and promising a future utopia; this is epitomized by the imprisonment and killing of millions of people by the totalitarian regimes of the Soviet Union headed by Joseph Stalin, of Nazi Germany headed by Adolph Hitler, of the People's Republic of China led by Mao Zedong, and of the Cambodian Khmer Rouge headed by Pol Pot.[25]

The content of rules governing conflict engagement is crucial. International norms regarding human rights and democracy have influenced the rules established in countries that are in transition away from authoritarian control.[26] The rules often help provide safeguards for individual and group security and also procedures to challenge the privileges of the dominant political party, class, ethnicity, or other groups. Many international governmental and nongovernmental organizations are influential in helping establish such rules, including the Organization for Security and Cooperation in Europe, the United Nations Development Programme, and the European Union.

The term *conflict regulation* refers to the rules that govern the contending parties' conduct in a dispute. But rules that are unilaterally imposed cannot be regarded as regulations, nor can policies that allow one party to violently suppress another and that are used as a mask for partisan struggle. Authentic regulation exists insofar as the contending parties recognize each other's legitimacy and regard the rules governing their conflict as legitimate.

Degree of Institutionalization

Institutionalized rules of conflict are generally sanctioned by legitimate authority, appear to exist external to those in conflict, and are internalized by members of the contending parties.[27] The existence of legitimate sanctions to punish violations and sanctions to reward compliance are crucial elements of the institutionalization of regulations and their maintenance. Sanctions that may be employed by officials, religious leaders, charismatic leaders, or friends include punishments such as fines or incarceration and rewards such as social acclaim or the promise of everlasting life in heaven. Rules embodied in written form or orally transmitted beyond one generation take on an independent quality that helps maintain and foster adherence to them. Persons accorded the authority to do so may codify these rules, making the rules less vulnerable to differing interpretations by contending parties. Institutionalization is increased when all the adversary parties as well as the other members of their social system internalize the pertinent regulations.[28] When the rules are internalized through socialization and other social learning, people generally police themselves and anticipate feeling guilty or ashamed if they violate the rules.

Bases of Regulation and Institutionalization

The fundamental factor underlying the content of the rules governing conflict behavior and the institutionalization of the rules is prior recurrent practices. Repeated actions come to be expected and deviations become not only violations of these expectations but also illegitimate.[29] The social logic for such codification is compelling: the way things are done is the way they should be done because that is the way they have been done. In the United States, for example, it would be unthinkable for a political party that loses an election to take up arms in order to prevent the prevailing party from assuming office. Yet in many places in the world such practices do occur.[30]

The adversaries' anticipation of continuing relations fosters regulation of conflicts; the absence of expected ongoing relations removes an important constraint on how a conflict is waged. Furthermore, insofar as the contending parties expect that they will have recurrent conflicts, they tend to develop shared understandings about how they should each pursue their goals, and other ways of fighting come to be regarded as wrong.[31] It follows that those patterns of conflict behavior that are stable and expected to remain stable tend to become institutionalized.

Several aspects of the relationship between the contending parties greatly affect the development of rules regarding their conflict behavior. Insofar as the parties are integrated with each other and have a shared culture, their conflict behavior will be regulated, while great separation and autonomy hampers conflict regulation. The level of inequalities between the adversaries also affects the regulation of their conflict behavior, but in contradictory ways. On the one hand, insofar as the parties are equal, rules governing their conflict behavior will be more equitable and adherence to them will be more acceptable to all parties. (It was the increased power of the U.S. trade unions, aided by political influence in the 1930s, that resulted in the widespread institutionalization of rules governing collective bargaining.) On the other hand, insofar as some parties have greater resources to shape the rules, those rules tend to serve their interests. Furthermore, the likelihood that rules will be enforced is greater when it appears to be in the interest and capability of particular persons to enforce them. Consequently, not only do the rules themselves tend to serve the interests of those who are dominant in the social system but also those rules that particularly favor the dominants are the ones most likely to be enforced.

The particular characteristics of the contending parties also affect the development of conflict rules and their institutionalization. Thus, the culture of a party affects the likelihood that some procedures and not others will be considered legitimate and amenable to institutionalization. Many of the Catalan people in Spain, for example, think of themselves as "deal makers" who have always tended to negotiate about issues in dispute. They offer that as an explanation for their successful negotiated achievement of regional autonomy.[32] More generally, in Western societies disputants in a controversy tend to have internalized expectations that disputes only have winners and losers, and their contentious behavior is guided by that expectation. In many traditional societies, and often in Asian cultures, generally the goal is to restore harmonious relations between the contending parties, and participants and intermediaries have internalized those expectations so that conflict becomes a search for resolutions that will enable the parties to resume coexistence in reasonable tranquility. Such broad cultural generalizations should not be overdrawn; there are individual and group variations within every culture. Furthermore, cultural patterns change over time and vary in different circumstances.[33]

The structure of governance within a social system also profoundly affects the content and institutionalization of conflict rules. In all social systems legitimate agents of an overarching social system seek to impose rules governing conflict between constituent contending parties. Such efforts are most successful in situations where governance bodies collaboratively fashion rules, have the capacity to enforce them, and enjoy legitimacy in the eyes of the affected social groups. Where these conditions are absent, social systems may suffer from fragmented, decentralized, or ineffective modes of conflict management. For example, at the international level supranational institutions have increasingly used international treaties and institutions to manage spheres of social, political, economic, and military affairs, notably evident in the area of human rights violations. The establishment and functioning of the International Court of Justice, ad hoc tribunals, and the International Criminal Court are illustrative of that trend.[34] However, in a world where state sovereignty is a major legal norm, supranational institutions often lack the capacity to enforce the principles that they champion. The International Court of Justice, for example, has no ability to force states to appear before it nor can it force states to submit to its judgments. On the other hand, those who violate laws within countries having well-developed legal systems can be compelled by local or state authorities to conform to the institutionalized rules.

Globalization, in its many dimensions, not only helps in ameliorating large-scale conflicts but also unleashes and exacerbates such conflicts. Groups from different societies that lack shared understandings encounter each other and generate intense antagonisms with few shared rules about how to handle the consequent conflicts. The reaction of some Muslim Salafists to Western influence can spur efforts to revitalize a radical Islam transnationally.[35] Consequently, international networks, such as al Qaeda, can emerge, whose members, based on their own self-reinforcing understandings, can feel justified in extreme attacks against alien others.

Finally, the kind of issues in contention profoundly affects the degree to which conflict behavior is controlled by institutionalized regulations. For example, conflicts in which the contending parties do not think their vital interests or fundamental identities are at stake tend to be relatively susceptible to institutionalized regulation. Also, some contentious issues seem relatively divisible, which makes them more amenable to negotiated resolution.

ILLUSTRATIVE STRATEGIES

To illustrate how coercive, rewarding, and persuasive inducements may be combined in various ways to constitute a strategy of struggle, we discuss five sets of strategies that employ different combinations of inducements. The strategic approaches are reframing enactments (Re), nonviolent actions (Nv), terrorist actions (Tr), coengagements (Ce), and problem-solving meetings (Ps). See figure 4.1.

Reframing Enactments (Re)

Persons in stable relations generally share expectations and understandings about their interactions, viewing them from similar subjective frames.[36] Those understandings in turn sustain their patterns of peaceful interaction. Members of a conflict party may try to change those relations by trying to get the others to agree that the relations should be viewed in a new way. But to affect others to change the social relationship usually requires more than persuasive words, it also requires a change in circumstances so that the old way of thinking loses its seeming inevitability.

The profound revolution in relations between men and women that began in the 1960s in the United States and elsewhere in the world is in good measure the result of a reframing enactment strategy with a large persuasive component. See Re(1) in figure 4.1. Changing economic and social conditions provided the bases for the rapid growth and acceptance among many women of new feminist thinking.[37] Betty Friedan's book *The Feminine Mys-*

tique, published in 1963, was vastly influential. Soon, a torrent of books and articles documented the ongoing inequities of women's social position and held out the vision of a society without rigid gender roles and with equal rights for women and men. Individual women and small groups of women interrupted, in innumerable ways and places, the previously traditional ways men treated women. In a remarkably short time, laws were enacted and new ways of thinking and behaving became evident among men as well as women. Such a radical and relatively fast change suggests that the new feminist ideas fit new social conditions very well, and the props supporting traditional patriarchal thinking were already weakened. The partisans of the struggle for equal rights also achieved so many gains due to the ingenuity of their tactics and to the persuasive argument made by many feminists that men as well as women would benefit by being liberated from highly prescribed gender roles.

Obviously, everything that feminists envisioned in the early years of the women's movement in the United States has not been realized. Moreover, some of what was achieved has generated new problems and conflicts. Consequently, the struggle for equality continues, but the struggle has been transformed and in a significant degree has become institutionalized in a transformed country (see table 10.1 and discussion in chapter 10).

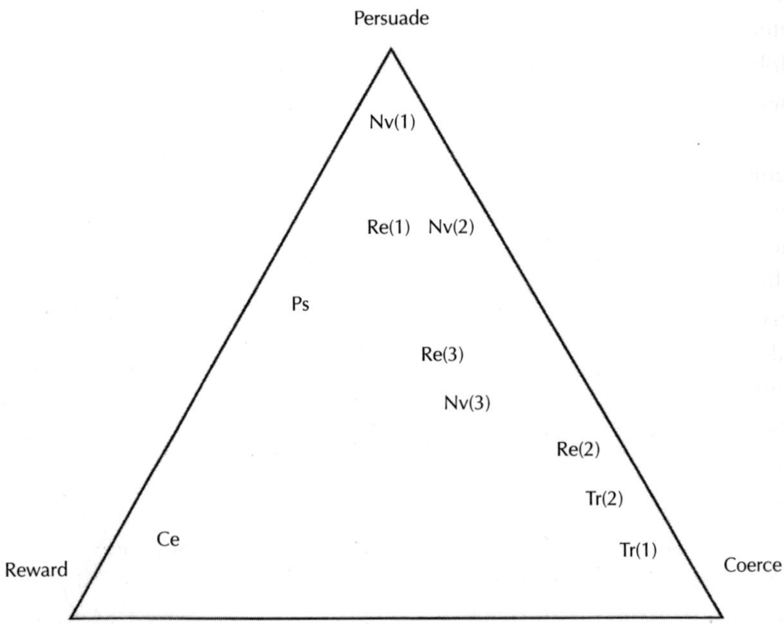

Figure 4.1. Types of Inducements

The struggle of the Zapatistas in Mexico, noted in chapter 3, provides another illustration of reframing enactments, opening with major coercive components; see Re(2) in figure 4.1. The immediate response of the Mexican government to the armed uprising in Chiapas that began on January 1, 1994, was to militarily suppress the insurrection.[38] Troops were dispatched and shots were exchanged; then the Ejército Zapatista de Liberación Nacional (EZLN) disappeared into the jungle. However, by January 12 Carlos Salinas de Gortari, the president of Mexico, declared a unilateral cease-fire and called on the Zapatistas to put down their arms and negotiate. Indeed, on February 21 peace talks began.

The speedy cessation of Mexican military actions is attributable to the social and political context and of the EZLN strategy. For several years, nongovernmental organizations (NGOs) had been rapidly increasing in Mexico, many working in the area of human rights generally and particularly of indigenous peoples' rights. They had worldwide electronic links so that news of the events in Chiapas quickly spread within and beyond Mexico, evoking a rapid mobilization of people in support the EZLN. Furthermore, the Zapatistas message was brilliantly articulated by one of the leading EZLN figures, Subcomandante Marcos. His analyses of the terrible conditions of indigenous peoples and ways of correcting them were written in a style that delighted the intellectuals of Mexico City and were electronically forwarded through the global NGO networks. In the context of all this attention, the Mexican government halted its effort to militarily destroy the EZLN.

In many of the struggles to transform authoritarian rule into substantial democratic governance, reframing enactment strategies were used. They mixed the promise of reward with persuasion and nonviolent coercion in the form of noncompliance with oppressive rules; see Re(3) in figure 4.1. Alternative social institutions and relations were established that provided services and produced goods autonomously, independently of the opposing sides. Some of the organizations fighting for such changes also embodied democratic practices in their own governance.[39] Such organizations are the core of a civil society, which constitutes the base for making peace and for a viable democratic order.[40] In varying degrees, these kinds of reframing enactments were elements in the struggle to end apartheid in South Africa, the first Palestinian intifada to end Israeli occupation of the West Bank and Gaza,[41] and in the transformation from authoritarian rule in Egypt in 2011. The new social media, cell phones, and other information technologies enhance dissenters' ability to express their views and share them despite government disapproval.

Nonviolent Actions (Nv)

Nonviolent actions are often used to bring about and to resist political, cultural, economic, and other major changes.[42] Sometimes participants in these nonviolent efforts, and often the resisting authorities, have resorted to violence as well. Participants in large-scale struggles employ a variety of nonviolent actions, combining different degrees of coercion, persuasion, and reward.[43] For example, a demonstration in which protesters march and carry banners expressing their views is largely an effort at persuasion, but it may also convey some threats, perhaps of electoral opposition. Many such actions would be located about the point Nv(1) in figure 4.1. In most societies, such protests are regulated, and government authorities may give or deny permission for demonstrations. And most, but certainly not all, demonstrations are carried out within authorized limits. Many demonstrations are rallies in support of one side in the struggle and may then be directed at intimidating the opponent.

More typically, nonviolent action refers to activities that have larger and more severe coercive components. This includes withholding purchases, goods, or services, as in boycotts and strikes—located at point Nv(2) in figure 4.1. Such actions are often intended to communicate how important the goal is to those making the claim and are executed in compliance with institutionalized rules.

Other nonviolent actions are based on noncompliance to laws that the challengers regard as unjust, such as laws upholding segregation between ethnic communities. Similar to reframing enactments, such noncompliance can be carried out in ways that disrupt or prevent those who practice segregation from doing so—located at point Nv(3) in figure 4.1. This was the case with battles to desegregate public accommodations in the U.S. South, waged by civil rights organizations during the early 1960s. Their actions had coercive components but embodied persuasive elements as well, since they were conducted in a manner to avoid hurting the people whose actions they sought to change, even at the cost of enduring violence themselves. The actions were presented as demonstrating the importance of ending segregation. The demonstrators expressed their view of segregation as immoral, but their demonstrating was done without hate and with the promise that once the segregated practices were ended, mutual benefits would follow.

Practitioners of nonviolent actions usually represent their efforts as not solely coercive, since they seek to persuade opponents of the mutual benefits in changing their objectionable conduct. The opponents are told, for example, that they will better satisfy their own value commitments to their country or to God.

Mohandas Gandhi developed a comprehensive approach to principled nonviolence in the struggle he led for the independence of India from Great

Britain.[44] His approach, termed *satyagraha*, or "truth force," has been influential throughout the world. Three concepts are fundamental in satyagraha: truth, nonviolence, and self-suffering. For Gandhi, truth is God; it is an end we seek, but since we cannot know absolute truth, its pursuit excludes the use of violence. Nonviolence does not imply the negative action of not harming, but positive love, of doing good to the evildoer. It does not mean acquiescence to the wrong, but resistance to the wrongdoer, even if that does injure the wrongdoer. Self-suffering means a willingness to endure suffering, not out of weakness but out of courage to refrain from violence even when it is possible to use violence. It is directed at moral persuasion.

Other advocates and practitioners of nonviolent action argue for its use on pragmatic grounds, asserting it is effective and ultimately less costly in human life. They examine which strategies have contributed to reaching particular goals.[45] Conflict analysts recognize that in actual struggles, violent actions often occur in conjunction with nonviolent behavior.[46] Different organizations within each side may use alternative and often complementary nonviolent means, the mixture changing within the course of a conflict.

Whether principled or pragmatic, some features of nonviolent strategies tend to foster constructively waged rather than destructively waged struggles. Certainly, the adversary tends to be less dehumanized by the process; indeed, nonviolent action often appeals to the empathy and reasonableness of the adversary. It can even garner respect from the adversary, often a goal of a people who have been viewed as inferior. As Martin Luther King Jr. wrote in 1963 about the civil rights struggle, "The Negro's method of nonviolent direct action is not only suitable as a remedy for injustice; its very nature is such that it challenges the myth of inferiority. Even the most reluctant are forced to recognize that no inferior people could choose and successfully pursue a course involving such extensive sacrifice, bravery, and skill."[47]

Nonviolent action often gains effectiveness by attracting support and allies who are impressed by the demonstration of commitment and the lack of generalized threat such action seems to convey. This may be seen in trade union organizing and strike efforts. For example, in the 1960s, Cesar Chávez effectively mobilized consumer boycotts against grapes to support the strike efforts of the National Farm Workers Association.[48]

In international relations, economic sanctions are increasingly used and regarded as a nonviolent form of coercion. The suffering imposed on the general population and the limited effectiveness of sanctions have led to proposals to employ narrowly targeted or "smart" sanctions.[49] Targeted sanctions are directed at decision makers and include freezing of financial assets, arms embargoes, flight bans, and travel bans. They effectively contributed to the step-by-step transformation of Libyan relations with the United States, having been applied for many years following the indictment of two Libyan officials for the terrorist bombing of the passenger airplane Pan Am Flight 103 over Lockerbie, Scotland, on December 21, 1988. Neither the sanctions nor the ending of sanctions transformed Libyan society. The domestic failures and repression of Muammar al-Qaddafi's government engendered the revolutionary challenge in 2011.

More recently the United States has tried to impose targeted sanctions on leaders of the Revolutionary Guard in Iran and on key leaders involved with North Korea's nuclear arms program. As with all international economic sanctions, their effectiveness depends on a number of factors, one of which is adaptation by a broad cross-section of the international community.[50] The more fundamental factor affecting the impact of sanctions is the intended goal and what the target of the sanctions believes is the goal. If the targeted group believes the goal is its elimination, it will resist what it regards as an existential threat and not yield to the demands of the sanctioning parties.

Terrorist Actions (Tr)

Since the attacks in the United States of September 11, 2001, and the ensuing efforts by the U.S. government to counter terrorist attacks, a great many people have tried to account for terrorism and propose ways to respond to it. Yet there is no universal agreement even about defining terrorism. Persons identifying with the targeted people generally use the term *terrorism* pejoratively in order to condemn certain antagonistic actions by an enemy and to justify strong countermeasures. Such usage is relevant for understanding the course of many large-scale conflicts, but it hampers comprehensive analyses of the phenomenon.

The solution taken here is to start with a broad definition of terrorist actions and then distinguish different aspects of such actions, which various groups use to label certain actions as terrorist. A broad definition is: acts or threatened acts of violence in order to create fear and compliant behavior in a victim or audience for some collective purpose.[51] Terrorism so defined fits in the coercion corner of figure 4.1, see Tr(1). Various groups use particular qualities of such acts to further delimit what they judge to be "terrorism," including qualities of the act, its target, the perpetrator, and the context of the actions.

For many people, to be designated terrorist, the actions must be unusually gruesome and frightening. This may mean not just killing someone, but desecrating the body and exhibiting the result. Thus, when the Ku Klux Klan (KKK) acted to restore white domination of African Americans in the U.S. South after the Civil War, KKK members publicly lynched African Americans. Bodies were left hanging from tree limbs and were sometimes mutilated.[52]

We must consider which kinds of violent behavior are so outrageous and terrifying that significant numbers of people regard them as terrorist. Obviously, what people regard as abhorrent and beyond the conventional limits depends on their normative standards. The capacity of humans to commit atrocities and still believe they are acting properly certainly helps propel conflicts destructively.

Terrorism is also defined according to the targets of the action. Violent attacks on noncombatants are widely regarded as terrorism. For instance, the Center for International Development and Conflict Management (CIDCM), at the University of Maryland, defines terrorism as "the intentional targeting of civilian, noncombatant populations."[53] This view is so widespread that violence directed against ordinary citizens and particularly children is likely to be counterproductive for the perpetrators' cause. Particularly if an individual or small group commits such actions, they and their cause often are discredited, as happened after the bombing of the federal building in Oklahoma City on April 19, 1995.

On the other hand, a wide variety of military actions, such as shelling, bombing, setting booby traps, or planting landmines, if directed against warriors or other combatants, tend not to be regarded as terrorist even if many noncombatants are the victims. In contemporary warfare, rules have been established to limit civilian casualties and ill treatment of combatants, but violations of those rules, for example, by killing or starving prisoners, tend to be regarded as crimes or atrocities, but not terrorism.

For many groups, however, the target alone does not always distinguish violence as terrorist. Thus, even when noncombatants have been subjected to bombing in their homes and workplaces and deprived of life-supporting necessities, those who order or commit the acts claim that they are defensive and are necessary to end a war quickly and therefore save lives. Terror bombing of population centers in Europe and Japan were prevalent during World War II and regarded by their perpetrators as legitimate, even if regrettable. Not surprisingly, the people in the societies subjected to those actions tended to regard the actions as terrorism.

Furthermore, the very notion of who is or is not a combatant is not always clear. Thus, when the naval vessel USS *Cole* was attacked in the harbor at Aden, Yemen, on October 12, 2000, and seventeen sailors were killed, the U.S. government and public regarded the action as a terrorist attack even though the target was military. This characterization of the attack was made because the al Qaeda network led by Osama bin Laden conducted the action.[54]

Perpetrators of the targeted killing of noncombatants sometimes justify their conduct by arguing that they are merely reciprocating such atrocities committed by the enemy or that the so-called noncombatants are actually combatants. For example, immediately after the 9/11 attacks, a senior al Qaeda operative, who helped plan the attacks, Ramzi bin al-Shibh, defended them by denying that they were terrorist attacks:

> They are legally legitimate, because they are committed against a country at war with us, and the people in that country are combatants. Someone might say that it is the innocent, the elderly, the women, and the children who are victims, so how can these operations be legitimate according to sharia? And we say that the sanctity of women, children, and the elderly is not absolute. There are special cases. . . . Muslims may respond in kind if infidels have targeted women and children and elderly Muslims [or if] they are being invaded [or if] the non-combatants are helping with the fight, whether in action, word, or any other type of assistance, [or if they] need to attack with heavy weapons, which do not differentiate between combatants and non-combatants.[55]

The same complexities confound definitions of domestic terrorist actions. Governments usually regard violent attacks on police, soldiers, or civilians by organized opposition groups as terrorist actions. Such groups, waging a revolutionary or secessionist struggle, regard themselves as conducting a legitimate fight and using necessary violence. Noteworthy examples of such organizations include the Liberation Tigers of the Tamils in Sri Lanka, the Kurdistan Workers' Party of the Kurds in Turkey, and the Basque Fatherland and Liberty of the Basque in Spain.[56]

Some governments also at times resort to widespread arrests and even imprisonment, torture, assassinations, and "disappearance" of presumed opponents. This may be done to prevent or to suppress challenging organizations. Such government actions are often conducted covertly and sometimes through nonofficial militia groups. Such operations are generally regarded as "state terrorism," such as those carried out some years ago by assassinations and disappearances of citizens in Argentina, Guatemala, and Chile. In the latter two countries, the terrorism was conducted by military regimes that seized power after democratically elected governments were overthrown with the covert assistance of the U.S. Central Intelligence Agency as part of the struggle against Soviet Communism.[57] Terrorism also includes the massive killings, labor-camp incarcerations, and torture by "internal security" forces within Hitlerite Germany and the Stalinist Soviet Union.

States also sometimes support and provide havens for organizations waging revolutionary or liberation struggles within other countries. The organizations may be too weak to wage large-scale violent or nonviolent campaigns in those other countries, but the support enables them to conduct occasional terror attacks. This was the case made during the Cold War in support of

Soviet and U.S. covert conduct. It is also the case where a country provides a haven for organizations attacking military and civilian targets in a neighboring country. For example, this has reportedly been done at various times by Syria, Libya, and Pakistan.

Another standard used to characterize violence as terrorist is the nature of the perpetrator. A defining feature of a state is that it holds a monopoly on legitimate violence. By this logic, when agents of the state commit violence under orders from above, they are engaging in warfare or police action, which cannot be classified as terrorism. This is evident in the definitions of terrorism adopted by various U.S. government agencies.[58] The definition used by the CIA is contained in Title 22 of the U.S. code, Section 2656f(d):

> The term "terrorism" means premeditated, politically motivated violence perpetrated against noncombatants by subnational groups or clandestine agents, usually intended to influence an audience.

Nongovernmental actors, however, sometimes challenge the very legitimacy of a state. If they view a state as illegitimate, then the state's use of violence is illegitimate and their acts are criminal. The authority of a state may be diminished in another way. Members of an organization operating transnationally or citizens of another country can more readily reject obedience to the government of the country in which they are carrying out violent attacks.

Some individuals or groups may commit terrifyingly violent acts that are generally not regarded as constituting terrorism. This is the case, for example, for criminal gangs who terrorize people from whom they extort money. It is also true for individuals who are suffering severe mental illness and violently attack political figures.

Finally, the context of the violent actions also can affect whether or not the actions are regarded as terrorist. One aspect of the context is the degree of transparency shown by the persons committing the action. Some violent actions are covert; and the agents conducting the action deny carrying it out. This makes it difficult to understand what goals are being pursued or how the conflict might be settled. The mystery of who committed the violent activities often contributes to their terrifying quality. This was true with the appearance of anthrax spores in the U.S. mail in October 2001. Furthermore, persons engaging in covert operations generally are able to act with little accountability and few constraints on perpetrating atrocities.

Another aspect of context is the degree to which the violence is part of a wide array of other methods of struggle. It may be incidental in a large-scale struggle in which various nonviolent methods are also being used, in which case it is less likely to be regarded as terrorist, while if it is the primary method of conducting a conflict, it is likely to be labeled terrorist.

Sometimes terrorism is conducted as if the perpetrators seek to persuade the targeted opposition of the depth of their feelings and the strength of their convictions. That may also enhance the intimidating character of the action, signaling that such actions will persist and cannot be prevented. Terrorist acts carried out by people who commit suicide in the process are an extreme example of such demonstrations of commitment and are honored by some people in whose name they die.[59]

The extent to which the violent actions are carried out with the ultimate purpose to negotiate an agreement with the adversary is an additional aspect of the actions' context. Violent actions may even be used to gain the attention of the inattentive. A cause is being announced, and indeed, an audience is gained as people try to understand why such actions are taken. Various terrorist actions, then, may combine different degrees of coercive and persuasive inducements; see Tr(2) in figure 4.1. Sometimes, however, terrorism seems hardly instrumental and not calculated to win concessions. Rather, it appears intended to punish the other side for its past wrong deeds. Insofar as the terrorist actions are punishing and revengeful, they may stiffen the enemy's resolve rather than achieve any desired change. Indeed, the terrorist acts may be largely expressive for some of the perpetrators. These qualities of terrorism tend to make struggles in which it is used more intractable and destructive.

Certainly, terrorism has existed throughout human history, even as its character and frequency have varied. In the twenty-first century, however, several new conditions provide new opportunities for nonofficial as well as official organizations to conduct terrorist activities. First, technological developments provide particularly effective and frightening ways to kill people. Not only have explosives become more powerful and delivery systems more precise, but also weapons of mass destruction, including nuclear, chemical, and biological weapons, have proliferated. Second, the rapid means of communication and transportation make transnational organizations able to function effectively and make organizations that are structured as a network rather than in a hierarchical form increasingly feasible, which makes their incapacitation more difficult. Third, the growing social and political integration of the world facilitates the movement of peoples and the ease of foreign people to fit into different societies. Fourth, the greater connectedness of communication systems enables information and images to spread rapidly throughout the world, increasing the impact of a terrifying event anywhere. Finally, the growing integration of the global economy increases its vulnerability to widespread disruption by an attack at one junction point.

The terrorist attacks in the United States on September 11, 2001, exhibit many features generally characterizing terrorism. But they also demonstrate some novel features deriving from the new conditions of the twenty-first century. Members of the al Qaeda network assert their desire to return Muslims to what they claim to be traditional Islamic faith and practice. They utilize, however, the newest technologies to construct a transnational network for mobilizing personnel and funds and to conduct their violent activities. They adapt to local life in many countries to conduct covert activities as they prepare to execute their attacks. They select targets and attack them dramatically to maximize mass media attention and to frighten officials or those denounced as infidels, crusaders, and Zionists.

In short, terrorist actions vary immensely, and there is no consensus about which actions deserve that label. Often, adversaries in intense conflicts attach the label *terrorism* to the other side's violent deeds. Although the discussion of terrorism in this book gives particular attention to nonstate perpetrators, violent deeds against noncombatants committed by government agents are not to be ignored.

Coengagements (Ce)

Rewards are typically employed to help settle and transform conflicts and to prevent the eruption of destructive conflicts. They are often components of strategies to establish an ongoing relationship in which the opposing sides engage in activities that promise shared benefits. These strategies include co-optation, corporate codetermination, collaboration, and political power sharing and are often part of a broad strategy in waging a conflict and sustaining a post-settlement accommodation.

Phillip Selznick influentially used the term *co-optation* in his analysis of the Tennessee Valley Authority (TVA).[60] Soon after President Franklin D. Roosevelt's inauguration in 1933, the federal government established a public corporation to undertake a multipurpose river valley development program to produce electricity and provide water for irrigation. Groups and interests that might have opposed some of the developments were invited to participate in policy making and became supporters of the TVA. Similar strategies to involve stakeholders in policy making processes are now widely used by regulatory authorities and are credited with reducing public policy conflicts and instances of post-facto litigation.[61]

Various forms of co-optation can be discerned in diverse settings. In some regards, programs undertaken in the United States under the Economic Opportunity Act of 1964 are illustrative. As part of the government's War on Poverty, the act authorized community action programs (CAPs).[62] Urban disorders and riots had begun to erupt, partly in conjunction with the civil rights movement. The CAPs were to stimulate local communities to mobilize resources in a coordinated attack on poverty and to do so by including the poor to participate to the "maximum feasible" extent. Indeed, poor persons did participate in the many local programs to alleviate poverty that were undertaken. Nevertheless, discontent rose and urban riots occurred widely in the late 1960s. The authors of the 1968 Kerner report on civil disorders noted the demand for greater grassroots engagement in directing the programs affecting low-income neighborhoods and racial ghettos. They concluded, "meaningful community participation and a substantial measure of involvement in program development is an essential strategy for city government."[63]

For many persons, co-optation has bad connotations, implying that a group seeking to improve its conditions abandons their aims, or settles for very little, and joins the dominant view. Co-optation may also refer to the actions of a group's leadership, who soften their demands and derive personal benefits from the dominants. Indeed, a dominant group may make concessions in order to win acquiescence in the future. Certainly, co-optation takes many forms and can have contradictory consequences. In general, there are risks of forgoing greater gains that might be achieved by further struggle rather than securing the gains already won by institutionalizing them.[64]

Within industrial organizations, efforts to ameliorate labor-management strife have included formal systems of worker engagement in management. For example, in the Federal Republic of Germany after World War II the trade unions sought codetermination, that is, worker representation in each company's board of directors and executive committee.[65] This was achieved in 1951 in the coal and steel industries, and 1972 legislation extended worker representation to all companies with at least five workers.

Collaboration is a more informal process between relatively independent parties jointly developing rules and structures to govern their relations and decision making. This process is increasingly being adapted within and among governmental and corporate organizations about issues they must manage interdependently. This can avoid many incipient conflicts erupting destructively and help avert destructive escalations.

Finally, one or another power-sharing arrangement may be instituted to settle and transform conflicts in a society rent by fighting along ethnic, religious, or language lines. Power sharing is a governance system that ensures representation of diverse groups in policy making and in administrative institutions, particularly in the police and military services.[66] For example, in South Africa in 1994, in the first elections in which people of all races could vote, major opposition parties were guaranteed that they would have a seat in the government and in the cabinet, for a transitional period, and would hold parliament seats proportional to their numbers in the population.

In Northern Ireland, the process of reaching a power-sharing arrangement acceptable to the major parties with a stake in the conflict between the Protestant and Catholic communities is illuminating.[67] In 1968, the Catholic minority began a civil rights campaign against discrimination and for equality. The Royal Ulster Constabulary, the police of the Protestant-controlled government, forcefully broke up the peaceful demonstrations, which were also attacked by Protestant vigilante groups. The Irish Republican Army, which had been dormant, began to organize to defend the Catholic community and raised the old demand to reunite the island of Ireland. Thus the struggle intensified and the British government suspended the Protestant-controlled governing body and imposed direct rule from London. The British were unable to sustain a tentative power-sharing government when Protestant workers led a general strike. Then, in 1985 the British and Irish governments agreed to work together and this helped transform the conflict. Although violent fighting between armed groups continued, negotiations also continued and some agreements were reached, but did not endure. Finally, a comprehensive settlement, the Good Friday agreement, was achieved in April 1998 and gradually implemented, with many stops and starts. The agreement consisted of three strands: proportional representation and power sharing in the North, a linked ministerial council between the assembly and Ireland, and British-Irish ties, consisting of a British-Irish council and a standing intergovernmental conference.

Problem-Solving Meetings (Ps)

The final strategy selected for particular attention here is engagement in meetings to exchange information in order to solve what may be regarded as a shared problem. This is an important mode of conflict resolution, but also a way to wage a conflict constructively.[68] The essential features of the problem-solving mode are that members of the contending parties discuss the nature of their problem and their possibly shared responsibility; they propose various solutions and consider ways to implement the mutually preferred solutions. The participants recognize the concerns of each other and seek ways in which those can be addressed in a mutually acceptable settlement. In this approach, adversaries are not viewed as unitary actors whose leaders are the only significant policy makers. As Harold H. Saunders writes, "The power of citizens is most fully realized and demonstrated in the capacity to build and change relationships."[69]

Problem solving is typically tried at an early stage of a conflict and at various points when the parties in conflict are seeking to de-escalate it. As with the strategies of nonviolent action and terrorist actions, problem solving may be carried out by official agents of the contending parties or by other members of the adversary camps. Unlike the previously discussed strategies, however, intermediaries often participate in problem solving, for example, as facilitators or mediators. Further, problem solving involves a joint decision-making process, rather than a unilateral imposition. In the last decades of the twentieth century, many problem-solving conflict-resolution methods began expanding greatly. They include informal and formal exchanges and dialogues, as well as mediated problem-solving negotiations, NGOs spanning ethnic and other fault lines, and workshops facilitated by intermediaries. They have expanded, particularly as a result of experience with ethnic and other communal conflicts within one country and in protracted conflicts between countries. For example, facilitated workshops have been conducted with Catholics and Protestants from Northern Ireland; members of various religious communities in Lebanon; Greek and Turkish Cypriots; Jewish Israelis and Arab Palestinians; and, following the war over the Falkland/Malvina Islands, with Argentinean and British representatives.[70]

Even workshops among persons who lack authority to bind their respective parties may contribute over time to the de-escalation and resolution of a conflict. Nongovernmental agencies may help inform influential people on each side about the concerns of their adversaries. The understandings and options generated may become vitally relevant when the circumstances have changed and an opportunity for official de-escalating efforts arises. Sometimes the people with workshop experience become part of the official problem-solving negotiations.[71]

In traditional competitive negotiations, in contrast, each party usually seeks to maximize its gain, often at the expense of the other side. Such negotiations usually involve an exchange of persuasive inducements, directed at changing the other side's position. Although the negotiations sometimes include promises of benefits to the other side in exchange for benefits received, on the whole, each side takes a hard line, insisting on as much as it thinks it may get and threatening coercive consequences if it does not. Traditional negotiations may be accompanied by coercive actions, as when union-management negotiations are conducted while the union members are on strike.

In problem-solving negotiations, efforts are made to understand the interests or needs of the other side and to discover possible solutions that maximize all the parties' goals. Mutual benefits result. Coercive inducements are minimized, but the negotiating parties may both anticipate losses if their search for mutual gain fails. Such problem-solving negotiations are located at point "Ps" in figure 4.1.

Figure 4.2 presents another way of conceptualizing the problem-solving conflict mode. An adversary's approach to a conflict varies along two dimensions, concern for oneself and concern for the relationship.[72] A low concern along both dimensions would be expressed by a conflict-avoidance approach. A high assertiveness and low cooperativeness orientation would be expressed by taking a competitive strategy. A low concern for oneself, but high concern for the relationship, would be expressed as an accommodating orientation. Finally, a high concern in both dimensions would be characterized as a collaborating approach, including problem solving.

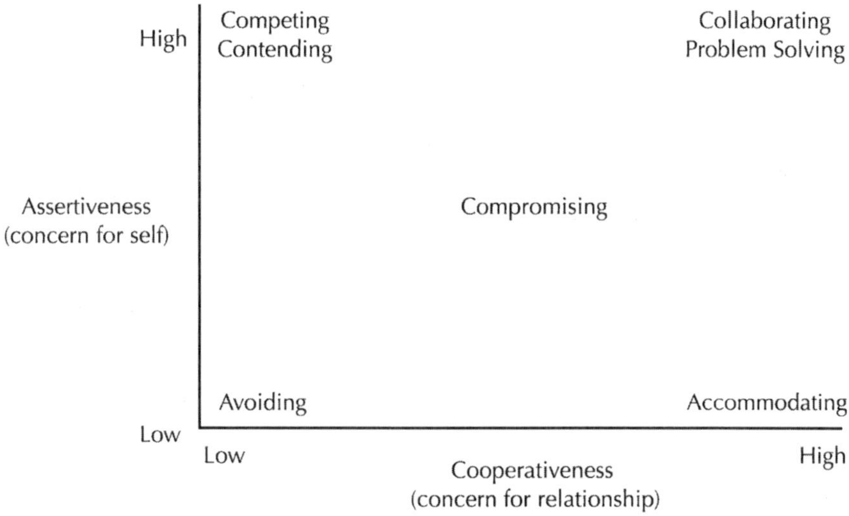

Figure 4.2. Conflict Modes

A problem-solving mode is more likely to be used in domestic conflicts than in international conflicts. For example, it may be seen even in attempts to find accommodations among peoples with ethnic, linguistic, religious, and other communal differences within a single society. Often, the efforts include negotiations among representatives of the different communities to find a constitutional formula to solve the problem they face. This may be seen in the negotiations leading to the transition of power in South Africa from a white-ruled country to one organized on the basis of equality in political rights of all peoples.[73] The problem-solving approach has also been advocated and utilized in labor-management relations and in regard to environmental issues.[74] Ps methods are increasingly employed in international conflicts by NGOs, but also by officials in conjunction with mediation undertakings.

CONCLUSIONS

The five kinds of conflict strategies discussed illustrate alternative ways inducements are combined at various conflict stages. Obviously, there are many other kinds of conflict strategies, and several of these diverse strategies are employed at the same time as well as sequentially in the course of a conflict's history. This complexity is especially likely for conflict parties that are large and loosely coordinated. A party may be a broad coalition of organizations that is working toward similar goals, using different approaches, and acting in competition as well as in concert with each other. For example, the 1960s U.S. civil rights movement included organizations using electoral political methods, judicial means, legal demonstrations, civil disobedience, and many other strategies and tactics.

Each major party in a large-scale conflict includes many subgroups, to some degree using different strategies with and against each other. Even in international conflicts between governments, nongovernmental and transnational organizations are often active, applying different strategies than those available to government officials. Moreover, governments include different departments and persons operating at different levels and engaging in different kinds of encounters with the adversary. This was evident, for example, in the buildup to the 2003 war between the Iraqi and U.S. governments, its execution, and its aftermath.

Strategies vary greatly in the likelihood that they are highly regulated and institutionalized. In this book, we are most attentive to strategies that typically are not greatly regulated or institutionalized. Many little-regulated or barely institutionalized strategies, however, are used by groups within broad systems of conflict management. Thus, social movement organizations may organize demonstrations and even engage in nonviolent disruptions in order to induce elected government officials to implement policies they desire. Often established electoral systems are the venue for covert and overt strategies that are outside or on the margins of the established system. For example, some groups may finance front organizations promoting policies benefitting the funders by making contributions to candidates for elective office, sometimes exceeding legal rules. Such actions may also constitute bribery or other forms of corruption. Leaders of social movement organizations may mobilize supporters by channeling popular grievances into support for policies that benefit persons and groups funding their efforts. The convergence of many circumstances may result in organizations outside the electoral system beginning to work influentially within it. In many ways this was the case for the surge of the Tea Party movement in the United States in 2009 and 2010.[75]

5

Adopting Conflict Strategies

The previous chapter considered the range of strategies available to participants who are engaged in a fight. In this chapter we examine why adversaries end up choosing certain strategies over others. Insights about this process require attention to four factors: (1) the partisans' goals, (2) the characteristics of each adversary, (3) the relations between the adversaries, and (4) their environment. Analyses of each of these factors can be useful for decision makers contemplating how the adversary will act and how their own choices may be unwittingly shaped. Considering alternative strategies that might be adopted will enhance examining how these conditions affect choices. This process can also help decision makers weigh which strategy is feasible and most likely to be effective.

PARTISAN GOALS

The relationship between ends and means in a social conflict is crucial in waging conflicts constructively and deserves serious attention. As adversaries make choices about how to best achieve their goals, they typically adopt strategies they believe will be efficacious. However, choosing is not a simple unidirectional matter; some goals may be eschewed if the means to attain them seem to be morally unacceptable, too costly in material matters, or otherwise insupportable. Some activists, for instance, reason that if a nonviolent, cooperative, and egalitarian relationship with another ethnic community is desired, a struggle using nonviolent methods and reframing enactments would be more likely to succeed than violent attacks. This was the reasoning of many activists in the 1960s civil rights movement in the U.S. South. Members of the Solidarity movement in Poland provide another illustration. When Solidarity was suppressed by the Communist-led government in 1981, many members simply "acted as if they were free." In many ways, they spoke, wrote, and met as they pleased, but discretely, while the government pretended not to notice.[1]

Some generalizations about the relationship between particular kinds of goals and various strategies may be ventured, but understanding that the strength of the relationship depends on many factors. In general, strategies with significant components of persuasive inducements tend to be used in conflicts that are largely dissensual rather than consensual. After all, in highly dissensual conflicts an alteration in the values or beliefs of the adversary is what is often sought, and in that case, some degree of conversion of the opponent is needed. However, when the dissensual conflicts are embedded within relations between groups who view each other as alien and threatening core values, persuasive inducements tend to be regarded as fruitless. Furthermore, if members of one side feel they have been or anticipate being extremely harmed by an opponent, they may go so far as to characterize the opponent as evil, and when defending against evil, negotiation may seem not only doomed to failure but also immoral. Violently destroying the evildoers may be seen as the only reasonable strategy to adopt.

In consensual conflicts, the possibilities of trade-offs between issues in contention with differing priorities makes negotiation, even problem-solving negotiation, feasible and often attractive, particularly when common interests and values are recognized. However, when the perceived incompatibility of the goals in a consensual conflict is great, the preferred strategies tend to incorporate coercive and often violent components. For example, data from a study of the strategies used by U.S. social-movement organizations challenging the status quo from 1800 to 1945 indicate that the goal of displacing or destroying the target was moderately correlated (.36) with accepting the ideology that violence was legitimate or necessary under some circumstances.[2] More specifically, in the civil rights struggle in the 1960s, many members of the Congress of Racial Equality (CORE) believed that their goals could be achieved with nonviolent action and its persuasive power because they believed that discrimination rested on isolated attitudes that were not deeply rooted and grounded in material interests.[3] Another example may be seen in a study of strikes and mutinies; those in which secession or seizure of power was sought were likely to use violence, imprisonment, or killing of superiors, while those in which improvement of interests was sought used work stoppage as their main weapon.[4]

Goals also vary in either desiring the adversary to initiate a new policy or in desiring the adversary to stop doing what it has undertaken. Strategies with positive sanctions rather than threats are likely to be regarded as appropriate for the former goals, while threats are likely to be seen as more suitable for the latter goals, since rewards might be seen as a form of bribery.

A conflict group may have goals that primarily benefit nonmembers (e.g., to end slavery) or that benefit members either as a collectivity (e.g., to establish cultural autonomy for an ethnic community) or as an aggregation (e.g., to provide for equality of individual opportunity). Goals for members as an entity are more likely to require coercion than are goals for individual constituent members.

One or both of the adversaries may be seeking either greater separation or greater integration between them. Thus, in communal struggles one ethnic group may be striving for greater autonomy or even secession from the polity controlled by another ethnic group, as have Kurds in Iraq and in Turkey. One group may even seek to expel or destroy another group by ethnic cleansing or genocide. Clearly, such extreme goals require brutal means to be attained. On the other hand, an ethnic community may strive for closer integration with other groups within the larger society. Specifically, they may seek equal opportunities within the economic and political systems in which they have been subordinated, as did many African Americans during the civil rights struggle. If members of an adversarial group seek a more integrated relationship, they are more likely to try using persuasion and take a problem-solving approach.

Finally, to the degree that one or more sides believes its vital interest or its very survival is at stake in the conflict, there is a greater likelihood that resorting to the most drastic strategies is selected. As noted in chapter 3, even seemingly high-ranking and strong collectivities may fear that their existence in high rank is threatened, leading them to apply the maximum force necessary to survive.

In short, conflict partisans select strategies that they believe will help them attain what they seek. Nevertheless, different members of conflict groups frequently disagree in values and beliefs about which strategy is best for the goal sought. The differences arise from variations in ideology, personality, past experience, interests, and many other circumstances, which influence the goals chosen and the means believed to be efficacious in attaining them. For example, consider the alternative approaches that various black liberationists and women's liberationists have taken in the United States. Some emphasize the consensual nature of their struggle against racial or gender inequalities, respectively, arguing that both sides want the same benefits and the other side is taking more of them at the expense of the exploited, deprived side. Based on this way of thinking, these strategists are likely to favor conflict modes with significant coercive components. Other liberationists, however, emphasize the dissensual nature of the conflict, arguing that both sides are the losers under the prevailing ways of thinking, and liberation from stereotypes and prejudice would be liberating and beneficial for everyone. On the basis of that view, conflict modes with large components of persuasion and reward would be favored.

PARTISAN CHARACTERISTICS

The means of conflict that partisans actually adopt often appear to observers as inappropriate for the goals they ostensibly seek. The choice often seems driven by other, unstated considerations, of which the partisans may not be aware. Inevitably, however, a strategy is chosen partly on the basis of a conflict group's internal predispositions, ideology, social structure, and resources, which we discuss in turn.

Predispositions

Much public and scholarly attention is given to the idea that members of conflict parties have specific cultural traditions, socialization experiences, and other characteristics that predispose them to prefer some conflict methods rather than others. But what appear to be predispositions may be merely the group's logical response to their persistent situation. Therefore, predispositions are not permanent, but change in varying degree with circumstances and experience. To the extent they exist, the predispositions interact with other circumstances in shaping the conflict choices made. Assessing the strength and sources of such predispositions can be enhanced by analyzing preferences for various conflict strategies that are favored by different categories of people. In this section, for example, we compare people of different socioeconomic statuses and different genders.

Very generally, persons of low income, education, ethnic status, and other indicators of socioeconomic rank appear to be somewhat more likely than persons of high rank to act violently in family and other interpersonal disputes.[5] That the patterns also extend to large-scale conflicts is indicated by many public opinion surveys, which support the generalization that higher-ranking persons tend to favor institutionalized and nonviolent modes of conduct, compared with low-ranking persons.[6] Evidence supports several explanations for these patterns, including subcultural socialization, learning by witnessing interpersonal violence, situational stress, lack of skills to use alternatives, and limited access to institutionalized conflict-resolution methods or levers of political power. A closer examination of the patterns can help explain them.

These patterns actually vary over time and in regard to different conflicts. Thus, when it comes to waging a war, higher-ranking citizens are often more likely to be supportive than are persons of lower ranks. A reason for this seems to be that lower-ranking persons tend to have less confidence in the leadership of established institutions and are more skeptical of the policies they pursue.[7] For example, at the outset of U.S. military engagement in Vietnam, respondents with many years of education were much more likely than those with few years of education to support "taking a stronger stand." As the war went on, however, the consensus among the elites broke down and support for the war fell. The educational differences lessened, as the college-educated respondents' support for the war markedly dropped, in concert with dissenting political leaders.[8]

Following the attacks of September 11, 2001, the U.S. public overwhelmingly supported the initiation of U.S. military action in Afghanistan. Shortly after the U.S. air attacks began in early October 2001, respondents across the country were asked whether they favored or opposed the United States using ground troops in Afghanistan. Among persons with a college education, 84 percent supported the use of ground forces compared to 75 percent of those with a high school education.[9] Again, the more educated persons seemed more accepting of the official consensus.

In the Israeli-Palestinian conflict, lower-status Israeli Jews have been relatively more militant in opposition to Palestinians than higher-ranking Jews. For example, in a survey conducted in January 1995, during a difficult period in Israeli–Palestine Liberation Organization (PLO) negotiations, respondents were asked: "Should talks be stopped or continued if terrorism continues?" The respondents with fewer years of education were slightly more likely than those with more education to answer: "Stop the talks."[10] In this case, the less-educated public tended to be more affiliated with the more hawkish political parties. On the other hand, among Palestinians in the occupied territories and in Gaza-Jericho, the more educated Palestinians were somewhat more likely to oppose continuing negotiations and more likely to support armed attacks against Israeli targets, compared with the less educated.[11] Probably the more educated persons were more attentive to the Palestinian political leadership at the time.

These varied findings indicate no consistent or strong tendency for persons of higher educational and class standing to support institutionalized rather than noninstitutionalized conflict strategies and of nonviolent rather than violent strategies, when engaged in large-scale external conflicts. Insofar as such relationships are found, they are not likely to be substantially due to subcultural differences in these regards. Rather, the differences are more likely explained by differences in trust of societal institutions and in the leaders of those institutions. It turns out that ideological beliefs and political party affiliations affect preferences about different strategies for specific conflicts more significantly than educational or economic levels.

Gender differences often seem to be a pervasive source of significant variation in predispositions regarding conflict methods. Males are somewhat more likely than females to act aggressively in domestic relations and other interpersonal interactions.[12] Presumably, this derives from the socialization into gender roles, based on the biological differences between males and females. These roles are socially constructed and vary from culture to culture. Feminists and other analysts of gender point out that in the United States and in many other societies, masculinity popularly stresses competitiveness, dominance, assertiveness, and readiness to inflict and accept pain and even death for honor, while femininity tends to emphasize relationships with others, nurturance, caretaking, and warmth.[13]

Masculine and feminine are more accurately regarded as overlapping socially constructed tendencies. Variations along many dimensions prevail rather than a set of qualities with little overlap between males and females. In most analyses of the relationship between gender and preferences regarding conflict methods, however, women and men are compared as separate categories, not as persons varying in degree of femininity and masculinity. A variety of evidence indicates consistent, but often small, differences between men's and women's preferences about modes of conflict.

We focus here on views regarding the use of military force. Public opinion surveys show women usually less likely to support the use of military means than are men. But the magnitude of the differences between men's and women's views varies with particular circumstances.[14] In general, analyses of numerous surveys reveals that women are more sensitive to the risk of casualties and tend to withhold support for military action more than do men, particularly as casualties mount. Thus, in a national survey conducted immediately following the attacks on September 11, 2001, support for military retaliation by the United States was extremely high: 90 percent among men and 88 percent among women.[15] As conditions are specified in the interviews, however, gaps between men and women appear. For example, support for military retaliation drops greatly to 76 percent among men and to only 55 percent among women if one thousand U.S. troops would be killed. When asked whether the United States should punish the groups involved in the attack or mount a long-term war on terrorism, 64 percent of the men chose the second alternative and only 42 percent of the women did.

In addition to sensitivity to casualties, men and women differ in their support for military action depending upon its stated purpose. Four purposes of U.S. military action were distinguished in analyzing 484 surveys conducted about the use of force by the United States, 1990–2003.[16] They are, in the order of their support, (1) humanitarian intervention, (2) coercion of a state or nonstate actor that threatens U.S. interests or allies, (3) change political order in another country, and (4) peacekeeping operations. The largest gender difference is for threatening or taking military action to advance U.S. interests that are threatened (men 68 percent and women 55 percent supportive) and the smallest gender difference is for humanitarian intervention (men 68 percent and women 63 percent supportive). The media reports of violence against women in some of the cases of humanitarian intervention probably contributed to relatively high support for intervention among women.

The effects of gender on the preferences about how to contend have also been examined in research about smaller-scale conflicts, in which the use of alternative conflict approaches is examined. Research includes observations, simulations, and self-reports regarding the alternatives used in various kinds of conflicts. The research includes studies of the choice of the conflict-handling styles identified in figure 4.2: competing, collaborating, compromising, avoiding, and accommodating. Interestingly, very few differences between men and women are consistently found.[17] For example, research using self-reports finds only small differences, with women reporting competing less and compromising more than men.[18] The popular expectations of large gender differences in conflict-handling strategies well may lead people to incorrectly perceive and attribute differences in conduct to gender and so confirm their expectations.

Women do tend to take action opposing violence. For example, they have frequently been engaged in peace movement organizations and peace work. Elise Boulding documents the "extraordinary creativity women have shown through time in creating not only public spaces for peaceful interaction in the midst of violence but also new ways of thinking and acting."[19] She describes, for example, the great density of transnational women's networks.

Research indicates that societies with greater gender equality are less likely to engage in international violence. A quantitative analysis of international crises from 1945 to 1994 finds that as domestic gender equality increases, a state's use of violence significantly decreases.[20] Similarly, more recent large-scale quantitative analyses of women's empowerment, controlling for many other variables, find that societies in which women are more empowered are less likely to use force in international relations, and societies with less subordination of women are more likely to have lower levels of armed conflict.[21]

Predispositions are not static, since they and their effects depend partly on circumstances, which are susceptible to change. Thus, in many societies the statuses of men and women have become more equal, as a result of public policies and changes in their economies. Relatedly, gender roles have become less sharply drawn and feminist perspectives more influential, shifting the predispositions of the men and women conducting conflicts. Such changes, however, may not alter political conduct so much as modify the justifications for traditional militancy. Thus, U.S. political leaders often justify resorting to military action in terms that appeal to feminine sensibilities, for example by emphasizing the need to protect women from offensive treatment by the Taliban in Afghanistan.

Group Ideology

Clearly, in many conflicts a group's established ideology drives and channels conflict behavior. Broadly conceived, ideology refers to general ways of thinking, often implicit, that offer interpretations of the social world in which the group members function and by which their conduct is guided. Narrowly conceived, ideology provides an explicit analysis of a group and its place in a larger social context, and it prescribes conduct to advance the values and interests of the group and its members. The discussion here focuses on ideology, narrowly defined.

In general all groups hold distinct ideological views that are articulated and institutionalized by group elites to varying degrees. In the extreme cases, ideologies are articulated by leaders of totalitarian political parties and used to control the societies they rule. In the cases of German Nazism and Soviet Communism, an ideology extolled a particular race or class and provided reasons for its dominance; it set forth goals and the means to achieve the goals. It also provided the rationale for a leader and a political party to have the absolute right to interpret the ideology. But ideologies are usually less comprehensive and authoritarian, with adherents debating the analysis and the prescriptions their ideology seems to set forth.

Ideologies, as understood here, also include religious as well as secular interpretations of the world and how to live in it. Religions usually provide a general vision of how individuals and communities should treat each other, including guidelines for engaging in conflicts.[22] The universalistic religions that are prevalent in the contemporary world all proclaim the equal and shared humanity of everyone. This principle provides the ethical basis for seeking solutions to conflicts that incorporate the partial truths known by the disputants in a more comprehensive shared truth. Some conflict transformation projects, for instance, bring together Christians, Jews, and Muslims by focusing on the shared religious values that are central to each faith.[23] It also may foster a problem-solving approach, whether as a partisan or as an intermediary. The belief in a common humanity also can provide an important basis for rejecting violence and killing. It is central in some religious denominations whose members adhere to pacifism; for example, within Christianity the historic peace churches include the Society of Friends (Quakers), Mennonites, and the Church of the Brethren.[24] Pacifist traditions are also found among a small proportion of followers of Catholicism, Judaism, Islam, Hinduism, Buddhism, and other major religions.

Other interpreters of the same holy writings, however, find support for the use of violence in the service of God's will. Undoubtedly, many wars have been fought by followers of one religion against adherents of another, and by one religious sect against another. Nonreligious identities and interests usually significantly overlap with religious ones, and the religious beliefs may largely provide a justification for fighting to secure political and economic gains.

In many battles and struggles, members of each side expect their prayers for God's blessing to be answered, and the religious beliefs may help to demonize the enemy, encouraging its destruction. Religious leaders help legitimate, for their followers, the actions taken by political leaders. They may sometimes interpret religious beliefs to require engagement in the struggle and promise a place near God after martyrdom; bolstered by such beliefs, individuals may be recruited to commit terrorist actions.

For example, in Israel, members of the messianic Gush Emunim believed that the Israeli government, by signing the 1978 Camp David Accords with Egypt, was committing an error that might stop a divine promise and process.[25] As disciples of Rabbi Zvi Jehuda Kook, they believed that the messianic age was at hand and formed an underground terrorist group within Gush Emunim to counter Palestinian attacks on Jewish settlers in the occupied territories. It planned and carried out several terrorist operations beginning in 1980 with attacks on Palestinian mayors. In 1984, the Israeli secret service discovered and disrupted plans to blow up five Arab buses full of passengers, and the group was put on trial and its members imprisoned.

Within Islam, too, some groups believe it is their religious obligation to wage a violent struggle to establish and defend a true and faithful Islamic society. For example, Osama bin Laden and his associates interpreted elements of the Islamic tradition and set goals and strategies to reach them, which had some appeal to Muslims. They were thus able to raise money and mobilize personnel to establish a transnational network organization that could conduct large-scale terrorist activities. The statement issued by bin Laden and his associates in February 1998, the "Jihad against Jews and Crusaders," condemns the wrongs committed by the United States against Muslims. They are:

> First, that for over seven years the United States has been occupying the lands of Islam in the holiest of places, the Arabian Peninsula, plundering its riches . . . humiliating its people. . . . Second . . . the great devastation inflicted on the Iraqi people by the crusader-Zionist alliance. . . . Third, if the Americans' aims behind these wars are religious and economic, the aim is also to serve the Jews' petty state and divert attention from its occupation of Jerusalem and murder of Muslims there. . . .
>
> On that basis, and in compliance with God's order, we issue the following fatwa to all Muslims: The ruling to kill the Americans and their allies—civilians and military—is an individual duty for every Muslim who can do it in any country in which it is possible to do it.[26]

The strategy al Qaeda used in attacking the United States was undertaken with the faith that it would damage American interests and provoke U.S. reactions that would strengthen al Qaeda, thereby forcing the United States to withdraw from Islamic regions.

Secular ideologies can also justify the use of violence or even extol it. Many ideologies analyze why their people continue to suffer injustice, using that analysis to formulate a winning strategy. Frantz Fanon's writing, influential in the 1960s and 1970s, offers a powerful illustration.[27] He examines how the colonizer dehumanizes the natives, turning them into animals. To overcome this violence, the colonized people must also use violence, and through violent struggle the colonized free themselves and gain a new sense of power and self-respect. This process was considered essential in winning national liberation from colonialism anywhere. For example, in the Basque region of Spain during the 1960s the Basque Fatherland and Liberty evolved as an organization of Basque nationalism. Influenced by Fanon's analysis, it undertook a strategy of violent actions that continues into the twenty-first century. So too did Che Guevara, following his engagement in the Cuban revolution, pursue a violent revolutionary strategy as the way to reveal injustice, create a revolutionary situation, and win a revolution.

Social and Political Organization

Among the many aspects of a group's social structure affecting the choice of a conflict strategy, the primary one for analyzing and resolving social conflicts is the relationship among those who represent one of the adversaries in a conflict and the constituent groups who support, challenge, or otherwise seek to influence them. This is what distinguishes intergroup conflicts from interpersonal ones. In intergroup conflicts, a leader or a group of them represent and commit their constituencies to the struggle, while in interpersonal conflicts the antagonists act largely independent of any constituency.

The relations among those who claim to speak for an adversary in a conflict vary greatly. In some adversaries, for some goals, and in some periods, leaders are easily able to mobilize constituent support for the conflict strategies they choose. During crisis periods when group members collectively confront an external threat, for instance, leaders are often able to elicit broad group support for what might be considered extreme measures during "normal" times.[28] For other adversaries, goals, and times, various coalitions of elite constituent groups shape the external policy and determine the modes to be used. For still other adversaries, goals, and times, rank-and-file constituents narrowly constrain the conflict strategies employed. The nature of these internal relationships matters because the various component groups tend to have different preferences and interests regarding strategic approaches. Furthermore, as the relationships among them change, shifts in the adversary's goals and strategies drive the conflict toward escalation or de-escalation.

Group relationships, and the constraints that they place on strategic choices, are not just socially derived but are politically derived as well. In any political entity there is a group of actors who, if they agree, have both the ability to commit the resources of the entity and the power to prevent other people, groups, or institutions from overtly reversing their position. The unit having this authority may (and frequently does) vary with the nature of the problem. For instance, in governments for issues of vital importance the highest political authorities often constitute the decision unit; there is a contraction of authority to those most accountable for the choices. For less dramatic, more technical issues, the decision unit generally varies depending on the type of problem the government is facing, whether military, economic, diplomatic, scientific, and so on. In governments where policy normally involves multiple bureaucratic organizations, the problem may be passed among different units—within one agency, across agencies, or between interagency groups.[29]

The preferences of the many constituent groups within a conflict party also vary with the character of the struggle. For example, in highly regulated conflicts, with contentious matters managed routinely, leaders are more prone than their followers to prefer to use the established conflict management procedures, while followers or important segments of them tend to favor relatively antagonistic and coercive modes. On the other hand, when the conflicts are not highly regulated, particularly if the conflict party is becoming mobilized, the leaders tend to resort to relatively confrontational strategies. To illustrate, a study of trade union leaders in the United States finds that the highest trade union leaders tend to be less militant than lower-ranking union officials.[30] Lower-ranking officials are more suspicious of management intentions, while the national leaders are more deeply involved in negotiations and other interactions with management, developing mutual dependence and understanding.

More generally, studies of elite groups' preferences regarding ways to conduct foreign policy reveal variations reflecting self-interests, general orientations, political ideology, network alliances, and other factors.[31] Their different positions and influence relative to the public and to elected national officials vary with the foreign policy issue and with the time frame being considered. Thus, analyses of U.S. foreign policy indicate that the public is likely to be involved and have some autonomy in forming opinions over time about foreign policy issues where national security and economic security are important.[32]

Consider the large changes in the U.S. government's use of armed force and shifts in American public opinion. In the early 1970s, public opinion turned against increased military expenditures in reaction to the war in Vietnam. In the 1980s, support for military spending rose again, but U.S. military action carefully took the form of covert or very limited interventions. In the 1990s, the use of military force became more legitimate as it was used in multilateral engagements. After the 9/11 attacks, highly militarized and unilateral U.S. military operations were undertaken.[33] U.S. government military policy and American public opinion do not change in unison; U.S. government policy can change abruptly and initially win public support, while public opinion has influence over a longer time frame. Both are also influenced by external events and long-term developments. For instance, the global economic downturn of 2008–2011 has created new budget realities for the U.S. government, leading even senior officials to the conclusion that a significant cut to defense expenditures is both inevitable and necessary.[34]

An examination of the continuities and discontinuities in American foreign policy goals and methods pursued in the administrations of President George W. Bush are illuminating. Since the U.S. entry into World War II, a high degree of consensus has been sustained that the United States should be engaged in international affairs, in concert with other nations.[35] Strikingly, the public's foreign policy goals that are most widely regarded as very important tend to be self-protective and are neither imperialist nor unselfishly humanitarian. And the public also seems cautious and does not give high importance to goals that are hugely ambitious. Evidently, some of the goals that were deemed to be so very important by leaders in the Bush administrations were not so regarded by most Americans. The grandiosity and risk-taking character of the Bush administration's foreign policy goals were remarkable in that context and appear to reflect both the political ideology of the neoconservative movement as well as the opportunity for a more assertive American foreign policy brought about because of the 9/11 attacks.[36] The high costs of the wars in Afghanistan and Iraq, and the failure to achieve the U.S. goals stated at their outset, have contributed to public support shifting back to more modest goals and less reliance on military means.

The methods the American public believes should be used to advance U.S. goals also are varied. These methods are widely discussed in terms of acting multilaterally in cooperation with allies or else acting unilaterally. In this matter, too, strong divergences appeared between the general public and the leaders in the Bush administration during the initial post–9/11 period. At the time, polls indicated that most Americans favored their government acting multilaterally in international affairs. Moreover, a 2005 survey found that most respondents reported that the experience with the Iraq war had made them feel worse about the possibility of using military force to bring about democracy.[37] These shifts contributed to Barack Obama's election to the presidency in November 2008.

An important aspect of internal social organization is the leaders' need to sustain constituency support. Having an external enemy may appear to leaders to be an effective way of rallying support. North Korean leader Kim Jong-il, for instance, frequently employs highly partisan language when referring to the United States and South Korea and the threats they pose. Furthermore, using certain conflict methods can help commit the constituencies to the course undertaken by the leaders. The leaders of a terrorist group, a state, or an ethnic separatist organization, by engaging their followers in violence against persons designated as enemies, make it difficult for the members to withdraw. They need to justify their bloody actions; they risk retribution from the enemy if they fail; and their compatriots in violence are bonded by their actions to continue the struggle. This pattern may be especially likely for ethnic groups that are culturally similar to the groups from which they seek to distinguish themselves, for example, the Kurds, Basques, and Croats.[38]

Finally, in large-scale conflicts adversaries are likely to have established units specialized to conduct extremely coercive actions and they tend to play important roles in the choice of strategies. These units include police departments, military organizations, and sometimes groups engaged in covert operations. They typically use coercive methods and often have standard operating procedures for applying them. Since they are expected to be prepared for action and have contingency plans, when a fight erupts, officials and leaders are likely to turn to them for guidance and often delegate responsibility to respond to them. Frequently, this leads to a rapid escalation and sometimes a destructive conflict. Thus, following standardized procedures, police may try to control a crowd or a riot but act in ways that intensify the confrontation. Procedures are designed to counter serious attacks, and when military personnel are asked to respond to a threat they usually apply the method they have prepared to use.

Cognizant of these risks, political leaders, members of specialized agencies, and other concerned persons have tried to develop responses that are less likely to result in destructive escalation. Some progress can be cited. Thus, nonprovocative techniques for police intervention in various crises have been developed and increasingly employed.[39] For example, when hostages are taken, police responses often utilize specialists in negotiation. Similarly, officials operating at the international and at the national level sometimes call on or readily accept intervention by persons or groups that provide experienced mediating or peacekeeping services.

Resources Available for Struggle

Adversary groups vary greatly in the resources they possess to use for particular conflict strategies. Hence, each group is careful to select from among the strategies it believes it has the capacity to employ. Consider the implications of the numerical size of the conflict group as a resource. Members of a small group, believing they lack the capability of openly challenging their adversary with other means, sometimes resort to terrorism.[40] They recognize that to wage even guerrilla warfare the group needs relatively large numbers of fighters and a supporting social environment. Similarly, nonviolent direct action requires a large number of participants to be effective, and a goodly number is also needed for mutual support and protection. The costs of nonviolent action are likely to decrease and the gains to increase the greater the number of participants.[41] The same is true for a strategy of reframing enactments,[42] which usually requires popular participation to interrupt ongoing social patterns. Rioting, too, requires a large number of participants at a given locality, assuring a sense of security and support. For example, research about racial disorders in the United States between 1961 and 1968 found that the absolute number of nonwhites in a city was by far the single most important factor in accounting for riotous disorders.[43] When the grievances of blacks were sufficiently widespread and protests were an accepted form of action, there were more incidents that might trigger a riot. Riots, depending in part on milling and contagion, require congeries of people: streets filled with people who are young enough to feel they can take risks may begin engaging in protest activity that draws in other participants and results in a riot.[44]

In general, a group's capabilities channel its selection of a conflict means. Groups with resources that can be conditionally awarded to an adversary, such as continued service or electoral votes, may choose to offer or withhold that resource. For example, a government representing the economically dominant class may offer concessions to members of the relatively deprived class to prevent or restrain challenging actions. Groups skilled in manipulating symbols are likely to try strategies with high degrees of persuasion, as is frequently done among environmental groups that seek to protect endangered species.

Finally, groups with powerful military capabilities are likely to depend on coercive conflict strategies. For example, since World War II, the U.S. Department of Defense has become a powerful and influential actor in U.S. foreign affairs. At the same time, and particularly in recent years, the Department of State's influence on foreign affairs has diminished. The vast capabilities of the military establishment make it an attractive tool to be used in a wide array of circumstances; consequently, U.S. foreign policy has become greatly militarized.[45] The global reach of American military forces is illustrated by the power and influence of regional commanders in chief (CinC).[46] The Department of Defense divides the world into geographical regions, and a CinC commands all U.S. military forces in each region. The Department of State has only regional "desks" in Washington, D.C.

Although each adversary has a repertoire of conflict techniques available, the repertoire tends to be limited to the methods previously used. Even using a method effectively once can make it a precedent for the future.[47] Many methods emerge from the members' routine conduct, for example, as a coercive inducement, factory workers can stop working, withholding their labor. Of course it is necessary to conceptualize first that such action might be a weapon.

An implication of these observations is that expanding the repertoire of conflict methods that adversaries possess increases the likelihood that a more constructive means of struggle will be adopted. This can include a wider array of novel means of violence. But it also means that adversaries with the resource of problem-solving conflict-resolution skills will be able to select a conflict mode that incorporates them. The growing use and success of these methods is a strong argument for increased training of social-movement organizations in nonviolent strategies, of schoolteachers and students in mediation skills, of police in nonprovocative methods of crowd control, and of military personnel in negotiation and collaborative decision-making skills for their peacekeeping, peace observation, and humanitarian-assistance duties. Trained persons charged to apply mediation and other problem-solving techniques in conflict situations increasingly staff special units within many kinds of organizations.

RELATIONS BETWEEN ADVERSARIES

Each adversary's choice of strategy greatly affects the other side's choice, since their conflict is a relationship. The effects of three underlying aspects of the adversaries' relationship will be discussed: (1) the level of integration between the antagonists, (2) how they perceive and feel about each other, and (3) the degree of symmetry in the resources each controls.

Integration between Adversaries

Adversaries are mutually integrated insofar as their degree of interaction with each other is high relative to their interaction with other parties, and insofar as they have common and complementary interests compared to conflicting ones. The degree and nature of integration affects not only the emergence of a conflict but also how it is waged.

Among highly integrated adversaries, violent conflict modes tend to be avoided for several reasons. The cross-cutting ties usually associated with integration reduce support for choosing means that presume animosity. The interdependence that is inherent in integration raises the costs of resorting to conflict methods that damage the relationship. And the greater likelihood of shared understandings and institutionalized rules for managing conflict among integrated adversaries increases the probability that they will use modes of conflict that are nonviolent and relatively low in coercion.

A variety of research results indicate that cross-cutting ties and other aspects of integration inhibit the use of highly coercive conflict or illegitimate means between adversaries and even provide the basis for the use of problem-solving conflict modes. For example, a study of the rate of strikes in eleven industrial countries found the propensity to strike to be high in mining and the maritime industries; medium-high in lumber and textiles; medium in the chemical and printing industries; medium-low in clothing and services; and low in railroad, agriculture, and trade.[48] The authors conclude that one important determinant of the inter-industry differences in the propensity to strike is the location of the workers in society. Workers who form "isolated masses" are particularly prone to strike, as has been the case for miners, sailors, and longshoremen, who tend to have separate communities, relatively homogenous work roles, and low mobility out of the occupation.

An example of another kind of cross-cutting mechanism is provided by a study of cities in India that experience recurrent intercommunal riots, between Hindus and Muslims, and the many cities that do not have such riots.[49] Localities with organizations that bring people from the two communal groups together to work for a common cause, such as traders' cooperatives or community-development committees, tend not to have intercommunal riots.

Certain kinds of cross-cutting ties inhibit or facilitate particular conflict modes. For example, since men are most often the warriors in external conflicts, cross-cutting bonds among the potential warriors is particularly relevant to the choice of war or other modes of violent conflict. This can be seen in cross-cultural research that found that societies with matrilocal residence patterns tend to have a sense of solidarity and lack inter-village warfare, while patrilocal residence societies are plagued by more dissension, fights, and feuds.[50] This occurs because among societies with the patrilocal residence pattern, the bride moves to the husband's village; while in societies with a matrilocal residence pattern, the husband moves to the bride's village. Consequently, in patrilocal societies the men live in the same village with their brothers, while in a matrilocal society they live with their in-laws and face the possibility of fighting against their brothers if they engage in a fight with another village.

In interstate conflicts, too, integration provides the basis for applying negative sanctions short of violence and increases the likelihood that problem-solving approaches will be tried and found effective. A variety of research findings support these expectations. For example, Karl W. Deutsch and his colleagues analyzed the emergence of "security communities," peoples within a territory who have a sense of community and have institutions that ensure, for a long time, that social problems will be resolved without recourse to large-scale physical force.[51] Examples of such security communities include "amalgamated" cases, such as the United States since 1877, England and Scotland since 1707, and Switzerland since 1848, and "pluralistic" cases, such as Norway and Sweden since 1907 and the United States and Canada since the 1870s. Three conditions seem essential for the success of both amalgamated and pluralistic security communities: the compatibility of major values relating to political decision making, the capacity of the participating units to respond to each other, and mutual predictability of behavior. Furthermore, in amalgamated security communities they find unbroken links of social communication both geographically between territories and socially between different strata, and there is a wide range of communication and transactions between the peoples.

Other research examines relations between trade and severe conflicts. For example, a study of wars between 1870 and 1975 found that countries that were more involved in foreign trade were less likely to be involved in wars.[52] Several other studies examine the relationship between trade and conflict among pairs of states, also finding that higher levels of trade lead to lower levels of conflicts.

Low levels of integration reduce many options that adversaries might otherwise employ, such as nonviolent coercive inducements exemplified by trade sanctions or severances of cooperative arrangements. This has been the case, for example, for the United States in trying to influence either North Korea or Iran following the Iranian revolution of 1979; the low level of integration with those countries seems to leave few inducements available aside from coercion or threats of coercion. It is true that many noncoercive sanctions are conceivable, although politically awkward; however, starting at such low levels, even steps toward normalized relations could be a strong inducement.[53]

Although high integration between parties reduces the likelihood that they will use violence against each other, it does not preclude it. A shared culture may actually allow for certain kinds of violence, as is the case where family or clan feuds are traditional. Furthermore, once a conflict erupts between integrated parties, the use of coercion may escalate into violence, even of a brutal kind, as the parties endure severe losses resulting from the special vulnerability arising from their mutual dependency and as the parties feel betrayed by those previously close. Such factors contributed to the extremely brutal fighting with the breakup of the former Yugoslavia.

Adversaries' Views and Feelings Regarding Each Other

A critical feature of adversary relations influencing the choice of conflict strategies is the degree to which each party respects the other. If the opponents regard each other as legitimate and are responsive to each other, then problem-solving modes of conducting their emerging conflicts are likely. This is supported by one of the few well-documented empirical findings about the occurrence of war: democratic societies rarely if ever make war on each other.[54] Furthermore, democratic dyads are much less likely than nondemocratic dyads to engage in any kind of militarized dispute.[55] The leaders and peoples of such societies tend to recognize important common values, shared norms, and common interests. Legitimacy is probably granted to the policies each government pursues, and they have shared understandings about how conflicts are to be managed. Some American political leaders have used these findings to justify waging war to install democratic governments elsewhere in the world, although the evidence does not support the efficacy of unilateral forceful impositions as a way of establishing democracies.

The content of the understandings and expectations that adversaries share affects which strategy each party will use. For example, traditional U.S. employer hostility to trade unions helps account for the violent and often bloody history of trade union organization in the United States.[56] In the past, collective bargaining has been less institutionalized in the United States than in other industrialized, democratic societies. Consequently, U.S. union members have been involved in more strikes and for longer periods than union members in other pluralistic industrial societies.[57]

Adversaries nearly always have a past history with each other or with others they regard as similar. They bring that past experience to bear in deciding how to act toward one another. Thus, it might be expected that countries that have been wartime allies would subsequently be less likely to make war on each other. However, quantitative analysis of pairs of countries that have fought wars against each other does not indicate a strong tendency for countries to sustain former relations either as allies or as enemies.[58] On the whole, they often shift from being antagonists in one war to allies in another.

Some enmities do persist, but that requires additional circumstances. If people on one side feel they have been humiliated in a prior fight, they may later seek revenge.[59] Generations of young people may be taught about such humiliations and learn to demonize their enemy, opening up the possibility of using dehumanizing conflict modes. Some ethnic conflicts have been plagued by such traditions, providing political leaders with sentiments that could be mobilized, as between the Hutus and Tutsi in Rwanda and the Serbs, Croats, and Bosnians in the former Yugoslavia.

Sometimes, one conflict party holds views about an adversary that justifies its use of particularly harsh conflict modes. Those views may derive from political or religious ideologies or accounts of past atrocities.[60] Consequently, the adversary may be considered subhuman or evil and therefore its interests and concerns can be di regarded with self-defeating results. For example, during World War II, in accord with Nazi racist ideology, Germans treated even the anti-Soviet Russians and Ukrainians as racial inferiors, driving them to support the Soviet government.[61]

Resource Balance between Adversaries

The abundance of resources a conflict party has available as possible inducements, relative to its adversary, affects not only the emergence of a conflict but also the choice of conflict strategies. Analyses of this matter tend to focus on the balance of capabilities to commit violence and the resort to physical force. Two contrasting views of coercive power differences as an explanation for resorting to violence have often been argued. According to one line of reasoning, a large power imbalance is expected to inhibit or deter the weaker party from coercively challenging the stronger one. By the same reasoning, the stronger party may be able to attain its goals merely by its dominance and the threat of coercion. Consequently, relationships in which one party has a clear preponderance of power are not likely to be marked by violent conflict. On the other hand, some analysts argue that it is a symmetrical balance of power that will inhibit either side from instigating a violent conflict, for unless one of the parties has considerable certainty that it will win a violent struggle, it will avoid initiating one.

The area in which these contrasting views have been most thoroughly examined pertains to the incidence of wars. Much of this work presumes a "realist" perspective, viewing each state as a unitary actor, rationally calculating the costs and benefits of waging war to maximize its power, and considering military force as the primary means to serve that end.[62] Each of the two lines of reasoning regarding power preponderance and power balance can be argued by using the "realist" approach. The research results, however, do not consistently support either argument.[63]

Reasons for not finding a consistent association between state power relations and initiating wars abound. Many of them flow from criticisms of the "realist" approach. For example, states are not really unitary actors; rather, governments respond to diverse domestic pressures and themselves include persons and groups with varied interests and perspectives. Also, power cannot be measured only by the capability of doing violence and cannot be assessed without relationship to the goals toward which it is directed.

Even putting aside these problems of the "realist" approach, another reason for the failure in finding a consistent relationship between power differences and the onset of war is suggested by Bruce Bueno de Mesquita.[64] He explains the onset of war by utilizing two influential theoretical approaches. First, he postulates that a leader seeks to maximize his or her expected utility; in other words, the policy maker tries to maximize the net benefits expected from his or her policy choices. Bueno de Mesquita further argues that the decision to go to war is generally made by an individual, a strong leader. Second, he utilizes the theoretical approach emphasizing the importance of uncertainty in decision making and variations in preferences regarding risk taking. Uncertainty refers to the degree to which the probability of a course of action being successful is unknown. Individuals have their own preferences regarding risk and uncertainty. Persons who are risk averse require much more confidence of success than do those who are risk acceptant. Increased uncertainty enhances the differences between persons who tend to avoid risks and those who tend to accept risks. An implication of this reasoning is that individuals, even having the same expectations about the outcome of a war, may rationally make different choices about going to war. Therefore, even for rational actors, the immediate external conditions do not altogether determine the choices of conflict mode.

Despite the considerable research about wars, many disagreements about explaining the incidence of wars remain. One difficulty in achieving consensus is that wars are not homogenous; they vary greatly and different explanations probably pertain to different kinds of wars.[65] Some are between rival states, or between complex alliances, or between a large expanding empire and a small neighboring people. They are fought for varying goals and by diverse means.

Although wars are usually studied in order to learn how to avoid them, relatively little research has been done about wars that have actually been averted.[66] In the present analysis, we consider how conflicts emerge and the alternative ways in which they are conducted. Shooting wars, in their manifold variety, are only one way among many to wage interstate struggles.

It is also useful to examine evidence from conflict domains other than interstate relations regarding the way resource differences affect the choice of conflict modes. Labor-management relations is another relatively well-studied domain. On the basis of reasoning about power differences, trade unions would be expected to strike when their chances of success are greatest. Indeed, strikes do tend to be more frequent during upturns in the economy, and therefore, when labor is in shorter supply.[67] This indicates that it is not increased grievances alone that account for the choice of institutionalized coercive means to wage a conflict; rather, it is the greater likelihood of being successful if attempted.

The increased integration of the world economy in many ways reduces the strength of workers and of labor unions relative to corporate managers.[68] The increased ease of moving investments and the growth of the global market makes it easier for managers to drive a hard bargain with workers by threatening to close a plant and open a new one somewhere else in the country or the world. The threat does not have to be explicit to be understood and carry weight. The gradual decline in trade union strength and militancy, of course, is due to many other factors such as political ideologies and shifts in the composition of the labor force away from industrial jobs. Indeed, the transnational growth of corporate activities does not always strengthen the hand of management relative to the workers. The worldwide integration of a company with specialized components of the production located in different parts of the world makes the whole company vulnerable to a stoppage at one locality. For example, in June 1988, 3,400 members of United Automobile Workers local 659 walked off their jobs at a General Motors (GM) metal-stamping plant in Flint, Michigan.[69] This quickly stopped production of parts essential for producing GM vehicles throughout North America.

This discussion of resource differences affecting selection of conflict strategies casts additional light on the findings that revolutions and uprisings often occur when previously improving conditions take a downturn. As discussed in chapter 3, this unrest is usually interpreted as expression of increased dissatisfaction resulting from an increased gap between attainments and expectations. But increased dissatisfaction alone does not lead to such actions. Some group must be held responsible, and action to change them must seem possible. It is when the ruling government is held responsible that noninstitutionalized coercive means tend to be undertaken. This is even more likely when the deterioration in conditions is attributable to the incompetence of the authorities. Such incompetence not only reduces their legitimacy but also makes them appear weak and vulnerable, inviting rebellion. The deteriorated conditions and the authorities' reduced legitimacy also mean that they have fewer resources to be traded for continued obedience. Thus, the French, Russian, and Chinese revolutions broke out when the governments had been weakened by their international overextension.[70]

An authoritarian government that allows for greater freedom of communication among its citizens in order to win support by reducing the citizen's sense of oppression risks greater opposition and sometimes protest, demonstrations, and uprisings. This occurs in part because the government may be seen as showing its weakness and revealing its internal division. The vastly speedier and more widespread interpersonal communication resulting from new social media technologies makes it possible for previously oppressed individuals to become aware of their shared discontent and take increasingly bold collective actions.[71] Indeed, new social media has been credited with greatly facilitating protests against authoritarian rule during the "Arab Spring" in 2011.

Although coercive power differences affect the choice of coercive strategies, they do not do so strongly and consistently. The asymmetry of noncoercive dimensions of power also needs to be considered, since that affects the choice of strategies with significant components of persuasion and rewards. Thus, partisans who believe they occupy the moral high ground tend to use moral claims to persuade not only allies to support them but also members of the adversary side who might come to agree with them. To illustrate, Palestinians won many resolutions in the UN General Assembly supporting their claims against Israel regarding the rights of Palestinians.[72] Despite those successes on the world stage, the Palestinian leadership was less effective in its persuasive efforts toward Israelis because such efforts were for so long contradicted by violent attacks on Jewish noncombatants and ambiguities about acceptance of the State of Israel. The leadership of the South Africans struggling against apartheid and the exclusion of blacks from the governance of South Africa more successfully won UN resolutions that placed economic pressure on the South African government. Moral condemnations of apartheid by the world community affected many white South Africans, some of whom felt shame and embarrassment. The impact of these external acts was great because they were accompanied by the black leadership's reassurances that whites were regarded as South Africans and their civil rights would be protected if apartheid were abolished.[73] Furthermore, the leaders of the struggle against apartheid carefully avoided what might be regarded as terrorist attacks on whites, foreseeing that such attacks would make negotiations much harder.

Finally, parties with control of resources that members of the adversary side desire possess rewards that might be used to co-opt opponents or otherwise win their compliance or agreement. Of course, the resource-rich party can use those assets to induce supporters of the opposing leadership to defect or to induce allies to remain aligned.

SOCIAL CONTEXT

Four aspects of the adversaries' social context significantly affect the adversaries' strategic choices: (1) the institutions of the opponents' social system, (2) the norms and ways of thinking prevailing in their environment, (3) the roles of other parties, and (4) other systemic features of their environment.

Institutions

Adversary relations are embedded within larger social systems and play out through various societal institutions. For example, in countries with well-established governments, judicial, legislative, and executive institutions are used extensively to manage conflicts within a family, a factory, a community, or across a country. Where a government is open to popular participation and regarded by its citizens as legitimate, even conflicts with the potential of breaking up the country may be successfully managed using the existing political system, with little or no violence, and often incorporating ad hoc negotiations among representatives of the contending parties. For example, this has been true in Canada, between largely French-speaking Quebec and the rest of Canada, and in Belgium, between its French-speaking and Flemish-speaking citizens. However, where a less inclusive or legitimate government presides, ethnic, linguistic, religious, and other communal divisions have been the basis for unchecked violence in struggles for control of the state or for secession from the state.

When the state itself represents one of the contending communal groups or there is a single ruling elite, problem-solving modes are much less likely to be used. If opponents seriously challenge the government's authority and domination, the response can include resorting to violence by the state. This is illustrated by the very severe, long-lasting violence in Sri Lanka between the government, dominated by the Sinhalese, and the Liberation Tigers of Tamil Eelam, the secessionist organization of the Tamil population.[74] The Sudan provides another instance of great violence, between the government dominated by Muslims in the north and the non-Muslim peoples in the south.[75]

Under extreme conditions of a government unable to govern, conditions of a failed state, violent conflicts among contending groups are likely to be persistent.[76] The resulting mass violence and great refugee flows often produce anguished cries for external intervention, which sometimes occur with dubious consequences, as discussed in later chapters. At present, the world lacks global institutions with the authority to reach and enforce binding decisions regarding conflicts among states or between states and nongovernmental groups. States often resolve their conflicts by themselves, often with coercion and even through wars. But transnational governmental and nongovernmental organizations increasingly contribute to problem-solving settlement modes.[77]

Norms and Prevailing Ways of Thinking

Members of a social system often share general understandings about the appropriate means to be used in pursuing and settling various conflicts. In the international domain, for example, ideas about national sovereignty and the right of governments to monopolize the legitimate use of violence internally are widely shared. Consequently, countries have long considered war a legitimate way to pursue foreign policy. Furthermore, governments have widely asserted the right to treat people in their territory as they deem correct, without other governments having any right to intervene. However, in recent decades ideas of sovereignty have been changing, as international norms limiting the rights of states to harm their citizens or to act aggressively against other states have been evolving. Consensus about human rights, for example, has been growing and with it a legitimate basis for intervention in the internal affairs of countries. This is exemplified by the United States and NATO's intervention in the wars breaking up Yugoslavia and the subsequent trials of Slobodan Milosevic and others in the International Criminal Tribunal for the Former Yugoslavia, established by the United Nations Security Council in 1993. As discussed in later chapters, there is growing international discussion about the governments' responsibility to protect people.[78]

Certainly, within a society norms and understandings about how various groups should conduct themselves when in conflict are widely shared and often quite detailed. Those can constrain even a powerful adversary's choice of conflict modes, making some choices unlikely while increasing the likelihood of others. The context of such norms varies with the culture and social system of different populations.

Other Parties

Protagonists in a fight are never isolated. Each has possible allies and additional enemies who may join the conflict. In addition, groups who are part of the constituency of one protagonist may defect or may shift their involvement in the struggle. Other groups may seek to intervene to pursue a mediating role. All these groups also help, wittingly and unwittingly, to shape the changing choices of a conflict mode.

An adversary's beliefs about these other parties and their possible actions profoundly shape the methods adopted in waging a conflict. Actions are often avoided in fear of alienating allies or of driving uninvolved parties to the opponent's side. Often, actions are chosen in hopes of getting the attention and sympathy of potential allies.

Thus, for the leaders of the U.S. civil rights movement of the later 1950s and early 1960s, large demonstrations and nonviolent direct action appeared to be an effective means because these were persuasive to many citizens and government leaders who might support legislation and other actions to end discrimination and to foster integration and equal opportunity. Police attempts at repression in 1963 in Birmingham and elsewhere, as well as vigilante terrorism, vividly revealed the prevailing oppression.[79] Those violent responses to the nonviolent struggle of the civil rights movement evoked widespread support for the 1964 civil rights legislation passed by the U.S. Congress.

On the other hand, separatist or other challenges by ethnic groups that have resorted to strategies with high components of violence, particularly involving noncombatants, receive little support or sympathy from external actors. Outside governments, international governmental organizations, and the attentive public may even condone harsh repressive actions against the challenging "terrorists." The highly destructive conflicts in Chechnya and in Sri Lanka are illustrative.

External actors intervene in diverse ways that contribute to the course of most large-scale conflicts. They may intervene as supporters of one side or as advocates and supporters of some means of struggle and not others. They may also play a variety of intermediary roles. Intervention for one side may hasten an imposed settlement, but it may also help escalate and prolong a destructive conflict as other external actors join the fray on the opposing side. One of the destructive features of the East-West Cold War was that the Soviet Union and the United States supported and sometimes directly engaged in violence in many regions and counties, including Korea, Vietnam, Nicaragua, southern Africa, Afghanistan, and the Middle East.

Interventions that contribute to determining conflict trajectories include promoting and supporting particular conflict strategies. Advocates of particular strategies of conflict have written about the virtues and effectiveness of those strategies and have influenced others to try them out.[80] This has been true of nonviolent direct action, guerrilla action, as well as police suppression. Some advocates have visited locales where conflicts were emerging in order to consult and provide training in particular conflict strategies. Sometimes governments provide training to soldiers, police, or terrorists from other countries to enhance their use of coercive methods in their home countries. For example, al Qaeda operated training camps for militants in Taliban-ruled Afghanistan, and the United States has provided training for anti-insurgency troops to help governments in Latin America. Often, without support from such outside groups, large-scale organized resistance, insurgencies, or repression could not be undertaken or sustained.

Finally, intermediary intervention, including mediation, advocacy, and other "third side" actions can greatly affect the trajectory of a conflict.[81] Domestically, intermediary intervention includes government agencies providing labor-management mediation and facilitation services and protection in civil rights cases. Intermediary interventions are also made by nongovernmental organizations, such as interreligious councils and the American Civil Liberties Union. Internationally, this includes mediation by the UN secretary general's special representatives, national governments, and also unofficial channels of diplomacy.

Systemic Features

Whether the social context for a conflict is the world, a country, or a local organization, it displays features of a social system. We will discuss four features of those systems that significantly affect the choice of conflict mode and that have received particular scholarly and policy attention: the distribution of resources among the constituent members, the changing relevant technologies, the degree of integration among the members, and the collective responses to social and nonsocial stress.

Resource Inequality

The earlier discussion of the preponderance or balance of power inhibiting the recourse to violence and war is applicable to the system level as well as to the dyadic relationship between two or more adversaries. The research about the incidence of wars in relationship to different power systems, whether unipolar, bipolar, or multipolar, however, has not yielded consistent results.[82] One reason for this may be that research focusing on polarity regards polarity as a discrete variable, often treated as dichotomous. That assumes a monotonic relationship between the incidence of war and either power preponderance or balance. But it may be that either extreme power concentration or extreme power diffusion reduces the likelihood of war, whereas a moderate degree of power dispersion increases the likelihood of war, the relationship being not monotonic but curvilinear.

Some research, using an index of power concentration among the major states in the international system, treats concentration as a continuous variable. Evidence of a curvilinear relationship between concentration and the incidence of wars among major states was found, wars being less likely with either high or low levels of concentration. The evidence is less clear for other kinds of wars.

Clearly, the relationship between any one measure of systemic power inequality and all kinds of violence cannot be large. There are too many dimensions of power and kinds of violence for that. Moreover, many other dimensions of inequality, as well as the other aspects of the system as a whole, affect the choice of a conflict mode.

Changing Relevant Technologies

Technological developments that are relevant for waging conflicts have always received great attention, particularly as related to making war. For example, in recent years this has included the increased possibility of inflicting great damage with weapons of mass destruction, and some governments and nongovernmental organizations seek to counter governments that possess them. Readily available small but powerful weapons can be adopted by militia groups to undertake violent attacks. Advanced delivery systems and smart bombs seem to enable powerful governments to undertake limited wars that inflict great destruction but avoid massive collateral damage and with little risk of deaths on their side. These and other war-making technological developments probably tend to make reliance on military force more attractive.

Many other technological developments, however, can foster reliance on relatively constructive means of struggle. For example, as noted elsewhere in this book, increased global integration and shared information, based on new technologies, generate the interest and capability to effectively intervene to avoid or constrain destructive conflicts. Particular interest in recent years has focused on the new information technologies and social media and how they may facilitate mobilization of nongovernmental actors who might undertake nonviolent protests and other coordinated challenges to authoritarian rulers. That capacity may have somewhat increased, but dominant groups also have increased capabilities to limit and contain the effectiveness of reliance on social media.

In the context of this book, it should be noted that the increased visibility of struggles nearly everywhere enhances the effectiveness of nonviolent strategies when they are undertaken. Moreover, the broad use of many means of communication increases the importance of persuasive inducements in conflicts. Governments and nongovernmental actors increasingly rely on persuasive arguments to justify their actions and causes and gain support for them from broader audiences. The new information technologies and social media also increase the possible adoption of strategies involving, for example, coengagement and co-optation. Conflict settlements may be better sustained and destructive conflicts avoided by enhanced organizational transparency, accountability, and engagement. There is some evidence of this, but the effects are uneven across cases.

Integration

The general level of integration in the system as a whole may affect adversaries' choices of conflict modes, even aside from the degree of integration between them. Higher overall levels of integration increase the interest and capability of other actors to affect the adversaries' choice of mode. In general, we expect that high levels of integration generate an effective interest in members of the system to constrain adversaries from choosing disruptive conflict modes such as wars or other organized violent actions.

Research relevant to these arguments has been conducted regarding the incidence of international wars. One set of studies examines the possible effects of the general level of integration, measured by the growth of international governmental and of international nongovernmental organizations. The results have not consistently supported the expectations about the level of integration so measured inhibiting wars.[83] It is likely the level of integration at the international level, indicated by the network of international organizations, is simply not great enough to markedly impact on the likelihood of wars in the system as a whole.

Many thinkers have argued that the growth of world trade would inhibit recourse to international wars. States would avoid wars when they are especially likely to be disruptive of trade benefits. Indeed, there is evidence that the level of international trade is inversely related to the incidence of wars among major states and among smaller states.[84] That relationship is quantitatively large and statistically significant.

Responses to Stress

Social systems are sometimes subjected to great stress from large-scale changes that impact contending parties. These may be demographic changes that result from epidemics or changes in birth rates that affect the overall capacity of the system to materially and politically sustain itself. Societal institutions may be overwhelmed and the management of conflicts break down. Natural disasters such as earthquakes or hurricanes may be followed by looting, riots, and intensified contentions between different ethnicities or classes. More resilient social systems may cope well with such crises, and a resulting sense of solidarity can override previous antagonisms.

There is growing concern that global climate change will exacerbate emerging conflicts. For example, the brutal fighting in the Darfur region of the Sudan is attributable in part to the increasing desertification in that region that has pitted farming people against nomadic people, peoples who also tended to differ in ethnicity and religion.[85] Periods of severe drought in recent decades forced nomads, many of Arab ethnicity, to migrate southward, resulting in conflicts with sedentary tribes, including the Fur and the Masalit. The Sudanese government's engagement in a civil war with rebel movements further contributed to the violent escalation of the conflicts in Darfur.

CONCLUSIONS

Four sets of factors jointly determine the choice of a conflict strategy: the goal sought, the characteristics of the adversary, the relations between the adversaries, and their social environment. The factors combine in various ways, changing in the course of a struggle, to constrain the choice of subsequent strategies and resulting conflict modes.

Adversary predispositions and characteristics also influence the selection of conflict means. But usually, they are less significant than characteristics pertaining directly to employing particular strategies, for example, adhering to an ideology legitimating a particular conflict method and having the capability to execute it. Furthermore, the proximate circumstances that the adversaries face are especially important. These significantly include the adversaries' conduct toward each other, which is particularly relevant to developing constructive strategies. The actions that each side takes affect the opponent's choices and thus the course of their conflict. The use of terrorism by one side, for example, is likely to arouse strong reactions, which themselves may then contribute to destructive escalation.

Knowledge of the many factors and processes that shape the selection of a conflict strategy is needed to account for conflict escalation and de-escalation, as examined in subsequent chapters. That knowledge also has policy relevance, indicating possible levers to move in order to bring about the adoption of conflict strategies that are likely to yield more constructive rather than more destructive actions. The analysis also indicates the severe obstacles to making those moves. Nevertheless, intermediaries with such knowledge can more effectively mediate, train negotiators, and consult with groups in each side of a conflict.[86]

6

Escalation of Conflicts

As illustrated in the previous chapter, partisans can choose to wage their conflicts in more or less constructive ways. When relatively destructive conflict strategies are adopted conflicts may become entrenched and persist at great cost to all parties. Partisans themselves often feel dismay that a conflict has so badly deteriorated, even as they continue to engage in rhetoric or take actions that do severe injury to the other side. In this chapter we examine how such escalation occurs, why it sometimes develops a "life of its own," and how that can be averted.

DIMENSIONS OF ESCALATION

Conflict escalation is manifested along two dimensions: the intensity of coercive and noncoercive inducements used to wage a conflict, and the breadth in the scope of a conflict's impacts. Increased severity of coercion occurs when one or more sides make greater threats and/or execute harsher sanctions. Most often, the level of coercion is indicated by increases in direct violence, typically the number of persons killed. Increasing nonviolent coercive inducements are also important markers of conflict escalation and include withdrawal of cooperation and imposition of economic sanctions. Increases in the application of persuasive inducements or of positive sanctions are very difficult to measure, but they also can increase in magnitude and contribute to constructive escalation.

Escalation also occurs when more people become engaged in a struggle or are impacted by it. The unionization of workers, for example, can escalate labor-management conflicts because a greater number of workers become parties to negotiations and can be more easily mobilized to wage a struggle. But scope also refers to increases in the proportion of people in each party who are directly engaged in the fight. For example, total war means that a high proportion of the state's citizens are engaged in waging the war or in bearing its costs. In limited wars, the scope is smaller since a relatively small proportion of the country's population is participating in the fight.

Changes in these two dimensions often occur together; as more people are mobilized for a fight, they are then able to undertake greater coercive action. Changes, however, can take different forms and directions. For instance, as numbers dwindle for one of the adversaries, the remaining members may desperately resort to more extreme methods. On the other hand, expanding participation may incorporate persons with less commitment to the struggle's cause.

Conflict escalation is not necessarily always destructive, as indicated in table 6.1. For example, the unionization of workers has the potential to escalate labor-management conflicts through work stoppages, strikes, and retaliatory mass lay-offs. But the collective power of unions may also serve as an inducement for management to negotiate agreements that they would otherwise reject. The result may be a more equitable, mutually beneficial, and sustainable relationship.

Often the destructiveness of escalation is related to the degree to which the parties feel themselves superior to or exclusive of each other. For example, the Nazi's racist identity had highly destructive implications, including

TABLE 6.1. Conflict Components and Destructiveness

Components	More Destructive	More Constructive
Identity	Exclusive of other Ethnonationalism Defining self by opposing other	Inclusive of other Civic nationalism Defining self independently of other
Grievance	Believe existence is threatened Feel humiliated by others Historical trauma	Believe existence not threatened Issues appear negotiable
Goals	Assume to be in zero-sum conflict Seek destruction of other Seek revenge	Assume to be in mixed-sum conflict Other side's needs given legitimacy Seek cooperative solution
Methods	Believe violence only recourse Indiscriminate violence allowed	Believe noncoercive means possible Use of violence greatly limited

for themselves. The Nazis articulated grievances in terms of threats to their perceived racial and moral purity; they set goals that entailed the destruction of those who embodied those threats; and they glorified their recourse to violence and its use to terrorize and kill opponents. More generally, nationalist identities vary in the degree to which ascribed qualities, such as ethnic origins, are emphasized or acquired qualities, such as allegiances, are stressed. The term *ethnonationalism* is often used when the former is emphasized, while *civic nationalism* is used when the latter is stressed. In actuality, these qualities tend to be blended everywhere, with citizens of a country differing in how they combine them.

PROCESSES OF ESCALATION

The escalation of conflicts has long been a major topic of scholarly analysis.[1] Escalation may occur inadvertently, step-by-step, without the opponents having carefully considered the implications of their actions. However, escalation may also be a calculated policy to raise the pressure against an opponent, either gradually or abruptly. Escalation is driven by changes within each of the conflict parties, by evolving interactions between the adversaries, and by changing involvement of other parties.

Internal Changes

Processes of escalation internal to one of the adversaries include those occurring within individual minds and within organizational structures. Those developments may result in well-calculated or ill-considered escalation. The latter is of special interest here.

Social Psychological Processes

Many theories and research findings in social psychology provide insights, helping to explain conflict escalation. Cognitive dissonance theory, for example, suggests that individuals seek consistency between what they do and what they think they should do.[2] Consequently, once having committed an action they seek to justify it in their own mind. After one has suffered an ordeal in order to join a fraternity or a military unit, the value of being a member of that group must be regarded as great so as to maintain self-respect for having put up with the ordeal. It follows that as persons expend resources to hurt or to support other humans, they tend to regard the cause for which those actions were taken as very important. As the cause becomes more valued, ever more harmful or helpful acts are justified. This dynamic occurs within groups as well as individuals. The "rally around the flag" phenomenon, for instance, demonstrates that during foreign policy crises the public will generally show strong support for its leaders, even as they escalate conflicts.[3]

Entrapment also contributes to conflict escalation. It refers to "a decision making process whereby individuals escalate their commitment to a previously chosen, though failing, course of action in order to justify or 'make good on' prior investments."[4] We can experience entrapment when telephoning if we are put on hold; the longer we wait the more we want to hang up but the more reluctant we are to do so, having already invested so much time. Having sunk resources into a fight, investing more resources seems called for in order to justify what has already been expended in money, honor, or blood. This ever-increasing commitment and allocation of resources may go beyond the original value of the goal, but the combatants on both sides may feel trapped into continuing and even escalating the struggle. Frequently cited examples of this dynamic include the escalation of commitment on the part of the Lyndon Johnson and Richard Nixon administrations during the Vietnam War and the escalation of commitment in Iraq by George W. Bush.[5]

In addition, selective perception occurs in ways that often contribute to conflict escalation. People tend to notice phenomena that fit their expectations, so that once a struggle has entered a serious stage of mutual recrimination and contentiousness, even conciliatory conduct by the adversary is likely not to be noticed, or if noticed, to be discounted and considered deceptive.

Having a sense of urgency during a conflict can also contribute to its escalation. Thinking is often impaired when people feel they are threatened and must respond with urgency. Policy makers embroiled in what they regard as a crisis experience such pressures.[6] Under those circumstances, fewer alternatives are considered, and, curiously, previous conduct, even if ineffective, tends to be repeated. This dynamic is sometimes called "groupthink" to signify the tendency of all members of a decision unit to quickly coalesce around one course of action without considering alternative courses of action.[7] Where groupthink is occurring, a group tends to disregard the views of those members who are critical to what is emerging as agreement; often then the would-be dissenters quickly go along in order to "get along." The 9/11 Commission report pointed to groupthink within and among intelligence agencies and policy makers that fostered communication breakdowns between agencies and the missing of important clues, partly due to resistance to views and information that did not fit into the already formed understandings.[8]

Emotions, then, play significant roles in the development of struggles that are protracted and destructive. Fear, anxiety, and anger are likely to be aroused when people feel attacked, and the tendency to express those emotions by inflicting harm on the presumed attacker certainly contributes to conflict escalation. Shame and humiliation and the resulting desire for revenge are other emotions that fuel many struggles.[9] These may be culturally elaborated and channeled, as in the institutions of duels, blood feuds, and wars. Unacknowledged, these feelings may hamper making decisions that can help wage a struggle constructively.

Calculation of Gains and Loses

Partisans may sometimes choose to escalate a conflict based on the belief that they must; they believe they are acting defensively to avoid great harm. The classic game of Prisoner's Dilemma (PD), for instance, shows that it often feels rational for adversaries to escalate a conflict even when that escalation may cause greater injury to them. The hypothetical story for this game is that two men have been arrested on suspicion of committing a serious crime. Although they are guilty, there is insufficient evidence for conviction of the serious offense but enough for a lesser one. Held in jail, they are not allowed to talk with each other. They have the following possibilities: If they both confess, they will be convicted of the serious offense, but their sentence will be reduced slightly for their cooperation. If one confesses and incriminates his accomplice, he gets off without punishment and his confederate gets the maximum sentence of twelve years. If they both hold out and do not confess, they can only be convicted for the lesser offense and be sentenced for one year.

This payoff choice poses a dilemma for the prisoners. Each would be better off if both held out and did not confess. Yet, if each considers what the other might do, there is compelling reason to confess. Thus, if B confesses, A is better off confessing. If B does not confess, A is again better off if he confesses. In other words, if each assumes the other prisoner cannot be tiusted and acts in his individual self-interest, they both will lose. The dilemma can be resolved only if the prisoners could trust each other not to confess. How such cooperative conduct can emerge is examined in chapter 7.

Many actual conflict escalation situations appear to unfold according to the PD logic. Consider two countries in an arms race with each other and suppose each has good reason to fear the other. If one government increases its arms expenditures and the other side does not, it believes it will triumph. According to the payoff matrix presented in figure 6.1, one side would gain twelve and the other loses twelve. The side that does not increase its arms expenditures when the other side does would fear that it would be at a military disadvantage and become subject to domination by the other side. If both sides continue to increase their arms expenditures, both suffer some loss, since they cannot employ the resources used for arms for other purposes, each side losing nine. If both sides would not increase arms spending, they would therefore both be better off, each side gaining six. Again, if each side does not believe cooperation is possible and pursues its own interest independently, they will both be worse off than if they acted cooperatively.

		A: Increase Arms	A: Not Increase Arms
B	Increase Arms	−9, −9 (a)	−12, +12 (b)
B	Not Increase Arms	+12, −12 (c)	+6, +6 (d)

Figure 6.1. Arms Race Payoffs

Of course, actual conflicts do not have such simple payoffs, and the payoffs are not stable or known. But the logic of these simple games is intriguing. If the game has a zero-sum payoff matrix, one side must inevitably lose and only one can win. Antagonists in a conflict generally see themselves in such zero-sum situations, as did the United States and Soviet Union during the height of the Cold War. In a mixed-motive game, each side can win or lose, but there is also the possibility of a win/win or a lose/lose outcome. Thus, if each side acts only in its self-interest, both will be worse off than if they acted cooperatively.

Organizational Developments

As a conflict persists and particularly as coercive inducements are used, the internal organization of the adversaries often changes in ways that tend to escalate the struggle destructively. Three interrelated developments are particularly noteworthy: leadership identification with external conflict, mobilization of partisans, and raised expectations.

Since leaders generally represent their constituents in conflicts with outsiders, they are predisposed to become identified with the group's already-established goals and the means being used to pursue them. They are prone to entrapment because the costs are particularly high for them to admit that their policies are failing. Usually, they have publicly claimed the course of prevailing action to be correct; to admit they were mistaken might subject the leaders to charges of weakness and submission to the enemy. Failing policies in external conflicts seem easier to obscure than in internal affairs because the constituents have less ground for forming independent judgments.

Competition and rivalry among alternative leaders may also foster conflict escalation. For example, a study of civil rights leaders in fifteen U.S. cities in the 1960s found that militancy was lower among leaders in cities with minimal competition and higher in cities with competition.[10] Demonstrations, although short lived, were also more frequent where there was rivalry. However, when relatively moderate alternative leaders challenge the established leaders, they may reduce their militancy. This is more likely to occur in later stages of a struggle, in particularly heterogeneous conflict units, with adversaries who are consistently conciliatory, and in relatively regulated conflicts.

In any hierarchy, there is a tendency for subordinates to support what they think their superiors already believe. For example, as it became evident to more and more people in the Bush administration that the president had decided to go to war to change the regime in Iraq, even those who had doubts about the policy yielded to the inevitable and did not question the decision that would soon be turned into action. The argument cutting off dissenting views was, "it's going to happen."[11] There were very few protest resignations.

A growth in the influence of leaders who are "hard-line" and who advocate coercive inducements also contributes to conflict escalation. As a fight persists and increasing reliance is placed on coercive means, the advocates and managers of those means tend to gain influence. For example, once the armed forces become engaged in an interstate conflict, military leaders assume greater dominance.[12] Usually, as the fight goes on those who are reluctant or who are critical of the means being used are silenced, are forced out of the leadership circle, or withdraw. The remaining leaders can then escalate the struggle, with less and less challenge. This happened within Iran after the disputed 2009 presidential election when moderate politicians were stripped of a number of leadership posts.

Even within less highly organized adversaries, as a conflict intensifies, shifts in the leadership can occur that enhance the influence of more intransigent persons. The new members of the leadership circle may be less likely than the established leaders to have nonconflicting relations with the adversary, and they are less likely to have a stake in the status quo. For example, in community conflicts if the new leaders are not former community leaders, they may lack the constraints of maintaining previous community relations and be less subject to the cross-pressures ordinarily felt by members of community organizations.[13] However, as discussed in the next chapter, changes in the leadership often importantly help turn a conflict into a more constructive or de-escalating direction.

The second set of internal developments contributing to conflict escalation is related to changes among the members of each adversary organization. At the early stages of a conflict, as members begin to share their experiences, their information about deprivations and their sense of grievance tend to increase. For example, as part of the U.S. women's liberation movement in the 1970s "consciousness-raising" groups played an important early role. In these small groups, women shared accounts of their lives as women. Hearing each other's stories, they learned that some difficulties that had seemed personal and singular were really general and societal, and therefore required societal solutions, not simply personal accommodations. The emergence of the social media enables non-face-to-face groups to experience similar "consciousness-raising" experiences regarding social, political, and economic issues.

The membership composition of partisan groups also often changes in ways that foster conflict escalation. As a fight goes on, and as participation widens, persons who are predisposed to use more intense means join the struggle. One reason this happens is particularly pertinent for members of oppressed groups. The most deprived members of such groups generally do not become involved in a struggle until possible gains have become credible. But their feeling of grievance, once aroused, is likely to be greater than among persons who had the resources to initiate the struggle. The newly aroused also tend to be more radical because they are less constrained by understandings earlier arrived at with the adversary and are less likely to have experienced compromises with opponents. Evidence for elements of this argument can be seen in a 1966 national survey of blacks and of black civil rights leaders.[14] The leaders, compared with blacks in general, were less satisfied about the progress being made and were more militant about the goals to be pursued, but nevertheless were less likely to say they would engage in violent conduct.

When geographically distant persons join a struggle, they are likely to be highly motivated fighters, due to political ideology or religious faith. Such motivation tends to give them tenacity and a commitment to support conflict escalation. Prior to his death, the ability of Osama bin Laden and his associates to build the transnational al Qaeda network illustrates the coercive potentialities of such recruitment. That network has been built through the social affiliations of like-minded persons, and their militancy was intensified within closely linked groups.[15]

Finally, as conflict behavior escalates, the members who prefer not to engage in higher magnitudes of conflict behavior tend to withdraw, and those willing to engage in more severe behavior become increasingly dominant. But such intensification may reduce the scope of the conflict, measured by the number of persons or groups engaged in the fight.

The third organizational change that contributes to conflict escalation is the heightened commitment to the goal and the increased conviction that it is attainable. This can bolster reliance on constructive strategies as well as destructive ones. Increasing commitment is likely to occur at an early stage of a struggle as a conflict party rallies its forces but has not yet experienced the other side's punishing sanctions. Before difficult tests of strength occur, a group's conviction of victory is likely to grow as its forces mobilize. Within the insularity of the partisan group, mutual reassurances go unchecked, reinforcing a sense of power. If there are also some initial gains, the support for escalation is likely to grow rapidly. Such swellings of feelings may be short lived, but they can escalate swiftly in the form of mass mobilization, riots, strikes, and nonviolent protests. The heightened commitment dynamic was clearly at play throughout Egypt, Tunisia, Libya, and Yemen during the so-called Arab Spring in early 2011. In each of these countries the sense that revolutionary transformation was at hand appears to have escalated the commitment of the protestors to the cause, leading to the rapid mobilization of additional groups of protestors. The preparation for the mobilization and the protest strategies varied and sparked different reactions by the government leaders. In the case of Tunisia nonviolent protests rapidly escalated to the point that the government fell and the leadership fled the country in only four weeks.[16] In Egypt, massive protests resulted in the crisis escalating to the point of the resignation of the president, but not overall government collapse. In Libya and Yemen government reaction to mass mobilization was much more repressive and regime change stalled. Leaders, intellectuals, and activists often employ the social psychological processes earlier discussed to mobilize partisans for the perpetuation and escalation of a conflict. Leaders may "wave the bloody shirt," exclaiming how much has already been sacrificed in the struggle and urging that those losses should not be in vain, that the struggle must be continued until victory is won. The pain already suffered is used to spur further struggle.

Leaders of a gang, a guerilla army, or a country sometimes commit followers to the struggle by requiring them to participate in acting violently against enemies. In accord with cognitive dissonance theory, noted previously, those recruits will tend to justify their actions and come to believe in their positive value. At the very least, they are likely to feel compromised and unable to return to their former position.

Finally, adversaries with agencies specialized for coercive engagement in conflicts, such as armies or police, may escalate coercive behavior quickly once those units begin operations. These agencies, following their standard operating procedures, sometimes pursue policies that are inappropriate for the particular circumstances in which they are undertaken, resulting in unforeseen self-defeating escalation.[17] Once military forces engage in operations, whether or not ordered to do so by civilian authority, the level of coercion is often much greater than had been anticipated. This has been true in civil wars and in military replacement of civilian governments, as well as in waging interstate wars.[18] The outbreak of World War I is a frequently cited example of how plans for mobilization and military actions, once triggered, seemed to generate uncontrolled escalation, hence, the image of unconstrained wildness when "the dogs of war are unleashed."[19]

Changes in Relations between Adversaries

Once a conflict erupts, the relations between the adversaries often change in ways that escalate the fight. Three such changes are fundamental: (1) the logic of contentious interaction, (2) the expansion of the issues in contention, and (3) the polarization of relations.

Contentious Interaction

Even initially moderately contentious actions, when responded to harshly, can ignite an extraordinary escalation if the underlying conditions are already heated and organizational linkages have been formed. For example, U.S. student strikes erupted in May 1970 in reaction to the U.S. military invasion of Cambodia and the subsequent killing of student protestors at Kent State University and at Jackson State University.[20] Quickly, across the country, about 1.5 million students left classes, campuses were barricaded, and sit-ins were conducted, forcing many colleges to close down and some to actually end the school year.[21]

As adversaries exchange punitive behavior, each reasonably expects that the other will increase its pressure unless it is prevented or deterred by even greater coercion. In these contentious interactions, the expectations become self-fulfilling prophecies. Acting on the premise that the other side is guided only by a drive for power and can be influenced only by coercion tends to produce confirming results.[22] This appears particularly evident when issues of social identity are central to the conflict. In these cases greater coercive efforts by one side often reinforce the social cohesion—and willingness to fight—of the other side.[23]

Exaggerated emotional responses contribute to the reverberation of coercive acts between opponents. If one party is harmed or even threatened by a rival, the likely reaction would be hostile rather than acquiescent.[24] That hostility is then reciprocated, after which the parties may come to feel that revenge has become a goal in itself. Runaway escalation then ensues.

Furthermore, as one side imposes negative sanctions on the other, those sanctions themselves become issues. For example, when U.S. women were struggling for suffrage, they picketed the White House in 1917. Police harassed them, and many were arrested. When maltreated in prison, they went on hunger strikes that resulted in forced feeding.[25] For members of the women's movement, such behavior by the opposition created new issues of contention and grievances. In addition, many passive observers became supporters of the women's cause.

Tragically, such expansion of issues is often inadvertent. One party misperceives how the opponents will respond and commits acts that result in greater escalation than was intended by either party.[26] This may occur when one party tries to intimidate its opponent and instead provokes a harsh counteraction. It also can occur when a threat is made with the expectation that that will suffice. Then, if the opponent is not intimidated, the threatening party may appear to have been bluffing and has an additional reason to carry out the threat or lose credibility and face. Both sides have taken a step up the escalation ladder that was not intended, and the conflict has risen to a higher coercive level than either believed appropriate for the original subject of their quarrel.

If one of the parties commits extreme coercive acts, the other is likely to perceive the perpetrator as brutish and subhuman, and perhaps as evil. Such views then allow or even justify harsh countermeasures. The brutish enemy presumably can only understand brutish acts. Soon, each side is treating the other inhumanly, but feels it is acting out of necessity. The identities attributed to the other side become characteristic of their own identities.

It is even possible that humiliating and brutalizing an enemy makes them appear despicable and less than human, and thus their further degradation is made more justifiable. For example, this may occur in prison camps, or even in battle, when pleas for pity by the vulnerable soldier make him seem contemptible.[27]

Finally, once a struggle has begun to deteriorate destructively, even efforts to dampen the conflict may feed the flames of escalation. If one of the parties makes a conciliatory gesture or responds less aggressively than anticipated, the other may interpret that as a sign of weakness. The weakness then serves as an invitation to escalate demands and pressure. As a result, to restore credibility and demonstrate resolve, the previously conciliatory party may stiffen its posture and raise its own demands. And so the conflict escalates again, as the stakes are raised.

Expansion of Issues

Once a struggle has begun about one issue, additional and more general ones usually surface. Contentious issues that had been denied or hidden are frequently raised when parties have begun to fight each other. There is less need to deny them, and the overt struggle may seem a good time to "settle accounts."[28] And so the goals expand.

Such issue expansion is particularly likely when there are deep cleavages of fundamental values or interests among members of a community, organization, or other social system. For example, a community controversy over the inclusion of particular books in the school library may become generalized to a fight about educational, moral, or political philosophies.[29]

So a relatively minor issue in dispute may take on great symbolic significance once a struggle has gotten under way. What might be a minor matter between friends has great significance between enemies. For example, control of a piece of land might seem easily divisible or a matter for which compensation could be made. But in a dispute with an enemy, the piece of land may be endowed with symbolic value and be prized even more because denying it to the enemy would be gratifying.

Polarization of Relations

As a conflict emerges and develops, the adversaries tend to disparage each other, viewing themselves as moral and the opponents as immoral and unreasonable.[30] Furthermore, adversaries generally become increasingly isolated from each other. For example, before war actually erupts between governments, they tend to have withdrawn from joint membership in international organizations.[31] As conflict parties reduce the number of nonconflicting relations, they are less constrained by cross-pressures and cross-cutting ties and are freer to indulge in more severe conflict strategies. This lack of contact also reinforces and may even institutionalize negative attitudes held by each group toward the other.[32]

Polarization is aggravated by the tendency of partisans to try winning bystanders to their side. Insofar as a party feels morally superior and confident that the people not yet engaged in the struggle will be their allies if they must choose sides, it will urge them to do so. If it believes it can, it may even insist that other parties join with it. For example, the German Nazis asserted, "If you are not for us, you are against us." The striking coal miners in Harlan County, Kentucky, sang in the 1930s, "You either are a union man or a thug for J. H. Blair. Which side are you on, man, which side are you on?" Eldridge Cleaver said during the civil rights struggle, "If you're not part of the solution, you're part of the problem." In reaction to the September 11, 2001, terrorist attacks, President George W. Bush declared, "Either you are with us or you are with the terrorists." Such formulations deny legitimacy to any neutrals or possible intermediaries who might play a role in containing or moderating the conflict.

Involvement of Other Parties

Once an overt struggle has begun, parties not initially engaged may envision significant benefits by joining the fray.[33] The struggle may provide an opportunity to inflict harm and weaken an old foe, or it may be an opportunity to win a portion of the spoils that a victory might yield. Sometimes a party will intervene out of obligation to support its friends or allies who are in the fight.

External interveners can contribute to conflict escalation by providing weapons, funds, or other implements of struggle, which enable the combatants to raise the magnitude of the means being used and to sustain the struggle. Thus, a study of civil strife in 114 countries found that external support for dissidents correlated .37 with the length of the civil strife and .22 with its pervasiveness.[34] During the Cold War, many local conflicts in Africa, Central America, Asia, and the Middle East were exacerbated and perpetuated by the superimposition of the conflict between the Soviet Union and the United States. Each superpower lent support to the enemy of the government supported by the other. Another example is provided by ethnic groups struggling for autonomy or independence that are sustained through both political and economic support by members of the same ethnicity in other countries, as has been the case in Northern Ireland, Sri Lanka, Ethiopia, and numerous other conflict zones.[35]

Other parties also tend to become engaged in a struggle because as the partisans pursue their goals, they sometimes infringe on the interests of parties not engaged. For example, in World War I, Germany used submarines to attack shipping to Great Britain and began sinking U.S. vessels prior to American entry in the war.[36] Furthermore, the German government secretly telegrammed the Mexican government proposing an alliance such that if the United States entered the war, Mexico would reconquer its lost territories. The secret telegram was discovered in March 1917 and, together with the submarine warfare, created such outrage in the United States that on April 2, the U.S. Congress declared war against Germany.

In summary, as a fight escalates, the means of waging it tend to become increasingly removed from the underlying conflict. Consequently, the conflict may be considered to have more and more "unrealistic" qualities. Or as the partisans are likely to argue, the objective conflict has shifted and the adversaries have more at stake now that the way of waging their fight has escalated.

Nevertheless, escalations can be conducted so as to be constructive. Thus, in numerous countries with authoritarian rulers, large-scale nonviolent demonstrations have quickly grown, reaching massive size, and forcing the heads of the government to yield power.[37] Often, this has followed elections that were widely regarded as fraudulent, as occurred in 1986 in the Philippines, in 2000 in Serbia, in 2003 in Georgia, in the winter of 2004–2005 in the Ukraine, and in 2011 in Côte d'Ivoire. Success in one country can raise the conviction among people in another country that similar actions can yield similar results. The relatively sudden success of nonviolent demonstrations against the Tunisian President, Zein el-Abedine Ben Ali, in December 2010 and January 2011 contributed to the conviction of many Egyptians that nonviolent demonstrations would succeed in ending Hosni Mubarak's presidency. At another level, for two years before the January 2011 demonstrations in Egypt, Tunisian and Egyptian youth exchanged information and shared experience in developing and employing strategies and tactics of nonviolent action; the ideas of the leading analyst of nonviolent action, Gene Sharp, proved influential.[38] Furthermore, worldwide mass media coverage of the demonstrations and some external assistance to the demonstrators enabled the protests to continue and helped avert their forceful suppression.

POLICIES AND CONDITIONS SHAPING ESCALATION

Processes of escalation tend to produce long-lasting destructive struggles under particular conditions. Enduring struggles are often referred to as "protracted" or "intractable" conflicts. Protracted conflicts refer particularly to deep-rooted, identity-based conflicts. For Edward E. Azar, it is "the prolonged and often violent struggle by communal groups [religious, ethnic, racial, or cultural] for such basic needs as security, recognition and acceptance, fair access to political institutions, and economic participation."[39] More generally, intractable conflicts refer to prolonged conflicts in the case of large-scale conflicts, those that persist for more than a generation. They are deemed destructive by many partisans and outsiders but resist efforts at resolution. They persist for an accumulation of reasons in addition to whatever the original reasons may have been. Often vested interests in waging the struggle develop; hence the conflicts tend to be waged in a self-perpetuating pattern and, of particular interest here, are marked by destructive interaction.[40]

Even highly intractable conflicts vary in their severity and destructiveness. For example, the Cold War between the United States and the Soviet Union was particularly intense in three periods: in 1948–1950, with the Soviet blockade of West Berlin and the North Korean invasion of South Korea; in 1962 with the Cuban missile crisis; and in the early 1980s, with the Soviet intervention in Afghanistan and the militant anti-Communist U.S. policy.[41] The conflict also had many periods of thaw, including 1955, with the end of the occupation of Austria; 1963, with the Partial Nuclear Test Ban agreement; and 1972, with the signing of several arms control agreements. Beginning in 1985, when Mikhail Gorbachev was chosen to lead the Soviet Union, the conflict was transformed, as was evident when the Berlin Wall fell in 1989; and was ended with the dissolution of the Soviet Union in 1991.

As seen in the previous chapter, the conflict strategies chosen, the issues in contention, the changes within the adversaries, the interaction among the adversaries, and the social context all affect how some conflicts become destructively prolonged. No single factor or policy wholly determines the course of a struggle, and therein lie many possibilities for averting or transforming a prolonged and destructive struggle.

Strategy Chosen

The conflict strategy of each adversary profoundly affects the likelihood of a struggle escalating destructively, since it influences the opponent's choice of response strategy. It also impacts the party that has undertaken the strategy as well as the kind of intervention made by other parties. Some strategies tend to limit escalation and others to foster it, either constructively or destructively. The selection too often is made with little attention to the long-term consequences of alternative strategies.

Impact on Self

Any strategy in pursuit of contentious goals has costs for the party applying it, and those costs tend to constrain the escalation of a conflict. The more burdensome the costs, the less potential there is to sustain, let alone escalate, the conflict. Strategies that impose heavy costs affecting large proportions of the conflict unit cannot be borne indefinitely, despite any entrapment. But assessing costs is difficult and objective indicators may fail to capture the subjective experience of costs. Even mounting deaths or casualties are not always good indicators of how long adversaries continue a war or escalate it.

Furthermore, the means of struggle in themselves can provide gratifications, some of which are emotional: feelings of collective solidarity, excitement, pride in one's bravery, pleasure in making history, and satisfaction in proving oneself are all exhilarating. For some people, being involved in a war is wonderfully exciting, giving meaning to life.[42] Such feelings enable participants to endure great discomfort and pain, and to risk death. Although such emotions cannot be sustained for long, they leave feelings of loyalty, obligation, and commitment, which help the group sustain terrible losses.

When a conflict party becomes differentiated enough to have persons whose careers are devoted to waging conflicts and using a particular method or of providing the infrastructure for it, the development of a vested interest in continuing the struggle and employing that means has begun. How important such vested interests become depends on the costs they impose, the access they have to policy making, their control of resource allocation decisions, and what the alternatives are for the partisans. In some countries, being engaged in armed struggle, whether as military officers or as guerrilla leaders, provides relatively attractive careers.

Use of certain conflict modes fosters antagonism toward the opponent. Harming the opponent needs to be justified, especially if partisans must be mobilized for a sustained campaign of inflicting injuries. Having undertaken such a strategy, the conflict party will tend to depict the opponent as not merely wrong on the issue in contention, but also as evil and posing a great threat. Pressure may even be brought to bear on those who question such depictions, calling them traitors.

After the end of World War II, many U.S. leaders wanted to ensure U.S. military, economic, and political engagement in Europe and the world generally. The Soviet military threat was dramatized in order to mobilize support for maintaining U.S. military forces in Europe and for the establishment of NATO. This break with traditional U.S. policies needed to be justified by a transcendent threat, and the Soviet threat was exaggerated to provide the needed justification.[43]

After the end of the Cold War, the absence of a major threatening enemy made many in the U.S. national security establishment feel that their work would become irrelevant. There were explicit discussions about possible new threats to American security, including security against environmental threats, security against nuclear proliferation, and against disorder within and between countries emerging from the Cold War structure. The specters of China and of Islam also were raised, but no clear consensus emerged about who or what was the country's enemy.[44] The attacks of September 11, 2001, provided a new enemy, but one whose character was unclear.

Conflict strategies that do not engender vested interests in the struggle or that do not dehumanize the opponent are less likely to result in prolonged, destructively waged conflicts. This is one of the arguments made for nonviolent strategies that oppose an adversary's policy or actions but do not demonize the opponents.

Impact on the Adversary

The conflict strategy chosen by one party significantly affects its adversary's actions. The conflict strategy may be varyingly severe, adhering to or crossing boundaries of what the adversary regards as legitimate. Strategies that the targets regard as outrageous often provoke severe countermeasures. Moreover, efforts at intimidation generally provoke responses of defiance.

For example, research on serious interstate disputes from 1863 to 1964 indicates that the use of threats tended to produce extreme responses, either of defiance or of compliance.[45] The inducements the researchers examined were: threats of violence, promise of reward, and both carrots and sticks. The responses were comply, placate, defy, mixed placate and defy, and ignore.

Inducements involving promises were somewhat less likely than those with threats to produce extreme responses of comply or defy; rather, the responses tended to be placate, mixed, or ignore. Placation or mixed responses may be the start of negotiations toward a mutually acceptable settlement. Among relatively evenly matched adversaries, threats were particularly likely to produce defiance, and defiance was associated with escalations leading to war. Threats or promises, when specified, tended to be reacted to by compliance or defiance, and if unspecified, those inducements were disproportionately ignored.

Some strategies tend to be unspecified and ambiguous even in regard to who is acting and with what purpose. For example, persons carrying out terrorist actions often keep their identities secret. Specific goals are not always articulated, unless there is an overt agency that is understood to speak for the underground elements. In the case of riots or covert resistance, there may be no authoritative interpreters of the actions. The target persons and groups are then relatively free to define who is committing the acts and for what objectives and not engage in negotiations or other noncoercive means of settling the conflict. Moreover, attacks on noncombatants may seem to imply rejecting the target group's right to exist. Consequently, many members of the target group are likely to regard the alleged perpetrators and their supporters as impossible negotiating parties and indeed as inhuman.

Nevertheless, tactics directed at civilians, such as airplane hijackings, have at times been embraced by some organizations. For example, after the failure of the Arab countries in their war with Israel in 1967, George Habash, a Palestinian physician, formed the Popular Front for the Liberation of Palestine (PFLP). In the spirit of Che Guevara, one of the leaders and theoreticians of the Cuban revolution, he declared, "Revolutionary violence as the highest expression of the people's struggle is not only the path, but it is the most concrete and the most direct potential for the defeat of imperialism."[46] In July 1968, he initiated a long period of airplane hijackings. The Palestinian hijackings and other attacks on Jews did gain considerable attention for the Palestinian cause, but also hampered support for it.

Finally, some violent strategies are intended to provoke the adversary in order to escalate the conflict. The expectation is that when the other side escalates, allies and supporters will be gained, offended by the escalating leap. For example, the Cuban revolutionaries, led by Fidel Castro, were a small group that committed acts that provoked the government. The government forces, under the direction of Fulgencio Batista y Zaldívar, the self-appointed president, undertook increasingly harsh and indiscriminate countermeasures, antagonizing many segments of the population. The government became isolated and fell in January 1959. Che Guevara considered this strategy to be an effective way to create a revolutionary situation, and he and many others attempted to follow the strategy in several countries, but it failed, as governments avoided overreacting.[47]

Effects on Other Parties

The conflict strategies adopted also affect the likelihood of other parties joining the fight and so increasing its scope. Certain actions are so offensive to people not engaged in the fight that they enter the struggle to stop the outrageous acts. Such increases in the conflict's scope tend to speed its end if those who join the fray add overwhelming resources to impose an ending. In international affairs, the atrocities generally must reach a very high persisting level of destruction before forceful officially sanctioned intervention occurs.[48] For example, in 1975, Indonesia invaded and then annexed East Timor and brutally suppressed any resistance, despite UN support for self-determination by the people of East Timor. Finally, in 1999, global pressure led to an agreement for a referendum, but with continuing Indonesian military control. The people of East Timor voted overwhelmingly for independence, despite Indonesian-instigated violence intended to intimidate them from doing so. Subsequently, as had been widely predicted, Indonesians unleashed widespread military retaliation. Only then did forceful UN-sponsored intervention occur, initiating UN transitional administration of the country.

Interventions lacking broad international consensus often contribute to prolonging conflicts destructively. Thus, when external parties support different adversaries, the interventions enable the contending parties to persist in the fight. The result can then have devastating consequences, as happened in many struggles, particularly during the Cold War when the U.S. and Soviet governments, and governments associated with them, gave assistance to opposing sides. This was the case in the Korean War and the Vietnam War, and indirectly in the prolonged Arab-Israeli conflict. Afghanistan exemplifies a case of American engagement that had severe "blowback" consequences.[49] The Soviet Union invaded Afghanistan in 1979 to maintain a friendly Marxist government, which was being attacked by local militant Islamic groups. The U.S. government expanded its small measures of aid to the Islamic resistance, which had begun months earlier. Then, in President Ronald Reagan's administration, the CIA greatly expanded its support of the mujahedeen; as the fighting went on, Muslims from many other countries, including Osama bin Laden from Saudi Arabia, joined the struggle. Even after Gorbachev signaled and then acted to withdraw Soviet forces, U.S. aid continued to the militant Islamic groups. Cooperative actions with the Soviets to assist the now nationalist Afghan government in defending itself from the mujahedeen attacks were not taken. The CIA aim to "get even" for the Soviets' actions against them in Vietnam seems to have been preeminent. When the Afghan government finally fell, the various militia groups fought against each other, the U.S. government disengaged, and ultimately the Taliban took control of most of Afghanistan, providing a haven for al Qaeda.

Partisans often portray their actions in ways intended to gain supporters and dissuade parties not yet engaged in the conflict from supporting their adversaries. Thus, even violent terrorist actions are often clothed in attempts at justifications and persuasive appeals. Depending on the values and interests of possible entrants to the conflict, such considerations may be effective in obtaining support or denying support to the other side. Of course, the conflict methods being used may also bring about efforts by those not engaged to enter as intermediaries to impose a cessation of the conflict. Thus, within a society certain methods of conducting a fight are regarded as illegal, and the government and its agents are seen as legitimate imposers of the legal limits. The existence of institutions to manage fights also usually means that if the adversaries fail to settle the fight between themselves within institutionalized channels, appropriate authorities will ensure a settlement is reached, as in labor or environmental disputes.

Issues in Contention

Matters in contention vary greatly in their disposition for escalation. Those that are regarded as of vital interest naturally have great potential for severe escalation. The party defending what it believes to be essential is likely to use whatever means that it believes will be effective against a threat to its existence. Thus, labor strikes about union recognition or about attempts to weaken the union are more likely to escalate into violence than are strikes about wages and hours.[50]

What is regarded as a vital interest may differ among various factions within each side of a large-scale conflict. What is of prime consequence is whose interests receive the highest priority. This may more readily be recognized in coalitions where the vital interest of a minor member binds other members whose vital interests are not as directly engaged. For example, during the Vietnam War the survival of the South Vietnamese government was certainly in its vital interests and the U.S. government persisted in the war in part in deference to those interests. In a different instance, the Cuban missile crisis in 1962 did not escalate more than it did in good measure because the Soviet leadership negotiated a deal with the U.S. government without including the unyielding Cuban government as a negotiating partner.[51]

In international affairs, issues involving many states are more prone to escalation, as indicated by systematic studies of interstate disputes. For example, a study of militarized disputes between 1816 and 1992 found that multiparty disputes have a significantly increased probability of escalating to war than do bilateral disputes, particularly when the dispute is over issues related to territory.[52] However, in domestic public-sector disputes, for example relating to environmental matters, the involvement of many parties can limit escalation due to cross-cutting ties, increased likelihood of finding trade-offs, and the increased likelihood of having superordinate goals.

Dissensual issues have a higher escalating potential than issues that are largely consensual. Disputes involving ideological and abstract value or moral issues can attract more parties than those involving concrete consensual matters. Indeed, contention about important values and beliefs often appear to the partisans themselves as not amenable to compromise. Dissensual issues also foster escalation because the opponent is often viewed as wrong in principle and not merely on the wrong side of an issue. Therefore, constraints on conduct may be reduced, particularly if the other side is considered immoral. Once one is engaged in a struggle, the advancement of one's side against an evil "other" can be supported by the fervor of exclusivist religious or nationalistic faith.

Matters regarded by adversaries as being integral to their personal or collective identities are particularly prone to escalation and resistant to resolution.[53] This is a source of the intensity and destructiveness with which ethnic or religious conflicts are sometimes waged. Thus, in a country with two or more ethnic communities whose people speak different languages, the state may be dominated by one ethnic group and require that educational and cultural activities be conducted in its language. Some members of the other group may well view this as an effort to destroy them as a people and vigorously resist the policies and those who would impose them.

The adversaries' goals also have varying escalating dispositions. Thus, insofar as the goals are collective rather than individualistic, escalation is more likely. Collectivist goals generally require group reallocations of resources, and that appears more threatening to the targeted adversary than the accommodations required to satisfy aggregated individualistic goals. Furthermore, collective goals require a relatively open acceptance of the claims of those working to achieve the goals. Finally, institutionalized and minimally coercive means are more likely to be seen as appropriate and effective by those seeking aggregated individualistic rather than collectivist goals. For example, an ethnic group's struggle for equal opportunity and even the possibility of assimilation are often more amenable to problem-solving conflict modes than an ethnic group's struggle for autonomy or independence.

In addition, the greater the number of issues in contention and the greater the grievances, the more fuel there is to feed the fire of escalation. Thus, a study of the outbreak of urban riots in the 1960s found that although community variations in the social conditions of blacks were not related to the riots' outbreaks, their eventual severity was.[54]

Finally, the nature and magnitude of the incompatibility between the adversaries' goals profoundly affect the course of their struggle. In some conflicts, one side may threaten the very existence of the other or opponents may pose existential threats to each other, at least for their ruling groups. The degree to which such threats may be actual, however, often is misperceived; if the opponents misperceive or exaggerate the threat and act on the basis of their perceptions, they may unduly perpetuate and escalate the conflict.[55]

Internal Developments

Many internal circumstances and policies affect the previously discussed social psychological and organizational processes so that they contribute to conflict escalation. The following discussion is limited to homogeneity and differentiation.

Homogeneity

Adversaries with little internal diversity tend to better sustain increases in the severity of a conflict. The social psychological processes and organizational developments fostering escalation tend to reinforce each other. Given the similarities within the conflict party, members are likely to respond similarly to events and to drown out dissident voices. Conversely, internal diversity can provide a basis for limiting escalation and fostering de-escalation since various segments of a heterogeneous party tend to have different priorities relating to the struggle.[56] Furthermore, the costs of waging the struggle are likely to be unevenly experienced, and such differences can provide the grounds for opposing conflict escalation and prolongation.

Leaders are likely to foster homogeneity, instituting policies to build support for the goals of the struggle and portraying the enemy as a grave threat to vital interests and identities. Insofar as they are effective in these policies and alternative voices are absent, their constituency is less open to divisive efforts, and to conciliatory overtures, by the opposing side.[57] Thus, challenging revolutionary and other political movements often set broad goals and try to mobilize diverse constituencies in a common cause against a narrow isolated opponent. For example, the popular 2011 Egyptian movement against the Hosni Mubarak regime rallied Copts and Muslims; traditional Islamists and relatively secular Egyptians; women and men; old and young; and members of business, professional, and other occupational strata. Of course, once the movement succeeded, divisions among the victors again emerged. This is often the case in post-revolutionary societies as a winning faction imposes its preferences on many of its former allies, as happened after the Russian, Cuban, and Iranian revolutions.

In any case, within any large conflict party some variations in orientation toward the adversary are generally present. In international relations, the differences between hard-liners and accommodationists have been frequently noted.[58] The differences are derived not only from personality characteristics but also from varying beliefs about the efficacy and legitimacy of threats and violence and about the possibility of compromising goals. Where hard-liners alone direct foreign policy, destructive escalation is more likely.

Differentiation

Opponents with specialized agencies to wage struggles are more capable of increasing the severity of a conflict without widespread constituency support. This is an advantage professional armies have over conscript armies for waging wars that lack popular appeal. More generally, training, discipline, threat of punishment, a sense of honor, and loyalty to comrades in arms combine to keep combatants risking their lives, even when the odds of avoiding death or injury are poor.

In some circumstances, it is the very lack of coordination and control that can result in escalating events, since the persons in direct confrontation are not under effective control by their superiors, which often results in conflict escalation. Wartime atrocities such as massacres, looting, and raping sometimes are carried out by individual soldiers or militia or by small groups acting without orders; but atrocities are much more extensive when higher authorities condone such behavior as a way of intimidating and punishing the enemy. Indeed, in the former Yugoslavia rape was an instrument of a genocidal policy by Serb officials against Bosnians and Croats.[59] The recourse to gross human rights abuses, whether due to official orders, overzealousness, or lack of supervision, often has grievous escalatory consequences that are counterproductive for the perpetrators. This occurred, for example, with the instances of torture and other abuses by U.S. personnel at detention facilities in Guantanamo Bay, Cuba, in Abu Ghraib, Iraq, and other locations in Afghanistan and Iraq.[60]

Interaction between Adversaries

How adversaries respond to each other's contentious conduct makes the most immediate contribution to a conflict's escalation. The skill and judgment of representatives of the antagonistic sides matters greatly, as indicated in the following discussion of nonresponsiveness, of acting overly harshly, and of acting with too great accommodation.

Nonresponsiveness

When a group that is satisfied with the current situation substantively ignores an adversary's contentious behavior, the result sometimes is little or no change in the status quo and no escalation. The quiet rebuff may be followed by the adversary's quiescent acceptance of the situation, for a time. This has happened in various times and places in the United States and Canada in regard to aboriginal nations' claims about land and autonomy. On occasion, an aboriginal group will undertake a territorial blockade or file a legal case in order to get some substantive action.[61]

Conversely, nonresponsive conduct can also result in escalating a conflict, as the adversary resorts to more extreme actions in order to get a response from the opposing party that is ignoring its claims. Sometimes, a contending party believes the other side is stalling and not treating its issues seriously, even if negotiations have begun. Furthermore, nonresponsiveness is often experienced as a denial of significance and is therefore humiliating and seems to demand increased pressure.

Violent and nonviolent struggles for civil rights, economic justice, autonomy, independence, or many other goals typically begin with requests and demonstrations. Failing to be taken seriously, the demonstrations often expand and some advocates of the cause may resort to nonviolent or even violent actions. For example, opponents of the way the global economy was being structured by North American free trade agreements and international organizations such as the International Monetary Fund and the World Trade Organization held demonstrations that had little impact. Dubbed anti-globalists by their detractors, they saw themselves being dismissed as they struggled for global justice and democracy. Only when they mounted massive demonstrations in Seattle, November 29–December 3, 1999, did they receive widespread recognition. Their nonviolent actions, isolated violent conduct, and the tough police responses provided publicity that led to subsequent large-scale demonstrations and attention to their messages.[62]

Starting negotiations does not guarantee progress toward a mutually agreed-on settlement. The side making claims against a government or other powerful body may come to believe that the other side is stalling the negotiations, not being responsive to its concerns, or even creating conditions to weaken it. Members of the side believing they are being strung along may escalate the conflict in order to get the other side to negotiate seriously. Some members of the relatively powerful body may indeed act to interrupt progress in the negotiations by escalating coercive pressures. Thus, the Mexican government's negotiations with the Ejército Zapatista de Liberación Nacional (EZLN, Zapatista Army of National Liberation) of Chiapas begun soon after the uprising on January 1, 1994, made little progress. By February 1995, the situation had deteriorated following the Mexican army's occupation of territory tacitly accorded to the EZLN. Only after the national congress intervened did serious negotiations occur, resulting in the Accord of San Andres, signed in February 1996. However, the government did not implement the accords.[63] Subsequent developments are discussed in chapter 10.

Sometimes even a war may be undertaken after negotiation efforts have been rebuffed or have failed. For example, shortly after Anwar al-Sadat succeeded Gamal Abdel Nasser as president of Egypt in 1970, he began to reduce reliance on the Soviet Union and improve relations with the United States. He proposed that Israel withdraw from a portion of the occupied Sinai and that Egypt reopen the Suez Canal for shipping. The U.S. officials tried to broker such an interim agreement, but despite some negotiations, no agreement on the terms of the settlement was reached. Sadat believed he had made great concessions but that the U.S. government had failed to induce the Israeli government to change its position sufficiently to reach a settlement. "Frustrated and humiliated, Sadat decided to abandon the interim-settlement idea."[64] In October 1973, Egypt and Syria attacked Israel, and after the war ended, such an Egyptian-Israel interim agreement was reached, with mediation by U.S. secretary of state Henry Kissinger.

Overreacting and Overreaching

Strong coercive countermeasures sometimes are effective in terminating a violent struggle. They may suppress the other side, destroying its ability to continue the struggle, or they may induce members of the other side to turn to nonviolent and less coercive means.[65] Channeling the other side to use nonviolent or legitimate institutionalized procedures is likely to be effective when punitive actions are narrowly focused and limited, and particularly if legitimate channels for protest and attaining desired changes are available. For example, consider the evolution of the Puerto Rican national independence movement. Shortly after World War II, the U.S. Congress, President Harry S. Truman, and the Puerto Rican Legislative Assembly took steps to establish commonwealth status for Puerto Rico.[66] Some Puerto Ricans, however, favored independence, and formed a political party, the Partido Independentista Puertorriqueño (PIP). But in 1950 and 1954 a group of nationalists, unsatisfied with the electoral strategy of the PIP, carried out armed attacks in Puerto Rico and in Washington, D.C. Although the PIP dissociated itself from those nationalist tactics, it garnered few votes in subsequent elections. Instead, support for statehood as an alternative to commonwealth status increased, although that has not reached majority support.

Social and economic developments in Puerto Rico, suppression of violent attacks, avoidance of general repression, and the openness of the electoral political process have limited the appeals of Puerto Rican independence and channeled the struggle within the existing political system. Furthermore, in many circles the intellectual climate at the beginning of the twenty-first century increasingly characterized nationalism in cultural terms relating to language and the arts more than in matters of governance.

Too often, however, once adversaries are engaged in a conflict, their contentious interaction tends to escalate in severity, as one side or both seeks to impose a settlement by increasing coercive pressure. Escalation is particularly likely if the step up in severity exceeds the normative expectations of the other side. The reaction may be of such outrage that the acts are rendered counterproductive—they fail to intimidate and instead provoke intensified and broader opposition. For example, this tends to be the case for terrorist attacks against civilians when conducted by marginal social groups and for wide-ranging arrests and killings by authorities with a narrow base of support. Within the context of U.S. civil society, severe reactions against social protest can result in the protest's escalation.[67] For example, a study of colleges that had demonstrations against Vietnam War–related campus recruitment in 1967 found that the more severe the control measures used against civil disobedience, the more likely was the protest to expand. The violent police actions to suppress the civil rights demonstrations of 1963 in Birmingham, Alabama, resulted in expanding protests and intervention by the federal government (see table 6.2).

Repression of violent protest can be effective under certain conditions, at least for a time. This is consistent with resource-mobilization, political-process, and rational-choice approaches to the study of social movements, which stress the opportunities and capabilities to engage in protest actions. These approaches suggest that domestic political violence tends to be greatest in societies with intermediate levels of repression. In countries with relatively high levels of consistent repression, dissent and opposition would be suppressed. In societies with relatively little repression, opposition could be expressed more easily and nonviolently. There is consistent evidence of such a curvilinear relationship between the repressiveness of governments and domestic political violence. For example, several cross-national, quantitative studies have related political violence to regime repression and other factors. Typically, regression analysis has been used, sometimes for the same years and sometimes lagging violence five years after the measure of repressiveness.

TABLE 6.2. Major Events in the Civil Rights Struggle, 1954–1968

1954	In *Brown v. Board of Education*, developed and argued by the National Association for the Advancement of Colored People (NAACP), the U.S. Supreme Court bans segregation in public schools.
1955	To end bus segregation, the Montgomery Improvement Association, with Dr. Martin Luther King Jr. as president, launches bus boycott in Montgomery, Alabama.
1956	December 21, after more than a year of boycotting and legal actions, the Montgomery buses are desegregated.
1957	At previously all-white Central High School in Little Rock, Arkansas, 1,000 paratroopers are called by President Eisenhower to restore order and escort nine black students.
1960	February, the sit-in protest movement begins at a Woolworth's lunch counter in Greensboro, North Carolina, and spreads across the nation.
1961	Freedom rides begin from Washington, D.C. Groups of black and white people ride buses through the South, challenging segregation.
1962	Two killed, many injured in riots as James Meredith is enrolled as the first black student at the University of Mississippi.
1963	Police arrest King and other ministers demonstrating in Birmingham, Alabama, and turn fire hoses and police dogs on the marchers. 250,000 attend the March on Washington, D.C., urging support for pending civil rights legislation. Sept. 15, four girls killed in bombing of the Sixteenth Street Baptist Church in Birmingham, Alabama.
1964	Three civil rights workers are murdered in Mississippi. July 2, President Johnson signs Civil Rights Act of 1964.
1965	Selma, Alabama, voting rights campaign waged. August 6, President Johnson signs Voting Rights Act of 1965, authorizing federal examiners to register qualified voters and suspend devices aimed at preventing African Americans from voting. August 11–16, Watts riot leave thirty-four dead in Los Angeles.
1968	King assassinated in Memphis, Tennessee, unleashing riots in more than a hundred cities.

The expected curvilinear relationship has consistently been found.[68] The quiet order of a society with a repressive regime is considered here to be a relatively destructive condition. Struggles resulting in overturning a repressive regime could therefore contribute to a more constructive relationship.

Regarding interstate conflicts, a great deal of theorizing and research has been done about the effectiveness of military strength as a way of preventing wars. On the one hand, the argument of traditional "realists" is that having the military strength to deter attack prevents wars. On the other hand, critics of that approach argue that as each side arms to deter the other, the resulting arms race generates mutual fear and hostility and escalates disputes into wars. The evidence indicates that arms races increase the likelihood that serious interstate disputes will escalate to war.[69] This is the case when the dispute is between states who are rivals and contiguous. The evidence does not indicate that an arms race by itself results in a war, but that it contributes to the tendency to resort to war in the context of an ongoing crisis or militarized dispute. Furthermore, bullying strategies in militarized situations tend to escalate disputes into war.[70]

One form of overreaction is a result of failing to adequately recognize differences within the enemy side. In those circumstances, employment of violence may be indiscriminate or threats to use violence broad, injuring or threatening to harm persons who are not directly engaged in the struggle. Those impacted by the broadness of the attack are made parties to the fight, thus increasing the scope and probably the severity of the struggle. Efforts at countering terrorist attacks from within or outside a country are susceptible to overreaction.

Another danger is that of overreaching. As a conflict party's leaders believe they are winning, they often raise their demands. However, that may well intensify resistance, resulting in a protracted destructive conflict. For example, after the Communist North Korean military forces crossed the 38th parallel in June 1950, U.S. military forces, under UN authority, came to the aid of the South Korean forces. After falling back, they quickly advanced back up the Korean peninsula but did not stop when they reached the old border. Instead, they continued up, approaching the Yalu River bordering the People's Republic of China. As Richard Neustadt observes, "Appetites rose as the troops went forward."[71] Consequently, the Chinese troops crossed the Yalu River and drove the U.S., South Korean, and allied forces back to about the 38th parallel, and the war continued on and on until a cease-fire was reached in 1953.

The decision of President Bush and his close associates to invade Iraq and remove the Saddam Hussein regime was eased by the quick U.S.-led attack that overthrew the Taliban regime in Afghanistan in October 2001.[72] This victory was accomplished by a small number of American personnel with few casualties, which gave the decision makers greater confidence that they would be successful in Iraq as well. The Afghan triumph also made public willingness to attack Iraq more likely. Moreover, public support for a war against al Qaeda's Afghan haven could be transferred to supporting the war on Iraq if it were presented as part of the war on terrorism. The government leadership so portrayed the war despite the lack of sound evidence, and the media gave little attention to dissenting views.

Overaccommodating

At times of a crisis, accommodative reactions to demands and threats can end the crisis and prevent a conflict from escalating, but sometimes at the cost of losing. Over longer time periods, conciliatory responses even to significant demands can result in new, mutually acceptable relationships, without having escalated to highly destructive encounters. Thus, during the depression of the 1930s in the United States, large-scale movements and demonstrations arose, demanding assistance in the face of loss of income. The administration of President Franklin D. Roosevelt and the U.S. Congress introduced many welfare measures to satisfy the needs underlying the protests.[73] These assuaging measures averted greater demonstrations and radicalization of the demonstrators.

However, sometimes concessions or too mild responses can result in conflict escalation, since the party making the demands insists on even more, sensing weakness on the other side. Those making the concessions then fear even greater demands and increase their resistance; what is then demanded is seen as intolerably excessive and a highly intense fight may ensue. The 1938 meeting in Munich where the British and French governments yielded to Nazi Germany's demands regarding its incorporation of the Sudetenland region of Czechoslovakia is the most notorious example of the escalating consequences of appeasement.

In a variety of circumstances, acting in a conciliatory fashion in the face of demands and threats can be followed by raised demands by the adversaries and weakening resistance. Thus, when the East European governments led by Communist parties faced waves of demonstrations in 1989, concessions did not stem growing demands for fundamental change. For example, the president of the German Democratic Republic (GDR) made the concession of resigning on October 18, 1989. His successor, another Communist Party leader, Egon Krenz, yielded to many popular demands, but the moves were too late and insufficient. The end came quickly with the rupture of the Berlin Wall, which resulted from the conjuncture of bumbling mistakes, misunderstandings, and the actions of East Berlin crowds. The Krenz government drafted new travel laws for GDR citizens wishing to travel outside East Germany. Krenz gave an outline of the new laws to Günter Schabowski who was about to hold a press conference, on November 9, 1989, to announce the composition of the new Politburo. Asked about the travel laws, Schabowski, being unfamiliar with the material given him, said that GDR citizens could travel abroad at the border crossings, without passports, starting immediately. News of this spread quickly and East Germans rushed to crossings at the Berlin Wall. West Berliners hurried to the wall to greet them. As people rushed to the crossing points, they called out that the gates be opened. The East German border guards had no orders, and they opened the gates. There was no violence. East and West Berliners danced, sang, and drank together.[74] Krenz resigned on December 3, 1989, and the East German Communist system soon collapsed.

Social Context

As discussed in chapter 5, the social context of a struggle greatly affects the adoption of conflict strategies by providing models of effective policies and also as the source of interventions. Those and other contextual processes and factors also significantly affect the shift from less to more destructive struggles.

Linkages

The extent to which each partisan in a fight is linked with other persons, groups, and organizations is critical in the expansion of a struggle's scope. Thus, friends and relatives tend to be drawn into interpersonal fights as partisans. This is evidenced in a study of men incarcerated for a homicide or aggravated assault who described the dispute that resulted in the criminal violence and another dispute that each had that did not so escalate.[75] In conflicts where other persons were present who had close ties with one of the disputants and not with the other, the fight was likely to escalate into criminal violence. Similarly, as suggested by resource mobilization theory, organizations allied by ideology, previous alliances, or other network connections tend to be mobilized for assistance once a struggle has begun. This is also demonstrated by the evidence that interstate alliances tend to spread a dyadic militarized dispute or war to a multiple-party war or world war.[76]

Other Conflicts

Another important aspect of the context surrounding a particular conflict is the partisans' engagement in other struggles. Thus, when an additional conflict becomes superimposed on a given struggle, both tend to escalate and be prolonged. For example, the 1936–1939 Spanish Civil War was long and bloody, in part because both internal adversaries thought they could persist and triumph with external support.[77] The fascist rebels led by General Francisco Franco sought to overthrow the elected Spanish government and were aided by the fascist states of Germany and Italy. The Loyalists for their part were aided by anti-fascist organizations from many countries in the world.

How conflicts are linked depends in part on the ideological and other ties among the partisans in specific fights and the analyses made by partisans about those ties. Thus, Dr. Ayman al-Zawahiri, an Egyptian surgeon and a leader of Egyptian Islamic Jihad, which had de facto merged with al Qaeda in 1998, became al Qaeda's theorist and planner.[78] His initial goal had been to overthrow the secular and oppressive Egyptian government headed by Hosni Mubarak and bring about a revival of Islam there. He came to believe that the West upheld the Mubarak government, thereby corrupting and humiliating Islamic society. Therefore, to succeed in overthrowing the oppressive non-Islamic governments in Muslim-populated countries, the West's and particularly American support of those governments had to be ended. Thus, individual militant jihadist actions have a much wider context.

Sometimes, too, a minor conflict within one of the major adversaries escalates rather than being subordinated in the general struggle against the common enemy. One or both sides in the subordinate conflict may regard the larger struggle as an opportunity to escalate its own fight. In the shadow of that larger struggle, brutal suppression or genocidal policies may be undertaken, as happened in the Ottoman Empire during World War I to the Armenians, and in many civil wars around the world since then.

Intervention

Outside parties often significantly affect the course of a struggle. They not only can act to escalate or prolong a conflict by joining the struggle on one side, they may alternatively pursue policies to contain the conflict, barring support to all sides in the struggle. In addition, they may provide intermediary services to facilitate a de-escalation of a destructive struggle or assist in a shift to a constructive escalation. Some specialized units can provide alternatives to violent escalation and channel escalation to be constructive. For example, within the United States agencies such as the National Labor Relations Board oversee union recognition and other collective bargaining conflicts. The work of the Community Relations Service of the U.S. Department of Justice is also illustrative, using mediation and other forms of conciliation to help adversaries ease or settle their conflicts, minimizing a destructive escalation.

Some interventions can help prepare for relatively constructive escalations of conflicts. For example NGOs may help provide training or resources that develop the capacity for challengers in countries dominated by repressive regimes to conduct well-considered nonviolent struggles. For example, for many years, the Fellowship of Reconciliation (FOR) and the Servicio Paz y Justicia en America Latina (SERPAJ-AL) have been conducting training in nonviolence in Latin America.[79]

The U.S. Department of State provides support to civil society organizations in many countries with authoritarian governments, which includes aiding nongovernmental organizations pushing for social and political reforms.

For example, The Middle East Partnership Initiative's mission is to create partnerships that help build pluralistic, participatory, and prosperous societies in the Middle East and North Africa. It was founded in 2002 and expanded in president Obama's administration. Its program includes bringing young academics and young activists from the region to the United States where they can learn possible ways to foster the changes they are seeking to make in their respective countries. Many of them are likely to effectively participate in the long-term transition started by the Arab Spring.[80]

When actors outside a given struggle affect the struggle's escalation and likely outcome, it can be by their inaction as well as action. Partisans, particularly those who feel weak, seek assistance from those not yet involved in the struggle. The failure to intervene, then, appears at least as acquiescence in the way the conflict is going. How intermediaries help transform and end destructive conflicts is the subject of chapter 8.

CONCLUSIONS

Numerous processes and conditions variously combine to prolong struggles and escalate their destructiveness. The policies pursued by partisans and outsiders sometimes intentionally contribute to such effects, but frequently the policies were not so intended. Better analyses of how various policies affect the likelihood of destructive escalation can help reduce its occurrence.

The welter of variables combining to determine the destructiveness of a conflict's escalation betokens the fact that many different actors affect that development. This can be illustrated by considering the initiation of the war on Iraq by the U.S. government in March 2003.

Many different reasons for the United States militarily attacking Iraq have been given; the war advocates gave shifting priorities to these reasons.[81] The justifications include: to ensure the destruction of weapons of mass destruction (WMDs) in Iraq, to end the tyranny of the Saddam Hussein regime, to foster the transformation of Iraq and other countries in the region into democracies with free-market economies, to counter the terrorist threat to the United States, to demonstrate U.S. military dominance and establish an enduring military presence in the Middle East, to put an end to a fight that had gone on too long, to ensure U.S. global preeminence, and to maintain domestic political power.

President Bush initially framed the necessity of resorting to war in terms of the threat Iraq's possession of WMDs presented; he did so because the prior UN resolutions were about such weapons, and they provided a veil of legitimacy. When no WMDs were found after the invasion, other reasons were stressed, including that it was better to fight the terrorists over there than in America.

The opponents of the war against Iraq raised many objections.[82] Some traditional realists argued that the president's foreign policy goals were too idealistic, too grandiose, and ultimately unachievable. They and others insisted that a higher priority be given to countering terrorism by focusing on the ongoing conflict in Afghanistan and the fight against al Qaeda, rather than drain American resources and arouse more Islamic antagonism by invading Iraq. Many persons objected to the way the decision was made, insisting on greater public participation and legitimation resulting from a congressional debate about a declaration of war and/or a UN Security Council resolution mandating military action. The war opponents reasoned that Iraq posed no imminent threat and that UN-supported inspections and multilateral actions could effectively contain Saddam Hussein. These views were expressed by then current and by former members of the U.S. foreign policy establishment, as well as by academics, advocacy organizations, and political figures. They urged all sorts of alternatives.[83] Many of them recommended acting multilaterally with UN approval to disarm Iraq, and others campaigned for muscular inspections by a multinational military force. Some observers argued that Hussein would be more cooperative if he and his regime were assured survival in power.

People throughout the world thought that invading Iraq was wrong and would have terrible consequences.[84] Massive demonstrations occurred in cities around the world, and several closely allied governments withheld their support. Governments in the region attempted mediation efforts. Public opinion polls in many countries indicated widespread opposition to the United States invading Iraq.

Iraqis also were major actors in the escalation. Saddam Hussein and his government asserted that Iraq did not possess WMDs and had no programs to develop them, but Iraqi officials were not fully compliant in demonstrating that truth. Perhaps Hussein thought that if the hostile powers believed he possessed the WMDs, they would be deterred. He certainly was not given any assurance that he and his government would survive if he fully sought to prove that the WMD programs had ended. Numerous persons in Iraq had died in trying to overthrow the regime and many others were intimidated. Iraqi diaspora groups lobbied the U.S. government to overthrow the Iraqi regime, arguing that it was a threat and assuring American officials that the Iraqi people would welcome the U.S. military.

Despite all the opposition, the U.S. government took the country to war. The UN Security Council might have tried to block such action, but it had already moved far along the path with implied threats of military action. Despite considerable reluctance and even some resistance, the U.S. Congress voted to give the president broad leeway to do what he thought best.[85]

Many U.S. government leaders, it appears, had larger goals than ensuring safety from Saddam Hussein's regime. They believed that the victorious end of the Cold War had established American global preeminence, and they wanted to bolster spreading democracy and free markets around the world. American military dominance seemed a powerful instrument to advance that goal, and the readiness to use it would enhance the dominance. The overwhelming U.S. military capability seemed to promise a way to swiftly resolve conflicts. Thus, there was little post-invasion planning, which contributed to the war's destructiveness and prolongation.

To many observers, such goals and means demonstrated great hubris, likely to result in overreaching and failure.[86] Some critics did stress the dangers of such arrogance, but that did not resonate with the public. Furthermore, Saddam Hussein and his government had behaved abominably for many years, and he could have no defenders in American society in 2003.

Many American civic organizations did raise cautions about what was clearly the determination by the president and his close associates to launch a preemptive war. However, in the aftermath of the attacks of September 11, 2001, emotions of fear and anger, the desire for retribution, and the wish to take strong actions were readily aroused. The news media could have done better, at least by noting the lack of evidence of imminent danger or of Iraqi culpability in the 9/11 attacks, by reporting the reasons for widespread opposition to going to war, and by reporting on alternatives to war that were being suggested. After the fall of the Saddam Hussein regime and the failure to find WMDs, a few writers examined the failure of the news media to report reasonable doubts about the existence of WMDs in Iraq before the war. For example, the editors of the *New York Times* investigated their coverage and acknowledged on May 26, 2004, that, "In some cases, information that was controversial then, and seems questionable now, was insufficiently qualified or allowed to stand unchallenged."[87]

More institutional constraints, greater civic engagement, and wider and deeper awareness of the destructive consequences of various kinds of escalatory strategies might have averted the way the war was undertaken and conducted, and also how the unwelcome consequences were managed. The later chapters in this book provide the context for considering those possibilities.

7

De-escalation of Conflicts

Conflict de-escalation takes many different forms. Sometimes, though relatively rarely, one side may simply compel the other to yield on the issues in dispute, or even destroy it as an organized entity. Other times de-escalation is imposed by a powerful external actor. Still other times de-escalation is achieved through recourse to institutionalized conflict management entities, such as courts, regulatory agencies, or law enforcement bodies.

The speed at which conflict de-escalation occurs also varies significantly. Oftentimes in large-scale conflicts, de-escalation occurs only slowly and is punctuated by periods of renewed escalation as elements within the adversary camps seek to "spoil" the progress toward resolving their conflict.[1] Other times the course of de-escalation is steady and stakeholders achieve negotiated agreements on particular contested matters but not on others. Finally, de-escalation can be marked by abrupt episodes, as with the steps ending the Cold War between the United States and the Soviet Union.

In this chapter, as with previous chapters, we concentrate largely on constructive avenues for conflict de-escalation. We find that even in the most destructive and intractable conflicts it is possible for members of one or both sides to begin considering more constructive conflict behavior as a prelude to the conflict's de-escalation. In the following pages we focus on three areas: (1) the de-escalation processes, (2) changing conditions, and (3) policies that foster de-escalation.

PROCESSES OF DE-ESCALATION

Processes fostering de-escalation occur within each adversary, in the relations between the adversaries, and also among other parties in the social environment. In the case of large-scale, long-lasting struggles, generally the effects of these various processes must converge and reinforce each other for significant de-escalation to proceed.

Internal Processes

Within each adversary, social psychological and organizational developments can advance conflict de-escalation.

Social Psychological Processes

As discussed in chapter 6, cognitive dissonance theory suggests that people seek to avoid incongruity between their attitudes and their behavior.[2] Thus, they find ways to justify actions they feel they are compelled to take, although they would generally regard the actions as distasteful or even abhorrent. In short, committing bad deeds needs to be self-justified. Cognitive dissonance can, however, also support and reinforce de-escalation moves. Dramatic collective moves toward peace, for instance, at least initially will gain approval as an expression of solidarity with the collectivity. They can encourage groups to develop new cognitions about their enemy that justify conciliatory moves and serve to reinforce subsequent peacebuilding efforts. Survey evidence, for instance, indicates that public approval of a U.S. president rises once the president undertakes a peace initiative, as illustrated by the approval won by President Richard M. Nixon for his conciliatory initiatives in the early 1970s toward the Soviet government and the Chinese government that prompted rapid movement toward détente between the United States and the Soviet Union and between the United States and the People's Republic of China (PRC).[3]

Thus, it appears that once actions toward de-escalation have been taken, attitudes may be altered to increase consistency and processes of de-escalation may be further strengthened. The grand contentious goals previously sought may become devalued when action to reach it is abandoned. Thus, in an Aesop's fable, a fox gave up trying to get the grapes it could not reach, explaining they were sour anyway. This "sour grapes" mechanism helps explain how at least some people handle desiring an outcome that is ultimately unattainable. In chapter 6, we also noted how the process of entrapment often fosters escalation. However, there can be a slippery path to peace as well as to destructive war. Having taken steps that entail an investment in de-escalation, there is a tendency to persevere to make the investment pay off. This is particularly the case when a major de-escalation step has been taken. For example, consider the commitment made by Egyptian president Anwar el-Sadat when he went to Jerusalem in November 1977. This phenomenon helps explain Sadat's continuing to negotiate with Israel and sign a peace treaty with it in 1979, despite failing to reach a fundamental result that would incorporate peace for the Palestinians.

Other emotional and cognitive processes, whose conflict-escalating effects were previously discussed, can also be controlled and actually contribute to constructive transformation and de-escalation. For example, the effects of earlier personal negative experiences with antagonistic individuals or groups do not have to result in long-term bias against them, obstructing constructive transformation. Insights about such bias can be learned from training in workshops, personal therapy, new experiences, and by reflection. Furthermore, persons who represent conflict groups in adversarial relations may be selected in ways that reduce the likelihood that they are greatly affected by negative emotional processes, which dispose them to engage in destructive conflict. Thus, persons selected through open, nonviolent democratic means are less prone to engage in destructive conflict escalation than those who have won leadership by their manipulative and violent conduct.

Sympathizing and empathizing with others are social psychological processes that significantly contribute to conflict de-escalation. Certain policies and experiences can trigger and sustain these processes, even between enemies. A person sympathizing with another person feels along with that other human, and is emotionally moved by the other's feelings.[4] Being sympathetic to members of another group tends to inhibit acting to inflict harm on them; indeed, it would evoke actions to help them. For example, the 1999 earthquakes in Greece and Turkey and the 2005 earthquake in Kashmir, a territory disputed by Pakistan and India, prompted sympathy and joint assistance between these pairs of adversaries for a while.

The construct of empathy, compared with sympathy, stresses taking the role of the other without losing one's identity.[5] Among the several components often noted as constituting empathy, four are particularly relevant for ameliorating destructive conflict escalation. First, empathy includes accurately perceiving the other persons' feelings and thoughts relating to the conflict. Second, empathetic persons experience those feelings and thoughts as if they were their own. Third, persons distinguish their own thoughts and feelings from those of the persons with whom they empathize. Finally, empathy includes communicating that experience to the others. This may be most fully realized in a therapeutic or intimate interpersonal relationship, but some degree of these various components can also occur even in social conflicts.

Varying proportions of the members of a conflict party may empathize, in different degrees, with their adversary. Signs of empathy were visible in the novels, plays, and statements by whites in South Africa regarding the circumstances of blacks there under apartheid.[6] Empathy can occur among some members of each side toward members of the other, for example, between some Israeli Jews and Arab Palestinians. Such empathy, more common among women, helps construct plausible and credible de-escalating steps.[7] Particular cultural patterns are varyingly conducive to experiencing empathy and sympathy.

Organizational Processes

Several organizational processes within large adversarial parties can also contribute to constructive de-escalation. Under certain conditions, leadership competition may foster de-escalation rather than escalation. The development of a constituency for accommodation is an important condition for the emergence of a viable alternative leadership; the emergence of alternative leadership, in turn, tends to give legitimacy to further dissent from the hard-line policies sustaining destructive conflict.

Constituencies for de-escalation arise from many sources. The costs of continuing a fight grow as the struggle goes on, raising doubts about the benefit of the goals sought. Such appeared to be the case with U.S. military intervention in Afghanistan as mounting costs to U.S. lives and treasure eroded public support for the mission. Moreover, the burdens of a long, escalating struggle often become increasingly unequal. Those suffering the inequities may dissent and withdraw support; in a war, this may take the form of draft riots, desertion, and flight. For example, in World War I, the Russian people's increasing losses yielded growing opposition to the war against Germany and generated support to the Communist party, which was able to seize power and take Russia out of the war.

Dissent and opposition to official hard-line policies can be mobilized readily insofar as groups of people favoring accommodation with an adversary are already present and are linked by existing communication networks. Thus, American opponents to the U.S. intervention in Vietnam and to the invasion of Iraq were able to mobilize demonstrations and other acts of resistance by their ties to previous peace movement organizations, to traditional peace churches, to student organizations, and to civil rights organizations.[8] Indeed, the ability of peace constituencies to mobilize through various social networking means is becoming a significant area of academic research.[9]

Even the increased severity of the means used by an individual or faction within a conflict organization, as a struggle escalates, can become a turning point toward de-escalation. If the actions cross the boundary of what most people regard as acceptable conduct, then the perpetrators and their cause suffer. In these cases even other members of the organization to which the perpetrators belong may be so outraged as to withdraw support.

This happened in the struggle for Quebec independence from Canada.[10] In the 1960s, the Quebec separatist movement grew rapidly, and the Front de Libération du Québec (FLQ; Quebec Liberation Front), a tiny Maoist organization, carried out bombings and conducted robberies for funds. These actions culminated in October 1970 with the kidnapping of two officials, one of whom was killed. Prime Minister Pierre Trudeau invoked the War Measures

Act, and the FLQ was made illegal. Since that time the separatist movement has used electoral and negotiation methods, while violence as a means of winning independence has been widely repudiated.

In the 1990s and 2000s, many acts of violence in the United States were directed at physicians who performed abortions and at clinics where abortions were provided. For a time, such tactics prompted reactions that tended to marginalize the more extreme groups within the right-to-life movement and encouraged moderation in means; even efforts to search for common ground with supporters of the freedom-of-choice movement were advanced. Whether an outrageous coercive action becomes a catalyst for a de-escalating transformation rather than for a greater escalation depends significantly on the reaction of the targeted party, as discussed later.

Although a crisis may engender further escalation due to the escalating processes discussed in the previous chapter, a crisis can spur de-escalation under certain circumstances. This was famously the case as a result of the great dangers of nuclear escalation that the 1962 Cuban missile crisis made evident to the U.S. and Soviet leaders. Less well known, the U.S.-Soviet crisis in 1983 contributed to the transformation of the Cold War in subsequent years. The Cold War had escalated in the early years of Ronald Reagan's presidency, due to the policies of confronting the Soviet Union rhetorically and in military actions. Within this context, a Korean Airlines 747 passenger plane strayed over Soviet territory on September 1, 1983. Soviet commanders, believing the plane to be on a U.S. intelligence mission, ordered the plane to be shot down by Soviet fighter planes, killing 269 people.[11] Reagan condemned the shoot-down as an act of barbarism. Then, in November, U.S. ground-launched cruise missiles began arriving in Britain and Pershing II missiles in West Germany. Also during this time, U.S. military exercises probed and tested Soviet defensive systems. Some Soviet officials became convinced that the U.S. was about to launch a nuclear attack. Warsaw Pact forces in East Germany, Poland, Czechoslovakia, and the Baltic republics were placed on heightened alert.

Reagan was briefed by CIA director William Casey that Soviet leaders actually feared that the U.S. might launch a surprise attack. Reagan grasped the frightening implications of such beliefs. Some analysts mark this as the turning point in Reagan's thinking. Reagan wrote in his memoirs that recognizing Soviet fears made him "even more anxious to get a top Soviet leader in a room alone and try to convince him we had no designs on the Soviet Union and the Russians had nothing to fear from us."[12]

Once de-escalation has gotten under way, several organizational processes can come into play that advance the process of de-escalation and make turning back difficult. Particularly if a major agreement has been reached, the signers have a stake in pursuing the path they began. For example, as discussed in chapter 4, the Good Friday agreement signed in April 1998 helped resolve the protracted conflict in Northern Ireland, even though implementing the agreement has been an arduous process. Although in a referendum 70 percent voted yes (with just over 50 percent among the unionists), resistance among many opponents remained strong. Thus, in August 1998 twenty-eight persons were killed in an explosion in Omagh; the Real Irish Republican Army, a splinter group of the Provisional IRA, claimed responsibility. Nevertheless, despite such acts, and despite delays in implementation and even threats of withdrawal from the agreed-on process, the supporters persevered, the institutions foreseen in the agreement were established, and the provisions of the agreement were slowly fulfilled.[13]

Reaction and Interaction Processes

Some unilateral reactions to an adversary's escalating coercive thrusts can blunt, interrupt, or reduce such attacks and so contribute to de-escalation. Some defensive actions raise a shield or otherwise reduce the vulnerability to an adversary's blows without increasing the threat to the antagonist, for example, by hardening possible terrorist targets. Other relatively nonprovocative reactions to threats or attacks sometimes occur, such as increasing the capacity to absorb or rebuff the opponents' coercive sanctions.

Unilateral actions can also take the form of directly implementing some of what is being sought from the opponent. If this is done in a way that minimizes threatening the other side, it can be effective and constructive. It can sometimes be done so as to demonstrate that mutual benefits may result. The Palestinian Authority's attempt in this regard, given the failure to make progress in direct negotiations with the Israeli government, is an interesting example. The overall objective is to build the infrastructure and attributes of a Palestinian state alongside Israel. An early step in this process was to improve internal security within the West Bank, which the PA largely controlled. Begun in George W. Bush's presidency, U.S. Lt. General Keith Dayton was detailed to the Department of State to lead a program training Palestinian security forces to serve in the West Bank.[14] The program was intended to thwart criminal groups and Hamas actions in the West Bank, and personnel were vetted by U.S. and Israeli officials. The trained forces have been deployed and greatly significantly enhance everyday security in Nablus and other West Bank areas, which has improved local economic conditions.

The PA prime minister, Salam Fayyad, has been working to develop the Palestinian economy, provide basic social welfare services, and build up the physical and social infrastructure. With assistance from Western states, progress in these regards was and is being made, as is evident in Ramallah and

Nablus.[15] In April 2011, the IMF reported that the PA was "now able to conduct the sound economic policies expected of a future well-functioning Palestinian state, given its solid track record in reforms and institution-building in the public finance and financial areas."[16]

Political moves toward statehood also were made. In May 2011, with Egyptian mediation, Hamas and Fatah reached a reconciliation pact, lessening the split among the Palestinians that could be viewed as a barrier to making peace with Israel.[17] Finally, Mahmoud Abbas, president of the PA, mobilized support for a UN General Assembly resolution recognizing a Palestinian state at the 1967 borders.[18] All these developments strengthened the Palestinian bargaining position and could do so without attacking or threatening Israel. These projects enhance effectiveness and are more constructive insofar as they are placed more fully within a context of potential mutual benefits.

Turning to interactive processes, we discuss three that often contribute to mutual de-escalation: reciprocity in interaction, issue containment, and developing ties between adversaries: these processes oppose the three escalating patterns discussed in chapter 6: the logic of contentious interaction, the expansion of the issues at stake, and polarization.

Reciprocity in Interaction

This analysis of reciprocity builds on the previous chapter's discussion of the possible escalating consequences of over- and underreaction. In certain circumstances, a severe counteraction may actually suppress the adversary; the severe negative sanctions effectively force the other side to lower its resistance or to discontinue the struggle. Underreaction may also bring about the de-escalation or even the termination of a struggle. Thus, one side may make such concessions to its adversary that the adversary's goals are sufficiently satisfied and escalation does not occur; the struggle then de-escalates. Some de-escalating strategies incorporate both processes, for example, attacking the opponent's leadership harshly while offering concessions and positive inducements to the rank-and-file members of the opposing side, as discussed in chapter 9.

The discussion here focuses on mutual de-escalations, which are more likely to be constructive than are unilaterally imposed terminations. Three related processes of adversary interaction help avoid destructive escalation and unilateral imposition: reacting equivalently, learning about the struggle and the adversary, and developing shared norms. In the first process, reacting equivalently, each side reacts in a measured and equivalent level to the other. In this scenario, one or both sides avoid acting in ways they think may be provocative or may invite an aggrandizing move by the other side. The response selected by President Kennedy to the Soviet emplacement of missiles in Cuba in 1962 was "quarantine." It was not a dismissal of the matter as of little consequence or simply a protest at the United Nations, nor was it a provocative air strike or an invasion of Cuba. President Kennedy had recently read Barbara Tuchman's book *The Guns of August*, which analyzed the swift escalation to World War I, and he was determined to allow time for discovering acceptable ways out of the crisis, thereby avoiding a runaway escalation of words and deeds.[19] Having drawn that lesson from history, he took what he regarded as a measured response, which would not provoke an escalating interaction. He also communicated directly with Soviet premier Nikita Khrushchev and closely monitored the operations of the U.S. quarantine.[20] Each side's actions during the crisis were roughly equivalent.[21]

The second interaction process that can have de-escalating effects is acquiring information and insight from research and from experience with the adversary.[22] As each side learns more about the other, about differences within it, and their views of themselves and their situation, each makes better estimates of how the other side will react to its initiatives, which reduces the likelihood of unintentional and ineffective escalation.

Learning occurs at the collective level as well as at the individual level, and over a period of months or years. For example, the U.S. and Soviet governments, over several years, became more familiar with each other's thinking about arms control and nuclear nonproliferation and developed ways to cooperate in these areas. Studies also indicate that officials representing their government in international conflicts over time learn much about their counterparts on the other side through informal exchanges as well as formal negotiations.[23]

Finally, adversaries sometimes develop shared norms guiding conduct in the particular arenas in which they are contending. The rules themselves may be matters of dispute for a time, but once agreed upon, they provide guidance for waging a conflict that constrains the antagonists from escalating very far. Thus, collective bargaining between management and union representatives is carried out concerning certain matters, but not all matters about which workers and managers may disagree. In international affairs, normative regimes sometimes develop that help stabilize and manage particular areas of recurrent disputes.[24]

Issue Containment

Taking steps to make sure that a struggle is contained to a specific goal also facilitates de-escalation. In 1963, Martin Luther King Jr. and the Southern Christian Leadership Conference led the blacks of Birmingham, Alabama, in an economic boycott, in demonstrations, in sit-ins, and into jail.[25] Although the local civil rights leaders did expand their goals to include national concerns, the local goals remained paramount. King's group kept focused on what they sought from Birmingham's economic elite: desegregation of public facilities in downtown department stores, fair hiring procedures in retail stores and city departments, and appointing a biracial commission to set a timetable for the desegregation of the public schools. A variety of tactics were used, but the focus on specific goals was sustained.

As a struggle persists, issues can even begin to contract. One of the adversaries, failing to attain its grand goals, may find settling for what it can get to be its best option. A conflict party that believes it is unable to impose its preferences will come to recognize that it must deal more realistically with its adversary. In such cases, the great matters in contention between them tend to be broken down into more manageable sub-issues. When adversaries fractionate the conflict into specific issues, some may appear easily settled and trade-offs among several issues become possible.[26]

Finally, inflammatory issues may be contained by the development of superordinate goals, shared goals that are given primacy over the contentious ones.[27] One kind of superordinate goal that sometimes emerges, when antagonists believe they are mired in a situation that is increasingly destructive, is to find an acceptable mutual escape. Adversaries often decide to de-escalate their conflict and even agree upon a settlement when both believe that the continued destructive encounter risks a worst outcome. Superordinate goals also may arise as a result of the rising salience of a perceived common enemy or of a shared identity.

Developing Ties between Adversaries

As a struggle persists and escalates destructively, some members of the opposing sides sometimes communicate with each other in order to facilitate a de-escalation of the conflict. They serve as quasi mediators, conveying information and suggestions between the antagonistic parties.[28] They may also develop bonds with each other and thus form an interest group within their own camps for de-escalation. Often, the leaders of one or more sides try to isolate the leaders of the other camp, making overtures to the subordinates and to supporters as well as dissenters within the other camp. This strategy may entail formulating objectives that are attractive to important groups within the opposing camps.

If the conflict persists with recurrent confrontations, the representatives of the opposing sides can develop shared expectations about how the next confrontation will be handled, and if previous confrontations were contained and settled in a mutually acceptable fashion, the next one tends to be guided by the positive previous experience. This is particularly likely in a setting with an ongoing personal relationship between the adversaries, for example, within a given business organization, members often have problems in common.[29]

Processes of Involvement with Other Parties

Adversaries contend with each other within a social context involving many other parties, and those other parties often foster de-escalation. First, they sometimes provide models of the way de-escalation may occur, or at least provide the vision that de-escalation is feasible. Thus, to bring about the transformation of colonial Rhodesia into independent Zimbabwe and end internal warfare, a system of transition was negotiated in 1979, mediated by Lord Carrington. This helped provide a model for arrangements in Namibia and other countries, as well as to establish a system of transition for implementing cease-fires and providing procedures to legitimate new governments, for example, through monitored elections.[30]

Second, outside parties often set limits to the escalation of a conflict and intervene to enforce those limits. Domestically, the state generally enforces certain constraints on the struggles between groups within a society. Such outside intervention may impose a cessation of the use of particularly destructive means to ensure that one of the adversaries is not too badly damaged. Increasingly, international governmental organizations (IGOs) and individual governments have intervened within a country whose government has exercised extreme violence on its own people.

Finally, other parties frequently serve as intermediaries to assist the contending parties in finding a way to de-escalate their conflict, as examined in chapter 8. They may assist the antagonists to de-escalate their struggle, for example, by providing a face-saving way out of the fight. This includes offering a peace proposal that an adversary would reject if made by its enemy but accepts when suggested by a mediator. The intermediaries may also forcefully intervene and help impose a settlement of the conflict, but such intervention sometimes only freezes the conflict at its current status.

CHANGING CONDITIONS

De-escalation, in large measure, occurs as a result of actual changes in the conditions that underlay the emergence of conflicts and that sustained their escalation. Changing conditions arise in three settings: within one of the adversaries in a struggle, within the relations between them, and among other parties not directly engaged in the struggle. This discussion draws illustrative material particularly from major conflicts that have been variously transformed after many decades of struggle: the conflicts (1) between the United States and the Soviet Union, (2) between Israeli Jews and Arab Palestinians, and (3) between blacks and whites in South Africa. The U.S. government was a primary protagonist in the first, a major mediator in the second, and more peripherally involved in the third.

Internal Changes

Since adversaries generally are sustained by confidence in the justness and morality of their cause, a waning of that conviction greatly contributes to de-escalating a struggle. Such a weakening can be seen in the gradually declining faith among Soviet citizens in Communist ideology and the Soviet system.[31] It can also be seen in the undermining of apartheid's legitimacy among whites in South Africa. This was attested to, for example, by the Dutch Reformed Church's resolution in 1986 that the forced separation of peoples cannot be considered a biblical imperative. In the Israeli-Jewish and Arab-Palestinian struggle, however, Jews have not slackened in their faith in Zionism and the Palestinians have not lost their sense that they have suffered a great injustice by the establishment of a Jewish state in Palestine. Nevertheless, many people in each camp had come to acknowledge the authenticity of the other's claims, and that helped initiate the de-escalation steps of 1993. The limitations of that acknowledgment and of a change in self-identity, however, contributed to the subsequent breakdown of negotiations.

The transition to transformation often arises from a realization that the coercive, often violent, means that had been used were not achieving what was intended. Indeed, some partisans may come to believe that past militant strategies undermined the attainment of the ends they sought. For example, American public support for the war in Iraq declined greatly starting in 2004, as Americans increasingly viewed the occupation as reducing U.S. security and well-being. Another example is evident in the Palestinian leaders and public largely rejecting reliance on violence as a means to gain an independent state following the disastrous consequences of the second intifada.

In the conflict over the maintenance of white domination in South Africa, both sides' efforts at unilateral imposition by the mid-1980s were clearly failing. The armed struggle by the African National Congress (ANC) had not forced an end to apartheid, but nonviolent actions were increasing. The South African government's police repression and military attacks clearly had failed to suppress the ANC, and white youths' opposition to military service was rising. Furthermore, integration and mutual dependence among the so-called racial communities was increasing despite the apartheid policy. Indeed, some actions of the South African government were undertaken to reduce black-white inequality.[32]

Certain changes in the relative influence among the constituent parts of an adversary group are important precursors of a de-escalating transition. The emergence into prominence of groups interested in an accommodation with the adversary may lead to a shift in goals and means. The Palestinian uprising, the first intifada, which began in December 1987, provides a paradoxical example. It escalated the intensity of the struggle against the Israeli occupation but also contributed to a moderating shift in the position of the PLO. The PLO leadership, seeking to represent all Palestinians, outside as well as inside the Israeli-occupied territories, had long stressed the desires of those Palestinians outside to return. This was viewed as especially threatening by the Israeli government. Furthermore, the PLO leaders had undertaken harsh means of struggle to compel Israeli change; consequently, the fighters in the armed struggle were an important component of the PLO. The intifada, however, increased the relative importance of the Palestinians in the occupied territories and their emerging local leadership. For those Palestinians, shaking off Israeli control over their lives was the primary objective. The PLO leaders needed a new political role to sustain their position. To represent the Palestinians within the occupied territories in their struggle, the PLO leadership sought recognition from the U.S. government as the representative of the Palestinians. Extensive negotiations through several channels were conducted to formulate a PLO statement satisfying certain U.S. government conditions. Finally, on December 14, 1988, Chairman Yasir Arafat said he accepted, "the right of all parties concerned in the Middle East conflict to exist in peace and security . . . including the state of Palestine, Israel and other neighbors according to resolution 242 and 338. . . . We renounce all forms of terrorism, including individual, group and state terrorism."[33] Thus, a year after the intifada had begun, the U.S. government agreed for the first time to open a dialogue with the PLO (see table 7.1).

Shifts in the relative influence of various groups within each party are crucial to the strengthening of the de-escalation process and to its reversal. Some persons and groups in each adversary camp are likely to oppose a de-escalating transformation or the terms of the likely settlement. They may even try to overthrow the leaders pursuing a de-escalation course or otherwise try to prevent such movement. These rejectionists, or spoilers, can stop a de-escalation movement if not effectively countered.[34]

For example, in the Israeli-Palestinian case, some Jewish nationalists and religious zealots opposed limiting their rights in any part of Jerusalem and the right of Jews to settle in the West Bank and Gaza. They successfully pressured the Israeli government to subsidize housing in territories under Israeli

TABLE 7.1. Israeli-Palestinian Chronology, 1978–2011

1978, Sept.	Framework for Peace in the Middle East signed at Camp David, mediated by Jimmy Carter
1987, Dec.	Intifada I (Palestinian uprising) begins
1988, Dec	United States and PLO enter into direct communications
1991, Oct.	Middle East Peace Conference in Madrid
1993, Jan.	Start of secret meetings in Oslo, Norway, between PLO and unofficial Israelis
1993, Sept.	The PLO and Israeli government sign Declaration of Principles; Yasir Arafat and Yitzhak Rabin shake hands
1994, May.	Cairo Agreement for Palestinian "self rule" in Gaza and Jericho
1995, Sept.	Israel and PLO sign interim agreement to transfer control of major Palestinian populated areas in the occupied territories
1995, Nov.	Yitzhak Rabin assassinated by Israeli zealot
1998, Oct.	Wye River Memorandum signed by Benjamin Netanyahu and Yasir Arafat
2000, July	Camp David II, Israeli and Palestinian negotiations, mediated by Bill Clinton
2000, Sept.	Intifada II begins
2001, Feb.	Ariel Sharon elected prime minister of Israel
2003, April	Quartet issues: A Performance-Based Roadmap to a Permanent Two-State Solution to the Israeli-Palestinian Conflict
2003, Dec.	Yossi Beilin and Yasser Abd Rabbo release Geneva Accord
2004, Nov.	Yasir Arafat dies
2005, Jan.	Mahmoud Abbas (Abu Mazen) elected President of Palestinian National Assembly
2005, Sept	Israel unilaterally withdraws from Gaza Strip
2006, Jan.	In election for Palestinian Legislature, Hamas wins majority
2007, June	Fatah takes control of West Bank and Hamas takes control of Gaza Strip
2010, Sept.	Direct negotiations by Israeli government and Palestine Authority (PA) briefly renewed
2011–	PA prepares to request UN General Assembly recognition of Palestinian state

military occupation. Subjected to attacks by Palestinians in those territories, large bypass roads were constructed to link the settlements and the State of Israel. Some settlers harassed Palestinians and violently retaliated for Palestinian attacks. At the same time, some Palestinian nationalists regarded the peace process begun in 1993 by the PLO leadership and the Israeli government as unacceptable, and this strengthened oppositional groups including

Hamas, Islamic Jihad, and Hezbollah. Some of their members attacked Jewish soldiers and civilians, at times resorting to suicide bombings. These actions by Israeli Jews and by Palestinians against their own leaders' peacemaking policies lent support to the arguments and mobilizing efforts of the hard-liners on the opposing side.

Finally, some internal changes demand attention from the adversary's leaders and divert them from pursuing antagonistic external relations. Beginning in the mid-1970s, the Soviet economy was clearly stagnating and living conditions were deteriorating. Life expectancy actually began to decline, unlike in any other industrially developed country.[35] Improving relations with the West offered the prospect of limiting the immense military defense expenditures and gaining access to Western technological developments and more and better consumer products. In 1985, Mikhail Gorbachev was chosen by the Communist Party to lead it and the Soviet Union into a period of domestic reforms, and an accommodation with the West was regarded as a requisite for that.

Within Israel, a change in the population in the 1990s also contributed to altering the Israeli government and increasing its willingness to be more forthcoming in negotiations with the Palestinians. This partly resulted from one of the Soviet actions, which aimed at winning approval in the West: the Soviet government increased the freedom of movement of the Soviet people. Consequently, the number of Russian Jews who entered Israel rapidly grew, rising further after the demise of the Soviet Union. The costs of absorbing them in Israel competed with the costs of subsidizing Jewish settlers in the occupied territories. The Labor Party, promising greater attention to the needs within Israel itself, won the election in 1992, aided by the votes of the Jews from the Soviet Union. The Labor Party government undertook more earnest negotiations with the Palestinians than had been the case earlier and reached an accord with the PLO in September 1993. The increased number of Jews from the former Soviet areas also enhanced Israelis' confidence about their future in the Middle East, easing the risk of conceding more to the Palestinians.

Changes in the Relationship

Changes in the relations between adversaries that undermine their prospects of unilaterally imposing a solution help turn them toward de-escalation. This frequently comes when the adversaries are in a stalemate and neither party anticipates that the balance of forces will change to enable it to triumph, and if the stalemate is highly unsatisfactory, they are in a "hurting stalemate."[36] Such circumstances can be a prelude to a negotiated settlement, but only if the prospect of a better alternative—one that provides a mutually acceptable solution that does not threaten each party's most significant interests—is envisioned.

For seemingly intractable destructive conflicts to pass through a transition to a mutually acceptable de-escalation, each side minimally must believe that the other does not threaten its collective existence. The nature of that collectivity and the form of its existence, however, can take many shapes. The bargaining about the character of each side can go on for a long time, even as part of a constructive struggle within the context of a legitimate political system. It should also be recognized, however, that the parties contending about their nature and their relations are generally not symmetrical.[37] The adversaries differ in resources, and one side usually attains more of what it wants than the other side does, even in a mutually accepted agreement.

Many of these points can be illustrated in the de-escalating transition of the Israeli-Palestinian conflict. The acceptance by each side of the other's collective legitimacy took decades. But many in the PLO leadership over the years came to accept as an unalterable fact what they had wished had never happened: the creation of a Jewish state in part of what they regarded as their land—Palestine. They had come to reconcile themselves to a Palestinian state alongside Israel, a two-state solution. Some Palestinians continued to reject that solution, and many others claimed more for their state than the Israelis were offering.

As for the Israelis, prior to the 1967 war, before the Israeli army took possession of the Gaza Strip, the Sinai, the West Bank, the Golan Heights, and East Jerusalem, they might well have accepted a two-state solution or would have agreed to the control of those territories by various Arab states. But after the war, the options shifted. Jerusalem was unified and incorporated into Israel, and Jewish settlements were increasingly established in the occupied territories, particularly after the Likud Party victory in 1977.

Gradually, Israeli consensus about a possible settlement of the conflict with the Palestinians broke down. Many Israelis wanted to retain control over the West Bank, providing the Palestinians only with limited autonomy there, a solution that was unacceptable to the PLO when it was offered in the course of many exploratory negotiations in the 1980s. Other Israelis increasingly came to believe that a more fundamental separation was desirable, allowing more of what the Palestinians were willing to accept. Those Israelis came to believe that Israel could not remain a democratic Jewish country and also rule or incorporate the Palestinians in the occupied territories. They preferred to be democratic and Jewish rather than to retain the land and undemocratically rule the Palestinian inhabitants.

By the early 1990s, the latter view was strengthened by the experience with the first Palestinian intifada. It helped achieve recognition by Israeli Jews of the national character of the Palestinians. In the occupied territories, an infrastructure separating Jews and Palestinians was being constructed. The changing position of the PLO was increasingly acknowledged, and Hamas rose as a more intransigent adversary. For Jewish Israelis, the PLO now seemed a more acceptable negotiating partner.

In South Africa, the social and economic relations between blacks and whites had been undergoing a fundamental change in the 1980s. Despite the official policies of apartheid, the racial communities were becoming increasingly interdependent. Blacks had migrated to the urban centers and integrated industry and residential areas, violating the official pass requirements.[38] Significantly, although the ANC demanded the transfer of power to a government chosen by a majority of the people, it "recognized the equal right of whites to South Africa as their native land."[39] That reassurance was available to be recognized by whites (see table 7.2).

The U.S.-Soviet relationship also underwent many profound social, political, and economic shifts in the course of the Cold War. The United States had overwhelming global dominance at the outset, but that gradually declined as more centers of economic power developed. The Soviet Union, although

TABLE 7.2. South African Chronology, 1948–1995

1948, May	National Party wins election, institutes apartheid policy
1955, June	Freedom Charter proclaimed by Congress of the People
1959, Mar.	Massacre of anti-pass demonstrators in Sharpeville
1964, June	Nelson Mandela and associates sentenced to life imprisonment
1976, June	Violent suppression of students in Soweto protesting ruling that half of secondary school classes must be taught in Afrikaans
1983, Aug.	United Democratic Front formed to link local resistance groups
1984, Dec.	Afrikaner academic facilitates meeting between ANC officials and Afrikaner newspaper editors in Lusaka, Zambia
1985, April	Repeal of prohibition of marriages between whites and others announced
1986, April	Law requiring blacks to carry pass books repealed
1986, Oct.	The general synod of the Dutch Reformed Church resolves that the forced separation of peoples cannot be considered a biblical imperative
1989, Aug.	Frederik Willem de Klerk elected president of South Africa
1990, Feb.	Nelson Mandela unconditionally released from prison
1991, June	Group Areas Act and Population Registration Act repealed
1991, Sept.	National Peace Accord signed
1992, Mar.	Whites-only referendum supports negotiations to end white minority rule
1994, April	Mandela elected president of South Africa
1995, July	Truth and Reconciliation Commission authorized

lacking the global economic and military reach of the United States, by the end of the 1960s had achieved the capability of waging a nuclear war that could destroy much of the United States, and so a balance of terror came into existence. At the same time, neither side had immediate goals that threatened vital interests of the other. With détente in the early 1970s, arms control agreements and many other measures appeared to demonstrate a mutual acceptance of each other as superpowers. After years of negotiation in the Conference on Security and Cooperation in Europe (CSCE), the Helsinki Final Act was signed in 1975. This included a major trade-off. It provided assurance to the Soviet Union of the inviolability of the borders established in Europe after the end of World War II, including the western shift of Soviet borders and the division of Germany. On the other hand, it also opened the Soviet Union and the East European countries it dominated to Western influence and obligated the Soviet Union to honor fundamental human rights, which proved to be of great consequence.

Changes in Context

Shifts in the salience of other conflicts with which a pair of adversaries are associated can profoundly contribute to the de-escalation of their struggle. For example, the shift to U.S.-Soviet détente in the early 1970s was fostered by changes in the prominence of other conflicts.[40] Thus, the Soviet-Chinese antagonism had intensified, demonstrated by bloody border skirmishes in 1969. That provided an incentive for each of those powers to be less intransigent toward the United States. Concurrently, the U.S. engagement in the Vietnam War was an overwhelming concern when Nixon was elected president in 1969. He and his advisors reasoned that an acceptable way out of Vietnam might be found by being more accommodating to the Soviet Union and the PRC, playing one against the other and isolating North Vietnam. Furthermore, the newly elected Social Democratic government of West Germany undertook a policy of accommodation with the Soviet Union, East Germany, and other countries of Eastern Europe, which eased and indeed fostered U.S.–Soviet accommodation.

The final end of the Cold War, marked by the fall of the Berlin Wall in 1989, and then the dissolution of the Soviet Union in 1991, impacted many conflicts throughout the world, including the struggles in South Africa and the Middle East. Many of these conflicts had been linked to the Cold War, with Soviet and American support going to the opponents waging bloody wars. The end of the Cold War required the local combatants to change their ways, hastening the end of their wars.

In South Africa, the collapse of communism in Europe undermined the National Party's argument that it was fighting communism by its anti-African

National Congress (ANC) policy and its armed intervention in neighboring countries. Consequently, the South African government could expect more opposition to its policies from the U.S. government. Moreover, the ANC's reassurances about the economic policies it would pursue if it gained political power seemed more credible under the new conditions. A new government strategy was needed, and the path toward accommodation with the ANC was taken.

How a conflict has been conducted and its outcome profoundly affect the possibility of transforming other conflicts in which one or more of the adversaries has been implicated. A victor may have added resources, and obligations, to help de-escalate other associated conflicts. For example, the Iraqi attempt to incorporate Kuwait unleashed an intense war as U.S. and allied forces drove the Iraqi army out of Kuwait. The war divided the Arabs, particularly weakening the positions of the Palestinians, the PLO, and Jordan, who had not joined the anti-Iraqi government coalition. Furthermore, the threat Saddam Hussein raised by appealing to popular anti-Israeli sentiments became an incentive for the U.S. government to promise efforts to settle the Israeli-Arab conflict, hoping to maintain the Arab governments' cooperation in the war against Iraq. The war also appeared to leave the United States as the dominant regional and global power. The U.S. government's incentive and ability to play a major intermediary role after the war were strong and led to the Middle East Peace Conference in Madrid, according to a formula brokered by U.S. secretary of state James Baker.[41]

Many other contextual developments affect the possible de-escalation of conflicts, including changes in the protagonists' economies. The increasingly integrated global economy impacted the conflicts being discussed. For example, growing global integration meant that the international economic sanctions against South Africa became more and more burdensome. The increasingly integrated global economy also contributed to the pressure felt by Soviet leaders to change their stagnating economy in order to function effectively within the world system.

Beginning in the early 1980s, economic conditions in many Arab countries deteriorated for most people. The great flow of income that the success of the Organization of Petroleum Exporting Countries had generated for some Arab countries in the 1970s had slowed down. This contributed to the felt need to settle the Arab-Israeli conflict.

Economic expansion, which is a goal shared by most adversaries, encourages cooperation, and its increased attainment facilitates finding win-win outcomes. For example, the growth of the economy in the United States in the 1960s facilitated the integration of women, blacks, and other minorities into the economy and, hence, into the general society.

Summary

A combination of several changes is generally needed to bring about a transition into a de-escalating movement, particularly for extended destructive conflicts. The changes may occur within one or more adversary, in their relations, or in the social context. Different degrees and combinations of changed conditions can bring about the shift toward de-escalation. Thus, if a stalemate is very painful, then the formula to escape from it need not be as attractive as when the stalemate is more bearable.

The nature of the de-escalation and the resulting outcome is also likely to differ, depending on the particular combination of conditions. There is little reason in theory or in experience to believe that the result of conflict de-escalation or termination will be equitable for all the adversaries. Some adversaries are likely to fare better than others, but none is likely to gain all that it wanted at the start of the struggle.

Changing conditions create opportunities, but no guarantees, for successful de-escalating efforts. In each of the major de-escalations described here, many counterforces and events were evident; they created a quite different set of expectations for many of the participants and observers at the time. The adverse circumstances as well as those conducive to constructive de-escalation must be recognized. No single kind of de-escalating effort will work for every conflict in every situation. A particular set of policies and a particular set of conditions must match if de-escalation is to succeed, as discussed next.[42]

DE-ESCALATION POLICIES

To this point we have discussed the processes and changes in conditions that can advance de-escalation. For each engaged part, however, de-escalation can also be sought through a variety of concrete policies. Effective and appropriate de-escalation policies vary, depending on the level of escalation that a conflict has already attained, on who is to implement the policy and on the time span considered for the de-escalation goal sought.[43] After considering these conflict parameters, we discuss illustrative de-escalation strategies for conflicts at different levels of escalation, for different actors, and over different time spans.

Analytic Parameters

Seemingly intractable destructive conflicts do not begin that way, but become so over time as a result of the actions committed and of actions not taken—by adversaries and by possible intermediaries.[44] This discussion differentiates among three starting levels: little escalation, sharp escalation (or crisis), and protracted stalemate. These levels tend to be mixed in actual struggles; for example, a crisis may erupt in the context of a low level of struggle or in the context of a protracted stalemate. Furthermore, various segments of a large-scale conflict may be in different stages simultaneously. For example, while at the societal level a struggle may be relatively stalemated, in one community one side may be sharply escalating the fight.

At their outset, conflicts generally exhibit expressions of dissatisfaction, assertions of demands, and probing behavior. That often leads to mutual exploration of the issues in contention and possible settlements. Sometimes, however, the conflict escalates with increasing threats and applications of coercive sanctions. As a conflict begins to become destructive and intractable, the adversaries, with or without the assistance of intermediaries, may implement policies that effectively prevent further deterioration. This can transform the conflict constructively, as happened in Latvia, Romania, and elsewhere in Eastern Europe in the 1990s.[45] Clearly, averting destructive escalation at this early stage is generally less costly and more likely to be enduring than after the conflict has become protracted.

More strenuous efforts at de-escalation are necessary when a conflict has markedly escalated. Among the many forms of sharp escalation, one form is much examined in international relations—the crisis. Crises occur in all kinds of relations, including between a state and a challenging organization within a country, such as a separatist party, and between nonstate actors, such as contending organizations and individuals. In these cases, military hostilities may not be likely, but a radical escalation in the intensity of the antagonistic exchanges and a rupture of the relationship is threatened and sometimes occurs. For example, confrontations have sometimes escalated tragically as the members of a religious community and government authorities reject the claims made by the other. This was the case in 1993 when the compound of the Branch Davidians near Waco, Texas, was besieged for fifty-one days by officers of the United States Bureau of Alcohol, Tobacco, Firearms, and Explosives (ATF); it was then stormed on April 19, resulting in a fire that consumed the people in the compound.[46] Two years later, on April 19, 1995, Timothy McVeigh carried out a terrible bombing of the Alfred P. Murrah Federal Building in downtown Oklahoma City.

In addition to crises, escalation surges occur when one of the parties greatly intensifies its means of struggle. In community and societal conflicts, this may take the form of disorderly outbursts such as riots and widespread demonstrations. Within organizations, it may occur when subordinates refuse to follow orders, such as in a military mutiny or when buildings are seized by protesting persons and groups or when prisoners take control of parts of a prison or students occupy and hold college buildings.

The third starting level is that of a seemingly intractable struggle, a stage receiving increasing attention by scholars and policy makers.[47] In these long-standing struggles, neither side is able to impose a settlement on the other, and neither is willing to accept the terms insisted on by the other.

Finally, some conflicts are at a stage where one side is increasingly dominating the other and is able to impose its preferred settlement. We give relatively little attention to how one side defeats or destroys the other because analysts and activists alike overemphasize that outcome, to the neglect of other courses of development. In large-scale conflicts, even if one side defeats the other, the adversary can and often does renew the fight at a later time. The relationship, in any case, generally persists in some form, and one or another kind of mutual accommodation ensues. Admittedly, in the short run for many conflicts and particularly for interpersonal and small-scale conflicts, a total defeat of one side or an end of the relationship may occur.

De-escalation policies can be examined in terms of short-term and long-term goals. Short-terms goals tend to focus on stopping ongoing violence and preventing imminent escalation. Long-term goals tend to emphasize changing the underlying conflict conditions, developing constructive alternative methods of struggle, building and institutionalizing conflict management norms, and reaching stable mutual accommodations. Table 7.3 identifies a variety of de-escalation policies that may be used by different actors for short- and long-term goals, in conflicts at varying levels of escalation.

TABLE 7.3. Policies for Constructive De-escalation

Starting Situation	Short-Term Goals		Long-Term Goals	
	By Partisans	By Intermediaries	By Partisans	By Intermediaries
Low-level Escalation	De-link issues; Nonviolent action; Measured reciprocity.	Provide mediation; Isolate conflict.	Reduce inequalities; Foster shared identities.	Develop supportive norms, institutions; Introduce more stakeholders.
Sharp Escalation	Allow time; Face-saving.	Mediation; Face-saving; Suggest formula. Sanctions.	Reframe conflict; Avoid provocation; CBM.	Mediation; Develop cross-cutting ties.
Protracted Struggles	Conciliatory signals; Track II; Accept responsibility; Reassure adversary.	Mediation; Isolate conflict. Observers.	GRIT; TFT; Training in conflict resolution; CBM; Introduce more stakeholders.	Develop superordinate goals; Foster communication.

From Low Level of Escalation

It is easier to stop a conflict from escalating destructively if the struggle has not persisted for a long time and not escalated greatly. This underlies the high interest among conflict resolution practitioners in the potential of early warning and preventive diplomacy. Much of this interest in early intervention is focused on parties who are possible interveners.

Despite the interest in early warning, the problem is not so much ignorance that a conflict is likely to escalate badly, but that the political will to act is low when the salience of a conflict is low.[48] First, this is because intervention even at an early stage generally calls for the use of resources, and there usually are many more pressing claims on resources. Second, potential interveners tend to believe there is a good chance that intervention will not be necessary. Third, what action actually will be effective is uncertain, a good reason for caution. Fourth, ineffectively interfering will be regarded as a failure. Finally, little credit is likely to be won by preventing a conflict from deteriorating, since most people will hardly have noticed or believed that a disaster was averted. Many of these considerations, of course, also affect the leaders of each adversary group, reducing the chances that they pursue de-escalatory policies. The presentation of effective early de-escalation policies, then, should not only contribute knowledge about what to do to prevent destructive escalation but also address the lack of popular and official support for such efforts.

Short Term

Conflict partisans and intermediaries can pursue a variety of policies that tend to prevent conflicts from escalating destructively and thus turn them toward constructive de-escalation.

As earlier discussions have shown, how a challenging group pursues its goals and how the other side responds will greatly affect the likelihood that a struggle will de-escalate constructively. For example, conflicts in which challenging groups use relatively nonprovocative methods, such as conventional protest or nonviolent resistance, are less likely to escalate destructively than those in which challenging groups resort early on to violence, especially terrorist actions. Similarly, conflicts in which the challenged parties respond in an equivalent way rather than by overreacting tend not to escalate destructively.

Early de-escalation is likely to be fostered insofar as the partisans keep the issues in contention narrowly focused and isolated from other issues about which they might also fight. Destructive escalation tends to be limited if participation by other parties does not spread, for instance through inflammatory rumors of outrages. Therefore, in periods of rioting, urban organizations may provide centers where citizens can seek verification about stories they had heard.

In the case of international conflicts or communal conflicts with transnational links, outside parties may strive to prevent the conflict from spreading into neighboring countries or try to stop or limit the sale of weapons in the country where the struggle is under way. Policies aimed at stopping a conflict spreading are illustrated by the conduct of the United Nations and other international organizations and governments in limiting the scope of the wars in the former Yugoslavia. Thus, at the request of the president of the Yugoslav Republic of Macedonia, in December 1992 the UN Security Council authorized the deployment of troops under command of the UN Protection Force along the Macedonian border with Albania and the successor Yugoslavia (Serbia and Montenegro). The troops not only acted as a deterrent to the spread of war but also mediated border encounters and succeeded in achieving a withdrawal of soldiers on both sides.[49] Unfortunately, external intervention was not so effective and sometimes even counterproductive in preventing or quickly stopping many bloody wars as Yugoslavia broke apart.[50]

Within many social systems, agencies frequently exist that provide mediation, information-gathering, facilitation, and consultative services to defuse nascent conflicts, exemplified in the United States by the Community Relations Service of the U.S. Department of Justice, the National Labor Relations Board, and community human rights commissions. In addition, political and religious leaders, acting informally, may also intervene to help settle community disputes. They often have bonds crossing religious and ethnic lines and can use such connections to bring together leaders from disputing communal groups.

Long Term

Long-term de-escalation policies include the promotion of cross-cutting ties; institutionalized procedures for resolving conflicts; improvement of the social, economic, and cultural way of life of the disadvantaged within the social system; and the creation of shared identities and vested interests in advancing those shared identities.

Within a society, policies fostering those conditions include establishing an electoral system that is conducive to participation by broad political parties, which are not based on a single ethnic, religious, or other exclusive identity. They also include educational systems and curricular material that emphasize shared identities, without denigrating minority ones. They further include the development of legitimate procedures for protecting fundamental rights of all members of the society.

From Sharp Escalation

Policy makers, analysts, and the public at large generally exhibit great interest in the outbreak of crises and other sharp escalations. Considerable research about policies and procedures that enable adversaries to avoid abrupt destructive escalations during crises has been done, at least in some arenas.[51]

Short Term

One of the essential qualities of a crisis is the sense of urgency engendered among the partisans. That urgency often hampers taking actions that would avoid a disastrous escalation. One way to increase the likelihood of crisis de-escalation is for one or more adversaries to allow time for the other side to reflect on its course of action and not be pushed into a corner and face humiliation if it backs down. This is exemplified in some degree by the U.S. government's responses in the Cuban missile crisis of 1962.[52] In that grave crisis, sufficient time was allotted to find a formula for a way out of the crisis. The final formula included the withdrawal of the Soviet missiles from Cuba, the promise that the U.S. government would not try to overthrow the Cuban government, and the covert understanding that the United States would close its missile base in Turkey.

In domestic crises, hostages are often a crucial component, since they provide leverage for a small, relatively powerless group to counter the overwhelming power of state forces. The common understanding among police officers and other officials in responding to hostage situations is to be patient and to negotiate with those holding hostages, but not to accede to their demands. For persons not part of a larger group who have seized a hostage in desperation, this strategy generally results in a nonviolent resolution. With persons who are acting as part of larger organizations and identities, the negotiations are more difficult, since government officials are concerned about precedents and sometimes use the negotiations as ruses in preparation for storming the location where the hostages are held.

Crises may also erupt in the course of de-escalating conflict transformation, when rejectionists try to disrupt the movement. During the transformation ending apartheid in South Africa such a threat arose. In April 1993, Chris Hani, a popular ANC leader, was assassinated by an immigrant from Poland, a member of the right-wing Afrikaner Weerstandsbeweging. The assassin was captured after an Afrikaner woman telephoned the police, providing his license plate number. Nelson Mandela and Frederik Willem de Klerk quickly acted together to isolate the event and move the transformation forward. Mandela spoke that evening on national television to prevent the negotiations under way from being derailed, saying,

> Tonight I am reaching out to every single South African, black and white, from the very depths of my being. A white man, full of prejudice and hate, came to our country and committed a deed so foul that our whole nation now teeters on the brink of disaster. A white woman, of Afrikaner origin, risked her life so that we may know, and bring to justice this assassin. . . . Now is the time for all South Africans to stand together against those who, from whatever quarter, wish to destroy what Chris Hani gave his life for—the freedom of all of us.[53]

The ANC organized protest demonstrations to allow for nonviolent expressions of anger and resentment; and the government, for its part, arrested a member of the Conservative Party in connection with the murder.

Long Term

Among the many ways to foster de-escalation from sharp escalations is to develop institutions and procedures that constrain escalation. This may take the form of improving communication between the adversaries, making it swifter and better understood. For example, in 2004 India and Pakistan created a hotline that provides a direct and immediate connection between the foreign ministries of each country in order to reduce the threat of a nuclear confrontation.

Another long-term strategy is to develop groups, networks, or organizations that include persons from opposing sides, often engaging primary representatives or their advisors. Their getting to know each other reduces the likelihood of misunderstandings that may exacerbate emerging conflicts. Such cross-cutting networks also provide channels for quickly considering alternative paths out of a sharp escalation when it occurs. For example, many communities have labor-management councils and interreligious and interethnic dialogue groups for these very purposes. Such organizations also exist in international relations and have played a role in the transformation of the U.S.-Soviet conflict. The Pugwash movement and the Dartmouth meetings are particularly noteworthy in this regard.[54]

In addition, confidence-building measures (CBMs) were developed in East-West relations in Europe to reduce the chances of sharp escalations. These measures included each side notifying the other in advance of large-scale military maneuvers and each side allowing representatives of the other to observe the maneuvers. Such measures provided reassurance, avoided misunderstandings, and thus contributed to the end of the Cold War. These methods have been discussed and to some extent implemented between other sets of international and domestic adversaries.[55]

Finally, of course, a basic policy for the prevention of conflicts from escalating destructively is to prevent provocative acts from happening. General agreements, even among unfriendly parties, can implement methods to reduce or even stop particular provocative actions. For example, politically motivated airplane hijackings were widespread in the 1960s, but they were greatly reduced by improved security measures at airports and by international agreements to deny havens to hijackers. Such measures, however, are not so effective against hijackers who plan to commit suicide.

From Protracted Struggle

Many large-scale conflicts persist generation after generation, appearing to be intractable; they persist in self-perpetuating ways with varying degrees of destructiveness. We will discuss some of the many strategies that enable adversaries to move out of such conflicts and into more constructive ways of conducting or of resolving their fights.

Short Term

Even profound and long-term conflict transformations have small beginnings, so tactical policies are crucial in initiating and sustaining long-term change. A fundamental issue in protracted struggles is that at least one side feels that its basic interests are threatened and it must fight on to sustain them. A crucial step in turning away from such fears is for at least one side to undertake actions that counter those feelings. When such actions are made on a reciprocal basis, appear credible, and seem irreversible, then the seemingly intractable conflict is in transition. Large variations in such actions exist among the three cases of intractable conflicts discussed here. The transformation in U.S.-Soviet relations that brought about the end of the Cold War occurred very unevenly over many years. There were periods of thaw and with them the normalization of some aspects of U.S.-Soviet relations; specific actions of both sides and the treaties they signed indicated accepting each other's continuing survival and even mutual recognition of superpower status. But occasions of intensified antagonism also arose, as happened after the Soviet invasion of Afghanistan in 1979. The subsequent renewal of Cold War rhetoric and conduct by the Reagan administration was brief, largely confined to his first term.

The threat to each other's collective existence was felt most intensely by the Israeli Jews and the Palestinians. For decades, officials of each did not recognize the other's legitimacy and would not meet with each other. The PLO, under the leadership of Chairman Arafat, gradually moderated its goals so that it came to accept the continuing existence of a Jewish state in Palestine. The Israeli government, even while led by the nationalist Likud Party, came to acknowledge the existence of a Palestinian people, though it continued to resist negotiating with the PLO as the representative of the Palestinians. The Israeli political leaders had for decades characterized the PLO as a terrorist organization, so their mutual recognition, manifested in the signing of the Declaration of Principles (DOP) and the handshake of Chairman Arafat and Prime Minister Yitzhak Rabin on September 13, 1993, were transforming events.[56] However, the transformation failed to be sustained.

In South Africa, too, whites and blacks lived together, but blacks generally felt that their basic rights were denied to them collectively and individually, while whites generally felt that to recognize those rights would undermine their own existence in the country. Yet, here too, many steps were taken that enabled leaders of each side, finally, to undertake direct, problem-solving negotiations. Notable among those early steps was the 1990 unconditional release of Nelson Mandela, the leader of the previously banned ANC, after twenty-seven years in prison. The release was celebrated in public ceremonies that made the commitment to peaceful negotiations appear irreversible. Public spectacles and media events are useful in making such commitments enduring.[57] Furthermore, Frederik Willem de Klerk expressed regrets and apologized for the harm done to blacks by whites in South Africa by apartheid, which was certainly a major conciliatory gesture that enhanced his credibility among the blacks.

Policies that build support for de-escalation among members of the adversary parties also are necessary for transforming large-scale intractable conflicts, particularly communal ones, which are especially dependent on the sentiments of the rank-and-file members of the opposing sides. Leaders of major institutions as well as members of grassroots organizations often do undertake such policies. The mobilization effort may be part of a long-term policy or a short-term effort to rally support for a particular action. Mobilization may be attempted, for example, by social movement organizations arranging a demonstration or a campaign against officials reluctant to change. Ceremonies and celebrations provide other ways to mobilize and sustain support for the transformation process. Officials may also hold a referendum to gain constituent support and campaign to get it. This was done, for example, in South Africa, and the government won a referendum in March 1992, in which only whites voted, to negotiate the end of white minority rule.

Of course, significant internal opposition to ending a protracted conflict, on terms not unilaterally imposed, is very likely. Once the transition toward a joint solution has begun, opposition often intensifies, and how leaders handle that opposition to continuing with de-escalating moves is crucial. They may attempt to suppress it, placate it, or co-opt it, with varying degrees of success.[58] Yet, having entered this path, the leaders of both sides have a mutual interest in helping their negotiating partners stay in power and maintain support from their constituents. This poses a fundamental dilemma. The leaders must reassure their own followers that the course taken will yield what they want and convince their opponents that they will not lose what is critical for them.

In South Africa, de Klerk and Mandela, each facing challenges from within their camps, used a wide array of tactics to maintain credibility with the opposing side, to mobilize support from their own side, and to block disruptive actions by opponents of accommodation. Opposition to the movement toward resolving the struggle in South Africa, nevertheless, included many threats and acts of violence.

Indeed, when the transition toward nonracial democracy began in 1990, political violence soared. From mid-1990, when negotiations for the transition began, to April 1994, when elections were held, about 14,000 South Africans died in politically related incidents.[59] Some deaths arose from the use of lethal force by security forces in public order policing, but much of the violence arose among black groups, particularly between two ethnic groups, the Xhosa and the Zulu, and two political organizations, the ANC and the Inkatha Freedom Party (IFP), associated with the Zulu. A "third force," consisting of right-wing white elements linked to the government security forces, supported violence perpetrated by some of the IFP. According to the Truth and Reconciliation (TRC) Report, the government began the transition in a de facto alliance with the IFP, which it abandoned in June 1992.

The extensive violence threatened the democratic transformation of South Africa and its social stability. Appeals to stop the violence and even the meetings of Mandela and other ANC leaders with Mangosuthu Buthelezi and other IFP leaders were ineffective. No single person or organization could stop the violence or even was accorded the legitimacy to convene a conference that might formulate a way to end it. Only the South African Council of Churches and the Consultative Business Movement, acting together, were able to call such a conference. They formed a facilitating committee and invited representatives of all major groups in the society to a closed meeting on June 22, 1991. A preparatory committee was selected that established five working groups and tasked them to write reports for the National Peace Convention to meet on September 14, 1991. The reports were discussed at the convention and the result was the National Peace Accord (NPA). Twenty-seven government, political, and trade union leaders signed the NPA; three white right-wing parties did not participate; and two Africanist groups on the left declined to sign but declared their support for the objectives of the accord.

Thus the NPA not only presented a vision of democracy, peace, and stability for South Africa but also established a national network of structures to attain those objectives. It included a code of conduct for political parties and organizations, a code of conduct for security forces, a national peace committee, a national peace secretariat, regional and local dispute resolution committees, a commission of inquiry regarding the prevention of public violence and intimidation, socioeconomic reconstruction and development, and a police board. These structures provided settings for persons from opposing sides to get to know each other and to work together at the national, regional, and local levels.

A contrasting picture emerged during the Israeli-Palestinian de-escalation phase of 1993–1999, when the leadership of both sides faced intense challenges. For example, following the announcement of the DOP in September 1993, Chairman Arafat was bitterly attacked by many Palestinians for negotiating the agreement privately and even more fundamentally for surrendering so much to the Israelis. Strong opposition was mounted by an organization rivaling the PLO, the Islamic-based organization Hamas. On the other side, Prime Minister Rabin was criticized for risking too much; he was opposed vigorously by the Likud Party and by some of the Jewish settlers in the occupied territories. For a variety of reasons, leaders on neither side had acted decisively enough to overcome dissent from within their camp, as had the leaders in South Africa.[60] That eroded each side's ability to sustain support for the long-term de-escalating strategy they had formally embraced.

Many Israeli critics of the Oslo peace process vilified Prime Minister Rabin, condemning him as a traitor to the Jewish people. The attacks intensified until his assassination in October 1995 by a Jewish religious extremist. His assassination shocked nearly all Israelis. Those who had been particularly vehement in the denunciations of Rabin and the peace process initially were somewhat marginalized, and the new prime minister, Shimon Peres, led the government in a speedy implementation of the interim agreement that had been signed shortly before Rabin was killed.[61]

To make progress in the de-escalating transformation of the Cold War, opposition in the Soviet Union and in the United States had to be overcome. When Gorbachev was chosen to head the Communist Party and the Soviet government early in 1985, his initial actions were not radical.[62] When he did initiate significant changes domestically and internationally, he encountered some popular resistance in the Soviet Union. The initial response in the United States was great skepticism and resistance to reciprocation by the traditional Cold Warriors in the Reagan administration and outside it. But the earlier widespread opposition to the Reagan administration's renewed Cold War policies offered alternative responses, and President Ronald Reagan himself was ready to quickly recognize the changed Soviet stance, even crediting his own earlier militant policy as a cause.[63]

Particularly in seemingly intractable struggles, when the adversaries are frozen in mistrust, mediators and other intermediaries often play critical roles in facilitating de-escalating negotiations. In the Israeli-Arab-Palestinian conflict, the U.S. government has often played such mediating roles. This has included helping to construct a formula that would enable adversaries to begin negotiations, a particularly challenging task when the opposing parties do not recognize each other and therefore do not officially meet. Thus, the U.S. government, following the first war against Iraq, sought to initiate comprehensive peace negotiations between the Israeli government and the neighboring Arab governments as well as the Palestinians. After much shuttle diplomacy, Secretary of State Baker and his associates constructed a complex negotiation formula. It consisted of three arenas for negotiation: first, a general conference (preferred by Arab governments), then, bilateral meetings between Israel and each neighboring Arab government (long sought by the Israelis), followed by regional meetings on issues of common concern such as water, security, and refugees (to provide a wider mix of countries and matters of possible mutual benefit). Palestinians were represented within the Jordanian delegation, and their relationship to the PLO was veiled. The general conference was held briefly in Madrid in October 1991; bilateral negotiations followed, as did the regional meetings somewhat later. A breakthrough of sorts had been achieved, but progress then languished until the Israeli government changed in the election of June 1992, when the ruling Likud Party was defeated by the Labor Party, led by Rabin.

Making little progress in bilateral negotiations between the Israelis and the Palestinians (but only indirectly with the PLO), a back channel for negotiations was secretly opened.[64] The negotiations began in unofficial conversations between Yair Hirschfeld, an Israeli Jewish academic, and Abu Alaa, a prominent PLO official and Arafat's director of finances.[65] Their first secret meeting was in London in December 1992, arranged by the Norwegian Terje Rod Larsen. Hirschfeld's previous contacts with Palestinians and with Israeli government officials made the meeting possible and hopeful. Soon the Norwegian government was supporting small regular meetings between Hirschfeld and the historian Ron Pundik, with Alaa and two aides, Hassan Asfour and Maher al Kurd. The Israelis sent reports of their meetings to Yossi Beilin, the new deputy foreign minister, who read them but offered no advice. The small group, in intensive discussions, developed the idea of a joint declaration of principles envisaging free elections in the occupied territories and the gradual establishment of Palestinian authority. Beilin informed Foreign Minister Peres and Prime Minister Rabin; Peres was enthusiastic and Rabin skeptical but open to new suggestions. Later, Israeli officials joined the talks and the intense negotiations continued until the DOP was initialed on August 20, 1993. By giving their tacit, but secret, go-ahead, both the PLO and Israeli leadership could explore and construct the formula for a major peacemaking move without arousing internal resistance until a deal had been struck.

Long Term

Moving out of large-scale, protracted struggles, barring one side's collapse, generally takes a long time. Many small steps usually must be taken before more significant ones can be made. The effectiveness of each action is likely to be enhanced if actions are considered as a series of steps along a path toward a shared objective. In addition, to be effective in large-scale struggles many de-escalating actions often must be taken by many elements of the opposing sides and by intermediaries in mutually supportive ways and in an appropriate sequence.

Two different strategies partisans may adopt to change from a confrontational relationship to a more cooperative one warrant discussion. One is graduated reciprocation in tension-reduction (GRIT), as set forth by Charles E. Osgood, and the other is a tit-for-tat (TFT) strategy, as discussed in the work of Anatol Rapoport and of Robert Axelrod.[66] Using the GRIT strategy, one of the parties in conflict unilaterally initiates a series of cooperative moves; these are announced and reciprocity is invited, but the conciliatory moves continue for an extended period, whether or not there is immediate reciprocity. GRIT was first prescribed in the early 1960s as a strategy for the United States to induce reciprocation from the Soviet Union.

While GRIT strategy was inferred from social psychological theory and research, the TFT strategy was derived from game theory, particularly work on the prisoners' dilemma (PD) game. The strategy reasons that in a series of PD games, the payoffs are cumulative and the player's strategy can be based on the other player's prior behavior. Experimental research and computer simulations of iterated games of PD indicate that cooperative relations often emerge, and the most successful strategy for developing cooperative relations and yielding the highest overall payoff is for one player to initiate the series of games by acting cooperatively and afterward simply reciprocating the other player's actions, whether a cooperative or a noncooperative action.

Analysts have assessed these strategies by examining actual de-escalating interactions, particularly in the protracted U.S.-Soviet conflict. For example, Amitai Etzioni interprets the de-escalation in U.S.-Soviet antagonism in 1963 as an illustration of the GRIT strategy.[67] He views it beginning with President Kennedy's June 10 speech at American University announcing a unilateral halt to the atmospheric testing of nuclear weapons; the Soviets reciprocated and other cooperative moves soon followed, including the signing of the Limited Nuclear Test Ban in August 1963. These initial moves, however, were to some extent orchestrated by indirect communication between President Kennedy and Premier Khrushchev.[68] The GRIT and the TFT explanations were compared in an analysis of reciprocity in relations between the United States and the Soviet Union, between the United States and the PRC, and between the Soviet Union and the PRC for the period 1948–1989.[69] It is ironic that GRIT was proposed by an American academic as a strategy to be undertaken by the U.S. government to break out of the Cold War, but it was a Soviet leader who undertook its most spectacular enactment. Gorbachev announced a change in policy toward the United States and Western Europe and made many conciliatory moves. It resulted in transforming relations with the United States, although initially, when the Soviets offered concessions, U.S. demands were raised. But Gorbachev's policy of saying "yes, yes" until the U.S. government could no longer say "no, no" successfully resulted in cooperative moves by the U.S. government. The Soviet's GRIT strategy also led to normalized relations with the PRC.

Another long-term de-escalation policy is to strengthen shared identities. This was important in the South African transformation where the many peoples of the country did share a salient South African identity. The ANC consistently proclaimed a nonracial policy, regarding whites as another African tribe. The Israelis and Palestinians, in contrast, have only a few, and relatively nonsalient, unifying identities—such as being Middle Eastern or having an Abrahamic faith. Moreover, as Zionism became state doctrine, it became exclusive, insisting that the Land of Israel is for Jews. Arab and Palestinian nationalism has tended to be exclusive as well, even if less sharply articulated than Zionism; but more recently, some Islamic activism has become quite exclusive.

Policies pursued by nongovernmental persons and organizations are also important in long-term de-escalating strategies. In South Africa, the gradual shift from confrontation to negotiation was fostered by changes in the white establishment's economic thinking. The increasing emphasis on the free market and efficiency undermined the wish to maintain white domination. Even blacks, if they shared the business ideology, were increasingly incorporated into the establishment, and this was regarded as a way of preserving the existing socioeconomic system. In December 1984, Hendrik W. van der Merwe, based at the University of Capetown, facilitated the first meeting of ANC officials and Afrikaner newspaper editors; it was held in Lusaka, Zambia. Then, in 1985 and 1986 "more than two dozen delegations of white and black South African businessmen, academics, church leaders and others met with the ANC in Lusaka."[70]

South African blacks used a variety of strategies to end apartheid and gain political rights in a unified South Africa. Generally, the strategies pursued were chosen with consideration of their effects on the long-term relationship between whites and blacks in South Africa. The ANC at the outset pursued a nonviolent strategy, but experiencing suppression, the decision was made in the early 1960s, with Mandela's urging, to sanction the formation of the Umkhonto we Sizwe (Spear of the Nation) to conduct an armed struggle. This led to the imprisonment of Mandela and the banning of the ANC in 1964. Mandela explains the kind of violence he advocated: "For a small and fledgling army, open revolution was inconceivable. Terrorism inevitably reflected poorly on those who used it. . . . Guerrilla warfare was a possibility, but since the ANC had been reluctant to embrace violence at all, it made sense to start with the form of violence that inflicted the least harm against individuals: sabotage. Because it did not involve loss of life it offered the best hope for reconciliation among the races afterward."[71] Mandela thus illustrates how violence can be modulated and constrained by long-term considerations.

Actually, the struggle waged by black South Africans was largely nonviolent, and it became more extensive and intensive in the 1980s.[72] The blacks carried out frequent labor union strikes to improve working conditions and withheld rent payments to force improvements in housing conditions. The United Democratic Front (UDF), established in 1983, emphasized the practical advantage of developing nonviolent options for resisting the state. UDF affiliates actually began to replace state authority, as local structures provided administrative, judicial, welfare, and cultural services. Despite growing efforts at state repression, the decentralized network of local organizations persisted, and nonviolent resistance grew.

Paralleling the ANC strategy in South Africa, the first Palestinian intifada was largely nonviolent.[73] It included extensive boycotts of Israeli products and the development of alternative economic and social structures. The stone throwing by the youth provided drama that won media attention, and knives and guns were not to be used. But in the opinion of Israeli Jews, the intifada was a challenge to the occupation and stone throwing was extremely violent, threatening their lives when driving in the occupied territories. The Israeli military response to the stone throwing generated the image seen around the world of soldiers catching Palestinian youth, beating them, and breaking their bones. This was effective in gaining attention and sympathy for the Palestinians, but it further embittered their relations with the Jews.

It needs to be emphasized that efforts by segments within an adversary group to influence the leadership's policy toward the group's common opponent are also important. For example, after Sadat's visit to Jerusalem in November 1977, the Peace Now social movement arose within Israel to pressure the Likud-led Israeli government to be more forthcoming in its negotiations with the Egyptians.[74] Opposing groups pressured the Israeli government not to yield land held by Israel to the Palestinians; notable among such groups were those of religiously motivated settlers, such as the Gush Emunim, discussed in chapter 5.

Sometimes even the dominant faction in an adversary party can be the source of long-term policies to bring about fundamental changes in relations with its opponent. Dramatically, this was the case in the Soviet Union starting in 1985 with the ascension to power of Gorbachev. He and his associates believed that reform of the Soviet system was necessary to sustain itself as a superpower. The changes they instigated were not widely popular and indeed were not radical, but they did create the opportunity for those who desired reform to generate pressure for more change. Clearly, the forces for change soon gained enough strength to transform the Soviet Union, and they could not be stopped.

Finally, it should be noted that the failure to control and coordinate action sometimes undermines de-escalation once it has been undertaken. Insofar as the struggle has generated hostility and mistrust between the antagonists, de-escalating efforts must be clear and consistent to be effective. Internal opponents of a de-escalation policy, however, may attack the policy and its advocates in extreme ways and even attempt to sabotage it, making consistency more difficult. Policy opponents may violently attack the adversary and so provoke responses that will escalate the conflict again. Leaders in the de-escalation effort may try to placate the internal opposition in order to retain credibility with their constituents, but doing that then undermines their credibility with members of the other side.

The Israeli-Palestinian peacemaking efforts following the 1993 DOP provide many examples of the difficulties of resolving these dilemmas and the tragedies of failing to do so.[75] Many steps were taken to fulfill the promise of the DOP, including the establishment of the Palestinian Authority (PA) in Gaza and Jericho in 1994, Palestinian elections, and steps of Israeli-Palestinian security cooperation.

The skeptics and opponents on both sides remained unconvinced by the progress that was made, and even the initial widespread support for the Oslo process gradually declined, on both sides. The essence of the Oslo bargain was security for Jews in Israel and a state for Palestinians, but supporters on each side began to question the realization of that bargain. Many Palestinians did not find their life greatly improved and resented the continuing growth of Jewish settlements in the occupied territories, the construction of more bypass roads linking the settlements, harassment, and restrictions on their movement. All this raised their doubts of ever achieving a viable Palestinian state. For their part, many Israeli Jews were concerned at the failure of the PA to stop fomenting anti-Israeli feelings and to stop extremist groups from conducting terrorist actions. This raised their doubts that the existence of Israel was truly accepted.

The PA and the Israeli government headed by Rabin, nevertheless, continued negotiating and making agreements. In September 1995, an interim agreement was signed for Israel to transfer control of the major areas of Palestinian population to the PA. Although Rabin was assassinated the next month, Peres, who succeeded Rabin as prime minister, moved quickly to implement the agreement. At the same time, the Israeli government demonstrated its toughness in January 1996 by assassinating Yahya Ayyash, a Hamas leader held responsible for some suicide bombings. In response, Hamas launched a series of suicide bombings that in five days killed more than sixty persons. Subsequently, in the May 1996 Israeli elections, Benjamin Netanyahu, the leader of the hard-line Likud Party who claimed he would bring security to Israel, was elected prime minister. He then stalled the peace process. Thus we see that even within the context of de-escalating movement, episodes of violent escalation may occur. In an escalating exchange, each side's militancy bolsters the hard-liners in the opposing camp and undermines the developing de-escalation.

This pattern was repeated even more devastatingly after the Israeli electorate rejected Netanyahu and elected Ehud Barak as prime minister in the elections of May 1999. Barak soon moved to begin negotiations with the PLO to conclude a comprehensive peace agreement. He put matters that had not been broached as part of official negotiations on the negotiating table, notably the status of Jerusalem and limits to the number of Palestinians who could enter Israel to live there. As discussed in the next chapter, even with U.S. mediation, these negotiations failed as a new violent intifada erupted.

Outside actors often foster de-escalation, for diverse reasons. They may do this as interested parties to support groups they favor or to stop what they regard as abhorrent conditions.

The United Nations, the United States, and many IGOs and nongovernmental organizations increasingly pressured the South African government with sanctions relating to trade, investment, and participation in cultural and sports events. These sanctions impacted not only the government but also the people in South Africa. The impacts were unequally borne and had a variety of effects, but they contributed to a widespread feeling among whites of being isolated and beleaguered. Blacks were encouraged by the external support, even though they also suffered economic strains.[76]

The Israeli government was subjected to pressure in the UN General Assembly; but generally, the U.S. government led in foiling sanctions, arguing that the Israeli government needed security reassurances so that it would feel safe enough to make concessions.

Intermediaries also often pursue long-term de-escalating strategies. These include actions to develop better mutual understanding and to foster recognition of possible mutual interests; the actions may be organizing dialogue groups and problem-solving workshops. They may also entail large-scale assistance programs to help develop institutions for managing social conflicts or to help reduce economic problems.

Intermediaries have played important roles in the transformation of U.S.-Soviet relations, but that is not widely acknowledged in the United States. For example, the CSCE, which formulated the Helsinki accords signed in 1975 by thirty-five countries including the United States, contributed immensely to the transformation of the Cold War. The neutral and nonaligned countries represented at the CSCE meetings played important roles in negotiating the agreement.[77]

CONCLUSIONS

This chapter examined the processes, conditions, and policies that affect how conflicts move toward settlement. As table 7.1 illustrates, the pathways for conflict de-escalation tend to take three forms and are driven by three different kinds of de-escalation processes: one party simply imposing its will on another; one or both parties engaging in a series of conciliatory probes and gestures; and an external actor prompting both parties to move into a de-escalatory process.

Success is never guaranteed when it comes to conflict de-escalation. As this chapter has illustrated, within each of the possible paths numerous developments can scuttle de-escalatory advances. Conciliatory probes and gestures may be unrecognized or go unanswered. Externally mediated or imposed processes often fail, and, as will be discussed in chapter 11, coercive, conciliatory, or externally driven de-escalatory processes often result in agreements that are not sustainable in the long term.

The choice of de-escalating policies should be contingent upon the goals sought and the existing circumstances if they are to be effective. It is easier and certainly less costly to the antagonists to avoid destructive escalation in the first place than to attempt de-escalation after the conflict has been raging for a long time. But there may also be costs to taking actions before a conflict has visibly deteriorated. For potential intermediaries, de-escalating interventions may seem unnecessary, or at least difficult to mobilize support for. Furthermore, the preventive action may fail and those undertaking it are likely to bear the blame for further deterioration. For representatives of one of the adversaries, the risks and costs of premature de-escalation are even greater. They are likely to appear weak and be accused of losing what they might have won if only the struggle had been continued and even intensified. A better understanding of ways to escalate and de-escalate a fight constructively can contribute to reducing those risks and costs.

Of course, de-escalation strategies, even constructive ones, are not implemented smoothly, since no party is wholly in charge and none gets all that it wants. Each party has many components, and the policies pursued by an adversary are manifold and often inconsistent. At the same time, the fundamental external conditions keep changing. Consequently, de-escalating transformations are usually long processes and do not move in a unidirectional fashion. Indeed, that a transformation has actually occurred is frequently recognizable only retrospectively.

The analysis here also suggests that an important component of successful de-escalating policies is envisioning a new relationship between the adversaries. This may be the result of new ways of thinking, perhaps arising from changes within one or more adversaries, changes in the concrete broader situation, and changes in the relationship between the adversaries. After all, conflicts are socially constructed, and they often can be restructured and reframed so they become a shared problem that requires a joint solution.

Such visions may be expressed in new ways of conducting the relationship between the erstwhile enemies. They may also be expressed in alterations in the set of parties primarily engaged in the conflict and its resolution, excluding intransigent parties or including accommodative new parties. The addition of accommodative new parties is particularly manifest in the interventions of intermediaries, discussed in the next chapter.

The de-escalation process most effectively proceeds in a broad step-by-step fashion, preparing for and sustaining any agreements reached. What is also especially important is that the changes be done consistently and unequivocally, be in depth, and not be attempts to squeeze as much as possible from the adversary. For leaders in each party, however, it is important to balance consideration of relations with adversaries with concern for their own constituents. Maintaining the support of their constituents is critical, but that is best thought of in terms of the constituents' long-term interests. In actuality, de-escalations of large-scale conflicts often stall and regress, which requires skill and determination to overcome.

A basic finding of this analysis is that transforming transitions come about when a new way of thinking about their conflict becomes dominant in each of the primary adversaries. They each come to believe that the strategy they had been pursuing cannot triumph or they cannot gain more by continuing it, while an accommodative strategy promises better alternatives. This is a more general statement than the suggestion that a negotiated settlement is reached when the adversaries are in a hurting stalemate and a formula for a settlement seems possible and acceptable.[78]

While force and coercion are sometimes critical, the evidence here is that the de-escalation of intractable conflicts is not necessarily the result of immutable, large-scale forces or of the actions of a few brave and wise persons. Many circumstances need to converge, and these must be combined with new interpretations in order for a seemingly intractable conflict to pass beyond a transition favoring de-escalation and become fundamentally transformed. Resistance and reversals are likely, and they too must be overcome.

8

Mediation in Conflicts

In the previous chapter we briefly introduced mediation as an important and frequently used tool for conflict de-escalation. In this chapter we look in detail at mediation: what it entails, what different forms it takes, and its uses and limitations as a conflict transformation tool. That we have a separate chapter on mediation in this book reflects the central role that it plays in contemporary conflict management. Just a few decades ago mediation as a formal conflict management method was limited largely to labor-management relations. Today, mediation is applied across virtually all conflict domains from international relations to environmental disputes to interethnic relations to divorce proceedings and to fights among students.[1] Many communities in the United States have institutionalized mediation programs as a central component of the justice system, and mediation is often viewed as a way to enhance civic engagement and empower citizens.

MEDIATION DEFINED

Mediation is a conflict management process whereby an outsider intervenes in a conflict to help the adversaries to negotiate an agreement themselves.[2] Mediators are generally expected to help the adversaries construct a mutually acceptable agreement and to avoid being advocates for one side or one solution. As such, mediation differs from arbitration, where the intermediary formulates the terms of a conflict's settlement; often the disputants agreeing in advance that they will abide by the arbitrator's decision. It also differs from other kinds of intermediary activities, such as fact-finding or conciliation, in which the intermediary plays a much less active role and which does not require interaction among the disputing parties. Although this chapter is focused on mediation, other kinds of intervention also are discussed later in the chapter, as they are associated with and sometimes supportive of intermediary services, including mediation.

Advocates of mediation argue that it has many advantages over traditional power and rights-based approaches to conflict management.[3] Many argue that it contributes to speeding an escape from a destructive struggle, that it is more efficient and less costly than litigation, that it helps the parties reach an agreement that reflects a broader range of interests than would otherwise be apparent, and that it increases the likelihood that an agreement between the adversaries is fair and enduring.[4] During times of international crisis mediation appears to increase the likelihood of achieving agreement, reduces the length of the crisis, and increases the partisan's satisfaction with the outcome.[5]

Specific mediation activities vary with the conflict stage. As the conflict emerges, they may include transmitting information between the adversaries about the risks of escalation and possible options for preventing destructive escalation. Keeping lines of communication open and utilized is an important activity as a conflict emerges and begins to intensify. Once a conflict escalates mediators may be called in to provide an informal and/or unofficial venue for communication between partisan leaders that might not be possible at the official level. As conflicts de-escalate mediation can lend legitimacy to an adversary party that is excluded from negotiations to reach a settlement. For example, in 1994 and 1995, when negotiations about the status of Northern Ireland were stalled, President Bill Clinton met with Gerry Adams, the leader of Sinn Fein, thereby raising Adams's status and helping him enter negotiations. In November 1994, Clinton visited Northern Ireland and was welcomed by enthusiastic crowds. These actions spurred negotiations by throwing a bright light on the situation and the wide support to reach a settlement. Finally, when the adversaries in a struggle move to settle their fight, they may be open to a wide variety of mediating activities. These include convening meetings, facilitating communication, suggesting options, and mobilizing support for the agreement to be reached. Mediators may also be enlisted to provide various kinds of guarantees that make it more likely that agreements will be sustainable in the long term.

Services

Mediators perform a wide range of activities to help parties transform a conflict. The specific services provided are a product of the stage of the conflict, the degree of hostility held by each side toward the other, and the conditions that either favor or make less likely constructive interaction among them.

Provide Opportunities for Communication

An important, and minimally intrusive, mediating service is to provide a place for adversaries or their representatives to meet. Sometimes adversaries want to meet to explore possible de-escalating moves but do not want this known until they work out an understanding about the move. This was the case for the 1993 meetings between the Palestine Liberation Organization (PLO) and Israelis in Oslo. Sometimes each adversary prefers not to meet in the other's space, fearing that it would appear to be the supplicant. A neutral location avoids that symbolic loss of face.

A helpful service for enemies who refuse to communicate directly with each other is to discretely transmit messages between them. A mediator may provide a channel for indirect communication, for example, by traveling between the enemy camps without public attention. Other times, however, one side of a conflict may wish to use a mediator in a very public way in order to gain attention, recognition, or status. This appears to be the case with North Korea's use of former U.S. presidents Jimmy Carter and Bill Clinton to help it resolve various political crises with the United States over the last decade.

Provide Information

As a struggle escalates, the antagonists are increasingly likely to misinterpret each other's actions and words, exaggerating the hostility and intransigence. It is difficult to cross those barriers, so transmitting information from one side to another with relatively little distortion can contribute significantly to constructive de-escalation. Information about how the struggle is viewed by the other side is an essential component of constructive de-escalation. The information conveyed may be about the other side's readiness to de-escalate, the terms of a possible settlement, or the risks of escalating the struggle.

Providing such information so that representatives of each side can hear it from and about the other requires that the transmitter have the confidence of both sides. It may require considerable skill on the part of the mediator, for example, making the transmission more acceptable by omitting particularly provocative elements of the message or by explaining the context from the other side's point of view.

Information gathered by an intermediary may be presented as facts or rules that can be used to help settle disputes. Such fact-finding services may be sought and the findings accepted by disputants.[6] For example, in a labor-management conflict, information presented by one side about prevailing wages and working conditions may be contested, while independently presented information is more likely to be accepted.

Help Adversaries to Enter Negotiations

Where conflicting parties have little or no interaction or trust, mediation can be used as a conduit to "soften up" hardened positions and make way for formal negotiations later on.[7] In these cases one or both parties may explicitly ask for mediation assistance as they struggle to find viable avenues for peacemaking. The Basque separatist group ETA, for instance, followed up their September 2010 truce with the Spanish government with a request for international mediation to permanently end the conflict in the Basque region.

Various mediating activities can also help adversaries undertake negotiations by making success seem more likely and by reducing the costs of failure. Mediators can explore with representatives of the antagonists what set of negotiating partners, agenda, and context would make negotiation seem worth trying. The formula for negotiations, presented by the mediator, is likely to have more appeal and legitimacy than if proposed by one of the partisans alone. This is illustrated by the effectiveness of Secretary of State James Baker in arranging the comprehensive 1991 Middle East peace conference held in Madrid.

Mediation can reduce the risks for adversaries of entering into negotiations with each other in several ways. The adversaries generally indicate to the mediator that they are serious in their effort to find a mutually acceptable settlement, and that becomes a kind of commitment to the mediator, aside from any commitment they may make to each other.

In addition, mediators may help determine who the negotiating partners will be. The choice of parties to be engaged in any de-escalating effort involves three competing principles. One is to exclude the intransigents so a deal can be made. The second is to include all those who have the capability to disrupt an agreement if one is reached. The third is to maximize participation by all those with a stake in the outcome. Difficult choices often must be made about the relative weight given to each principle, but the choice can change after the initial negotiations are undertaken, as has happened in regard to Northern Ireland.

Some external actors have the authority to simply convene a meeting of the adversaries or invite themselves to talk to each party and transmit information. Thus, the secretary general of the United Nations can interject himself into a conflict even when one or more sides would prefer no such intervention. The president of the United States may convene a meeting that one or more parties regard as untimely. This was the case when President Clinton called Israel and the Palestinian Authority to come to Camp David in July 2000, although Yassir Arafat had told him he was not ready for such a meeting.[8] Domestically, national and local governmental officials often have the authority to intervene and bring opponents together to settle their dispute.

Help Penetrate Social-Emotional Barriers

Mediators and other intermediaries may act in many ways that help lessen the hostile feelings and antagonizing interactions that hamper members of one side accurately perceiving the other side or believing that its leaders are trustworthy. A mediator sometimes meets with each side privately, sympathetically listening to expressions of anger, hate, or fear. Members of an adversary party, having vented such emotions out of the enemy's hearing, are then better able to carry on without showing such feelings and provoking the other side.

Mediation also includes making suggestions that help build mutual appreciation between the adversary representatives. Thus, a mediator may suggest to one side that it make a unilateral gesture or symbolic gift that would be difficult for the other side to misinterpret. Gestures as simple as acknowledging the bravery of persons in the adversary camp or recognizing their sacrifices may be moving and effective in de-escalating a conflict. Such gestures can win the adversary's attention and prompt a fresh look at the other side.

Mediators may introduce methods that help penetrate social-emotional barriers.[9] They can set interaction rules that enable disputants to discuss differences, yet minimize adversarial argument. They may suggest that representatives from each side take turns listening to each other and summarizing what the other side's representative said. The exercise improves hearing what the other side says and also enhances the other side's feeling that it has been heard. Another, less formal, technique is to work together on some collective task (preparing a meal or arranging an excursion) and having teams with members from different sides undertake various aspects of the task.

Help Stop Deterioration

If a conflict persists in escalation, it generally rises in destructiveness. Mediation services can help halt further conflict deterioration by assisting adversaries to envisage a possible settlement option that is better than continuing the ongoing level of fighting. More coercive interventions also can sometimes help stop the deterioration, perhaps freezing the conflict until a more opportune time develops to move toward a substantive de-escalation. Interveners may impose sanctions that raise the costs of escalating violence or may intercede to help implement a cease-fire agreed upon by the antagonists. The numerous UN peacekeeping missions exemplify this kind of service. In some domestic arenas, such as labor-management disputes, institutionalized arrangements may provide for cooling-off periods in which escalations such as lockouts or strikes are not allowed for a fixed period of time.

Save Face

Once in a fight, each side finds it difficult to appear to accept the ideas of the enemy. If a mediator voices an idea, it can be accepted without seeming to yield to the adversary. Furthermore, the idea may be accepted out of respect for the mediators or in deference to the relationship with them. Recognizing these considerations, an adversary, rather than offer an idea on its own, sometimes suggests that the mediator make it.[10] Similarly, a commitment can be made to a mediator without appearing to bow meekly to an opponent's demands.[11] To illustrate, in the 1973 negotiations between the Israeli and Egyptian governments mediated by Henry Kissinger, the Israelis wanted a commitment from Egypt to reopen the Suez Canal and allow Israeli shipping to use the canal. President Anwar al-Sadat, not willing to appear to be limiting Egyptian sovereignty, refused. The commitment to allow passage was made to the U.S. government, which conveyed this commitment to the Israeli government.[12]

Another way for adversaries to save face is to have the mediator take the blame for a mistake. If something goes wrong in the negotiation arrangements, the relationship between the adversaries is less likely to be damaged if the mediator accepts responsibility than if one of the adversaries is accused of a blunder or a deception.

Change Procedures

Negotiators sometimes become frozen in unproductive procedures, and suggesting new procedures may break the impasse. Bringing in high-ranking representatives of the opposing sides, who have more authority to take new positions than lower-level negotiators, is a significant procedural change. Or difficult issues frequently are delegated to specialists on the issues in contention to discuss options in small working groups. Establishing small negotiation groups to work on a subset of issues is a way to fractionate a conflict, resolving pieces of the total conflict one at a time.

Altering seating arrangements may affect social interaction patterns, perhaps making them more informal. Altering the format, perhaps by having a facilitator, in addition to a chair, can change the style of discussion.[13] The facilitator moderates the discussion of proposals, at first allowing only clarifying questions. The facilitator then summarizes what has and has not been agreed to, setting the stage for new proposals to deal with the matters not yet in agreement.

Help Invent New Options

Once a conflict has persisted or has become severe, the adversaries tend to become locked into the positions they have previously staked out. Each side sees the other's preferred outcome as unacceptable and thus sees continuing or escalating the struggle as better than accepting those terms. Mediators often can help reframe the struggle and suggest ways to construct new options for consideration.

Mediators can sometimes be more inventive than the opposing sides because they recognize more clearly the underlying interests that the negotiators for each side are trying to advance. Furthermore, they are not likely to be committed to the previous terms of settlement offered by the adversaries themselves and therefore are freer to think of new alternatives.

Mediation often helps adversaries themselves to think of new options. One way this is done is to bring together a few members of the opposing sides to informally discuss their relationship and identify a variety of possible solutions to the problem they face. This may occur in the context of problem-solving workshops, discussed later in this chapter. It may also be promoted by setting aside time for brainstorming. Members of the negotiating sides are encouraged to suggest possible solutions, putting aside likely difficulties in implementing them. The rule is to be imaginative and uncritical of one's own or of each other's suggestions. Only after many options have been mentioned can the necessary critical discussion begin.[14]

Finally, mediators may encourage a different style of discussion.[15] For example, when a person says "no, no, no" to a proposal from another party, the mediator may ask, "What if the other person had said such and such; would that be better?" Then, if the person says, "That's better, but it's not enough," the mediator may ask, "What would you add to improve it?" The idea is to show participants how to get beyond rejecting a proposal to thinking about how to make it acceptable.

Represent Persons Not Represented in the Negotiations

Conflicts generally affect many more parties than those represented in any set of negotiations, and those parties have a stake in the outcome. Mediators may be able to represent the more diffuse interests of others by upholding general norms of fairness or of human rights.[16] Mediators may also be expected to represent the interests of absent others, for example, the general public, consumers, taxpayers, or future generations.

Construct Deals

Often, mediation entails actively shuttling between opposing sides, learning what each side wants, what each will give up, and what each will not abandon. On that basis, a mediator may develop a possible settlement and propose it to the opposing sides. This may become the basis for further negotiations as the mediator modifies the proposed plan, taking into account the criticisms of each side. The mediator repeatedly modifies the plan and presents all negotiating parties this single negotiating text, which each side is asked to accept as a whole.[17] The mediator may be more or less active in formulating the proposals, varying from combining elements of the positions of both sides to creatively constructing a deal that he or she tries to sell.

Add Resources

Since expanding the size of the pie makes it easier to divide, mediators sometimes help the adversaries find additional resources that they can use. To illustrate, community groups contending about access to limited sport facilities may be encouraged to go together to city hall requesting increased facilities that they would share. Sometimes, the mediation can directly assist in those efforts.

Some mediators themselves contribute resources that sweeten the settlement deal, resources that none of the adversaries will or can credibly contribute to the settlement. Thus, in 1979 when an Israeli-Egyptian peace treaty was finally negotiated with the Egyptian government, the assistance to each side and the monitoring services promised and provided by the U.S. government were crucial in reaching and sustaining the agreement.

The explicit or implicit promise of assistance by external organizations, such as the United Nations or the European Union, to recover from the devastation of internal strife can encourage former adversaries to end their fight and reap benefits for doing so. Benefits may be targeted to gain the acquiescence of persons and groups who might be threatened by the conflict's outcome. Thus, external actors may promise them safety, and even funds they previously hid in other countries, as part of the agreement to end a civil conflict.[18] They may also facilitate post-conflict power-sharing agreements in order to further incentivize peacemaking. Each of the above is referred to in the literature as "commitment enhancing provisions" and are often found to make a difference in the durability of peace agreements.[19]

Finally, in domestic conflicts about environmental issues such as building a waste disposal facility, siting a wind farm, or drilling for natural gas, reaching an agreement may entail external assistance to reimburse persons who would have to move their homes. Sometimes in these cases a pool of funding is set aside as a result of the mediation process to protect citizens in the event of a future environmental claim. Other times resources are added by having developers agree to pay additional taxes to support public works, schools, or community projects as an "offset" to potential environmental damage down the road.[20]

Generate Pressures for an Agreement

Mediators sometimes pressure one or more of the adversaries to reach an agreement. One mild source of pressure is the obligation felt by the adversaries toward the mediators with whom the parties have a friendly relationship. Aware of the investment of time and the risk taken by the mediator by trying to help bring about a settlement, the adversaries frequently hesitate to abandon the negotiations, as this may seem disrespectful of the mediator's efforts.

Mediator pressure is sometimes much more direct. Time constraints may be imposed, as when the mediator sets a time to stop mediation in the near future. President Carter, for example, set a deadline for his mediation of the negotiations between President Sadat and Prime Minister Menachem Begin at Camp David.

The mediation pressure may be applied to one side more than another. One way this is done is to threaten public accusations that the failure to reach agreement is due to the intransigence of one party. In addition, a powerful mediator may more or less directly threaten to impose negative sanctions on the recalcitrant party.[21] Carrying out the threat, however, interferes with continuing to serve as a mediator afterward. Thus, when the Israeli-Palestinian negotiations at Camp David II in July 2000 failed to reach an agreement, President Clinton, who had mediated the negotiations, was critical of Arafat's failure to be more receptive to the Israeli offers. The Palestinian side felt it had been treated unfairly.

Rally Support for an Agreement

Mediation often provides support for an agreement, which helps give it legitimacy in the eyes of the negotiators' constituencies. A mediator may even testify how well the negotiators for each side strove to protect the interests of their respective constituencies.

Mediators, insofar as they represent a broader community, frequently are seen as validating the fairness of the agreement. Furthermore, the negotiating sides are likely to regard the mediator's engagement in the negotiations as helping to guarantee that the agreement reached will be honored, since the mediator has an interest in ensuring that its efforts appear successful.

In short, many mediating services can enhance the de-escalating process. These activities may speed initiating and concluding settlements and may contribute to the fairness of a resulting agreement and help ensure its implementation. Some activities, however, are difficult for the same person or group to perform simultaneously. Other activities are readily combined by the same person and tend to be carried out by incumbents of particular social roles.

SOCIAL ROLES

The mediation services reviewed above are, in fact, carried out by a wide variety of individuals and organizations with different resources, backgrounds, skills, degrees of neutrality, and levels of authority. Some mediators, for instance, represent states, others international organizations, others NGOs, and still others are simply private citizens. Some mediators bring with them formal powers to commit resources while others are private individuals with few resources to bring to the table. In this section numerous mediator and other intermediary roles are discussed, including roles that some analysts and practitioners do not regard as embodying true or good mediation. We begin with a discussion of the conditions and contexts that impact mediator neutrality. We then discuss the variety of mediator roles and the kinds of services they tend to provide. Next we discuss the factors that help shape the roles. We conclude with a discussion of ways to assess the impacts that mediators have on social conflicts.

Mediator Neutrality

The realities of mediator neutrality are often a matter of contention.[22] Many mediators and analysts of mediation stress that mediators should be neutral while playing mediator roles. Others argue that neutrality is not possible, and in any case is not necessary. Being trustworthy and honest with the disputants is sufficient to play the role effectively. To clarify this debate, we should recognize that neutrality in this context has a variety of meanings.

Neutrality of the mediator may refer to feelings and intentions, to conduct as perceived by the disputants or observers, or to effects on the disputants and the course of the conflict. Some mediators may be genuinely disinterested in the conflict or the disputants; this is more likely among mediators who play their role largely as facilitators. But even they may have strong interests in the use of particular processes and/or in reaching an agreement. Such concerns are likely to mean that whatever their neutrality about the dispute, their actions will have implications for the kind of settlement reached.

More often, the mediators are likely to have feelings and interests that are the bases for sympathy toward one party compared with another. How they act on such convictions, however, is another matter. Some may strive to act evenhandedly or to be an advocate for both sides, while others act to assist one side more than another or to advance their own interests.

In addition, how the disputants perceive the mediators' intentions and actions influences the mediators' effectiveness. Some mediators, with past histories of relations with one or more of the parties in a conflict, may be regarded as too biased or untrustworthy to serve as a mediator. In many circumstances, particularly for potential mediators with great resources, disputants do not expect or want disinterested neutrality. One or more sides may prefer a mediator who can enlarge the pie to be divided, who can leverage the other side, or who can ensure the compliance with any agreement reached. This is one of the attractions of U.S. official mediation for antagonists in the Middle East and in other regions.

Whatever the intentions or perceived conduct of mediators, the consequences of their efforts are not likely to be neutral. By their very act of mediation, they give some legitimacy to all the parties among whom they are mediating. Of course, this is a reason for a party that does not recognize the legitimacy of an opposing side to refuse mediation. This is particularly the case for official mediation. By according legitimacy, the mediators tend to provide a measure of equality, at least in rights, to the adversaries.

Finally, mediators may enhance adherence to societal and international norms about human rights and other principles of proper human relations.[23] Doing so can provide guidelines that help construct an acceptable agreement and also improve the quality and the durability of any agreement reached. Thus, the Organization for Security and Cooperation in Europe (OSCE) has a High Commissioner on National Minorities (HCNM) with the authority to intervene at the earliest possible stage in response to a crisis related to national minority issues that threaten international peace. Max van der Stoel, during his tenure as the first HCNM, 1993–2001, helped avert escalating conflicts and resolve them consistent with international norms. For example, this was accomplished by his quiet mediation regarding the language and education rights of the Hungarian minority in Romania and the citizenship rights of ethnic Russians in the newly independent Estonia.

Mediator Roles

Mediators play many different roles, at different times, and with different degrees of intrusiveness. Nine diverse roles are reviewed here.

Quasi Mediator

At one pole of the wide range of mediator roles are members of one of the adversary parties who carry out some go-between activities. They usually are not recognized as mediators and are referred to here as quasi mediators.[24] Nevertheless, they frequently convey information from the adversary back to their own side. In international relations, ambassadors are expected to inform their home government about the thinking of the government to which they are assigned. In the light of their insights, they may even suggest new options to their home government.

In the course of negotiations, one or more members of the negotiating team may explore the possibility of the other side accepting a particular option and then seek their own side's acceptance of the idea. They may help breach the barriers of mistrust within their side by testifying to the sincerity and trustworthiness of members of the opposing side. For example, during the 1978 Camp David negotiations between the Israeli and Egyptian governments, some members of the Israeli delegation, such as Israeli defense minister Ezer Weizman, helped to convey confidence in President Sadat's trustworthiness to Prime Minister Begin.[25]

Ad Hoc Informal Go-Betweens

In all kinds of large-scale conflicts, persons acting as individuals or as representatives of religious, political, or other organizations often convey messages between adversaries whose hostility makes direct communication difficult. To be accepted as go-betweens they may severely limit the range of activities they will perform. This has been the case for the work of a few Quakers in the protracted and severe struggle between the Sinhalese-dominated government of Sri Lanka and the now defeated separatist organization of the minority Tamils.[26] Conditions of their mediation include that the adversaries respect the confidentiality of the intervention and that each can veto continuing the mediation. This helps ensure that the mediators have no agenda of their own beyond helping the adversaries negotiate with each other.

Often, conflict resolution centers serve as a channel of communication between adversaries (see appendix A). For example, when Hendrik W. van der Merwe, an Afrikaner, became director of a new center on intergroup relations at the University of Cape Town in 1968, he did research and organized intergroup workshops, but also actively opposed apartheid.[27] With his background and experience, he initiated and facilitated meetings between Afrikaner and African National Congress leaders and between leaders of the Inkatha Freedom Party and the United Democratic Front, rival black organizations.

Consultant and/or Trainer

Increasingly, also, persons and organizations provide training and consultation services in conflict resolution methods. They are based in academic, governmental, business, religious, and philanthropic settings. The training includes developing skills in negotiation, active listening, mediation, strategic planning, nonviolent action, and other aspects of conducting a constructive struggle. The consultation often includes such training and also helps in developing conflict-management systems, including democratic organizational and societal systems. Such intermediary activity is often carried out with one of the sides engaged in a struggle, but sometimes is provided to all sides. The training and consultation may foster mediation and other ways to manage conflicts among the groups making up the party or coalition constituting one side in a larger conflict.

Such intermediary efforts are often undertaken before intense struggles erupt, but they may be introduced even when a struggle has become protracted, and increasingly are used after a settlement has been reached to help transform adversarial relations and avert renewed violence. For example, the Federal Mediation and Conciliation Service (FMCS), an independent agency of the U.S. government, was established in 1947 to mediate domestic labor-management disputes. In the 1990s it was authorized to expand its conflict resolution services in the United States and in other countries.[28] It now accepts invitations to provide training, facilitation, and consultation relating to a wide range of community and societal conflicts, as well as to labor-management disputes.

Training in conflict resolution and alternatives to violence are increasingly offered in schools at all levels, in prisons, in governmental and business organizations, and in churches and other voluntary associations. The training may be part of managing adaptations to changes in the composition of memberships, for example, as women and minorities become more significant participants in organizations.

Facilitator in Problem-Solving Workshops

An important form of conflict resolution utilizes a workshop structure. Typically, a convener brings together a few members of the opposing sides and guides their discussions about aspects of the conflict in which they are engaged. Some workshops are designed to improve mutual understanding of each side's views and feelings, while others are designed to tackle particular issues in contention and generate possible mutually acceptable solutions to the contention. The participants' experiences and/or the possible solutions they construct may be directly or indirectly transmitted to the official representatives of the opposing side, to other elite groups, or to the attentive public. For instance, in the early 2000's Professor Alexis Keller at the University of Geneva convened a series of dialogues between former Israeli and Palestinian officials, among them Yossi Beilin and Yasser Abed Rabbo. These dialogues eventually resulted in the publication of the Geneva Accords in 2003, which proposed concrete solutions to the Israeli-Palestinian conflict on issues ranging from the right of return for Palestinian refugees and the political control of Jerusalem. Although unofficial, the Geneva Accords showed that Israelis and Palestinians could reach consensus on final status negotiations. One copy of the Geneva Accords was provided to every household in Israel.

Participants in problem-solving workshops are often persons with ties to the leadership of their respective parties or have the potentiality to become members of the leadership in the future. The workshops usually go on for several days, moving through a few stages of discussion. The workshops have evolved through the experience of John Burton, Leonard Doob, Herbert C. Kelman, Edward Azar, Harold H. Saunders, Ronald J. Fisher, and others.[29] Workshops often have been held in connection with protracted international and intranational struggles, such as those in Northern Ireland, in Cyprus, in the United States, and between Jewish Israelis and Arab Palestinians.

Former members of workshops, however, sometimes act as quasi mediators on returning to the adversary group to which they belong. Furthermore, some later become participants in official negotiations, as has been the case with former members of some of Kelman's workshops who subsequently participated in the early negotiations between the PLO and the Israeli government.[30]

Problem-solving, interactive workshops are one kind of what is often referred to as "track-two diplomacy" in international relations.[31] Track one is the official mediation, negotiation, and other exchanges conducted by governmental representatives. Track-two channels include much more than problem-solving workshops and are best viewed as multitrack.[32] Among the many nonofficial channels are transnational organizations within which members of adversarial parties meet and discuss matters pertaining to the work of their organizations.[33]

Facilitators and Members of Dialogue Groups

A few members of adversary groups sometimes conduct an ongoing series of meetings at which they discuss particular aspects of the struggle in which their groups are engaged.[34] Such nonofficial, regular meetings between well-connected persons from adversary parties can provide a channel of communication and a means to discuss possible solutions to contentious issues. Members act as unofficial mediators, but their actions are done consciously and are known to the leaders and others in the groups to which they belong. Finally, some organizers of workshops have extended their problem-solving workshops into a series of meetings, becoming a kind of dialogue group between representatives of opposing sides. Examples of each of these kinds of dialogue groups can be found in many domestic conflict arenas, including industrial relations and community interreligious and interethnic relations, as well as in the international arena.

In 1957, nuclear physicists and others involved in the development of nuclear weapons and strategies about their possible use, working in the United States, Great Britain, and the Soviet Union, began to meet and exchange ideas about ways to reduce the chances of nuclear warfare. The first meetings were held in Pugwash, in Nova Scotia, Canada, and evolved into the Pugwash Conferences on Science and World Affairs.[35] In the 1950s, 1960s, and 1970s, discussions at these meetings contributed to the later signing of the Partial Test-Ban Treaty, the Nonproliferation Treaty, the Biological Weapons Convention, and the Antiballistic Missile Treaty. Later meetings helped build consensus for the Strategic Arms Reduction Treaties I and II, the Intermediate Nuclear Force Treaty, and the Chemical Weapons Convention. In 1995, the Pugwash conferences and Joseph Rotblat, its executive director, won the Nobel Peace Prize for their work. It continues to be transnationally active in organizing conferences and in issuing reports relating to regional global security threats.

Another important example of international track-two diplomacy is the Dartmouth conference.[36] At the urging of President Dwight D. Eisenhower, Norman Cousins, then editor of the *Saturday Review*, brought together a group of prominent U.S. and Soviet citizens as a means of keeping communication open when official relations were especially strained. The first meeting was at Dartmouth College in 1960, and many meetings followed, providing a venue for the exchange of information and ideas such that participants could serve as quasi mediators.

After the Cold War, a more direct mediating role evolved through one of the task forces that the Dartmouth conference established in 1982. Following the deterioration of détente at the end of the 1970s, members of the conference established task forces to examine what had gone wrong. Reflection on the process and the phases of development of the Dartmouth conference provided the basis for two members of the task force on regional conflicts, Gennady I. Chufrin and Harold H. Saunders, to cochair another set of conferences, called the Tajikistan Dialogue.[37] Meetings among a wide range of Tajikistanis were begun in 1993, following a vicious civil war that erupted after the Soviet Union dissolved and Tajikistan became independent. Meeting frequently, the sustained dialogue group contributed to building interpersonal relations and developing ideas that aided a settlement of the civil war.

More recently the Pacific Forum, a nonprofit institute under the direction of the Center for Strategic and International Studies, has sponsored ongoing track-two exchanges among Pacific Rim countries to foster regional stability and security through dialogue. This venue, known as the Council for Security Cooperation in the Asian Pacific, allows senior foreign and defense ministry officials to regularly gather for unofficial talks on WMD proliferation, preventive diplomacy, and economic cooperation.

Finally, some communities have labor councils, at which management and union representatives meet regularly, and associations, such as the Industrial Relations Association, nationally and locally that provide a forum for ongoing discussions. In the United States, local and national interreligious organizations provide a way for leaders of different religious communities to get to know each other and help avert destructive conflict eruptions.

Facilitators and Nonaligned Parties in Conferences

Large, multilateral meetings are often a setting in which conflicts involving many parties are negotiated. Some participants in such conferences play important intermediary roles, but more frequently, some parties provide intermediary services without filling explicitly defined roles.

Delegations in multilateral conferences sometimes coalesce into two camps that form clearly opposed coalitions, while a few delegations do not align with either side and tend to perform mediating functions. In international affairs, this proved to be the case for the UN General Assembly and the negotiations about arms control during the Cold War. Neutral and nonaligned powers have also been quite significant in the case of negotiations related to the Conference on Security and Cooperation in Europe, which concluded with the 1975 Helsinki Accords, and has since evolved to become the Organization on Security and Cooperation in Europe.[38]

Local conflicts relating to environmental issues such as water usage, disposal of radioactive waste, or the location of a garbage-burning facility usually involves numerous parties. A variety of conference formats are used to bring many of the stakeholders together in order to find acceptable solutions.[39] For example, between 1981 and 1990 the management of the South Platte River in Nebraska and Colorado evoked great controversy among persons engaged in sport fishing, raising cattle, and farming, as well as residents desiring fresh water for household uses and environmentalists desiring the preservation of the natural habitat for sandhill cranes and endangered whooping cranes.[40] In the late 1970s, the state of Colorado initiated plans to build a large reservoir where the north fork joined the main stem of the South Platte River. The conflict escalated in 1985 when the U.S. Army Corps of Engineers joined the Denver Water Board in supporting the dam project.

As the protests mounted, then Colorado governor Richard Lamm convened a meeting of business, environment, and government leaders to discuss the issue. As a kind of coengagement, a series of conferences were also held at several Colorado universities involving scientific, recreational, agricultural, business, and environmental interests. At these meetings, the implications of the project for various parties were analyzed and alternatives discussed, including water conservation and small-scale development projects. In part because of this, when the Environmental Protection Agency's director, William Reilly, ordered a full review of the project in 1989 and then terminated plans for the dam in 1990, the interested parties considered the conflict to be acceptably resolved.

Quite differently, the conflict over the habitat of the spotted owl in the forests of Oregon escalated into a very intense and protracted struggle between the timber industry and environmentalists. Extensive meetings and conferences were not held at the beginning of the conflict; rather, the conflict began with confrontations and escalated. In 1990, the Fish and Wildlife Service declared the spotted owl to be an endangered species, and several months later a forest service biologist released a report noting that the Sierra National Forest habitat was critical to the spotted owl's survival. In response to lawsuits brought by national environmental organizations, a federal court ordered that five million acres of the eight million acres of federal forest be set aside to protect the spotted owl. Later, when President George H. W. Bush's administration acted to ease those federal restrictions and open another two million acres to logging, the fight escalated further. The struggle was at a high level of tension when Clinton took office as president. He convened a conference at which the many interested parties could meet and try to identify possible compromises. Shortly thereafter, the president announced a compromise, but it failed to satisfy either side and the issue remained before the country. The struggle had persisted in being viewed as a zero-sum conflict and as ideologically significant. Furthermore, organizations from outside the immediate region had entered the fight, lending it great symbolic importance. Once a conflict has so far escalated, many people feel embittered even after a settlement is reached and their resentments may exacerbate the next conflict.

Institutionalized Mediator

In many large-scale social systems mediators operate within the context of a legal system, with specified obligations for the mediator and the disputants. In many countries, institutionalized mediation is most developed in the realm of labor-management relations. Even in such contexts, there are important variations in the social roles and how they are played. For example, Deborah M. Kolb compared official labor mediators in two organizations: the Federal Mediation and Conciliation Service (FMCS) and a state board of conciliation.[41] She finds that the mediators of the FMCS thought of themselves and acted as orchestrators, assisting the union and management to reach an agreement. The mediators in the state board regarded themselves and acted as deal makers, actively constructing a package acceptable to both sides and using persuasion and even manipulation to win acceptance.

In recent years, alternative dispute resolution (ADR) has greatly expanded in many conflict arenas. Thus, throughout the United States ADR is conducted in neighborhood conflict-resolution centers. In some judicial districts, mediation is mandated as part of the judicial process, as in child custody disputes between divorcing parents.

When the mediator functions within a highly institutionalized setting, the failure to reach a negotiated agreement tends to be followed by conflict-settlement procedures that are even less under the control of the parties to the dispute. Recourse to judicial proceedings is likely to follow or an executive branch agency imposes a settlement. Sometimes, however, the conflict escalates to a struggle in which each adversary resorts to coercion, attempting to unilaterally impose its desired outcome.

Ad Hoc Mediator

On occasion, when conflicts erupt or their escalation is anticipated, a well-regarded person or organization is requested, by the disputants or by a governmental body with the requisite jurisdiction, to serve as a mediator. The nature of the social role of these mediators and the services they provide is quite variable. In many urban conflicts, a mayor or governor may request that someone serve as a mediator to help manage or resolve the conflict. Usually, there is little preexisting consensus about the kind of mediator role the designated person will assume. Sometimes, in a difficult conflict a series of mediators may be asked to try to help settle the dispute.[42]

Some religious organizations are highly engaged in humanitarian work in various parts of the world, and some of their members provide informal, facilitative mediation. For example, various members of the Society of Friends have served in this way in several conflicts around the world. This was true in the deadly 1967–1971 Nigerian civil war, when the eastern region struggled unsuccessfully for independence as the Republic of Biafra.[43]

Former U.S. senator George Mitchell provided mediating services that contributed greatly to reaching the Good Friday agreement of April 1998, regarding the status of Northern Ireland.[44] In 1995, he chaired an international committee to make recommendations on the issue of decommissioning (disarming) underground organizations. In September 1997, peace negotiations began in Belfast with an extraordinarily wide range of groups represented and Mitchell as chair. Besides chairing the sessions, he acted as a go-between for parties that would not talk to each other directly, and he helped provide norms for the discussion, creating a safe space for negotiations. He also helped establish rules to reach decisions by significant consensus, and in addition he had access to President Clinton, who at times spoke directly to the parties.

Ad Hoc Deal Maker

In many community or societal settings, an influential personage is called on to help settle a dispute, with more authority to act than as facilitating mediator. The intermediary may have the authority to act as an arbitrator but more often acts as deal-making mediator. The deal maker may have resources with which to offer benefits or threaten losses, but he or she often relies largely on persuasion and manipulation.[45]

In international relations, often the deal-maker mediator has many resources that can be used to help reach an agreement. These are mediators with muscle, or clout. President Carter was such a mediator at the 1978 Camp David negotiations between the Israeli and Egyptian governments, which resulted in the peace treaty between Israel and Egypt. The president could provide political cover for the concessions that each side felt it would otherwise be fearful to make, could provide Israel with alternative sources of oil and military security if needed, and could provide Egypt with the prospects of badly needed economic assistance.

Richard Holbrooke at meetings in Dayton, Ohio, in 1995 provides an extreme example of mediator as deal maker.[46] As U.S. assistant secretary of state for Europe, Holbrooke practically imposed a settlement for Bosnia, which had been largely divided by Serbia and Croatia in terrible fighting. The meeting followed NATO bombing and U.S. assisted military advances against Serbian forces. Holbrooke cajoled, threatened, and promised assistance in brokering a deal among the leaders of Serbia, Croatia, and Bosnia.

Summary

Mediator roles vary greatly in their degree of intrusiveness.[47] At one extreme, some mediation roles involve only facilitative activities, and at the other extreme, they include deal making or even near-imposition of settlements. Activities at different ends of this continuum generally do not mix well within a single mediator role. This is one reason that different kinds of mediation are often carried out by different mediators in sequence or in parallel.

Many advocates of mediation in the context of the recent growth of conflict resolution practice stress that mediators should only facilitate the disputants reaching an agreement themselves. The power to make an agreement should lie in the disputants' own hands. This is counterpoised to a legal system in which judges and jurors determine the outcome of the dispute. But many other kinds of mediation also occur and are advocated. For example, some analysts stress the transformative potential of mediation that works for empowerment and recognition of the disputants.

Although the parties to a dispute are the ones who ultimately select the mediator role and sometimes the person(s) who occupy the role, they frequently face some degree of pressure to accept mediation and to reach an agreement. In large part, this depends on the institutional setting. In certain areas of labor-management relations, laws require a governmental effort at mediation. Once parties enter into a mediation process, the degree of external pressure and influence varies greatly.

SHAPERS OF MEDIATOR ROLES

Although members of the social system in which mediator roles are played have varying influence, they jointly construct the norms for the roles. Furthermore, mediator roles are negotiated anew among the parties undertaking an actual mediating effort. Four major kinds of determinants of mediator roles warrant examination here: the cultural setting, the institutional context, the characteristics of the conflict, and the characteristics of the mediator.

Cultural Setting

Every social system, whether a society or an organization, has a culture with rules about how conflicts should be managed, including rules about mediation.[48] In traditional societies, mediators tend to be political or religious leaders of their communities, and they use the resources of their positions to help resolve conflicts. In many small traditional societies, the goal is to heal the rupture that a conflict may have caused and to ensure that cooperative relationships within the community are sustained. For example, in traditional Hawaiian culture interpersonal conflicts are regarded as entanglements, which are unfortunate, as when fishing lines or nets become entangled.[49] Conflict resolution, therefore, is called *ho'oponopono*, or disentanglement. In this process, still in practice, the disputants are gathered together by a high-status community member who knows them. Prayers are offered, a statement of the problems is made, and for each problem, the leader asks questions and a discussion follows, channeled through the leader. After a period of silence, confessions are made to the gods (or God) and to each disputant, and then restitution is arranged. Each problem is dealt with in this fashion, and then the disputants forgive each other, releasing each other from guilt. After a closing prayer, the participants share something to eat.

In highly differentiated societies, especially in Western societies, the judicial system tends to focus on the disputants and strives to determine who is right and who is wrong. Yet even in such societies, mediation is often used to discover or construct a mutually acceptable agreement between the disputants. Nevertheless, the mediation process is different in large societies from small, traditional societies. Within larger societies, disputes usually are treated in relative isolation, the mediator roles tend to be professionalized, and the value of mediator neutrality is emphasized. The previous discussion of the various mediator roles should demonstrate, however, the great variability among kinds of mediation in every society.

Institutional Context

Mediator roles range greatly, also due to their diverse institutional settings. Some mediator roles are part of the same hierarchical structure as the disputing parties. The mediators in those roles operate with considerable authority deriving from their position. A conflict unresolved by mediation is likely to be decided by other processes, such as litigation or administrative authority.

Many mediator roles, even in highly differentiated societies, are quite informal and without institutional support, so that the resources such mediators have at their disposal are generally small. Sometimes they consist of little more than personal ties with each side, the knowledge brought from previous mediating experience, and the information attained in the very process of the mediation. Thus, in interpersonal conflicts, even in large, bureaucratized societies, a local priest, a bartender, or coworker may mediate informally and represent the concerns of the local set of social relations.

In many settings, the institutions are relatively sparse or weak for managing certain conflicts among particular adversaries. Thus, in some societies institutionalized procedures are not well developed for family disputes, since these are considered private. Communal conflicts are relatively inchoate and therefore often lack institutionalized ways to be managed.

Characteristics of the Conflict

The scale and stage of a conflict and the nature of the adversaries and their relationship all affect the kind of mediation that is used. In large-scale conflicts, many kinds of persons are likely to be engaged in the mediation, sometimes at the same time. In small-scale conflicts, more often a single person serves as the mediator, whether in a facilitative or deal-making role.

Increasing attention is being given by analysts to specifying the kind of intermediary intervention that is appropriate for various stages of a conflict.[50] For example, unofficial mediation that is largely facilitative is most common and effective at early stages of a conflict. Furthermore, as mediation efforts come closer to a deadline, mediators tend to increase pressure tactics and/or provide compensations.

Finally, the adversaries and the relationship between them strongly affect the kind of mediation practiced and the impact of the mediation. One important dimension of the relationship between adversaries in a conflict is the symmetry in resources between them. If adversaries differ greatly in resources, including legitimacy, the party with more tends to refuse mediation that seems to place the adversaries on an equal level. Official mediation tends to make visible that recognition. Consequently, an informal and relatively facilitative kind of mediation is more likely to occur under those circumstances.

Adversaries with an ongoing relationship and with high levels of integration tend to utilize mediation or even arbitration in seeking to settle their disputes. Mediation or arbitration is expected to help reach a settlement quickly and prevent the escalation of antagonism, and so preserve the social relationship.

Characteristics of the Mediator

Each kind of person or group can play only a particular variety of mediator roles. For example, mediators with considerable material resources are likely to find it difficult to restrict themselves to facilitator roles; the adversaries tend to anticipate that such mediators will use their resources to help fashion a deal.

The proliferation of mediation channels, including various official and unofficial mediator roles, raises the importance of understanding which ones are most appropriate for different conflicts at various stages.[51] Generally, track-two mediation is facilitative rather than deal making and occurs at early rather than later stages of conflict de-escalation.

In addition to organizational base and sponsorship, individuals obviously differ in style, as a result of past mediating training, experience, and personality. Such individual differences make some kinds of mediation especially congenial to particular persons and provide a strong reason that no single way of filling a role will prove to be effective for every incumbent. Effective training for mediation takes that variability into account.

ASSESSING MEDIATION CONTRIBUTIONS

Having noted many of the services that mediators and related intermediaries may provide to foster constructive conflict de-escalation, we must consider what their actual contributions are. Although intermediaries can help adversaries in many ways, the adversaries must first agree to accept the services of a mediator if someone is to play that role. If one or more of the adversaries refuses to do so or does so only begrudgingly, a mediator cannot act effectively.

Consequently, one might argue that when the adversaries want to de-escalate their conflict, they will do so, and the contributions of mediators are therefore only marginal. The evidence regarding the nature and magnitude of the contributions mediation efforts make toward conflict de-escalation and settlement must be critically examined.

For many analysts, the ambiguities of the terms *effectiveness* and *success* have led them to categorize simply reaching a settlement with the participation of a mediator to be a successful mediation.[52] If the overt struggle continues, the mediation is regarded as failed. Other analysts use several criteria of effectiveness, including durability of the agreement, fairness of the agreement, and speed of reaching an agreement. The assessment of each of these dimensions varies in difficulty. Measuring durability may seem relatively straightforward, but even that can be uncertain when we consider the disputes that often arise about adherence to an agreement. Determining justness and efficiency are even more problematic, yet very important.[53]

A general problem in assessing the contributions of mediation efforts is that the agreement, when it does come, depends on many factors in addition to whatever an intermediary has done. It is extraordinarily difficult to separate out the value added by an intermediary's actions. For some purposes, the testimony of the adversaries is an important indicator. Research findings indicate high rates of user satisfaction with mediation, typically 75 percent or higher.[54] But to make an independent assessment of the contributions mediation makes, an analyst must use various kinds of comparative evidence of other mediating efforts in the same conflict at other times, of mediating conflicts in other similar conflicts, and of the consequences of similar conflicts lacking mediation.

Success is never complete for any single mediation effort to settle, resolve, or transform a large-scale conflict. Even if an agreement is reached, some people on each side are likely to reject it and some will become dissatisfied as the agreement is carried out; indeed the agreement may fail to be implemented and be followed by renewed and even more intense struggle. Furthermore, agreements are rarely reached without prior efforts, and earlier mediation efforts may have contributed to changes that ultimately resulted in reaching a mutually satisfactory agreement. Therefore it is advisable to consider the specific consequences of various mediating actions for different people on the opposing sides.

In trying to assess what kinds of mediation affect a conflict's movement toward greater constructiveness, another question should be posed: Compared to what? In the realm of many interpersonal, family, or public disputes, mediation is generally compared to adjudication. Within hierarchical organizations, the comparison may be to arbitration by higher authority, and in international relations the comparison may be to coercive diplomacy or to efforts at coercive imposition. All these matters have not yet been systematically examined in a comprehensive fashion to assess what effects different kinds of mediation have in various circumstances. Pieces of relevant theory and research are noted here to indicate important empirically grounded generalizations and patterns. The discussion focuses on five issues: (1) gaining mediator entry, (2) helping reach an agreement, (3) enhancing the quality of the agreement, (4) contributing to the implementation and durability of the agreement, and (5) coordinating mediation efforts. This discussion is about persons enacting mediator roles that are so recognized by the adversaries. Too little research is available to make a comparable examination of informal mediation and of quasi mediation.

Gaining Entry

The intervention of mediators is anticipated and generally realized in many spheres of societal life, so that mediation entry is not problematic. For example, in countries with institutionalized labor-management collective bargaining, mediation is generally available and frequently used. In the rapidly growing arena of disputes mediated through community dispute-resolution centers, between one-third and two-thirds of the disputants to whom mediation is offered refuse it.[55] In some matters where mediation is required, interestingly, the likelihood of agreement and of user satisfaction is about the same for mandated and elective mediation.

Even in international conflicts, mediation by international organizations or by governments not engaged in the conflict frequently occurs. Thus, an analysis of 310 international disputes between 1945 and 1974 found that a mediator was involved in 82 percent of the cases.[56]A study of the 72 more severe international conflicts between 1945 and 1984 with at least 100 deaths found that 61 percent were mediated.[57] Highly serious conflict episodes, in the context of protracted conflicts, are even less frequently mediated. Thus, in a study of international conflicts between 1945 and 1995, 18 cases of intractable conflicts were identified; they lasted more than fifteen years, had recurrent violent episodes, and resisted conflict management efforts.[58] Among those 18 cases, 75 serious militarized conflicts occurred, and only 44 percent were mediated. However, some of the conflicts received numerous mediation efforts and others only a few. Thus there were 87 mediation efforts in the 4 militarized conflicts in the Greece-Turkey relationship and only 4 such efforts in the 5 militarized conflict eruptions between the Soviet Union and the United States. The two superpowers were able to keep formal mediators from intervening, and did so.

Contributing to the Attainment of Agreements

Settlement rates for mediated disputes vary greatly across domains, ranging between 20 and 80 percent.[59] Analyses of international conflicts indicate that the involvement of intermediaries is associated with reduced likelihood that the conflict will escalate and result in violence. Thus, an analysis of 72 major international conflicts between 1920 and 1965 found that only 28 percent of those that were handled through procedures involving intermediaries had outcomes determined by violence, compared with 76 percent for those conflicts in which the adversaries did not use intermediaries.[60]

However, taking mediation events as the unit of analysis reveals that they frequently fail to produce an agreement. In an analysis of the 97 international disputes between 1945 and 1990, with more than 100 fatalities, 346 separate mediation attempts were made.[61] Only 6 percent of the mediation attempts yielded a full settlement, 12 percent a partial settlement, and 10 percent a cease-fire, while 72 percent were deemed unsuccessful. Clearly, the nature of the conflict at the time of the mediation limits the possibility of success. This analysis found that mediation was much more likely to be successful in conflicts with low complexity and few fatalities, and that had only recently begun.

Research findings indicate that mediators make contributions aside from succeeding in producing a signed agreement. They tend to speed reaching an agreement for several reasons. Thus, in social experiments when a mediator intervened to make suggestions, the subjects made larger and more frequent concessions.[62] Apparently, the interventions enabled the adversaries to make concessions without considering themselves weak for doing so.

Observations and analyses of industrial disputes indicate that mediators are able to make suggestions and generate pressures that tend to result in concessions that hasten reaching an agreement.[63] A study of negotiations involving municipal governments and police and firefighter unions found that mediators using a relatively aggressive strategy of making suggestions were associated with narrowing the differences between the bargainers, particularly about nonsalary issues.[64]

Although mediators often contribute to the reaching of an agreement, they certainly do not ensure it. Even powerful mediators can fail to produce an agreement at a particular mediation endeavor, as illustrated by the failure of Israeli and Palestinian leaders to reach an agreement at Camp David meetings in July 2000 mediated by President Clinton.[65] This failure is partly attributable to the attempt to reach a final status agreement within severe time constraints regarding issues about which the two sides held significantly different positions. Prime Minister Barak was facing elections and President Clinton was soon to leave office. Major issues had not been subjected to official negotiations by the most senior leaders of the two sides, including those pertaining to the disposition of Jerusalem and of Palestinian refugees.

Contributing to the Quality of Agreements

Reaching a settlement is not the only standard of success. The settlement should be regarded as a good one by the disputants and by other stakeholders it affects. A variety of evidence indicates that mediators often help produce agreements that are regarded as fair by analysts as well as those with a stake in the conflict. Experimental evidence, for example, indicates that third-party observers or mediators making even small interventions increase the pressures toward adhering to norms of fairness and equity.[66] Furthermore, experimental research indicates that mediators who are perceived to have high ability are especially likely to help produce settlements that yield high gains for the negotiators, perhaps because their suggestions can be readily accepted without losing face.[67]

There is evidence that mediated disputes result in agreements involving more equal sharing of resources and more compromise than adjudicated agreements. For example, divorce mediation resulted in more joint (rather than sole) custody agreements, and small claims disputes resulted in "awards going entirely to the plaintiff in almost 50 percent of the adjudicated cases, but in only 17 percent of the mediated ones."[68]

Observations and interviews with negotiators indicate several ways that mediators may help to produce relatively fair agreements and outcomes. One reason for this is that the presence of a trusted mediator who is considered skillful in mediation facilitates a fuller discussion of contentious issues.[69]

Contributing to the Implementation and Durability of Agreements

Compliance to mediated agreements appears to be relatively high. Thus, agreements reached in neighborhood justice centers have compliance rates of 67 to 87 percent; in the small claims area, full compliance was reported for the mediated cases, compared with 48 percent through adjudication.[70]

Several reasons for the relatively high compliance and durability of mediated agreements can be suggested. First, insofar as the disputing sides have participated in reaching an agreement, they are likely to feel that the agreement is fair and represents their interests, hence worthy of implementation and maintenance. The disputants' relations to the mediator are also important bases for honoring an agreement; disputants may have obligations to the mediator or wish to sustain their reputation with the mediator and therefore believe they should honor the agreement made with the assistance of that mediator. Particularly for mediators who have actively supported an agreement and have great resources, such considerations are important. For example, this has played an important role in the honoring of the 1979 Israeli-Egyptian peace treaty mediated by President Carter.

Mediating and other intermediary actions are increasingly geared to the post-settlement period and to sustaining the agreements reached, as discussed further in chapter 10. This increased activity follows from the recognition that agreements in large-scale conflicts frequently break down, in part due to inadequate external engagement in supporting the implementation and enabling further conflict transformation. Despite the many workshops, dialogue groups, and track-two negotiations that had attempted to de-escalate the Israeli-Palestinian conflict, not enough was done to transform the parties in the conflict and to fully implement the agreements previously made.[71] This contributed greatly to the failure of U.S. mediation of the Israeli-Palestinian negotiations in 2000 and the subsequent outbreak of the second intifada, years of violence, and greater mistrust.

When the mediation is limited, the adversaries' leaders grapple to improve their position, spoilers act to undermine the agreement, and external actors support rejectionist groups, an agreement is likely to fail. This happened disastrously in the case of the mediated 1993 Arusha Peace Agreement for Rwanda. The United Nations, the Organization of African Unity, and Tanzania were to aid in the implementation but were unable to prevent the genocide that killed 800,000 Tutsis and moderate Hutus.[72]

Coordinating Intermediary Peacemaking Efforts

Whether consciously intended or not by the several intermediaries in large-scale conflicts, their activities often support each other, making them more effective jointly than each would have been alone.[73] However, different activities performed by various intermediaries sometimes unfortunately interfere with each other, impairing their effectiveness.

Two major types of coordination should be distinguished: sequential and simultaneous, and the many varieties of each. Intermediary activity may be coordinated over time in several ways. Thus, many times one intermediary prepares the ground or even initiates de-escalating negotiations and then the negotiations are taken up by a different set of intermediaries. Many instances of effective sequential complementarity can be cited, usually involving non-official or track-two methods preceding more traditional diplomacy.[74] Track-two operations may prepare the way for official negotiations, as noted earlier regarding ANC and Afrikaner meetings about apartheid in South Africa. Thus, too, workshops involving Israeli Jews and Palestinian Arabs contributed to the later direct official negotiations between the Israeli government and the PLO.[75] For example, the understandings about each other's points of view and concerns, and possible ways to reconcile them, provided the basis for officials on each side to believe a mutually acceptable formula could be found. Some of the members of the Israeli and Palestinian negotiation teams had participated in such workshops.

In addition, negotiations may be initiated in a nonofficial track and then handed off to an official negotiating channel. Sometimes the traditional diplomatic channel has reached an impasse and a new track is opened informally. When progress is made, the negotiations are returned to the official channel. This is illustrated in the 1993 negotiations between Israelis and the PLO, conducted in Oslo, Norway.[76]

Simultaneous as well as sequential coordination may result from unofficial meetings and official back-channel conversations that complement relatively traditional diplomatic activities.[77] One way this occurs is when unofficial tracks parallel official negotiating tracks. For example, this was the case for the Pugwash and Dartmouth meetings during the years of U.S.-Soviet negotiations regarding arms control measures.

In large-scale conflicts, various intermediaries and approaches generally need to be blended together to be effective. If they are well coordinated, their effectiveness enhances the efforts of each approach, as illustrated in the 1989–1992 peace process ending Mozambique's war.[78] Coordination may occur through regular gatherings of representatives from intermediary groups, at which they exchange information about what each is doing. Some organizations are acknowledged by others to be the "lead" organization, and some have the capacity and interest to give direction to many other organizations. This is increasingly the case as the U.S. government and other governments, as well as international governmental organizations, contract out much of the work in peacemaking. However, when a national government has a very strong interest in the political developments in another country, it may pursue those interests, hampering efforts by the United Nations or other governments in mediation efforts that are responsive to the concerns of a wide range of people in that country. This happened with the U.S. occupation of Iraq in 2003–2004, to the detriment of the political transformation in Iraq.[79]

The destructive and protracted character of many communal conflicts, despite multiple efforts to intervene and resolve them, indicates that the interventions are often ineffective. We must consider why they fail. To what extent is failure due to the nature of the conflict and the existing conditions, and to what extent is it due to inappropriate intermediary actions? Was the time not ripe for the kind of interventions that were tried?[80] Does the multiplicity of intermediary efforts hamper effective de-escalation and reaching enduring mutually acceptable agreements? Does this occur because poorly coordinated efforts undermine each other as they convey inconsistent messages to the adversaries about what needs to be done? Were the wrong kinds of intermediaries used for the kinds of adversaries in the conflict? Under what circumstances do adversaries use one intermediary against another? Do intermediaries compete for attention and strain the capability of the adversaries' representatives to make appropriate responses?

Previous experience, theorizing, and research suggest answers to some of these questions.[81] Thus, possible intermediaries vary in the likelihood of effectively intervening in different kinds of conflicts. For example, conflicts within a country, between the government and challengers to the government, tend to be resistant to peacemaking interventions by other states, and even by international governmental organizations. Therefore, unofficial, facilitating interveners are probably more likely to gain access.[82] The difficulty that governments and governmental organizations have in intervening in domestic conflicts has created a void that nongovernmental organizations increasingly fill, for example, the center established by Jimmy Carter in Atlanta and International Alert, based in London.[83] Once negotiations have been initiated, however, intermediaries with resources are relatively more effective than are nonofficial intermediaries in bringing about an agreement and to help implement it.[84]

Various intermediary activities also differ in their likely effectiveness for different kinds of conflicts and at different phases of a conflict. Thus, consulting and conveying information between the adversaries is likely to be more effective than strong, deal-making activities at the pre-negotiation stage of a conflict.[85]

CONCLUSIONS

This chapter has indicated that mediation is more or less effective, depending on the nature and stage of the conflict, the disputants, and their relations with each other, as well as the skill and appropriateness of the mediation effort. On the whole, the less antagonistic and the more integrated the relations between the adversaries, the better are the prospects for mediation.[86] The more intensely and destructively a conflict has been waged, the greater is the difficulty in undertaking mediation and doing so effectively. But if the antagonists believe they are unable to impose a victory and begin to search for a way out, mediation begins to appear attractive.

Conflicts in which one side is more powerful than the other are more difficult to mediate than are conflicts in which the adversaries are relatively equal. The ethical dilemmas of trying to mediate asymmetrical conflicts can be reduced by championing international norms, as illustrated in the work of Max van der Stoel as HCNM.[87] The growing consensus about the primacy of human rights norms therefore can aid conflict resolution practitioners in reaching more equitable outcomes in asymmetric circumstances. Some kinds of contentious issues are more amenable to mediation (and to resolution) than are others. For example, conflicts deriving from dissensus, value differences, or matters of principle are often more difficult to mediate than are conflicts deriving from consensus, or substantive matters that are more susceptible to compromise. Evidence supporting this generalization can be found in studies of international conflict, labor relations, and community mediation regarding environmental issues. Furthermore, mediation is more difficult under conditions of resource scarcity, as noted in studies of labor mediation and in divorce mediation. Finally, mediation is more difficult the greater the disparity in goals and the greater the sense by any side that its vital interests are threatened.

Many other conditions relating to the mediation process, the mediators, and the adversaries' relations with possible mediators influence the effectiveness of mediating efforts. In certain cultural and institutional settings, mediation is likely to be seen as widely appropriate to help resolve conflicts. Furthermore, mediation is more likely to occur and be effective if mediators are available whom the adversaries regard as legitimate and with whom they have ongoing relations.

Certainly, mediation is not a panacea for all conflicts. It can make significant contributions, however, to preventing or controlling destructive conflicts. It can contribute to the transition from escalation or stalemate to de-escalation, to constructing a mutually acceptable outcome, and to improving the equity and stability of the outcome. The size of such contributions depends on many conditions of a conflict; the kind of mediation efforts undertaken; and, most significantly, the match between them.

Knowledge about the applicability of various mediating strategies and methods can enhance mediators' effectiveness. Research, reflection, and experience can indicate useful principles for mediators. For example, Chester A. Crocker, Fen Osler Hampson, and Pamela Aall offer the following checklist for mediating intractable conflicts:

1. Protect and exploit good formulas, repackaging earlier potentially winning ideas.
2. Anticipate troublesome and destructive negotiating behavior from the parties.
3. Isolate the spoilers and reward the risk takers by extracting reciprocal, conditional offers.
4. Mobilize the tools for transforming the post-settlement conditions.
5. Maintain home-base support for the mediation.
6. Keep an eye on the clocks running for the many parties involved.[88]

Intermediary actions other than mediation also contribute to the amelioration and resolution of conflicts. These include interventions to separate contending groups. Sometimes this is done with the agreement of the adversaries, as is generally the case with UN peacekeeping forces; other times this occurs without such agreement, as when police break up family or community fights. Other intermediary efforts are intended to reduce the presumed grounds for the conflict or to mitigate the damages caused by the fighting, as is attempted by the interventions of organizations advocating human rights or providing humanitarian assistance.

The great expansion of the Internet contributes enormously to the contributions that intermediaries can make toward waging conflicts constructively. Many organizations engaged in training, consulting, and mediating have websites that provide information about their services (see appendixes A and B). Many websites are also sources of information about a wide variety of conflicts and of methods of peacemaking. In addition, numerous networks exist globally, sustained by listservs linking people who share interests in particular conflicts and ways of building peace. For example, TRANSCEND: A Network for Peace and Development is directed by Johan Galtung; its members provide training and consultations around the world.[89]

Certainly, the immense variety of intermediary actors and actions are a great resource for those who would wage conflicts constructively. They may help avoid, limit, or end the destructive qualities of conflicts, when the appropriate actions by the appropriate actors are taken under suitable circumstances.

9

Settling Conflicts through Negotiated and Nonnegotiated Means

Constructive conflicts tend to be settled through means that do not rely on severe violence, that engage the partisans in direct interaction, and that encourage the exploration of each side's aspirations and interests. Yet not all conflict settlements are viewed by all sides as fair or mutually beneficial, and many are achieved through varying degrees of coercion by one or more of the adversaries. Moreover, there is often disagreement among both partisans and analysts about when a conflict has actually been settled, particularly when no explicit agreement or widely recognized symbolic event occurs. Some conflicts gradually melt away as partisans give up their fight, engage in a different struggle, or accept an accommodation they cannot change. In other cases, even major actions signaling the settlement of a struggle are contested since spoiler factions may continue the struggle that the authorized leadership has agreed to settle.

In this chapter we consider these and other issues related to settlement outcomes and means. We first examine variations in settlement outcomes. We then explore five nonnegotiated pathways to settlements that are frequently found across conflict settings. Finally, we look in depth at negotiation as a central tool for constructively ending a fight.

VARIATIONS IN SETTLEMENT OUTCOMES

Partisans in a fight usually think about a conflict as ending in victory or defeat. Indeed, that is what parties themselves often proclaim after a fight, and those designations have important consequences. Such characterizations affect who will seek future redress and which conflict modes will be tried in the future. They do not suffice, however, to portray the social reality, since they do not allow for the multidimensional quality of actual outcomes. Below we first consider the distributive aspects of settlements: the degree of relative gains and losses between the adversaries, not assuming one side wins all and the other loses all. We then discuss joint outcomes: the extent to which the adversaries share benefits as well as costs. Outcomes with a high degree of shared benefits are often termed "integrative."[1] The set of distributive and joint outcomes are shown in figure 9.1. Finally, we consider an additional settlement dimension: the degree of engagement or separation between the former adversaries.

Distribution of Gains and Losses

Adversaries often view the outcome of a fight in terms of the relative gains each side won at the expense of the other. This view of conflict is usually taken, particularly regarding consensual conflicts, for example, about the allocation of money or land. Furthermore, the gains and losses are generally considered in terms of what was sought by each side as the conflict arose. Therefore, to make a demand and then fail to have it met is generally regarded as a loss and will be so considered here. Of course, one side rarely wins everything it sought; some degree of compromise is almost inevitable. Even the Egyptian opposition's successful demand that President Hosni Mubarak step down in 2011 was tempered by their acceptance of Mubarak's Egyptian military assuming control once he resigned. Therefore, the losing side may not lose as much as it feared it might, and can claim some success. Gains and losses are rarely total, but one side usually gets more of what it sought than does the other side.

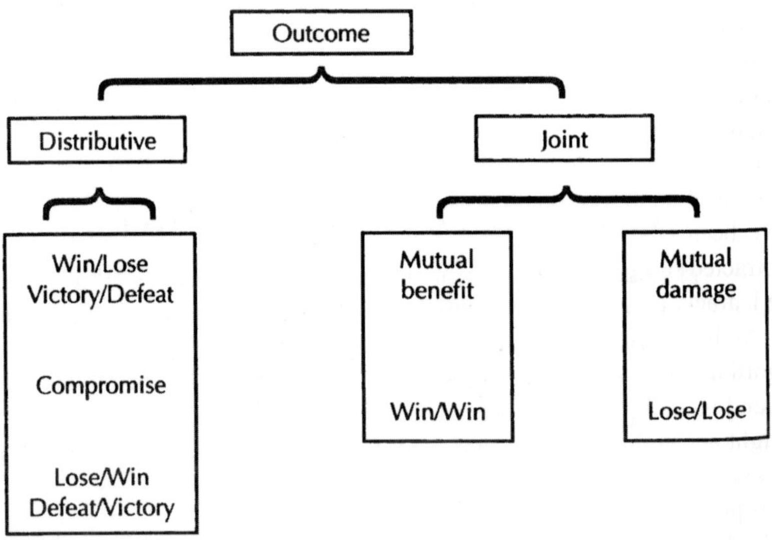

Figure 9.1. Types of Outcomes

Assessing relative gains and losses is difficult because for many matters in dispute, the goals of the opposing sides are not clear, and various persons and groups within each side have somewhat different goals. Furthermore, the goals are likely to shift in the course of a struggle. Thus, adversary leaders tend to expand their goals when they are doing well in the struggle but contract their goals when they believe they are doing poorly.

Another possible anchoring point to assess gains and losses is the circumstance of each adversary when the conflict erupted. One or more of the parties in a struggle may end up worse off after the struggle has settled than they were before it began. Or one or the other may think it is better off, even if it did not achieve what it set out to achieve in the struggle. Admittedly, the circumstances at the time the conflict erupted are ambiguous in retrospect and may also be disputed. Furthermore, the parties generally start off in unequal circumstances, and the fight may modify the balance without fundamentally changing the relative positions of the opponents. The party advantaged by the modification, however, may assert that it has gained.

From still another perspective, each side may regard its gains and losses relative to those of its opponent, so a party that inflicted pain on its opponent or prevented the opponent from attaining all that it sought may claim a victory.

Finally, sometimes merely resisting fiercely, under great odds, is proclaimed to be a defining event and a great achievement. It becomes the basis for mobilization in renewed later battles. For example, many Serbs celebrate the Battle of Kosovo, fought in 1389, in which they unsuccessfully resisted the invading Turkish army.

Generally, in this analysis losses and gains are assessed by comparing them with the adversaries' ostensible goals at the outset of their struggle. This conception is closest to the partisans' sense that they won or lost. Nevertheless, the other considerations noted are often useful in interpreting the significance of various endings for the adversaries in the struggle. Furthermore, they allow leaders to interpret a settlement in a favorable light, even if the losses have been heavy. Indeed, even a defeat in a campaign embedded within a protracted struggle can contribute to victory in subsequent campaigns: lessons are learned, allies are rallied, and constituents are aroused.

An important implication of these observations is that each adversary may regard the settlement as having given it some benefits. Indeed, most conflicts do end in a kind of compromise with each side gaining something of what it sought and failing to gain everything. The compromise may be the result of an exchange of concessions, sometimes reflecting a trade-off with gains in high-priority areas traded for concessions in low-priority areas. In ideologically driven conflicts and in some cultures, compromise has connotations of betraying sacred commitments. Although adversaries in such circumstances may deny they have agreed to a compromise, outside observers may view the outcome as embodying an exchange of concessions.

The ambiguities of outcomes and the rarity of one side totally overwhelming the other makes the attainment of a mutually acceptable outcome more feasible than it might otherwise appear. The changing character of goals and their varying importance for different elements within each side help adversaries find settlements with some joint gains and minimal joint loses.

Joint Damages and Benefits

In addition to relative losses and gains for each side, settlements vary in the degree to which the parties have joint gains and losses. That is, one can look at the outcome in terms of the benefits and damages accruing to the opposing parties together. However, the settlement may be more or less mutually damaging or mutually beneficial, not simply in an additive sense, but as a shared result. Such joint possibilities are present in every conflict ending, but often are not part of either adversary's goals when entering a fight. They become more significant when the adversaries begin to consider ending a fight and are generally more salient when a problem-solving approach is taken in conducting the struggle.

For example, Richard E. Walton and Robert B. McKersie, in a classic analysis, describe a union-management dispute regarding the issue of promotion that was transformed into a problem and then solved. Only a few senior employees were being promoted because management said they lacked the requisite skills. The union wanted to improve the promotional chances of employees with most years of service. Initially, the employees said they wanted more weight to be given to seniority. "After considerable discussion, it was agreed that the company would inaugurate a 'self-help' program for employees. It would pay for outside education and do everything possible to help the employees improve their skills in advance of promotion opportunities."[2]

Damages

A severe struggle is usually costly to all of the adversaries. Each is hurt by the coercion inflicted by the other, and each loses the resources expended in coercing the other. Furthermore, the losses are mutual in the sense that all sides have had to forgo the benefits that might have accrued to them if they were acting cooperatively to achieve whatever shared objectives they had. Thus, revolutions often cause great damage to a society's economy, which takes decades to overcome.[3]

A fierce struggle may end with the adversaries so weakened that outside parties, not primarily engaged in the struggle, are able to gain at the expense of the contending parties. For instance, the outcome of civil strife may be the domination of the contenders in one country by the government of another country. The outcome of the very long civil war waged among many Lebanese groups between 1975 and 1991, for example, was largely imposed and enforced by the Syrian government. In some cases, the opposing parties contribute to each other's destruction, as was the case in World War I, the outcome of which included the end of the German, Austro-Hungarian, Ottoman, and Russian ruling dynasties.

Mutual losses also take the form of embittered relations, mutual fear, mistrust, and hatred, so it is difficult afterward to engage in the cooperation that may be essential for either side to regain some of what it lost. This is often the legacy of communal fights, where members of each side experienced atrocious acts perpetrated by members of the other side.

Benefits

Some conflict endings, on the other hand, are integrative, yielding the opponents much of what they most sought when they entered the fight. They discover trade-offs that allow members of each side to gain what has high priority for them in exchange for concessions on low priority matters. Given the opponents' different sets of preferences, a formula often can be found that maximizes the benefits they can achieve together.[4] A labor-management agreement, for example, may provide enhanced job security, improved opportunities for training and advancement, and for management experimentation to increase productivity, yielding higher profits. Such outcomes are often called "win-win" because they involve mutual rather than unilateral gains.[5]

Another important source of mutual benefits is the avoidance of mutual losses. Stopping a fight reduces the costs each side would bear in continuing the struggle. Even an outcome that favors one side more than the other may yield important mutual benefits. Thus, an agreement for power sharing among various ethnic communities, even if dominated by one as was the case with the formation of a coalition government dominated by Shiites in Iraq in late 2010, may be seen as mutually beneficial because the resulting stability allows for economic prosperity, which disorder would undermine. Similarly, the accommodation in Malaysia between the politically dominant Malays and the economically successful ethnic Chinese minority allowed them all to "make money."[6]

Finally, mutual benefits may be attained at the expense of outsiders to the conflict. Adversaries may negotiate an agreement that gives them much of what they regard as important and passes on the costs to others. For example, labor-management negotiations in a company operating in a market that it tends to monopolize may reach an agreement whose costs of increased wages, salaries, and/or profits are largely paid for by the consumers of the company's products. In a sense, collusion between the representatives of the opposing sides may be integrative for them but yield a one-sided gain for the constituency of one side. For example, negotiators for one side may accept an unfavorable contract in exchange for personal gains awarded by the opposing side. While outcomes with high levels of joint benefits are regarded as constructive, this is not the case when the benefits are gotten at the expense of other legitimate parties.

Degree of Engagement or Separation

A quite different dimension of conflict settlements is the degree to which the outcome betokens movement toward greater engagement or toward greater separation. To illustrate, ethnic or other communal groups within a society may move toward increased integration and away from segregation in the use of public facilities, in residential locations, and in occupational positions. Integration may extend to a gradual assimilation or to the preservation of group diversity. At the other extreme, separation may extend to expulsion or to population transfers between states, and it may include the division of territory into separate states. In between are various forms of societal coexistence with varying degrees of segregation, power sharing, or federal systems with local autonomy. Relations between countries also vary in their degree of integration, with varying rates of trade, movements of people, or shared consumption of popular culture.[7]

Certainly, there are many dimensions of integration, and persons and groups may be very close along some dimensions and separated along others. Clearly, too, one side may largely impose the degree of interaction or separation, or it may be a matter of mutual preference. Finally, and importantly, the parties to large-scale conflicts are never unitary actors. Consequently, some elements of each side may feel that they gained much of what they wanted, while other factions feel they received little.

Constructive and Destructive Settlements

Conflicts ending with great joint damages are widely recognized as destructive. Conflicts ending with considerable mutual benefit are generally regarded as constructive, unless, as noted above, the benefits are accrued at the expense of legitimate parties not agreeing to the ending of the struggle. The degree to which conflicts ending with one side gaining more than the other should be regarded as constructive or destructive is not obvious. Victors are quick to proclaim that the outcome has enhanced many widely shared values and is constructive, and their interpretation often prevails.

In this book, we temper such judgments by taking into account the aspirations of all the parties affected by the struggle and their claims for equity and justice.[8]

An improved relationship between the former adversaries is another marker of constructive outcomes. Usually, but not necessarily, this means that outcomes with increased engagement between the adversaries are regarded as constructive. Separation when it is mutually sought and does not impose severe unequal costs on one side can also be regarded as constructive, but more frequently one side imposes separation on the other.

Since conflicts are not neatly bounded, the constructiveness of their endings should not be assessed only in regard to those most directly engaged in ending a struggle. All the stakeholders are rarely involved in settling a fight; yet in determining how constructive the conflict outcome is, the more distant stakeholders should also be considered. Finally, characterizations should give weight to long-term considerations as well as short-term ones.

PATHS TO SETTLEMENT

There exist many paths to settlement that can be pursued by stakeholders in a conflict. One way to distinguish between them is to separate settlements achieved through nonnegotiated processes from those achieved through negotiation.

Nonnegotiated Paths to Conflict Settlement

There are several nonnegotiated ways to end a fight, each of which can be combined in diverse ways. Most small-scale disputes between neighbors, within extended families, and among members of work organizations are resolved without written agreements. Even large-scale struggles sometimes quietly subside to low-level contention after threatening to erupt into violent confrontation or after intense struggle. Sometimes unilateral actions are taken, modifying the status quo, and the other side acquiesces to them.

Six types of nonnegotiated endings are distinguished here.[9] First, a settlement may be externally imposed, with varying degrees of concurrence between the adversaries. This includes, for example, arbitration, judicial proceedings, police intervention, or forceful intervention by an international organization.

Second, one side in the conflict may unilaterally force the other side to capitulate or destroy it as an organized entity. Mutinies, uprisings, and other disruptive challenges to authority are often simply suppressed. Capitulation may also arise from a restructuring of one of the parties so that its representatives no longer contest the goals of the other side. This may result from a change in the leadership of one of the adversaries, especially a leadership whose policies were not supported by major elements of its constituency.

Third, a fundamental conversion of one or both sides may arise from the experience with the conflict. Important members of one side may become convinced that the views of the adversary have great merit, undermining faith in their previous ideology or religious beliefs. Thus, many white South Africans who had believed in the propriety of apartheid became convinced in the course of the struggle against apartheid that it was wrong and inconsistent with Christianity. Similarly, in the 1980s many persons in the Soviet Union increasingly found fault with the workings of the Soviet system and viewed the Western democratic and free market system as attractive.[10]

Fourth, a conflict may be settled by implicit bargaining, as each adversary takes actions, partly in response to what the other side has done, until a new mutual accommodation has been reached. The actions are left to speak for themselves, and each side makes its own interpretations of what has happened. This may reflect a kind of stalemate that neither side can overcome but that is preferred by the adversaries to acknowledging the reality and giving it legitimacy. Thus, in some civil wars the government may for years control the capital and many regions of the country while insurgents control a segment of the country, as has often been the case in Afghanistan.[11]

Fifth, one party to a conflict may raise and pursue a contentious issue, but meeting strong resistance it may abandon the pursuit and the conflict becomes dormant. The challenge withdrawn, the overt struggle dwindles away. Or a diffuse conflict may erupt in a demonstration or other protest in which demands are voiced but no settlement of the ostensible issues is reached, and yet the protests cease. The grievance may remain, but the other factors essential to sustain the struggle are lacking.

Finally, one side may be exterminated or expelled from the social system that the victor controls. This may entail genocide or ethnic cleansing or other forms of driving people out of the organization, territory, or society ruled by the victors. A conflict may also end as one party in the conflict ceases to exist in a coherent form and with a clear identity as a significant contender. It may have overreached, or its ideology and strategy, which had been timely and seemingly effective, ill fits new times. The dissolution of the Soviet Union as the outcome of the Cold War may be viewed this way, and the waning of al Qaeda as a major global threat to the United States is becoming another example.

Note that in many of these terminations, the adversaries themselves may not openly acknowledge that the conflict has ended. This means that the belligerents in a struggle may disagree about when (or whether) a conflict has ended and what the terms of its settlement were. In addition, outside analysts or observers sometimes use their own criteria and judgment for regarding a conflict as terminated. For example, Uppsala University's Conflict Data Program (UCDP) maintains a conflict termination dataset that contains information on how armed conflicts of different type and intensity have been terminated.[12] The UCDP program identifies six different kinds of conflict terminations: peace agreement; cease-fire with conflict regulation; cease-fire agreement; victory; and low level, which indicates that conflict activities continued but did not reach the UCDP "threshold" number of fatalities per year; and other (termination did not fit any of the above criteria). The dataset also identifies four types of conflicts in its dataset: extrasystemic (wars of colonial independence), interstate, internal, and internationalized internal. For the period 1946–2009 the UCDP data indicate that across all conflict types 24 percent of the conflicts were terminated with a peace agreement, 21 percent of the conflicts were terminated due to the victory of one side over the other, 12 percent were terminated though cease-fire with conflict regulation, 3 percent were terminated through cease-fire alone, and 40 percent were terminated because deaths resulting from the conflict simply dropped below the UCDP threshold. When the data are broken down according to conflict type, interesting variations in this pattern emerge. For instance, within extrasystemic conflicts peace agreements are the most frequent means of conflict termination (48 percent). For internal conflicts the most frequent means of conflict termination is low activity (41 percent). For internationalized internal conflict, victory by one side over the other accounts for the largest percent of terminations (35 percent). Finally, for interstate conflicts there is no dominant means of termination, although the most infrequent type of termination is victory (12 percent).

Negotiated Paths to Conflict Settlement

In struggles in which the stakes are not as high as in civil wars or where adversaries regard legitimate institutionalized ways of managing the conflict to exist, negotiated endings are highly likely. Most interpersonal and intergroup community and societal conflicts have those characteristics. More particularly, negotiated agreements are generally used to settle economic and political conflicts in most domestic settings. The highly contentious issue of protection of endangered species in the United States, for instance, has gone through many rounds of negotiation in the U.S. Congress. Specifically, reviews of the landmark Endangered Species Act of 1973 have been carried out through highly institutionalized means that have resulted in a series of negotiated amendments over the years meant to accommodate the interests of various stakeholders impacted by the Act.[13] In such cases institutionalized mechanisms for settlement are usually seen as legitimate by partisans on both sides of the conflict. Negotiated agreements are emphasized in this book because they are more likely than nonnegotiated outcomes to reflect mutual accommodation. Negotiations increase the chances that the conflict settlement will be constructive.[14] They also are expected to increase the likelihood that the negotiators' constituents will support the agreement and hence that the settlement will be enduring. The growing literature on how negotiations can be done to maximize efficiency, mutual gain, social justice, and durability contribute to understanding why those expectations are fulfilled in some cases but not in others.

Negotiation occurs in every aspect of social life, between companies buying and selling materials needed in production, among family members deciding where to spend a vacation, between a supervisor and a worker settling how long it will take to finish a task, or between governments setting the conditions to end a crisis.[15] The negotiating parties, in all these cases, are trying to find the terms they will mutually accept to act jointly: either to transfer ownership of a house or to cease firing weapons at each other.

Negotiating to end a fight, however, tends to be unlike negotiating a sale of a commodity in several ways. First, in negotiating a sale the seller usually has alternative buyers and the buyer typically can find alternative sellers. An agreement to end a fight, however, must be made between existing adversaries; peace is negotiated with enemies. Second, negotiations to end a fight usually occur after interactions with the adversary have aroused anger and mistrust. But this is typically not the case in purchasing a car or a house. Third, in a conflict the alternative to not reaching an agreement is often to continue the fight and suffer ongoing costs. In a business transaction, the alternative usually is to find another negotiating partner.

Negotiations to de-escalate or to end struggles, nevertheless, share some qualities with trading kinds of negotiations. For example, the logic of the search for a mutually acceptable agreement is generally shared in all negotiations. Furthermore, negotiations generally move through various stages: including each party preparing its positions; the parties arranging who will negotiate and what the agenda will be; and the sides setting forth their positions, exploring possible options, exchanging concessions, reaching an agreement, and implementing the agreement.[16] In addition, the nature of negotiations varies considerably, unrelated to whether they are part of an effort to settle a conflict or to sell a commodity. For example, the negotiating partners may anticipate an ongoing relationship with recurrent negotiations, or they may anticipate that after the agreement is reached their interactions will largely cease. The negotiations may also vary in their scope, being about a narrow matter, part of a larger set of negotiations, or about a wide range of matters at the same time. In examining negotiations to settle a struggle, therefore, some lessons can be drawn from other kinds of negotiations, but that should be done thoughtfully, taking into account the peculiarities of negotiations in the context of a fight and the degree to which the particular conflict or exchange context differs.

Theories and Strategies of Negotiation

People have reflected about negotiations for a very long time, since they are a universal aspect of social life. The reflections have produced general theories, suggested rules of conduct, and provided many observations about how negotiations are conducted.[17] Much theorizing has been based on the analysis of actual behavior, seeking to predict or explain negotiating conduct. Some theorizing also has been deductive, based on assumptions about human nature or the logic of mathematical games. In either case, the reflections often take the form of admonitions, prescribing good negotiating behavior. One variation in these prescriptions underlies much discussion about negotiations and is particularly relevant here. At one extreme, negotiation is treated as a way of waging a contest, and the prescriptions are about how to win for yourself and your side. At the other extreme, negotiation is considered a way to reach mutually acceptable and even beneficial agreements, and the prescriptions aim to efficiently and effectively attain such outcomes for all parties in the negotiations.

Maximizing One Side's Advantage

In conflicts, people often view negotiations as a way to continue their fight. Consequently, each side tries to gain as much as it can, expecting that the gains will be at the expense of the other side. Some theorists reason that this is inherent in negotiations and therefore each side must pursue this effort or risk being badly exploited. Others argue that negotiators generally believe that this is so and therefore act on that belief, making it effectively true, but that they might be led to believe otherwise.

Adherents of this conventional approach tend to take a hard line in negotiations, arguing that by firmly staking out a desired position and holding to it, negotiators will maximize their benefits. Conversely, making concessions will be viewed as indicating weakness and will invite increased demands or rigidity by the other side. From this perspective, conflicts are essentially zero-sum in character, and negotiations typically take the form of a series of concessions moving toward convergence somewhere between the initially stated positions.

In this approach, much attention is accorded to tough bargaining strategies. The advantages of staking out a relatively high opening position are emphasized. This follows from the negotiating parties' belief that a series of concessions by opposing sides will be made and an agreement most likely will be reached somewhere between the opposing opening positions, around the midpoint between them. The midpoint assumes salience as a focal point, barring other bases for making a particular division seem natural and legitimate.[18]

Persons using this approach give attention to the strategy of convincing the other side that significant concessions cannot be made. Tactics that seem to commit the negotiator to the position staked out and leave little room for maneuver are frequently made. For example, leaders may make their positions public, and even announce them prior to negotiations, so that they would suffer a loss of face if they later backed down. They may also say that they cannot change their positions because of constraints imposed by their constituency, who would not support any concession. Negotiators may also assert that they are under strict instructions and are not authorized to make any concessions. Consider how Soviet intransigence in negotiations with the United States during the Cold War was often attributed to the inability of Soviet negotiators to deviate from strict instructions.[19]

This conventional approach also tends to emphasize that one side may use or threaten to use coercion in order to convince its adversary that the alternatives will be more costly than the terms being offered. Indeed, in many cases negotiations are conducted while a mutually coercive struggle is being waged, as happens when collective bargaining is conducted while a strike is on or peace negotiations are conducted while a war continues, as has been the case in Afghanistan where the United States engaged in nascent talks with representatives from the Taliban even while fighting a war against them.

One side may even intensify the struggle to increase its bargaining power, whether by harming the adversary, increasing its coercive capacity, or strengthening support among coalition partners, as was the case with U.S. President Ronald Reagan's aggressive pursuit of "star-wars" anti-missile technologies even as U.S.-Soviet nuclear arms negotiations began in earnest. Such re-escalations of a conflict sometimes appear to succeed but other times may severely damage the process of reaching a negotiated settlement, as occurred with the second Palestinian intifada that erupted in September 2000.

Duplicity is not so widely discussed in the scholarly literature, but its significance is noted by practitioners and feared by many members of each adversary party. One or more sides often provide deceptive or misleading information about their capabilities, alternatives, and preferences. The degree to which this is done, and is expected, varies by personality, social role, culture, and subculture.[20]

Maximizing Mutual Benefit

The problem-solving approach has developed in part from critiques of the relatively traditional one-sided maximizing style. The approach, derived from many analyses and practices, has become increasingly adopted beginning in the early 1980s.[21] Game-theory models and social psychological experiments have revealed the many self-defeating dangers of seeking immediate unilateral gains. Prescriptions for an alternative approach that would serve the best interests of all or most of the negotiating parties began to emerge. These were skillfully set forth in the vastly influential book *Getting to Yes* by Roger Fisher and William Ury, originally published in 1981.[22]

Fisher and Ury named their approach to negotiation "principled" and located it between the hard-line and soft-line negotiation approaches. They argued that with positional bargaining, negotiators play either a soft or a hard game, but that negotiators should change the game and negotiate on the merits. For example, the goal for those following a soft line is agreement, and the goal for the hard-liners is victory, but the goal for those negotiating on the merits is a wise outcome reached efficiently and amicably. This means, for example, separating the people from the problem, focusing on interests and not positions, inventing options for mutual gain, and insisting on objective criteria in choosing options.

Advocates of this approach (presently often identified as interest-based negotiations) contend that in traditional negotiation, bargaining positions are often set forth without adequate reflection about the underlying interests the positions are supposed to satisfy, so that gaining the positions becomes the goal rather than satisfying the underlying interests. Indeed, more than one way to satisfy underlying interests frequently exists. If both sides examine their interests and explore various options to meeting them, it is often possible to discover options that substantially meet the underlying interests of all the negotiating partners. A variety of tactics can facilitate such a problem-solving strategy. For example, negotiators may ask questions, search to understand what the other side's interests are, and try to communicate their recognition of how the other side sees them. Making such efforts contributes to converting a hostile negotiation session into a problem-solving discussion.

Another important technique is to generate many possible options to solve the problem. Special brainstorming periods may be used for this purpose, in which all participants are encouraged to suggest solutions and these ideas are not to be critiqued or discussed until very many options have been introduced. Only then are ideas that seem to be the basis for actual solutions selected, examined carefully, and modified in discussion. A related basic idea is that a conflict can be reconfigured, under certain conditions, so that a mutually beneficial or at least mutually acceptable agreement can be reached. Reframing the conflict and constructing a formula in order to enter negotiations can help reach an agreement.[23]

To undertake negotiations, each adversary must come to believe that a joint settlement of some contested issues is possible. Moreover, joint action is needed, a unilaterally imposed settlement is not considered feasible, and each side acknowledges that the interests of the other side must be given some recognition. The diagnoses need not be totally shared, but they must be compatible for serious negotiations to be undertaken. As I. William Zartman and Maureen Berman state: "Negotiation is appropriate when the parties see that a problem can only be resolved jointly and when they have the will to end an existing situation they consider unacceptable, while admitting the other party's or parties' claim to participate in that solution."[24]

Such diagnoses come about by reframing the conflict so that it is no longer viewed as purely zero-sum; rather, some common interests will be served by a joint solution. Along with the redefinition, possible formulas for settling the conflict emerge. The formulas may begin to be constructed in the prenegotiation stage of a conflict or in the early negotiation sessions. The formula may be the result of mutual concessions, as that which occurs in negotiations following a traditional bargaining model. But they also may be constructed by reference to a general conception or principle. A combination of a general framework with concessions and trade-offs is likely for complex, multidimensional problems.[25]

This new formula may be related to a redefinition of the primary parties involved in the conflict. Conflicts that appear nonnegotiable for one set of parties may become negotiable for a subset of those parties or by including additional parties with a stake in the outcome.[26] To illustrate, the several interlocked conflicts in the Middle East offer many examples of shifting diagnoses and formulas for settlement. One recurrent difference in the diagnoses of the conflict and of the possible formulas for resolution is whether the conflict is to be considered as a single, multifaceted conflict requiring a comprehensive settlement or a set of related conflicts best dealt with in a step-by-step fashion. Various parties have at different times stressed one or the other formulation regarding the Arab-Israeli conflict. Generally, prior to the Egyptian-Israeli peace treaty of 1979, the Arab governments had sought comprehensive negotiations, including Palestinian representation, while the Israeli government tended to seek bilateral negotiations with one Arab government at a time.

In 1977, President Jimmy Carter sought a comprehensive settlement and worked to organize a peace conference including Israel and all the neighboring Arab countries and Palestinian representatives within the Jordanian delegation. Anwar al-Sadat, president of Egypt, came to believe that such a comprehensive meeting was doomed to fail because too many intransigent parties would participate. He decided to break open the barrier to peace by going to Jerusalem and opening a dialogue with Israel, and to the amazement of the world he did this in November 1977.[27] Afterward, with the help of President Carter and the U.S. team of mediators, a treaty was negotiated and signed in March 1979. Sadat also tried to represent the Palestinians and to link Egypt's peace treaty with a resolution of the Palestinian issue, but he failed to do so.

Sadat was hailed as a great leader and peacemaker in Israel and most of the world, receiving the Nobel Peace Prize along with Israeli Prime Minister Menachem Begin. But Sadat was widely condemned by Arabs as a traitor, and Egypt was ostracized by the Arab world. Clearly, different combinations of disputants will produce different formulas resulting in different solutions. Making agreements among those finding a formula to do so may also outrage many others with a stake in the conflict.

Formulas, in a similar way, may be based on one or two issues from the many in contention or by aggregating many issues to seek a more comprehensive settlement. Each strategy can be effective under particular circumstances. By disaggregating or fractionating a conflict, particular issues may be selected that appear relatively easy to solve.[28] They may appear to be less contentious and less risky. Once successfully negotiated and implemented, they often become stepping stones to agreements regarding more fundamental issues.

Aggregating several issues can also be the basis for a formula because linking issues facilitates trade-offs among them.[29] Although negotiating parties may have opposing interests on many issues, the priority they assign to each issue is likely to be different. By linking the issues, party A may give up to party B what is much more valuable to B than to A and in exchange, party B will give up what is more important to the other side than to itself.[30] For example, after the Israeli army seized and occupied all of the Sinai in 1967, the territory became a matter of contention between Egypt and Israel. The Israelis wanted security from military threats from Egypt, and Egypt wanted to regain sovereignty over its territory. Among other matters, the Egyptian-Israeli peace treaty of 1979 encompassed a trade-off: Egypt regained sovereignty over all of the Sinai, and Israel's security concerns were assuaged by the treaty provision severely limiting the presence of Egyptian military capability in the Sinai.

Finally, a formula may be based on a shared image of the future or an agreed-on conception of the conflict as a problem.[31] Particularly, in ethnic conflicts, having a shared vision of the future relationship between the contending communities is critical. The negotiators may anticipate an outcome in which their communities will become separate countries, establish a system of autonomous regions, or construct a political structure providing power sharing among the different communities. In the case of an international environmental dispute, a problem-solving process is aided if the negotiators agree that they are confronting a shared ecological problem. This likelihood is enhanced when the negotiators from different countries share common professional outlooks, have developed personal relationships, and are joined by nongovernmental representatives in the negotiations.[32]

What is critical in the problem-solving approach is working together to find solutions. Innovative thinking can often make conflicts that seem nonnegotiable open to joint solutions, but such thinking must be convincingly communicated to significant segments of each side's members if the agreement is to be implemented and sustained.

Combining One-Sided Maximizing and Problem-Solving Approaches

In the minds of some advocates of the traditional one-sided maximizing approach and of some advocates of the problem-solving approach, the two perspectives are incompatible. Some traditionalists argue that ultimately one side wins and the other loses and negotiation simply reflects and ratifies that reality. They dismiss the adherents of the other approach as being naive and unrealistic. Moreover, some critics of the problem-solving approach argue that it often fails to deal with the existing asymmetries of power and enduring injustices.[33]

On the other hand, some advocates of the integrative problem-solving approach contend that every conflict can be converted into a set of negotiable interests and then reconfigured in a way that is mutually beneficial to those with a stake in the solution. They dismiss the adherents of the traditional approach as rigid and enamored with toughness such that each side seeks to advance its interests unilaterally, which fosters reliance on force and sustains injustice.

In actuality, the two approaches are often complementary, one being more appropriate and effective under some circumstances than others. Most analysts and practitioners believe that each of the two approaches can be carried too far and think that in practice negotiators tend to synthesize the approaches and their prescriptions derived from both. Some commonalities and complementarities deserve attention.

Analyzing the conflict that is to be settled by negotiations is an important first step to effective negotiation of any kind.[34] Such analyses also require attending to the alternatives each side has if a negotiated agreement is not reached. For rational calculation, the best nonnegotiated alternative sets the minimum terms a party is willing to accept in negotiations. One or more side, however, may not fully estimate what its best alternative would be; its members may get caught up in the process of negotiation and consider not reaching an agreement to be necessarily a failure. A prescriptive admonition of many trainers and consultants of negotiation, therefore, is that a negotiating team must carefully consider what its best alternative to a negotiated agreement (BATNA) is.[35]

Advocates of the one-sided maximizing and of the problem-solving approaches tend to differ in how to affect the other side's BATNA. Persons utilizing the traditional approach tend to believe that it is necessary to change the external reality, often by increasing the costs to the other side of failing to accept the terms offered or by enhancing its options to satisfy its interests in other ways. Problem solvers, however, tend to argue that changing the other side's BATNA may be affected by changing the frame within which the conflict is viewed. Such changes may be brought about by persuasive efforts and by insights gained from exploring the perspectives of the opposing sides.

Another matter of significance to analysts and practitioners of negotiations is the appropriate time for undertaking de-escalating efforts. There is widespread consensus that the effectiveness of de-escalating efforts, whether by partisans or by interveners, depends on the timing of such efforts. But there is much less consensus about what is the ripe moment for various strategies. Those taking a traditional approach tend to argue that until the adversaries have exhausted the coercive alternatives, de-escalating efforts are not likely to be effective. Ill-timed efforts to de-escalate a conflict will not be successful and can have undesired consequences.[36] On the other hand, problem-solving advocates tend to emphasize the value of de-escalating attempts in a wide variety of circumstances, arguing for finding an attractive possible outcome in the prevailing circumstances.[37] An emphasis on constructing an acceptable formula in combination with a hurting stalemate having been reached between the adversaries provides a synthesis of the two approaches.[38]

Some negotiating techniques fit within either approach. For example, one negotiating partner may offer a "side payment" to the other, which provides some compensation to the other side for a concession in the matter being negotiated. This is feasible when there are significant asymmetries in the relationship between the negotiating sides. For example, a country that is located higher on a river running through another state has a geographic advantage over its downstream neighbor.[39] Although that situation is prone to conflict, it is the basis for many international treaties entailing significant cooperation. The Mekong River Commission, for example, has successfully coordinated international cooperation among the six countries that populate the Mekong Basin.[40] There are many issues relating to flood control, hydropower, and pollution that would be well served by up-stream and down-stream cooperation, whose achievement is attributable to compensation or side-payments by one state to the other to balance off the costs and benefits of the cooperative arrangement.

Ethical issues confound the choice of either negotiating approach, as indicated by the moral critiques that can be made of each approach. Critics of the one-sided maximizing approach, for example, may argue that the failure to attend to possible mutually acceptable solutions tends to perpetuate struggles destructively and often results in imposed oppressive outcomes. On the other hand, critics of the problem-solving approach may argue that in the rush to find an accommodation between adversaries, evildoers are rewarded and injustices perpetuated or de-escalating efforts fail and reduce the chances for an agreement when the times are more suitable. As discussed in chapter 11, ethical issues need to be considered in specific empirical conditions, partly because the weighting given to various ethical considerations is influenced by the perceived probabilities of diverse conflict endings.[41]

According to the perspective taken in this book, the problem-solving approach should be broadly understood to include strategies of constructive struggle. Those strategies may foster conditions that encourage conducting problem-solving negotiations and reaching outcomes that minimize injustice. Such strategies may also include escalating a conflict by mobilizing broad support and adhering to policies that do not deny the humanity of the opponents. The inducements used in such strategies include large components of persuasion, the offering of rewards, and coercion that is minimally violent.

Finally, we acknowledge that not all negotiations are serious attempts to resolve a conflict. Sometimes leaders of one party enter negotiations simply to demonstrate to their constituents, to a wider audience, or even to elements in the opposing side that they are devoted to peace; and they actually seek only to reveal the intransigence and unreasonableness of their opponents. They may formulate positions they expect to be rejected but that appear plausible to their own side. This was the case in the early years of the Reagan administration arms-control negotiations with the Soviet Union.[42] In the disarmament negotiations in the early years of the Cold War, both sides engaged in such tactics.[43]

Some negotiations, even those pursued for years, then, may be fraudulent. Nevertheless, even these may be transformed and become serious. Changes within one of the parties or changes in the ongoing struggle may produce a shift that facilitates earnest negotiations. The preceding negotiation sessions then may turn out to have been useful, for example, by constraining the tendency toward escalation. Moreover, the negotiators may have established interpersonal relations with each other and each side may have learned enough about the other side's concerns that when the time is more suitable, they can move speedily toward a mutual agreement. This happened when Mikhail Gorbachev led the Soviet Union into the pursuit of a new foreign policy.

This suggests that one side may be able to transform the course of negotiations, even when the other side entered into them for duplicitous reasons.

Treating a stated position, even one suspected of insincerity, as a serious offer and subject to modification may commit the side making the offer to become engaged in serious negotiations. Mediators sometimes are helpful in this regard, as was examined in chapter 8. They take a proposal submitted by party A, objected to by party B, and ask what changes would make it acceptable. They then take the modified proposal back to party A to discover what additional modifications the proposal requires to be acceptable.[44]

Cultural Considerations

One-sided maximization and problem-solving approaches share similar cultural limitations. They tend to focus on independent actors engaged in episodes of social interaction and that may reflect a particular cultural orientation. But other cultural views can be found. Thus, in some cultures, such as the traditional Chinese culture, conflict is viewed as a disruption of community relationships. Negotiation and accommodation is then seen as the right way to restore relations within the community in which the antagonistic parties live.

More generally, the distinction is often made, in this context, between individualistic and collectivist world outlooks.[45] European and North American societies are regarded as generally having individualistic cultures, emphasizing personal freedom and achievement. Many non-Western societies, in contrast, tend to be collectivist, according high respect to authority and giving group welfare precedence over individual welfare. Conflicts within individualistic societies tend to be adjudicated within a legal framework based on individual rights, and that framework tends to characterize one side as right and the other as wrong. Conflicts in societies with collectivist cultures tend to be handled through conciliation in order to sustain group affiliation.

Regard should be given to such cultural orientations, but they should not be made into stereotypes, assuming that all members of a given society share the identical culture and there is no overlap among cultures. Within every society, individual differences exist as well as do subcultural variations by class, area of residence, gender, and many other factors. Moreover, all cultures include a broad range of conduct, and persons in each culture are familiar with a wide variety of ways of conducting themselves, differing in their tendencies to act in a particular way in specific circumstances. For example, U.S. negotiators are often reported to go directly to the issues to be negotiated and try to reach an agreement quickly, while negotiators from many non-Western cultures think it is important to build a relationship within which the negotiations can be conducted and therefore take time to build that potential relationship.[46] But obviously there are circumstances when Americans, too, recognize that building a relationship is important and takes time, for example, in courting a potential customer or spouse.

As we consider negotiation and other paths to conflict termination, cultural variations should be kept in mind. We will treat one-sided maximization and problem-solving approaches broadly in order to minimize the cultural bias that otherwise would limit their applicability.

FORMS AND STAGES OF NEGOTIATION

Negotiations sometimes are completed in a single session, but generally, to settle large-scale conflicts a series of sessions are conducted over a period of months or even years. The negotiations are conducted in a wide variety of forms and generally proceed through several stages. Before discussing the consequences of different negotiation approaches, these contexts need to be mapped out, because the likelihood and consequences of pursuing one or another strategy differ in those various settings.

Forms of Negotiation

Negotiations vary in their institutionalization, size, scope, isolation, privacy, and conflict setting. The variations reflect differences among struggles and their context, and they have significant implications for the results of the negotiations. The various characteristics of negotiations are varyingly intertwined, but they are discussed separately here.

Institutionalization of Negotiation Procedures

Every society has procedures for settling disputes, generally embodied in political institutions and judicial proceedings. Informal negotiations often are integral to the working of these formal procedures. This obviously is the case in the negotiations among legislators drafting a law. It occurs in adversarial legal proceedings when the lawyers, frequently with the encouragement of the judges, negotiate a settlement of the case before it goes to trial.[47] Afterword, the agreement frequently is made binding by the court.

Those formal legal and political procedures available to resolve disputes are the almost universal context for the relatively unofficial and informal methods, generally referred to as alternative dispute resolution (ADR).[48] The disputants often recognize that if the informal procedures they are using do not result in an agreement, they have recourse to legal proceedings or to political action. ADR, then, serves as a complement to the formal and official procedures.

In the United States, and increasingly in many other societies, provisions are made for disputants to negotiate directly or with the support of mediators. The arenas in which such direct negotiations are conducted often function with legally enacted rules about procedures. In the case of collective bargaining, legislation and previous contracts define what is good faith bargaining and specify what is negotiable. In recent decades, understandings about informal conflict resolution procedures have developed in public policy disputes concerning environmental issues and alleged discrimination by gender, age, or minority status.

The form of institutionalization, reflecting culture and institutional structures, influences which negotiation approach is used. For example, in the United States the adversarial style is deeply embedded in the political and legal culture. The founding document of the U.S. government, the Constitution, is based on a system of checks and balances, presuming that a struggle between different government units will preserve and protect liberty. A society in which individuals and groups seek their own advantage is thought best managed by having other individuals and groups contest them in an adversarial manner. This is evident in the way the U.S. electoral and judicial systems function.

Elements of collective solidarity, mutual support, and shared responsibilities, of course, are also to be found in U.S. society. In recent years, conscious efforts have been made to promote less adversarial methods to manage possibly disputatious relations and specific conflicts. This has been true within work organizations, among groups differing in religion or ethnicity, and between groups differing in policy positions, for example, about environmental matters.[49] The conflict resolution movement and the promotion of the problem-solving approach to negotiation in many ways have been part of those developments.[50]

Scale of Negotiations

Negotiations vary in scale by the number of parties engaged and by the number of persons representing each party. Although most theorizing about negotiations assumes two parties are engaged, actual negotiations increasingly include more than two parties. In international affairs, multilateral negotiations are becoming more frequent and are conducted in large conferences. For example, the UN Convention on the Law of the Sea was negotiated with more than 150 governments represented.[51]

The participation of many parties often enables some of them to provide intermediary services and so to foster a problem-solving approach. Some participating parties may not have interests at stake as vital as those of the primary adversaries in the conference, and hence they are subjected to appeals for support from the major antagonists. This also encourages persuasive efforts, couched in terms of shared principles and objective criteria, appeals consistent with a problem-solving approach. This was evident in the extended Conference on Security and Cooperation in Europe negotiations, culminating in the 1975 Helsinki Accords.[52]

In negotiations involving large entities, each delegation is often numerous, with representation of diverse constituencies. Hence, in interstate negotiations technical specialists, even military specialists, in each delegation may discover some commonalities in perspectives and experience not as well shared with other members of their own delegation. This can become the basis for alliances or at least increased channels of communication across delegation lines.

Scope of Negotiations

Everything about the relations between adversaries cannot be settled at the same time. A subset of issues can be jointly chosen for negotiation, although often the parties may not agree about which matters should be subject to bargaining. Negotiations vary greatly in the significance and number of issues that are considered. They may include matters of vital concern to one or more parties or matters regarded as of insubstantial consequence, and they may include only a few items or encompass a great number and variety of issues.

Negotiations covering many significant matters pose difficulties, particularly for traditional negotiations, but bring opportunities for newer integrative negotiations, since the multiplicity of issues on the table enhances the likelihood of finding advantageous trade-offs. Constructing a formula for a solution becomes increasingly important and hence more likely, since it will be more energetically sought.

Isolation of Negotiation Sessions

Negotiations vary in their degree of isolation in several senses. Some negotiations are brief, one-time sessions, while others are conducted in a series of sessions over many years. Some negotiations result in agreements in a relatively short time and are regarded as unique agreements, some are viewed by the negotiating partners as part of a series of possible agreements, and some are considered to be one in a series of recurrent negotiations to renew expiring prior agreements. When agreements are viewed as the product of recurring negotiations, expectations about trade-offs over time may develop.

Some negotiations are conducted through one set of representatives in a single negotiating channel. For example, there may be only one official, highly visible channel and the negotiators take instructions and report back to the central authority of each negotiating party. But others are conducted through more than one channel. Thus, an official, but private "back channel" may be used in addition to the official and relatively public negotiation channel. Such a dual format was made famous (or infamous) when Henry Kissinger, while the official Strategic Arms Limitation Treaty (SALT I) negotiations were being conducted, met privately with the Soviet ambassador to the United States and shaped the terms of the SALT I agreement. He was criticized for keeping U.S. officials in the dark and not drawing on their expertise about the terms of the agreement. He later justified what he did by pointing out that he discussed SALT I in conjunction with several other matters in U.S.-Soviet relations, and explicit as well as implicit trade-offs were developed during those talks.[53] Such back channels have notable advantages in facilitating reaching agreements but also disadvantages in getting the agreements enacted and implemented.[54]

In international relations and other conflict arenas, various negotiation channels are used sequentially and concurrently with the official channel, as discussed in chapter 8. Among the many nonofficial channels are transnational organizations within which members of adversarial parties meet and discuss matters pertaining to the work of their common organizations. Another kind of track includes occasional meetings or ongoing dialogue groups with members from the adversary parties discussing the issues in contention between their respective countries (or communities or organizations). Such meetings were held between whites and blacks in Rhodesia beginning before official negotiating efforts were attempted for the transition to majority rule and the establishment of Zimbabwe.[55]

Privacy

Negotiations are conducted with varying degrees of confidentiality. Some are conducted in public; for example, community members may be important witnesses to a political or religious leader's mediation of a dispute between neighbors. Even negotiations between large-scale entities may be public, with news media providing coverage and the negotiators discussing their positions with the general public. On the other hand, many negotiations are conducted in private and they are considered confidential until they are concluded. Some negotiations are so confidential that only the participants and a few others are aware of them, and even the negotiators' constituents are not informed of them; the proceedings and sometimes even the agreements are considered secret.[56]

Several advantages accrue with confidential negotiations. The negotiators are able to be more flexible in considering each other's ideas and suggesting possible options, thus encouraging a relatively problem-solving approach.

They are also able to be more flexible in making concessions, thus facilitating traditional negotiation. These arguments are supported by social psychological experiments indicating that if negotiators are subject to attention and evaluation by their constituencies, they are more intransigent in their bargaining.[57]

In general, secrecy is particularly useful in the preliminary, prenegotiation stage. Explorations of possible agreements and steps to reach them can determine whether or not the time is ripe to undertake serious negotiations. Secret negotiations can also be useful when formal open negotiations become stalemated and positions appear frozen. This was the case when the official Israeli-Palestinian negotiations became stalemated in 1992 and another channel was opened in Oslo for meetings that explored options and constructed a package agreement unbeknown to the official delegations. The resulting 1993 Declaration of Principles was a startling surprise to the people on both sides.[58]

Secret negotiations, however, also can have severe drawbacks. The negotiators may reach agreements acceptable to them that do not reflect the interest of their respective constituents or that may be neglectful of implications damaging to all sides. Furthermore, mobilizing the necessary support to ratify and implement an agreement tends to be hampered by secrecy. A full and open discussion of the agreement reached and a legitimate ratification process are ways to minimize those risks.

Negotiation Stages

That negotiations move through several stages is generally recognized, even if there is no consensus about identifying them. Here, we discuss seven stages: prenegotiation, planning, initial presentations and analysis, search for options and formulas, drafting agreements, ratifying, and implementing. Different negotiation approaches and strategies are varyingly effective at each phase of negotiation.

Prenegotiation

In recent years, considerable attention has been devoted to the processes and conditions that bring adversaries to the negotiating table. In chapter 7, we considered the circumstances and policies that move adversaries toward de-escalation and ultimately toward settlement. Here, the proximate actions prior to direct negotiations are discussed, particularly after protracted struggle.

An early phase of this prenegotiation stage is the signaling by one of the adversaries to the other that it is interested in reaching a negotiated settlement.[59] This is not an easy matter. Adversaries often are mutually suspicious, and each side has been mobilized to sustain the positions staked out as its goals. Therefore, a leadership group thinking about making a conciliatory gesture as an overture to begin negotiations faces several risks. The other side may construe the overture as a sign of weakness and raise its demands; consequently, the leaders will appear foolish or weak to their followers. Another possibility is that the other side rejects the overture as a trick, aimed at appearing good to various audiences, but not serious; consequently, the overture may seem inept and be counterproductive.

Several policies can help minimize the risks associated with signaling a readiness to start negotiations. One is to use unofficial intermediaries to discover whether the basis for negotiations exists for the parties engaged in the struggle. Another tactic is to conduct secret meetings between high-ranking representatives of each side to probe for possible formulas for negotiations. Such communications help ensure that the overture will be appropriately reciprocated. For example, prior to President Sadat's dramatic visit to Jerusalem in November 1977, the Israeli foreign minister, Moshe Dayan, and the Egyptian deputy premier, Hassan Tuhami, discussed formulas for peace at a secret meeting hosted and facilitated by the king of Morocco in September 1977.[60]

Other policies involve taking a risk and by doing so making the overture particularly attractive and credible. The fundamental transformation of the Cold War between the blocs led by the United States and the Soviet Union was initiated in a series of statements and acts carried out by the government led by Premier Gorbachev. In many ways, the actions and their effects on President Reagan, his administration, the U.S. public, and the West generally were in accord with the idea of graduated reciprocation in tension-reduction (GRIT), discussed in chapter 7. The Soviet actions, however, did entail substantial risks to the Soviet Union, much greater than those recommended by Charles E. Osgood, who directed his articulation of GRIT at the United States. Gorbachev had reason to believe that the risks of the West taking unilateral advantage of the Soviets' military downsizing and restructuring were manageable, given the U.S. and Western opposition to the heightened militancy of the Reagan administration.[61] Gorbachev, however, underestimated the internal risks to the Soviet system.

The covert exploration and the grand public commitment can also be effectively combined. The adversary leaders can give each other some assurances, and then the apparently bold public gesture can win over mistrusting elements within the antagonistic side and rally constituents to the new course the gesture seems to initiate. The spectacle of the president of the largest Arab nation flying to Jerusalem in 1977 and addressing the Israeli Knesset was highly dramatic and constituted an irrevocable act. The prior secret direct and indirect communications ensured a warm response when President Sadat publicly expressed his readiness to go to Israel.

Some grand gestures can actually change the structure of the conflict and help transform it. This was true of the unconditional release of Nelson Mandela from prison by the Frederik Willem de Klerk government, in February 1990. It was a powerful transforming message for all people in South Africa that the struggle to end apartheid had entered a new phase.

Another prenegotiation aspect is the formulation of the structure for negotiations: this includes agreeing on the parameters of the negotiations, on the participants, and on the possible outcomes. Adversaries will avoid entering negotiations if they are convinced that the likely negotiated agreement will be worse than the status quo and deny them what they regard as minimally acceptable. Consequently, exploratory talks, through various intermediaries or directly between the adversaries' representatives at several levels, are often necessary before negotiations can begin.

Planning

Each negotiating party, before entering talks, generally reflects on what it seeks and how it proposes to reach its goals from the negotiations. In large-scale parties, difficult and complex negotiations are generally conducted among the various groups within each side that have a stake in the outcome. The goals of any large entity are always manifold, with varying priorities accorded different goals. The positions articulated for negotiation by each side reflect the relative influence of groups within that side.

It seems wise for each party entering negotiation to work out what it wants, what it will ask for, and what it will settle for prior to meeting with its negotiating counterparts. The negotiators will then enter discussions with detailed instructions about what they should try to get. But this fosters the traditional one-sided maximizing negotiation approach and makes problem-solving negotiation more difficult. The difficulties in combining the internal and external negotiations are severe. Roger Fisher suggests a strategy to reconcile them so as not to hamper a relatively problem-solving approach.[62] According to this strategy, the initial instructions should not include commitments, but directives, for example, to learn the other parties' views of their interests and concerns, to explain their own side's interests and concerns, and to generate a range of options that might satisfy both sides.

Initial Meetings and Analysis

What happens in the initial meetings varies with the negotiation approach being followed. In the relatively traditional approach, representatives of each side argue their positions. When these sessions are public, the staking out of commitments may subsequently hamper reaching a mutually acceptable agreement. In confidentially held negotiations and when the negotiations are anticipated to be lengthy, the initial sessions may involve a good measure of housekeeping matters, such as getting acquainted and agreeing on ground rules. The procedural understandings may pertain to confidentiality, ensuring space for informal socializing and scheduling some shared activities.

In these initial meetings, attention may be given to discussing the issues in contention and the concerns underlying the stated positions in order to ensure that each side understands how the other views the matters being negotiated. A shared analysis of the conflict may then emerge that sets the stage for viewing the conflict as a common problem the negotiators will seek to solve, rather than a contest each will try to win. Obviously, this is particularly important for the problem-solving approach. Regardless of the approach used, initial sessions of negotiations that are anticipated to be conducted over many meetings are often devoted to establishing an agenda and common priorities.

Inventing Options and Constructing Formulas

At various times in extended negotiations, sessions may be devoted to thinking of new options and constructing possible formulas for an agreement. Such sessions may be held at junctures in the extended negotiation process when an impasse seems to have arisen. Changing the venue or composition of the negotiating teams, for example, by having subgroups of technical experts meet or by adding outsiders to discuss the issues or to help facilitate the sessions may enhance the effectiveness of such sessions. In addition, discussions of possible trade-offs and formulas may occur in informal conversations over drinks at the bar or in side-channel meetings.

Drafting an Agreement

The product of a negotiated agreement is nearly always a written document, and the processes of negotiation are directed at finding the words the negotiating parties can all accept. The more detailed and precise the terms of the agreement are, the more difficult the task of writing is, as provisions for likely but unwanted contingencies are considered and ways to counter them fashioned. An agreement that uses vague and ambiguous terms to paper over differences can be written much more easily. But of course, precisely written documents reduce the likelihood of later misunderstandings and alleged violations. Negotiators try to balance the urgencies of reaching an agreement with their concerns to forge an enduring agreement; as noted later, mechanisms can be instituted to minimize future disagreements arising from inevitable ambiguities in any document.

To reach complex agreements involving many items, another set of choices among approaches must generally be made. According to one strategy, a disposition is first reached on particular items and these are treated as settled. They may be the relatively easy items, but agreeing on them helps create a sense of confidence and trust. Another approach sets aside the items settled early on but allows them to be reintroduced later when they may be renegotiated in the context of a larger trade-off among several items. A quite different approach is to agree on general principles and then work out solutions to specific issues based on those principles. Finally, the agreement may be negotiated as a whole with changes made incrementally to a single negotiating text. The latter strategies fit better than the former with the problem-solving negotiation approach, but the best strategy may well vary from struggle to struggle and from its cultural, historical, and social context.

Finally, the style of discourse used in negotiations can affect the speed with which an agreement is reached and its equity. Undoubtedly, there are cultural variations in how positions are put forward, discussed, accepted, and rejected. The style in the United States is generally viewed as direct, matter of fact, even hasty.[63] But even in the United States, effective negotiators are not confrontational. There is evidence that effective negotiators tend to ask more questions of their counterparts than do less effective negotiators, and they do not preface their remarks with "I disagree."[64] They tend not to attribute feelings and motives to the other side but clearly identify their own thoughts and feelings.

Signing and Ratifying

The negotiation process is not over, even when the negotiators have finalized an agreement. Often, the heads of governments or organizations that the negotiators represented formally sign the agreement, frequently at a public event. This gives visibility to the agreement and further commits the signatories to honor the agreement; like a wedding ceremony, its public nature announces the new status of the relationship and serves to bind the parties who have jointly reached the agreement.

Frequently, in addition, the people represented by those signing the agreement must ratify it. For example, a treaty signed by the president of the United States must be ratified by two-thirds of the U.S. Senate for the treaty to be legally binding on the United States. A labor contract signed by a union president usually must be approved by a majority of the union's members for the agreement to commit the union.

Concessions to significant constituency groups to gain their support for ratification may seem necessary; but they sometimes undermine the purpose of an agreement. For example, during the Cold War, after an arms control agreement was reached, promises of weapons modernization were often made to those whose support was important but who were reluctant to provide it. This was the case with the ratification of SALT I, and the result was a continuing increase in the number of nuclear warheads after the number of missile launchers was capped.

Implementing

Finally, attention must be given to the degree to which an agreement is adhered to and the signatory parties believe it is faithfully implemented. An agreement that is violated is a source of mistrust and renewed struggle. A sound agreement is one that is self-enforcing, giving both sides reason to comply with the agreement. In addition, committees and other mechanisms may be established to monitor compliance and to reconcile discrepant interpretations of the agreed-on document. The absence of such mechanisms contribute to the mutual recurrent recriminations between the North Korean and U.S. governments regarding agreements reached about nuclear weapons in North Korea. Implementation of agreements is increasingly recognized as a vital component in conflict resolution and is analyzed in chapter 10.

Summary

As we have seen, negotiations incorporate several interrelated stages. Furthermore, various forms of negotiation tend to be suitable at different negotiation stages. Being aware of these many possibilities helps those engaged in negotiations to conduct them more effectively. Experience and exchanging stories of past negotiations help expand negotiators' repertoires and so improve their skills. Of course, research and training can supplement and specify prior experience.

CONCLUSIONS

Problem-solving negotiation is always conducted within the context of many other conflict-ending processes. They are also conducted with the awareness that one or more of the protagonists may resort to more coercive means at various stages of the negotiation process. These relatively coercive means include recourse to the judicial process, to traditional one-sided maximization negotiations, and even to the use of violence.

Nevertheless, a struggle's ending is not shaped only by the threat of coercive and legal controls. The termination process itself alters the context in which the struggle is viewed. Through negotiation, enemies can become persons with concerns that are appreciated, and the conflict becomes a problem to be solved by joint action. The complexities of a conflict and the negotiation processes can be recognized as often providing opportunities to fashion a mutually acceptable settlement.

10

Outcomes and Post-Termination Sequences

A terminated conflict, through either negotiated or nonnegotiated processes, may seem as if it has vanished. Partisans demobilize, the media moves its attention to other matters, and public concern ebbs as the sense of urgency and threat surrounding the conflict subsides. In reality, however, conflicts are rarely resolved forever. In most cases, the "end" of conflict simply marks its transformation from one state to another by addressing some issues of contention but not others, by restructuring social and political power into new forms, and by eliminating some actors from the stage but not others. Sometimes the new conditions that emerge after a fight ends are significantly constructive, as when former enemies develop more equitable and stable relations, develop closer ties and less dehumanizing narratives about each other, or find ways to institutionalize their fight through nonviolent means, such as courts. Other times, however, a conflict outcome turns out to be only a pause in a protracted destructive struggle. The losing side may regroup and rise again, trying to regain what it lost in honor, land, freedom, or material wealth. Alternatively, new grievances are created by the agreement and its implementation. Thus, all outcomes, whether largely constructive or severely destructive, have consequences that themselves contain the seeds for new fights and struggles. In this chapter we consider different kinds of settlements and post-settlement sequences, the factors that help explain why one post-settlement sequence is likely to occur but not another, and how conditions at the end of a fight can be altered in order to maximize the chances for sustainable and constructive forms of conflict transformation.

VARIATIONS IN OUTCOMES

The outcomes at the end of a fight vary in many substantive ways, including (1) the degree to which they are part of a fundamental change in the adversarial relationship, (2) the degree to which they foster closer integration, (3) the way benefits are distributed among the major groups engaged in the fight on both sides, (4) the balance of vested interests to sustain or to change the outcomes, and (5) the degree to which the outcomes reached are regarded as one in a series or as final and irrevocable. The discussion in the chapter gives particular attention to outcomes embodied in explicit agreements.

Changes in Relations

A conflict termination is part of a fundamental change in relations when it is consistent with the transformation that has occurred, for example, when the collective identity of one side is redefined such that many no longer regard themselves as excluding their adversaries, who had been treated as outsiders. Confirming such a change can provide the major adversaries with the sense that the loss of former dominance enhances justice. To a significant degree, the transformation of Germans after Nazism, of Russians after Communism, and of South African whites after apartheid made the outcome in many senses a victory for their new self-understandings.

Yet even without such transformations, constructive conflict resolution may yield outcomes that are seen by the former adversaries as equitable and conflict transforming. Each side may have achieved something close to its aspirations, after a long, costly struggle. More often, in actual conflict settlements the result is one step in an already improving relationship. Issues of contention remain, but they may be pursued in a less antagonistic way than previously. This is illustrated in the relations between African Americans and European Americans in the southern states after the federal civil rights legislation starting in the mid-1960s (see table 6.2).

Most outcomes, or even explicit agreements, however, are not regarded as equitable by the partisans of each side. Generally, one adversary suffers what it must, accepting what it can get. It may bide its time, waiting for more opportune circumstances to renew its struggle. Sometimes an adversary settles after gaining only some of what it sought while still aspiring to win more in the future. Even members of the triumphant side may seek new conquests, finding that the fruits of victory are not as sweet as they expected, or because they are emboldened by recent victories. Finally, as the glow of victory passes, the awareness of remaining injustices and unfulfilled expectations rise in salience.

Partisans of the side that has been largely defeated often experience an increased sense of injustice. Relations and values they took for granted have become disrupted in painful ways. They feel that the other side has gone too far and they may try to mobilize support for a renewed fight to regain what they consider lost ground. There is a backlash. For example, in the United States social changes resulting from several interrelated struggles in the 1960s and early 1970s constituted a cultural revolution profoundly affecting social relations between men and women and between persons of different ethnicity, sexual orientation, and other social identities.[1] Many persons adhering to relatively traditional values and practices became deeply offended by these changes, and they mobilized to restore what they regarded as dangerous losses. In that context, some issues became matters of intense struggle, such as abortion, gun control, rights of gays and lesbians, prayer in the schools, and affirmative action. Organizations quickly arise, seeking to reverse some of the changes or to block further movement; for example, the effort to add an amendment to the U.S. Constitution providing for equal rights for women (ERA) was defeated in 1982. However, the expansion of opportunities for women and minorities had become embedded in American society and continues (for a history of the women's rights movement see table 10.1).

TABLE 10.1. Major Events in Women's Rights Movement, 1963–2010

1963	Report of the President's Commission on the Status of Women published. Betty Friedan's *Feminine Mystique* published.
1964	U.S. Congress passes the Civil Rights Act, including Title VII, prohibiting discrimination in employment on the basis of sex.
1965	National Organization for Women (NOW) is founded.
1968	New York NOW members picket the *New York Times* to end sex-segregated classified advertising.
1970	Kate Millet publishes *Sexual Politics;* Robin Morgan edits the book *Sisterhood Is Powerful.*
1972	Congress passes the Equal Rights Amendment (ERA), ratification by states required. Congress passes Title IX of Educational Amendments to the Civil Rights Act, enforce sex equality in education. *Ms*. magazine initiated.
1973	Supreme Court in *Roe v. Wade* decision establishes a woman's right to abortion. First U.S. battered women's shelters open.
1974	The Coalition of Labor Union Women is formed.
1975	The United Nations sponsor: First International Conference on Women, in Mexico City.
1987	U.S. Congress declares "Women's History Month." Fund for the Feminist Majority founded to support feminists running for office.
1993	Congress passes the Family and Medical Leave Act, providing men and women protected unpaid leave for family emergencies.
1994	Congress passes the Violence Against Women Act.
2000	UN Security Council Resolution 1325 passed calling for increased representation of women at levels regarding peace and security.
2004	Some 1.1 million join March for Freedom of Choice, Washington, D.C.
2009	Lily Ledbetter Fair Pay Restoration Act signed by President Obama, allowing for signing complaints after last paycheck.
2010	UN General Assembly creates new UN Entity for Gender Equality and Empowerment of Women, uniting four earlier agencies and offices.

Events of 1963–1994 adapted from Ruth Rosen, *The World Split Open* (New York: Viking, 2000).

Closer Integration

The second noteworthy variation among outcomes is along the dimension of integration and separation of the parties. Toward the integration end of the continuum, the parties interact relatively frequently, are mutually dependent, and have important shared identities and interests. Toward the separation end, the parties have little contact with each other, function independently, and have little shared identity or interests. Nevertheless, the form of this variation necessarily differs for diverse kinds of relationships within and between countries.

In the chapters on the emergence and escalation of conflicts, evidence was cited indicating that integration between potential adversaries tends to prevent the outbreak and escalation of destructive conflicts. But once a destructive conflict has been waged, this is not so clear. After animosities and grievances have increased and mutual fears have been raised, outcomes that entail close integration might seem to be fraught with the danger of renewed strife. In those circumstances, perhaps separation is more likely to avoid a renewal of destructive conflict.

Some analysts of post-combat settlements, following destructive ethnic or other communal civil wars, have made this argument. For example, Chaim Kaufman stresses the security dilemma that arises as one community confronts another that distrusts it: As members of one community act to increase their security, members of the other community will perceive the actions as threatening.[2] This follows from the experience of mobilization, stories of atrocities, and heightened exclusive ethnic or other communal identities.

There are many examples of war recurrence after a civil war ended without partition, such as Algeria and Congo/Zaire. In other cases, partitions were not followed by wars, as in the Pakistan-Bangladesh situation. On the other hand, war followed the partition of India and Pakistan, while peace without partition followed the bloody ethnic wars in South Africa and Uganda. In a careful quantitative analysis of many factors, Nicholas Sambanis does not find that partition significantly reduces the risk of war recurrence following civil wars.[3] He finds only weak support for the hypothesis that partitions contribute significantly to ending low-level ethnic violence after civil wars.

These findings should not be surprising. How terminations entailing integration or partition affect the occurrence of violent conflict depend on the quality of the integration, of the partition, and on many other aspects of the settlement. The degree to which the settlement reflects the preferences of the opposing sides and is not unilaterally imposed is crucial. A mutually acceptable accommodation becomes possible as one or both sides modify their identities, grievances, conflict goals, and beliefs about ways to achieve their goals and so transform their conflict with each other.

Distribution of Benefits

The third important aspect of a conflict outcome to be considered is the way benefits are distributed between the adversaries. The issue is whether the settlements embody a net alleviation of grievances for each side. What is particularly important is the extent to which any terminating provisions and understandings, as well as how they are implemented, reduce grievances and avoid generating new ones. The effects of this variation on the subsequent course of the conflict are relatively straightforward: if the grievances turn out to remain or even increase, a recurrence of intense conflict is more likely. This appears to be the case in post–civil war countries where challengers have gained a "seat at the table" through power-sharing provisions. Recent research by Mattes and Savun, for instance, shows that such provisions are positively correlated with the durability of peace agreements in forty-six civil wars that occurred between 1945 and 2006 where a peace settlement was reached.[4] Power sharing tends to alleviate post-termination grievances because it gives former rebels the ability to address remaining grievances through nonviolent political processes.

Some ways that terminating arrangements affect the level of satisfaction are indirect and not so obvious. Having ended a fight, expectations about future benefits are often raised; consequently, the actual results are generally disappointing. This problem is aggravated by the tendency of leaders to try to mobilize constituent support for a concluding agreement by extolling the benefits it will bring. They oversell the agreement. Furthermore, leaders on each side may stress the benefits to be derived, but those benefits from the other side's point of view are contingent on the partners' conduct.

The Declaration of Principles agreed to by the PLO leadership and the government of Israel in September 1993 seemed to promise to each side much of what it desperately wanted. For the Palestinians, the prospect of a state of their own in the territories occupied by Israel seemed imminent. For the Israelis, the acceptance of Israel in the region promised security in their own country. These expectations were not quickly realized, and evidence that they would not be soon appeared.[5] Palestinians grew mistrustful as Jewish settlements expanded in the occupied territories and Israelis grew mistrustful as the Palestinian Authority (PA) exceeded limits on armed officials and as terror attacks continued. Hard bargaining had characterized the negotiations and now the implementation of agreements was generally tardy, giving rise to doubts of good faith. The agreements of September 1993 became a source of grievance for many persons on both the Israeli and Palestinian sides.

Vested Interests

The fourth aspect of an outcome that affects its durability is the extent to which vested interests in maintaining it arise within each side. Agreement provisions to dismantle the structures that had perpetuated the struggle enhance the balance favoring the agreement's durability. More directly, mechanisms embodied in an agreement may create vested interests in its preservation. Finally, practices and institutions may be established to manage the disputes that arise in implementing the terms of the agreement.[6]

Dismantling the structures that had perpetuated the struggle is often critical in maintaining a de-escalatory agreement or in raising the chances that it will be a step toward a full peace and mutual accommodation. In any protracted struggle, particularly between large-scale adversaries, a significant problem is the redeployment of those who made a career of waging the struggle. In the aftermath of civil wars, for example, the disarming of the militias and large military forces and finding employment for the former combatants is a severe challenge. Consequently, procedures and institutional safeguards for reducing the weapons of war have been incorporated in the settlement package ending the civil wars in Namibia and in El Salvador, including a land-for-arms exchange to former combatants.[7]

The problem is particularly difficult when some groups, sometimes acting covertly, conduct terrorist acts and gross human rights violations. Sometimes they are assured of amnesty from prosecution in order to gain their cooperation in reaching a settlement and complying with it, and that would seem to undermine the justice the settlement is expected to advance. We will return to this issue when discussing reconciliation.

Creating vested interests for a new accommodation between former adversaries is also important to sustain a de-escalatory agreement. This may take the form of creating organizations with paid staffs whose job it is to implement and monitor the provisions of an agreement, as was done in the United States to fulfill legislation barring discrimination. Vested interests may also be created by coengagement, taking the form of institutions that bring representatives of the former adversaries to work in a common enterprise. A particularly notable example of this is the European Coal and Steel Community.[8] Established in 1952 by France, West Germany, Italy, Belgium, the Netherlands, and Luxembourg, it was a supranational institution with authority over the production of coal and steel in the six countries. In accord with the logic of functional integration, transnational nongovernmental organizations (NGOs) and actions followed. Slowly and with interruptions, integration among the six European countries grew and then expanded into a wider European Union.[9]

Ensuring compliance to an agreement ending or managing a conflict obviously is critical to the survival of the agreement and constructive relations between the former adversaries. Compliance and full implementation of agreements can be made more certain by several mechanisms and conditions. Thus, the signatories to an agreement may establish an ongoing agency to consider differing interpretations of the agreement, receive charges of violations, and discuss possible revisions under changing circumstances. For example, as part of the 1972 agreement to limit the number of strategic nuclear weapons (SALT I), a Standing Consultative Commission was established.[10]

Conclusiveness

Finally, the fifth important variation in outcomes is the degree to which the adversaries regard them to be part of an ongoing series of contentions or as a relatively irrevocable conclusion. Thus, in collective bargaining between labor and management, each negotiated agreement is generally regarded as one in a never-ending series of negotiations. In general, in large-scale, protracted conflicts, beginning with efforts to reach a comprehensive settlement is not likely to be successful. Rather, an overall peace is more likely to be achieved on a step-by-step basis. This seems to have been the case for the transformation of the U.S.-Soviet relationship over many years, which contributed to the fundamental change within the Soviet Union. In a quite different way, the transformation of the Egyptian-Israeli conflict occurred in the course of two partial agreements between Egypt and Israel, building on each other and culminating in the 1979 treaty of peace. Domestically, the negotiations between the South African government and the ANC resulted in a series of agreements cumulatively marking the fundamental South African transformation.

In the case of Israeli-Palestinian relations, however, the series of agreements beginning in September 1993 collapsed as a violent struggle erupted in September 2000. Certainly, the negotiation of limited agreements step-by-step does not guarantee steady progress to a comprehensive peace agreement. A great many factors converged to account for the failure in this case; at this point we cite those pertaining to the relations between the Israeli Jews and the Palestinians.[11] The leaders of the PLO and the Israeli government led by the Labor Party did not convince their respective populations to accept the ultimate deal that would have to be reached. They could not bring along the rejectionist groups in their respective camps nor marginalize their capacity to preclude a final agreement. So the leadership of each side tried to placate the opponents of the emerging final agreement, but in doing so raised suspicion and mistrust from their negotiating partners on the other side. Although some peacemaking activities at the grassroots and elite levels were pursued, they were limited compared to the opponents' incitement against the likely final agreement. As a consequence, the agreements that were reached were not implemented in a timely fashion and each side could point to the other side's violations of previous agreements.

In order to avoid undermining progress toward a stable mutually acceptable accommodation, legitimate channels for modifying and improving the terms of an agreement are helpful. That also tends to incorporate more members of each side in the peace process.

VARIATIONS IN POST-TERMINATION SEQUENCES

Generally the outcome conditions reviewed above result in six different types of conflict sequences, following the termination of a particular conflict. First, an outcome may help prevent a conflict from deteriorating into a protracted destructive struggle by settling one contested issue among many or by managing how future conflicts are waged. A conflict may escalate moderately and be settled and then escalate constructively again and be settled again repeatedly. The struggle remains within bounds the adversaries regard as legitimate or as acceptable, oscillating in moderate intensity. Thus, labor-management negotiations often reach agreements more to the liking of one side than to the other. The struggle continues, nevertheless, relatively institutionalized. Communal struggles in some countries can also take that course, as has been the case between blacks and whites in the United States after the civil rights struggle and between the Walloon and Flemish peoples of Belgium.[12] Struggles regarding environmental issues often have this quality too; many arise in local areas over local issues and are settled locally, even as overarching tensions between environmental and development priorities remain.

Second, some conflicts may have deteriorated into a seriously destructive struggle but finally begin to de-escalate, with the opponents reaching a settlement that serves as a stepping-stone toward increasingly comprehensive agreements and constructive relations. These partial agreements can lead to a fundamental and enduring transformation of the relationship. Thus, the struggle in South Africa about the issue of apartheid and white domination was fundamentally transformed with a series of agreements, each built on the preceding ones.

Third, after a protracted destructive struggle, some conflicts seem to de-escalate as the adversaries reach a partial settlement that leads to further agreements. But this progress is halted; some factions blow on the smoldering embers and a destructive reversal flares up. For example, despite years of seeming progress toward a mutually agreed-on accommodation between Israelis and Palestinians, in the fall of 2000 the negotiations broke down and years of anger, fear, and violence followed.

Fourth, some conflicts persist at intense levels of hostility with episodic efforts at reaching agreements that turn out to be very short-lived. Adversaries seem locked in a self-perpetuating violent cycle that sustains an intractable conflict.[13] The struggle between the various political factions in Somalia over the past decades is an example.[14]

Fifth, the agreement can become the basis for a new conflict, as groups that feel offended or adversely affected by the settlement try to reverse or otherwise change the terms of the settlement. This may be seen in the campaigns against affirmative action programs, which were one of the achievements of the American civil rights struggle. On the other hand, the gains one side makes can be the impetus to strive for even further gains, igniting new struggles. For example, the Tea Party's success in the 2010 mid-term elections in the United States led to their adherents' even bolder subsequent efforts to limit the size of government and roll back various federal regulations.

Sixth, some conflicts are terminated with a unilaterally imposed settlement. One side in the conflict triumphs and the other is defeated. The defeated side may surrender or cease to be an organized entity. Thus, in World War II the allies insisted on unconditional surrender by the German government to end hostilities. In 1945, the German government surrendered and ceased to exist; two new German governments were soon formed. Domestically, adversary organizations also may cease to exist. For example, in August 1981 U.S. air traffic controllers, organized in the Professional Air Traffic Controllers Association (PATCO), went on strike.[15] President Ronald Reagan fired those who would not return to work and declared a lifetime ban on rehiring the strikers. New air controllers were hired and PATCO ceased to exist. But the issues that led to the strike remained and in six years the employed air traffic controllers organized a new union, the National Air Traffic Controllers Association.

What explains why conflicts go down one of these roads and not the others? Why do some conflicts appear to be settled for good only to emerge again? To answer these questions we must examine the consequences that the conflict outcome has on each party and on the broader sociopolitical context. Certain consequences appear to make it more likely that a conflict will re-emerge in new forms, while other consequences appear to dampen that likelihood. The following discussion focuses on internal and sociopolitical consequences in turn.

INTERNAL CONSEQUENCES

Every struggle of great magnitude has wide-ranging, long-term effects on the internal relations among members of each party. These effects are a consequence of both the methods used in waging a struggle and the outcomes of that struggle. The way a conflict is waged helps set precedents, form preferences, and shape expectations about whether and how to engage in further struggles. We examine the effects particularly on internal equity and stability.

Consequences of Conflict Methods: Equality and Stability

Three developments affect the sense of equity among members of a collectivity who have engaged in a struggle: increased solidarity with each other; the development of new internal grievances; and the development of new policies that reduce the differential between group members who had benefited during the struggle and those who suffered losses.

The idea that external conflict fosters internal solidarity is one of the often-noted generalizations in conflict analysis. As Coser reformulated Georg Simmel, "Conflict with another group leads to the mobilization of the energies of group members and hence to increased cohesion of the group."[16] Another important proposition is "Conflict with other groups contributes to the establishment and reaffirmation of the identity of the group and maintains its boundaries against the surrounding social world."

A strong sense of solidarity and common identity can mitigate the feelings of injustice at unequally shared costs, and they can foster compensations, to some degree, for the losses that some members of the group suffered. Compatriots, comrades, and survivors of persons who died fighting against an enemy are themselves celebrated and often awarded financial assistance. This may include benefits for the immediate family members of uniformed soldiers who were killed, suicide bombers who died, and victims of state repression. Honors and compensations are also often given to those who had participated in the past fight and may have suffered thereby. This is particularly evident in the various programs that provide benefits to war veterans.

Several processes can help overcome the internal dissension that external conflict might otherwise have exacerbated. Feelings of loyalty are aroused and called on by leaders, supported by group norms, and often fostered by interpersonal networks, all evident in the United States after the attacks on September 11, 2001. Furthermore, the increased prominence of an external conflict tends to reduce the salience of internal fights, and striving for a shared purpose tends to subordinate internal discord. For example, during the civil rights campaigns in the United States, aggressive crimes among blacks decreased.[17] That decrease may have resulted from the civil rights struggle by absorbing energy and attention, by appearing to provide alternative ways of attaining what was sought, and by actually achieving improvements in rights and opportunities.

When the major basis for solidarity is a common enemy, increased hostility toward that foe will tend to strengthen solidarity. Thus, military alliances tend to have less internal dissension when confrontations with an adversary intensify. This was the case during the Cold War for changes in NATO solidarity.[18] However, internal solidarity may quickly dissolve once the external conflict loses salience or is terminated through agreement. This phenomenon can be seen in the tendency for previous allies to fight over the spoils after a victory has been won.

Relatively constructive modes of conflict tend to produce a sense of group pride and solidarity and may be more enduring. For example, after the negotiations for a new constitution in South Africa were completed and the transition to a new, freely elected government accomplished, white South Africans, as well as nonwhites, were generally proud of what they had accomplished. This helped the transition through very difficult challenges.

On the other hand, many persons who commit atrocities during a struggle, or are members of collectivities that do, later come to regard those actions as wrong and blame their leaders, assume responsibility, and feel guilty, while some deny what happened.[19] For example, in Bosnia and Herzegovina after the brutal fighting marked by "ethnic cleansing" was ended and the peace agreement forcefully mediated by the U.S. government began to be implemented, many former Bosnian Serb combatants expressed shame and bewilderment about what they had done. As one young man in a small rural town in what had become a Serb republic within Bosnia and Herzegovina said in January 1996, "I don't remember what we were trying to do with this war, and now I don't care. I got out alive, and now I want to leave the Serbian republic. I'll go almost anywhere else."[20]

An external conflict, then, may become a source of subsequent internal dissension and intense conflict. The externally induced internal cohesion tends to weaken as the conflict persists as the burdens of waging the struggle rise, and particularly as those costs are unevenly borne. In addition, the insistence on loyalty sometimes is experienced as repression and a reason for increasing opposition to those pursuing the struggle against an external enemy.

The sense of equity is likely to be affected by the actual distribution of the costs of conducting a struggle and of its outcome. Given the internal differences in rank and power within any large-scale adversary group, it might seem reasonable to expect that the costs would be disproportionately borne by members of the low-ranking strata. There is abundant evidence supporting this generalization.

Where the fighting is intense and burdens great, often the relatively disadvantaged are further harmed. For example, during World War I, the health of the working class on the European continent suffered.[21] The effects of poor health are long lasting, particularly on children. Furthermore, many people, especially those who have few resources, become desperate refugees as a result of international wars, civil wars, and severe state repression. The number of forcibly displaced persons varies from year to year and consists of different categories of people, but however considered, the number of persons is large. In 2009, the total number for displaced persons was 43,300,000, which included 10,400,000 refugees under the mandate of the United Nations High Commissioner for Refugees and 27,100,000 conflict-generated internally displaced persons.[22]

Under certain circumstances, nevertheless, the waging of a struggle and its outcome do reduce the previous inequalities within an adversary party. Thus, in large-scale conflicts involving high levels of mobilization, the previously disadvantaged within an adversary party actually may improve their circumstances. In protracted international civil wars, minority groups, women, and other previously underutilized persons tend to become more valuable and gain new advantages. Thus, quantitative cross-national analyses indicate that countries with relatively high military participation ratios tend to have more income equality, holding other factors constant.[23] Erich Weede argues more generally that interstate conflict has tended to empower the middle and lower strata of the societies in Europe and contributed to the development of capitalism and freedom.[24] More particularly, research indicates that in the United States during World War II and in the Korean and Vietnam Wars wages increased relative to profits.[25] Other research finds that overall income inequality decreased in the United States during the Civil War and the two world wars, but not during the U.S. engagement in the Korean and Vietnam Wars.[26] The impact of war on societal inequality undoubtedly varies with the war's duration and the degree of mobilization associated with it. Furthermore, increased equality is not necessarily perceived as fair; the dominant groups may find this change wrong and threatening and then seek to restore their relatively higher rank.[27]

Particular advantaged groups, in some circumstances, actually suffer disproportionate costs of a fight. By taking the lead, they sometimes expose themselves to greater risks. In World War I, the British elite suffered casualties greater than the rest of the population.[28] The sons of the elite, graduates of Oxford and Cambridge, volunteered, and as military officers had very high mortality rates. This contributed to the subsequent anti-militarist and pacifist sentiments in Great Britain in the 1920s and 1930s.

Finally, how costs and benefits are distributed within an adversary party is not mechanically translated to varying feelings of equity. What appears to be fair depends on standards of judgment and on how the benefits and costs are presented. Thus, the appearance of profiteering in wartime, of corruption by greedy individuals personally benefiting by the way the struggle is waged or how it is settled, may arouse feelings of outrage. Public campaigns to control such behavior increase the sense of fairness among the members of a conflict party. On the other hand, if leaders and their families flaunt their personal gains, they risk repudiation and the discrediting of the cause they claim to lead, as illustrated by the opposition to some of the leaders after the wars in the former Yugoslavia.

Until recent decades, young men were particularly likely to bear the heaviest burdens in warfare, and that was often viewed as natural and inevitable. The decline of interstate wars waged on battlefields and the ferocity of civil wars has meant that casualties have become very high for civilian noncombatants, including children, women, and elderly men. Such casualties are widely regarded as horribly unjust and often produce a legacy of bitterness and hatred.

Class and ethnic differences associated with unequal sacrifices are traditional and often regarded as unfair. For example, during the U.S. Civil War a draft was instituted in the North, including the provision that a drafted man could hire a substitute or pay $300 and so escape service. Opposition was widespread and riots broke out in many cities.

In the U.S. engagement in the Vietnam War, blacks suffered higher casualties than whites. While blacks averaged about 9.3 percent of the total active duty personnel in 1965–1970, they suffered 12.6 percent of the deaths, "35.5 percent in excess of their percentage in the U.S. armed forces and 30 percent in excess of their percentage in Indochina."[29] This contributed to blacks' sense of injustice within U.S. society even after the war was over. But the protests against the war, while it was being waged, were more evident among white college students when they were subject to the draft.

The destructiveness with which a conflict is waged and ended affects the chances that the relations among the members of each adversary party will be destructively renewed. Insofar as equity is increased, or at least not damaged, the chances of no hostile relations among the members of an adversary party are increased. Three other matters pertaining to stability warrant discussion: first, changes in social and material conditions within a conflict party; second, the previous use of particular conflict methods; and third, the degree of joint decision making in settling the conflict.

First, severe conflicts involving significant proportions of the members of the adversary parties generally disrupt routine life for many people within each adversary camp. When the disruptions are at a moderate level, they can produce new opportunities for many persons as they change roles and locations. The disruption may foster a spurt of growth, spurred by new ideas, combinations, and innovations arising from the experience of the struggle itself. The expansion may compensate for some of the losses of those who had suffered hardships. More generally, social systems confronting recurrent threats of conflict develop internal discipline and organizational efficiencies that tend to enhance their productivity in many arenas.

Large-scale violence in waging wars or revolutions, however, often imposes heavy burdens and significant declines in the well-being of populations in one or both sides of the conflict. The resulting disruptions are likely to create hardships for many persons, and if severe enough, produce social disorder resulting in widespread violence, famine, and flight. The decline can persist because the material and social bases for productive lives have been destroyed. This occurred in Somalia, Rwanda, Cambodia, and Lebanon. It may take years or even decades to overcome those losses. The costs are not only economic but also social, such as fostering official secrecy, undermining social trust, reducing tolerance for dissent, and distracting attention from other social problems. These conditions threatened even the United States as people reacted to the 9/11 attacks.

Societal disruptions following large-scale, protracted violence sometimes are so great that government institutions fail to function adequately. Corruption and criminal conduct may become rampant and institutionalized, and consequently extremely difficult to overcome.[30]

A cross-sectional analysis of countries during the period 1960–1989 found that economic performance was negatively associated with engagement with interstate and with civil wars.[31] However, post-war economic performance was positively associated with wars, particularly civil wars. The wars' disruptions of entrenched coalitions and the engagement of many people in new experiences may be liberating and help account for this result. Such studies, however, do not compare wars with nonviolent revolutions or state breakups. It may be that the constructive consequences of war are due to the conflict in which the violent means are embedded, and if the conflict were waged with greater reliance on nonviolent means of struggle, more beneficial consequences would result. Moreover, attention must be given to the policies followed after a war; if they are directed at recovery, as happened so significantly in Europe after World War II but not after World War I, the consequences can be more constructive.

The second important factor affecting internal stability is the support developed for particular modes of conflict. Each adversary party, as a struggle goes on, becomes increasingly committed to its way of waging the fight. As it relies on armed attacks, covert actions, nonviolent protests, rent strikes, diplomacy, or persuasive appeals, it tends to devote more human and other resources to the chosen method. Even after the conflict is over, the resources devoted to the previously important mode tend to remain salient and be used again.

A variety of evidence demonstrates how these effects occur. For governments that have waged a war, the resources devoted to the military may decline afterward, but generally not to the prewar levels. There is frequently an upward ratchet effect, based on the vested interests created by past usage and on future expectations.

Despite what was written earlier about the energizing and equalizing effects of mobilizing resources to conduct a struggle, the effects are quite different if the mobilization is at a very high level and it is sustained for an extremely long time. In civil and in international wars, if large proportions of the youth are preparing for and engaging in violent struggle, they fail to learn the skills and knowledge needed for economically and politically productive participation in civil life afterward. Even sustained mobilization to maintain readiness for armed struggle can drain and divert intellectual and material resources in ways that undermine the goals that the mobilization is supposed to serve. The collapse of the Soviet Union is illustrative. For decades, by Central Intelligence Agency estimates, the Soviet Union devoted 12 to 15 percent of its gross national product (GNP) to military expenditures; by Soviet and Russian sources after the Cold War ended, estimates are even higher, with percentages, in the 25 to 30 percent range. This allocation of resources greatly contributed to the failure of the Soviet system to satisfy the basic needs of the Soviet peoples. Even in the United States, a much smaller percentage of a much larger GNP devoted to the military has contributed to a slower growth than many other advanced industrialized countries that devoted smaller proportions of their GNP to military expenditures.[32]

The use of nonviolent and noncoercive means of struggle, on the other hand, often enhances internal stability. For example, large-scale participation in nonviolent campaigns can be exhilarating and tends to build solidarity among the participants. Although difficult to sustain, it provides models and encourages approaches for settling internal disputes, which reduce the likelihood of destructive escalation of the conflict. Where nonviolent strategies are employed, popular engagement in political life is fostered. For example, the Zapatista movement in Chiapas fostered popular education and includes a variety of local organizations engaging in civic and economic affairs, which are independent of the dominant political and economic structures; these endeavors provide the bases for effective political engagement.[33]

Third, negotiated endings of conflicts can have their own problematic consequences for internal stability. If leaders secretly agree to an ending, internal dissension may arise at a later time, particularly if an internal opposition group exists and was excluded. Dissension tends to occur when the constituents have not participated in the transformative interactions among the persons engaging in the actual negotiations.[34] The way the Oslo meetings between PLO and Israeli representatives were conducted, while effective in reaching an accord, provoked resistance among many Palestinians and Israeli Jews who were surprised by the 1993 Declaration of Principles (DOP) agreement. The problem can be reduced by enabling more segments of the constituents to be informed and participate in the process of change, or having parallel processes at various levels. At a minimum, if the negotiations are publicly concluded and ratified, the chances of the agreement receiving continued support are increased.

In short, the particular conflict mode used in a struggle often has lasting impacts on the equity and stability for relations within the party using them, with unintended consequences. The effects of the means used may actually undermine the goals they were intended to serve. Thus, struggles are often waged to improve the material conditions of the constituency in whose name the struggle is conducted or to gain more freedom and control for them. But even victory may bring about only a little of what was sought and in some ways may lower attainments for years. This is particularly the case when the means of struggle create high levels of disorder and resentment and high degrees of centralization and control within the organization conducting the struggle. Such consequences have often been noted in regard to revolutions. As Martin Oppenheimer observed in the late 1960s, when romanticism about armed struggle and guerrilla warfare was relatively widespread, "the types of personalities, as well as the forms of organization that usually emerge in a violent revolutionary struggle . . . are those which undercut the humanistic hopes of such endeavors."[35]

The processes of waging and ending a conflict have diverse consequences for relations within each of the adversary parties, in some ways enhancing internal equity and stability, but in other ways reducing them. The consequences are also shaped by the outcome of the struggle, in interaction with the way the struggle was conducted.

Consequences of Conflict Outcomes: Equity and Stability

Conflict outcomes have long-term as well as immediate effects on the internal relations of the members of each side. The effects on equity and stability are likely to differ for the adversaries since the outcomes of conflicts are usually not symmetrical. Thus, the side that believes it lost much of what it struggled for will experience quite different consequences than its adversary.

Members of the side that has suffered greater losses as a consequence of a conflict are likely to believe that they are suffering an injustice and feel disappointment, resentment, and anger. Those feelings may be directed not at the adversary, but at some people on their own side, especially the leadership. Trade union leaders who fail to win benefits desired by their constituency, for example, are likely to face factional disputes and challenges to their leadership.[36] Leaders of the winning party, foreseeing such consequences, may try to avoid framing the outcome as a defeat for the opponent so as to preserve the opponent's leadership and to preserve the outcome. They avoid public gloating and help their defeated foe save face.

Nevertheless, a faction within the losing side is likely to accuse another of being responsible for the loss. The accusations may be well grounded, but frequently they are self-serving, explaining away the accusers' own responsibility or justifying the accusers' rise to power. A classic example of this phenomenon was the claim by Adolf Hitler and many German former military leaders that Germany's defeat by the allies in World War I was due to internal enemies who had "stabbed Germany in the back."[37]

A defeat may also result in ongoing burdens. The hardships are the consequence of damaged assets, of reduced capacity to function effectively, and of increased demands arising from the inequities resulting from the different harms suffered by various segments of the population. These consequences may contribute to harsh economic or social conditions, pitting subgroups against each other, which can contribute to scapegoating, blaming a relatively vulnerable person, group, or people who had little capacity to affect the outcome. Policies, however, can be implemented that help limit the adverse consequences of severe losses. For example, after World War II the West German state took many measures to incorporate the German refugees from Eastern Europe.[38]

On the other hand, the members of the winning side more often feel content with each other. Insofar as the members share a common identity, the victory of their side is gratifying. Those who led in the struggle are likely to be honored and their cause in the struggle vindicated. But the gains of victory are rarely evenly distributed, and that can be the source of changes in the relative position of groups within the winning side and a source of internal dissension. Thus, a collective bargaining agreement that gives all workers a fixed-sum increase will improve the relative position of the lower-paid workers, while an across-the-board percentage increase will be of greater benefit to the higher-paid workers. Either strategy if pursued consistently for a long time is likely to arouse opposition from the disadvantaged members.

Outcomes are rarely simply zero-sum; conflict outcomes generally have significant joint benefits and losses. The internal consequences of different combinations of benefits and losses vary greatly, depending on their characterization by the members of each side. Outcomes that have been regarded as failures for both sides are likely to produce high levels of cynicism and resentment among the rank-and-file members of each side. On the other hand, mutually beneficial outcomes, particularly if they seem to have averted anticipated disaster, tend to foster a sense of shared triumph and pleasure. This was the case for many of the people in South Africa as the transition to majority rule was made. Of course, many problems remain and new ones have arisen, requiring new problem-solving negotiations.

External conflicts that result in one-sided defeats are often the basis for internal revolts against the leadership of the defeated party. As the discussion about the emergence of overt struggle in chapters 3 and 5 indicated, research on revolutions demonstrates the importance of severe and failed external conflicts in explaining revolutionary challenges and their success.

Victories, however, can also be the source of internal dissension. Expectations may be raised by triumphs; and if the anticipated benefits are not forthcoming, the resulting disappointment may generate challenges against the leaders or the advantaged groups within the same side. This is particularly likely when the previously disadvantaged were mobilized to wage the struggle and therefore feel they have a special claim after victory. They may also have more capability than they had earlier to make their claims effectively. These factors contributed to the rise of the civil rights movement in the United States after World War II ended.

Win or lose, the end of a fight allows people to turn their attention to previously submerged internal conflicts. The loss of an external enemy generally raises the salience of internal fights since the need for internal solidarity is reduced. For example, during World War II the U.S. federal government had induced the trade unions to make a no-strike pledge. Nevertheless, strikes increased each year of the war, except 1942, perhaps because the tight labor market increased the power of the workers relative to the managers, presenting an opportunity for them. Some labor disputes may have been held in abeyance, as indicated by the wave of labor strikes immediately after the war ended. The increase in strikes may also have been driven by workers seeking to counter the post-war inflation and also by employers seeking to regain ground they lost when workers had greater bargaining power during the tight labor market of wartime.

After threats from a primary external enemy have disappeared, attention to new enemies often rises, in part from the tendency of some people to organize their lives around fighting against an enemy, so the loss of a major enemy produces a search for others. The new enemies may be internal as well as external. In the United States, after the end of the Cold War some groups sought support for their struggle against domestic enemies, including the federal government itself or ethnic minorities.[39] As discussed previously in chapters 2 and 6, the dangers of a clash of civilizations, particularly between the Western and Islamic civilizations, became salient after the end of the Cold War.

Combined Effects of Methods and Outcomes

The way a conflict is waged and the way it comes out have many interacting effects for the equity and stability of each adversary party. They are discussed in the context of the relationship between external and internal conflicts. Although the proposition that external conflict strengthens internal cohesion is often cited, the evidence is not generally supportive of it. Rather, the nature of the relationship depends on many factors, such as the previous condition of solidarity, the kinds of internal conflict, and the severity and duration of the external conflict.

Consider the differing responses within the United States to waging World War II and the Korean and Vietnam Wars. Examinations of changing public attitudes, evasive draft behavior, and protests and repression indicate increasing disaffection and dissent during the Korean and Vietnam Wars, but not during World War II. Several factors help account for these differences. First, World War II was a relatively total war, which tends to be more equally depriving than a limited war. Thus, income inequality decreased during World War II, but not during the Korean War.[40] Second, the circumscribed goals of the limited wars were less likely to submerge internal differences than was the greater shared threat against which World War II was seen to be waged. Third, internal solidarity was already relatively low prior to the escalation of the Vietnam War, as the emerging civil rights struggle and university student uprisings indicated. In addition, the Vietnam War was waged for a relatively long time.

Finally, the results of the limited wars were not generally viewed as successful as were those of World War II. Failure is reason enough to punish leaders and withdraw support, as the Argentine military junta found after its 1982 attempt to unite the Malvina/Falkland Islands with Argentina by military force was defeated by Britain.[41] Moreover, leaders of failed endeavors are likely to be seen as less competent and therefore more readily challenged than are leaders of successful efforts. Whether dissatisfaction comes to be expressed in overt struggles with the government or among different groups within the society depends on additional factors.

The rationale for a war also matters. Immediately after September 11, 2001, American consensus was high to make war to overthrow the Taliban and destroy the al Qaeda leadership and organization. However, the reasons for going to war in Iraq were more dubious, and disagreement about the wisdom of the war quickly grew, as did protests against it. This followed the shift from an alleged immediate threat to a long-term transformation of Iraq and the Middle East, the many mistakes in implementation, and the resulting failures.[42]

A study of five major wars in which the United States was engaged between 1890 and 1970 indicates that the wars were associated with increases in domestic violence.[43] This was most evident following World War I, with violence by whites against blacks in race riots, attacks by National Guard units against striking workers, and federal government raids during the "Red Scare" in 1919 and 1920. Not only were the differences within U.S. society exacerbated by the wars, but also resorting to violence appeared to be more acceptable.

Several studies find a positive relationship between external conflict and internal conflict.[44] Although the proposition that external conflict generates internal solidarity is not universally valid, it holds in some circumstances, depending on the way the external and internal conflicts are conducted and on the political character of the state.[45] External conflicts conducted for a short time and without recourse to violence tend to be associated with internal cohesion, at least in democratic countries. For example, considering increased approval for the president of a country as an indicator of internal cohesion, there is evidence that becoming engaged in a foreign conflict produces the "rally-round-the-flag" effect and a surge of support for the president.[46] However, engagement in peacemaking efforts also tends to have the same effect.[47]

Thus, moderate external challenges often foster internal equity and stability; on the other hand, destructive, protracted struggles result not only in heavy burdens at the time but also in internal changes perpetuating inequities and restrictions. Weede concludes from his analysis of the effect of interstate conflicts on revolutionary change and individual freedom that the "expansion of freedom seems best served by some modest amount of interstate conflict, by moderate threats to regime security rather than by extreme threats."[48]

CONSEQUENCES FOR THE SOCIAL CONTEXT

The outcome of a conflict and the mode of reaching it affect not only internal dynamics within each party directly engaged in the struggle but also the larger social systems of which they are a part. In addition, they often affect many other parties in the social environment who themselves were not participants in the previous struggle.

Consequence of Conflict Methods: Equity and Stability

The nature of a conflict's ending creates new conditions for many people, even if they had not participated directly in the struggle. A destructive conflict tends to create a variety of problems, as a result of the disruptions, dislocations, and traumas experienced not only by the combatants but also by those associated with them. Thus, civil strife in one society may disrupt trade relations or generate mass movements of people, imposing severe burdens on members of nearby societies. For example, beginning in the late 1970s the number of refugees in the world has sharply increased. A time-series analysis of refugees between 1971 and 1990 indicates that generalized violence such as genocides/politicides, ethnic rebellion, and civil war with foreign military intervention are the best predictors of refugee flows.[49] Other factors such as human rights violations, ethnic conflict, and poverty or underdevelopment did not generate the large numbers of refugees that widespread violence did.

The conflict means used in past struggles affect how the former adversaries wage other conflicts. Thus, national independence movements in countries that became independent during the de-colonization wave after World War II used varying amounts of violent and nonviolent actions preceding their independence. An analysis of those countries found a positive relationship between violence before independence and later external violent behavior.[50] In addition, the methods used in a conflict influence the choice of conflict methods by outside parties, adapting means that seemed effective. Thus, in the 1960s, nonelectoral methods of protest in the United States such as street demonstrations and nonviolent action spread among civil rights groups in different cities, to student groups on different campuses, to women's groups, and subsequently to many other identity and interest groups. Even people with quite different ideologies many years later have resorted to some of those nonelectoral tactics, for example Tea Party activists after the election of President Obama.

Extremely severe means of struggle affect persons who are not directly engaged in the primary conflict and often create new injustices and long-lasting injuries. Violence in which people are driven from their homes, killed, tortured, and raped inflicts enduring emotional impairments on the surviving victims of such trauma and their family members. Consequently, they may act with desperation to find security and protect themselves, individually and collectively. In an extraordinary case, the largely successful Nazi effort to destroy European Jewry contributed immensely to the drive among the survivors to get to Palestine and to fight to establish a Jewish state there. That in turn resulted in a disaster for Palestinians, which reverberated throughout the Arab world.

A demonstration of an effective conflict strategy by partisans in one conflict can affect the sense of equity among parties that had not been engaged in that conflict. Thus, knowing about strategies that have been successful can help a group that previously did not act to redress its grievances, because its members believed they could not succeed, to strive for greater equity. In 2011, for instance, nonviolent democratization protests in Tunisia inspired similar movements in neighboring states, with a domino effect occurring as each movement adopted slogans and tactics used by others. Conditions that may have seemed inevitable and therefore tolerated may come to be seen as alterable and therefore regarded as intolerable. However, in some of those other

Arab countries, such as Libya, the uprising lacked the preparation, planning, and adherence to a nonviolent strategy demonstrated in Tunisia and Egypt.

This rise of claims for justice by groups who have endured discrimination and disadvantages may improve their condition, as happened in the 1960s and 1970s in the United States, and in the 1990s in Eastern Europe. But some groups may seek gains antagonistically, and the absence of problem-solving methods results in too little consideration of the adverse effects on the opponents. That may then contribute to still other groups feeling that satisfaction of those claims puts them at a new disadvantage, and they try to counter those gains by raising their own cries for justice. The backlash against affirmative action for minorities and women beginning in the 1980s in the United States is illustrative. To some degree the rise of the movement favoring traditional social values and practices and its growing strength in the United States into the first decade of the twenty-first century is a well-organized reaction to the many changes in social values and practices that had been contested and achieved in earlier decades.[51] Persons, who were offended by tolerance for abortions, gay rights, and multiculturalism, came to believe that their concerns about moral issues mattered more than other issues and allied themselves with Republicans who seemed to share their moral concerns.

The way a conflict was conducted tends to have enduring consequences for those who engaged in the struggle; usually, the mode tends to be perpetuated. For example, college students who had been activists in social struggles continue to be relatively active in advocating political and social change in their later years.[52] Under particular circumstances, such as great losses, the mode will be rejected in future struggles.

Major conflicts often have strong and enduring impacts on those reaching political maturity while the conflicts were fought. Through processes examined in the work on political generations by Karl Mannheim and others, certain identities and ways of thinking may be enduringly internalized.[53] For example, the Americans who became politically mature in the great economic depression of the 1930s became more class conscious than other American generations.[54] Similarly, certain issues and ways of managing them become salient as a result of a generation's experience. Thus, the age cohorts who became politically mature at the time of World War I or of World War II (turning eighteen during either of the wars) tend to give higher salience to foreign policy matters and be more likely to favor recourse to war than are generations who became politically mature in the 1920s or 1930s.[55]

The Vietnam generation exhibits different consequences. Indeed, studies indicate that in 1973 and 1975, the Vietnam generation was disproportionately likely to say that the United States was spending too much on arms, while the World War II generation was likely to say that too little was being spent.[56] By

1978, however, the generational effects were no longer significant. The lack of consensus about the meaning of the Vietnam War probably reduced any enduring generational consequence of the experience.

If the struggle has brought severe and widespread destructive effects, attempts at developing a social-system solution to avoid its recurrence are likely to be made and generally be supported. For example, the devastating effects of World War II had many profound consequences for the global systems and for Europe, as well as for each of the countries of Europe. Thus, at the global level, the United Nations and many associated international governmental organizations were established to avert future wars. The presumed defects in the earlier structures, including the League of Nations, were to be avoided.

The devastating impact of World War II on the peoples in Europe followed many previous European wars and the failure of policies to prevent and control them. One consequence of these experiences, particularly on the Continent, was the increased salience of a pan-European identity and support for binding the peoples of Europe together. These widespread sentiments nourished the European movement and the support given, for example, to the establishment in 1952 of the European Coal and Steel Community and then the later steps toward the European Union. The results were remarkably successful in ending the long-enduring enmity among countries in Western Europe, most notably between France and Germany.

Within European societies, too, political, religious, and intellectual personages strove to contain and reduce extreme ethnonationalism that might threaten the rights of minority groups or might result in threats against neighboring countries. This was especially the case in West Germany where de-Nazification policies were implemented, laws banning Nazi activities were passed, and policies toward German refugees from former German territories were undertaken to counter possible irredentist mobilizations.

The application of a problem-solving approach in a struggle contributes to the chances of sustaining stable relations in the larger system. For example, consider alternative ways of conducting struggles regarding discrimination against ethnic and other minorities and against women in the labor market. If framed and waged as a struggle in which increased opportunities for some are won at the expense of reduced opportunities for others, the struggle takes on zero-sum qualities. The matter in many circumstances, however, can be viewed differently, stressing common values and interests. Thus, it may be argued that cultural diversity within occupations will provide better service and production than hiring policies that sustain traditional homogeneity. The police force, for example, will better protect the citizens if its ethnic composition reflects the ethnic diversity of the citizenry. In addition, if the labor pool decreasingly consists of white males, a labor policy that does not prepare people of diverse identities to work together collaboratively reduces productivity and damages the collective standard of living. Discriminatory practice, then, is a problem that needs to be solved to satisfy the shared interest in improving productivity and the quality of service. Since the 1980s, this kind of reasoning has influenced much social policy and private practice.

Consequences of Conflict Outcomes: Equity and Stability

A struggle's outcome, as well as how it was waged, affects many other parties in the former adversaries' social environment and impacts the social system of which they are a part. The consequences affect the sense of equity and the stability of the adversaries' other relationships and of the social system as a whole.

Many conflicts are waged to increase equity in relations between the adversaries in the struggle. However, the outcome of a struggle often creates new injustices for people who had not been directly involved in the conflict itself. This is particularly likely for destructively waged and disastrously terminated conflicts. Often, persons whose lives are endangered by widespread violence and disorder resulting from civil strife or wars flee to other places and impose severe hardships for the host peoples. Precarious demographic, cultural, and economic balances may be upset, causing violent conflicts to erupt, as has happened in Lebanon and in several central African countries.

Leaders of groups waging conflicts generally claim they do so for their constituencies; but that wider constituency often does not share the intense convictions of those leaders and fighters. The peripherally engaged, even if the struggle is victorious, may find that the outcome burdens their lives. This is an important matter in assessing the consequences of major historic revolutions.[57]

Research indicates that long-lasting violent revolutionary turmoil generally produces significant and relatively long periods of reduced production. For example, France did not regain its prerevolutionary (1789) levels of foreign trade until well after 1815.[58] The relative gains and losses of different segments of the population, however, even more directly affect their sense of justice. A comparative analysis of social revolutions in Mexico, Bolivia, Cuba, and Peru finds that low-income groups made relative gains in each country during the new regime's consolidation of power, and land reform in each country generally improved the position of the rural groups.[59]

Nevertheless, in subsequent years the interests of the lower-income groups suffered relative to the middle- and upper-income groups. In these developing countries, the global economy seemed to limit labor's gains by fostering government policies primarily aimed at attracting foreign investment and financial assistance rather than policies that more directly targeted social inequities.

The long-term consequences of revolution for society members vary not only with the country's place in the world economy and outside engagement in building peace after civil wars but also with the degree of destructiveness with which it is brought about and the character of the revolutionary change. Palace-guard revolutions, in which a ruling family or small faction is turned out and replaced by a similar small group, are not likely to have profound consequences. Such top-down revolutions may seem liberating at times, as when they are made in the name of national liberation, but their effects are likely to be disappointing and stultifying rather than economically and socially satisfying for the general population—perhaps partly because they were attained without popular involvement. For example, the countries that had been part of the Soviet Union or controlled by it became free of Soviet control with varying degrees of popular engagement. For most of the republics of the former Soviet Union, the union was dissolved by decisions made among a small group of officials. In a few countries, such as Lithuania, nonviolent demonstrations and other actions propelled the movement toward independence.

When a struggle is not destructive, it can be a catalyst for increased diffuse benefits, as indicated in the earlier analysis of external conflicts that are not very severe. This is also indicated by studies of the effects of trade union struggles. Labor leaders and some economists provide evidence that if workers increase labor costs to the employer, workers will be used more efficiently and the employer will also have more incentive to replace workers by machinery. The general economy will be improved by pressures on management to be more efficient, to introduce technical improvements, and to increase capital investments.[60]

Theoretical approaches stressing the centrality of power or of ideology raise the expectation that victors in one conflict tend to initiate additional conflicts. The victors, with confidence in their ability to fight, will have heightened conviction in the justness of their cause and greater resources to use in a fight. For example, triumphant revolutionary regimes often try to spread the doctrines that provided the ideological basis for their coming to power, as illustrated by the French, Russian, Cuban, and Iranian Revolutions.

Attention should also be given to the consequences for the social environment of what one side regards as defeat. As discussed earlier, a humiliating destructive loss may lead to renewed struggle against the victor to recover what was lost or to gain revenge. But if that path is effectively blocked by superior force, more vulnerable targets may be sought out.

The consequences are likely to be different insofar as members of a defeated group interpret their failure as indicating that their goals and their means were unrealistic or ethically wrong. To the extent that they have become persuaded about the erroneous nature of their past struggle, a new course of action will be chosen that makes possible constructive struggle or even a fundamental reconciliation.

When conflicts end with negotiated outcomes or otherwise incorporate the concerns of many of the previously struggling parties, the former adversaries are more likely to see the need and the possibility for continuing work with each other. That will tend to absorb their attention and energy. When the conflicts end without such inclusiveness, however, some groups are likely to regard themselves as losers and seek redress or withdraw to fight battles in other arenas, perhaps as mercenaries.

Successful accommodative solutions can serve as models for members of other societies and organizations. In social systems challenged by divisions along ethnic lines, for example, many kinds of arrangements have averted or mitigated destructive struggles, such as provisions for cultural autonomy, structures of confederation, educational integration, and norms of tolerance. In societies torn by ethnic-related struggles, successes elsewhere have been held up as exemplary ways out of their troubles. The achievements of the civil rights struggle in the United States, the establishment of a system of regional autonomy in Spain, and the ending of apartheid in South Africa have been so used.

Combined Effects of Methods and Outcomes

Conflicts may be expected to foster an ever-widening circle of additional conflicts, but they may also inhibit new conflicts. The research on the relationship between internal and external conflicts can help assess which is more likely. There are several reasons to expect that internal conflicts will generate external ones. Thus, it may be argued that domestic turmoil encourages leaders to engage in an external conflict as a distraction and a way to create solidarity. It may also be reasoned that when one domestic party triumphs over an internal enemy, it will believe itself able to defeat other groups who are holding the wrong ideas or exercising unjust domination. In addition, internal disorder may harm or endanger groups who have external ethnic, ideological, or economic ties with external groups who intervene to counter the threats. Finally, domestic conflict may weaken the party so much that it becomes an inviting target for aggressive action by external parties.

However, there are also reasons to expect that internal conflicts make external conflicts less likely. Thus, internal disorder can so weaken a party that it tries to avoid engagement in external conflicts, believing it will be defeated. Furthermore, posing little threat to external adversaries, the potential adversaries will not engage in threatening actions themselves and will pursue cooperative relations.

Quantitative analyses from the 1960s support each line of argument, depending on specific conditions, such as the nature of the countries' regimes and the kind of conflict behavior. Thus, for countries with authoritarian regimes, internal warfare is somewhat negatively correlated to external war one and two years later.[61] Internal war, however, is somewhat positively correlated to belligerence (anti-foreign demonstrations and severance of diplomatic relations) one and two years later. These findings suggest that leaders of authoritarian regimes, facing internal disorder, act belligerently against other countries, but not so far as to enter military clashes and wars. In countries with democratic regimes, however, internal war is related neither to subsequent belligerence nor to external war. Internal turmoil is somewhat positively correlated to belligerence one year later and more strongly to war two years later. Possibly, leaders of democratic regimes, facing moderate internal conflict, resort to external conflict behavior to divert internal dissension. Finally, in countries with dictatorial regimes, internal turmoil is positively correlated to belligerence a year later and internal war is positively correlated to external war one and two years later. Perhaps leaders in dictatorial regimes are particularly prone to resort to external conflict as a way of diverting attention from domestic difficulties or perhaps the victors of internal wars that are ideologically driven tend to spread their beliefs aggressively in other countries. It may also be that internal wars are particularly likely to invite external intervention.

Much recent research has focused on the efforts of external interveners to foster economic development and democracy as ways to regenerate peace after civil wars. These efforts are based on research on the relations between economic conditions and violent conflict and on the relations between democracy and war. There is systematic evidence that, overall, internal conflicts, external conflicts, and economic recessions are mutually reinforcing.[62] The findings suggest a self-perpetuating dynamic of violent conflicts breeding poverty and poverty breeding violent conflicts.

Since the end of the Cold War, there has been a great increase in multilateral interventions to stop civil wars and severe violent repressions and also to assist in building peaceful societies.[63] The results have been mixed.[64] Significant success was achieved in preventing a renewed outbreak of civil wars in Namibia and Mozambique, while renewed war quickly followed peace-building efforts in Angola and Rwanda. In some countries democratic institutions seem to have taken root and economic progress was made, but in other countries elections resulted in authoritarian rule and economic inequities increased.

The policies of external interveners affect the long-term consequences of how conflicts are conducted and ended. The degree of stability and equity that is achieved depends partly on the persistence of the external parties' engagement; overcoming the disasters of war takes time. Rushing to hold elections before the institutional base has been adequately developed and before demilitarization has sufficiently progressed does not yield dependably democratic societies. Insisting on moving quickly to a market economy characterized by privatizing state-owned enterprises, reducing government subsidies, liberalizing state regulations, and reducing government spending results in immediate economic hardships, whatever the long-term benefits may be. These hardships can undermine the nascent democracy. Recognition is increasing that policies need to be based on analyzing each society's particular problems and not be dominated by ideology or the immediate self-interests of the external interveners.[65]

CONSTRUCTIVE TRANSFORMATIONS

The discussion above examined the variety of conflict sequences that emerge after a fight seems to have ended and the factors that push sequences in one direction or another. We now turn to two processes that appear effective in fostering sequences that are relatively constructive; they are reconciliation and intermediary work.

Reconciling Adversaries

The recurrence of brutal struggles often related to communal identities demonstrates the importance of reaching an enduring and just accommodation between enemies.[66] Conflict partisans and analysts alike increasingly stress reconciliation as an important ingredient in achieving such accommodations and ending recurring destructive conflicts. Normative changes have raised expectations that reconciliatory actions be taken to help resolve differences even long after the direct violence of the conflict has ended.

The developments that tend to perpetuate destructive conflicts, as discussed earlier, include dehumanizing opponents, blaming the others for the harms that have been experienced, and denying the validity of the other side's experience. Reconciliation is a multifaceted process, often occurring over an extended period of time, which contributes to reducing or overcoming these phenomena. Progress in that process requires many people to undertake a wide variety of actions. The various aspects of reconciliation need to be distinguished before examining their implications for the subsequent course of conflicts.

Aspects of Reconciliation

One important aspect of reconciliation pertains to the entities that are being reconciled with each other. The reconciling parties, for example, may be individuals from the antagonistic sides who interact with each other in ways that demonstrate mutual regard and trust. They may be persons or groups who represent the antagonistic sides and express contrition for past acts of injury by members of the collectivity they are representing. They may be writers, religious leaders, or othe·s who address their own community and acknowledge that members of their community had injured people in another community. These persons or groups may be acting with little support from others in their community or they may be part of a mainstream consensus.

Reconciliation processes can occur in several domains, varying in scope and context. We focus this discussion on four important dimensions of reconciliation along which the process occurs.[67] The processes relate to truth, justice, regard, and security.

Truth is often noted as an important dimension of reconciliation, since members of antagonistic sides are so prone to deny what the other side experiences and believes to be true. At a minimal level, persons on each side may openly recognize that they have different views of reality. They may even acknowledge the possible validity of part of what members of the other community believe. At a fuller level, members of the different communities may develop a shared and therefore more comprehensive truth. Official investigations, judicial proceedings, scholarly research, and mass media reporting are all ways to expose and acknowledge abuses that had been hidden or denied. In some societies, formal truth commissions may seem unhelpful "talk-talk" to locals more concerned with immediate needs.

Recognizing the truth about past abuses ideally includes acknowledgment by those who belong to the collectivity that had inflicted the harm or benefited from it and acceptance of responsibility for what happened. Such acknowledgments may relate to individual perpetrators or to collective entities. The acknowledgment may incorporate offering apologies and expressing regrets and be part of discovering and facing the truth. This is difficult to achieve, particularly for members of the relatively victorious and dominant groups.

The second major dimension of reconciliation pertains to justice in its manifold meanings. Many persons who have suffered oppression and atrocities in the course of an intense struggle seek redress for the injustices they endured. Redress may be in the form of tangible restitution or compensation for what was lost; it may take the form of punishment for those who committed injustices; or it may be exhibited in policies that offer protection against future discrimination or harm. Many actions of the Federal Republic of Germany illustrate these methods in relation to the Jewish people.[68] For example, compensation has included payments to Jewish survivors of the Holocaust and assistance to the State of Israel. Trials have been held of persons charged with crimes against Jews and other victims of Nazism, and laws were enacted against organizations advocating racism and to provide asylum for victims of political repression.

The third important dimension in reconciliation involves expressions of regard and respect between victims and perpetrators. It includes expressions by those who have suffered the harms acknowledging the humanity of those who committed the injuries. Most extremely, the acknowledgment may convey mercy and forgiveness, stressed by some advocates of reconciliation. Expressions of forgiveness may be a way for some people to shed the burdens of hate, while for others it may be contingent on expressions of guilt, remorse and shame by members of the perpetrating community. The ability of humans to treat each other with respect is given support by widespread religious beliefs regarding the value of every human being before God.

Many instances of such conduct are reported at conferences held at Mountain House, established in 1946 in Caux, Switzerland.[69] It has served as a place where persons from countries and peoples who had warred against each other meet for unofficial dialogue and become open to reconciliation. In the first years of operation, many participants came from France and Germany and in many personal encounters and public statements reciprocated requests for forgiveness.

Frequently, recognition of the other side's humanity entails only recognizing that many members of the adversary community did not personally and directly carry out harmful actions and the next generation is not responsible for the acts of previous generations. Even less directly, persons from communities who had suffered injury may engage cooperatively in projects relating to past harms with members of the community that had inflicted the harm, but not express any apology or forgiveness.

The fourth dimension of reconciliation pertains to security. The adversaries have reason to believe they can look forward to living together without threatening each other, perhaps even in harmony and unity. This may be in the context of high levels of integration or in the context of separation and little regular interaction. The nature of the anticipated peaceful relations varies, but the realization of the mutual preferences is what is critical.

Clearly, all these aspects of reconciliation are rarely fully realized and certainly not at the same time. Indeed, they are often contradictory at a given time. Thus, forgiveness and justice often cannot be satisfied at the same time, although they may occur sequentially. Nevertheless, if done by different members of the previously antagonistic sides they may be compatible even simultaneously. In some ways, furthermore, these various elements are interdependent. If members of one party acknowledge that another community has suffered great injury by their actions, forgiveness or at least acceptance of their humanity becomes easier to be felt and expressed.

Reconciliation generally is not a one-sided matter, nor is it symmetrical. Some members of one side may seek justice from another party that is viewed as responsible for the injustice; but members of the other side deny responsibility and there is no reconciliation movement. Expressions of regret may be recognized by members of the injured party and not deemed fully adequate by some of them. Often, both sides have suffered injuries at the hand of the other, although not in equal measure. Reconciliation actions may reflect such asymmetries, but usually do not.

Implications

This discussion thus far stresses that there are many kinds and degrees of reconciliation, with different mixes of elements. We turn to particular implications of this complexity. In large-scale conflicts, full reconciliation among all members of the former adversaries is improbable. Some persons remain unreconciled and some claims that seemed impossible to achieve become feasible only at a much later time. The process of reconciliation, then, can go on for many generations, as standards of fairness change and the ability of various groups to make claims shift. Thus, indigenous peoples in Australia, Canada, and the United States toward the end of the twentieth century insisted that they had suffered injustices as Europeans settled what had been their land and the truth of what they suffered had been hidden in subsequent generations. Indeed, descendants of the European settlers in those countries have acknowledged some past abuses, such as placing children in boarding schools away from their families, and have provided monetary compensation for lands unlawfully taken from indigenous peoples.

Some people in Africa and in countries to which black Africans were brought as slaves have also called for recognition of the losses they currently suffer as a legacy of past injustice and exploitation. Some of them argue that reparations should be made. In April 1993, the first pan-African conference on reparations was convened in Abuja, Nigeria, and declared that the international community owed a moral debt to the African peoples that had yet to be paid. In the United States, the issue of compensation for the losses suffered by African Americans as a consequence of slavery, of legally enforced discrimination, and of informally imposed restrictions has become the subject of growing debate. On January 5, 1993, John Conyers, a black Democratic congressman from Detroit, introduced a bill in Congress "to establish a commission to examine the institution of slavery, subsequent de jure and de facto racial and economic discrimination against African Americans, and the impact of these forces on living African Americans, to make recommendations to the Congress on appropriate remedies, and for other purposes."[70] At the outset of the twenty-first century, Randall Robinson and others have undertaken a campaign to raise awareness of the debt owed to African Americans.

The failure to carry out any substantial measures of reconciliation endangers the stability in the relationship between former antagonists. For example, the atrocities committed during World War II in Yugoslavia, particularly by the Croat Ustasha forces against Serbs, were not explicitly and openly adjudicated or investigated by the Yugoslavian government headed by Josip Broz Tito. The government leaders, partly on ideological grounds and concerned about stirring up ethnic animosities, treated the internal struggles among Yugoslavs in terms of class and ideological differences. The unreconciled ethnic hostilities were available to be aroused later and contributed to the breakup of Yugoslavia in bloody wars a generation later.

Actions that foster reconciliation need not await the ending of a specific fight. Even when a conflict is being waged and escalated, attention to future coexistence and ultimate reconciliation can affect the way a struggle is conducted. For example, if the opposing ethnic group is not treated as a single unit and all its members are not dehumanized, reconciliation will be more readily attainable when the fighting ceases. This was done in good measure by the ANC in South Africa and contributed greatly to the constructive transformation of South African society.

Occasionally, efforts to attain certain aspects of reconciliation sometimes hamper ending a conflict and establishing a stable relationship. Thus, demands for justice by the aggrieved party may seem to pose unacceptable demands to the dominant party. Requiring that leaders of the ruling group be charged with human rights violations or held accountable for economic corruption and put on trial is likely to be resisted by those leaders. In Egypt, for instance, the 2011 effort to put former President Hosni Mubarak and his sons on trial for the actions of the Egyptian security forces during the successful pro-democracy uprising was initially resisted by some members of the military elite. But without some measure of justice, the resulting outcome may be the imposition of injustice and a relationship that is far from equitable and therefore prone to renewed destructive struggle.

The earlier analyses of the course of struggles and their outcomes indicate that reconciliation is not an inevitable stage in every conflict. Mutual recriminations can persist, as they do in the relations between the United States and Iran and the United States and North Korea. Furthermore, the reconciliation that does occur is often fundamentally one sided, incorporating only a few elements of a full and mutual reconciliation. Other groups use that reality to justify their own brutalities.

Acts intended to advance the process of reconciliation do not necessarily do so. This is exemplified by developments relating to the ethnic Germans who were expelled from the Sudetenland area of Czechoslovakia at the end of World War II, because they had been instrumental in the Nazi dismemberment of Czechoslovakia.[71] After Vaclav Havel was elected president of Czechoslovakia in 1990, he denounced the expulsions as deeply immoral. The post-Communist Czech leaders made other reconciliatory gestures. But this reconciliation process broke down in an escalating exchange of charges and demands between the Sudeten Germans living in Germany and the Czechs. Public exchanges of recriminations endangered the emerging rapprochement between Germany and the Czech Republic. In secrecy, senior Czech and German officials tried to fashion a declaration that could be acceptable to both countries. On January 21, 1997, Czech premier Vaclav Klaus and German chancellor Helmut Kohl signed a joint declaration, which was approved by both countries' parliaments. Ultimately, the government policies helped attain a higher level of mutual accommodation and reconciliation than existed earlier.

The establishment and functioning of the Truth and Reconciliation Commission (TRC) in South Africa is rightfully well regarded throughout the world. Yet, many South Africans have not agreed that it was so good, as may be seen in the findings of a national public opinion survey conducted in November 1998.[72] While overall 57 percent said they thought the TRC has been good for the country and 72 percent of the black South Africans agreed, only 44 percent of the Colored, 40 percent of the Indians, and merely 25 percent of the whites responded favorably. Clearly, particularly for many whites, the revelations of the TRC were difficult to accept. The TRC hearings and findings received wide public attention, aroused much discussion, and helped promote reconciliation and the emergence of a common history. Consensus is high on the value of reconciliation in principle, but differences between whites and blacks about what is needed for reconciliation remained.

Intervening Constructively

Settlements at the end of a conflict can be very fragile and subject to failure. Between 1949 and 2005, for instance, violent conflicts that ended in peace agreements were subject to failure in nearly 40 percent of the cases.[73] Conflicts in the contemporary world are seldom isolated. Many kinds of interventions by various actors are widespread, and they are often crucial in sustaining accommodations that have been achieved. Since the variety of intermediary activities that contribute to transforming conflicts was examined in chapter 6, this discussion of interventions is relatively brief. It focuses on peace-building interventions after an accommodation has been reached, not emphasized earlier.

Kinds of Interveners

The government is generally the pivotal actor in settling and managing grave domestic conflicts. States usually maintain the institutions by which innumerable conflicts are settled, including labor-management, intercommunal, and environmental fights. However, the state itself is often a party to such fights, as in the case of civil strife and civil wars. In such cases, external intervention is increasingly likely. Civil wars have usually ended by one side defeating the other, but after the Cold War, the United Nations, the United States, and other international actors more actively intervened to avert or stop genocidal killings or massive refugee flows. Such interventions contributed to more negotiated endings and consequently increased ongoing international engagement to preserve the peace.

The number of external actors who might help sustain a conflict settlement is now large and growing. They include the United States and many other countries so acting when their officials believe that their countries' national interests would otherwise suffer. They include numerous global and regional international governmental organizations, such as the United Nations, the World Bank, the Organization on Security and Cooperation in Europe, the Organization of American States, and the European Union. The growth in the role of transnational NGOs is especially striking.[74] What is particularly relevant in the context of intervention efforts is the expansion of NGOs working in the fields of humanitarian assistance, human rights, democratization, and other programs of advocacy, as well as conflict resolution.

Contributions of Intervention

Intermediaries often perform valuable services in reaching and sustaining an agreement.[75] They may help produce agreements that are relatively fair, and they may provide some representation for stakeholders who are not sitting at the table. This may include rank-and-file constituents of the presumed leaders and representatives, for example, by including provisions for elections as a part of the settlement. To some extent, this can be seen in the mediating role that Oscar Arias, the Costa Rican president, provided in Central America and that U.S. assistant secretary of state Chester A. Crocker provided in linking the withdrawal of Cuban military forces from Angola with implementation of UN Resolution 435 in Namibia.[76]

Intervener organizations can provide a variety of resources that help stabilize an accommodation and contribute to a conflict's constructive transformation. They can provide material resources such as food, medical care, and funds for developing the infrastructure, and they can enhance skills to help rebuild social institutions. Intermediaries often play critical roles in implementing an agreement. They sometimes monitor agreements, and if violations occur, impose sanctions or provide compensation to the disadvantaged side. They may observe an election, prescribed in an agreement, to help ensure that it is fair and regarded as legitimate. Following protracted civil strife, demobilization of armed forces is generally needed, and intermediaries have assisted in this process, as in Namibia and El Salvador.

Often, factions on each side of the conflict continue to strive to better their position, which undermines an agreement. Mediators and other intermediaries are often needed to inhibit such undermining "spoiler" actions. However, interveners are likely to find that staying engaged after an accommodation is politically difficult. From the interveners' perspectives, support from the people who provide funds and personnel tend to decline after the conflict seems to have been settled. Furthermore, a variety of undesirable accidents and events are likely to occur over time as the interveners' engagement wanes. Yet, over time relations and understandings also can be built that give everyone confidence that an enduring transformation is underway.

No single way of intervening is likely to be effective in transforming large-scale destructive conflicts. The probability of effectiveness is enhanced when interveners pursue many strategies and not only military ones, when interventions involve many agents at various levels, and when they involve a variety of activities such as peacekeeping, economic development, and fostering legitimate political institutions. Since the early 1990s, multilateral engagement in societies that had been rent by civil wars greatly increased; the policies generally pursued attempt to speedily bring about democratic procedures and free market economies. These efforts, however, are often too quickly and too ideologically implemented; consequently, even if civil wars are not soon renewed, considerable inequalities and acts of violence result.[77]

The importance but also the difficulties in intervening effectively after the progress toward accommodation is broken by violent exchanges can be seen in the mistrust and anger in Israeli-Palestinian relations as the second intifada raged.[78] When George W. Bush took office as president in 2001, his administration decided to avoid dealing with Arafat and not engage in the high-level intermediary efforts that President Clinton had made and that ultimately failed to produce a settlement. As the fighting continued, domestic and international calls for U.S. engagement grew and some limited efforts were made.[79] President Clinton tasked George Mitchell to investigate the breakdown and propose a plan for progress; the report was issued in April 2001, but under the circumstances, had little effect. The Bush administration sent George Tenet, director of the CIA, to mediate a cease-fire, but the agreements reached were short-lived. Finally, a more comprehensive, multilateral effort was made. The

United States, the UN, the EU, and Russia—the "Quartet"—set forth a roadmap for progress toward a permanent two-state solution. This was accepted with qualifications by the Israeli government and the PLO, but again it was not implemented.

Only after much more violence, the Israeli suppression of Palestinian attackers, the death of Yassir Arafat in November 2004, and the election of Abu Mazen as the new president of the Palestinian National Assembly in January 2005, did direct negotiations and high-level active U.S. engagement begin again. However, the Israeli government had begun a policy of unilateral separation; it began building a fence/wall between the major Jewish areas and the largely Palestinian territories, beyond the cease-fire lines established in 1967, and it withdrew Jewish settlements and military forces from the Gaza Strip and some small settlements in the West Bank.

Nevertheless, track-two activity continued, with more emphasis upon mobilizing public support among Jews and Palestinians for a two-state solution on the terms that had been almost agreed upon when the negotiations broke down. One such widely noted effort was associated with the release of the Geneva Accord, in December 2003, by a group led by Yossi Beilin and Yasser Abd Rabbo. The unofficial accord conveyed plausible details about ways to resolve complex contentious matters such as those related to security, Jerusalem, the borders, and Palestinian refugees.

Without any sustained official movement toward realizing a two-state solution to the Israeli-Palestinian conflict, popular belief in the possibility of achieving it had collapsed among Jews and Palestinians. Among Palestinians, this contributed to increasing Palestinian support for Hamas, an Islamic organization opposing a two-state solution that had been designated a terrorist organization by the U.S. government. In January 2006, in an election in the West Bank and Gaza, urged by the Bush administration, Fatah was defeated by Hamas. The resulting Hamas-led government was short-lived, and in June 2007, violent fighting between Fatah and Hamas supporters resulted in Hamas rule in Gaza and Fatah rule in the West Bank.

U.S. intervention, particularly during the Bush administration, was intermittent and generally ineffectual.[80] This was attributable to inattention, undue reliance on official Israeli interpretations, and viewing the issue in the context of waging a global war against terrorism. Such faults were the product of conventional political thinking and concern about domestic support for Israeli policies.[81] Of course the asymmetries in Israeli-Palestinian capacities and strategies to win American support also played roles in the Israeli advances on the ground and the failure to reach an enduring Israeli-Palestinian peacemaking agreement.

President Obama upon taking office seemed determined to move quickly to renew substantive Israeli-Palestinian talks, and he took some measures to distinguish his new approach. In June 2009, he spoke at Cairo University, expressing his intention: "to seek a new beginning between the United States and Muslims around the world, one based on mutual interest and mutual respect." In July 2009, Obama met with leaders from major Jewish-American organizations and discussed his policies relating to Israel, and particularly to Jewish settlements in the West Bank and Jerusalem.[82] He won acquiescence and some support for his efforts to halt further expansion of Jewish settlements in Palestinian territories.

Obama promptly appointed George Mitchell to be the special envoy to renew Israeli-Palestinian negotiations. Obama tried to address Israeli concerns by stressing the interconnections among Middle East conflicts to attain the trade-offs he desired. He linked Israeli concerns about the threat from Iran with reaching an accommodation with the Palestinians. He noted that while Iran posed an existential threat to Israel, halting settlement construction did not, and he assured the Israeli government that the U.S. would handle the Iranian problem.

The mediation effort was focused on restarting direct negotiations between the PA and the Israeli government.[83] The primary issue in accomplishing this was halting the expansion of Jewish settlements in the occupied territories. Secretary of State Clinton and Obama became intensely engaged in achieving Israeli agreement to such a freeze, but won only a ten-month partial freeze, which Netanyahu announced in November 2009. The United States then convinced the Palestinians to renew negotiations on that basis, and direct negotiations began. Despite some progress, the Israeli government would not extend the freeze, which expired on September 26, 2010, and the negotiations were broken off as the PA said they would be without a settlement freeze.

These negotiation failures produced a Palestinian focus on developing the infrastructure for a Palestinian state and turning to a more international setting, the UN General Assembly, to resolve the conflict with Israel.[84] In May 2011, aided by Egyptian mediation, Fatah and Hamas leaders reached an agreement to form a unity government and to hold elections. All these moves were designed to reduce the asymmetries in the conflict relationship, to directly improve Palestinians' circumstances, and to achieve statehood.

CONCLUSIONS

No agreement can forever end conflicts between large-scale adversaries. Some agreements, however, are part of the transformation of a conflict such that the adversaries can engage in largely cooperative relations. An agreement, however, is only a part of that process; internal developments within each adversary party and changes in their environments impact the course of each conflict. Whether or not a settlement is effective in the long term depends on the difficulty that the conflict poses for settlement and how strong the interest of major external actors in preserving it is.

The nature of a struggle's consequences depends significantly on how the former adversaries and others interpret the way the conflict ended. Thus, the consequences vary with the degree to which protagonists regard the outcome as fair and reached through a joint process. For example, diverse American views of how the Cuban missile crisis was settled and how the Cold War was ended have different implications for subsequent U.S. foreign policy. We note here elements of problem-solving strategies in the way these struggles were transformed, elements that are too often unrecognized.

Thus, U.S.-Soviet relations became somewhat more accommodating after the Cuban missile crisis, and not simply because both sides were frightened by getting to the brink of a nuclear war. The crisis was resolved in negotiations between President John F. Kennedy and Premier Nikita Khrushchev.[85] The U.S. official policy carefully avoided appearing to humiliate the Soviet Union for withdrawing its missiles from Cuba. The Soviets were able to claim they had achieved what was essential: the assurance that the United States would not try to overthrow the Cuban government. In addition, the U.S. missile base near the Soviet border in Turkey was closed.

The Cold War did not end because of its intensification in the early 1980s and the added pressure of the Reagan administration. It was basically the result of fundamental problems within the Soviet Union. However, the course of action chosen to manage those problems was greatly influenced by the preceding years of growing U.S.-Soviet accommodation.[86] The prior years of cultural exchange, economic transactions, and other kinds of communication and interdependence made Western solutions seem increasingly attractive. At the same time, the fundamental interests of the Soviet Union seemed to be assured by previous agreements accepting the permanence of the borders established at the end of World War II.

Conflicts waged and terminated destructively tend to perpetuate destructive relations. Such persisting cycles, however, can be broken. To interrupt and alter these tendencies requires wise transforming policies that are resolutely pursued. Intermediaries based outside of the primary adversaries can be crucial in undertaking and carrying out such policies. In addition, individuals and groups within one or more of the antagonistic sides can initiate and help implement such policies. Of course, conducting a struggle constructively in the first place makes the task easier and can contribute afterward to stronger cooperative relations between former adversaries. Elements of constructive struggle are often present in the settlement of conflicts, increasing the likelihood of building stable and equitable relations.

11

Synthesis, Specifications, and Challenges

In this final chapter three matters pertinent to waging constructive conflicts will be discussed. First, the conflict cycle presented in the first chapter needs to be reexamined, synthesizing the analyses presented in the later chapters in order to better understand the conditions and context that lead to the emergence, escalation, de-escalation, and sustainable transformation of social conflicts. Second, the main findings will be specified for different kinds of conflicts. Third, two challenges related to the application of the constructive conflict approach will be identified and addressed.

SYNTHESIS

The idea that conflicts move through a series of stages is useful, so long as each stage is not treated as rigidly bounded and sequenced. Throughout this book we have considered the stages as broad phases through which struggles tend to move, varying greatly in how long each stage lasts, in the nature of the transition from one to the other, and in the reversals of their sequence. The designation of each stage also depends on the characterization of the parameters of the conflict being considered, since fights are generally embedded in larger and more enduring struggles and also encompass smaller and briefer disputes, and each of the interlocked conflicts may be at a different conflict stage. Furthermore, the members of each side do not all move in unison from one stage to another.

Underlying Conditions

The bases for the emergence of a conflict include factors within one or more of the adversaries driving their members to contend with others, as well as aspects of the relationship between possible adversaries. A conflict, then, may arise not only from what an analyst regards as objective conflict relations, such as the distribution of formal political power among stakeholders, but also from what the analyst considers mistaken understandings of the relationship by the antagonists, or from a combination of both.

Differences in rankings in terms of class, status, or power, as well as differences in values or cultural markers between categories of people, are major bases for struggles. Conflicts generally are waged about a combination of such consensual and dissensual issues. Interdependence between possible adversaries makes it difficult for them to escape these differences, but such integration also tends to inhibit the emergence of a conflict, especially destructive ones.

The social context of the adversaries is another important set of conditions. Changes in those conditions often generate shifts in the relations between various categories of people, thus creating the bases for a manifest struggle. Thus, economic and demographic changes in cities, countries, and global regions, by affecting migration patterns or relative political power, may intensify the interactions between people of different classes and cultures so that they come to view each other as competitive and even antagonistic.

The conditions for an infinite number of conflicts are always present; yet relatively few conflicts become manifest, and even fewer become destructive. This is the case partly because there are also many integrating processes and conditions within which possible conflicts are embedded and there are many constructive ways to remedy the conditions that are the bases of a struggle. Such factors usually inhibit the emergence and destructive escalation of a struggle largely outside institutionalized channels.

Manifestation

In the initial conflict stage, a struggle becomes manifest. Four components must be minimally present for that to occur. First, at least one protagonist has a sense of its identity, distinguishing itself from other parties. Second, members of one or more of the adversary parties believe they have a grievance, some aspect of their situation being unsatisfactory and unjustified. Third, members of one or more sides, believing that their grievance would be reduced by a change wrought by another person or group, formulate a goal to bring about the changes in the other side so that their grievance will be reduced. Fourth, those asserting the goal must believe that they can act to help attain it.

A conflict emerges as one or both sides express these beliefs by mobilizing supporters or by directly trying to affect the opposing side so as to achieve their goal. All the adversaries need not explicitly articulate each of these component beliefs. If one side acts in these terms, the other side will likely see itself as engaged in a struggle. Indeed, members of the aggrieved party often experience as provocative the other side's denial that there is any conflict.

As diagramed in figure 1.1, a conflict arises as those underlying conditions change and become conducive to the eruption of a struggle. The arrows from outside the conflict cycle indicate that factors and actors external to the primary adversaries also affect the likelihood that a conflict becomes manifest and changes in its course. Thus, external actors not considered to be the primary adversaries may intrude and exacerbate a struggle. They may introduce new ideologies or standards of evaluation and they may provide support for particular adversaries. The arrows from inside the conflict cycle indicate that factors and groups within each adversary also affect the emergence and subsequent changes in the conflict.

Many strategies can be pursued to prevent a conflict from becoming manifest. They include efforts by the dominant side to intimidate those who seek to force a change they desire, to deprive or reduce their resources for effecting change, and to convince them that they cannot achieve the alteration they seek. Other strategies entail trying to convince those who feel aggrieved that their condition is fair or is the result of their own actions. More constructively, the actual amelioration of injurious conditions can reduce the likelihood of a struggle arising to correct those conditions. Another strategy is to promote an identity shared by the potential adversaries, for example, as members of the same nation, country, or organization. In addition, intermediaries may help contending groups find acceptable solutions to their disagreements and avert manifestations of severe conflict, as the earlier discussions of the work of the OSCE illustrates. Finally, strategies may utilize largely institutionalized ways of conducting conflicts, such as legal and electoral procedures.

Escalation

The next stage of a conflict, escalation, is often lengthy. In this phase, each side increases its efforts by intensifying the means used and rallying support for its cause. The early efforts may rely on attempts at persuasion and perhaps promises of future benefits for yielding what is sought. In addition, relatively mild kinds of coercion may be employed or threatened. Reliance on coercion, and especially on violent coercion, occurs if the conflict escalates greatly. Conventional understandings may act as barriers to escalation, but once crossed, a much higher level of antagonism may be reached and sustained.

Conflicts become destructive and seemingly intractable as they escalate because of the interactions between the adversaries, the processes internal to one or more sides, and the developments in the adversaries' social context. Adversary interactions and their views of those interactions are primary sources of escalation and destructiveness. Insofar as antagonists view themselves as struggling within a clearly bounded system that they constitute, they are likely to see themselves involved in a zero-sum conflict. This compounds the incompatible nature of their goals.

The adversaries' treatment of each other in waging the fight greatly contributes to the destructiveness of their struggle. Inhumane treatment deepens the antagonism and the desire to continue fighting and even to seek revenge. The callous and indiscriminate use of violence, intended to intimidate and suppress the enemy, is frequently counterproductive, prolonging a struggle and making an enduring peace more difficult to attain.

Another important policy affecting the increasing destructiveness of a conflict is the rejection of the adversary's claim to fundamental human rights and minimal living conditions. Related to this, another important policy affecting a conflict's destructiveness is the refusal to recognize the other side as a legitimate collectivity and the consequent refusal to directly communicate with the other side.

Conflict destructiveness often expands when a party that believes it is winning overreaches. Its goals become more grandiose and it gives little attention to the interests and concerns of opponents. This tends to stiffen the resistance of the opponents and increase their sense of outrage and desperation, which prolongs and intensifies the struggle. Furthermore, overextension based on arrogant or unwitting hubris often results in failure and defeat, in a battle, in a war, or in sustaining an empire.[1]

Various developments within one or more of the adversary parties can also contribute to escalation and destructiveness. For example, widespread adoption of an ethnonationalist ideology by members of one or more adversaries is a likely source of intractability. Some political leaders, intellectuals, and mass media producers at times promote such ideologies, often through the manipulation of culturally significant symbols and myths, seeking to arouse emotions of fear and hatred toward ostensible enemies.[2] They may not only extol particular qualities claimed by members of their own community but also condemn qualities attributed to an enemy.

For some members of a contending side, the sense of belonging to a larger entity engaged in a struggle provides meaning and significance to their lives. For others, it provides a livelihood as well as a sense of identity, and for still others, it provides a vehicle for power and influence. Thus, the struggle itself creates a vested interest for some people to continue the fight. Furthermore, the process of entrapment tends to lock some people into persisting in a destructive course of action. Fighting on seems to justify what has already been expended in money, honor, or blood.

In addition, some organizational developments contribute to a conflict escalating destructively. For example, members of small groups, including elite decision-making circles, tend to pressure each other to conform to the prevailing views of the group. Dissenters are likely to withdraw or be excluded; consequently, dissenting voices are silenced and alternatives to continuing on the chosen path are not considered.

Every conflict is embedded in a larger social system and interlocked with other conflicts. Consequently, the nature of that larger social system and the interlocking conflicts also contribute greatly to a conflict's escalation and destructiveness. In some cases, the larger social system fosters a resort to destructive means of struggle, either by creating a high sense of mistrust and lack of security or by upholding norms of honor and revenge that tend to perpetuate fights. On the other hand, legitimate institutions for managing conflicts provide alternatives to destructive coercion, and norms of tolerance and restraints on violence constrain a conflict from escalating destructively.

A struggle also tends to destructively escalate as one conflict becomes superimposed on other conflicts. Thus, insofar as class, ethnic, religious, ideological, and other cleavages coincide rather than cross-cut each other, the struggles will be more intense and more difficult to resolve. For example, the Cold War was superimposed on many conflicts in the Middle East, Central America, Africa, and Asia. The U.S. and Soviet governments each justified its support of contending local parties as necessary to counter the actions of the other. Consequently, a governmental or nongovernmental actor may have acted provocatively to gain regional goals, anticipating support from one of the superpowers. Once engaged in struggle, local adversaries were able to continue fighting, sometimes using powerful weapons, as each side gained support from an opposing superpower. The resulting local struggles were then made more intense, and peace agreements were often difficult to reach and sustain.

De-escalation

After varying duration, a transition to de-escalation eventually occurs in every struggle. De-escalation arises from changes in the relationship between adversaries, from changes within one of the major adversaries, and from changes in the external context.[3] Often, elements from two or three of these sources converge and transform a struggle. De-escalation usually entails the interaction between a set of changing conditions and of new policies, both long and short term.

Certain changes in adversarial relationships are particularly important sources of de-escalation and movement away from destructiveness. One such change is the weakening of resolve or the inability to sustain resistance by members of one side; consequently, the more vulnerable party yields and the victorious side largely imposes its terms of settlement. A precursor to such changes may be an intensification of the struggle by the challenging party, raising the cost for the dominant group until a settlement seems attractive. This is often the rationale used by the challenging party for resorting to violence, even terrorism. Nonviolent coercive means may also be employed, including demonstrations, refusal of cooperation, and boycotts. In addition, the challenger may seek assistance from external supporters, thus shifting the balance of power and increasing coercive threats or experiences against the dominant party. These nonviolent coercive means more readily result in a mutually agreed-upon accommodation than do more purely violent means of struggle, as the people-powered revolutions in the Philippines and in Tunisia attest.

In addition to such coercive means, or in conjunction with them, noncoercive methods also help de-escalate conflicts. These include new ways of thinking about the relationship developed from mutual interchange, growing interdependency, or confidence-building measures, as illustrated by the steps taken in de-escalating the Cold War well before the collapse of the Soviet Union. Change within one of the parties is also an important source of shifts toward de-escalation. The change may include new political leaders, new thinking, and realignments in domestic forces, as occurred among the South African whites before apartheid was abolished. Changes in the social context of the focal conflict provide another set of possible factors fostering de-escalation. Such changes include according new salience to common enemies and impositions by external actors. The change may also be the cessation of competitive interventions, as happened with the end of the Cold War, which helped transform conflicts within southern Africa and Central America.

In short, there are many possible paths away from a destructive struggle; which one is taken depends on many factors. First, it hinges on where the antagonists start from—whether from the defeat of one side, a protracted Cold War, or a violent stalemate. Second, it is affected by the adversaries' goals. Thus, movement may be toward the utter defeat of one side, or it may be toward mutual acceptance and accommodation. Unlikely as it seems, the defeat of one side sometimes can be followed by reconciliation, as in Franco-German relations after World War II.

Finally, an assessment of the pathway taken depends on the time frame that is used. The same road segment, when viewed alone, appears quite different than when seen as part of a long highway. For example, even an intensification of a conflict may appear as a step toward reconciliation when considered over a fifty- or hundred-year span.

Different parties with a stake in a struggle pursue varying strategies to achieve de-escalation. Some of these efforts are planned, and others may be considered strategic only in hindsight by outside analysts. The strategies involve selecting parties for the de-escalating efforts, choosing the issues to be emphasized, and selecting the combination of inducements to be used.

Various combinations of actors may undertake the strategies over the span of months or of years. For example, Anwar al-Sadat, upon becoming president of Egypt in 1970, began a series of steps that, taken with others, led to the 1979 peace treaty with Israel.

Fresh thinking about possible options and new combinations helps the construction of new formulas for possible settlements. Ideas by outsiders, new players, or dissidents sometimes help provide the new thinking. The formulation of possible agreements, in conjunction with a hurting stalemate, often presents a mutually acceptable outcome. This often entails reframing the conflict and drawing attention to common interests and values.

In the course of a long struggle, changes inevitably occur within each side, and some of those changes foster de-escalation. Under certain circumstances, people weary of the struggle and the burdens it imposes, so the goals seem less and less worth the effort. As fervor for fighting declines, more dovish leaders may challenge or replace hawkish leaders, resulting in conciliatory probes toward members of the opposing side and acknowledgement of some of their needs and rights.

Finally, external intermediaries often contribute to the de-escalation of even destructive and seemingly intractable conflicts. Their contributions include (1) arranging package deals to end the conflict, (2) expanding the pie to be divided by adding resources, (3) giving legitimacy to possible new options, and (4) helping implement and sustain the agreement that is reached. The availability of such intermediaries facilitates a transformation when other conditions are favorable. The intermediaries can also help produce more propitious circumstances, for example, by lending support to one party or cutting off assistance to another, or by helping to reframe the conflict and fashion the vision of mutually acceptable options for the adversaries.

Changed contextual conditions also affect one or more of the adversaries and the relations between them. This includes changes in economic, demographic, and social conditions. In addition, informational, normative, and ideological changes affect the sense of what alternatives are possible. For example, in the post–World War II era, many whites in the United States increasingly lost their conviction regarding the inherent inferiority of blacks as racist beliefs decreased in legitimacy and credibility. After the Cold War, recognition and respect for basic human rights deepened and became more widespread. This increased challenges to authoritarian rule and also made the challenges more likely to be effective as some members of authoritarian regimes began to share those norms. This was evident in some of the countries in Eastern Europe as the Soviet Union dissolved and in some Arab countries in 2010 and 2011. In some cases, reform could avert violent revolutionary struggles.

Short-term policies include initiating conciliatory gestures to the other side. These range widely in word and deed and include offering concessions, acknowledging the legitimacy of the other side's concerns, and accepting responsibility for having inflicted injury.[4] Making gestures that are credible to the opposing side without exposing oneself to appear foolish and weak if rebuffed is challenging. To overcome the difficulties, intermediaries may be used to test possible responses or secret overtures may be ventured. It is also important to mobilize constituency support for conciliatory moves and to develop strategies for dealing with constituency opposition, whether by suppression, co-optation, or persuasion. Finally, bottom-up strategies that pave the way for broad public acceptance of elite-level deals, such as people-to-people exchanges or similar second-track initiatives, are often beneficial.[5]

Settlements

Every conflict ends, but each one has a different ending. Sometimes the challenging party abandons its efforts to change its relationship with the adversary. Sometimes one party is largely able to impose the resolution it wants, more ready to destroy an old relationship than to construct a new one. More often, none of the contending sides obtains all that it sought, but each comes to accept a compromise yielding some of what it wanted. In some cases, a creative, mutually beneficial outcome is reached. The outcomes, however, are rarely symmetrical, and disagreements about assessing the relative gains are likely to persist among some factions. These outcomes are frequently tacitly reached and only gradually become evident.

Conflicts are often settled through explicit processes, generally involving negotiations between the adversaries. Certainly, the outcome of negotiations is greatly dependent on the way a struggle has been waged and the resulting relative standing of the adversaries when the negotiations are undertaken. Nevertheless, negotiations have their own dynamics and can be conducted more or less effectively to produce mutually acceptable and enduring agreements.

Intermediaries often play important roles in helping adversaries negotiate to settle or resolve their conflicts. They can provide critical services at each stage of negotiations: exploring the possibility of initiating negotiations, influencing the agenda and choice of negotiating partners, transmitting information about positions and underlying concerns, formulating possible trade-offs, helping to gain support for the agreements reached, and assisting in their implementation. Persons playing an official mediator role can provide these services, but so can quasi mediators.[6] In negotiating endings of large-scale conflicts, a wide variety of agents are likely to perform intermediary activities.

The movement from de-escalation to termination is rarely a smooth, uninterrupted passage. The changed conditions supporting de-escalation and termination may change again and undermine the movement, the terms of the conflict's settlement may appear unacceptable on closer inspection, and parties to the fight who are excluded from the termination proceedings may obstruct and sabotage the process. This was illustrated in the discussions in earlier chapters of the difficulties in making peace between the Israeli government and the Palestine Liberation Organization (PLO), even after the 1993 Declaration of Principles. Unlike the leaders of the ANC and the Nationalist Party in South Africa, the Israeli government and PLO leaders were not seeking a common political union, but separation. Therefore, the leaders had less immediate interest in appealing to the constituency on the other side and building a cooperative relationship.

Outcomes and Post-Termination Sequences

What seems the end of a conflict may indeed be so, but it often marks the change to a renewed conflict or is the basis for a new one. Whatever the end, a conflict never returns to the circumstances before it began; the struggle has consequences that cannot be undone. In this sense, the metaphor of a conflict going through a cycle is misleading, insofar as it is understood as coming back to the starting place. A spiral is a more apt image, with each linked loop varying in the degree of escalation as the conflict is waged in a different historical setting.

Certain kinds of outcomes and transformations from one conflict to another deserve special attention. Here we emphasize mutually acceptable transformations and their sources in changes within one or more of the adversaries, in their relationship to each other, and in their social context.

Internal Changes

Some struggles result in the demise of one of the adversaries. This may occur by the destruction of one of the parties as a physical entity, an identifiable collectivity, or as a functioning social organization. Thus, a social movement organization may cease to exist when it is broken up and its members incapacitated, dispersed, or converted by rival organizations or by government repression. For example, the Black Panther Party erupted onto the U.S. scene in 1966, proclaiming that it sought power to determine the destiny of the black community, restitution for slavery, freedom for all black men held in prisons and jails, and several other goals.[7] After a few years of militant multifaceted struggle, the organization, beset by dissension, was suppressed by police and other government actions. Nevertheless, the constituencies that the Black

Panther Party sought to represent did not disappear and other organizations would in varying degrees try to serve their needs, or the needs would likely be left unaddressed. An adversary may also cease to be antagonistic because its internal structure is radically transformed. Thus, the leaders may change, and the character of the collectivity proclaimed by the former leaders is rejected. This can occur as a result of a revolution and the replacement of the old leadership by a new ruling group.

Sometimes, even when an external enemy has overthrown the leadership, the former supporters of the fallen leaders respond as if they too had been victims and were now liberated, as happened to a large degree in Germany after the defeat of Nazism. On occasion, the election of a new leadership marks a transformation that enables a resolution and reconciliation of an intractable conflict to be reached. This was the case in the ending of British colonial rule in India. In 1945, as World War II was coming to an end, the British electorate voted against the governing Conservative Party, led by Winston Churchill, choosing the Labor Party, led by Clement Atlee. The Labor government quickly moved to offer independence to India. Spain provides another example: after the death of Francisco Franco in 1975, the authoritarian centralized regime he led was replaced by a liberal democratic system that allowed for regional autonomy, thus helping to resolve the conflicts arising from Catalan, Basque, and other regional demands.

In addition, significant members of one of the partisan sides, in the course of a struggle, may become convinced of the correctness of specific previously contested views of their former antagonists. Such a change certainly would greatly contribute to resolving their conflict, as happened in the 1970s in the United States for many men during the women's rights struggle and for many heterosexuals during the gay rights struggle.

A change in the character of an adversary takes many forms. It may be marked by an ideological transformation, by a reorientation of alliances, by a shift from one political economy to another, or by a shift in the ethnicity of the dominant faction. Such changes often mark a definitive end of the previous conflict, but may also be the basis for the emergence of new ones.

Adversary Relationship Changes

The conflict outcome may help forge a new, shared identity for the adversaries, new interdependencies, and therefore vested interests in maintaining good relations. The need to recover from the damages of a destructive encounter can foster cooperation, and if that goes well, the resulting increase in resources can enhance the incentive and the ability for greater cooperation. In large-scale conflicts, however, relations cannot all go so positively.

Some members of the side that regards itself as having been defeated are likely to seek to recover from their losses. The side that felt the gains it had made were secure then may experience a backlash from their erstwhile opponents. The opponents may try to become stronger by finding new allies or reframing their persuasive arguments. For example, Barack Obama's election as president of the United States reinforced the feeling of some right-wing activists and Christian fundamentalists, concerned about matters such as abortion, the teaching of evolution, and the rights of nonheterosexuals, that they were losing electoral ground in recent decades. They allied themselves with the Republican Party and with people who want lower taxes, less regulation of business, and a smaller footprint for government. The groups support each other's preferences and together they have great power, as witnessed by the rise of the Tea Party in the United States.[8]

Even the demise of the opposing collectivity does not mean its total disappearance. A significant constituent group is likely to retain a sense of continuity with its past identity. For example, the Soviet Union ceased to exist in 1991 and the successor country, Russia, was politically transformed. Nevertheless, many Russian citizens, although not viewing themselves as ideological enemies of the United States and believing they now share many common interests with the United States, also hold some opposing goals. The conditions for overt struggles are present but are subordinated to other matters and are waged in a relatively problem-solving manner.

Even within one country, the destruction of a contending party does not obviate the need to build integrative relations between the supporters of the previously contending parties. For example, in May 2009, the LTTE was crushed by Sri Lankan military forces, and its paramount leaders were dead. The Sri Lankan government undertook several measures related to the demobilization of the 12,000 ex-LTTE combatants, the reintegration of Tamils who lived in the areas formerly controlled by the LTTE, and the reconstruction of the destroyed infrastructure of those areas. However, these efforts have not dealt directly with many of the issues that had been the source of the grievances felt by many Tamils in Sri Lanka and in the diaspora. Furthermore, the lack of information and accountability regarding the very large numbers of Tamil civilians who were killed and/or disappeared in the closing months of the civil war hampers reconciliation or a generally acceptable accommodation between the Sinhalese and the minorities in Sri Lanka.[9]

Restructuring of Social Contexts

The social system within which adversaries have struggled frequently is affected, sometimes profoundly, by a conflict or series of conflicts taking place within it. These changes in the social system or in the more diffuse social environment then impact the character of subsequent struggles. Many conflicts are destabilizing for the larger social order as weakened institutions and normative controls foster conflicts and the use of violence. As a consequence, in societies disrupted by protracted civil strife, the state may become unable to provide basic services and rebuilding a political order often takes a very long time.

Struggles, however, sometimes result in strengthening the institutions for managing conflicts. Some evidence for this can be seen in the growth of international governmental and nongovernmental organizations after the two world wars. It also can be seen in the development in the United States of laws and institutions relating to collective bargaining between unions and management. The civil rights struggles by women and minorities in the United States also resulted in the establishment of legal procedures and institutions for countering discrimination in employment, in schooling, and in other spheres of social life.

Major conflicts also affect the social and political environment so as to shape future contentious issues as well as how the struggles about them are waged. Thus, in the United States the various struggles of the 1960s about the U.S. engagement in the Vietnam War and about the rights of university students, African Americans, and women often relied on nonelectoral means of struggle. Recourse to nonelectoral methods gained more legitimacy. In later decades, persons fighting for other causes, including right-leaning ones, relied more on direct action and less on electoral or judicial procedures. This contributed to the weakening of the political party system because it opened space for political struggles to be waged by organizations based on special interests and narrow identity concerns, more than between and within broad coalitions constituting each major party.

Globally, the dissolution of the Soviet Union enhanced the ideological, economic, and military dominance of the surviving superpower, the United States. In the 1990s, this contributed to the increased effectiveness of international governmental organizations, led by the United States, as can be seen in the increase of multilateral interventions to end civil wars and to counter international aggression.

After the 9/11 attacks against the United States, however, that dominance also enabled the administration of George W. Bush to act unilaterally in many arenas, relying greatly on America's sophisticated military capabilities. That was particularly evident in the way the war in Iraq was undertaken and conducted.[10] It was pursued with little international support and considerable opposition in the United States and elsewhere around the world. The goal of transforming the Middle East, advanced by the influential neoconservatives, was widely regarded as unrealistically grandiose. The costs of the war for the

United States, in lives, influence, and good regard were greater and the gains were much less than the officials who decided to wage the war anticipated.

SPECIFICATIONS

As illustrated above, the conditions and context that lead to various kinds of conflict sequences vary in many regards. Accordingly, it is not reasonable to expect that specific processes operate the same way in all kinds of conflicts. More needs to be known about the way particular processes function in different kinds of conflicts. We distinguish conflicts in terms of several general qualities by which they differ: the issues in contention, the characteristics of the adversaries, the relations between the adversaries, and the social context. This discussion focuses on the implications of those qualities for processes affecting the destructive and constructive ways that struggles are conducted.

Issues in Contention

Since the end of the Cold War, considerable attention has been given to ethnic, religious, or other intercommunal conflicts within and between countries. They are often regarded as especially prone to being waged destructively. Indeed, some struggles for ethnic dominance have resulted in genocidal conduct, as in the fierce wars in Rwanda and in parts of the former Yugoslavia. Not all communally associated struggles, however, become destructive. Many are conducted and settled largely through legitimate institutionalized means, as has been true in Malaysia, Canada, Belgium, and India.[11]

Furthermore, conflicts not associated with communal differences, but with differences in political ideology, class position, or relative power also have been destructive and protracted. For example, this was the case for the Cold War between the Soviet Union and the United States, the struggle waged by the Khmer Rouge in Cambodia, the repression by the government of Guatemala, and the fighting among the major clans in Somalia.[12]

Some analysts have argued that conflicts based on value or identity differences or more generally dissensual conflicts are particularly difficult to resolve or to settle. However, this does not seem to be inherently the case. Much depends on many other aspects of the conflict that are related to the adversaries, their relationship, and their social context.

Adversary Characteristics

Many attributes of each adversary in a conflict affect the course of any struggle they wage against each other. Thus, the degree to which an adversary is clearly bounded impacts the course of a conflict, but in different ways at each conflict stage. For example, the likelihood of a conflict emerging is reduced when one or more of the adversaries are not clearly bounded, due to the difficulties in mobilizing partisans. Once the conflict has escalated, however, the absence of clear boundaries can increase the chances of de-escalation since partisans may more readily drift away when the burdens of the struggle become very great.

Negotiating an explicit ending of a conflict, however, is often more difficult when the membership and leaders of one or more sides is not clear and readily changes. This can be seen in the surges of confrontation in the United States during the late 1960s, in many environmental disputes around the world, and in the transnational conflicts related to economic globalization. It is also evident in the transnational Islamic network of Salafist revivalists striving to establish the true Muslim state, some of whose members violently attack the United States because it protects the local false Muslim governments.[13]

The effects of the degree of internal differentiation also have paradoxical effects at different stages of a conflict. Thus, conflicts are prone to become manifest if one or more of the adversaries is highly differentiated, particularly with subgroups that have obligations to contend against external adversaries. On the other hand, highly differentiated parties tend to be hierarchically organized. Consequently, although leaders are often able to make decisions that result in a rapid escalation, they can also spur moves toward de-escalation and a decisive settlement of a conflict.[14]

The relationship between constituents and representatives within each side is a particularly significant aspect of internal differentiation. Thus, the leaders or representatives are varyingly constrained or guided by their constituents. In democracies or other systems in which the followers influence policy decisions, the leaders try to stay attuned to their followers. Where leaders control many resources and are not subject to selection by their constituents, they can be autocratic in their decisions. Of course, these polar differences are imbedded in complex situations and vary in different cultures, about diverse issues, and at different times.

The implications of constituency considerations for the course of a struggle are extremely important. Those in authority are not always more bellicose or more conciliatory than are their constituents, since various mechanisms favor each direction. Thus, leaders regularly dealing with an external adversary have reasons to be restrained and even accommodative in their conduct. These include interdependence with their counterparts (each can help or hurt the other) and mutual understanding that occurs from recurrent interactions. Their constituents are less likely to have such interests or experiences. On the other hand, leaders dealing with an external adversary have reasons to be more antagonistic than are their constituents for other reasons. These include an interest in rallying support for themselves by attacking outsiders and seeking gains for their constituents at the expense of outsiders. Strategies fostering the former mechanisms rather than the latter contribute to waging a struggle constructively.

More consistently, leaders or representatives who tend to be independent of their constituents tend to be capable of making relatively sudden moves, whether to escalate or to de-escalate a conflict. For example, Adolf Hitler and the Nazi leadership of Germany and Joseph Stalin and the Communist Party leadership of the Soviet Union had commanding control of their respective constituents in the summer of 1939. As a central tenet of their ideologies and policies, each had mobilized fierce constituent support against the other. But they signed a nonaggression pact in August 1939, and Nazi Germany and Soviet Russia quickly occupied and divided Poland between them, igniting World War II. The implacable German-Soviet conflict, as far as public utterances were concerned, was suddenly ended. Of course, it was revived with ferocious intensity when Nazi military forces suddenly invaded the Soviet Union in June 1941.

Gross violations of international laws and international human rights laws are not likely to be sustained without the complicity or direction of those in authority. Destructive episodes may erupt at the local level, executed by low-ranking persons within a group, organization, or community. But even then, someone in authority is likely to provide leadership for the outbreak or fail to implement policies that avoid atrocities. This can be seen in the case of the Rwanda genocide, massacres of civilians by soldiers in combat, and in intimidating violence directed against African Americans in the reign of Jim Crow laws in the U.S. South.[15]

Conversely, to stop, reduce, or prevent destructive aspects of a struggle, initiatives from the grass roots and local leadership often pressure the higher levels of authority to move toward de-escalation, settlement, and reconciliation. Of course, de-escalating initiatives are also undertaken by persons with high-level authority in a country or organization, and by persons at the middle or sub-elite levels of an adversarial entity. Cooperation, or at least acquiescence, among different levels is generally necessary for major transitions from one stage of conflict to another. Even in the great transforming breakthroughs, seemingly led by top leaders such as Anwar al-Sadat of Egypt, Mikhail Gorbachev of the Soviet Union, or Frederik Willem de Klerk of South Africa, the leaders were responding to constituency concerns. Their responses were creative and constructive toward an outside adversary as part of the solution for their immediate domestic problems.[16]

Finally, each adversary's self-conception significantly impacts the course of a social conflict and the likelihood that it will be waged with relative constructiveness. One aspect of a group's self-conception that is particularly relevant to how destructively a fight is waged is its sense of specialness. On the grounds of religious faith, ideological beliefs, myths about the past, or presumptions about race differences, some persons or groups claim that they are inherently superior to their adversaries. They may believe that God, history, or nature has chosen them to lead, convert, civilize, subdue, or destroy others. They may consider this to be true universally or only within a particular domain such as a particular territory. When an adversary is armed with such beliefs, genocidal acts may be committed with a sense of self-righteousness.[17] For example, racist views have contributed to genocidal killing, not only by Nazis in Europe but also in Rwanda and in the former Yugoslavia.[18]

Not surprisingly, the interpretation of the meaning of such self-conceptions is often contested. For example, many Americans celebrate that they are a chosen people in a promised land, with a manifest destiny. Such self-conceptions may serve as American justifications for domination and the denial of rights for other peoples in North America and throughout the world.[19] It is when pride in family, group, or nation incorporates the belief that one's claims take complete precedence over those of other humans that they become destructive. Those beliefs may justify claims for exclusive rights in particular territories, even places others regard as sacred, for example, by indigenous peoples in the United States. Denying the legitimacy of the claims made by others prepares the ground for destructive treatment of the adversary.

Adversary Relations

Throughout this book, the relations between the adversaries have been found to be crucial for the way a conflict is conducted and ended. Among the many variations in those relations affecting a conflict's trajectory, we return to the three discussed in the first chapter: numbers, integration, and dominance.

Numbers

We usually think of every conflict as having two sides, but there are always more than two parties in a struggle. This follows from the likelihood that each party has internal diversity in addition to allies and enemies who have a stake in the struggle and are varyingly engaged in it with their own concerns and interests. Moreover, each party may act and be reacted to as if it were part of a larger party or itself consisted of several actors, and so each fight may be regarded as interlocked in many others. Related to the likelihood that each fight is embedded in many others, the issues in contention are numerous and they shift in salience in the course of a struggle.

Given these many possibilities, agreement among analysts about how many adversaries are engaged in any particular conflict is not likely. In considering the numbers engaged in a struggle, therefore, we give priority to the way the adversaries themselves view their struggle. Some parties try to dominate these views, seeking to rally parties to their side and trying to simplify the fight so that it is regarded as being waged between only two sides.

The more moderate factions within the opposing sides may find a satisfactory arrangement and conclude an agreement, shutting out the more extreme groups who would hold out for better terms. For example, in many public policy disputes relating to environmental issues, the number of affected parties is very large. Some with relatively radical positions may raise demands that opponents reject, but others who also have a stake in the problem but desire to find a solution without an escalated struggle can sometimes impose a compromise.

Once escalation has gone far, however, having many parties directly engaged in a struggle can increase the difficulty of settling it. Each party has somewhat different interests and concerns, and a formula acceptable to all the parties on each side may be difficult to construct. For example, in World War II the allied governments waging war against Germany and Japan insisted on unconditional surrender, partly because they understandably feared that trying to set surrender terms might break up the anti-fascist alliance. This probably prolonged the war but also resulted in a more unilateral victory than would otherwise have been the case.

Reaching out to the moderates in the opposing camp may mean appealing to or even undertaking negotiations with elements of the enemy side, even when that side is regarded as evil. For example, efforts by the United Sates and the Afghan government to reach out to moderate members of the Taliban are a central component of the long-term strategy to bring peace to Afghanistan.

Degree of Integration

High mutual interaction and interdependence between actors tends to limit the emergence of conflicts and their escalation into severe struggles.[20] Integration between possible adversaries militates against frictions between them becoming an overt conflict because issues that might be in dispute are viewed in a relatively cooperative context. Furthermore, increased mutual understanding and shared norms tend to limit conflict escalation, even when it becomes manifest.

The absence of shared understandings and norms is related to the degree of cultural differences between peoples, organizations, and classes. Such differences contribute to the emergence and escalation of conflicts in several ways. They may be the basis of denigrating the persons with a different culture and result in efforts to correct or reject them. Furthermore, cultural differences may result in misunderstandings and miscommunications, which help to generate and perpetuate conflicts. In addition, the absence of shared cultural understandings and common institutions reduces the likelihood that rules that tend to mitigate the destructive course of a conflict exist and will be enforced, and do not provide a basis for a shared identity.[21]

Knowledge about each other's cultures, gained through training, experience, or the work of intermediaries, can help overcome these difficulties. Recognizing that no civilization, society, organization, social class, or group is culturally homogenous reduces the dangers of stereotyping and increases the possibilities of finding common bonds across cultural cleavages.

Higher levels of integration also increase the alternatives in conducting a struggle. Inducements of persuasion and possible rewards and of nonviolent coercion are more available because of the mutual dependency resulting from integration. Furthermore, the costs of disrupting the mutual dependency tend to inhibit escalating the means of struggle. There is strong evidence supporting these generalizations in the research about the relationship between international trade and wars.[22]

Dominance

The effects of integration vary depending on the degree to which one side dominates another. There is evidence indicating that asymmetry in dyadic relationships, for example, in trade, is a source of conflicts and that those sometimes escalate.[23] Inequalities in resources, making it possible for one side to dominate the other, naturally affect the emergence and course of every conflict. Inequality between adversaries in controlling resources is an important source of grievance and therefore a basis for an underlying conflict becoming manifest, but this is not a linear relationship. Low levels of inequality tend to reduce a sense of grievance, and extremely high levels of inequality tend to result in domination by one side that inhibits those who might have a grievance from believing they can correct the situation by struggling against it. The domination may be exercised in hegemonic ways, so that the subordinates internalize the legitimacy of their position.[24] Furthermore, great power differences permit great abuses of power.[25] When a conflict erupts, the power concentration contributes greatly to the kind of escalation that follows. Thus, genocides tend to occur when the target group is isolated and vulnerable.

In general, mutually perceived symmetry in the ability to act and to be free of the other side's domination increases the likelihood that the struggle to correct inequities will be conducted in a less destructive manner, and under many conditions, even constructively.

The degree of resource asymmetry between groups, it should be recognized, is not always clear and unchanging.[26] Adversaries in a protracted struggle tend to see themselves as beleaguered and threatened by the powerful other, and feel they must fight hard to defend themselves. During the years of apartheid, South African whites generally saw themselves as threatened by the much more numerous blacks, while the South African blacks regarded themselves as militarily, economically, and politically dominated and exploited by the whites. Israeli Jews generally saw themselves as surrounded by a vast Arab world, while Palestinians saw themselves as dominated by the militarily mighty Israel, backed by Western imperialism. Similar patterns of perceived insecurity can be noted for the Greek and Turkish Cypriots and for the Serbs and Muslims in Bosnia.

Such different views of power and vulnerability help explain the protracted nature of many conflicts. They can also suggest ways out of intractable conflicts if the context and the parties to a conflict are altered. For example, in the 1980s several Central American countries were wracked by long-lasting and interlocked conflicts, making it difficult to settle any one of them in isolation. A large step toward resolution was made by the accord reached among the presidents of the five Central American countries, meeting in Esquipulas, Guatemala.[27] The accord is often called the "Arias Plan" to recognize the great mediating contributions of Oscar Arias, the president of Costa Rica. The accords included three components to be implemented simultaneously and a fixed time schedule in the countries devastated by civil wars. The components provided for ending the violent conflicts, promoting democracy, and fostering economic integration.

System Context

The particular social system within which a conflict is waged provides a conventional way to identify different kinds of conflicts. Families, large-scale formal organizations, residential neighborhoods, countries, and regions of the world each have their own peculiarities that are relevant for the course of struggles within them. These system settings differ along several conflict dimensions, variously combined. Focusing on the dimensions themselves helps in comparing different conflicts, theoretically and practically. For example, resource differences tend to be greater within countries than within neighborhoods, but countries and neighborhoods also vary greatly in the degree to which control of resources is concentrated. We will consider the course of a conflict in the light of four aspects of social systems: culture and institutions, scarcity, resource distribution, and consistency and stability.

Culture and Institutions

In addition to the degree to which culture is shared, discussed previously, the specific content of the conflict-relevant rules of the shared culture and institutions is particularly important in affecting the course of conflicts. For example, the shared values may be conducive to competitiveness, individualism, and machismo. They may encourage revenge-seeking, feuds, and other practices that tend to perpetuate conflicts. On the other hand, beliefs in the oneness of the human species or valuing tolerance or celebrating diversity help mitigate the destructive implications of cultural differences. Furthermore, culturally prescribed procedures may provide for problem-solving ways to manage conflicts. The UN Educational, Scientific, and Cultural Organization (UNESCO), for several years, conducted a variety of programs in many countries to foster a "culture of peace."[28]

The field of peace education, associated with fields of peace studies and of conflict resolution, has a large number of analysts and practitioners. Work in the field includes early childhood socialization, primary and secondary curriculum effects, socialization into gender roles, effects of mass media programing, and many other topics.[29]

The system may encourage and enable interventions. The involvement of parties that are not the primary antagonists provides opportunities to explore possible solutions to a conflict before it escalates. Such parties may serve as mediators, helping to discover plausible mutually acceptable formulas. They may help sustain norms of decent conduct by punishing violators. That has been the hallmark of states and their governments, but absent at the global level. However, the propriety of external intervention into the territory of sovereign states, under certain conditions, has been slowly increasing at the global level.

Scarcity

Conflicts are often viewed as contests over scarce resources.[30] If there were enough to go around, common sense suggests, people would not fight each other. Indeed, families, organizations, and societies vary in the general level of material endowments and in trends of their growth and decline. Higher and increasing levels of such resources do tend to reduce the manifestation of conflicts and facilitate the waging of constructive struggles, as indicated by the cross-national research on income distribution and violent conflicts.[31] To some extent, however, material goods and social attributes such as prestige or power are valued relatively, compared with how much others have. Insofar as that is true, the ameliorating effects of abundance and its growth are reduced.

Scarcity is not inherent in particular circumstances. Rather, the experience of scarcity depends on the parameters of the social system being considered.

Even prestige, which is relative, can be accorded to many people at the same time in different arenas. Consequently, even in apparent conditions of scarcity, the stated conditions underlying a struggle may be reconfigured. This can occur by increasing the number of significant subsystems, for example, in diverse social realms or in local and regional settings. Thus, the diversification of ranking systems provides more opportunities for people to excel.

Resource Distribution

The adversaries, whatever the symmetry of their resources, exist in a larger social context, characterized by differing kinds of resource distributions, with varying implications for how a conflict is conducted. Within a hierarchical system in which the challengers are relatively low ranked, the way they conduct a struggle will be greatly affected by the rules and interventions of the superordinate group. On the other hand, in a system of numerous, relatively equal, autonomous parties, the rules are more likely to reflect all the parties in the system, but the rules are less likely to be precise or to be enforced.

Consistency and Stability

Inconsistencies among different aspects of a social system and the lack of stability tend to generate conflicts and to foster their escalation, particularly in combination. For example, research on genocide and politicide indicates that they occur when the political opportunity structure permits.[32] Already-occurring disorder and violence frees some people to engage in other struggles destructively. Thus, in the shadow of military operations, a ruling group is more able to implement policies that limit civil liberties or even result in killings, as was true for the removal of U.S. residents and citizens of Japanese descent from the U.S. West Coast to relocation camps during World War II and the genocide of Armenians in Turkey during World War I.[33]

This discussion of the many ways conflicts differ indicates too that they vary in their predispositions to escalate destructively or constructively. Such predispositions affect the consequences of pursuing policies to foster constructive struggle. For some conflicts, the challenge of finding ways to conduct a conflict constructively is relatively easily met; but for others, the challenge may be insurmountable, at least in the short run.

CHALLENGES

Perhaps the primary reason that people study how social conflicts are waged is to mitigate their destructive effects. It is widely presumed that knowledge about specific struggles and general understandings about the bases of conflicts and their destructive escalation can be useful. Such knowledge could be effectively applied to avoid conflicts, to conduct struggles constructively, to resolve them cooperatively, or to advance good causes, such as freedom, equity, or peace. Applying knowledge to advance such values, however, presents two main challenges: first, determining how partisans can apply general knowledge about social conflicts to a particular case, and second, determining under what circumstances conflict interventions are both constructive and moral.

Implementing Effective Practices

Persons working in applied conflict resolution are usually concerned about specific conflicts and what to do in each case. Medical practice offers a tantalizing metaphor. Physicians generally value their clinical skills: the ability to diagnose what is happening to a particular patient at a specific time and to decide on the most effective therapy to treat that particular patient. In doing so, they draw on general theories of physiology, pharmacology, and many other disciplines. But it is the peculiar and unique interactions of many general processes that account for the particular condition of each patient. On the other hand, scientists studying a specific process try to isolate and hold constant other variables that affect that process. Their knowledge is generally presented in probabilities, the likelihood that particular consequences will result from specific conditions, everything else being equal. Furthermore, theorists often emphasize relatively immutable conditions and processes affecting many conflicts rather than the factors that may be manipulated in individual cases, which are of greater interest to practitioners.

An important difference between medical practitioners and conflict resolvers is that there is a widely shared consensus about the meaning and desirability of good health rather than poor health, of living rather than dying. Such consensus is lacking about conflicts, at least among the adversaries. A particular conflict may be valued insofar as it is viewed as a means to a better outcome for one of the contending parties.

In the practice of conflict resolution, the clinical approach is preeminent. Conflict resolvers use their moral standards and draw from their general knowledge about relevant conflicts to prescribe actions for the adversaries and for themselves in particular struggles.[34] Analysts of conflict resolution sometimes also indulge in prescribing policies, applying their understandings of general truths and morality to specific cases. They usually seek general patterns of effective mediation, negotiation, and constructive struggle and in that way may provide general prescriptions for classes of conflicts.

There is no single conflict resolution formula for ameliorating every conflict or preventing each from becoming more destructive; however, being able to select from a large repertoire of methods increases the chances of choosing an appropriate method. Thinking about each case as freshly as possible, and not assuming it is just ike another struggle, is a good rule to follow.

In order to apply general knowledge about conflicts to specific struggles, researchers and practitioners should analyze the struggle carefully, considering how it is like and unlike other struggles. But there is no agreed-on comprehensive theory of conflicts that can specify the consequences of every act any partisan might take. Any assertion is likely to be contested and each tends to be quite abstract and valid only in a probabilistic sense.

General knowledge can be applied more readily to large sets of similar conflicts than to a single case. This is like using a public health model rather than a clinical medical model. Using a public health approach, the systemic causes of a disease are treated in order to reduce the incidence of that disease. For example, having a good sewage system prevents illnesses, but it does not cure someone already sick.

Many public health policies entail public engagement such as eating a proper diet, reducing transmission of illnesses by washing hands, and regulating products, services, and behavior that might cause accidents. Similarly, waging conflicts constructively, at every level, depends on the persons engaged in the conflict, with or without the assistance of professional conflict resolvers. Therefore a primary mission of workers in the field of conflict resolution and transformation is to teach, inform, train, and otherwise convey the ideas and practices that foster doing conflicts constructively. To some extent this is happening through programs teaching alternatives to violence to inmates of prisons, peer mediation to students in elementary schools, negotiation and mediation skills to corporate and government managers, and facilitation and discussion methods to the public at large. Of course, in many circumstances it is important that the diffusion of particular techniques or methods happens in conjunction with the underlying ideas and evidence of the constructive conflict approach. Without that, the words and practices of the conflict resolution approach may be misapplied and ineffective, or worse.[35]

Conflict resolvers increasingly are concerned with designing systems to prevent conflicts from becoming manifest or from escalating destructively. They seek to fashion constructive ways to manage conflicts in particular settings such as corporations, churches, schools, factories, or municipalities.[36] This may include developing grievance procedures, training members of such organizations in ways to negotiate or to mediate conflicts before they escalate.

This meshes well with the growing interest in and practice of collaboration.[37] Collaboration occurs between relatively autonomous actors when they jointly develop rules and structures to govern their relations and decision making about issues they must manage interdependently. This usually occurs in circumstances of shared norms and possible mutual benefits. This can bring under control many incipient conflicts and help avert destructive escalations. Conversely, the ability to wage conflicts constructively enhances the effectiveness of collaboration.

In applying theoretical understanding to ameliorating conflicts, whether individual struggles or recurrent fights, it is useful to recognize the variety of stages and types of conflicts and to consider the diverse methods that tend to be effective at each stage of different kinds of conflicts.[38] Certainly, increasing attention is being given to preventing destructive conflicts, to interrupting them, to getting adversaries to the negotiating table, to negotiating agreements, and to building cooperative relations.

Research to assess the consequences of various kinds of conflict interventions and of various policies related to waging conflicts is rapidly growing. As the practice of conflict resolution has expanded, practitioners and their funders more often seek assessments of the work that is done. Studies are also increasing about the ways various strategies and methods, undertaken by many different actors, complement and sometimes interfere with each other in different conflict circumstances.[39] In addition, we need to learn what methods can be used by different kinds of people, since actors, whether partisans or intermediaries, vary in their skills and resources to apply different methods.

Issues of Subjectivity and Morality

Questions about when and how to engage in particular conflicts necessarily involves subjective judgments about values and morality. People engaged in a conflict as partisans or as intermediaries must wrestle with moral dilemmas. We begin our examination of these matters and possible grounds to stand on in making moral judgments by discussing violence in conflicts.

The field of conflict studies tends to contain a strong normative bias against the use of violence. Considerable literature in the field is devoted to an examination of nonviolent tactics, conditions that facilitate peaceful interaction between adversary groups, and the conditions that foster sustainable peace.[40] In this book we have often labeled use of violence by partisans as an example of a destructively waged fight. We have argued that severe means of struggle affect persons who are not directly engaged in the primary conflict and often create new injustices and long-lasting injuries. Violence in which people are driven from their homes, killed, tortured, and raped inflicts enduring emotional impairments on the surviving victims of such trauma and their family members. Consequently, they may act with desperation to find security and protect themselves, individually and collectively. In an extraordinary case, the largely successful Nazi effort to destroy European Jewry contributed immensely to the drive among the survivors to get to Palestine and to fight to establish a Jewish state there. But there are always consequences that flow from the choice of conflict tactics chosen by adversaries. Applying overwhelming coercive pressure to force an adversary to yield may hasten the end of a conflict in the short term, but such tactics may make the resumption of the conflict more likely in the long term.

That violence can beget violence, that it causes enormous suffering, and that it can prolong destructive episodes of conflict is beyond dispute. However, whether violence as a conflict management tactic can ever be considered constructive is subject to debate. There is a long tradition in social conflict studies that justifies the use of violence in cases of extreme injustice as an appropriate and even necessary vehicle for upending political and social orders which themselves use destructive tactics to protect the power and privilege of one group over another. Some authoritarian regimes and police states, so the argument goes, will only adjust their behavior when confronted by violence or the threat of violence. Hence, the story of British Prime Minister Neville Chamberlain's signing of the 1938 Munich Agreement with Adolf Hitler's Germany has come to symbolize the folly of appeasement and the limitations of nonviolent tactics when it comes to confronting "evil." Indeed, the specter of Adolf Hitler has been used by U.S. presidents over the years to justify violent campaigns against authoritarian leaders ranging from Saddam Hussein to Mullah Mohammad Omar. As President Barack Obama stated when accepting his Noble Peace Price in 2009:

> For make no mistake: evil does exist in the world. A non-violent movement could not have halted Hitler's armies. Negotiations cannot convince al Qaeda's leaders to lay down their arms. To say that force is sometimes necessary is not a call to cynicism—it is recognition of history; the imperfections of man and the limits of reason.[41]

In the end the debate over the morality and use of violence and its relationship to post-conflict sequences is both an empirical and a normative question. Empirically researchers have measured such relationships by looking at the effectiveness of adopting nonviolent methods. For example, a recent research project by Maria Stephan and Erica Chenoweth demonstrated that nonviolent campaigns are on the whole more successful at achieving their aims than are armed campaigns.[42] Furthermore, some of these studies support the proposition that nonviolent strategies tend to produce more peaceful relations subsequently. Thus, a comparison between national independence movements that used varying amounts of violent and nonviolent actions preceding their independence found a positive relationship between violence before independence and later external violent behavior.[43] However, there are many stories to be told in the field of social conflict studies, and some of them suggest that violent tactics or the threat of violence has led to outcomes that might be considered constructive.

There are many efforts to provide solid ground upon which such moral judgments can rest. Religious faith is widely believed to provide the source of morality. As discussed in chapter 5, pacifist strains are to be found in many religious traditions, but the mainstreams of these religions tend to support the conflict choices made by civil authorities in the countries where the religious organizations are based. In conflict matters they tend to take rather parochial stands rather than universal ones that encompass enemies. Sometimes, indeed, some people draw on their religious faith to characterize certain other people as evil and damnable. Undoubtedly, for many people in the world, religious faiths do provide moral guidance in engaging in conflicts. There are religious imperatives shared by many religions, for example about doing onto others as they would have done to themselves, which are congruent with a constructive conflict approach. Persons holding offices of authority in religious organizations often take and are expected to take actions that serve to avoid or stop destructive conflict escalation. They may mediate between antagonistic parties or counsel one side to take peacemaking courses of action.

There are also some specific guidelines for particular kinds of conflicts that have philosophical and religious origins. For example, the just war doctrine is often claimed to be a justification for government actions in deciding whether or not to go to war and how to wage it once war has begun.[44] Traditionally, just war thinking pertains to the right to go to war and the right conduct in making war. According to this reasoning, the right to go to war requires a just cause, the probability of success, a legitimate public authority, proportionality, that it be a last resort, and that it is undertaken with a right intention. According to just war interpreters, combatants should not conduct war actions against noncombatants and not use weapons such as mass rape or weapons whose effects are uncontrolled, war actions should be proportional and militarily necessary, and prisoners of war should be fairly treated.

Problem-solving conflict resolution efforts also require attention to moral issues.[45] For example, mediators and other kinds of interveners face choices about whether to intervene, when to intervene, and how to intervene. Moreover, the partisans waging a struggle endeavor to morally justify their actions to themselves, to their constituents and allies, and also to their adversaries. If they take a problem-solving conflict-resolution approach, the moral issues are particularly salient. Some conflict resolvers, concerned about the morality of various kinds of interventions, declare particular basic values or moral principles that should guide conflict resolution work. James Laue, for example, argued that conflict resolution ethics rest on "the basic premise . . . that persons are inherently valuable, and to be treated as ends-in-themselves."[46] He derived three core values from this premise: proportional empowerment, justice, and freedom; and on the bases of these values, he derived several ethical principles for interveners. Helpful as such directives may be, the parties in a conflict may not accept them, or different priorities are given to these values and principles by various partisans and interveners.

Another ground for moral assessments is related to the idea that there are universal basic human needs whose lack of fulfillment is a fundamental cause of deeply-rooted conflicts. This idea was discussed in chapter 2. One reason for the attraction of this idea is that it suggests an empirically grounded basis for moral judgments. It is also attractive to conflict resolvers doing interactive, problem-solving workshops because it not only helps explain the emergence and persistence of protracted conflicts, but it also is congruent with ways to overcome them. Since such conflicts derive from unsatisfied basic human needs, it is argued that they can be resolved when adversaries in a conflict, aided by facilitators, recognize that condition and thereby change it. As discussed in chapter 2, however, there are severe limits to relying on the idea of universal basic human needs to account for the variations in social conflicts' emergence, escalation, and transformation.

The profound difficulties in discovering or creating a widely shared, firmly grounded basis for moral judgments relating to social conflicts lead many people to assert that morals are a matter of personal taste or of social conventions. An influential view of morals and values is that they are relative, deriving from culture and personal experience. Admittedly, there is no universal consensus about any absolute standards that provide a ranking of values to be honored. Morality is traditionally based on value preferences, and according to an important social science tradition, value preferences cannot be derived from beliefs about reality. Morality is articulated in the form of "should" statements, not factual statements.[47] It is given authority by shared understandings, for example, about God or human nature. For many social scientists this has meant that morality is a matter of faith and convictions that are socially constructed. It follows that morality is variable; it is culturally relative and cannot be judged by absolute standards.

However, according to a related social science tradition, there is an objective reality that can be approached by empirical methods of research. Full and accurate understanding of the objective reality may never be attained, but by seeking it, much can be learned about it. That is the goal of the social as well as the natural sciences and of all policy makers and policy analysts.

These conceptions of beliefs and values have been subjected to severe criticisms, and newer views warrant consideration here, because they help lessen the dilemmas about acting morally in resolving a conflict.[48] The existence of a reality separable from the observation of it is now widely questioned. The argument is that what we know must derive from our observations and those must be filtered through our senses, even as they are augmented by instruments.[49] It follows that reality can be known only under specific conditions of observation, and therefore reality varies under different conditions and from differently situated perspectives. However, this does not mean that we can construct reality any way we like. Matters vary in the strength of their predispositions to be perceived one way rather than another. Some matters are generally viewed similarly, regardless of the bases of observations.

Our understanding of morality has also been affected by recent social experience and thought. One development has been the growing sense that certain kinds of conduct are almost universally deplored. Even those persons who perpetrate condemned acts often hide or deny that they or members of their group committed them, or they construct them as different kinds of acts. But sometimes they even come to acknowledge that their group was wrong or that they themselves did wrong. The extension of shared norms may be seen in the growing acceptance of the existence of universal human rights and the condemnation of torture, rape, and genocidal acts.[50] The study of normative regimes in international affairs also reveals the existence of moral standards that influence the conduct of governments sharing those standards.[51] Furthermore, there is growing codification of the circumstances under which international intervention should occur when a government does not meet its responsibilities to serve and protect its citizens. The UN-supported "Responsibility to Protect" doctrine spells out the procedures for the international community to appropriately intervene.[52]

The attention to shared normative standards provides a broad basis for moral imperatives. This is exemplified by the argument for conventionalism as the basis for ethics in international relations and other domains. Ethics is based on principles that people use to justify and win acceptance from others for their actions. To be effective, the concerned parties must share the principles. Rather than promulgating any particular ethical tradition as the foundation for moral theory, as David A. Welch writes, moral obligation can be and is based on agreement to regard "certain rules as authoritative, and certain practices as legitimate. . . . Whatever the parties concerned agree to regard as just or legitimate is just or legitimate," according to this view.[53] The present discussion is based on this conventionalist approach. Accordingly, we neither assert that there is a universally agreed-on moral code, nor assume that a particular moral code is supreme. But the argument does not assert that every conventional moral code is equally supportable.

In addition, new insights have emerged from the application of social policies to promote human welfare. In recent decades, increased use has been made of social science research to help formulate social policies; but that has not ensured that the policies have the desired effects and avoid undesired ones. We are too often reminded that good intentions do not guarantee good results. One response may be skepticism about trying to implement any public policies, but another is to examine even more carefully the consequences of alternative policies. Knowledge of the consequences of different ways of fighting and of intervening helps ground morality in empirical and practical realities.

The expanding work in problem-solving conflict resolution has stimulated practitioners and analysts to reflect on the nature of their knowledge and of their morality. These concerns compel attention to the varying interpretations of the past and the present that adversaries construct, even about the same events. Moreover, many practitioners of nonviolence and conflict resolution believe that through mutual probing all parties can gain a more complete truth.[54] The probing takes many diverse contexts, including interactive workshops, confrontations in a nonviolent campaign, or community meetings.

The study of conflicts makes evident that no means of struggle and no settlement has purely good or bad consequences. Every course of action embodies a mixture of moral characteristics. Thus, people may be struggling for a future with greater social justice, but in doing so they reduce freedom for many, engage in killing, and suffer severe losses; or a settlement may end the killing, but only briefly and in a way that engenders new injustices. Indeed, to insist on the primacy of one's own value-ordering and moral principles seems to contradict some aspects of the problem-solving conflict-resolution perspective. We are convinced that reflecting on the growing empirical evidence about social conflicts can help guide partisans and intermediaries to more effectively mitigate the destructiveness of conflicts.

Simply avoiding conflicts is not the solution. They are inevitable; and furthermore, they often are necessary to advance important values. Even after relatively successful struggles, which were pursued constructively, injustices often persist. Thus, despite the great achievements of the civil rights struggle in the United States in the 1950s–1970s, African Americans at the beginning of the twenty-first century have much higher rates of unemployment, poverty, incarceration, and fatherless families than do European Americans. The workings of the conventional political processes seem inadequate to correct these inequities. More creative constructive approaches to address these problems are needed, ones that would arouse widespread engagement of African Americans and other Americans to overcome the obstacles to greater equity.

Dilemmas cannot be avoided, for three major reasons. First, everyone holds a variety of values, and maximizing one is often done at the expense of another. Thus, people generally believe that preserving life, maintaining order, advancing justice, and promoting freedom are good, but are uncertain about how much of each should be sacrificed for the other in a particular historical circumstance. For would-be conflict resolvers, a frequent moral dilemma is whether they should seek a settlement under existing conditions or support continuing the struggle in the hope that future conditions will yield a more equitable agreement.

Another source of dilemmas is that everyone has many identities, and each offers a different vantage point, providing different priorities and meaning to the values each person holds. For example, some people may share identities with an oppressed minority struggling for greater equality, or with all the citizens of the country in which the minority lives, or with others who believe all humans are equally children of God, or with adherents of a political ideology extolling individual liberty. Thus, the priority and interpretation of the many values each person holds are likely to differ depending on the salience of the various identities held.

Third, moral dilemmas arise from the intertwining of struggles, so that resolving one may hamper resolving another. For example, in the United States after the Civil War the whites of the former Confederacy were reincorporated into the Union against which they had rebelled.[55] The reconciliation was made partly at the expense of the Southern blacks, the former slaves. The Southern whites were allowed to dominate the former slaves after the reconstruction policy slackened and ended.

CONCLUSIONS

In the contemporary world, constructive methods of waging conflicts are more important than ever. A conflict waged destructively in one place is often the result of faraway, interacting linkages and has wider implications. The attacks in the United States on September 11, 2001, are tragically illustrative.

The world is always in flux and in never-ending transition, so that many old paradigms are no longer valid, but neither are they wholly irrelevant. For example, a world divided among sovereign states with persons largely interacting within each country is less the world in which many people actually live than it was a century ago. Conflicts based on universal ideologies or narrow economic interests seem less salient than they had been, as struggles related to identity issues have become more urgent.

Furthermore, globalization links people all over the world. This is manifested in the growth of international trade, in the expansion of investments from several countries to much of the world, and in the movement of people from one region to another as laborers, technicians, professionals, and as refugees from war and disorder. It is also manifested in people's exposure to the same information and entertainment generated by the mass media. In addition, the newer technologies of communication enable people to quickly communicate with each other, forming new networks and sustaining old ones over long distances. Finally, changes in the environment and populations constitute growing problems threatening everyone. We face common problems in our neighborhoods, countries, and planet.[56]

In addition, the changes in weapons technologies also increase the possibility that struggles will be waged with even greater destructive consequences. Weapons capable of inflicting immense harm are increasingly accessible to more people. Even small nongovernmental groups may threaten attacks with weapons of mass destruction. The increasing global integration multiplies the vulnerability of people everywhere to such attacks.

These developments converge to exacerbate old conflicts and generate new ones. These developments also implicate each of us in each other's affairs, giving each of us a stake in the way others behave. They therefore provide an impetus to find and pursue constructive ways of waging struggles. They encourage us to recognize that no person or group is in sole possession of truth or morality. Therefore, increased reliance on constructive conflict strategies can enhance benefits for all.

Another consequence of these developments is that intermediaries have become more important than ever in managing conflicts. More parties than before have a stake in a conflict and therefore have incentives to intervene and try to avert its destructive escalation. Furthermore, intervention is increasingly expected and considered proper. There is less tolerance for conduct, even in large-scale conflicts, that violate increasingly shared understandings of human rights. These and related developments help explain the significant decrease in domestic and international wars since the end of the Cold War, noted at the beginning of this book.

The analysis presented here indicates that everyone can contribute something to the amelioration of struggles of any magnitude. This is true whether we are working at the grassroots level, the middle range, or as system leaders. This is the case because of the interconnectedness of many conflicts and the ever-growing interdependence of people throughout the world.

The participation of citizens everywhere in promoting methods, goals, and identities that foster constructive conflicts is important. Further information about how this occurs is increasingly available. Sources of such information are presented in this book's endnotes and also in appendixes A and B. Appendix A lists many organizations engaged in intermediary and partisan activities seeking to foster the constructive waging of struggles. Appendix B lists websites providing information about numerous specific conflicts and also about various ways conflicts are conducted.

We humans are not doomed to endless and all-pervasive destructive struggles. We may not escape them all, but we can certainly reduce and limit them. Awareness that conflicts can be waged constructively is increasing, but much more information is needed about how to do so under various circumstances. This includes understanding how to avoid destructive overreaching and how and when to employ methods that are not very likely to result in destructive escalations, such as nonviolent actions, reframing enactments, coengagements, and problem-solving meetings. We also need more and better knowledge about constructive approaches at every stage of a conflict from emergence to sustaining accommodations after the fighting has ceased. Such knowledge will help raise the chances that conflicts will be constructively waged, even if all parties are not prepared to do so.

Appendix A

Selected Organizations in the Field of Constructive Conflicts

This list suggests the diversity of organizations contributing to the constructive waging of conflicts. It provides a sampling of centers, associations, and institutions engaging in relevant activities, including

- education (EDU): degree-granting and certificate programs, outreach
- intermediary services (INT): mediation, facilitation, and consultation
- research and theory building (RTB): reporting, analyzing data
- training (TRA): workshops in conflict resolution applications

ACCORD, African Centre for the Constructive Resolution of Disputes (EDU, INT, RTB, TRA)
Private Bag X018, Umhlanga Rocks, 43320, South Africa
Tel: 27 (31) 502-3908
http://www.accord.org.za/us/contact/contact-details.html

American Arbitration Association (INT)
140 W. 51st Street, New York, NY 10020
Tel: 212-484-4000 Fax: 212-765-4874
www.adr.org

Association for Conflict Resolution (EDU)
1015 18th Street, NW, Washington, DC 20036
Tel: 201-464-9700
http://www.acrnet.org/webforms.aspx?ekfrm=534

Berghof Conflict Research (RTB, TRA)
Altensteinstraße 48a
D-14195 Berlin
Phone +49 (0)30 844154-0
http://www.berghof-conflictresearch.org/en/

The Carter Center of Emory University (INT, RTB)
One Copenhill, Atlanta, GA 30307
Tel: 404-420-5151 Fax: 404-420-5196
www.cartercenter.org

CDR Associates (INT, TRA)
100 Arapahoe Avenue, Suite 12, Boulder, CO 80302
Tel: 303-442-7367
www.mediate.org

Centre for Conflict Resolution (EDU, RTB, TRA)
Department of Peace Studies, University of Bradford,
Bradford, BD7 1DP, UK
Tel: +44(0)1274-23-5235
www.bradford.ac.uk/acad/confres/

Conflict Research Consortium (EDU, RTB)
University of Colorado, Campus Box 327, Boulder, CO 80309
Tel: 303-492-1635 Fax: 303-492-2154
www.colorado.edu/conflict

Department of Dispute Resolution (EDU, RTB, TRA)
Nova Southeastern University, 3301 College Avenue, Ft. Lauderdale, FL 33314
www.nova.edu/CWIS/centers/ssss/index.html

Educators for Social Responsibility (EDU, TRA)
22 Garden Street, Cambridge, MA 02138
Tel: 617-492-1764
www.esrnational.org

Fellowship of Reconciliation (TRA, INT)
Box 271, Nyack, NY 10960
Tel: 914-358-4601 Fax: 914-358-4924
www.nonviolence.org/~nvweb/for

Global Partnership for the Prevention of Armed Conflict (GPPAC)
Laan van Meerdervoort 70—6th floor
2517 AN The Hague
The Netherlands
Telephone: +31 (0)70 311 0970
http://www.conflict-prevention.net/index.html

Heidelberg Institute for International Conflict Research (RTB, TRA)
Bergheimer Str. 58
69115 Heidelberg
Germany
+49.6221.54.3198
http://www.hiik.de/en/index.html

Kroc Institute for International Peace Studies (EDU, RTB)
University of Notre Dame, P.O. Box 639, Notre Dame, IN 46556-0639
Tel: 219-631-6970
http://kroc.nd.edu/

Mennonite Conciliation Service (INT, TRA)
21 South 12th Street, P.O. Box 500, Akron, PA 17501-0500
Tel: 717-859-3889
http://conciliationserv.mennonite.net

Ohio Commission on Dispute Resolution and Conflict Management (INT, TRA)
77 S. High Street, Columbus, OH 43266-0124
Tel: 614-752-9595
http://disputeresolution.ohio.gov/

The Program for the Advancement of Research on Conflict and Collaboration (PARCC) (EDU, INT, RTB, TRA)
Syracuse University, Syracuse, NY 13244
Tel: 315-443-2367 Fax: 315-443-3818
http://www.maxwell.syr.edu/parcc.aspx

Program on Conflict Resolution (EDU, INT, RTB, TRA)
University of Hawaii at Manoa, 2424 Maile Way, Honolulu, HI 96822
Tel: 808-956-7792 Fax: 808-956-921
http://www.hawaii.edu/graduatestudies/fields/html/departments/cd/conflictres/conflictres.htm

Program on Negotiation at Harvard Law School (EDU, INT, TRA, RTB)
500 Pound Hall, Cambridge, MA 02138
Tel: 617-495-1684 Fax: 617-495-7818
http://www.pon.harvard.edu/?floater=99

School of Conflict Analysis and Resolution (EDU, INT, RTB, TRA)
George Mason University, 4400 University Drive, Fairfax, VA 22030-4444
Tel: 703-993-1300 Fax: 703-993-1302
www.gmu.edu/departments/ICAR/

Search for Common Ground (INT, TRA)
1601 Connecticut Ave., NW, Washington, DC 20009
Tel: 202-265-4300 Fax: 202-232-6718
www.sfcg.org

SIPRI Stockholm International Peace Research Institute (RTB)
Signalistgatan 9, SE-169 70 Solna, Sweden
Tel: 46-8-655 97 00
www.sipri.org

TRANSCEND: A Peace and Development Network (EDU, INT, TRA)
Tel: 914-773-3400; email: transcend@transcend.org
http://www.transcend.org/

United States Institute of Peace (EDU, RTB, TRA)
1550 M Street, NW, Washington, DC 20005-1708
Tel: 202-457-1700 Fax: 202-429-6063
www.usip.org

Uppsala Universitet
Department of Peace and Conflict Resolution (EDU, DTB, TRA)
SE 751 20 Uppsala, Sweden
Tel: 46 (0) 18 471 00 00
www.pcr.uu.se

Appendix B

Selected Websites Relating to Social Conflicts

A growing number of websites are providing a major resource for learning about social conflicts, how they are waged, and how they might be conducted less destructively. Official and unofficial analysts and intermediaries who are concerned about particular conflicts or general kinds of conflicts have established websites with information about how the conflicts can be conducted to minimize their destructiveness. The sites listed below exemplify some of these possibilities.

In addition, partisans on different sides of a struggle construct websites that give the visitor insights about the conflict and a sense of how leaders on each side try to mobilize their constituencies. Information about current conflict developments also can be accessed readily on the Internet. Finally, many of these sites offer simulations or other exercises that may be very useful to students and teachers.

METHODS OF CONDUCTING AND SETTLING CONFLICTS

http://beyondintractability.com/
Beyond Intractability

www.crinfo.org
The Conflict Resolution Information Source

http://www.everyday-democracy.org/en/index.aspx
Every Day Democracy

http://mediate.com
Information about resolution, training, and mediation

www.ijc.org
International Court of Justice

www.international-alert.org
International Alert

http://www.aeinstein.org/
Albert Einstein Institution

www.c-r.org
Conciliation Resources

http://www.un.org/peace/peacebuilding/pbso.shtml
United Nations Peacebuilding Commission

DOMAINS OF CONFLICT (COMMUNAL, ENVIRONMENTAL, ORGANIZATIONAL)

www.incore.ulst.ac.uk/cds
INCORE

http://www.uga.edu/islam/
Islamic studies

www.hrw.org/
Human Rights Watch

www.ecr.gov/
U.S. Institute for Environmental Conflict Resolution

www.fmcs.gov
Federal Mediation and Conciliation Service

www.crisisgroup.org
International Crisis Group

http://ictj.org/
International Center for Transitional Justice

www.osce.org
The Organization for Security and Co-operation in Europe

http://www.ipcri.org/IPCRI/Home.html
Israel/Palestine Center for Research and Information

www.mideastweb.org
Information on dialogues, maps, etc., relating to the Middle East

www.usip.org
United States Institute of Peace

Notes

CHAPTER 1

1. In 1980, after nearly a decade of litigation, the Passamaquoddy and Penobscot people received federal recognition and a cash settlement of over eighty-one million dollars for the purchase of land in the state of Maine. The agreement, known as the Maine Indian Claims Settlement Agreement, is one of the most far-reaching of its kind and is one of the few large-scale land-claim settlements in the United States. For a discussion of the history of the conflict, the obstacles to its settlement, and the deal that was reached, see D. J. Kotlowski, "Out of the Woods: The Making of the Maine Indian Land Claims Settlement Act," *American Indian and Culture Journal* 30(4) (2006): 62–97.

2. Lewis A. Coser provisionally defined conflict as "a struggle over values and claims to scarce status, power and resources in which the aims of the opponents are to neutralize, injure or eliminate their rivals." See L. A. Coser, *The Functions of Social Conflict* (New York: Free Press, 1956), 8.

3. R. Dahrendorf, *Class and Class Conflict in Industrial Society* (Stanford, CA: Stanford University Press, 1959); K. Marx, *The Poverty of Philosophy* (New York: International Publishers, 1963).

4. R. E. Park and E. W. Burgess, *Introduction to the Science of Sociology* (Chicago: University of Chicago Press, 1924), 574. Also, K. Boulding, *Conflict and Defense* (New York: Harper & Row, 1962).

5. The term *zero-sum* derives from game theory and refers to the payoff matrix in which each cell, in a two-by-two table, adds up to zero. Imagine a game of two persons matching pennies; each person may toss a head or a tail of the coin. One person wins both coins if the pennies match, and the other person wins both coins if they do not match. The loser gets nothing; the winner gets two cents. Further explanation can be found by referring to table 6.2 in chapter 6.

6. B. W. Dayton and L. Kriesberg, *Conflict Transformation and Peacebuilding: Moving from Violence to Sustainable Peace* (London: Routledge, 2009).

7. S. G. Jones and M. C. Libicki, *How Terrorist Groups End: Lessons for Countering al Qaida* (Santa Monica, CA: Rand Corporation, 2008).

8. For example, various web-based discussion groups have formed to engage diaspora communities and policy makers in dialogue about conflict management, reconciliation, and conflict transformation. See, for example, the work of Syracuse for Sri Lanka at http://www.syracuse4srilanka.org/. A diaspora is a transnational ethnic community that defines itself by its emigration from an original homeland.

9. L. Kriesberg, *The Sociology of Social Conflicts* (Englewood Cliffs, NJ: Prentice-Hall, 1973); O. J. Bartos and P. Wehr, *Using Conflict Theory* (Cambridge, UK: Cambridge University Press, 2002).

10. For a discussion see M. Rubin and M. Hewstone, "Social Identity, System Justification, and Social Dominance: Commentary on Reicher, Jost, Sidanius et al.," *Political Psychology* 25(6) (2004): 823–44. See also M. Brewer, "Inter-Group Identification and Inter-Group Conflict," in *Social Identity and Intergroup Conflict Reduction*, ed. L. J. R. Ashmore and D. Wilder (Oxford: Oxford University Press, 2001).

11. For example, see J. Galtung, *Global Projections of Deep-Rooted U.S. Pathologies* (Fairfax, VA: George Mason University, 1996).

12. G. Delanty, *Citizenship in a Global Age* (Buckingham, UK: Open University Press, 2000).

13. K. R. DeRouen, "Presidents and the Diversionary Use of Force," *International Studies Quarterly* 44(2) (2000): 317–28.

14. H. Raiffa, *The Art and Science of Negotiation* (Cambridge, MA: Harvard University Press, 1982).

15. B. Russett and J. R. Oneal, *Triangulating Peace: Democracy, Interdependence, and International Organization* (Princeton, NJ: Princeton University Press, 2001).

16. C. R. Mitchell, "Asymmetry and Strategies of Regional Conflict Reduction," in *Cooperative Security: Reducing Third World Wars*, ed. I. W. Zartman and V. A. Kremenyuk, pp. 25–57 (Syracuse, NY: Syracuse University Press, 1995); L. Kriesberg, "Changing Conflict Asymmetries Constructively," *Dynamics of Asymmetric Conflict* 2(1) (2009): 4–22.

17. A. Gramsci, *Selections from the Prison Notebooks* (New York: International Publishers, 1971).

18. In addition to the power over others and the power *with* others to accomplish collective tasks, the power *from* others (autonomy) is an important kind of power. Power *over* others presumes a zero-sum relationship. See C. W. Mills, *The Power Elite* (New York: Oxford University Press, 1956); H. M. Blalock Jr., *Power and Conflict: Toward a General Theory* (Newbury Park, CA: Sage, 1989). Power with others has been a meaning of power used by some structural functionalists: T. Parsons, *Politics and Social Structure* (New York: Free Press, 1969). A related meaning is found in feminist approaches to social theory. See L. M. Woerhle, Social Constructions of Power and Empowerment: Thoughts from Feminist Approaches to Peace Research and Peace-Making, in *Social Theory and Nonviolent Revolutions: Rethinking Domination and Rebellion*, ed. N. Bell and L. R. Kurtz (Austin: University of Texas Press, 1992).

19. K. E. Boulding, *Three Faces of Power* (Newbury Park, CA: Sage, 1989).

20. G. Sharp, *The Politics of Nonviolent Action* (Boston: Porter Sargent, 1973).

21. Kriesberg, "Changing Conflict Asymmetries Constructively."

22. See www.incore.ulst.ac.uk/cds/countries/srilanga.html.

23. See associated websites at www.incore.ulst.ac.uk/.

24. This was evident in the development of the student protests of the 1960s, as at the University of California, Berkeley. See M. Heirach, *The Spiral of Conflict: Berkeley 1964* (New York: Columbia University Press, 1968).

25. P. M. Blau, *Exchange and Power in Social Life* (New York: Wiley, 1964).

26. Crime rates are lower when the certainty of punishment is higher, see C. R. Tittle, "Crime Rates and Legal Sanctions," *Social Problems* 16 (1969): 409–23.

27. R. N. Lebow and J. G. Stein, *We All Lost the Cold War* (Princeton, NJ: Princeton University Press, 1994).

28. Human Security Report Project (2008), *Human Security Brief 2007*. Vancouver, Canada: Simon Fraser University.

29. S. A. Stouffer, A. A. Lumsdaine, et al., *The American Soldier: Combat and Its Aftermath* (Princeton, NJ: Princeton University Press, 1949), 166.

30. L. Harbom, Stina Högbladh, and Peter Wallensteen, "Armed Conflict and Peace Agreements," *Journal of Peace Research* 43(5) (2006): 617–13.

31. M. Deutsch, *The Resolution of Conflict: Constructive and Destructive Processes* (New Haven, CT: Yale University Press, 1973).

32. Accounts of the horrors of genocide can only partially convey how destructive conflicts can become. Even with genocide, however, there are social and personal variations that warrant attention. See H. Fein, *Accounting for Genocide: National Responses and Jewish Victimization during the Holocaust* (New York: The Free Press, 1979).

CHAPTER 2

1. President George W. Bush, Address to a Joint Session of Congress, September 20, 2001.

2. H. Putnam, *Reason, Truth, and History* (New York: Cambridge University Press, 1981), xi. This discussion draws from H. Putnam, *The Many Faces of Realism* (LaSalle, IL: Open Court, 1987).

3. H. H. Kelley, "The Process of Causal Attribution," *American Psychologist* 28 (1973): 107–28; also, C. Mitchell, *Gestures of Conciliation: Factors Contributing to Successful Olive Branches* (New York: St. Martin's Press, 2000).

4. For example, see R. Ardrey, *The Territorial Imperative* (New York: Dell, 1966).

5. John A. Vasquez reviews this literature and also the research reporting the high frequency of territorial issues in international wars. He concludes that humans are not "hard-wired" with an instinct for territoriality, but, quoting Albert Somit, may be "'soft-wired' to favor certain behaviors and cultural options." See his *The War Puzzle* (Cambridge: Cambridge University Press, 1993), 139–52; and Albert Somit, "Humans, Chimps, and Bonobos: The Biological Bases of Aggression, War, and Peacemaking," *Journal of Conflict Resolution* 34 (September 1990): 553–82.

6. A. Mazur, "A Cross-Species Comparison of Status in Small Established Groups," *American Sociological Review* 38 (October 1973): 513–30.

7. For a discussion of in-group favoritism and out-group bias, see M. Rubin and M. Hewstone, "Social Identity, System Justification, and Social Dominance: Commentary on Reicher, Jost, Sidanius et al.," *Political Psychology* 25(6) (2004): 823–44.

8. M. Rothbart and S. Lewis, "Cognitive Processes and Intergroup Relations: A Historical Perspective," in *Social Cognition: Impact on Social Psychology*, ed. P. G. Devine, D. L. Hamilton, and T. M. Ostrom (San Diego: Academic Press, 1994). The work that generated much subsequent research is T. W. Adorno, E. Frenkel-Brunswik, et al., *The Authoritarian Personality* (New York: Harper Brothers, 1950).

9. B. Bettleheim and M. Janowitz, *Dynamics of Prejudice* (New York: Harper, 1950).

10. J. Burton, *Conflict: Resolution and Provention* (New York: St. Martin's, 1990).

11. A sociological statement on war and peace, endorsed by the Section on Peace and War of the American Sociological Association in 1992, stresses that social conditions account for the great variations in degrees and varieties of violence. It appears in R. Elia and J. Turpin, eds., *Re-Thinking Peace* (Boulder, CO: Lynne Rienner, 1994), 66.

12. An early formulation of the idea is to be found in J. Dollard, L. W. Doob, et al., *Frustration and Aggression* (New Haven, CT: Yale University Press, 1939). A review of research is in L. Berkowitz, ed., *Roots of Aggression* (New York: Lieber-Atherton, 1969).

13. For reviews of related literature, see P. G. Devine, D. L. Hamilton, et al., eds., *Social Cognition: Impact on Social Psychology* (San Diego: Academic Press, 1994).

14. For an application of this principle to the Israeli-Palestinian conflict, see A. Bizman and M. Hoffman, "Expectations, Emotions, and Preferred Responses Regarding the Arab-Israeli Conflict," *Journal of Conflict Resolution* 37(1) (1993): 139–59.

15. M. H. Ross, *The Culture of Conflict* (New Haven, CT: Yale University Press, 1993). Also see V. Volkan, *The Need to Have Enemies and Allies: From Clinical Practice to International Relationships* (New York: Jason Aronson, 1988).

16. See Ross, *The Culture of Conflict*. See also B. B. Whiting and J. W. M. Whiting, *Children of Six Cultures: A Psycho-Cultural Analysis* (Cambridge, MA: Harvard University Press, 1975).

17. Research and theorizing are less developed on these matters than on the processes making for antagonistic feelings and conduct. Feminist writers note this neglect and direct attention to social relationships and caring for others. For example, see C. Gilligan, *In a Different Voice: Psychological Theory and Women's Development* (Cambridge, MA: Harvard University Press, 1982) and J. Tronto, "Beyond Gender Difference to a Theory of Care," *Signs: Journal of Women in Culture and Society* 12(4) (1987): 644–63; see also A. P. Goldstein and G. Y. Michaels, *Empathy: Development, Training, and Consequences* (Hillsdale, NJ: Lawrence Erlbaum Associates, 1985).

18. Ross, *The Culture of Conflict*, 61–62; and A. Montagu, ed., *Learning Non-Aggression* (New York: Oxford University Press, 1978).

19. This effect is emphasized by analysts of mass societies, where many people are isolated and alienated. W. Kornhauser, *The Politics of Mass Society* (New York: Free Press, 1959).

20. A. Inkeles and D. Levinson, "National Character: The Study of Modal Personality and Sociocultural Systems," in *Handbook of Social Psychology*, vol. 2, ed. G. Lindzey (Reading, MA: Addison-Wesley, 1954).

21. Theodore Schwartz writes, "Culture consists of the derivatives of experience, more or less organized, learned or created by the individuals of a population, including those images or encodements and their interpretations (meanings) transmitted from past generations, from contemporaries, or formed by individuals themselves." See T. Schwartz, "Anthropology and Psychology: An Unrequited Relationship," *New Directions in Psychological Anthropology*, ed. T. Schwartz, G. White, and G. Lutz (Cambridge: Cambridge University Press, 1992), 324.

22. B. A. Reardon, *Sexism and the War System* (Syracuse, NY: Syracuse University Press, 1996).

23. President Eisenhower said, "In our councils of government we must guard against the acquisition of unwarranted influence, whether sought or unsought, by the military-industrial complex. The potential for the disastrous rise of misplaced power exists and will persist." Cited in C. W. Kegley and E. R. Wittkopf, *American Foreign Policy Pattern and Process* (New York: St. Martin's Press, 1982), 255. Also see C. W. Mills, *The Power Elite* (New York: Oxford University Press, 1956); S. J. Rosen, ed., *Testing the Theory of the Military-Industrial Complex* (Lexington, MA: Heath, 1973); and D. R. Herspring and I. Volgyes, eds., *Civil-Military Relations in Communist Systems* (Boulder, CO: Westview, 1978).

24. A. J. Bacevich, *The New American Militarism: How Americans Are Seduced by War* (New York: Oxford University Press, 2005); R. J. Wheeler Leng and H. Wheeler, "Influence Strategies, Success and War," *Journal of Conflict Resolution* 23 (December 1979): 655–84.

25. M. Glenny, *The Fall of Yugoslavia* (New York: Penguin, 1992); J. Pickering and E. F. Kisangani, "Democracy and Diversionary Military Intervention: Reassessing Regime Type and the Diversionary Hypothesis," *International Studies Quarterly* 49 (2005): 23–43.

26. L. A. Coser, *The Functions of Social Conflict* (New York: Free Press, 1956).

27. K. Avruch, *Culture and Conflict Resolution* (Washington, DC: United States Institute of Peace, 1998). Cultural similarities help account for the finding that democratic countries do not wage wars against each other.

28. A. Rapoport, *Fights, Games, and Debates* (Ann Arbor: University of Michigan Press, 1960).

29. L. Diamond, *Squandered Victory* (New York: Henry Holt, 2005).

30. Beginning in 1938, the Swedish social scientist Gunnar Myrdal led a large number of social scientists to examine the conditions of blacks and the attitudes of whites in the United States. See G. Myrdal, R. Sterner, et al., *An American Dilemma: The Negro Problem and American Democracy* (New York: Harper & Brothers, 1944).

31. J. S. Coleman, *Community Conflict* (New York: Free Press, 1957). For theories about strain generating social movements, see N. Smelser, *The Theory of Collective Behavior* (New York: Free Press, 1963).

32. C. Johnson, *Revolutionary Change* (Boston: Little, Brown, 1966), 60.

33. Many characteristics can be selected to serve as a basis for coordination, as a way for people to group themselves for their mutual benefit. See R. Hardin, "Self Interest, Group Identity," in *Perspectives on Nationalism and War*, ed. J. L. Comaroff and P. C. Stern (Amsterdam, The Netherlands: Gordon and Breach, 1995).

34. See R. Dahrendorf, *Class and Class Conflict in Industrial Society* (Stanford, CA: Stanford University Press, 1959).

35. K. Marx and F. Engels, *The Communist Manifesto* (Chicago: H. Regnery, 1954); M. Weber, *The Theory of Social and Economic Organization*, trans. A. M. Henderson and Talcott Parsons (New York: Oxford University Press, 1947); and Dahrendorf, *Class and Class Conflict*.

36. The distinction between consensual and dissensual conflicts is based on the work of V. Aubert, "Competition and Dissensus: Two Types of Conflict and Conflict Resolution," *Journal of Conflict Resolution* 7 (March 1963): 26–42.

37. P. L. Berger and T. Luckman, *The Social Construction of Reality* (New York: Doubleday, 1966); E. Goffman, *Frame Analysis* (New York: Harper Colophon, 1974); and M. J. Shapiro and H. R. Alker, eds., *Challenging Boundaries* (Minneapolis: University of Minnesota Press, 1996).

38. K. Manheim, *Essays on the Sociology of Knowledge* (London: Routledge and Kegan Paul, 1952); and L. Kriesberg, H. Murray, et al., "Elites and Increased Support for U.S. Military Spending," *Journal of Political and Military Sociology* 10 (Fall 1982): 275–97.

39. A. J. Bacevich, *American Empire: The Realities and Consequences of U.S. Diplomacy* (Cambridge, MA: Harvard University Press, 2002).

40. S. P. Huntington, "The Clash of Civilizations?" *Foreign Affairs* 72 (Summer 1993): 22–49; and B. Russett, J. R. Oneal, and M. Cox, "Clash of Civilizations, or Realism and Liberalism Deja Vu? Some Evidence," *Journal of Peace Research* 37(5) (September 2000): 583–608.

41. B. W. Dayton, "In Between Science and Decision: Policy Frames and the Global Climate Discourse" (PhD dissertation, Syracuse University, 1999); S. Hunter, "The Roots of Environmental Conflict in the Tahoe Basin," in *Intractable Conflicts and Their Transformation*, ed. Louis Kriesberg and Stuart J. Thorson (Syracuse, NY: Syracuse University Press, 1989); and B. Moyers, "Welcome to Doomsday," *New York Review of Books*, March 24, 2005, 8–10.

42. C. Gilligan, *In a Different Voice: Psychological Theory and Women's Development* (Cambridge, MA: Harvard University Press, 1982); and A. Nye, *Feminist Theory and the Philosophies of Man* (New York: Croom Helm, 1988).

43. A comprehensive assessment of the literature on ethnocentrism is available in R. A. Levine and D. T. Campbell, *Ethnocentrism: Theories of Conflict, Ethnic Attitudes, and Group Behavior* (New York: Wiley, 1972).

44. M. Hewston and K. Greenland, "Intergroup Conflict," *International Journal of Psychology* 35 (2000): 136–44.

45. L. Kriesberg, *The Sociology of Social Conflicts* (Englewood Cliffs, NJ: Prentice-Hall, 1973); J. Bar-Siman-Tov, "Interlocking Conflicts in the Middle East," *Conflict and Conflict Resolution in Middle-Eastern Societies: Between Tradition and Modernity*, ed. H.-J. Albrecht et al. (Berlin: Duncker & Humboldt, 2006).

46. R. L. Garthoff, *Reflections on the Cuban Missile Crisis* (Washington, DC: The Brookings Institution, 1989); and R. N. Lebow and J. G. Stein, *We All Lost the Cold War* (Princeton, NJ: Princeton University Press, 1994), 19–145.

47. M. Eastman, ed., *Capital, The Communist Manifesto and Other Writings by Karl Marx* (New York: The Modern Library, 1932), 321.

48. Thus, when ethnic groups in a society are hierarchically ranked, conflicts are likely to be more intense than in societies in which the ethnic groups are not ranked. D. L. Horowitz, *Ethnic Groups in Conflict* (Berkeley: University of California Press, 1985), 21–36.

49. L. Kriesberg, *International Conflict Resolution: The U.S.-USSR and Middle East Cases* (New Haven, CT: Yale University Press, 1992).

50. M. L. DeVault, "Conflict over Housework: A Problem That (Still) Has No Name," *Research in Social Movements, Conflict and Change,* ed. L. Kriesberg (Greenwich, CT: JAI Press), 12 (1990):199.

51. A. Gramsci, *Letters from Prison* (New York: Harper & Row, 1973); and M. Carnoy, *Education as Cultural Imperialism* (New York: David McKay, 1974).

CHAPTER 3

1. D. Little, *Sri Lanka: The Invention of Enmity* (Washington, DC: United States Institute of Peace Press, 1994); M. Hermann and B. W. Dayton, "Transboundary Crises through the Eyes of Policymakers: Sense Making and Crisis Management," *Journal of Contingencies and Crisis Management* 17(4) (2009): 232–41.

2. Initially, these components may become manifest within one party in the conflict, but once that party begins to take actions to achieve its goals, the target of the actions generally counters them and the conflict emerges for it as well.

3. R. D. Ashmore, L. J. Jussim, et al. *Social Identity, Intergroup Conflict, and Conflict Reduction* (Oxford: Oxford University Press, 2001); P. G. Coy and L. M. Woehrle, eds., *Social Conflicts and Collective Identities* (Lanham, MD: Rowman & Littlefield, 2000); T. A. Northrup, "The Dynamic of Identity in Personal and Social Conflict," in *Intractable Conflicts and Their Transformation*, ed. L. Kriesberg, T. A. Northrup, and S. J. Thorson (Syracuse, NY: Syracuse University Press, 1989); and G. H. Herb and D. H. Kaplan, eds., *Nested Identities: Nationalism, Territory, and Scale* (Lanham, MD: Rowman & Littlefield, 1999).

4. In 1948, the Communist Party of the Soviet Union accused Josip Broz Tito, the leader of the Yugoslav Communist Party and government, of deviating from Communism. Tito defied the Soviets, and relations between them were ruptured. Yugoslavia developed its own form of market socialism, with factories comanaged by the workers and managers.

5. Thus, the percentage of the adult population of Yugoslavia identifying themselves as Yugoslavs increased from 1.7 percent in 1961 to 5.4 percent in 1981. The percentage varied, in 1981, from 8.2 percent in Croatia and in Vojvodina, to 7.9 percent in Bosnia-Her-

zegovina, to 1.4 percent in Slovenia, to 0.7 percent in Macedonia, and to only 0.1 percent in Kosovo. See D. Sekulic, G. Massey, et al., "Who Were the Yugoslavs? Failed Sources of a Common Identity in the Former Yugoslavia," *American Sociological Review* 59 (February 1994): 85. How identities were changed and extreme acts of brutality were perpetrated are examined in F. Wilmer, *The Social Construction of Man, the State, and War: Identity, Conflict, and Violence in the Former Yugoslavia* (New York: Routledge, 2002).

6. R. Hardin, "Self Interest, Group Identity," in *Perspectives on Nationalism and War*, ed. J. L. Comaroff and P. C. Stern (Amsterdam, The Netherlands: Gordon and Breach, 1995).

7. R. H. Thompson, *Theories of Ethnicity: A Critical Appraisal* (New York: Greenwood Press, 1989). For constructionist approaches, see B. Anderson, *Imagined Communities: Reflections on the Origin and Spread of Nationalism* (London: Verso, 1991); and P. R. Brass, *Ethnicity and Nationalism: Theory and Comparison* (Newbury Park, CA: Sage, 1991). A hybrid approach that views ethnic consciousness as a potentiality that is realized only under certain conditions is articulated by J. L. Comaroff, "Humanity, Ethnicity, Nationality: Conceptual and Comparative Perspectives on the U.S.S.R.," *Theory and Society* 20 (1991): 661–87; and D. Conversi, ed., *Ethnonationalism in the Contemporary World* (London: Routledge, 2002).

8. For a discussion of the distinction between these three forms of identity formation, see N. G. Jessee and K. P. Williams, *Ethnic Conflict: A Systematic Approach to Cases of Conflict* (Washington, DC: CQ Press, 2011).

9. T. Parsons, *The Social System* (Glencoe, IL: Free Press, 1951), 63–65.

10. P. L. van den Berghe, *Race and Racism: A Comparative Perspective* (New York: Wiley, 1978); Ashmore, Jussim, et al., *Social Identity*.

11. D. M. Smith and E. Wistrich, ed., *Regional Identity and Diversity in Europe: Experience in Wales, Silesia and Flanders* (New York: Palgrave Macmillan, 2008); J. T. Checkel and P. J. Katzenstein, eds., *European Identity* (Cambridge: Cambridge University Press, 2009); J. Aaker and A. Smith, *The Dragonfly Effect: Quick, Effective and Powerful Ways to Use Social Media to Drive Social Change* (San Francisco: Jossey Bass, 2010).

12. C. Offe, "New Social Movements: Challenging the Boundaries of Institutional Politics," *Social Research* 52(4) (1985): 817–68. On the culture wars in the United States, see A. J. Bacevich, *The Limits of Power: The End of American Exceptionalism* (New York: Metropolitan Books, 2008).

13. S. Perlman, *A Theory of the Labor Movement* (New York: Augustus M. Kelley, 1928); and D. C. Bok and J. T. Dunlop, *Labor and the American Community* (New York: Simon & Schuster, 1970), 30.

14 W. H. Form, "Conflict within the Working Class: The Skilled as a Special-Interest Group," in *The Uses of Controversy in Sociology*, ed. O. N. Larsen (New York: Free Press, 1976).

15. For example, faculty heterogeneity was correlated with disputes among high school teachers and administrators. See R. G. Corwin, "Patterns of Organizational Conflict," *Administrative Science Quarterly* 14 (December 1969): 507–20.

16. For evidence that the husband's class location is a major determinant of the wife's subjective class identity, see J. Baxter, "Is Husband's Class Enough? Class Location and Class Identity in the United States, Sweden, and Australia," *American Sociological Review* 59 (April 1994): 220–35.

17. T. Skocpol, *States and Social Revolutions: A Comparative Analysis of France, Russia, and China* (Cambridge: Cambridge University Press, 1979), 92.

18. E. Flexner, *Century of Struggle* (Cambridge, MA: Harvard University Press, 1959), 23–40.

19. Dual citizenship is increasingly common. See T. A. Aleinikoff and D. Klusmeyer, ed., *Citizenship Today: Global Perspectives and Practices* (Washington, DC: The Carnegie Endowment for International Peace, 2001); also see G. Delanty, *Citizenship in a Global Age* (Buckingham, UK: Open University Press, 2000).

20. J. D. Clark, ed., *Globalizing Civic Engagement: Civil Society and Transnational Action* (London: EarthScan, 2003).

21. B. Stanislawski, ed., "Para-States, Quasi-States, and Black Spots: Perhaps Not States, but Not 'Ungoverned Territories,' Either," *International Studies Review* 10 (2008): 366–96.

22. J. Seidman, J. London, et al., *The Worker Views His Union* (Chicago: University of Chicago Press, 1958).

23. C. Tilly, *From Mobilization to Revolution* (Reading, MA: Addison-Wesley, 1978); S. G. Tarrow, *Power in Movement: Social Movements and Contentious Politics* (Cambridge: Cambridge University Press, 1998); and D. McAdam, J. D. McCarthy, et al., ed., *Comparative Perspectives on Social Movements* (New York: Cambridge University Press, 1996).

24. A. D. Morris, *The Origins of the Civil Rights Movement* (New York: Free Press, 1984).

25. J. Smith and H. Johnston, ed., *Globalization and Resistance: Transnational Dimensions of Social Movements* (Lanham, MD: Rowman & Littlefield, 2002). For websites with reports of Seattle and other locations of protests relating to globalization, see www.globalexchange.org/ and www.infoshop.org/no2wto.html.

26. See M. Sageman, *Understanding Terror Networks* (Philadelphia: University of Pennsylvania Press, 2004).

27. The term *jihadist* is generally understood among Muslims to refer to the inner struggle to be faithful to Allah. Many non-Muslims use the phrase *waging jihad* to mean a war against nonbelievers. We qualify *jihadist* here with the term *militant* to indicate we are referring to groups of Muslims resorting to violence to advance Salafism, a particular brand of Islam that they regard as traditional and correct.

28. For example, in the 1950s and 1960s, with colonial rule losing its legitimacy and European empires dissolving, the incidence of ethnonationalist conflicts rose. T. R. Gurr, *Minorities at Risk* (Washington, DC: United States Institute of Peace, 1994); and J. Fox, "The Rise of Religious Nationalism and Conflict: Ethnic Conflict and Revolutionary Wars, 1945–2001," *Journal of Peace Research* 41 (2004): 715–31. For a discussion of Arabs, see L. Wedeen, "Beyond the Crusades," *Items & Issues* 4(2–3) (Spring/Summer 2003): 1–5.

29. F. Barth, ed., *Ethnic Groups and Boundaries* (Boston: Little, Brown and Company, 1969).

30. R. A. Levine and D. T. Campbell, *Ethnocentrism: Theories of Conflict, Ethnic Attitudes, and Group Behavior* (New York: Wiley, 1972); and W. A. Elliott *Us and Them: A Study of Group Consciousness* (Aberdeen: Aberdeen University Press, 1986).

31. M. Brewer, "Inter-group Identification and Inter-group Conflict," in *Social Identity and Intergroup Conflict Reduction*, ed. L. J. R Ashmore and D. Wilder (Oxford: Oxford University Press, 2001).

32. D. Druckman, "Social Psychological Aspects of Nationalism," in *Perspectives on Nationalism and War*, ed. J. L. Comaroff and P. C. Stern (Amseterdam, The Netherlands: Gordon and Breach, 1995), 56–59.

33. See J. T. Borhek, "Ethnic-Group Cohesion," *American Journal of Sociology* 76 (July 1970): 33–46.

34. M. B. John Jost and Brian Nosek, "A Decade of System Justification Theory: Accumulated Evidence of Conscious and Unconscious Bolstering of the Status Quo," *Political Psychology* 25(6) (2004): 881–919.

35. C. A. Johnson, *Peasant Nationalism and Communist Power* (Stanford, CA: Stanford University Press, 1962).

36. *Race* popularly refers to genetically determined differences among major groupings of humans. Biologically, however, the only meaning to *race* is to broad, overlapping genetic pools, lacking clear boundaries. On the basis of selecting some traits, people in many societies construct "social races." These are often bounded by social rules, allowing for the classification of individuals. See J. Nagle, "Constructing Ethnicity: Creating and Recreating Ethnic Identity and Culture," *Social Problems* 41(1) (February 1994): 152–76.

37. B. Barber, "Jihad vs. McWorld," *Atlantic Monthly*, March 1992, 53–63.

38. B. Klandermans, "The Social Construction of Protests and Multiorganizational Fields," in *Frontiers in Social Movement Theory*, ed. A. Morris and C. Mueller (New Haven, CT: Yale University Press, 1992).

39. T. R. Gurr, *Why Men Rebel* (Princeton, NJ: Princeton University Press, 1970).

40. C. Brinton, *The Anatomy of Revolution* (New York: Vintage, 1955); and J. C. Davies, "Toward a Theory of Revolution," *American Sociological Review* 27 (February 1962): 5–19.

41. D. Snyder, "Collective Violence Processes: Implications for Disaggregated Theory and Research," *Research in Social Movements, Conflicts and Change*, vol. 2, ed. L. Kriesberg (Greenwich, CT: JAI Press, 1979).

42. D. Lerner and L. W. Pevsner, *The Passing of Traditional Society: Modernizing the Middle East* (Glencoe, Il: Free Press, 1958).

43. R. Wright, "Will Globalization Make You Happy?" *Foreign Policy*, September/October 2000, 54–64.

44. J. S. Ellsworth, *Factory Folkways* (New Haven, CT: Yale University Press, 1952).

45. M. Weber, *The Theory of Social and Economic Organization* (New York: Oxford University Press, 1947).

46. G. E. Lenski, *Power and Privilege* (New York: McGraw-Hill, 1966).

47. Self-assessed happiness or well-being is based on the balance of positive and negative feelings. A person may have a lot of both, a lot of one and a little of the other, or little of both. N. M. Bradburn, *The Structure of Psychological Well Being* (Chicago: Aldine, 1969).

48. A. Inkeles, "Industrial Man: The Relation of Status to Experience, Perception, and Value," *American Journal of Sociology* 66 (July 1960): 1–31.

49. R. Blauner, *Alienation and Freedom: The Factory Worker and His Industry* (Chicago: University of Chicago Press, 1964).

50. Bradburn, *The Structure of Psychological Well Being*; and N. M. Bradburn and D. Caplovitz, *Reports on Happiness* (Chicago: Aldine, 1965).

51. W. Buchanan and H. Cantril, *How Nations See Each Other* (Urbana: University of Illinois Press, 1953).

52. B. P. Karon, *The Negro Personality* (New York: Springer, 1958); and S. Parker and R. J. Kleiner, "The Culture of Poverty," *American Anthropologist* 72 (June 1970): 516–27.

53. An analysis of interstate wars between 1820 and 1964 finds that national capability correlated 0.64 with war initiation. J. D. Singer, Stuart A. Bremer, and John Stuckey, "Capability Distribution, Uncertainty, and Major Power War, 1820–1965," in *The Correlates of War I: Research Origins and Rationale*, ed. J. D. Singer (New York: Free Press, 1979).

54. The Project for the New American Century, "Rebuilding America's Defenses," September 2000, available at http://cryptome.org/rad.htm; I. H. Daalder and J. M. Lindsay, *America Unbound: The Bush Revolution in Foreign Policy* (Washington, DC: Brookings Institution Press, 2003); and J. Mann, *Rise of the Vulcans* (New York: Viking, 2004).

55. R. K. Merton and A. S. Kitt, "Contributions to the Theory of Reference Group Behavior," in *Studies in the Scope and Method of "The American Soldier,"* ed. R. K. Merton and P. F. Lazarsfeld (New York: Free Press, 1950), 70–105; W. G. Runciman, *Relative Deprivation and Social Justice* (Berkeley: University of California Press, 1966); M. H. Kuhn, "The Reference Group Reconsidered," in *Symbolic Interaction: A Reader in Social Psychology*, ed. J. Manis and B. Meltzer (Boston: Allyn and Bacon, 1967).

56. E. C. Hughes, "Dilemmas and Contradictions of Status," *American Journal of Sociology* 50 (March 1944): 353–59; and G. E. Lenski, "Status Crystalization: A Non-Vertical Dimension of Social Status," *American Sociological Review* 19 (August 1954): 405–13. Also see J. Galtung, "A Structural Theory of Aggression," *Journal of Peace Research* 2 (1964): 95–119; and R. Moss Kanter, *Men and Women of the Corporation* (New York: Basic Books, 1977).

57. A. Falk and M. Snell, "Choosing the Joneses: On the Engogeneity of Reference Groups" (working paper, University of Zurich, 2000).

58. S. M. Lipset and E. Raab, *The Politics of Unreason: Right Wing Extremism in America 1790–1970* (New York: Harper & Row, 1970); J. A. Geschwender, "Continuities in Theories of Status Consistency and Cognitive Dissonance," *Social Forces* 46 (December 1967): 160–71; and E. Jackson, "Status Consistency and Symptoms of Stress," *American Sociological Review* 27 (August 1962): 469–80. Workers with inconsistent ranks who are underrewarded tend to exhibit symptoms of individual unrest. See J. A. Geschwender, "Status Inconsistency, Social Isolation, and Individual Unrest," *Social Forces* 46 (June 1968): 477–83; D. H. Bennett, *The Party of Fear: From Nativist Movements to the New Right in American History* (New York: Vintage, 1995).

59. In addition, the identification problem arises from the difficulty in distinguishing an additive effect from an interactive effect of two or more variables. See H. M. Blalock Jr., "Status Inconsistency and Interaction: Some Alternative Models," *American Journal of Sociology* 73 (November 1967): 305–15.

60. Surveys conducted in fourteen countries reveal a high rank correlation between the socioeconomic level of the country and the average level of current satisfaction. See H. Cantril, *The Pattern of Human Concerns* (New Brunswick, NJ: Rutgers University Press, 1965); and P. J. Stone, "Expectations of a Better Personal Future," *Public Opinion Quarterly* 34 (Fall 1970): 346–59.

61. W. S. Landecker, "Status Congruence, Class Crystallization and Class Consciousness," *Sociology and Social Research* 54 (April 1970): 343–55.

62. See W. G. Runciman, *Relative Deprivation and Social Justice* (Berkeley: University of California Press, 1966); and for the latter point see S. M. Lipset, *Agrarian Socialism* (Berkeley: University of California Press, 1950).

63. T. Shibutani and K. M. Kwan, *Ethnic Statification* (New York: Macmillan, 1965).

64. P. H. Rossi and R. A. Berk, "Local Political Leadership and Popular Discontent," *Annals*, September 1970, 111–27.

65. Sri Lanka is an island in the Indian Ocean, southeast of India. The population consists of the predominantly Buddhist Sinhalese (75 percent), the predominantly Hindu Tamils (18 percent), and Muslims who are largely Tamil speaking (7 percent). Some Christians are in the Sinhalese and Tamil communities. D. Little, *Sri Lanka: The Invention of Enmity* (Washington, DC: United States Institute of Peace Press, 1994).

66. L. A. Coser, *The Functions of Social Conflict* (New York: Free Press, 1956).

67. M. Covell, "Belgium: The Variability of Ethnic Relations," in *The Politics of Ethnic Conflict Regulation*, ed. J. McGarry and B. O'Leary (London: Routledge, 1993).

68. For Rwanda, see www.incore.ulst.ac.uk/cds/countries/rwanda.html; and for Sri Lanka, see www.incore.ulst.ac.uk/cds/countries/srilanka.html.

69. E. Lindner, *Making Enemies: Humiliation and International Conflict* (Westport, CT: Praeger Security International, 2006).

70. V. Fontan, *Voices from Post-Saddam Iraq: Living with Terrorism, Insurgency and New Forms of Tyranny* (Westport, CT: Praeger, 2008).

71. D. Powers and C. G. Ellison, "Interracial Contact and Black Racial Attitudes: The Contact Hypothesis and Selectivity Bias," *Social Forces* 74 (1995): 205–26.

72. D. Ronfeldt, John Arquilla, Graham E. Fuller, and Melissa Fuller, *The Zapatista Social Netwar in Mexico* (Santa Monica, CA: RAND Arroyo Center, 1998). For Internet material, see the links provided by the United States Institute of Peace Library, http://www.usip.org/publications/chiapas-web-links. J. Mueller, "American Public Opinion and the Gulf War," in *The Political Psychology of the Gulf War*, ed. S. A. Renshon (Pittsburgh: University of Pittsburgh Press, 1993).

73. I. P. Bell, *CORE and the Strategy of Non-Violence* (New York: Random House, 1968); Kerner Commission, *Report of the National Commission on Civil Disorders* (New York: Bantam, 1968).

74. E. Azar and N. Farah, "The Structure of Inequalities and Protracted Social Conflict: A Theoretical Framework," *International Interactions* 4 (1981): 317–35.

75. The earlier findings are in M. A. East, "Status Discrepancy and Violence in the International System: An Empirical Analysis," in *The Analysis of International Politics*, ed. J. N. Rosenau, V. Davis, and M. A. East (New York: Free Press, 1971). The later findings are in T. J. Volgy and S. Mayhall, "Status Inconsistency and International War: Exploring the Effects of Systemic Change," *International Studies Quarterly* 39 (March 1995): 67–84.

76. The terms *left* and *right* are used with different meanings in different historical contexts. For example, in the initial post-Soviet period in Russia, *left* sometimes meant those favoring radical change and increased freedom and sometimes those favoring maintaining a great deal of socioeconomic equality and much of the old state apparatus. In the United States, at the end of the twentieth and beginning of the twenty-first century, left and right differences also pertained to issues of morality, with the right often advocating the use of state power to ensure adherence to what were claimed to be traditional values.

77. Tilly, *From Mobilization to Revolution*.

78. Demanding the abolition of private ownership of large agricultural estates is proclaiming a unitary goal, while a demand for a 10 percent increase in wages is a divisible goal. See J. M. Paige, *Agrarian Revolution: Social Movements and Export Agriculture in the Underdeveloped World* (New York: Free Press, 1975).

79. E. J. Hobsbawm, *Primitive Rebels* (New York: W. W. Norton, 1965).

80. B. B. Hughes, *The Democratic Context of American Foreign Policy* (San Francisco: W. W. Freeman, 1978), 38; see also J. E. Mueller, *War, Presidents and Public Opinion* (New York: Wiley, 1973); and Mueller, "American Public Opinion and the Gulf War."

81. M. J. Hetherington and M. Nelson, "Anatomy of a Rally Effect: George W. Bush and the War on Terrorism," *PS: Political Science and Politics* 36 (2003): 37–42; and B. Woodward, *Plan of Attack* (New York: Simon & Schuster, 2004).

82. Hetherington and Nelson, "Anatomy of a Rally Effect."

83. T. Branch, *Parting the Waters: America in the King Years, 1954–63* (New York: Simon & Schuster, 1988).

84. G. T. Marx, *Protest and Prejudice* (New York: Harper & Row, 1968).

85. R. G. Braungart, "The Utopian and Ideological Styles of Student Political Activists" (paper presented at the annual meeting of the International Society of Political Psychology, Washington, DC, May 24, 1979).

86. D. R. Schmitt, "An Attitudinal Correlate of the Status Incongruency of Married Women," *Social Forces* 44 (December 1965): 190–261; and L. Broom and F. L. Jones, "Status Consistency and Political Preference: The Australian Case," *American Sociological Review* 35 (December 1970): 989–1001.

87. For information about the activities of the American Jewish Committee, see www.ajc.org, and of the American-Arab Anti-Discrimination Committee, see www.adc.org.

88. For analyses of the decline in take-home earnings from wages and the growing income inequality in the United States, see D. Braun, *The Rich Get Richer* (Chicago: Nelson-Hall, 1991); P. Blumberg, *Inequality in an Age of Decline* (New York: Oxford University Press, 1980); and T. Smeeding, "America's Income Inequality: Where Do We Stand?" *Challenge*, September–October 1996, 45–53.

89. Gurr, *Why Men Rebel.*

90. See K. Millet, *Sexual Politics* (New York: Doubleday, 1970), 125–27; and R. Collins, *Conflict Sociology* (New York: Academic Press, 1975), 225–85.

91. Many other economic and cultural factors contributed to the Iranian revolution and to the appeal of anti-Westernism. See F. Moshiri, "Iran: Islamic Revolution Against Westernization," in *Revolutions of the Late Twentieth Century*, ed. J. A. Goldstone, T. R. Gurr, and F. Moshiri (Boulder, CO: Westview, 1991), 116–35; and M. Parsa, *Social Origins of the Iranian Revolution* (New Brunswick, NJ: Rutgers University Press, 1989).

92. Daalder and Lindsay, *America Unbound.*

93. R. S. Wistrich, *Antisemitism: The Longest Hatred* (New York: Pantheon, 1991); M. Barkun, *Religion and the Racist Right: The Origins of the Christian Identity Movement* (Chapel Hill: University of North Carolina Press, 1994).

94. Gurr, *Why Men Rebel*, 125–26.

95. R. N. Rosecrance, *Action and Reaction in World Politics* (Boston: Little, Brown, 1963).

96. Such considerations affect changes in goals as well. For example, the relatively radical Palestinian organization the Popular Democratic Front for the Liberation of Palestine published a circular in 1969 arguing that its goal of "throwing the Jews into the sea" had done "grave damage" to the Arab position and argued for creating a "democratic Palestinian state" in which Arabs and Jews would live in peace. Y. Harkabi, "Liberation or Genocide?" *Transaction* 7 (July/August 1970): 63.

97. M. N. Dobkowski and I. Wallimann, eds., *On the Edge of Scarcity: Environment, Resources, Population, Sustainability, and Conflict* (Syracuse, NY: Syracuse University Press, 2001).

98. J. H. Mittleman, *The Globalization Syndrome: Transformation and Resistance* (Princeton, NJ: Princeton University Press, 2000).

99. J. M. Ayres, *Defying Conventional Wisdom: Political Movements and Popular Contention Against North American Free Trade* (Toronto: University of Toronto Press, 1998); and A. Starr, *Naming the Enemy: Anti-Corporate Movements Confront Globalization* (New York: Zed Books, 2000).

100. R. Pagnucco, "The Transnational Strategies of the Service for Peace and Justice in Latin America," in *Transnational Social Movements and Global Politics: Solidarity Beyond the State*, ed. J. Smith, C. Chatfield, and R. Pagnucco (Syracuse, NY: Syracuse University Press, 1997).

101. For accounts of Jewish-Palestinian relations, see B. Kimmerling and J. S. Migdal, *Palestinians: The Making of a People* (New York: Free Press, 1993). Similarly, in Sri Lanka, Tamil nationalism grew in response to Buddhist revivalism. See Little, *Sri Lanka*.

102. Paige, *Agrarian Revolution*, 361.

103. In the language of economists, this is called vicarious utility. See S. Valavanis, "The Resolution of Conflict When Utilities Interact," *Journal of Conflict Resolution* 2 (June 1958): 156–69.

104. T. Lodge, "Revolution Deferred: From Armed Struggle to Liberal Democracy," *Conflict Transformation and Peacebuilding: Moving from Violence to Sustainable Peace*, ed. B. W. Dayton and L. Kriesberg (London: Routledge, 2009).

105. M. N. Zald and J. D. McCarthy, *The Dynamics of Social Movements* (Cambridge, MA: Winthrop, 1979); and D. McAdam and D. A. Snow, *Social Movements: Readings on Their Emergence, Mobilization, and Dynamics* (Los Angeles: Roxbury, 1997).

106. P. F. Lazarsfeld, B. Berelson, et al., *The People's Choice* (New York: Columbia University Press, 1944); and M. Kriesberg, "Cross-Pressures and Attitudes," *Public Opinion Quarterly* 13 (Spring 1949): 5–16.

107. E. Jackson, "Status Consistency and Symptoms of Stress," *American Sociological Review* 27 (August 1962): 469–80.

108. S. Alinsky, *Reveille for Radicals* (New York: Vintage, 1946).

109. L. Kriesberg, *International Conflict Resolution: The U.S.-USSR and Middle East Cases* (New Haven, CT: Yale University Press, 1992).

110. G. Steinem, "A New Egalitarian Life Style," *New York Times*, August 26, 1971, 37.

111. K. Marx and F. Engels, *The Communist Manifesto* (Chicago: H. Regnery, 1954), 44.

112. J. D. Medrano, *Divided Nations: Class, Politics, and Nationalism in the Basque Country and Catalonia* (Ithaca, NY: Cornell University Press, 1995).

113. Ronfeldt, Arquilla, Fuller, and Fuller, *The Zapatista Social Netwar in Mexico*, 37.

114. S. Coll, *Ghost Wars: The Secret History of the CIA, Afghanistan, and bin Laden, from the Soviet Invasion to September 10, 2001* (New York: Penguin, 2004).

115. Skocpol, *States and Social Revolutions*. Revolutions often follow wars for other reasons as well. Walter Laqueur writes that the "general dislocation caused by war, the material losses and human sacrifices, create a climate conducive to radical change. A large section of the population has been armed; human life seems considerably less valuable than in peacetime." See W. Laquer, "Revolution," in *International Encyclopedia of the Social Sciences*, vol. 13, ed. David L. Sills (New York: Macmillan, 1968), 501.

116. M. C. Ruppert, *Crossing the Rubicon: The Decline of the American Empire at the End of the Age of Oil*. (Gabriola, BC: New Society Publishers, 2004); Bacevich, *The Limits of Power*.

117. Some conflict analysts combine particular components in order to distinguish different kinds of conflicts. For example, identity conflicts refer to struggles about dissensual issues such as the core values and values held by the contending parties, while interest conflicts are based on what is regarded here as consensual issues. See J. Rothman, *Resolving Identity-Based Conflict in Nations, Organizations, and Communities* (San Francisco, CA: Jossey-Bass, 1997).

CHAPTER 4

1. Psychologists and economists have called this dynamic the sunk cost fallacy. See H. Arkes and C. Blumer, "The Psychology of Sunk Costs," *Organizational Behavior and Human Decision Processes* 35(1) (1985): 124–40. The relationship of such entrapment to sustaining and escalating conflict is examined in J. Brockner and J. Z. Rubin, *Entrapment in Escalating Conflicts: A Social Psychological Analysis* (New York: Springer Verlag, 1985).

2. Analysts of social conflicts use many different terms to make these or similar distinctions. "Influence," "threats," and "promises" are the terms used by M. Deutsch, *The Resolution of Conflict: Constructive and Destructive Processes* (New Haven, CT: Yale University Press, 1973). "Persuasion," "inducements," and "constraints" are used by W. A. Gamson, *Power and Discontent* (Homewood, IL: Dorsey Press, 1968). "Persuasion," "coercion," and "bargaining" are distinguished by R. H. Turner, "Determinants of Social Movement Strategies," in *Human Nature and Collective Behavior: Papers in Honor of Herbert Blumer*, ed. T. Shibutani (Englewood Cliffs, NJ: Prentice-Hall, 1970). "Coercive," "utilitarian," and "normative bases of compliance" are distinguished by A. Etzioni, *A Comparative Analysis of Complex Organization* (New York: Free Press, 1961). And "threat," "exchange," and "love forms of power" are distinguished by K. E. Boulding, *Three Faces of Power* (Newbury Park, CA: Sage, 1989). Other writers stress the differences between threats and promises or between negative and positive sanctions. See, respectively, D. Singer, "Inter-Nation Influence: A Formal Model," *American Political Science Review* 57 (June 1963): 420–30; and D. A. Baldwin, "The Power of Positive Sanctions," *World Politics* 24 (October 1971): 19–38.

3. J. Galtung, "Violence, Peace, and Peace Research," *Journal of Peace Research* 3(3) (1969): 168.

4. Galtung, "Violence, Peace, and Peace Research," 171.

5. For popular views on violence, see M. D. Blumenthal, R. L. Kahn, et al., *Justifying Violence* (Ann Arbor: University of Michigan Press, 1972).

6. D. Cortright and G. A. Lopez, eds., *Economic Sanctions: Panacea or Peacebuilding in a Post-Cold War World* (Boulder, CO: Westview, 1995).

7. M. H. Ross, *The Culture of Conflict* (New Haven, CT: Yale University Press, 1993). A. Montagu, ed., *Learning Non-Aggression* (New York: Oxford University Press, 1978).

8. L. V. Sigal, "Look Who's Talking: Nuclear Diplomacy with North Korea," *Items (Social Science Research Council)* 51 (June–September 1997): 31–36; and L. V. Sigal, *Disarming Strangers: Nuclear Diplomacy with North Korea* (Princeton, NJ: Princeton University Press, 1998).

9. President Lyndon B. Johnson during the war against North Vietnam offered aid for reconstruction, linked to ending the war, but this was not wholly credible and in any case reflected a grave cultural and political misunderstanding. D. Kearns, *Lyndon Johnson and the American Dream* (New York: New American Library, 1977), 278–82.

10. J. S. Nye, *Soft Power: The Means to Success in World Politics* (New York: Public Affairs, 2004).

11. S. J. Stedman, "Spoiler Problems in Peace Processes," in *International Conflict Resolution after the Cold War*, ed. P. Stern and D. Druckman (Washington, DC: National Academies Press, 2000).

12. One definition that incorporates many shared ideas is that persuasion is "symbolic activity whose purpose is to effect the internationalization or voluntary acceptance of new cognitive states or patterns of overt behavior through the exchange of messages." See M. J. Smith *Persuasion and Human Action* (Belmont, CA: Wadsworth, 1982), 7.

13. M. Kleiboer, *The Multiple Realities of International Mediation* (Boulder, CO: Lynne Rienner, 1998); and J. P. Lederach, *Building Peace: Sustainable Reconciliation in Divided Societies* (Washington, DC: United States Institute of Peace Press, 1997).

14. S. Allard, *Russia and the Austrian State Treaty* (University Park: University of Pennsylvania Press, 1970), and L. Kriesberg, *International Conflict Resolution: The U.S.-USSR and Middle East Cases* (New Haven, CT: Yale University Press, 1992).

15. F. Rose, *Coalitions across the Class Divide: Lessons from the Labor, Peace, and Environmental Movements* (Ithaca, NY: Cornell University Press, 2000).

16. J. T. Tedeschi, "Threats and Promises," in *The Structure of Conflict*, ed. P. Swingle (New York: Academic Press, 1970).

17. C. Simpson, *Science of Coercion: Communication Research and Psychological Warfare* (New York: Oxford University Press, 1994).

18. As reported in K. H. Nakamura and M. C. Weed, *U.S. Public Diplomacy: Background and Current Issues* (Washington, DC: Congressional Research Service, 2010), 26.

19. M. Mead, "Warfare Is Only an Invention—Not a Biological Necessity," *Asia* 40(8) (1940): 402–5.

20. P. H. Gulliver, *Disputes and Negotiations: A Cross-Cultural Perspective* (New York: Academic Press, 1979).

21. J. Nef, *War and Human Progress* (Cambridge, MA: Harvard University Press, 1950).

22. For the texts of the Geneva conventions regarding warfare, see the International Committee of the Red Cross website: www.icrc.org/eng.

23. J. Miller and L. Mylroie, *Saddam Hussein and the Crisis in the Gulf* (New York: Times Books, 1990).

24. See G. Prunier, *The Rwanda Crisis: History of a Genocide* (New York: Columbia University Press, 1996). See also B. Steidle and G. S. Wallace, *The Devil Came on Horseback: Bearing Witness to the Genocide in Darfur* (New York: Public Affairs, 2007).

25. B. Kiernan, *The Pol Pot Regime: Race, Power, and Genocide in Cambodia under the Khmer Rouge, 1975–1979* (New Haven, CT: Yale University Press, 1996).

26. L. Diamond, *Developing Democracy: Toward Consolidation* (Baltimore: Johns Hopkins University Press, 1999).

27. P. M. Blau, *Exchange and Power in Social Life* (New York: Wiley, 1964).

28. R. Axelrod, "An Evolutionary Approach to Norms," *American Political Science Review* 80 (December 1986): 1095–111; and M. Foucalt, *Power-Knowledge* (New York: Pantheon, 1980).

29. W. G. Sumner, *Folkways* (Lexington, MA: Ginn, 1906).

30. For instance, on the frequency of political coups in Africa, see A. B. Assensoh and Y. M. Alex-Assensoh, *African Military History and Politics: Coups and Idealogical Incursions, 1900–Present* (New York: Palgrave, 2001).

31. L. R. Sayles and G. Strauss, *The Local Union: Its Place in the Industrial Plant* (New York: Harper & Brothers, 1953).

32. The observation is based on my interviews with Catalans in Barcelona conducted in 1994. Also, J. D. Medrano, *Divided Nations: Class, Politics, and Nationalism in the Basque Country and Catalonia* (Ithaca, NY: Cornell University Press, 1995).

33. K. Avruch, *Culture and Conflict Resolution* (Washington, DC: United States Institute of Peace, 1998).

34. The International Court of Justice, which sits at The Hague, Netherlands, was established in 1945 under the Charter of the United Nations. Its predecessor was the

Permanent Court of International Justice (1922–1946). See www.icj-cij.org/. The International Criminal Court was established in 2002 to prosecute individuals' crimes against humanity, genocide, and war crimes; however, the United States, China, and a few other countries have not joined the ICC.

35. M. Sageman, *Understanding Terror Networks* (Philadelphia: University of Pennsylvania Press, 2004); and M. Palmer and P. Palmer, *The Heart of Terror: Islam, Jihadist, and America's War on Terrorism* (Lanham, MD: Rowman & Littlefield, 2004).

36. On frames and reframing, see D. A. Snow and R. D. Benford, "Ideology, Frame Resonance, and Participant Mobilization," in *International Social Movement Research*, vol. 1, ed. H. K. Bert Klandermans and Sidney Tarrow (Greenwich, CT: JAI Press, 1988).

37. On the rise of new feminist thinking and the women's movement arising in the 1960s, see B. Friedan, *The Feminine Mystique* (New York: W. W. Norton, 1963); and R. Rosen, *The World Split Open* (New York: Viking, 2000). For an analysis of the numerous legal restrictions suffered by women, and by men under the U.S. legal system that the women's movement strove to change, see K. DeCrow, *Sexist Justice* (New York: Random House, 1974).

38. On the Zapatistas, see D. Ronfeldt, John Arquilla, Graham E. Fuller, and Melissa Fuller, *The Zapatista Social Netwar in Mexico* (Santa Monica, CA: RAND Arroyo Center, 1998).

39. M. Pace and D. Kew, "Catalysts of Change: Applying New Forms of Practice to the Context of Nigeria's Democratic Development," in *Cutting-Edge Theories and Recent Developments in Conflict Resolution*, ed. Rosemary O'Leary, Rachel Fleishman, and Catherine Gerard (Bingley, UK: Emerald Press, 2008).

40. A. Wanis-St. John and D. Kew, "Civil Society and Peace Negotiations: Confronting Exclusion," *International Negotiation* 13 (2008): 11–36.

41. These are discussed in later chapters. On comparing the first and second intifadas, see R. Hammami and S. Tamari, "The Second Uprising: End or New Beginning," *Journal of Palestine Studies* 30(2) (Winter 2001): 5–25.

42. P. Wehr, H. Burgess, et al., eds., *Justice without Violence* (Boulder, CO: Lynne Rienner, 1994); and R. S. Powers, W. B. Vogele, et al., eds., *Protest, Power, and Change: An Encyclopedia of Nonviolent Action from ACT-Up to Women's Suffrage* (New York: Garland, 1997).

43. G. Sharp, *The Politics of Nonviolent Action* (Boston: Porter Sargent, 1973); and G. Sharp, *Waging Nonviolent Struggle: 20th-Century Practice and 21st-Century Potential* (Boston: Porter Sargent, 2005).

44. M. K. Gandhi, *An Autobiography of My Experiments with Truth* (Almedabad, India: Nvajivan, 1940); and J. V. Bondurant, *Conquest of Violence: The Gandhian Philosophy of Violence* (Berkeley: University of California Press, 1965).

45. P. Ackerman and C. Kruegler, *Strategic Nonviolent Conflict* (Westport, CT: Praeger, 1994).

46. C. Tilly and D. Snyder, "Hardship and Collective Violence in France 1830–1960," *American Sociological Review* 37 (October 1972): 520–32.

47. M. L. King Jr., *Why We Can't Wait* (New York: The New American Library, 1963).

48. D. C. Reitzes, *The Alinsky Legacy: Alive and Kicking* (Greenwich, CT: JAI Press, 1987).

49. D. G. L. Cortright with Richard W. Conroy, Jaleh Dashti-Gibson, and Julia Wagler, *The Sanctions Decade: Assessing UN Strategies in the 1990s* (Boulder, CO: Lynne Rienner, 2000); and D. Cortright, G. A. Lopez, et al., *Sanctions and the Search for Security* (Boulder, CO: Lynne Rienner, 2002).

50. For a discussion of the challenges and possibilities of targeted sanctions, see P. Wallensteen, C. Staibano, et al., *Making Targeted Sanctions Effective: Guidelines for the Implementation of UN Policy Options* (Uppsala, Sweden: Uppsala University Department of Peace and Conflict Research, 2003).

51. M. Stohl, "Demystifying the Mystery of International Terrorism," in *International Terrorism: Characteristics, Causes, Controls*, ed. C. W. Kegley Jr. (New York: St. Martin's, 1990), 83. For a taxonomy of definitions, see A. P. Schmid, "Frameworks for Conceptualising Terrorism," *Terrorism and Political Violence* 16(2) (Summer 2004): 197–221; and for the U.S. Department of State's definition of terrorist activity, see www.state.gov/s/ct/.

52. S. Kennedy, *After Appomattox: How the South Won the War* (Gainesville: University of Florida Press, 1995).

53. M. G. Marshall, *Global Terrorism: An Overview and Analysis*, report of the Integrated Network for Societal Conflict Research, University of Maryland, the Center for Systemic Peace, 2002.

54. In 1996, bin Laden issued a declaration of war, titled "Against the Americans Occupying the Land of the Two Holy Places (Expel the Infidels from the Arab Peninsula)." For the text, see http://www.pbs.org/newshour/terrorism/international/fatwa_1996.html; see also www.fas.org/irp/world/para/docs/980223-fatwa.htm.

55. Quoted from "The Truth about the New Crusade: A Ruling on the Killing of Women and Children of the Non-Believers," cited in A. Cullison, "Inside Al-Qaeda's Hard Drive," *Atlantic Monthly*, September 2004, 55–70.

56. In October 2005, the U.S. Department of State designated forty-two foreign terrorist organizations, including the Liberation Tigers of Tamil Eelam, the Basque Fatherland and Liberty, Hamas, Real IRA, Kahane Chai, and the Kurdistan Workers' Party. Source: www.state.gov/s/ct/rls/fs/37191.htm.

57. Among the numerous accounts, see V. Marchetti and J. D. Marks, *The CIA and the Cult of Intelligence* (New York: Dell, 1974); S. Chavkin, *The Murder of Chile: Eyewitness Acounts of the Coup, the Terror, and the Resistance Today* (New York: Everest House, 1961); and R. M. Carmack, ed., *Harvest of Violence: The Maya Indians and the Guatemalan Crisis* (Norman: University of Oklahoma Press, 1988).

58. CIA definition at: http://www.cia.gov/terrorism/faqs.html. The Department of Defense definition is: "The calculated use of unlawful violence or the threat of unlawful violence to inculcate fear; intended to coerce or intimidate governments or societies in the pursuit of goals that are generally political, religious or ideological." *U.S. Army CDSINT Handbook No. 1* (Version 3.0), "A Military Guide to Terrorism in the Twenty-First Century," August 15, 2001. See www.fas.org/irp/threat/terrorism/index.html.

59. For a discussion of the psychological motivations of suicidal terrorism, see M. Crenshaw, "The Psychology of Terrorism: An Agenda for the Twenty-First Century," *Political Psychology* 21(2) (2002): 405–20.

60. P. Selznick, *TVA and the Grass Roots* (Berkeley: University of California Press, 1949).

61. Such approaches come under the rubric of "regulatory negotiation." See L. Susskind and J. L. Cruikshank, *Breaking the Impasse: Consensual Approaches to Resolving Public Disputes* (New York: Basic Books, 1987).

62. K. B. Clark and J. H. Clark, *A Relevant War against Poverty* (New York: Harper & Row, 1969); and D. P. Moynihan, *Maximum Feasible Misunderstanding* (New York: Free Press, 1970).

63. Kerner Commission, *Report of the National Commission on Civil Disorders* (New York: Bantam, 1968), 279.

64. F. F. Piven and R. A. Cloward, *Poor People's Movements* (New York: Vintage Books, 1979), P. G. Coy and T. Hedeen, "A Stage Model of Social Movement Co-Optation: Community Mediation in the United States," *Sociological Quarterly* 46 (2005): 405–35.

65. C. Kerr, "The Trade Union Movement and the Redistribution of Power in Postwar Germany," *Quarterly Journal of Economics* 68 (November 1954): 535–64.

66. T. D. Sisk, "Democratization and Peacebuilding: Perils and Promises," in *Turbulent Peace: The Challenges of Managing International Conflict*, ed. C. A. Crocker, Fen Osler Hampson, and Pamela Aall (Washington, DC: United States Institute of Peace Press, 2001).

67. J. Holland, *Hope Against History* (New York: Henry Holt, 1999).

68. M. H. Ross, "Democracy as Joint Problem Solving: Addressing Interests and Identities in Divided Societies," *Nationalism & Ethnic Politics* 4(4) (Winter 1998): 19–46; H. H. Saunders, *A Public Peace Process: Sustained Dialogue to Transform Racial and Ethnic Conflicts* (New York: St. Martin's Press, 1999); and E. Weiner, ed., *The Handbook of Interethnic Coexistence* (New York: Continuum, 1998). For links to websites with basic information about conflict resolution, see www.crinfo.org/.

69. Saunders, *A Public Peace Process*, 31.

70. R. Fisher, *Interactive Conflict Resolution* (Syracuse, NY: Syracuse University Press, 1997); and J. Rothman, *From Confrontation to Cooperation: Resolving Ethnic and Regional Conflict* (Thousand Oaks, CA: Sage, 1992).

71. H. C. Kelman, "Contributions of an Unoffical Conflict Resolution Effort to the Israeli-Palestinian Breakthrough," *Negotiation Journal* 11 (January 1995): 19–27.

72. This formulation was introduced in R. R. Blake and J. S. Mouton, *The Managerial Grid* (Houston, TX: Gulf, 1964).

73. J. Kane-Berman, *South Africa's Silent Revolution* (Johannesburg: South African Institute of Race Relations, 1990); A. Sparks, *Tomorrow Is Another Country* (New York: Hill and Wang, 1995); H. van der Merwe, *Pursuing Justice and Peace in South Africa* (London: Routledge, 1989).

74. R. R. Blake, H. A. Shephard, et al., *Managing Intergroup Conflict in Industry* (Houston, TX: Gulf, 1964); and M. A. Rahim, *Managing Conflict in Organizations* (Westport, CT: Praeger, 1986).

75. See J. Mayer, "Covert Operations: The Billionaire Brothers Who Are Waging a War against Obama," *New Yorker*, August 30, 2010, 44–55.

CHAPTER 5

1. T. G. Ash, *The Magic Lantern: The Revolution of '89 Witnessed in Warsaw, Budapest, Berlin and Prague* (New York: Random House, 1990). In Poland in October 1985, when Solidarity was suppressed, Kriesberg participated in a conference about social movements and witnessed the faculty and students speaking openly of their engagement in Solidarity. L. Kriesberg, "Peace Movements and Government Peace Efforts," in *Research in Social Movements Conflicts and Change*, vol. 10, ed.. J. Mucha, L. Kriesberg and B. Misztal (Greenwich, CT: JAI Press, 1988).

2. The data are from H. R. Steedlly and J. W. Foley, "The Success of Protest Groups: Multivariate Analyses," in *The Strategy of Social Protest*, ed. W. A. Gamson (Belmont, CA: Wadsworth, 1990), 188, table 1.

3. I. P. Bell, *CORE and the Strategy of Non-Violence* (New York: Random House, 1968), 59.

4. C. J. Lammers, "Strikes and Mutinies: A Comparative Study of Organizational Conflicts between Rulers and Ruled," *Administrative Science Quarterly* 14 (December 1969): 558–72.

5. A. P. Goldstein and M. H. Segall, *Aggression in Global Perspective* (Elmsford, NY: Pergamon Press, 1982).

6. M. D. Blumenthal, R. L. Kahn, et al., *Justifying Violence* (Ann Arbor: University of Michigan Press, 1972).

7. S. M. Lipset and W. Schneider, *The Confidence Gap: Business, Labor and Government in the Public Mind* (New York: Free Press, 1983).

8. J. E. Mueller, *War, Presidents and Public Opinion* (New York: Wiley, 1973), 122–36; also: L. Kriesberg, Harry Murray, and Ross A. Klein, "Elites and Increased Public Support for U.S. Military Spending," *Journal of Political and Military Sociology* 10 (Fall 1982): 275–97.

9. The Gallup poll analysis of October 24, 2001, www.gallup.com/poll/releases/pr01024.asp.

10. A. Arian, *The Peace Process and Terror: Conflicting Trends in Israeli Public Opinion in 1995* (Tel Aviv: Tel Aviv University, Jaffee Center for Strategic Studies, 1995).

11. Among respondents with fewer than nine years of education, 17 percent opposed continuing negotiations, compared with 31 percent among those with university degrees. Similarly, among the respondents with fewer than nine years of education, 27 percent supported armed attacks against Israeli targets, compared with 47 percent of those with university degrees. Data from public opinion poll no. 16, conducted and reported by the Center for Palestine Research and Studies, Nablus, West Bank.

12. Goldstein and Segall, *Aggression in Global Perspective.*

13. T. A. Northrup, "Personal Security, Political Security: The Relationship between Conceptions of Gender, War, and Peace," in *Research in Social Movements, Conflicts and Change*, vol. 12, ed. L. Kriesberg (Greenwich, CT: JAI Press, 1990); and N. C. M. Hartsock, "Masculinity, Heroism, and the Making of War," in *Rocking the Ship of State*, ed. A. Harris and Y. King (Boulder, CO: Westview Press, 1989).

14. R. C. Eichenberg, "Gender Differences in Public Attitudes toward the Use of Force by the United States, 1990–2003," *International Security* 28 (1) (2003): 110–41.

15. CNN/USA Today/Gallup poll analysis by Jeffrey M. Jones, October 5, 2001, see www.gallup.com/poll/Releases/Pr011005.asp (accessed June 15, 2006).

16. Eichenberg, "Gender Differences in Public Attitudes."

17. L. Keashly, "Gender and Conflict: What Does Psychological Research Tell Us?" in *Conflict and Gender*, ed. A. Taylor and J. B. Miller (Cresskill, NJ: Hampton Press, 1994).

18. See T. L. Ruble and J. A. Schneer, "Gender Differences in Conflict-Handling Styles: Less Than Meets the Eye?" in *Conflict and Gender*, ed. A. Taylor and J. B. Miller (Cresskill, NJ: Hampton Press, 1994).

19. E. Boulding, *Cultures of Peace: The Hidden Side of History* (Syracuse, NY: Syracuse University Press, 2000), 107; and John Paul Lederach, *The Moral Imagination* (New York: Oxford University Press, 2005), 10–13.

20. M. Caprioli and M. A. Boyer, "Gender, Violence, and International Crisis," *Journal of Conflict Resolution* 45(4) (2001): 503–18.

21. M. G. Marshall and D. R. Marshall, "Gender Empowerment and the Willingness of States to Use Force," available at: http://www.systemicpeace.org/CSPpaper2.pdf; and E. Melander, "Gender Equality and Intrastate Armed Conflict," *International Studies Quarterly* 49 (December 2005): 695–714.

22. M. Gopin, *Between Eden and Armageddon: The Future of Religion, Violence and Peacemaking* (New York: Oxford University Press, 2000); M. Gopin, *Holy War, Holy Peace* (New York, Oxford University Press, 2001); M. Abu-Nimer, *Nonviolence and Peace Building in Islam: Theory and Practice* (Gainesville: University Press of Florida, 2003).

23. For examples see D. Little, ed., *Peacemakers in Action: Profiles of Religion in Conflict Resolution* (Cambridge: Cambridge University Press, 2007).

24. P. Brock, *Pacifism in the United States: From the Colonial Era to the First World War* (Princeton, NJ: Princeton University Press, 1968); and R. L. Holmes, ed., *Nonviolence in Theory and Practice* (Belmont, CA: Wadsworth, 1990).

25. E. Sprinzak, "Fundamentalism, Terrorism, and Democracy: The Case of Gush Emunim," *New Outlook* 31 (September/October 1998): 8–41.

26. For full text, see http://www.pbs.org/newshour/terrorism/international/fatwa_1996.html.

27. D. Conversi, "Domino Effect or Internal Developments? The Influences of International Events and Political Ideologies on Catalan and Basque Nationalism," *West European Politics* 16 (July 1993): 245–70; see also F. Fanon, *The Wretched of the Earth* (New York: Grove Press, 1966); M. Rejai, *The Comparative Study of Revolutionary Strategy* (New York: David McKay, 1977); and J. Castenero, *Companero: The Life and Death of Che Guevara* (New York: Knopf, 1997).

28. For an example of this principle as applied to Woodrow Wilson's leadership style, see C. E. Schulzke, "Wilsonian Crisis Leadership, the Organic State, and the Modern Presidency," *Polity* 37(2) (2007): 262–85.

29. M. G. Hermann, "How Decision Units Shape Foreign Policy: A Theoretical Framework," *International Studies Review* 3(2) (2001): 47–82.

30. C. W. Mills, *The New Men of Power* (New York: Harcourt, Brace, 1948).

31. C. W. Mills, *The Power Elite* (New York: Oxford University Press, 1956); and A. M. Rose, *The Power Structure* (New York: Oxford University Press, 1967).

32. B. B. Hughes, *The Democratic Context of American Foreign Policy* (San Francisco: W. W. Freeman, 1978).

33. L. Kriesberg, H. Murray, et al., "Elites and Increased Support for U.S. Military Spending," *Journal of Political and Military Sociology* 10 (Fall 1982): 275–97; W. Hyland, *Clinton's World: Remaking American Foreign Policy* (Westport, CT: Praeger, 1999); and A. J. Bacevich, *The New American Militarism: How Americans Are Seduced by War* (New York: Oxford University Press, 2005).

34. See, for example, Secretary of Defense Robert Gate's Defense Budget Recommendation Statement released on April 6, 2009. It can be found at: http://www.defense.gov/speeches/speech.aspx?speechid=1341.

35. Chicago Council on Foreign Relations, "Worldviews 2002, American Public Opinion and Foreign Policy," 13, figure 1.7, http://www.worldviews.org/index.html (accessed June 15, 2006).

36. I. H. Daalder and J. M. Lindsay, *America Unbound: The Bush Revolution in Foreign Policy* (Washington, DC: Brookings Institution Press, 2003); and J. Mann, *Rise of the Vulcans* (New York: Viking, 2004).

37. Chicago Council on Foreign Relations, "American Public Opinion and Foreign Policy," Figure 3.9; and The Chicago Council on Foreign Relations, "Americans on Promoting Democracy," September 29, 2005.

38. D. Conversi, "Violence as an Ethnic Border: The Consequences of a Lack of Distinctive Elements in Croatian, Kurdish and Basque Nationalism," in *Nationalism in*

Europe: Past and Present, ed. X. Beramendi, R. Maiz and X. M. Nunez (Santiago de Compostela, Spain: University of Santiago Press).

39. M. S. Miron and A. P. Goldstein, *Hostage* (Kalamazoo, MI: Behaviordelia, 1978); and K. Schonborn, *Dealing with Violence: The Challenge Faced by Police and Other Peacekeepers* (Spingfield, IL: Charles C. Thomas, 1975). Negotiating a resolution of a siege by police or other officials is not always successful. In the 1993 Waco standoff, differences in worldviews contributed to the failure. J. S. Docherty, *Learning Lessons from Waco: When the Parties Bring Their Gods to the Negotiation Table* (Syracuse, NY: Syracuse University Press, 2001).

40. In the case of state terrorism, government resources may be very great, and even if some terrorist acts may be conducted by factions of state police or security agencies, a policy of state terrorism requires the engagement of large numbers of people and authoritarian or totalitarian controls.

41. A. Oberschall, "The 1960 Sit-Ins: Protest Diffusion and Movement Take-Off," in *Research in Social Movements, Conflict and Change*, vol. 11, ed. L. Kriesberg (Greenwich, CT: JAI Press, 1989).

42. Discussed in chapter 4.

43. S. Spilerman, "The Causes of Racial Disturbances: A Comparison of Alternative Explanations," *American Sociological Review* 35 (August 1970): 627–49.

44. Youth tend to feel invulnerable, with fewer assets that are hostage to those with superior power, and therefore are disproportionately involved in violent disruptions. L. A. Coser, *Continuities in the Study of Social Conflict* (New York: Free Press, 1967); and Kerner Commission, *Report of the National Commission on Civil Disorders* (New York: Bantam, 1968).

45. Bacevich, *The New American Militarism.*

46. D. Priest, *The Mission: Waging War and Keeping Peace with America's Military* (New York: W. W. Norton & Co., 2003).

47. C. Tilly, *From Mobilization to Revolution* (Reading, MA: Addison-Wesley, 1978), 156. In Labrador, Canada, one community of indigenous people, the Inuit, had a history of passively responding in conflicts. After cooperating with another community, the Innu, in carrying out civil disobedience by successfully blockading a work project on their land, they were ready to threaten such actions again. Lawrence Albert Dunn, "Negotiating Cultural Identities: Conflict Transformation in Labrador" (unpublished PhD Social Science dissertation, Syracuse University, 2002).

48. C. Kerr and A. Siegel, "The Interindustry Propensity to Strike: An International Comparison," in *Industrial Conflict*, ed. A. Kornhauser and A. M. Ross (New York: McGraw-Hill, 1954). Other studies of inter-industry strike propensity in France and in Italy did not find the same pattern. See E. Shorter and C. Tilly, *Strikes in France, 1830–1968* (Cambridge: Cambridge University Press, 1974); and D. Snyder and W. R. Kelly, "Industrial Violence in Italy, 1878–1903," *American Journal of Sociology* 82 (July 1976): 131–62.

49. A. Varshney, *Ethnic Conflict and Civic Life: Hindu and Muslims in India* (New Haven, CT: Yale University Press, 2002).

50. G. P. Murdock, *Social Structure* (New York: Macmillan, 1949); and R. A. LeVine, "Socialization, Social Structure, and Intersocietal Images," in *International Behavior*, ed. H. C. Kelman (New York: Holt, Rinehart & Winston, 1965).

51. K. W. Deutsch, S. A. Burrell, et al., *Political Community and the North Atlantic Area* (Princeton, NJ: Princeton University Press, 1957); and A. M. Kacowicz, Yaacov Bar-Siman Tov, Ole Elgstrom, and Magnus Jerneck, ed., *Stable Peace among Nations* (Lanham, MD: Rowman & Littlefield, 2000).

52. W. K. Domke, *War and the Changing Global System* (New Haven, CT: Yale University Press, 1988). Also see M. Gasiorwski, "Economic Interdependence and International Conflict: Some Cross-National Evidence," *International Studies Quarterly* 30 (1986): 23–28; and S. W. Polachek, "Conflict and Trade," *Journal of Conflict Resolution* 24 (March 1980): 55–78.

53. J. Carter, "North Korea Wants to Make a Deal," *New York Times*, October 16, 2010, A31.

54. R. J. Rummel, "Libertarian Propositions on Violence within and between Nations," *Journal of Conflict Resolution* 29 (September 1985): 419–55; B. Russett, *Grasping the Democratic Peace: Principles for a Post-Cold War World* (Princeton, NJ: Princeton University Press, 1993); S. Gates, T. L. Knutsen, et al., "Democracy and Peace: A More Skeptical View," *Journal of Peace Research* 33(1) (1996): 1–10; and B. Russett, "Bushwacking the Democratic Peace," *International Studies Perspective* 6 (2005): 395–408.

55. For a statistical overview of conflicts dyadic conflicts between 1946 and 2007, see L. Harboom, E. Melander, et al., "Dyadic Dimensions of Armed Conflict, 1946–2007," *Journal of Peace Research* 45(5) (2008): 697–710.

56. P. Taft and P. Ross, "American Labor Violence: Its Causes, Character, and Outcome," in *Violence in America*, ed. H. D. Graham and T. R. Gurr (New York: Bantam, 1969); J. Haydu, "Managing 'The Labor Problem' in the United States ca. 1897–1911," in *Intractable Conflicts and Their Transformation*, ed. L. Kriesberg, T. A. Northrup, and S. J. Thorson (Syracuse, NY: Syracuse University Press, 1989).

57. A. M. Ross and D. Irwin, "Strike Experience in Five Countries, 1927–1947: An Interpretation," *Industrial and Labor Relations Review* 4 (April 1951): 323–42.

58. Lewis F. Richardson found that of the 186 pairs of opposed belligerents in wars from 1820 to 1929, 48 percent had fought against each other in the past and only 29 percent had been wartime allies. J. David Singer and Melvin Small, using somewhat different indicators, found that of the 209 who had ever fought in opposition between 1816 and 1965, 19 percent had fought in opposition at least once before, but 21 percent had been partners in the past. See L. F. Richardson, *Statistics of Deadly Quarrels* (Pittsburgh, PA: The Boxwood Press, 1960), 345.

59. T. J. Scheff, *Bloody Revenge: Emotions, Nationalism, and War* (Boulder, CO: Westview, 1994); and V. Volkan, *The Need to Have Enemies and Allies: From Clinical Practice to International Relationships* (New York, Jason Aronson, 1988).

60. See, for instance, T. Judah, *The Serbs: History, Myth and the Destruction of Yugoslavia* (New Haven, CT: Yale University Press, 2000).

61. G. Fischer, *Soviet Opposition to Stalin: A Case Study in World War II* (Cambridge, MA: Harvard University Press, 1952).

62. This topic is influentially developed in H. J. Morgenthau, *Politics among Nations* (New York: Alfred A. Knopf, 1950). Among recent discussions, see J. Vasquez, *The War Puzzle* (Cambridge: Cambridge University Press, 199[illegible]).

63. J. David Singer, Stuart A. Bremer, and John Stuckey find that in the nineteenth century, wars among major states were less likely when power was dispersed, consistent with the balance of power argument, but in the twentieth century, wars were less likely when capability was concentrated, consistent with the preponderance argument. See J. D. Singer, Stuart A. Bremer, and John Stuckey, "Capability Distribution, Uncertainty, and Major Power War, 1820–1965," in *The Correlates of War I: Research Origins and Rationale*, ed. J. D. Singer (New York: Free Press, 1979).

64. B. B. de Mesquita, *The War Trap* (New Haven, CT: Yale University Press, 1981).

65. Vasquez, *The War Puzzle*.

66. However, see James C. Juhnke and Carol M. Hunter, *Missing Peace: The Search for Nonviolent Alternatives in U.S. History*, 2nd ed. (Kitchner, Canada: Pandora Press, 2004).

67. Business upturns also tend to be accompanied by price increases and a fall or slowing down of real income; but the relative power interpretation seems particularly compelling in that strikes to organize unorganized workers show the same pattern as do strikes to secure wage increases and other benefits. See L. Christman, W. R. Kelly, et al., "Comparative Perspectives on Industrial Conflict," in *Research in Social Movements, Conflict and Change*, vol. 4, ed. L. Kriesberg (Greenwich, CT: JAI Press, 1981).

68. For information about the Workers in the Global Economy project of Cornell University's School of Industrial Relations, see www.laborrights.org/projects/globalecon/ See also the Institute for Policy Studies Global Economy Project: http://www.ips-dc.org/projects/global-econ (accessed June 15, 2006).

69. A. Herod, "Implications of Just-in-time Production for Union Strategy: Lessons from the 1998 General Motors–United Auto Workers' Dispute," *Annals of the Association of American Geographers* 90(3) (2000): 521–47.

70. T. Skocpol, *States and Social Revolutions: A Comparative Analysis of France, Russia, and China* (Cambridge: Cambridge University Press, 1979).

71. J. Aaker and A. Smith, *The Dragonfly Effect: Quick, Effective and Powerful Ways to Use Social Media to Drive Social Change* (San Francisco: Jossey Bass, 2010); C. Shirky, "The Political Power of Social Media," *Foreign Affairs* 90(1) (2011): 28–41. M. E. Keck and K. Sikkink, *Activists Beyond Borders: Advocacy Networks in International Politics* (Ithaca, NY: Cornell University Press, 1998).

72. F. J. Khouri, *The Arab-Israeli Dilemma* (Syracuse, NY: Syracuse University Press, 1985). With the expansion of UN membership by the admission of many newly independent countries, the economically developing countries were able to exercise their voting strength to pass resolutions they favored. African countries favored resolutions condemning South Africa's apartheid policy, and the Middle Eastern countries favored strong resolutions condemning Israeli policies relating to Palestinians. By joining together, each voting group was able to win many resolutions that it sought.

73. N. Mandela, *Long Walk to Freedom* (Boston, Little, Brown, 1994); and H. van der Merwe, *Pursuing Justice and Peace in South Africa* (London: Routledge, 1989).

74. The Sinhala, predominantly Buddhist, make up about 75 percent of the population of Sri Lanka, and the Tamil, mainly Hindu, constitute about 18 percent of the population. In addition, about 7 percent of the population is Muslim, mostly Tamil speakers. D. Little, *Sri Lanka: The Invention of Enmity* (Washington, DC: United States Institute of Peace Press, 1994). In 2009, the LTTE was militarily defeated by the government's armed forces.

75. In 2011, the results of an agreed-upon referendum in Southern Sudan signaled the independence of Southern Sudan.

76. R. I. Rotberg, *When States Fail: Causes and Consequences* (Princeton, NJ: Princeton University Press, 2003); N. Chomsky, *Failed States: The Abuse of Power and the Assault on Democracy* (New York: Metropolitan Books, 2006).

77. J. Goodhand, *Aiding Peace? The Role of NGOs in Armed Conflict* (Boulder, CO: Lynne Rienner, 2006).

78. K. Mills and C. O'Driscoll, "From Humanitarian Intervention to the Responsibility to Protect," in *The International Studies Encyclopedia*, ed. R. A. Denemark (New York: Wiley-Blackwell, 2010). Also available online at: http://www.isacompendium.com/subscriber/tocnode?id=g9781444336597_chunk_g97814443365978_ss1-28.

79. Martin Luther King Jr. and his associates thought about the effects on national opinions of demonstrations and the local reactions against them while planning and conducting their nonviolent actions. M. L. King Jr., *Why We Can't Wait* (New York: New American Library, 1963).

80. D. Conversi, "Domino Effect or Internal Developments?" and R. Pagnucco and J. D. McCarthy, "Advocating Nonviolent Direct Action in Latin America: The Antecedents and Emergence of SERPAJ," in *Religion and Politics in Comparative Perspective*, ed. B. Misztal and A. Shupe (Westport, CT, Praeger, 1992).

81. W. Ury, *The Third Side* (New York: Penguin, 2000).

82. D. A. Zinnes, "Empirical Evidence on the Outbreak of International Violence," in *Handbook of Political Conflict: Theory and Research*, ed. T. R. Gurr (New York: Free Press, 1980); and E. D. Mansfield, *Power, Trade, and War* (Princeton, NJ: Princeton University Press, 1994).

83. P. Smoker, "Nation State Escalation and International Integration," *Journal of Peace Research* 1 (1967): 60–74; and J. D. Singer and M. Wallace, "Intergovernmental Organization and the Preservation of Peace, 1816–1964: Some Bivariate Relationships," *International Organization* 24 (Summer 1970): 520–47.

84. Mansfield, *Power, Trade, and War*, 233.

85. R. S. O'Fahey, (2004), *Environmental Degradation as a Cause of Conflict in Darfur*. Conference Proceedings, Khartoum, University for Peace.

86. M. Palmer and P. Palmer, *The Heart of Terror:Islam, Jihadist, and America's War on Terrorism* (Lanham: MD: Rowman & Littlefield, 2004); and T. H. Hastings, *Nonviolent Response to Terrorism* (Jefferson, NC: McFarland, 2004).

CHAPTER 6

1. J. S. Coleman, *Community Conflict* (New York: Free Press, 1957); and T. A. Northrup, "The Dynamic of Identity in Personal and Social Conflict," in *Intractable Conflicts and Their Transformation*, ed. L. Kriesberg, T. A. Northrup, and S. J. Thorson (Syracuse, NY: Syracuse University Press, 1989).

2. L. Festinger, *A Theory of Cognitive Dissonance* (Evanston, IL: Row, Peterson, 1957).

3. J. R. Oneal and A. L. Bryan, "The Rally 'Round the Flag Effect in US Foreign Policy Crises: 1950–1985," *Political Behavior* 17(4) (1995): 379–401.

4. J. Brockner and J. Z. Rubin, *Entrapment in Escalating Conflicts: A Social Psychological Analysis* (New York: Springer Verlag, 1985), 5.

5. C. F. Hermann, "When Policy Is Failing: Applying Theories of U.S. Decision Making in the Iraq War" (paper presented at the International Studies Association Annual Convention, Chicago, 2007).

6. J. A. Robinson, C. F. Hermann, et al., "Search Under Crisis in Political Gaming and Simulation," in *Theory and Research on the Causes of War*, ed. D. G. Pruitt and R. C. Snyder (Englewood Cliffs, NJ: Prentice Hall, 1969); R. Cohen, *Threat Perception in International Crisis* (Madison: University of Wisconsin Press, 1979); and P. J. McGowan and C. W. Kegley Jr., eds., *Threats, Weapons, and Foreign Policy* (Beverly Hills, CA: Sage, 1980).

7. I. L. Janis, *Victims of Groupthink* (Boston: Houghton Mifflin, 1972).

8. National Commission on Terrorist Attacks upon the United States, T. H. Kean, et al., *The 9/11 Commission Report: Final Report of the National Commission on Terrorist*

Attacks upon the United States (Washington, DC: National Commission on Terrorist Attacks upon the United States, U.S. G.P.O, 2004).

9. T. J. Scheff, *Bloody Revenge: Emotions, Nationalism, and War* (Boulder, CO: Westview, 1994); V. Fontan, *Voices from Post-Saddam Iraq: Living with Terrorism, Insurgency and New Forms of Tyranny* (Westport, CT: Praeger, 2008).

10. G. A. McWorter and R. L. Crain, "Subcommunity Gladiatorial Competition: Civil Rights Leadership as a Competitive Process," *Social Forces* 46 (September 1967): 8–21.

11. Based on several informal conversations Kriesberg had with officials and former officials in the Department of State and Department of Defense in the months prior to the invasion of Iraq. Also, B. Woodward, *Plan of Attack* (New York: Simon & Schuster, 2004).

12. F. C. Ikle, *Every War Must End* (New York: Columbia University Press, 1971).

13. Coleman, *Community Conflict*.

14. W. Brink and L. Harris, *Black and White* (New York: Simon & Schuster, 1969).

15. M. Sageman, *Understanding Terror Networks* (Philadelphia: University of Pennsylvania Press, 2004).

16. International Crisis Group, *Popular Protests in North Africa and the Middle East (IV): Tunisia's Way*, Middle East/North Africa Report No. 106 (Tunis/Brussels: International Crisis Group, April 28, 2011).

17. For example, when the Soviet rocket units built the bases in Cuba for the nuclear-tipped missiles, they did so following their standard procedures, laying out their insignia on the ground. This revealed the bases to U.S. intelligence flights. See G. Allison, *The Essence of Decision* (Boston: Little, Brown, 1971).

18. Despite a long tradition of political civility in Chile, the democratically elected government led by Salvador Allende was subjected to destabilizing efforts, covertly assisted by the U.S. Central Intelligence Agency. A military junta led by General Augusto Pinochet Ugarte seized power on September 11, 1973, and unleashed a bloody repression. S. Chavkin, *The Murder of Chile: Eyewitness Acounts of the Coup, the Terror, and the Resistance Today* (New York: Everest House, 1961).

19. Thus, the German kaiser believed that once mobilization had been ordered, he was unable to halt or even modify the next steps, and the war came. See B. W. Tuchman, *The Guns of August* (New York: Macmillan, 1962).

20. The Ohio National Guard fired into a crowd of students at Kent State University, killing four persons and wounding nine others. K. J. Heinman, "Look Out Kid, You're Gonna Get Hit! Kent State and the Vietnam Anitwar Movement," in *Give Peace a Chance: Exploring the Vietnam Anitwar Movement*, ed. M. Small and W. D. Hoover (Syracuse, NY: Syracuse University Press, 1992).

21. C. DeBenedett and C. Chatfield, *An American Ordeal: The Antiwar Movement of the Vietnam Era* (Syracuse, NY: Syracuse University Press, 1990).

22. J. Vasquez, *The War Puzzle* (Cambridge: Cambridge University Press, 1993).

23. E. Cuhadar and B. W. Dayton, "The Social Psychology of Identity and Intergroup Conflict: From Theory to Practice," *International Studies Perspective* (Forthcoming 2011).

24. T. R. Gurr, *Why Men Rebel* (Princeton, NJ: Princeton University Press, 1970), 35; L. Berkowitz, ed., *Roots of Aggression* (New York: Lieber-Atherton, 1969).

25. E. Flexner, *Century of Struggle* (Cambridge, MA: Harvard University Press, 1959).

26. C. Lockhart, *Bargaining in International Conflicts* (New York: Columbia University Press, 1979), 140–41; and G. H. Snyder and P. Diesing, *Conflict among Nations: Bargaining, Decision Making, and System Structure in International Crises* (Princeton, NJ: Princeton University Press, 1977).

27. H. Near, ed., *The Seventh Day: Soldiers Talk about the Six-Day War* (London: Penguin, 1971).

28. Ikle, *Every War Must End.*

29. R. Shaplen, "Scarsdale's Battle of the Books," *Commentary* 10 (December 1950): 530–40.

30. D. Bar-Tal and Y. Teichman, *Stereotypes and Prejudice in Conflict: Representations of Arabs in Israeli Jewish Society* (Cambridge: Cambridge University Press, 2005).

31. K. Skjelsbaek and J. D. Singer, "Shared IGO Memberships and Dyadic War, 1865–1964" (paper presented at the conference on the United Nations, Center for International Studies, 1971).

32. M. Hewstone and K. Greenland, "Intergroup Conflict," *International Journal of Psychology* 35 (2005): 136–44.

33. H. Eckstein, ed., *Internal War: Problems and Approaches* (New York: Free Press, 1966).

34. Gurr, *Why Men Rebel.*

35. See for instance, T. Lyons, "The Ethiopian Diaspora and Homeland Conflict" (paper presented at the 16th International Conference of Ethiopian Studies, Trondheim, Norway, 2009).

36. B. W. Tuchman, *The Zimmermann Telegram* (New York: The Viking Press, 1958).

37. D. J. Elwood, "Philippines People Power Revolution, 1986," in *Protest, Power, and Change*, ed. R. S. Powers, William B. Vogele, Christopher Kruegler, and Ronald M. McCarthy (New York: Garland Publishing, 1997); K. Schock, "People Power and Political Opportunities: Social Movement Mobilization and Outcomes in the Philippines and Burma," *Social Problems* 46(3) (1999): 355–75; and G. Sharp, *Waging Nonviolent Struggle: 20th-Century Practice and 21st-Century Potential* (Boston: Porter Sargent, 2005).

38. D. D. Kirkpatrick and D. E. Sanger, "A Tunisian-Egyptian Link That Shook Arab History," *New York Times*, February 14, 2011, A1, A9–10. Gene Sharp's work is discussed in chapter 4.

39. E. E. Azar, "The Analysis and Management of Protracted Conflicts," in *The Psychodynamics of International Relationships*, vol. 2, ed. V. D. Volkan, J. V. Montville, and D. A. Julius (Lexington, MA: Lexington, 1991), 93.

40. L. Kriesberg, T. A. Northrup, et al., eds., *Intractable Conflicts and Their Transformation* (Syracuse, NY: Syracuse University Press, 1989); and L. Kriesberg, "Nature, Dynamics, and Phases of Intractability," in *Grasping the Nettle: Analyzing Cases of Intractable Conflicts*, ed. C. A. Crocker, Fen Osler Hampson, and Pamela Aall (Washington, DC: United States Institute of Peace, 2005).

41. L. Kriesberg, *International Conflict Resolution: The U.S.-USSR and Middle East Cases* (New Haven, CT: Yale University Press, 1992).

42. C. Hedges, *War Is a Force That Gives Us Meaning* (New York: Public Affairs, 2002). For pride in nonviolent action, see: I. P. Bell, *CORE and the Strategy of Non-Violence* (New York: Random House, 1968), 115.

43. T. J. Lowi, "Making Democracy Safe for the World: National Politics and Foreign Policy," in *Domestic Sources of U.S. Foreign Policy*, ed. J. Rosenau (New York: Free Press, 1967); J. D. Singer, ed., *Correlates of War*, vol. 1, *Research Origins and Rationale* (New York: Free Press, 1979).

44. S. P. Huntington, "The Clash of Civilizations?" *Foreign Affairs* 72 (Summer 1993): 22–49.

45. See R. J. Leng, "Influence Stategies and Interstate Conflict," *The Correlates of War*, vol. 2, ed. J. D. Singer (New York: Free Press, 1980).

46. W. J. Pomeroy, *Guerilla Warfare and Marxism* (New York: International Publishing Co., 1968), p. 291.

47. E. Guevara, *"Che" Guevara on Revolution* (New York: Delta, 1969). Guevara participated in another such attempt in Bolivia and was captured and killed there in 1967.

48. R. Thakur, *The United Nations, Peace and Security: From Collective Security to the Responsibility to Protect* (Cambridge: Cambridge University Press, 2006).

49. S. Coll, *Ghost Wars: The Secret History of the CIA, Afghanistan, and bin Laden, from the Soviet Invasion to September 10, 2001* (New York: Penguin, 2004); and T. G. Weiss and J. G. Blight, eds., *The Suffering Grass: Superpowers and Regional Conflict in Southern Africa and the Caribbean* (Boulder, CO: Lynne Rienner, 1992).

50. A. Oberschall, "Group Violence: Some Hypotheses and Empirical Uniformities," *Law & Society* 5(1) (1969): 61–92.

51. The Cuban government vehemently objected to the agreement. See O. R. Holsti, R. A. Brody, et al., "Measuring Affect and Action in International Reaction Models: Empirical Materials from the 1962 Cuban Crisis," *Journal of Peace Research* 3–4 (1964): 170–89.

52. K. K. Petersen, J. A. Vasques, et al., "Multiparty Disputes and the Probability of War, 1816–1992," *Conflict Management and Peace Science* 21 (2004): 85–100.

53. T. A. Northrup, "Dynamics of Identity," in *Social Conflicts and Collective Identities*, ed. P. G. Coy and L. M. Woehrle (Lanham, MD: Rowman & Littlefield, 2000); and D. L. Horowitz, *Ethnic Groups in Conflict* (Berkeley: University of California Press, 1985).

54. J. J. Wanderer, "An Index of Riot Severity and Some Correlates," *American Journal of Sociology* 74 (March 1969): 500–505.

55. W. A. Gamson and A. Modigliani, *Untangling the Cold War* (Boston: Little, Brown, 1971).

56. For an interesting discussion of the relationship between homogeneity and the escalation of violent conflict, see D. D. Laitin, *Nations, States, and Violence* (Oxford: Oxford University Press, 2007).

57. G. H. Quester, "Wars Prolonged by Misunderstood Signals," *The Annals of the American Academy of Political and Social Science* 392 (November 1970): 30–39.

58. Vasquez, *The War Puzzle*, 200–216; see also Snyder and Diesing, *Conflict among Nations*; and E. R. Wittkopf and M. A. Maggiotto, "Elites and Masses: A Comparative Analysis of Attitudes toward America's Role," *Journal of Politics* 45 (May 1983): 303–34.

59. B. Allen, *Rape Warfare: The Hidden Genocide in Bosnia-Herzegovina and Croatia* (Minneapolis: University of Minnesota Press, 1996).

60. J. Sifton, *"Enduring Freedom" Abuses by U.S. Forces in Afghanistan* (New York: Human Rights Watch, March 2004).

61. For example, L. Pertusati, *In Defense of Mohawk Land: Ethnopolitical Conflict in Native North America* (Albany, NY: State University of New York Press, 1997).

62. For various accounts, see www.globalexchange.org/wto/; http://www.infoshop.org/page/No2WTO.

63. See http://www.usip.org/publications/chiapas-web-links; J. Ross, *Rebellion from the Roots: Indian Uprising in Chiapas* (Monroe, ME: Common Courage Press, 1995); and P. L. Russell, *The Chiapas Rebellion* (Austin, TX: Mexico Resource Center, 1995).

64. W. B. Quandt, *Peace Process: American Diplomacy and the Arab-Israeli Conflict since 1967* (Washington, DC: The Brookings Institution / Berkeley: University of California Press, 1993), 128–29; and Yossi Beilin, interview by Kriesberg, Jerusalem, June 19, 1985.

65. K. Schock, "People Power and Political Opportunities: Social Movement Mobilization and Outcomes in the Philippines and Burma," *Social Problems* 46(3) (1999): 355–75.

66. A. M. Carrion, *Puerto Rico: A Political and Cultural History* (New York: W. W. Norton, 1983), 276ff.

67. W. R. Morgan, "Faculty Mediation of Student War Protests," in *Protest! Student Activism in America*, ed. J. Foster and D. Long (New York: Morrow, 1970); and T. Branch, *Parting the Waters: America in the King Years, 1954–63* (New York: Simon & Schuster, 1988), 756–802.

68. Regression analysis is a statistical method where one or more variables are predicted conditional on other variables. E. Weede, "Some New Evidence on Correlates of Political Violence: Income Inequality, Regime Repressiveness, and Economic Development," *European Sociological Review* 3 (September 1987): 97–108; and E. N. Muller, "Income Inequality, Regime Repressiveness, and Political Violence," *American Sociological Review* 50 (February 1985): 47–61.

69. Vasquez, *The War Puzzle*, 177–84; M. D. Wallace, "Armaments and Escalation: Two Competing Hypotheses," *International Studies Quarterly* 26 (March 1982): 37–51; and H .W. Houweling and J. G. Siccama, "The Arms Race–War Relationship: Why Serious Disputes Matter," *Arms Control* 2 (September 1981): 157–97.

70. R. J. Leng and H. Wheeler, "Influence Strategies, Success and War," *Journal of Conflict Resolution* 23 (December 1979): 655–84.

71. R. Neustadt, *Presidential Power* (New York: Wiley, 1960), p. 127.

72. Woodward, *Plan of Attack*, 66; and Snyder and Diesing, *Conflict among Nations*, 205–7.

73. F. F. Piven and R. A. Cloward, *Poor People's Movements* (New York: Vintage Books, 1979).

74. A. Stent, *Russia and Germany Reborn: Unification, the Soviet Collapse, and the New Europe* (Princeton, NJ: Princeton University Press, 1999), 99ff.

75. R. B. Felson, S. A. Ribner, and M. S. Siegel, "Age and the Effect of Third Parties during Criminal Violence," *Sociology and Social Research* 68(4): 452–62.

76. Vasquez, *The War Puzzle*.

77. H. Thomas, *The Spanish Civil War* (New York: Harper & Row, 1977); and S. M. Ellwood, *The Spanish Civil War* (Oxford: Blackwell, 1991).

78. J. K. Cooley, *Unholy Wars: Afghanistan, America and International Terrorism* (London: Pluto Press, 2002), 117–26; L. Wright, "The Man behind bin Laden," *New Yorker*, September 16, 2004, 56–85; and National Commission on Terrorist Attacks upon the United States (2004), T. H. Kean, et al., *The 9/11 Commission Report*.

79. R. Pagnucco and J. D. McCarthy, "Advocating Nonviolent Direct Action in Latin America: The Antecedents and Emergence of SERPAJ," in *Religion and Politics in Comparative Perspective*, ed. B. Misztal and A. Shupe (Westport, CT: Praeger, 1992). Also see www.aeinstein.org for information about the work of Gene Sharp, in providing information about nonviolence.

80. The Maxwell School of Syracuse University participates in two MEPI programs. The Leaders for Democracy Fellows come for six weeks of study at the Maxwell School and then go to Washington, D.C., on an assignment for six weeks in an organization of professional interest to them. The Civic Education and Leadership Fellowship provide an opportunity for academics from the region to have a four-month residency at the Maxwell School. Dayton and Kriesberg have been engaged in these projects for a few years.

81. For President Bush's speeches, go to: http://www.whitehouse.gov. Also see: K. M. Pollack, *The Threatening Storm: The Case for Invading Iraq* (New York: Random House, 2002).

82. M. Scheuer, *Imperial Hubris: Why the West Is Losing the War on Terror* (Washington, DC: Brassey's, 2004); J. J. Mearsheimer and S. Walt, "An Unnecessary War," *Foreign Policy*, January/February 2003, available at: http://www.mtholyoke.edu/acad/intrel/bush/walt.htm.

83. J. T. Mathews, "Is There a Better Way to Go?" *Washington Post*, February 9, 2003, B1.

84. See Pew Global Attitudes Project, "America's Image Further Erodes," released March 18, 2003. See http://people-press.org/2003/03/18/americas-image-further-erodes-europeans-want-weaker-ties/; Rebecca Solnit, *Hope in the Dark: Untold Histories, Wild Possibilities* (New York: Nation Books, 2004).

85. G. Packer, "A Democratic World," *New Yorker*, February 16 and 23, 2004, 100–108.

86. P. Beinart, P. *The Icarus Syndrome: A History of American Hubris* (New York: Harper, 2010).

87. They attributed the mistakes largely to relying on information from a circle of Iraqi informants and exiles whose accounts "were often eagerly confirmed by United States officials convinced of the need to intervene in Iraq." See: "From the Editors: The Times and Iraq," *New York Times*, May 23, 2004, 16; M. Massing, "Now They Tell Us," *New York Review of Books*, February 26, 2004, 43–49; and J. Steinberg, "Washington Post Rethinks Its Coverage of War Debate," *New York Times*, August 13, 2004.

CHAPTER 7

1. S. J. Stedman, "Spoiler Problems in Peace Processes," in *International Conflict Resolution after the Cold War*, ed. P. Stern and D. Druckman (Washington, DC: National Academies Press, 2000).

2. I. Deutscher, *What We Say/What We Do* (Glenview, IL: Scott, Foresman & Co., 1973).

3. S. Borker, L. Kriesberg, et al., "Conciliation, Confrontation, and Approval of the President," *Peace and Change* 11 (Spring 1985): 31–48.

4. A. P. Goldstein and G. Y. Michaels, *Empathy: Development, Training, and Consequences* (Hillsdale, NJ: Lawrence Erlbaum Associates, 1985). To take the role of other persons is a basic human capability and is essential for the development of a sense of self. G. H. Mead, *Mind, Self and Society* (Chicago: University of Chicago Press, 1934).

5. Goldstein and Michaels, *Empathy*, 4–7.

6. A. Paton, *Cry, The Beloved Country* (New York: Scribner's, 1948); and N. Gordiner, *July's People* (New York: Viking, 1981).

7. For example, R. Halabi, *The West Bank Story: An Israeli Arab's View of Both Sides of a Tangled Conflict* (San Diego: Harcourt Brace Jovanovich, 1985); and D. Grossman, *The Yellow Wind* (New York: Farrar, Staus and Giroux, 1988). On the role of women, see T. P. d'Estree and E. F. Babbitt, "Women and the Art of Peacemaking: Data from Israeli-Palestinian Interactive Problem-Solving Workshops," *Political Psychology* 19(1) (1998): 185–209; and S. Sharoni, *Gender and the Israeli-Palestinian Conflict* (Syracuse, NY: Syracuse University Press, 1995).

8. C. DeBenedetti and C. Chatfield, *An American Ordeal: The Antiwar Movement of the Vietnam Era* (Syracuse, NY: Syracuse University Press, 1990); S. Marullo and E. John Lofland, eds., *Peace Action in the Eighties* (New Brunswick, NJ: Rutgers University Press, 1990); D. S. Meyer, *A Winter of Discontent: The Nuclear Freeze and American Politics* (New York: Praeger, 1990).

9. S. Aday, H. Farrell, et al., "Blogs and Bullets: New Media in Contentious Politics," in *Peaceworks* (Washington, DC: United States Institute of Peace, 2010), 65.

10. K. McRoberts, *Quebec: Social Change and Political Crisis* (Toronto: McClelland and Stewart, 1988).

11. R. M. Gates, *From the Shadows: The Ultimate Insider's Story of Five Presidents and How They Won the Cold War* (New York: Simon & Schuster, 1996), 131–34, 143–49; and J. Suri, "Explaining the End of the Cold War: A New Historical Consensus?" *Journal of Cold War Studies* 4(4) (Fall 2002): 60–92.

12. R. Reagan, *An American Life* (New York: Simon & Schuster, 1990), 589.

13. J. Holland, *Hope against History* (New York: Henry Holt, 1999); and C. McCartney, ed., *Striking a Balance: The Northern Ireland Peace Process Accord: An International Review of Peace Initiatives* (London: Conciliation Resources, 1999); see also, cain.ulst.ac.uk/.

14. R. Dreyfuss, "US General Builds a Palestinian Army," *Nation,* The Dreyfuss Report, 2009, available at: www.thenation.com/blogs/dreyfuss/434494.

15. A. R. Green, "Economic Peace in the West Bank and the Fayyad Plan: Are They Working?" *Middle East Institute Policy Brief,* January 2010: 1–10.

16. E. Bronner, "Bid for State of Palestine Gets Support from I.M.F.," *New York Times*, April 6, 2011. The World Bank concurred in this assessment.

17. I. Kershner, "Drive for Palstinian Unity Exposes Fractured Society," *New York Times*, May 7, 2011, A6. As long as Hamas was not part of the Palestinian government, any agreement between the Israeli government and the PA might be viewed by Israeli officials as unreliable.

18. M. Abbas, "The Long Overdue Palestinian State," *New York Times*, May 17, 2011, A25.

19. R. F. Kennedy, *Thirteen Days: A Memoir of the Cuban Missile Crisis* (New York, W. W. Norton, 1971), 40.

20. R. N. Lebow and J. G. Stein, *We All Lost the Cold War* (Princeton, NJ: Princeton University Press, 1994),110–45.

21. O. R. Holsti, R. A. Brody, et al., "Measuring Affect and Action in International Reaction Models: Empirical Materials from the 1962 Cuban Crisis," *Journal of Peace Research* 3–4 (1964): 170–89.

22. G. W. Breslauer and P. E. Tetlock, eds., *Learning in U.S. and Soviet Foreign Policy* (Boulder, CO: Westview Press, 1991).

23. For example, Henry Kissinger, as national security advisor and then secretary of state in President Richard M. Nixon's administration, on the basis of his experience negotiating with Soviet officials, modified his thinking about how the various issues might be linked, taking a step-by-step approach and not trying to require particular linkages. D. W. Larson, "Learning in U.S.-Soviet Relations: The Nixon-Kissinger Structures of Peace," in *Learning in U.S. and Soviet Foreign Policy*, ed. G. W. Breslauer and P. E. Tetlock (Boulder, CO: Westview Press, 1991).

24. S. D. Krasner, *International Regimes* (Ithaca, NY: Cornell University Press, 1983).

25. A. D. Morris, "Birmingham Confrontation Reconsidered: An Analysis of the Dynamics and Tactics of Mobilization," *American Sociological Review* 58 (October 1993): 621–36.

26. R. Fisher, "Fractionating Conflict," in *International Conflict and Behavioral Science*, ed. R. Fisher (New York: Basic Books, 1964).

27. M. Sherif, *In Common Predicament* (Boston: Houghton Mifflin, 1996).

28. L. Kriesberg, "Varieties of Mediating Activities and of Mediators," in *Resolving International Conflicts*, ed. J. Bercovitch (Boulder, CO: Lynne Rienner, 1995).

29. H. Saunders, *Politics Is about Relationship: A Blueprint for the Citizens' Century* (New York: Palgrave, 2005).

30. S. J. Stedman, Donald Rothchild, and Elizabeth M. Cousens, ed., *Ending Civil Wars: The Implementation of Peace Agreements* (Boulder, CO: Lynne Rienner, 2002); and H. Wiseman and A. M. Taylor, *From Rhodesia to Zimbabwe: The Politics of Transition* (New York: Pergamon, 1981).

31. V. Shlapentokh, "Attitudes and Behavior of Soviet Youth in the 1970's and 1980's," *Reseach in Political Sociology* 2 (1986): 199–224.

32. J. Kane-Berman, *South Africa's Silent Revolution* (Johannesburg: South African Institute of Race Relations, 1990).

33. W. B. Quandt, *Peace Process: American Diplomacy and the Arab-Israeli Conflict since 1967* (Washington DC: Brookings Institution Press / Berkeley: University of California Press, 2005).

34. E. Newman and O. Richmond, ed., *Challenges to Peacebuilding: Managing Spoilers during Conflict Resolution* (New York: United Nations University Press, 2006).

35. C. Davis and M. Feshback, *Rising Infant Mortality in the USSR in the 1970s* (Washington, DC: US Department of Commerce, Bureau of the Census, 1980).

36. S. Touval and I. W. Zartman, ed., *International Mediation in Theory and Practice* (Boulder, CO: Westview Press, 1985); and L. Kriesberg and S. J. Thorson, ed., *Timing the De-escalation of International Conflicts* (Syracuse, NY: Syracuse University Press, 1991).

37. C. R. Mitchell, "Asymmetry and Strategies of Regional Conflict Reduction," in *Cooperative Security: Reducing Third World Wars*, ed. I. W. Zartman and V. A. Kremenyuk (Syracuse, NY: Syracuse University Press, 1995); L. Kriesberg, "Changing Conflict Asymmetries Constructively," *Dynamics of Asymmetric Conflict* 2(1) (March 2009): 4–22.

38. Kane-Berman, *South Africa's Silent Revolution.*

39. B. Neuberger, "Nationalisms Compared: ANC, IRA, and PLO," in *The Elusive Search for Peace: South Africa and Northern Ireland*, ed. H. Giliome and J. Gagiano (Cape Town: Oxford University Press, 1990), 65.

40. L. Kriesberg, *International Conflict Resolution: The U.S.-USSR and Middle East Cases* (New Haven, CT: Yale University Press, 1992).

41. Quandt, *Peace Process*, 383–412.

42. Kriesberg and Thorson, *Timing the De-escalation*; and I. W. Zartman, *Ripe for Resolution: Conflict and Intervention in Africa* (New York: Oxford University Press, 1985).

43. L. Keashly and R. J. Fisher, "Complementarity and Coordination of Conflict Interventions: Taking a Contigency Perspective," in *Resolving International Conflicts*, ed. J. Bercovitch (Boulder, CO: Lynne Rienner, 1996).

44. L. Kriesberg, "Nature, Dynamics, and Phases of Intractability," in *Grasping the Nettle: Analyzing Cases of Intractable Conflicts*, ed. C. A. Crocker, Fen Osler Hampson, and Pamela Aall (Washington, DC: United States Institute of Peace, 2005).

45. M. S. Lund, *Preventing Violent Conflicts* (Washington, DC: United States Institute of Peace Press, 1996); and P. C. McMahon, *Taming Ethnic Hatred: Ethnic Cooperation and Transnational Networks in Eastern Europe* (Syracuse, NY: Syracuse University Press, 2007).

46. D. J. Reavis, *The Ashes of Waco: An Investigation* (New York: Simon & Schuster, 1995); J. Tabor and E. V. Gallagher, *Why Waco?* (Berkeley: University of California Press, 1995); J. S. Docherty, *Learning Lessons from Waco: When the Parties Bring Their Gods to the Negotiation Table* (Syracuse, NY: Syracuse University Press, 2001).

47. E. A. Azar, P. Jureidini, et al., "Protracted Social Conflict: Theory and Practice in the Middle East," *Journal of Palestine Studies* 29 (Autumn 1978): 41–60; L. Kriesberg,

T. A. Northrup, et al., ed., *Intractable Conflicts and Their Transformation* (Syracuse, NY: Syracuse University Press, 1989); C. A. Crocker, Fen Osler Hampson, and Pamela Aall, ed., *Grasping the Nettle: Analyzing Cases of Intractable Conflicts* (Washington, DC: United States Institute of Peace Press, 2005).

48. L. Kriesberg, "The Phases of Destructive Conflicts: Communal Conflicts and Proactive Solutions," in *Peace in the Midst of Wars: Preventing and Managing International Ethnic Conflicts*, ed. D. Carment and P. James (Columbia: University of South Carolina Press, 1998).

49. United Nations, *United Nations Peacekeeping*, Update, December 1994, 31; United Nations, *The United Nations and the Situation in the Former Yugoslavia* (New York: United Nations Dept. of Public Information, 1995); A. Ackermann, *Making Peace Prevail: Preventing Violent Conflict in Macedonia* (Syracuse, NY: Syracuse University Press, 2000).

50. D. N. Gibbs, *First Do No Harm: Humanitarian Intervention and the Destruction of Yugoslavia* (Nashville, TN: Vanderbilt University Press, 2009).

51. See, for instance, A. McConnell and L. Drennan, "Mission Impossible? Planning and Preparing for Crises," *Journal of Contingencies and Crisis Management* 14(2) (2006): 59–70.

52. M. Brecher, *Crises in World Politics* (Oxford: Pergamon, 1993), 84–85, 250–53.

53. N. Mandela, *Long Walk to Freedom* (Boston: Little, Brown., 1994), 530.

54. L. Kriesberg, "International Nongovernmental Organizations and Transnational Integration," *International Associations* 24(11) (1972): 520–25; M. J. Pentz and G. Slovo, "The Political Significance of Pugwash," in *Knowledge and Power in a Global Society*, ed. W. M. Evan (Beverly Hills, CA: Sage, 1981); G. I. Chufrin and H. H. Saunders, "A Public Peace Process," *Negotiation Journal* 9 (April 1993): 155–77; and J. Rotbalt, *Scientists in the Quest for Peace: A History of the Pugwash Conferences* (Cambridge, MA: MIT Press, 1972).

55. S. Feldman, ed., *Confidence Building and Verification: Prospects in the Middle East* (Jerusalem: The Jerusalem Post / Boulder, CO: Westview, 1994).

56. In December 1993, Kriesberg traveled with a group of the U.S. Interreligious Committee for Peace in the Middle East to Israel, Syria, Egypt, and Jordan. The group met with government officials, academics, and other persons, with varying opinions about the DOP. Nearly everyone spoke of the irreversibility of what had happened.

57. See D. Dayan and E. Katz, *Media Events: The Live Broadcasting of History* (Cambridge, MA: Harvard University Press, 1992).

58. G. Duffy and N. Frensley, "Community Conflict Processes: Mobilization in Northern Ireland," in *International Crisis and Domestic Politics*, ed. J. W. Lamare (New York: Praeger, 1991).

59. See *Report of the Truth and Reconciliation Commission*, vol. 2, chapter 7, available at: http://www.justice.gov.za/trc/report/finalreport/Volume%202.pdf. For an account of the NPC, see P. Gastrow, *Bargaining for Peace* (Washington, DC: United States Institute of Peace, 1995).

60. Unlike the South African case, neither side had a widely shared view either of the past or of a common future together. K. Aggestam, *Reframing and Resolving Conflict: Israeli-Palestinian Negotiations, 1988–1998* (Lund, Sweden: Lund University Press, 1999); and A. Jamal, "Palestinians in Israeli Peace Discourse," *Journal of Palestine Studies* 30(1) (2000): 36–51.

61. The withdrawal of Israeli occupation forces from Hebron, however, was delayed and remained as a matter of contention when the Likud came to power in 1996, under the leadership of Netanyahu. See L. Kriesberg, "Negotiating the Partition of Palestine and

Evolving Israeli-Palestinian Relations," *Brown Journal of World Affairs* 7 (Winter/Spring, 2000): 63–80.

62. Kriesberg visited Moscow in the spring of 1985. In conversations with several academicians, with and without ties to the Communist Party and the government, he was often told that more radical action would be forthcoming. Gorbachev was securing his base before undertaking the needed wide-ranging reforms.

63. In 1989, while some Americans doubted that real changes were happening in the Soviet Union, some proclaimed the West had defeated the Soviet Union. See "Bulletin: We Won!" *Wall Street Journal*, May 24, 1989, A14. For alternative explanations of the ending of the Cold War, see Kriesberg, *International Conflict Resolution*; and R. K. Herrmann and R. N. Lebow, *Ending the Cold War: Interpretations, Causation, and the Study of International Relations* (New York: Palgrave Macmillan, 2004).

64. A. Wanis-St. John, *Back Channel Negotiations: Secrecy in the Middle East Peace Process* (Syracuse, NY: Syracuse University Press, 2010).

65. At the time of the first meeting, Israel law banned contact with the PLO; the Israeli Knesset abrogated the law on January 19, 1993. A. Elon, "The Peacemakers," *New Yorker*, December 20, 1993, 77–85; and D. Makovsky, *Making Peace with the PLO: The Rabin Government's Road to the Oslo Accord* (Boulder, CO: Westview, 1996).

66. See C. E. Osgood, *An Alternative to War or Surrender* (Urbana: University of Illinois Press, 1962); A. Rapoport, "Escape from Paradox," *Scientific American* 217 (1967): 50–59; and R. Axelrod, *The Evolution of Cooperation* (New York: Basic Books, 1984).

67. A. Etzioni, "The Kennedy Experiment," *Western Political Quarterly* 20 (June 1967): 361–80.

68. Based on Arthur Schlesinger Jr. interview by Kriesberg, New York, October 9, 1978; and Ted Sorenson, interview by Kriesberg, New York, March 20, 1979. See also N. Cousins, *The Impossible Triumverate* (New York, W. W. Norton, 1972); L. Kriesberg, "Noncoercive Inducements in U.S.-Soviet Conflicts: Ending the Occupation of Austria and Nuclear Weapons Tests," *Journal of Political and Military Sociology* 9 (Spring 1981): 1–16.

69. J. S. Goldstein and J. R. Freeman, *Three-Way Street: Strategic Reciprocity in World Politics* (Chicago: University of Chicago Press, 1990).

70. H. van der Merwe, *Pursuing Justice and Peace in South Africa* (London: Routledge, 1989), 102; and H. W. van der Merwe, *Peacemaking in South Africa: A Life in Conflict Resolution* (Cape Town: Tafelberg, 2000). See also, D. Lieberfeld, "Evaluating the Contributions of Track-Two Diplomacy to Conflict Termination in South Africa, 1984–90," *Journal of Peace Research* 39 (2002): 355–72.

71. Mandela, *Long Walk to Freedom*, 246.

72. K. Schock, *Unarmed Insurrections: People Power Movements in Nondemocracies* (Minneapolis: University of Minnesota Press, 2001); S. Zunes, "The Role of Non-Violent Action in the Downfall of Apartheid," *Journal of Modern African Studies* 37(1) (March 1999): 137–169.

73. D. Peretz, *Intifada* (Boulder, CO: Westview, 1990).

74. Kriesberg, *International Conflict Resolution.*

75. International Crisis Group, *Dealing with Hamas*, ICG Middle East Report No. 21 (Brussels: International Crisis Group, January 26, 2004).

76. W. Kemfer, A. D. Lowenberg, et al., "Foreign Threats and Domestic Actions: Sanctions Against South Africa," in *Justice without Violence*, ed. P. Wehr, H. Burgess, and G. Burgess (Boulder, CO: Lynne Rienner, 1994).

77. J. Leatherman, *From Cold War to Democratic Peace* (Syracuse, NY: Syracuse University Press, 2003). On the role of neutral countries in reaching the agreement on control

of arms on the seabed, see B. Ramberg, *The Seabed Arms Control Negotiations* (Denver, CO: University of Denver, 1978).

78. William I. Zartman, "Ripeness: The Hurting Stalemate and Beyond," in *International Conflict Resolution after the Cold War*, ed. Paul C. Stern and Daniel Druckman (Washington, DC: National Academy Press, 2000).

CHAPTER 8

1. L. Kriesberg, "The Evolution of Conflict Resolution," in *Sage Handbook of Conflict Resolution*, ed. Jacob Bercovitch, V. Kremenyuk, and I. W. Zartman (London: Sage, 2009).

2. D. M. Kolb, *When Talk Works: Profiles of Mediator* (San Francisco: Jossey-Bass, 1994); C. W. Moore, *The Mediation Process: Practical Strategies for Resolving Conflict* (San Francisco: Jossey-Bass, 1996); J. Laue, "Intervenor Roles: A Review," *Crisis and Change* 3 (Fall 1973): 4–5; R. A. B. Bush and J. P. Folger, *The Promise of Mediation: The Transformative Approach to Conflict* (San Francisco: Jossey-Bass, 2005).

3. For a discussion of the difference among interest, rights, and power as processes by which conflict is resolved, see chapter 1 in W. Ury, J. Brett, et al., *Getting Disputes Resolved: Designing Systems to Cut the Costs of Conflict* (San Francisco: Jossey-Bass, 1988).

4. Moore, *The Mediation Process*.

5. J. Wilkenfeld, K. Yong, et al., "Mediating International Crises," *Journal of Conflict Resolution* 47(3) (2003): 279–301.

6. Laue, "Intervenor Roles."

7. See J. M. Greig and P. F. Diehl, "Softening Up: Making Conflicts More Amendable to Negotiation," in *International Mediation: New Approaches and Findings*, ed. J. Bercovitch and S. S. Gartner (New York: Routledge, 2009).

8. Arafat told Clinton that he was not ready for Camp David II. A. Hanieh, *The Camp David Papers* (Ramallah, Palestine: Al-Ayyam Newspaper, 2000), 1–98; D. Ross, *The Missing Peace: The Inside Story of the Fight for Middle East Peace* (New York: Farrar, Straus and Giroux, 2004); R. Malley, "Israel and the Arafat Question," *New York Review of Books*, October 7, 2004, 19–23.

9. A. Garcia, "Dispute Resolution without Disputing: How the Interactional Organization of Mediation Hearings Minimizes Argument," *American Sociological Review* 56 (1991): 818–35; B. Wedge, "A Psychiatric Model for Intercession in Intergroup Conflict," *Journal of Applied Behavioral Science* 7(6) (1971): 733–61.

10. J. Carter, *Keeping Faith* (New York: Bantam Books, 1982).

11. J. Z. Rubin and B. R. Brown, *The Social Psychology of Bargaining and Negotiation* (New York: Academic Press, 1975).

12. M. Golan, *The Secret Conversations of Henry Kissinger: Step-by-Step Diplomacy in the Middle East* (New York: Bantam, 1976).

13. M. Doyle and D. Straus, *How to Make Meetings Work* (New York: Playboy Press. 1976).

14. Brainstorming was used in developing the National Peace Accord in South Africa at the planning meeting on June 22, 1991.

15. Ways that one mediator does this are reported in J. Forester, "Lawrence Susskind: Activist Mediation," in *When Talk Works: Profiles of Mediator*, ed. D. M. Kolb (San Francisco: Jossey-Bass, 1994).

16. E. F. Babbitt and E. L. Lutz, eds., *Human Rights and Conflict Resolution in Context* (Syracuse, NY: Syracuse University Press, 2009).

17. This was done in the Israeli-Egyptian negotiations mediated by President Carter and his associates at Camp David. See R. Fisher, "Playing the Wrong Game?" in *Dynamics of Third Party Intervention: Kissinger in the Middle East*, ed. J. Z. Rubin (New York: Praeger, 1981); and R. Fisher, Elizabeth Kopelman, and Andrea Kupfer Schneider, *Beyond Machiavelli: Tools for Coping with Conflict* (New York: Penguin, 1994), 126–32.

18. This happened as ,994 efforts to restore Bertrand Aristide to the presidency of Haiti were coming to a climax. Following a period of UN-imposed sanctions and failed negotiations, a U.S. invasion force was dispatched to force the transfer of power from the Haitian military rulers. Former President Carter, Senator Sam Nunn, and former chairman of the joint Chiefs of Staff Colin Powell were sent to Haiti and arranged a nonviolent transfer of power. The Haitian military leadership, General Raoul Cedras, General Philippe Biamby, and Chief of Police Lieutenant Colonel Michel Francois went into exile. Robert J. Tata, "Haiti," Microsoft Encarta Online Encyclopedia.

19. M. Mattes and Burcu Savun, "Fostering Peace After Civil War: Commitment Problems and Agreement Design," *International Studies Quarterly* 53 (2009): 737–59.

20. For example, in Pennsylvania and upstate New York efforts to manage conflict over the extraction of natural gas from shale deep below the surface through a process known as fracking has focused on finding the appropriate compensation for landowners and communities where fracking is being proposed.

21. Carter, *Keeping Faith*, 392; see also E. F. Babbitt, "Jimmy Carter: The Power of Moral Suasion in International Mediation," in *When Talk Works: Profiles of Mediator*, ed. D. M. Kolb (San Francisco: Jossey-Bass, 1994).

22. P. J. Carnevale and S. Arad, "Bias and Impartiality in International Mediation," in *Resolving International Conflicts: The Theory and Practice of Mediation*, ed. J. Bercovitch (Boulder, CO: Lynne Rienner, 1996); B. S. Mayer, *Beyond Neutrality: Confronting the Crisis in Conflict Resolution* (San Francisco: Jossey-Bass, 2004).

23. S. R. Ratner, "Does International Law Matter in Preventing Ethnic Conflicts?" *New York University Journal of International Law and Politics* 32(3) (2000): 591–698; Babbitt and Lutz, *Human Rights and Conflict Resolution in Context*; E. F. Babbitt, *Principled Peace: Conflict Resolution and Human Rights in Intra-State Conflicts* (Ann Arbor: University of Michigan Press, forthcoming); and E. Kaufman and I. Bisharat, "Introducing Human Rights into Conflict Resolution: The Relevance for the Israeli-Palestinian Peace Process," *Journal of Human Rights* 1(1) (March 2002): 71–91.

24. L. Kriesberg, "Varieties of Mediating Activities and of Mediators," in *Resolving International Conflicts*, ed. J. Bercovitch (Boulder, CO: Lynne Rienner, 1995). Also see the discussion of an important kind of quasi mediator, the insider-partial mediator in P. Wehr and J. P. Lederach, "Mediating Conflict in Central America," *Journal of Peace Research* 28(1) (1991): 85–98.

25. W. B. Quandt, *Camp David* (Washington, DC: Brookings Institution, 1986); and Carter, *Keeping Faith*.

26. T. Princen, "Joseph Elder: Quiet Peacemaking," in *When Talk Works: Profiles of Mediator*, ed. D. M. Kolb (San Francisco: Jossey-Bass, 1994); and C. H. M. Yarrow, *Quaker Experiences in International Conciliation* (New Haven, CT: Yale University Press, 1978).

27. H. W. van der Merwe, *Peacemaking in South Africa: A Life in Conflict Resolution* (Cape Town: Tafelberg, 2000).

28. A. Strimling, *The Federal Mediation and Conciliation Service: A Partner in International Conflict Prevention* (unpublished report, February 27, 2002).

29. R. Fisher, *Interactive Conflict Resolution* (Syracuse, NY: Syracuse University Press, 1997). See also R. J. Fisher, *Paving the Way: Contributions of Interactive Conflict Resolution to Peacemaking* (Lanham, MD: Lexington Books, 2005).

30. H. C. Kelman, "Contributions of an Unofficial Conflict Resolution Effort to the Israeli-Palestinian Breakthrough," *Negotiation Journal* 11 (January 1995): 19–27; C. E. Cuhadar-Gurkaynak, *Evaluating Track Two Diplomacy in Pre-negotiation: A Comparative Assessment of Track Two Initiatives on Water and Jerusalem in the Israeli-Palestinian Conflict* (Syracuse, NY: Syracuse University Press, 2004).

31. J. V. Montville, "Transnationalism and the Role of Track-Two Diplomacy," in *Approaches to Peace: An Intellectual Map*, ed. W. S. Thompson and K. M. Jensen (Washington, DC: United States Institute of Peace, 1991).

32. See J. W. McDonald, "Further Explorations in Track Two Diplomacy," in *Timing the De-Escalation of International Conflicts*, ed. L. Kriesberg and S. J. Thorson (Syracuse, NY: Syracuse University Press, 1991); J. Davies and E. Kaufman, eds., *Second Track Diplomacy* (Lanham, MD: Rowman & Littlefield, 2002); and Fisher, *Paving the Way.*

33. W. M. Evan, ed., *Knowledge and Power in a Global Society* (Beverly Hills, CA: Sage, 1981); and L. Kriesberg, "International Nongovernmental Organizations and Transnational Integration," *International Associations* 24(11) (1972): 520–25.

34. Many such dialogue groups have been organized between Jews and Palestinians in Israel and elsewhere in the world, working with Jews and Palestinians in the Diaspora. For discussions about the theory and practice of such groups, see Fisher, *Interactive Conflict Resolution*, 121–41.

35. M. J. Pentz and G. Slovo, "The Political Significance of Pugwash," in *Knowledge and Power in a Global Society*, ed. W. M. Evan (Beverly Hills, CA: Sage, 1981); and J. Rotblat, *Scientists in the Quest for Peace: A History of the Pugwash Conferences* (Cambridge, MA: MIT Press, 1972). For current activities see http://www.Pugwash.org.

36. G. I. Chufrin and H. H. Saunders, "A Public Peace Process," *Negotiation Journal* 9 (April 1993): 155–77.

37. H. H. Saunders, "Sustained Dialogue on Tajikistan," *Mind and Human Interaction* 6 (August 1995): 123–35; N. N. Rouhana and H. C. Kelman, "Non-official Interaction Processes in the Resolution of International Conflicts: Promoting Joint Israeli-Palestinian Thinking through a Continuing Workshop," *Journal of Social Issues* 50(1) (1994): 157–78; and N. N. Rouhana, "The Dynamics of Joint Thinking between Adversaries in International Conflict: Phases of the Continuing Problem-Solving Workshop," *Political Psychology* 16(2) (1995): 321–45.

38. J. Leatherman, *From Cold War to Democratic Peace* (Syracuse, NY: Syracuse University Press, 2003).

39. L. Susskind and J. L. Cruikshank, *Breaking the Impasse: Consensual Approaches to Resolving Public Disputes* (New York: Basic Books, 1987); L. Susskind, *Dealing with an Angry Public: The Mutual Gains Approach to Resolving Disputes* (New York: Free Press, 1996); and J. Forester, *The Deliberative Practitioner: Encouraging Participatory Planning Processes* (Cambridge, MA: MIT Press, 1999).

40. For an analysis comparing the Two Forks dam and spotted owl conflicts, see B. W. Dayton, "Sources of Escalation in Natural Resource Conflicts: The Spotted Owl and the Two Forks Dam" (unpublished paper, 1994), Syracuse University; see also G. Bingham, *Resolving Environmental Disputes* (Washington, DC: The Conservation Foundation, 1990).

41. D. M. Kolb, *The Mediators* (Cambridge, MA: MIT Press, 1983).

42. A. H. Raskin, "The Newspaper Strike: A Step-by-Step Account," in *The 50% Solution*, ed. I. W. Zartman (New Haven, CT: Yale University Press, 1983).

43. Yarrow, *Quaker Experiences in International Conciliation.*

44. J. Holland, *Hope Against History* (New York: Henry Holt, 1999); and G. J. Mitchell, *Making Peace* (Berkeley: University of California Press, 2000).

45. P. J. Carnevale, "Mediating from Strength," in *Studies in International Mediation*, ed. J. Bercovitch (New York: Palgrave Macmillan, 2002).

46. D. N. Gibbs, *First Do No Harm: Humanitarian Intervention and the Destruction of Yugoslavia* (Nashville, TN: Vanderbilt University Press, 2009); R. Cohen, "Taming the Bullies of Bosnia," *New York Times Magazine*, December 17, 1995, 58–63, 76–78, 90, 95; R. C. Holbrooke, *To End a War* (New York: Random House, 1998).

47. Many analysts make similar distinctions; for example, Tom Princen, *Intermediaries in International Conflict* (Princeton, NJ: Princeton University Press, 1995), distinguishes between neutral mediators and principal mediators. For a discussion of transformative mediation, Bush and Folger, *The Promise of Mediation*.

48. P. H. Gulliver, *Disputes and Negotiations: A Cross-Cultural Perspective* (New York: Academic Press, 1979); J. P. Lederach, *Preparing for Peace: Conflict Transformation across Cultures* (Syracuse: Syracuse University Press, 1995); P. J. Carnevale, Y. S. Cha, et al., "Culture and the Mediation of Disputes," in *Culture and Negotiation: Integrative Approaches to Theory and Research*, ed. M. Gelfand and J. Brett (Palo Alto, CA: Stanford University Press, 2003); P. J. Carnevale, Y. S. Cha, et al., "Adaptive Third Parties in the Cultural Milieu," in *Handbook of Negotiation and Culture*, ed. M. Gelfand and J. Brett (Palo Alto, CA: Stanford University Press, 2004). For a general discussion of culture and conflict resolution, see K. Avruch, *Culture and Conflict Resolution* (Washington, DC: United States Institute of Peace, 1998).

49. J. A. Wall Jr. and R. R. Callister, "Ho'oponopono: Some Lessons From Hawaiian Mediation," *Negotiation Journal* 11 (January 1995): 45–54; and E. Shook, V. Kwan, et al., "Ho'oponopono: Straightening Family Relationships in Hawaii," in *Conflict Resolution: Cross-Cultural Perspectives*, ed. K. Avruch, P. Black, and J. Scimecca (New York: Greenwood Press, 1991). Also see P. Salem, ed., *Conflict Resolution in the Arab World: Selected Essays* (Beirut: American University of Beirut, 1997).

50. L. Keashly and R. J. Fisher, "Complementarity and Coordination of Conflict Interventions: Taking a Contingency Perspective," in *Resolving International Conflicts*, ed. J. Bercovitch (Boulder, CO: Lynne Rienner, 1996); C. Mitchell, "The Process and Stages of Mediation," in *Making War and Waging Peace: Foreign Intervention in Africa*, ed. D. R. Smock (Washington, DC: U.S. Institute of Peace, 1993); L. Kriesberg, *International Conflict Resolution: The U.S.-USSR and Middle East Cases* (New Haven, CT: Yale University Press, 1992); and P. J. Carnevale and D. Conlon, "Time Pressure and Strategic Choice in Mediation," *Organizational Behavior and Human Decision Processes* 42 (1988): 111–33.

51. L. Kriesberg, "Mediation and the Transformation of the Israeli-Palestinian Conflict," *Journal of Peace Research* 38(3) (2001): 373–92.

52. M. H. Ross, "Creating the Conditions for Peacemaking: Theories of Practice in Ethnic Conflict Resolution," *Ethnic and Racial Studies* 23(6) (2000): 1002–34; M. H. Ross and J. Rothman, *Theory and Practice in Ethnic Conflict and Management: Theorizing Success and Failure* (London: Macmillan, 1999); and T. P. d'Estree, Larissa A. Fast, Joshua N. Weiss, and Monica S. Jakobsen, "Changing the Debate about 'Success' in Conflict Resolution," *Negotiation Journal* 17(2) (2001): 101–13.

53. For a general discussion of the challenges of evaluating conflict resolution interventions, see E. C. Gurkaynak, B. Dayton, et al., "Evaluation in Conflict Resolution and Peacebuilding," in *Handbook of Conflict Analysis and Resolution*, ed. D. J. D. Sandole, S. Byrne, I. Sandole-Staroste, and J. Senehi (London: Routledge, 2009).

54. K. Kressel and D. G. Pruitt, "Conclusion: A Research Perspective on the Mediation of Social Conflict," in *Mediation Research*, ed. K. Kressel and D. G. Pruitt (San Francisco: Jossey-Bass. 1989).

55. K. Kressel and D. G. Pruitt, *Mediation Research* (San Francisco: Jossey-Bass, 1989); and T. Hedeen and P. G. Coy, "Community Mediation and the Court System: The Ties that Bind," *Mediation Quarterly* 17(4) (2000).

56. R. Butterworth, *Managing Interstate Conflict 1945–1974* (Pittsburgh, PA: University of Pittsburgh Press, 1976).

57. J. Bercovitch, "International Mediation: A Study of the Incidence, Strategies and Conditions of Successful Outcomes," *Cooperation and Conflict* 21 (1986): 155–68.

58. J. Bercovitch, "Mediation in the Most Resistant Cases," in *Grasping the Nettle: Analyzing Cases in Intractable Conflicts*, ed. C. A. Crocker, F. O. Hampson, and P. R. Aall (Washington, DC: United States Institute of Peace Press, 2005).

59. Kressel and Pruitt, *Mediation Research.*

60. P. Wolf, "International Social Structure and the Resolution of International Conflicts," in *Research in Social Movements, Conflicts and Change*, vol. 1, ed. L. Kriesberg (Greenwich, CT: JAI Press, 1978).

61. J. Bercovitch and J. Langley, "The Nature of the Dispute and the Effectiveness of International Mediation," *Journal of Conflict Resolution* 37(4) (1993): 670–91.

62. Rubin and Brown, *The Social Psychology of Bargaining and Negotiation.*

63. A. Douglas, *Industrial Peacemaking* (New York: Columbia University Press, 1962).

64. T. A. Kochan and T. Jick, "The Public Sector Mediation Process," *Journal of Conflict Resolution* 22 (June 1978): 210–40.

65. J. Pressman, "Visions in Collision: What Happened at Camp David and Taba?" *International Security* 28(2) (2003): 5–43; Malley, "Israel and the Arafat Question."

66. Rubin and Brown, *The Social Psychology of Bargaining and Negotiation.*

67. D. A. Brookmire and F. Sistrunk, "The Effects of Perceived Ability and Impartiality of Mediators and Time Pressure Negotiation," *Journal of Conflict Resolution* 24 (June 1980): 311–27.

68. Kressel and Pruitt, *Mediation Research*, 397. Such outcomes are not necessarily more just or fair.

69. R. E. Walton, "Interpersonal Confrontation and Third Party Functions: A Case Study," *Journal of Applied Behavioral Sciences* 4(3) (1968): 327–50.

70. Kressel and Pruitt, "Conclusion."

71. L. Kriesberg, "The Relevance of Reconciliation Actions in the Breakdown of Israeli-Palestinian Negotiations, 2000," *Peace & Change* 27(4) (2002): 546–71. On the importance of public engagement in a peace process, see H. H. Saunders, *A Public Peace Process: Sustained Dialogue to Transform Racial and Ethnic Conflicts* (New York: St. Martin's Press, 1999). For examples of public participation in different countries, see C. Barnes, *Accord, Owning the Process: Public Participation in Peacemaking* (London: Conciliation Resources, 2002), 13.

72. G. M. Khadiagla, "Implementing the Arusha Peace Agreement on Rwanda," in *Ending Civil Wars: The Implementation of Peace Agreements*, ed. J. Stephen, D. Rothchild, and E. M. Cousens (Boulder, CO: Lynne Rienner, 2002).

73. C. A. Crocker, Fen Osler Hampson, and Pamela Aall, ed., *Herding Cats: Multiparty Mediation in a Complex World* (Washington, DC: United States Institute of Peace Press, 1999); L. Kriesberg, "Coordinating Intermediary Peace Efforts," *Negotiation Journal* 12

(October 1996): 341–52; S. A. Nan and A. Strimling, "Coordination in Conflict Prevention, Conflict Resolution and Peacebuilding," *International Negotiation* 11(1) (2006): 1–6.

74. McDonald, "Further Explorations in Track Two Diplomacy"; Montville, "Transnationalism and the Role of Track-Two Diplomacy"; Chufrin and Saunders, "A Public Peace Process."

75. Kelman, "Contributions of an Unofficial Conflict Resolution Effort."

76. H. Ashrawi, *This Side of Peace* (New York: Simon & Schuster, 1995); and U. Savir, *The Process: 1,100 Days That Changed the Middle East* (New York: Random House, 1998).

77. A. Wanis-St.John, *Back Channel Negotiations: Secrecy in the Middle East Peace Process* (Syracuse, NY: Syracuse University Press, 2010).

78. C. Hume, *Ending Mozambique's War* (Washington, DC: United States Institute of Peace, 1994).

79. L. Diamond, *Squandered Victory* (New York: Henry Holt, 2005).

80. I. W. Zartman, *Ripe for Resolution: Conflict and Intervention in Africa* (New York: Oxford University Press, 1989); and I. W. Zartman, "Conflict Reduction: Prevention, Management, and Resolution," in *Conflict Resolution in Africa*, ed. F. M. Deng and I. W. Zartman (Washington, DC: Brookings Institute, 1991); and L. Kriesberg and S. J. Thorson, ed., *Timing the De-Escalation of International Conflicts* (Syracuse, NY: Syracuse University Press, 1991).

81. M. S. Lund, *Preventing Violent Conflicts* (Washington, DC: United States Institute of Peace Press, 1996); S. Touval and I. W. Zartman, ed., *International Mediation in Theory and Practice* (Boulder, CO: Westview Press, 1985); E. Boulding, ed., *Building Peace in the Middle East* (Boulder, CO: Lynne Rienner, 1994); Carnegie Commission on Preventing Deadly Conflict, *Final Report* (New York: Carnegie Corporation, 1997); Kriesberg, "Coordinating Intermediary Peace Efforts."

82. Hume, *Ending Mozambique's War*.

83. D. E. Spencer and H. Yang, "Lessons from the Field of Intra-National Conflict Resolution," *Notre Dame Law Review* 67(5) (1992): 1495–1517; D. Brinkley, "Jimmy Carter's Modest Quest for Global Peace," *Foreign Affairs* 74 (November/December 1995): 90–100. International Alert, based in London, was established in 1985 by human rights advocates and others working in international development agencies and responding to ethnic conflict. See: http://www.international-alert.org.

84. Zartman, "Conflict Reduction."

85. Keashly and Fisher, "Complementarity and Coordination of Conflict Interventions"; and J. G. Stein, ed., *Getting to the Table: The Process of International Prenegotiation* (Baltimore: Johns Hopkins University Press, 1989).

86. Kressel and Pruitt, *Mediation Research*; J. Bercovitch and O. Elgstrom, "Culture and International Mediation: Exploring Theoretical and Empirical Linkages," *International Negotiation Journal* 6 (2001): 3–23.

87. C. R. Mitchell, "Asymmetry and Strategies of Regional Conflict Reduction," in *Cooperative Security: Reducing Third World Wars*, ed. I. W. Zartman and V. A. Kremenyuk (Syracuse, NY: Syracuse University Press, 1995); Babbitt and Lutz, *Human Rights and Conflict Resolution in Context*.

88. C. A. Crocker, Fen Osler Hampson, and Pamela Aall, eds., *Grasping the Nettle: Analyzing Cases of Intractable Conflicts* (Washington, DC: United States Institute of Peace Press, 2005).

89. J. Galtung, Carl G. Jacobsen, and Kai Frithjof Brand-Jacobsen, *Searching for Peace: The Road to TRANSCEND*, 2nd ed. (London: Pluto, 2002).

CHAPTER 9

1. R. E. Walton and R. B. McKersie, *A Behavioral Theory of Labor Negotiations* (New York: McGraw-Hill, 1965); and M. Deutsch, *The Resolution of Conflict: Constructive and Destructive Processes* (New Haven, CT: Yale University Press, 1973).

2. Walton and McKersie, *A Behavioral Theory of Labor Negotiations*, 132.

3. See reports on the outcomes of revolutions in J. A. Goldstone, ed., *Revolutions: Theoretical, Comparative, and Historical Studies* (San Diego, CA: Harcourt Brace Jovanovich, 1986).

4. H. Raiffa, *The Art and Science of Negotiation* (Cambridge, MA: Harvard University Press, 1982).

5. R. Fisher, William Ury, and Bruce Patton, *Getting to Yes: Negotiating Agreement Without Giving In*, 2nd ed. (New York: Penguin, 1991).

6. D. Mauzy, "Malaysia: Malay Political Hegemony and 'Coercive Consociationalism,'" in *The Politics of Ethnic Conflict*, ed. J. McGarry and B. O'Leary (London: Routledge, 1993).

7. H. H. Saunders, *A Public Peace Process: Sustained Dialogue to Transform Racial and Ethnic Conflicts* (New York: St. Martin's, 1999).

8. This discussion is beholden to many commentators on this subject, including J. Rawls, *A Theory of Justice* (Cambridge, MA: Harvard University Press, 1971); and J. Burton, *Conflict: Resolution and Prevention* (New York: St. Martin's, 1990).

9. P. R. Pillar, *Negotiating Peace: War Termination as a Bargaining Process* (Princeton, NJ: Princeton University Press, 1983).

10. D. Remnick, *Lenin's Tomb: The Last Days of the Soviet Empire* (New York: Random House, 1993). For an analysis of public opinion in the Soviet Union in the period of transformation, see N. Popov, *The Russian People Speak: Democracy at the Crossroads* (Syracuse, NY: Syracuse University Press, 1995).

11. I. W. Zartman, *Elusive Peace: Negotiating an End to Civil Wars* (Washington, DC: Brookings Institution, 1995).

12. J. Kreutz, "How and When Armed Conflicts End: Introducing the UCDP Conflict Termination Dataset," *Journal of Peace Research* 47(2) (2010): 243–50. Armed conflicts include wars, which are conflicts with one thousand or more battle-related deaths, and other conflicts with 25–999 battle-related deaths.

13. B. Czech and P. R. Krausman, *The Endangered Species Act: History, Conservation, Biology, and Public Policy* (Baltimore: Johns Hopkins University Press, 2001).

14. For a discussion of the relationship between the settlement terms reached through accommodation and those reached through other means, see C. Hartzell and M. Hoddie, "Institutionalizing Peace: Power Sharing and Post-Civil War Conflict Management," *American Journal of Political Science* 47(2) (2003): 318–32.

15. R. J. Lewicki, David M. Saunders, and John W. Minton, *Negotiation* (New York: McGraw-Hill, 1999); P. J. Carnevale, *Negotiation in Social Conflict* (Buckingham, UK: Open University, 2004).

16. P. H. Gulliver, *Disputes and Negotiations: A Cross-Cultural Perspective* (New York: Academic Press, 1979).

17. For an analysis of informal negotiations in many spheres of social life, see A. Strauss, *Negotiations: Varieties, Contexts, Processes, and Social Order* (San Francisco: Jossey-Bass, 1978). Reviews and analyses of formal negotiations include P. T. Hopmann, *The Negotiation Process and the Resolution of International Conflicts* (Columbia: Uni-

versity of South Carolina Press, 1996); Raiffa, *The Art and Science of Negotiation*; and T. C. Schelling, *The Strategy of Conflict* (Cambridge, MA: Harvard University Press, 1960). For an excellent collection of essays on negotiation in conflict management, see I. W. Zartman, *Negotiations and Conflict Management: Essays on Theory and Practice* (New York: Routledge, 2008).

18. Schelling, *The Strategy of Conflict.*

19. See P. E. Mosley, "Some Soviet Techniques of Negotiation," in *Negotiating with the Russians*, ed. R. Dennett and J. E. Johnson (Boston: World Peace Foundation, 1951), 288.

20. Some of these matters are examined, using data from India, China, Greece, Korea, the Netherlands, United States, and elsewhere, in Harry C. Triandis, Peter Carnevale, Michele Gelfand, Christopher Robert, S. Arzu Wasti, Tahira Probst, Emiko S. Kashima, Thalia Dragonas, Darius Chan, Xiao Ping Chen, Uichol Kim, Carsten de Dreu, Evert van de Vliert, Sumiko Iwao, Ken-Ichi Ohbuchi, and P. Schmitz, "Culture and Deception in Business Negotiations: A Multi-Level Analysis," *International Journal of Cross Cultural Management* 1(1) (2001): 73–90.

21. L. Kriesberg, "Contemporary Conflict Resolution Applications," in *Leashing the Dogs of War: Conflict Management in a Divided World*, ed. C. A. Crocker, Fen Osler Hampson, and Pamela Aall (Washington, DC: United States Institute of Peace Press, 2007); and Hopmann, *The Negotiation Process.*

22. R. Fisher and W. Ury, *Getting to Yes* (Boston: Houghton Miflin Company, 1981).

23. I. W. Zartman and M. Berman, *The Practical Negotiator* (New Haven, CT: Yale University Press, 1982).

24. Zartman and Berman, *The Practical Negotiator*, 66.

25. Hopmann, *The Negotiation Process*, 80; and J. K. Sebenius, *Negotiating the Law of the Sea* (Cambridge, MA: Harvard University Press, 1984).

26. L. Kriesberg, *International Conflict Resolution: The U.S.-USSR and Middle East Cases* (New Haven, CT: Yale University Press, 1992).

27. C. Mitchell, *Gestures of Conciliation: Factors Contributing to Successful Olive Branches* (New York: St. Martin's, 2000).

28. R. Fisher, "Fractionating Conflict," in *International Conflict and Behavioral Science*, ed. R. Fisher (New York: Basic Books, 1964).

29. Trade-offs in the context of complex environmental problems has been the subject of a large-scale MacArthur Foundation project called "Advancing Conservation in a Social Context: Working in a World of Trade-offs." See www.tradeoffs.org. Also see "Bulletin: We Won! Review and Outlook," *Wall Street Journal*, May 24, 1989, A14; P. D. Hirsch, W. M. Adams, et al., "Acknowledging Conservation Trade-offs and Embracing Complexity," *Conservation Biology* 25 (2011): 259–64.

30. This is the basic premise of exchange theory. P. M. Blau, *Exchange and Power in Social Life* (New York: Wiley, 1964). For applications to negotiations, see Raiffa, *The Art and Science of Negotiation.*

31. I. W. Zartman and V. Kremenyuk, eds., *Peace versus Justice: Negotiating Forward-and Backward-Looking Outcomes* (Lanham, MD: Rowman & Littlefield, 2005).

32. J. P. Manno, "Advocacy and Diplomacy: NGOs and the Great Lakes Water Quality Agreement," in *Environmental NGOs in World Politics*, ed. T. Princen and M. Finger (London: Routlege, 1994).

33. L. Nader, "Harmony Models and the Construction of Law," in *Conflict Resolution: Cross-Cultural Perspectives*, ed. K. Avruch, P. W. Black and J. A. Scimecca (New York: Greenwood Press, 1991).

34. J. Galtung, Carl G. Jacobsen, and Kai Frithjof Brand-Jacobsen, *Searching for Peace: The Road to TRANSCEND*, 2nd ed. (London: Pluto, 2002).

35. Fisher and Ury, *Getting to Yes*.

36. R. N. Haass, "Ripeness, De-Escalation, and Arms Control: The Case of the INF," in *Timing the De-Escalation of International Conflicts*, ed. L. Kriesberg and S. J. Thorson (Syracuse, NY: Syracuse University Press, 1991).

37. L. Kriesberg, "Introduction: Timing Conditions, Strategies, and Errors," in *Timing the De-Escalation of International Conflicts*, ed. L. Kriesberg and S. J. Thorson (Syracuse, NY: Syracuse University Press, 1991).

38. For a discussion of the hurting stalemate and a settlement formula, see S. Touval and I. W. Zartman, ed., *International Mediation in Theory and Practice* (Boulder, CO: Westview Press, 1985).

39. "Transboundary Rivers and Crisis Prevention," at www.bicc.de/water/rivers.php.

40. C. Sneddon and C. Fox, (2007), "Power, Development, and Institutional Change: Participatory Governance in the Lower Mekong Basin," *World Development* 35(12): 2161–81.

41. See L. Kriesberg, "On Advancing Truth and Morality in Conflict Resolution," *Peace and Conflict Studies* 6(1) (1999): 7–19.

42. S. Talbott, *Deadly Gambits* (New York: Knopf, 1984).

43. A. Myrdal, *The Game of Disarmament: How the United States and Russia Run the Arms Race* (New York: Pantheon, 1982).

44. J. Forester, "Lawrence Susskind: Activist Mediation," in *When Talk Works: Profiles of Mediator*, ed. D. M. Kolb (San Francisco: Jossey-Bass, 1994).

45. R. Cohen, *Negotiating across Cultures* (Washington, DC, U.S. Institute of Peace Press, 1997); E. T. Hall, *The Silent Language* (New York: Doubleday, 1959).

46. H. Binnendijk, ed., *National Negotiating Styles* (Washington, DC: U.S. Government Printing Office, Department of State Publication, 1987).

47. M. Provine, *Settlement Strategies for Federal District Judges* (Washington, DC: The Federal Judicial Center, 1986).

48. J. Lynch, "Beyond ADR: A Systems Approach to Conflict Management," *Negotiation Journal* 17(3) (2001): 207–16.

49. R. O'Leary and L. Bingham, *The Collaborative Public Manager: New Ideas for the Twenty-First Century* (Washington, DC: Georgetown University Press, 2009).

50. J. Lofland, *Polite Protestors: The American Peace Movement of the 1980s* (Syracuse, NY: Syracuse University Press, 1993).

51. Sebenius, *Negotiating the Law of the Sea*.

52. J. Leatherman, *From Cold War to Democratic Peace* (Syracuse, NY: Syracuse University Press, 2003).

53. See H. Kissinger, *White House Years* (Boston: Little, Brown, 1979); see also G. Smith, *Double Talk: The Story of the First Strategic Arms Limitation Talks* (New York: Doubleday, 1960); and J. Newhouse, *Cold Dawn: The Story of SALT* (New York: Holt, Rinehart and Winston, 1973).

54. A. Wanis-St.John, *Back Channel Negotiations: Secrecy in the Middle East Peace Process* (Syracuse, NY: Syracuse University Press, 2010).

55. The Rhodesian Prime Minister Ian Smith led the opposition to black political participation in the 1960s. His son Alec describes the regular meetings of white and black Christian leaders, which became known as the Cabinet of Conscience. It began to meet in 1975 and continued until Zimbabwe achieved independence in 1980. Alec Smith and

Arthur Kanodereka, a black resistance leader, traveled together and organized meetings attracting blacks and whites. A. Smith, *Now I Call Him Brother* (Basingstoke, UK: Marsalls Paperbacks, 1984); and A. Griffith, *Conflict and Resolution: Peace-Building through the Ballot Box in Zimbabwe, Namibia and Cambodia* (Oxford: New Cherwell Press, 1998). For the Rhodesian transformation, see H. Wiseman and A. M. Taylor, *From Rhodesia to Zimbabwe: The Politics of Transition* (New York: Pergamon, 1981).

56. During and after World War I, secret diplomacy was widely viewed as bearing major responsibility for the war. President Woodrow Wilson, in the Fourteen Points, proclaimed the goal of "open covenants of peace, openly arrived at, after which there shall be no private understandings of any kind, but diplomacy shall proceed always frankly and in the public view." H. J. Morgenthau, *Politics among Nations* (New York: Alfred A. Knopf, 1950).

57. See J. Z. Rubin and B. R. Brown, *The Social Psychology of Bargaining and Negotiation* (New York: Academic Press, 1975).

58. Y. Beilin, *Touching Peace: From the Oslo Accord to a Final Agreement* (London: Weidenfeld & Nicolson, 1999); and U. Savir, *The Process: 1,100 Days That Changed the Middle East* (New York: Random House, 1998).

59. L. Kriesberg, *International Conflict Resolution*; C. R. Mitchell, *A Willingness to Talk* (Fairfax, VA: George Mason University, Center for Conflict Analysis and Resolution, 1990); C. R. Mitchell, "Ending Conflicts and Wars: Judgement, Rationality and Entrapment," *International Social Science Journal* 127 (February 1991): 35–55; and Louis Kriesberg and Susan French, "Reactions to Soviet Initiatives" (paper presented at the annual meeting of the International Studies Association, London, March 1989).

60. M. Dayan, *Breakthrough* (New York: Alfred A. Knopf, 1981), 38–54; also Don Patir, interview by author, Washington, DC, June 17, 1982.

61. Kriesberg, *International Conflict Resolution.*

62. R. Fisher, "Negotiating Inside Out: What Are the Best Ways to Relate Internal Negotiations with External Ones," *Negotiation Journal* 5 (January 1989): 33–41.

63. Cohen, *Negotiating across Cultures.*

64. Huthwaite Research Group and Huthwaite, Inc., *The Behavior of Successful Negotiators* (Reston, VA: Huthwaite Research Group and Huthwaite Inc., 1982).

CHAPTER 10

1. J. D. Hunter, *Culture Wars* (New York: Basic Books, 1991).

2. C. Kaufmann, "When All Else Fails," *International Security* 23(2) (Fall 1998): 120–56.

3. N. Sambanis, "Partition as a Solution to Ethnic War," *World Politics* 52(4) (2000): 437–83.

4. M. Mattes and B. Savun, "Fostering Peace after Civil War: Commitment Problems and Agreement Design," *International Studies Quarterly* 53 (2009): 737–59.

5. Y. Beilin, *Touching Peace: From the Oslo Accord to a Final Agreement* (London: Weidenfeld & Nicolson, 1999).

6. G. Duffy and N. Frensley, "Community Conflict Processes: Mobilization in Northern Ireland," in *International Crisis and Domestic Politics*, ed. J. W. Lamare (New York: Praeger, 1991); M. Hoddie and C. Hartzell, "Signals of Reconciliation: Institution-Building and the Resolution of Civil Wars," *International Studies Review* 7(1) (2005): 21–40.

7. S. J. Stedman, Donald Rothchild, and Elizabeth M. Cousens, ed., *Ending Civil Wars: The Implementation of Peace Agreements* (Boulder, CO: Lynne Rienner, 2002).

8. E. B. Haas, *The Uniting of Europe* (Stanford, CA: Stanford University Press, 1958).

9. D. Mitrany, *A Working Peace System* (Oxford: Oxford University Press, 1944).

10. SALT I refers to the first Strategic Arms Limitation Treaty. SALT II refers to the talks resulting in the treaty signed in 1979 on the limitation of strategic offensive arms. Article 17 of SALT II provides for the continuing role of the Standing Consultative Commission. S. Talbott, *Endgame: The Inside Story of SALT II* (New York: Harper & Row, 1979).

11. A. Hanieh, *The Camp David Papers* (Ramallah, Palestine: Al-Ayyam Newspaper, 2000), 1–98.

12. M. Covell, "Belgium: The Variability of Ethnic Relations," in *The Politics of Ethnic Conflict Regulation*, ed. J. McGarry and B. O'Leary (London: Routledge, 1993).

13. L. Kriesberg, "Nature, Dynamics, and Phases of Intractability," in *Grasping the Nettle: Analyzing Cases of Intractable Conflicts*, ed. C. A. Crocker, Fen Osler Hampson, and Pamela Aall (Washington, DC: United States Institute of Peace, 2005).

14. For a discussion of the history of civil war, international intervention, and the possibilities of peace building in Somalia, see A. A. Elmi, *Understanding the Somalia Conflagration: Identity, Islam and Peacebuilding* (London: Pluto Press, 2010).

15. See Rebecca Pels, "The Pressures of PATCO: Strikes and Stress in the 1980s," at extext.lib.Virginia.edu/journals/EH/EH37/Pels.html.

16. See L. A. Coser, *The Functions of Social Conflict* (New York: Free Press, 1956), 95, 38; see also W. G. Sumner, *Folkways* (Lexington, MA: Ginn, 1906); and G. Simmel, *Conflict and the Web of Intergroup Affiliations* (New York: Free Press, 1955).

17. F. Solomon, "Civil Rights Activity and Reduction in Crime among Negroes," *Archives of General Psychiatry* 12 (March 1965): 227–36.

18. P. T. Hopmann, "International Conflict and Cohesion in the Communist System," *International Studies Quarterly* 11 (September 1967): 212–36; and O. R. Holsti, "External Conflict and Internal Cohesion: The Sino-Soviet Case," in *Communist Party-States*, ed. J. Triska (Indianapolis, IN: Bobbs-Merrill, 1969).

19. While living in Germany in the summer of 1950 and the academic year 1956–1957, Kriesberg heard many Germans express abhorrence at what the Nazis had done and bewilderment at their enthusiasm for Nazism. However, others denied awareness of the Holocaust at the time, and some even denied that it had happened on the scale revealed.

20. M. O'Connor, "Serbs in Bosnia See No Peace for Their Dead . . . and Are Angry at Leaders and Themselves," *New York Times*, January 18, 1996, A6.

21. The health of the British working class, however, improved during the war. See J. Winter, "The Impact of the First World War on Civilian Health in Britian," *Economic History Review* 30 (August 1977): 487–507.

22. Included in the total are 1,000,000 pending asylum seekers and 4,800,000 refugees under the UNRWA mandate (which covers Palestinian refugees and their descendants). UNHCR, *Asylum Levels and Trends in Industrialized Countries 2010* (Geneva, Switzerland, UNHCR, 2011).

23. See S. Andrzejewski, *Military Organization and Society* (London: Routledge and Kegan Paul, 1954); P. Cutright, "Inequality: A Cross-National Analysis," *American Sociological Review* 32 (August 1954): 562–78; M. A. Garnier and L. Hazelrigg, "Military Organization and Distributional Inequality: An Examination of Andreski's Thesis," *Journal of Political and Military Sociology* 5 (Spring 1977): 17–33; and E. Weede, "Military Participation, Economic Growth and Income Equality," in *Defense, Welfare and Growth*, ed. S. Chan and A. Mintz (London: Routledge, 1992).

24. E. Weede, "The Impact of Interstate Conflict on Revolutionary Change and Individual Freedom," *Kyklos* 46(4) (1993): 473–95.

25. Miroslav Nincic, "Capital Labor and the Spoils of War," *Journal of Peace Research* 17(2): 103–17.

26. L. Kriesberg, *Social Inequality* (Englewood Cliffs, NJ: Prentice-Hall, 1979), 58–65.

27. M. Stohl, *War and Domestic Political Violence: The American Capacity for Repression and Reaction* (Beverly Hills, CA: Sage, 1976).

28. J. M. Winter, "Britian's Lost Generation of the World War," *Population* 31 (November 1977): 487–66.

29. D. K. Phillips, "The Case for Veteran Preferences," in *Strangers at Home: Vietnam Veterans since the War*, ed. C. R. Figley and S. Leventman (New York: Praeger, 1980), 348. Charles Moskos notes different bases for calculating the relative death rate in combat of African Americans, yielding different implications. Charles Moskos, letter to author, November 1996. Indeed, in military operations since Vietnam (1975–1995) blacks comprised 15 percent of those killed in action, while they averaged 19 percent of active duty military personnel during that same period. See Charles Moskos and John Sibley Butler, "Overcoming Race: Army Lessons for American Society" (paper presented at the symposium honoring Robin M. Williams Jr., Ithaca, NY, October 1996).

30. Halvor Mehlum, Karl Ove Moene, and Ragner Torvik, "Plunder and Protection, Inc.," *Journal of Peace Research* 39 (July 2002): 447–59.

31. Vally Koubi, "War and Economic Performance," *Journal of Peace Research* 42 (January 2005) 67–82.

32. S. Melman, *The Permanent War Economy: American Capitalism in Decline* (New York: Simon & Schuster, 1974); R. W. DeGrasse Jr., *Military Expansion Economic Decline* (Amonk, NY: M. E. Sharpe, 1983); R. N. Lebow and J. G. Stein, *We All Lost the Cold War* (Princeton, NJ: Princeton University Press, 1994).

33. Alicia Claire Singer Swords, "The Power of Networks: Popular Political Education among Neo-Aapatista Organizations in Chiapas, Mexico" (PhD dissertation, Cornell University, 2005).

34. Larry Dunn notes that this sometimes occurs in labor-management negotiations "where the rank and file accuses the leadership of caving in or selling out and they are left with two choices: not supporting a contract or blindly supporting it without understanding how that's the best they can get." Larry Dunn, email to Kriesberg, April 1997.

35. M. Oppenheimer, *The Urban Guerrilla* (New York: Quadrangle/The New York Times, 1969), 71.

36. S. Weir, "U.S.A.: The Labor Revolt," in *American Society, Inc.*, ed. M. Zeitlin (Chicago: Markham, 1970).

37. See the characterizations of the great subversive power of Jews articulated in Adolf Hitler's 1924 book, *Mein Kampf* (New York: Reynal and Hitchock, 1941).

38. L. Kriesberg, "Transforming Conflicts in the Middle East and Central Europe," in *Intractable Conflicts and Their Transformation*, ed. L. Kriesberg, T. A. Northrup, and S. J. Thorson (Syracuse, NY: Syracuse University Press, 1989).

39. B. A. Dobratz and S. L. Shanks-Meile, *"White Power, White Pride!" The White Separatist Movement in the United States* (New York: Twayne, 1997); see also D. H. Bennett, *The Party of Fear: From Nativist Movements to the New Right in American History* (New York: Vintage, 1995); and M. Barkun, *Religion and the Racist Right: The Origins of the Christian Identity Movement* (Chapel Hill: University of North Carolina Press, 1994).

40. E. C. Budd, "An Introduction to a Current Issue of Public Policy," in *Inequality and Poverty*, ed. E. C. Budd (New York: W. W. Norton, 1967).

41. N. A. Femenia, *National Identity in Times of Crises: The Scripts of the Falklands-Malvina War* (New York: Nova Science, 1996).

42. M. Danner, "Taking Stock of the Forever War," *New York Times Magazine*, September 11, 2005, 45–53, 68, 86, 87; and L. Diamond, *Squandered Victory* (New York: Henry Holt, 2005).

43. Stohl, *War and Domestic Political Violence.*

44. For example, see R. J. Rummel, "The Dimensions of Conflict Behavior within and between Nations," *General Systems Yearbook* 8 (1963): 1–50; and R. Tanter, "Dimensions of Conflict Behavior within and between Nations, 1958–1960," *Journal of Conflict Resolution* 10 (March 1966): 41–64. For a review and interpretation of the studies, see Michael Stohl, "The Nexus of Civil and International Conflict," in *Handbook of Political Conflict*, ed. Ted Robert Gurr (New York: Free Press, 1980).

45. J. Wilkenfeld, "Some Further Findings Regarding the Domestic and Foreign Conflict Behavior of Nations," *Journal of Peace Research* 2 (1969): 147–56; and J. Wilkenfeld and D. A. Zinnes, "A Linkage Model of Domestic Conflict Behavior," in *Conflict Behavior and Linkage Politics*, ed. J. Wilkenfeld (New York: D. McKay, 1973).

46. J. E. Mueller, *War, Presidents and Public Opinion* (New York: Wiley, 1973).

47. S. Borker, L. Kriesberg, et al., "Conciliation, Confrontation, and Approval of the President," *Peace and Change* 11 (Spring 1985): 31–48.

48. Weede, "The Impact of Interstate Conflict."

49. S. Schmeidl, "Exploring the Causes of Forced Migration: A Pooled Time-Series Analysis, 1971–1990," *Social Science Quarterly* 78 (June 1997): 284–308; see also UN High Commissioner for Refugees, at www.unhcr.ch.

50. M. A. Dugan, *The Relationship between Pre-Independence Internal Violence and Nonviolence and Post-Independence Violence, External Belligerency, and Internal Governmental Repressiveness* (Syracuse, NY: Syracuse University, 1979).

51. T. Frank, *What's the Matter with Kansas?* (New York: Henry Holt, 2004).

52. J. M. Fendrich and E. S. Krauss, "Student Activism and Adult Left-wing Politics: A Causal Model of Political Socialization for Black, White, and Japanese Students of the 1960s Generation," in *Research in Social Movements, Conflicts, and Change*, vol. 1, ed. L. Kriesberg (Greenwich, CT: JAI Press, 1978); and B. Park, *Motivational Dynamics of Student Movement Participation in Contemporary South Korea* (Syracuse, NY: Syracuse University, 1995).

53. K. Mannheim, "The Sociological Problem of Generations," in *Essays on the Sociology of Knowledge*, ed. P. Kecskemeti (New York: Oxford University Press, 1952); and R. Braungart and M. M. Braungart, ed., *Life Course and Generational Politics* (Lanham, MD: University Press of America, 1993).

54. J. C. Leggett, *Class, Race, and Labor* (New York: Oxford University Press, 1968), 90–91.

55. N. E. Cutler, "Generational Success as a Source of Foreign Policy Attitudes," *Journal of Peace Research* 7(1) (1970): 33–47; and V. Jeffries, "Political Generations and the Acceptance or Rejection of Nuclear Warfare," *Journal of Social Issues* (30) (1974): 119–36.

56. L. Kriesberg and R. A. Klein, "Changes in Public Support for U.S. Military Spending," *Journal of Conflict Resolution* 24 (March 1980): 79–111.

57. J. A. Goldstone, ed., *Revolutions: Theoretical, Comparative, and Historical Studies* (San Diego: Harcourt Brace Jovanovich, 1986).

58. T. Skocpol, *States and Social Revolutions: A Comparative Analysis of France, Russia, and China* (Cambridge: Cambridge University Press, 1979), 176.

59. S. Eckstein, "The Impact of Revolution on Social Welfare in Latin America," in *Revolutions: Theoretical, Comparative, and Historical Studies*, ed. J. A. Goldston (San Diego: Harcourt Brace Jovanovich, 1986); see also M. S. Lewis-Beck, "Some Effects of Revolution: Models, Measurement, and the Cuban Evidence," *American Journal of Sociology* 84 (March 1979): 1127–49.

60. L. A. Coser, *Continuities in the Study of Social Conflict* (New York: Free Press, 1967); S. Melman, *Dynamic Factors in Industrial Productivity* (Oxford: Blackwell, 1956); and R. Levine and J. A. Gewschwender, "Class Struggle, State Policy, and the Rationalization of Production: The Organization of Agriculture in Hawaii," in *Research in Social Movements, Conflicts and Change*, vol. 4, ed. L. Kriesberg (Greenwich, CT: JAI Press, 1981).

61. Wilkenfeld, "Some Further Findings."

62. S. Brock Blomberg and G. D. Hess, "The Temporal Links between Conflict and Economic Activity," *Journal of Conflict Resolution* 46(1) (2002): 74–90; G. Junne and W. Verkoren, ed., *Postconflict Development: Meeting New Challenges* (Boulder, CO: Lynne Rienner, 2004).

63. Human Security Report Project *The Shrinking Costs of War* (Vancouver, Canada: Simon Fraser University, 2009).

64. R. Paris, *At War's End: Building Peace after Civil Conflict* (Cambridge: Cambridge University Press, 2004); R. Licklider, "Obstacles to Peace Settlements," in *Turbulent Peace*, ed. Fen Osler Hampson, Chester H. Crocker, and Pamela Aall (Washington, DC: United States Institute of Peace Press, 2001); W. J. Henisz, B. A. Zelner, et al., "The Worldwide Diffusion of Market-Oriented Infrastructure Reform, 1977–1999," *American Sociological Review* 70(6) (2005): 871–97; and T. Lyons, *Demilitarizing Politics: Elections on the Uncertain Road to Peace* (Boulder, CO: Lynne Rienner, 2005).

65. L. Kriesberg, "Challenges in Peacemaking: External Interventions," in *Peacemaking: A Comprehensive Theory and Practice Reference*, ed. A. Bartoli, S. A. Nan, and Z. Mampilly (Santa Barbara, CA: Praeger, 2011).

66. Y. Bar-Siman-Tov, ed., *From Conflict Resolution to Reconciliation* (Oxford: Oxford University Press, 2003); B. Pouligny, Simon Chesterman, and Albrecht Schnabel, ed., *After Mass Crime: Rebuilding States and Communities* (Tokyo: United Nations University Press, 2007).

67. J. P. Lederach, *Building Peace: Sustainable Reconciliation in Divided Societies* (Washington, DC: United States Institute of Peace Press, 1997); G. Millar, "Assessing Local Experience of Truth-Telling in Sierra Leone: Getting to 'Why' through a Qualitative Case Study Analysis," *The International Journal of Transitional Justice* 4: 477–96.

68. See N. J. Kritz, "Germany (After Nazism)," in *Transitional Justice*, vol. 2 (Washington, DC: United States Institute of Peace Press, 1995). See also Y. Auerbach, "The Role of Forgiveness in Reconciliation," in *From Conflict Resolution to Reconciliation*, ed. Y. Bar-Siman-Tov (Oxford: Oxford University Press, 2004).

69. M. Henderson, *The Forgiveness Factor* (London: Grosvenor Books, 1996); M. Minow, *Between Vengeance and Forgiveness* (Boston: Beacon Press, 1998).

70. R. Robinson, *The Debt: What America Owes to Blacks* (New York: Dutton, 2000), 201.

71. T. W. Ryback, "Dateline Sudentland: Hostages to History," *Foreign Policy* 105 (Winter 1996–1997): 162–78. In 1992, Czechoslovakia broke into the Slovak and the Czech Republics through negotiations.

72. G. Thiessen, "Object of Trust and Hatred: Public Attitudes towards the Truth and Reconciliation Commission," in *Truth and Reconciliation in South Africa,* ed. Audrey R. Chapman and Hugo van der Merwe (Philadelphia: University of Pennsylvania Press, 2008).

73. L. Harbom, Stina Högbladh, and Peter Wallensteen, "Armed Conflict and Peace Agreements," *Journal of Peace Research* 43(5) (2006): 617–13.

74. See, for instance, P. Aall, "What Do NGOs Bring to Peacemaking?" in *Turbulent Peace: The Challenges of Managing International Conflict*, ed. C. A. Crocker, Fen Osler Hampson, and Pamela Aall (Washington, DC: United States Institute of Peace Press, 2001). See also J. Goodhand, *Aiding Peace? The Role of NGOs in Armed Conflict* (Boulder, CO: Lynne Rienner, 2006).

75. C. A. Crocker, F. O. Hampson, et al., *Taming Intractable Conflicts: Mediation in the Hardest Cases* (Washington, DC: United States Institute of Peace Press, 2004). B. W. Dayton, "Useful but Insufficient: Intermediaries in Peacebulding," *Conflict Transformation and Peacebuilding*, ed. B. W. Dayton and L. Kriesberg (London: Routledge, 2009).

76. C. A. Crocker, *High Noon in Southern Africa: Making Peace in a Rough Neighborhood* (New York: W.W. Norton, 1992).

77. Paris, *At War's End.*

78. Former U.S. senator George Mitchell headed a five-member international fact-finding commission. See: http://www.palestinefacts.org/. L. Kriesberg, "The Relevance of Reconciliation Actions in the Breakdown of Israeli-Palestinian Negotiations, 2000," *Peace & Change* 27(4) (2002): 546–71.

79. For the text of the Geneva Accord and current work, see: http://www.geneva-accord.org. During the same period, Ami Ayalon and Sari Nusseibeh launched the People's Voice, a statement of broad principles for peace, for which they amassed tens of thousands of Israeli and Palestinian signatures.

80. D. C. Kurtzer and S. B. Lasensky, *Negotiating Arab-Israeli Peace: American Leadership in the Middle East* (Washington, DC: United States Institute of Peace Press, 2008).

81. S. Zunes, "The Israel Lobby: How Powerful Is It Really?" Foreign Policy in Focus, May 16, 2006, available at: http://www.fppif.org/fpiftxt/3270.

82. R. Kampeas, "At White House, U.S. Jews Offer Little Resistance to Obama Policy on Settlements," available at: www.jta.org/news/article/2009/07/13/1006510/obama-gets-jewish-support-on-peace-push-questions-about-style.

83. L. Susser, "Obama Sharpens His Focus," *Jerusalem Report*, February 15, 2010, 4–7.

84. L. Susser, "Countdown to a State," *Jerusalem Report*, May 23, 2011, 6–9.

85. R. L. Garthoff, *Reflections on the Cuban Missile Crisis* (Washington, DC: The Brookings Institution, 1989).

86. J. Suri, "Explaining the End of the Cold War: A New Historical Consensus?" *Journal of Cold War Studies* 4(4) (Fall 2002): 60–92; D. Cortright, *Peace Works: The Citizen's Role in Ending the Cold War* (Boulder, CO: Westview Press, 1993); M. Kaldor, "Who Killed the Cold War?" *Bulletin of the Atomic Scientists* 51(4) (July–August 1995): 57–60, and L. Kriesberg, *International Conflict Resolution: The U.S.-USSR and Middle East Cases* (New Haven, CT: Yale University Press, 1992).

CHAPTER 11

1. R. Collins, "Some Principles of Long-Term Social Change: The Territorial Power of States," in *Research in Social Movements, Conflicts and Change*, vol. 1, ed. L. Kriesberg (Greenwhich, CT: JAI, 1978); C. A. Johnson, *The Sorrows of Empire: Militarism, Secrecy, and the End of the Republic* (New York: Metropolitan Books, 2004); and P. M. Kennedy,

The Rise and Fall of the Great Powers: Economic Change and Military Conflict from 1500 to 2000 (New York: Random House, 1988).

2. F. Wilmer, *The Social Construction of Man, the State, and War: Identity, Conflict, and Violence in the Former Yugoslavia* (New York: Routledge, 2002); and D. I. Kertzer, *Ritual, Politics, and Power* (New Haven, CT: Yale University Press, 1988).

3. L. Kriesberg, "Nature, Dynamics, and Phases of Intractability," in *Grasping the Nettle: Analyzing Cases of Intractable Conflicts*, ed. C. A. Crocker, Fen Osler Hampson, and Pamela Aall (Washington, DC: United States Institute of Peace, 2005).

4. L. Kriesberg, *International Conflict Resolution: The U.S.-USSR and Middle East Cases* (New Haven, CT: Yale University Press, 1992); C. R. Mitchell, *A Willingness to Talk* (Fairfax, VA: George Mason University, Center for Conflict Analysis and Resolution, 1990), and C. R. Mitchell, "Ending Conflicts and Wars: Judgement, Rationality and Entrapment," *International Social Science Journal* 127 (February 1991): 35–55.

5. R. J. Fisher, *Paving the Way: Contributions of Interactive Conflict Resolution to Peacemaking* (Lanham, MD: Lexington Books, 2005).

6. L. Kriesberg, "Varieties of Mediating Activities and of Mediators," in *Resolving International Conflicts*, ed. J. Bercovitch (Boulder, CO: Lynne Rienner, 1995).

7. R. Major, *A Panther Is a Black Cat* (New York: William Morrow, 1971); and W. Foner, *The Black Panthers Speak* (New York: J. B. Lippincott, 1970). For an analysis of the decline of the 1960s social movements, see A. Oberschall, "The Decline of the 1960s Social Movements," in *Research in Social Movements, Conflicts and Change*, vol. 1, ed. L. Kriesberg (Greenwich, CT: JAI Press, 1978).

8. The growth of the Tea Party was aided by right-wing media commentators and also by the financial support given by David and Charles Koch and other billionaires. W. Bunch, *The Backlash: Right-Wing Radicals, High-Def Hucksters, and Paranoid Politics in the Age of Obama* (New York: HarperCollins, 2010); J. Mayer, "Covert Operations: The Billionaire Brothers Who Are Waging a War against Obama," *New Yorker*, August 30, 2010, 44–55.

9. Tamils in the diaspora and many international organizations called for an investigation of the events in the last months of the war. The Sri Lankan president appointed a Lessons Learnt and Reconciliation Commission in May 2010, but it was not generally accorded great credibility. The UN Secretary General appointed a panel of experts to examine the events. In its March 31, 2011, report it found credible evidence, which if proven, would show that war crimes and crimes against humanity were committed by the Sri Lankan military forces and by the LTTE. See: http://www.un.org/News/dh/infocus/Sri_Lanka/POE_Report_Full.pdf. Also see reports of the International Crisis Group, pertaining to Sri Lanka.

10. L. P. Bremmer III and M. McConnell, *My Year in Iraq: The Struggle to Build a Future of Hope* (New York: Simon & Schuster, 2006); J. Fallows, "Bush's Lost Year," *Atlantic*, October 2004, 68–84; J. Mann, *Rise of the Vulcans* (New York: Viking, 2004); and B. Woodward, *Plan of Attack* (New York: Simon & Schuster, 2004).

11. See R. Licklider, "The Consequences of Negotiated Settlements in Civil Wars, 1945–1993," *American Political Science Review* 89 (September 1995): 682.

12. Under the leadership of Pol Pot, the Khmer Rouge ruled Cambodia from 1975 to 1979. During this regime, an estimated 1.7 million Cambodians were killed or starved to death—21 percent of the population. The Khmer Rouge claimed to be advancing communism, and the killing was directed at ridding the society of imperialist influences, but the death rates varied by ethnicity. See B. Kiernan, *The Pol Pot Regime: Race, Power, and Genocide in Cambodia under the Khmer Rouge, 1975–1979* (New Haven, CT: Yale

University Press, 1996). The great inequalities in Guatemala were brutally sustained for decades by military governments, following the U.S.-backed military coup of 1954. R. M. Karmic, ed., *The Harvest of Violence: The Maya Indians and the Guatemalan Crisis* (Norman: University of Oklahoma Press, 1998). After Siad Barre's dictatorship in Somalia was overthrown and he fled the capital in January 1991, fighting among the many clan-families in Somalia escalated, producing large-scale killing and extensive famine.

13. G. Kepel, *The War for Muslim Minds: Islam and the West* (Cambridge, MA: Belknap Press of Harvard University Press, 2004); M. Sageman, *Understanding Terror Networks* (Philadelphia: University of Pennsylvania Press, 2004).

14. M. I. Handel, *The Diplomacy of Surprise: Hitler, Nixon, Sadat* (Cambridge, MA: Center for International Affairs, Harvard University, 1981), 97–175.

15. D. A Blackmon, *Slavery by Another Name: The Re-Enslavement of Black Americans from the Civil War to World War II* (New York: Random House, 2008). Also see the account of a communal riot between Hindus and Muslims in B. Roy, *Some Trouble with Cows* (Berkeley: University of California Press, 1994).

16. See L. Kriesberg, *International Conflict Resolution: The U.S.-USSR and Middle East Cases* (New Haven, CT: Yale University Press, 1992); J. Suri, *Power and Protest: Global Revolution and the Rise of Detente* (Cambridge, MA: Harvard University Press, 2003); and M. P. Colaresi, *Scare Tactics: The Politics of International Rivalry* (Syracuse, NY: Syracuse University Press, 2005).

17. L. Kuper, *Genocide: Its Political Use in the Twentieth Century* (New York: Penguin, 1981); M. Dobkowski and I. Walliman, *Genocide in Our Time: An Annotated Bibliography with Analytical Introductions* (Ann Arbor, MI: The Pierian Press, 1992); S. Totten W. S. Parsons, et al., ed., *Century of Genocide: Eyewitness Accounts and Critical Views* (New York: Garland, 1997); and B. Harff and T. R. Gurr, "Toward an Empirical Theory of Genocides and Politicides: Identification and Measurement of Cases since 1945," *International Studies Quarterly* 32 (1988): 357–71.

18. R. Hilberg, *The Destruction of the European Jews* (New York: Holmes and Meier, 1985); F. Wilmer, *The Social Construction of Man, the State, and War: Identity, Conflict, and Violence in the Former Yugoslavia* (New York: Routledge, 2002).

19. J. Galtung, *Global Projections of Deep-Rooted U.S. Pathologies* (Faifax, VA: George Mason University, 1996).

20. Integration, here, is as a characteristic of the relationship between possible adversaries, but it can also be viewed as a characteristic of a single actor or of the system within which the adversaries are acting. A. R. Stein, "Governments, Economic Interdependence, and Cooperation," in *Behavior, Society, and International Conflict*, vol. 3, ed. P. Tetlock, J. L. Husbands, R. Jervis, P. C. Stern, and C. Tilly (New York: Oxford University Press, 1993).

21. See the discussion of mediation in Nicaragua between the Miskitos and Sandinistas in L. L. K. Dunn, "Mediating Intermediaries: Expanding Roles of Transnational Organizations," *Studies in International Mediation: Essays in Honour of Jeffrey Z. Rubin*, ed. J. Bercovitch (London: Palgrave Macmillan, 2002).

22. J. R. Oneal and B. Russett, "The Classical Liberals Were Right: Democracy, Interdependence, and Conflict, 1950–1985," *International Studies Quarterly* 41 (June 1997): 267–94.

23. S. M. McMillan, "Interdependence and Conflict," *Mershon International Studies Review* 41 (May 1997): 33–58; L. Kriesberg, "Changing Conflict Asymmetries Constructively," *Dynamics of Asymmetric Conflict* 2(1) (March 2009): 4–22.

24. Roy, *Some Trouble with Cows*, 149–50.

25. R. J. Rummel, *Death by Government* (New Brunswick, NJ: Transaction Books, 1994), 1.

26. Kriesberg, "Changing Conflict Asymmetries Constructively."

27. P. T. Hopmann, "Negotiating Peace in Central America," *Negotiation Journal* 4 (1988): 361–80; and P. Wehr and J. P. Lederach, "Mediating Conflict in Central America," *Journal of Peace Research* 28(1) (1991): 85–98.

28. D. Adams, ed., *UNESCO and the Culture of Peace* (Paris: UNESCO, 1995); and E. Boulding, *Cultures of Peace: The Hidden Side of History* (Syracuse, NY: Syracuse University Press, 2000).

29. I. M. Harris and M. L. Morrison, *Peace Education*, 2nd ed. (Jefferson, NC: McFarland & Co, 2003).

30. M. N. Dobkowski and I. Wallimann, *The Coming Age of Scarcity: Preventing Mass Death and Genocide in the Twenty-First Century* (Syracuse, NY: Syracuse University Press, 1998); M. N. Dobkowski and I. Wallimann, ed., *On the Edge of Scarcity: Environment, Resources, Population, Sustainability, and Conflict* (Syracuse, NY: Syracuse University Press, 2001).

31. E. Weede, "Some New Evidence on Correlates of Political Violence: Income Inequality, Regime Repressiveness, and Economic Development," *European Sociological Review* 3 (September 1987): 97–108; E. N. Muller, "Income Inequality and Political Violence: The Effect of Influential Cases," *American Sociological Review* 51 (1986): 441–45.

32. M. Krain, "State-Sponsored Mass Murder," *Journal of Conflict Resolution* 41 (June 1997): 331–60.

33. V. N. Dadrian, "The Documentation of the World War I Armenian Massacres in the Proceedings of the Turkish Military Tribunal," *International Journal of Middle East Studies* 7(2): 173–201.

34. I am adapting the use of the term *prescription* from the comments of Allan T. Griffith.

35. L. Kriesberg, "The Current State-of-the-Art of the Conflict Transformation Field," *Berghof Handbook for Conflict Transformation*, ed. M. Fischer, J. Giessmann, and B. Schmelzle (Berlin: Berghof Forschungszentrum für Konstruktive Konfliktbearbeitung, 2011).

36. In the planning field, see J. Forester, *The Deliberative Practioner: Encouraging Participatory Planning Proceses* (Cambridge, MA: MIT Press, 1999).

37. A. M. Thomson and J. L. Perry, co-edited by Rosemary O'Leary, Lisa Bloomgren, and Catherine Gerard, "Collaboration Processes: Inside the Black Box," *Public Administration Review Supplement: Special Issue on Collaborative Public Management* 66 (December 2006): 20–32.

38. L. Keashly and R. J. Fisher, "Complementarity and Coordination of Conflict Interventions: Taking a Contigency Perspective," in *Resolving International Conflicts*, ed. J. Bercovitch (Boulder, CO: Lynne Rienner, 1996); C. Mitchell, "The Process and Stages of Mediation," in *Making War and Waging Peace: Foreign Intervention in Africa*, ed. D. R. Smock (Washington, DC: U. S. Institute of Peace, 1993).

39. L. Reychler and T. Paffenholz, *Peacebuilding: A Field Guide* (Boulder, CO: Lynne Rienner Publishers, 2001); S. A. Nan, "Track One-and-a-Half Diplomacy," in *Paving the Way*, ed. R. J. Fisher (Lanham, MD: Lexington Books, 2005); P. F. Diehl and D. Druckman, *Evaluating Peace Operations* (Boulder, CO: Lynne Rienner, 2010).

40. See for instance H. Miall, Oliver Ramsbotham, and Tom Woodhouse, *Contemporary Conflict Resolution* (Cambridge: Polity, 2008); D. J. D. Sandole, *Peacebuilding* (Malden, MA: Polity, 2010).

41. B. Obama, "Remarks by the President at the Acceptance of the Nobel Peace Prize," Washington, DC, 2009.

42. M. J. Stephan and E. Chenoweth, "Why Civil Resistance Works: The Strategic Logic of Nonviolent Conflict," *International Security* 33(3) (2008): 7–44.

43. M. A. Dugan, *The Relationship between Pre-Independence Internal Violence and Nonviolence and Post-Independence Violence, External Belligerency, and Internal Governmental Repressiveness* (Syracuse, NY: Syracuse University Press, 1979).

44. M. Waltzer, *Just and Unjust Wars: A Moral Argument with Historical Illustrations*, 4th ed. (New York: Basic Books, 1997).

45. Some critics of the problem-solving approach to conflict resolution argue that its advocates and practitioners too often ignore moral issues. See L. Nader, "Harmony Models and the Construction of Law," in *Conflict Resolution: Cross-Cultural Perspectives*, ed. K. Avruch, P. W. Black, and J. A. Scimecca (New York: Greenwood Press, 1991).

46. J. Laue, "Ethical Considerations in Choosing Intervention Roles," *Peace and Change* 8 (Summer 1982): 34; see also J. Laue and G. Cormick, "The Ethics of Intervention in Community Disputes," in *The Ethics of Social Intervention*, ed. G. Bermant, H. C. Kelman, and D. P. Warwick (Washington, DC: Halstead Press, 1978). The basic human needs approach as formulated by John Burton also posits a standard by which to judge intervenor and other conflict resolution efforts to satisfy those needs. See J. Burton, *Conflict: Resolution and Prevention* (New York: St. Martin's, 1971).

47. This important distinction was examined in Max Weber's essays, see M. Weber, "Politics as a Vocation" and "Science as a Vocation," in *From Max Weber: Essays in Sociology*, ed. H. H. Gerth and C. W. Mills (New York: Oxford University Press, 1946).

48. L. Kriesberg, "On Advancing Truth and Morality in Conflict Resolution," *Peace and Conflict Studies* 6(1) (1999): 7–19.

49. H. Putnam, *The Many Faces of Realism* (LaSalle, IL: Open Court, 1987). See also the distinction between operational environment and cognized environment, as discussed in R.A. Rubinstein, C. D. Laughlin, et al., *Science as Cognitive Process: Toward an Empirical Philosophy of Science* (Philadelphia: University of Pennsylvania Press, 1984).

50. J. Mueller, *The Retreat from Doomsday: The Obsolescence of Major Wars* (New York: Basic Books, 1983).

51. S. D. Krasner, *International Regimes* (Ithaca, NY: Cornell University Press, 1983).

52. L. Kriesberg, "Challenges in Peacemaking," in *External Interventions Peacemaking: A Comprehensive Theory and Practice Reference*, ed. A. Bartoli, S. A. Nan, and Z. Mampilly (Westport, CT: Praeger Security International, 2011).

53. D. A. Welch, "Can We Think Systematically about Ethics and Statecraft?" *Ethics & International Affairs* 8 (1994): 23–37.

54. E. H. Erikson, *Gandhi's Truth* (New York: W. W. Norton, 1969).

55. The abandonment of the policy of reconstruction was due to many other factors, including the resistance of white Southerners, the waning of Northern enthusiasm to overcome slavery, and increasing economic problems. J. Higham, "America's Three Reconstructions," *New York Review of Books*, November 6, 1997, 52–56; and E. Foner, *Reconstruction: America's Unfinished Revolution, 1863–1877* (New York: Harper and Row, 1988).

56. Dobkowski and Wallimann, *On the Edge of Scarcity*.

Subject Index

Note: Page numbers in italics refer to diagrams or tables.

Author Index

About the Authors

Louis Kriesberg is professor emeritus of sociology and Maxwell Professor Emeritus of Social Conflict Studies at Syracuse University. He is the founding director of the Program on the Analysis and Resolution of Conflicts and past president of the Society for the Study of Social Problems.

Bruce W. Dayton is associate director and senior research scholar at the Moynihan Institute of Global Affairs in The Maxwell School at Syracuse University, and coresearch director of the international and interstate conflicts research initiative at Maxwell's Program for the Advancement of Research on Collaboration and Conflicts.